Contributions to Economics

More information about this series at http://www.springer.com/series/1262

Simeon Karafolas
Editor

Credit Cooperative Institutions in European Countries

Springer

Editor
Simeon Karafolas
Western Macedonia University of Applied Sciences
Kozani, Greece

ISSN 1431-1933 ISSN 2197-7178 (electronic)
Contributions to Economics
ISBN 978-3-319-28783-6 ISBN 978-3-319-28784-3 (eBook)
DOI 10.1007/978-3-319-28784-3

Library of Congress Control Number: 2016935719

Printed on acid-free paper

This Springer imprint is published by Springer Nature
The registered company is Springer International Publishing AG Switzerland

Preface

At a recent ICA[1] conference, a speaker stated that he did not consider financial capital to be an important parameter in cooperative institutions, including credit cooperative institutions. Another speaker stated that on the contrary financial capital in a credit cooperative institution can have a crucial role; he referred to the case of Cyprus where the whole system has been jeopardized because of changes in the capital requirements for credit unions and to the case of Greece, where the Central Bank revoked the license of some cooperative banks which did not achieve capital adequacy.

The first speaker had the experience of a big European country with an old and well-established credit cooperative system, while the second speaker had the experience of a newly established credit cooperative system.

Different experiences of specialists result in very different views on similar issues. This book allows us to see the sharp contrasts between the credit cooperative systems throughout the EU. Credit cooperative systems do not have the same evolution or structure. Many differences exist between countries, including EU countries, not least in their appellation as cooperative bank, credit union, or credit cooperative.

In some countries, a minimum initial capital is required for the creation and function of a cooperative bank, while in others, there is no such requirement. Even in the same country, differences may exist across credit cooperative institutions. Historically, some European countries have an old and well-established credit cooperative system characterized by big credit cooperative institutions (even of a multinational character); other European countries have newly created credit cooperative systems, while countries in Eastern Europe had to abandon old cooperative systems and create new ones. In some cases, the credit cooperative system has a pyramid structure with local, regional, and national central institutions; in other

[1] International Cooperative Alliance.

cases, credit cooperative systems are characterized by independent local cooperative banks.

Differences within these systems can provoke problems in the application of common policies within the EU. Recent financial crises affected credit cooperative systems on different levels and to different extents, depending on the country and the system. Measures regarding supervision and solvency have been put in place, creating important changes in the function of the credit cooperative institutions, in some cases even ending the function of credit cooperative banks.

Knowledge of the different credit cooperative systems is highly useful and of significant scientific and practical interest, especially for policy makers.

The importance of these institutions to the European economy and society is obvious. Within the 20 European countries' members of the European Association of Co-operative Banks (EACB), 4229 cooperative banks have 67,954 branches in the home country, with 77.8 million members and 205 million clients.[2]

The aim of this book is to give a comparative presentation of the credit cooperative systems in 23 European countries. It is the most recent and most international collection of essays on the credit cooperative systems in Europe considering the number of examined countries.

The outline of each examined country case discusses the establishment and historic evolution of the credit cooperative system, the current model, and its importance to the national banking market and/or to the local market. The consequences of the financial crisis and thoughts on the future of the credit cooperatives are also presented. The establishment and evolution discusses when and how the system was created and how the system has evolved in terms of organization, function, legislation, number of banks, and numbers of members of credit cooperative institutions.

The discussion of the current model focuses on the actual structure and organization of the system, including the local or national hierarchy. This includes a discussion on minimum capital adequacy requirements, the role of the central bank, international or local networks, governance, policy on members and customers, and range of services offered. Whether cooperative financial institutions are mainly deposit takers or lenders is also considered. The role of the State in supporting the establishment and development of credit cooperative institutions is outlined. The importance of the credit cooperative system to the national and/or the local banking market is examined in one or more of terms as the number of banks, banking network, employees, assets, and deposits or loans.

The recent financial and economic crisis affected almost all European banking markets and European economies. We might expect that cooperative credit systems have performed better than their banking counterparts since they have not been exposed to the same high-risk speculative activities. But we can say with certainty that the economic crisis has affected cooperative banks as well. The essays explore the national or European financial supports provided and the extent to which the

[2] EACB, Annual Report for 2014.

crisis provoked mergers or closures. Examination of these issues enables thought on the future of the credit cooperative system.

The general outline of each essay helps with the homogeneity of presentation and comparison, but differences in the examined cases are expected due to historical reasons or country-level particularities. For example, it is of the same importance to understand why a system has not developed historically or has followed a different evolution compared to others and suffered more than others from the crisis.

Authors invited to participate in this book are specialists in the country cases. This book examines 23 country cases, 22 in the EU countries and Serbia which is an EU accession candidate. Thus, cases of different European regions are examined including Baltic, Balkans, British Isles, Central Europe, including France and Italy, Iberian Peninsula, and Scandinavia. Therefore, this book is unique.

The book is divided into two parts: the Western European countries and the former Eastern European countries. This distinction is related mainly to the fact that the Eastern European countries had to pass from a centrally planned economy to a liberal economy. During the planned economy period, cooperatives were integrated into the State's policy and philosophy on the economy but also into political and social life. The new socioeconomic environment required a new philosophy of cooperatives and public financing. In particular, European financing has assisted the development of cooperatives in these countries.

In most of the examined Western European countries, the credit cooperative system is well established with a long history. Countries with new credit cooperative systems are the exception, as in the Greek case. In a few European Union countries, such as Belgium, Denmark, Luxembourg, Malta, and Sweden, despite the existence of an important cooperative movement, a credit cooperative system is not really developed, even if some initiatives may be under way; consequently, the book does not refer to these countries.

The first part of the book examines the financial cooperative systems in Austria, Cyprus, Finland, France, Germany, Great Britain, Greece, Ireland, Italy, Netherlands, Portugal, and Spain.

The second part of the book examines the former Eastern European countries: Bulgaria, Czech Republic, Estonia, Hungary, Latvia, Lithuania, Poland, Romania, Slovakia, Slovenia, and Serbia.

Kozani, Greece Simeon Karafolas

Contents

Part I
Credit Cooperative Systems in Western Europe

Cooperative Banks in the Austrian Banking System

Johann Brazda, Holger Blisse, and Robert Schediwy

Abstract The two autonomous cooperative banking groups in Austria, Volksbanks and Raiffeisenbanks, have taken very different paths in their development. To understand the recent situation, it could be helpful and necessary to reflect the past and to describe the Austrian banking system as well as today's structure of the Raiffeisen banking group and the Volksbanken group. We conclude this paper by giving a short overview of the latest developments and the current situation.

1 Historical Development

The start of a credit cooperative movement in Austria fell into a period of profound and fundamental social and economic changes (1848–1859) and was marked by economic liberalism, but also by persistent lack of freedom in the civil-political area. These circumstances increased the pressure on traders, craftsmen, and farmers.

The oldest credit cooperatives were organized based on a guarantee system with the participation of wealthy patrons as sponsors. The first of these was founded in 1851, the "Aushilfskassenverein in Klagenfurt". It served as a model for later establishments. Since 1858, when the ideas of Schulze-Delitzsch became known in Austria, the founding of credit cooperatives have followed his principles e.g. of self-help.

In contrast to the development in Germany, the Austrian cooperative movement remained without any leading figure for a very long time. This was also a result of the political situation in Austria, because it was not possible to unite the cooperatives of all the different nationalities in the Austrian monarchy and even the cooperatives of German speaking people in Austria were not able to be united in

J. Brazda (✉) • H. Blisse • R. Schediwy
Department of Business Administration, Cooperative Studies, University of Vienna, Vienna, Austria
e-mail: johann.brazda@univie.ac.at; holger.blisse@univie.ac.at; Robert.schediwy@gmx.at

S. Karafolas (ed.), *Credit Cooperative Institutions in European Countries*, Contributions to Economics, DOI 10.1007/978-3-319-28784-3_1

Table 1 Number of cooperative banks (Volksbanks) in the Danube monarchy, since 1873 registered cooperatives

Year	Volksbanks	Year	Volksbanks
1851	2	1870	635
1860	10	1871	749
1861	35	1873	142
1862	90	1874	713
1863	141	1875	818
1864	174	1880	946
1865	224	1885	1.133

Source: Brazda and Todev (2001, p. 40, 65, 85)

a federation. So a general federation was established not until 1872. One year later, the most important legal pillar was passed: the cooperative law of 1873. This basic law was modified by important amendments in 1920, 1974, 1982, and 2005.[1]

In the second half of the 1870s, the number of new Schulze-Delitzsch credit cooperatives was stable but increased during the second half of the 1880s. This development is consistent with the upswing of the middle class in this period. However, the banks developed very differently: In the smaller villages and towns, they remained largely faithful to cooperative principles, whereas in cities they became small banks for the affluent middle-class. These cooperative banks financed the rise of larger manufacturers but tended to neglect more and more the financial needs of destitute artisans (Table 1).

In 1865, Raiffeisen cooperatives became known in Austria via German publications and since the Agricultural Congress held in 1873 in Vienna their introduction became part of the agenda of agricultural policy. It was not until 1885 that the government started a successful "founding wave", e.g. in Lower Austria. As in Germany, it was the aim of the introduction of Raiffeisen credit cooperatives to reduce the credit crunch for the rural population; similar to Germany, the rapid development succeeded with the help of public entities. The diet of Lower Austria was the first to provide assistance to self-help: The public sector took over the revision, monetary settlement, the starting aid, supported with training courses, the publication of manuals and the organization of study tours (Fig. 1).

During the Habsburg monarchy, until 1918, the Raiffeisen movement expanded to a largely comprehensive network of Raiffeisen credit cooperatives. Although its development started later, it surpassed that of Schulze-Delitzsch credit cooperatives already at the turn of the century. In the 1890s, the course was set for the three-tier-structure of the Raiffeisen organization with local, regional, and national entities.

After the end of the First World War, the entire Austrian economy faced a severe test: The close links with other regions of the Danube monarchy were shattered. The "rest of Old Austria" consisted of an oversized government bureaucracy in Vienna, a predominantly military-based manufacturing sector and a hypertrophic service sector. The ultimately unsuccessful attempt by large Viennese banks to maintain

[1] The most important documentations regarding cooperative law are probably Keinert (1988) and Dellinger (2005). See also Kastner (1986).

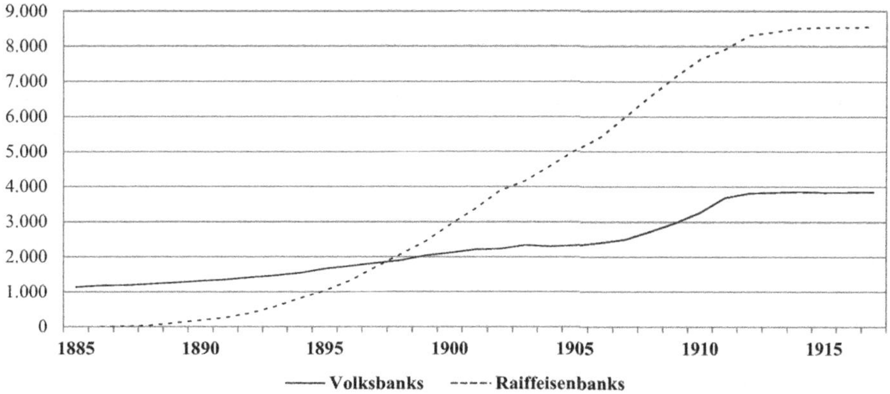

Fig. 1 Number of cooperative banks (1885–1917) in the Danube monarchy. *Source of data*: Brazda et al. (1997, pp. 73f.)

their regional position in the Danube region, led to a plethora of collapses and mergers that resulted in the crash of the Creditanstalt in 1931.

In this extremely difficult situation, the Austrian economy reached only for a short period the performance of the pre-war era. The Schulze-Delitzsch credit cooperatives passed the test quite well, but with only a small market share of 5 %. A decisive element of their success was the fact that they tended to avoid the speculative excesses of the period of inflation and the 1924 stock market boom. They did not succumb to the temptation of so many large banks: to retain the assets in illiquid investments, to borrow short and lend long term. Gradually, the name "Volksbank" became popular and was pushed increasingly in the dictatorial era after 1938, but it was also a longer period of a decrease of bank branches because of forced mergers.

In the 1920s, the representatives of agriculture used more and more the term of the "three pillars" on which agriculture was based on: the political representation by the farmers' federation, the lobbying organization by the Chambers of Agriculture and the economic aspect by the agricultural cooperative system. The dairy sector and the trade of agricultural products (warehouse cooperatives) were fully cooperatively organized. Agriculture was financed by Raiffeisen credit cooperatives. In 1929, they achieved a market share of 21 % of total deposits.

This period is also characterized by an important step towards strengthening sectoral networks: In 1922, the Schulze-Delitzsch credit cooperatives established the "Österreichische Zentral-Genossenschaftskasse" in the legal form of a cooperative as their central bank (today: Österreichische Volksbanken-AG). The creation of the Girozentrale österreichischer Genossenschaften (today: Raiffeisen Zentralbank Österreich AG) was created in 1927 as a corporation and became soon the central clearinghouse for the Raiffeisen credit cooperatives, which opened them the way to the Austrian money market.

During the period of the Nazi regime, the Austrian credit cooperatives were incorporated in the German cooperative organization, which led to significant changes. These were mainly related to the organizational structure, the self-administration and the cooperative audit. Successfully working structures were destroyed, but after the Second World War, the former structures could be quickly reactivated.

The reconstruction of the Austrian economy began soon after the Second World War. The strict state regulation of the Austrian banking system prevented, until the late 1970s, an organic growth of the Austrian banking sector. That meant a local stagnation for the Volksbanks, because their traditional customers were already satisfied with banking services before the war, whereas the inhabitants of rural areas were increasing their need for banking services as their income grew in the 1960s. This was positive for the Raiffeisen credit cooperatives and for the savings banks both of which catered to these customer groups. Above all, the Raiffeisen credit cooperatives also had an advantage by adapting their opening hours (opening times had been only on Sunday after church) to the regular opening hours of most banks. At the same time, a tighter network management was conducted. In the 1970s, only the Raiffeisen credit cooperatives expanded above the average compared to other types of banks, because the market potential of the people employed in the commercial industrial centers was almost exhausted, whereas it was still high in rural areas.

All banks expanded from their traditional customer groups to customers of other banking sectors. In the competition for deposits, the banks appealed to all customer groups at the same time, concentrating on both retail and private banking business and focusing on the national as well as on the international market. This trend to a global-universal bank displaced the old, long time characteristic bank type in the Austrian banking system—that of a universal bank offering all banking services, but only to a specific group of customers.

The trend to universal banking and to a further intensification of competition continued with the liberalization in 1977 that set up branches, the approval of business expansions of previously specialized banks and the abandonment of the regional principle for the Viennese large savings banks. The liberalization of banking activities was reinforced in the Banking Act of 1979 (obligatory full-time management) by abandoning the still partially practiced specialization and by favouring the legal form of a corporation. As a result, competition increased with decreasing revenues, a tendency which was reinforced by the accession of Austria to the EU.

The Volksbanks experienced significant problems in the 1980s in a highly competitive market, because they did not always follow the organizational and business principles of Schulze-Delitzsch. Local managers often made their own decisions, which caused detriments of their bank. However, the sector was able to overcome the crisis on its own, without taking state aid and thus sacrificing the autonomy and independence of the Volksbanks. A strategic reorientation and the establishment of a vertically integrated network in the early 1990s led to temporary success of the Volksbank group: For a while it was able to show the highest operating profit rate compared to the other banking sectors.

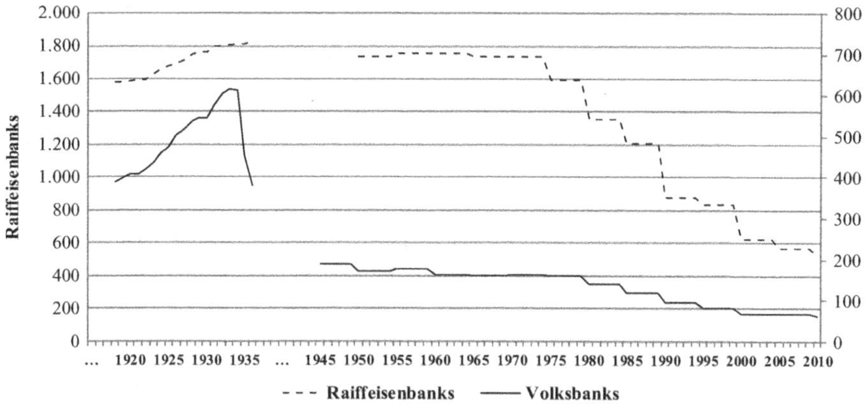

Fig. 2 Number of cooperative banks (1918–2010) in Austria. Since 1945 data for every 5 years. *Source of data*: Brazda et al. (1997, pp. 73f., 122, 244f.), ÖGV (2000, p. 128), ÖGV (2005, p. 29), ÖGV (2010 2011, pp. 7, 11), RZB (2005, p. 59), RZB (2010–2012, pp. 22, 28, 20), Bruckmüller, Werner (1998, p. 337)

The Raiffeisen Banking Group has expanded since the fall of the Iron Curtain in 1989, primarily by its national central bank, to an extremely successful broad-based network of banks in Central and Eastern Europe. A further expansion in this area assisted by a meaningful cooperation with a foreign partner has not been realized yet. The Raiffeisen banking sector grew more important by its acquisitions in non-banking sectors, but this is also a reason for dispute (Fig. 2).

2 Legal and Tax Framework

We would like to concentrate on the law of the legal form of the cooperative banks, the cooperative law, as well as on the specific law for banking, known as the Banking Act.

2.1 Cooperative Law and Taxation

Cooperative organization in Austria based on different important legal pillars: The most important of these is the cooperative law of 1873 (Gesetz vom April 9, 1873, über Erwerbs- und Wirthschaftsgenossenschaften, RGBl. Nr. 70/1873). The fact that many of the norms of this law of 1873 were not binding and thus could be modified by cooperative statutes (by-laws) has certainly contributed much to the continuing vitality and flexibility of that law. The cooperative auditing law of 1903, on the contrary, was strongly influenced by an already thriving cooperative sector and by specific pressure groups that had been formed within this sector. Instead of being extremely liberal this law acknowledged the necessity to control the existing cooperative sector via cooperative auditing associations according to the German model. This control was believed to be more efficient and thus to be preferred to state-control. Cooperative mergers were favoured; now the formation of new cooperatives due to a merger was possible (Genossenschaftsverschmelzungsgesetz 1980, BGBl. 1980/223). Previously, there had to be a receiving and thus "victorious" cooperative, which continued its existence, while the other had to lose its legal existence. In this way, the obstacle of members' irrationalism was reduced.

The changes of the last decades can be interpreted as a result of the progressive reduction of differences between cooperatives and other legal entities of commercial law; one can therefore speak of a certain banalization of the legal entity of a cooperative. The amendment of 1974 allowed explicitly the sale to non-members and the share-holding of cooperatives in firms of other legal entities, which were rights that had been more or less acquired by practice, but that were questioned from time to time by a rather purist jurisdiction.

In the 1970s and 1980s, certain tax privileges of cooperatives were eliminated, e.g. a reduced corporate income tax for cooperative banks (1977) and a tax-free cooperative refund, which reflected the level of intensity a member had used the bank's services (1988)—but also certain disadvantages with regard to other legal forms.[2] Today there are no tax privileges for cooperative banks compared to the tax regime for banks in other legal forms. Nevertheless, a number of cooperative banks, in particular Volksbanks, pay dividends to its shareholders (members).

The extremely deplorable collapse of the Konsum Austria consumer cooperative in 1995 led to a new round of cooperative reform demands: On January 31, 1997, the Austrian Ministry of Justice organized a public hearing on the topic of "The Reform of Austrian Cooperative Law" in Salzburg. A little later, the ministry published the contents of this hearing. This interesting publication still constitutes the most up to date overview of the various positions of Austrian experts on cooperative law and its problems. The quite controversial discussions of the hearing, however, can be used to reflect on the existing attitudes and the still unsolved problems. Therefore, we should discuss them at least briefly. The main divergence between the defenders of the present system and its critics seems to be the question of "Verbund" or sector unity. Should it be seen as an instrument to stifle grass roots spontaneity, independence and democracy? Thus, not much has come out of this whole debate. [3] A small reform of Austria's cooperative auditing law, Genossenschaftsrevisionsgesetz 1997, was the whole outcome of the debate. The tasks of auditing were put in more precise terms and to a certain extent strengthened the position of the individual auditor and improved the auditor's training, which now should fulfil EU standards. The law of 1997 sticks to the

[2] See Maurer in Dellinger (2005, pp. 88f.) and Schaschko (2010, pp. 53f.).

[3] See Bundesministerium für Justiz (1997).

principles of material auditing, not just formal control of orderliness, and it maintains the (marginal) possibility of cooperatives to exit from auditing.

In 2004, the Firmenbuchgesetz merged the Austrian trade register with the register of cooperatives. An amendment in 2006 (Genossenschaftsrechtsänderungsgesetz of 2006) transformed the EU's concept of a European Cooperative (Societas Cooperativa Europaea—SCE) into domestic Austrian law, [SCE-VO (EG) Nr. 1435/2003]—so far without any considerable impact. With the introduction of the European Cooperative, two new legal institutions were introduced into Austrian cooperative law: investing members and minimal capital. Both aspects have so far remained foreign to Austria's cooperative practice. The pertinent legal provisions are Art. 5a (2) No 1 and 2 GenG.

2.2 *Banking Law*

The Austrian Banking Act of 1993 (Bankwesengesetz, BWG), amending the Banking Act of 1979, is valid for Raiffeisenbanks and Volksbanks as well as for other banks. The rules require, among other things, a minimum capital of five million euros [Article 5 (1) no. 5 BWG] and a membership in a deposit insurance scheme. According to the sectorial structure (see Chap. 3), both cooperative banking groups have their own statutory deposit protection schemes with a deposit protection up to 100,000 euros per depositor (private client) (Art. 93 ff., 103 h and 103 k BWG).

In addition, each group has a voluntary protection: The Gemeinschaftsfonds (group fund) of the Volksbanken group is to protect the existence of each member of the ÖGV: Volksbanks and ÖVAG. The fund is due to the German guarantee fund, founded in 1937, and has consisted for the Austrian Volksbanks since 1938. The fund is comparable to the deposit protection fund of the German central organization of the cooperative banking group (BVR). If necessary, the Volksbanken-Beteiligungsgesellschaft Ltd improves the capital of Volksbanks and gives organizational, staffing and consultative assistance.

The Raiffeisen banking group set up the Raiffeisen-Kundengarantiegemeinschaft Österreich (RKÖ, deposit guarantee association) in 2000. The association guarantees up to 100 % of customer deposits covering all savers' deposits, including not only private individual customers but also businesses and foreign currency deposits as well as the member banks' own securities issues. The model has a regional and national level. About 80 % of the Raiffeisenbanks are members of the RKÖ, including RZB and Raiffeisen Bank International.

3 The Cooperative Banking Sectors in the National Banking System

Currently, Raiffeisenbanks and Volksbanks hold together more than one third of the total asset of Austria's banking system. Within the Austrian banking system, they form two of seven banking sectors: Depending on the nature of their activities, the banks can be divided into universal banks and specialized banks. Universal banks are the sectors of Joint Stock Banks and Private Banks (e.g. Bankhaus Carl Spängler & Co. AG, BAWAG P.S.K., Oberbank AG or UniCredit Bank Austria AG) as well as the Savings Banks, the State Mortgage Banks and the Raiffeisen Credit Cooperatives and the Volksbank Credit Cooperatives; Building and Loan Associations and Special Purpose Banks (e.g. Severance funds, Investment companies or the Oesterreichische Kontrollbank AG) as specialized banks.[4]

Measured by total assets held at the end of June 2015 (December 2010), the Raiffeisen sector holds a 30.0 (29.1) % market share and is the market leader, followed by the joint stock banks and private banks with 29.4 (24.9) %, the savings banks have 17.2 (16.7) %. The other banking sectors hold less than 10 % of the market share.[5] The Volksbanks achieved a market share of 4.6 (7.4) %. A characteristic for Austria is still the clear distinction between the banking sectors by the number of tiers. There are single-tier sectors, such as joint stock banks, state mortgage banks and building and loan associations and special purpose banks. There are also sectors with two tiers where a central institution is on top, which is responsible for the affiliated institutions in coordination and balance functions. This is the case of Volksbanks and savings banks. There is also the Raiffeisen sector with three tiers, which still includes a level with regional banks in addition to the local and the national level.

Noticeable for the Austrian banking market is the high density of branches with 1673 inhabitants per bank branch. The densest branch network is that of the Raiffeisen sector with a share of 44.3 % of all branches in Austria, followed by savings banks and joint stock banks with a share of 20.8 % and 16.0 %, while the Volksbanks are at 10.9 % (end 2010).[6]

The Austrian banking market is a mature market, in which any kind of domestic expansion is only possible by the acquisition of competitors. This route was followed by the Volksbank sector when its central bank bought the Investkredit Bank AG with its corporate customer businesses, municipal financing (Kommunalkredit Austria AG) and real estate (Europolis Real Estate Asset Management GmbH) in 2005.

Furthermore, there was a striking, long-term commitment of Austrian banks in Central, Eastern and South Eastern Europe (CEE) (2010: 314 billion,[7] more than the Austrian GDP), which has evolved over the past two decades as a central pillar

[4] See Brazda and Blisse (2010, p. 1096).

[5] See Böck et al. (2012, p. 210) and based on current OeNB-data.

[6] See Böck et al. (2012, p. 210).

[7] See Anonymous (2012).

of its business. This commitment created critical attention during the financial and economic crisis, but soon measures by central banks, governments, the International Monetary Fund, the European Commission and the World Bank were taken to provide help. However, it was one reason for a so-called banking package in early 2009 by the Austrian Government (Financial Market Stabilization Act) to strengthen bank capital, especially in the core capital, in particular the tier-1 capital.

In addition to the BAWAG PSK, the Erste Group Bank and Hypo Alpe Adria, the RZB Group received 1.75 billion and ÖVAG received one billion euros as participation capital from the state. Previously, the owners of the RZB supported a capital increase of their institution, whereas the Volksbanks, with approximately 58.2 % majority owner, and the DZ BANK (25 % plus one share) were not willing to accept a capital increase of ÖVAG. This is one reason why the ÖVAG was looking for a "strategic partner".[8] The DG BANK, the former DZ BANK, became partner and shareholder in 1996 when ÖVAG and the Austrian Association of Cooperatives (ÖGV) started to develop a common perspective for the cooperative banks in Europe.

By the end of July 2010, RZB was also one of the top institutions participating in the banking stress test and passed it successfully. ÖVAG was not included. It was burdened with a high annual loss for the year 2009 by the discharge of Kommunalkredit Austria to the state and the business of Investkredit Bank (Table 2).

Table 2 Statistical data on Austrian banks by sector

2010 2015[a]	Head offices	Branch offices	Employees	Assets (in million Euro)	Loans (customers')	Deposits (customers')
Joint stock banks and private banks	47	758	22,123	243,704.14	135,820.85	102,175.05
	41	1012	20,784	263,666,62	140,884,69	127,394.91
Savings banks	54	990	15,412	162,937.44	69,780.65	59.806.87
	49	905	14,770	153,950.11	71,471.64	61,830.14
State mortgage banks	11	162	4378	92,547.23	51,319.10	18,723.27
	10	147	3843	59,347,39	41,499,59	17,603,18
Raiffeisen credit cooperatives	539	1680	24,978	285,180.23	109,502.01	98,393.49
	498	1578	24,245	268,564.98	119,409.2	110,781.17
Volksbank credit cooperatives	67	479	6828	72,730.57	31173.81	22,723.23
	53	428	6166	41,209.84	23,149.4	21,379.64
Building and loan associations	4	90	1799	22,989.79	17,596.55	18,902.87
	4	81	1390	24,252.79	18,603.95	20,834.88
Special purpose banks	91	11	3350	87,039.96	14,761.37	3609.46
	75	8	3683	69,198.19	10,984.70	6307.59

[a]Without member state credit institutions, Data of June 2015, Employees' data of 2014
Source: Oesterreichische Nationalbank

[8] See Brazda and Blisse (2010, p. 1097).

3.1 Volksbanks

The Volksbanken sector represents the senior of the two cooperative banking groups. It is traditionally based on the principles of self-help, self-responsibility and self-government and emphasizes the aspect of freedom as a prerequisite to act in the market.[9] It is a two tier organisation. Its central institution the Volksbank Wien-Baden, and there are 41 regional Volksbanks. Important structural reforms took place in the sector in the mid-1980s when a horizontal structure concept was developed to form the 113 smaller local Volksbanks with their 385 branches (1985) to regional banks with of 60–90 employees each. Volksbanks had about 545,000 members (end 2012).

In recent years, the sector has witnessed difficult times. On several occasions, the Austrian state had to rescue the Austrian Volksbanken AG (ÖVAG), which used to serve as a central institution of the sector. The sale of four banking subsidiaries of the ÖVAG to the primary level Volksbanks was also undertaken to stabilise further the capital base of ÖVAG. Within the so called "project regio" the Volksbank Wien, Ärztebank and IMMO-BANK were sold to the local Volksbanks. This process was successfully completed in 2009. Volksbank Linz and Mühlviertel merged with Volksbank Wels in 2010.

ÖVAG announced the financial turnaround with a profit of 56.5 million euro in 2010. In order to repay the government's participation capital as stipulated in the contract, ÖVAG has actively initiated a search for strategic partnerships and sold Volksbank International, its subsidiary for banking activities in Central and Eastern Europe. Instead of expected 800–1000 million euros, the bank collected finally 500 million euros from the Russian Sberbank (2012)—without the Romanian subsidiary. ÖVAG had to reduce its assets so that the bank would not be regarded as a systemically important bank on European level and would not have to fulfill the new capital requirements.

The turnaround announced in 2010 was not sustainable. The annual loss in 2011 was more than 1300 million euro compared with 1200 million euro shareholders' capital. The Volksbanks discussed with the Austrian state, the Ministry of Finance, the Financial Market Authority (FMA) and the Oesterreichische Nationalbank new solutions controversially.[10] At the end, ÖVAG and Volksbanks were more closely connected and realized a model similar to the Dutch Rabobank in accordance with the new legal framework (Art. 30a BWG), which is called "Kreditinstitute-Verbund" (Integrated System of Banks) based on a contract ("Verbundvertrag") with a joint liability and joint liquidity scheme and authorising ÖVAG, the central organisation within the association, to issue directives to the affiliated credit institutions—the Volksbanks [Art. 30a (1) no. 3 BWG].[11] Accepted by the general

[9] See Hofinger (2007, p. 65).

[10] See Grabner (2012a, b).

[11] See Kischko and Trummer (2012).

meetings of the Volksbanks, the FMA approved the contract on September 18, 2012 and the new Association of Volksbanks became legally effective.

At the beginning of July 2015, the core functions of ÖVAG were transferred to the Volksbank Wien-Baden, the biggest primary co-operative of the system. At the same time, all property belonging to the non-core-segments of ÖVAG was transferred out of the co-operative group. These assets werde taken over by a "bad bank" that was formed under the name of "Immigon Portfolioabbau AG".

The systematic liquidation of the ÖVAG must be seen as a consequence of its risky expansion towards Eastern Europe and the concomitant losses. ÖVAG had to be rescued several times by the Austrian state. In spite of this help, it would not have passed the EU-stress test of 2014. Its leadership therefore announced its step-by-step liquidation even before the results of the stress test were published.

Although a few Volksbanks have opted for the legal form of a corporation, their statutes are designed as a cooperative corporation; most of the Volksbanks still operate in the cooperative form. The cooperatives oppose the shareholder value principle the member value and pay a dividend. Generally, one member has a maximum of ten votes depending on the number of shares.

3.2 *Raiffeisenbanks*

The Raiffeisen Zentralbank Austria AG (RZB) is the top-level institution of Raiffeisen Banking Group (RBG). It is the management holding for the entire RZB Group, including the Raiffeisen Bank International AG (RBI). "The RZB acts as the organiser of synergies and shared solutions between the RBG and the RBI and also of services, products and processes for the entire RBG."[12]

The RZB investment portfolio needs to be understood in the context of its role as the top-level institution of the RBG in Austria and as the hub connecting the RBG and the RBI with its international network.

The three-stage Raiffeisen Banking Group, with nearly 500 Raiffeisen banks, is based on approximately 1.7 million members. The Raiffeisenbanks are owners of the eight Raiffeisenlandesbanks on a regional level, which in turn hold together with the Zveza Bank an approximately 90 % majority share of RZB, approximately 79 % are combined in the R-Landesbanken Beteiligung Ltd Other owners of RZB with more than a 2 % rate are the ÖVAG (4.84 %), UNIQA Versicherungen AG (insurance company) (2.53 %) and RWA Raiffeisen Ware Austria AG (agriculture) (2.40 %). While the RZB has been a corporation since its formation, four Raiffeisenlandesbanks converted from the cooperative form to a corporation in

[12] Austrian Raiffeisen Federation (2011, p. 13).

the last decade. At the level of the Raiffeisenbanks, nearly all institutes operate as cooperatives (AG).[13]

Both sectors, Volksbanks and Raiffeisenbanks, have coordinated their business in Central and Eastern Europe by companies in Vienna which hold the majority shares of subsidiaries operating as banking corporations in the different countries of the CEE.

At present, the Volksbanks have only kept the deficit business of Volksbank Romania. On the other hand, in 2010, Raiffeisen International was transformed from a holding to a bank regarding the entire international business and serves more than 15 million customers in Austria and abroad. The shares of this institute have been listed since April 2005 with approximately 39.9 % free float, as the RZB has reduced its shares. RBI's total assets represent about 85 % of unconsolidated assets of the RZB group.[14]

4 Reorganization and the Future of the Cooperative Banking Sectors

Both central cooperative banks, RZB and ÖVAG, hold subsidiaries concentrating on different fields of financial services. In the financial crisis, both institutes got governmental aid in 2009 and recently had to strengthen their capital.[15] Therefore, the banks have been reorganized.

The Raiffeisen International Bank-Holding AG (RI), Vienna, is the largest and fully consolidated subsidiary of the RZB, holding the banking subsidiaries in Central and Eastern Europe (CEE),[16] and its shares have been listed on the Vienna stock exchange since April 2005.

In February 2010, RZB and RI announced that they were considering a merger as a strategic option. This merger should bring RZB's principal business areas — above all, its business with Austrian and international corporate customers — together with those of the RI. The merged bank would be strengthened in its position as one of the leading universal banks in CEE through the combination of

[13] See RZB (2010, pp. 18, 22) and http://www.rzb.at/eBusiness/01_template1/831197035645054749-831197001285316293_831201177604143970-834060609795856814-NA-1-NA.html, online available at October 20, 2014.

[14] See Raiffeisen Bank International (2013, p. 3) and RZB (2013, p. 153).

[15] Raiffeisen paid the capital aid back in 2014.

[16] The predecessor of RI for the purposes of company law was founded back in 1991. The name before 2003 was Raiffeisen International Beteiligungs AG. After the fall of the Berlin Wall (1989) Raiffeisen systematically expanded its presence in the countries of Central and Eastern Europe (CEE). The first banking subsidiary was founded in Hungary almost back in 1986 and started its operations 1987. Starting in 1999, the retail business with private individuals and small and medium-sized customers was added. With its network in CEE RI is one of the region's leading banking groups.

the Raiffeisen International's broad distribution network in the CEE region and RZB's comprehensive product portfolio and would have broad access to capital markets to fulfil further capital needs.[17] At the end of 2009, the RI-group served more than 15 million customers. The bank would remain listed on the Vienna Stock Exchange and would be active primarily in the areas of retail (in CEE), corporate and investment banking. The business associated with the RZB's function as central institution of the Austrian Raiffeisen banking group would continue to be conducted by the RZB. The shareholders at Raiffeisen International's general meeting on July 8, 2010 provided their approval for the merger of Cembra and RI in the way of a universal succession on the record date of 31 December, 2009. The shareholders also approved the associated share capital increase and the merger agreement.[18]

Since these transactions have been completed, the free float of Raiffeisen Bank International, which continues to be listed on the Vienna Stock Exchange, is around 21.5 %; Raiffeisen International's free float had stood at around 27.2 % and RZB's indirect shareholding in Raiffeisen Bank International amount to approximately 78.5 %. Previously, RZB's indirect shareholding in Raiffeisen International had stood at approximately 72.8 %. Those business segments and shareholdings associated with RZB's role as the central institution of the Austrian Raiffeisen banking group are not influenced by these steps and will remain incomplete in the RZB that will concentrate on customers' and service needs of the regional the Raiffeisen banks. RZB sharpens its profile as the central institute of the decentralized Raiffeisen banks in Austria and will be the interface in the liquidity reserve holdings of the affiliated institutions of the Raiffeisen banking group and will continue to hold the key subsidiaries of group interest, for example, Raiffeisen Capital Management (RCM), UNIQA Insurance or Raiffeisen Invest. The RBI should join the common liquidity compensation and belong to this system, too.[19]

Since 2015, there are discussions about a possible sale of some Eastern Europe banking activities. Although a more intense co-operation between the RZB, RBI and Raiffeisenlandesbank Niederösterreich-Wien is quite thinkable.

5 Development in Progress

As has been demonstrated above, Austrian credit co-operatives have been facing difficult times recently. Part of this development might be due to the well-known fact that central organisations of federative networks tend to be over-expansive in order to gain ground against the pressure from below (that is from their strongest member organisations).

[17] See Cembra Beteiligungs AG/Raiffeisen International Bank-Holding AG (2010, p. 17).

[18] See Raiffeisen International (2010).

[19] See Blisse and Zeitlberger (2010, pp. 241f.).

At the moment, the two central cooperative banks are preparing further steps: The RZB Group has to meet higher regulatory capital requirements, form two Institutional Protection Schemes in accordance with European regulations[20] and pay back the capital aid by the state. Those tasks, which the ÖVAG had to perform, because they were legal obligations in the context of the Volksbanken guarantee-system were transferred to Volksbank Wien-Baden. The service functions of the ÖVAG that are necessary for an organised banking activity were also transferred to the above mentioned. The number of Volksbanks should be reduced to eight Volksbanks and two specialized banks. This could be seen as a contribution to the 'consolidation' in the Austrian banking market. However, it would reduce the cooperative character of the Volksbanken sector, because the remaining institutes would operate as corporations. Holding cooperatives would become owners of the banks and therefore would indirectly represent the former members of the Volksbanks.

References

Anonymous (2012) Sieben Prozent der Ostkredite der Banken wackeln. In: Wirtschaftsblatt, 25.01., p 3

Austrian Raiffeisen Federation (Österreichischer Raiffeisenverband) (2011) Raiffeisen in Austria. In: IRU Courier, No 2 (December), pp 13–17. Available at: http://www.iru.de/wp-content/uploads/2011/03/IRU-2011-2-en.pdf. Accessed 20 Oct 2014

Baltzarek F (1986) Die geschichtliche Entwicklung der österreichischen Genossenschaften. In: Patera M (ed) Handbuch des österreichischen Genossenschaftswesens. Orac, Wien, pp 3–114

Blisse H, Zeitlberger R (2010) Weiterentwicklung des Konzerns der Raiffeisen Zentralbank Österreich AG. In: Zeitschrift für das gesamte Genossenschaftswesen, 60. Jg., S 236–242

Böck N, Fleischhacker W, Simhandl L (2012) Österreichs Kreditinstitute im Jahr 2010. In: Bank-Archiv—Zeitschrift für das gesamte Bank- und Börsenwesen, 60. Jg., pp 209–216

Brazda J (ed) (2001) 150 Jahre Volksbanken in Österreich. Schulze-Delitzsch-Schriftenreihe, Bd 23. Wien

Brazda J, Blisse H (2010) Veränderungen an der Spitze—Zur Neuordnung der genossenschaftlichen Bankenverbünde Österreichs. In: Zeitschrift für das gesamte Kreditwesen, 63. Jg., pp 1096–1098

Brazda J, Todev T (2001) Die gewerblichen Kreditgenossenschaften in der Donaumonarchie. In: Brazda J (ed) 150 Jahre Volksbanken in Österreich. Schulze-Delitzsch-Schriftenreihe, Bd 23. Wien, pp 5–131

Brazda J, Schediwy R, Todev T (1997) Selbsthilfe oder politisierte Wirtschaft—Zur Geschichte des Österreichischen Genossenschaftsverbandes (Schulze-Delitzsch) 1872–1997. Schulze-Delitzsch-Schriftenreihe, Bd 18. Wien

Brazda J, Dellinger M, Rößl D (eds) (2013) Genossenschaften im Fokus einer neuen Wirtschaftspolitik Bericht der XVII. Internationalen Genossenschaftswissenschaftlichen Tagung (IGT) 2012 in Wien, Teilband I: Hauptvorträge und Podiumsdiskussionen. Wien

Bruckmüller E, Werner W (Eds for Österreichischer Raiffeisenverband) (1998) Raiffeisen in Österreich—Siegeszug einer Idee. St. Pölten

[20] See Dellinger (2013).

Bundesministerium für Justiz (1997) Reform des Genossenschaftsrechts—Enquete des Bundesministeriums für Justiz, Salzburg, 31. Jänner 1997. Schriftenreihe des Bundesministeriums für Justiz, No. 87. Wien

Cembra Beteiligungs AG/Raiffeisen International Bank-Holding AG (2010) Gemeinsamer Verschmelzungsbericht der Vorstände der Cembra Beteiligungs AG und der Raiffeisen International Bank-Holding AG über die Verschmelzung der Cembra Beteiligungs AG mit der Raiffeisen International Bank-Holding AG (29.05.2010), Vienna. Available at: http://investor.rbinternational.com/fileadmin/ir/20100530_Verschmelzungsbericht_signed_Deutsch.pdf. Accessed 20 Oct, 2014

Dellinger M (ed) (2005) Genossenschaftsgesetz samt Nebengesetzen Kommentar. LexisNexis, Wien

Dellinger M (2013) Bankaufsichtsrecht, Kreditgenossenschaftsverbund und Sorgfaltspflicht der Organe. In: Brazda J, Dellinger M, Rößl D (eds) Genossenschaften im Fokus einer neuen Wirtschaftspolitik Bericht der XVII. Internationalen Genossenschaftswissenschaftlichen Tagung (IGT) 2012 in Wien, Teilband I: Hauptvorträge und Podiumsdiskussionen. Wien, pp 161–177

Frasl EJ, Haiden RA, Taus J (eds) (2007) Österreichs Kreditwirtschaft—Von der Reichsmark über den Schilling zum Euro. Neuer Wissenschaftlicher Verlag, Wien

Frasl EJ, Haiden RA, Taus J (eds) (2009) Österreichs Kreditwirtschaft in der Weltfinanzkrise—Fakten, Analysen, Perspektiven und Chancen. Neuer Wissenschaftlicher Verlag, Wien

Grabner R (2012a) Volksbanken verkaufen Flügel und Freiheit. In: Der Standard, 14.02. Available at: http://derstandard.at/1328507757495/Sberbank-Deal-Volksbanken-verkaufen-Fluegel-und-Freiheit. Accessed 20 Oct 2014

Grabner R (2012b) ÖVAG nimmt Volksbanken an kurzen Zügel. In: Der Standard, 01.03. Available at: http://derstandard.at/1330390151672/Schlechtes-Erwachen-OeVAG-nimmt-Volksbanken-an-kurzen-Zuegel. Accessed 20 Oct 2014

Hofinger H (2007) Der Volksbanken-Verbund seit 1945. In: Frasl EJ, Haiden RA, Taus J (eds) Österreichs Kreditwirtschaft—Von der Reichsmark über den Schilling zum Euro. Wien, S 65–96

Hofinger H (2009) Die Zukunft der genossenschaftlichen Volksbanken. In: Frasl EJ, Haiden RA, Taus J (eds) Österreichs Kreditwirtschaft in der Weltfinanzkrise—Fakten, Analysen, Perspektiven und Chancen. Wien, S 103–124

Kastner W (1986) Österreichisches Genossenschaftsrecht. In: Patera M (ed) Handbuch des österreichischen Genossenschaftswesens. Orac, Wien, pp 117–229

Keinert H (1988) Genossenschaftsrecht—Lehr- und Handbuch. Manz, Wien

Kischko I, Trummer P (2012) Volksbanken vor Zerreißprobe. In: Kurier, 17.01. Available at: http://kurier.at/wirtschaft/unternehmen/4481454-volksbanken-vor-zerreissprobe.php. Accessed 20 Oct 2014

Österreichische Bankwissenschaftliche Gesellschaft (ed) (1968) Das Kreditwesen in Österreich. Festschrift für Hans Krasensky—Zum 65. Geburtstag. Wien

Österreichischer Genossenschaftsverband (Schulze-Delitzsch) (ÖGV) (2000, 2005, 2010–2011) Jahresbericht. Wien

Raiffeisen International (2010) Raiffeisen International's Annual General Meeting Approves Merger, press release of July 8, 2010. Available at: http://www.rbinternational.com/eBusiness/rzb_template2/6772264136645151 43-677226413664515144_677923699994573261_681488699556356605-681487912235163959-NA-10-EN.html. Accessed 2 Feb 2012

Raiffeisen Bank International (2013) Annual Report 2013. Vienna. Available at: http://investor.rbinternational.com/fileadmin/ir/2013_FY/2014-03-27_2013_Annual_Report_RBI.pdf. Accessed 20 Oct 2014

Raiffeisen Zentralbank Österreich (2005) Geschäftsbericht 2005 (Vorabdruck). Wien. Available at: http://www.rzb.at/eBusiness/services/resources/media/677043205476211500-677043205476211501_679789700419741890_679796905764258277-302213974893454763-1-9-DE.pdf. Accessed 7 Feb 2012

Raiffeisen Zentralbank Österreich (2010–2012) Geschäftsbericht. Wien. Available at: http://www.rzb.at/eBusiness/01_template1/831197035645054749-831197001285316293_831201035333351966-831201035333351966-NA-1-NA.html. Accessed on 21 Jan 2014

Raiffeisen Zentralbank Österreich (2013) Jahresfinanzbericht 2013. Wien. Available at: http://www.rzb.at/eBusiness/services/resources/media/831197035645054749-831197001285316293_831201035333351966-985037425275370825-1-1-NA.pdf. Accessed 20 Oct 2014

Rothensteiner W (2007) Die Raiffeisenbanken Gruppe Österreich—Erfolg durch Dezentralität und Internationalität. In: Frasl, EJ, Haiden RA, Taus J (eds) Österreichs Kreditwirtschaft—Von der Reichsmark über den Schilling zum Euro. NWV Neuer wissenschaftlicher Verlag, Wien, S 109–124

Schaschko M (2010) Neugründungen von Genossenschaften in Österreich. Wiener Studien des Forschungsvereins für Genossenschaftswesen, Neue Folge, Bd 18. Eigenverlag des FOG, Wien

Schediwy R (2001) Die gewerblichen Kreditgenossenschaften in der Zwischenkriegszeit. In: Brazda J (ed) (2001) 150 Jahre Volksbanken in Österreich. Schulze-Delitzsch-Schriftenreihe, Bd 23. Wien

Todev T, Brazda J (2001) Die Volksbanken in Österreich seit 1945. In: Brazda J (ed) (2001) 150 Jahre Volksbanken in Österreich. Schulze-Delitzsch-Schriftenreihe, Bd 23. Wien

Werner W (2005) Auf der Straße des Erfolges—Zur Geschichte der österreichischen Raiffeisenbewegung von kleinen Ortsgenossenschaften zu international tätigen Netzwerken. Kooperation und Wettbewerb, Bd 4. Rainer Hampp Verlag, München, Mering

Co-operative Credit Institutions in Cyprus

Akis Kleanthous and Athanasios Hadjimanolis

Abstract Co-operative Credit Institutions, in Cyprus, were created in 1909 to save people from usurers and loan sharks, and have grown ever since. As a result of the financial crisis of 2013, and the subsequent lending of Cyprus by Troika, Co-operative financial institutions were forced to merge reducing their number from 100 to just 18 while 99 % of their ownership was passed to the Cypriot state as exchange for a capital injection of 1.5 billion euros and their supervision was passed from the Co-operative Societies Supervision and Development Authority to the Central Bank of Cyprus. Additionally, the Independent Commission on the Future of the Cyprus Banking Sector recommends the merge of all 18 Co-operative institutions to a single legal entity and its disposal to a foreign bank. It is the author's view that, if this happens, the true non-for-profit nature of Co-operative financial institutions will change and their members and the greater society will suffer, as the counterweight to investor owned banks that keeps them in balance will be removed.

1 The Establishment and Evolution of the Credit Cooperative System

The Co-operative movement in Cyprus was created later than in the rest of Europe because of the low education that farmers had and the lack of initial capital (Argyridou-Dimitriou and Kanaris 2012). The foundation of the Co-operative movement in the early twentieth century was the most effective reaction of the Cypriot society against the social and economic suppression of people and especially against usury (CSSDA 2014a). The long period of foreign ruling had its toll

A. Kleanthous (✉)
University of Glasgow, Glasgow, UK
e-mail: a.kleanthous.1@research.gla.ac.uk

A. Hadjimanolis
European University Cyprus, Nicosia, Cyprus
e-mail: a.hadjimanolis@euc.ac.cy

S. Karafolas (ed.), *Credit Cooperative Institutions in European Countries*, Contributions to Economics, DOI 10.1007/978-3-319-28784-3_2

on the Cypriot society, which created a social system that was against any individual initiative (CSSDA 2014a). Commercial banks were not willing to lend farmers (consisting the 80 % of population in 1881) because of the difficulty in selling the mortgaged property, thus leaving farmers in the hands of usurers who charged interest rates of 30–40 % instead of the legal rate of 9 % (Argyridou-Dimitriou and Kanaris 2012). Under these difficult conditions, the anthropocentric Co-operative idea played an important role both in the economic development and the social progress of Cypriots (CSSDA 2014a).

The first Co-operative company was set up in 1909 with the founding of the "Rural Bank of Lefkoniko" (CSSDA 2014a), aiming at providing short and longer term financing for agricultural purposes (Argyridou-Dimitriou and Kanaris 2012). Its founders were Mr. Ioannis Economides, the Director of the Bank of Cyprus, and Mr. Markos Charalambous, the headmaster of the elementary school of Lefkoniko (Clerides 1947, p. 5). At the beginning, it was feared that the Raiffeisen Credit System would not be effective in Cyprus due to the spendthrift, the illiteracy and the customization of people in being over indebted. Despite this fear, Co-operatives were created according to the Raiffeisen Credit System, as it was very successful in other countries (Clerides 1947, p. 6). This is because the members of credit unions, based on the Raiffeisen model, were generally poor and they had smaller, more seasonal and thus more unpredictable income (Guinnane 1994). Commercial banks were unwilling to service people in rural areas due to the small size of the loans involved, the high cost involved in monitoring their loans and the extreme difficulty in selling the property that was used as collateral (Guinnane 1994). This, rendered the repayment of the loans on fixed loan instalments very difficult, while the Raiffeisen model relied on the strong feelings of solidarity among villagers to put pressure on borrowers to repay and reduce the information asymmetry (on villager's character, competence and on the way money was spend) (Guinnane 1994).

Despite the law of 1914 (Law no. 13 "for Co-operative Financial Institutions"), the development of the Co-operative movement was minimal due to the lack of capital and educated people (CSSDA 2014a). In 1923, a new law was passed providing for the founding of new non-financial Co-operative companies (CSSDA 2014a), but again without any significant change. During the same period, the British ruler gave a loan of UK£20,000 to facilitate the development of Co-operatives and in 1925 the Agricultural Bank was founded, by the British ruler, in an effort to ease the financial problems that the First World War had created (CSSDA 2014a). These loans were granted through the Co-operative institutions, something that led to the steady increase in the number of Co-operatives from 24 in 1924 to 273 in 1935 (CSSDA 2014a). In 1937, the Co-operative Central Bank was founded, aiming to create capital for the Co-operative movement and to become self-financed, by borrowing from the wealthy and lending to the weaker Co-operative institutions (CSSDA 2014a). In addition, the Co-operative Central Bank acted as the government representative for the financing of various developmental agricultural programmes (CSSDA 2014a).

Table 1 Evolution of number of co-operative societies and their membership for the period 1925–1960

Year	No. of societies	Membership
1925	29	500
1930	326	10,000
1935	276	15,175
1938	282	21,172
1940	264	30,950
1947	413	59,000
1950	446	69,000
1955	484	87,300
1960	588	109,800

Taken from Phylaktis (1995, p. 32)

The number of Co-operative Credit Institutions and their membership for the period 1925–1960 can be seen in Table 1:

After Cyprus' independence, in 1960, and until the withdrawal from the government of the Turkish-Cypriot community, there were two Co-operative Development Departments, one for each community (Argyridou-Dimitriou and Kanaris 2012). Up until 1974, the Co-operative movement grew rapidly and contributed enormously to the development of the society and the economy of the new state (Argyridou-Dimitriou and Kanaris 2012). The Turkish invasion, in 1974, left Cyprus in a devastating situation and Co-operatives took a leading role in raising social cohesion and in providing for the housing of the one third of the population that was displaced by the Turkish army (even though 225 Co-operative societies were directly affected as well) (CSSDA 2014a; Argyridou-Dimitriou and Kanaris 2012). As part of the effort, the Co-operative Central Bank financed the founding of new industrial and construction Co-operatives but because of the financial situation and the poverty, these went bankrupt. Therefore, the Co-operative movement was assisted financially by the Cyprus government (with a loan of CY£17.8 million) and the commercial banks (with a loan of CY£4.5 million) or combined: 3 % of Cyprus's GDP of 1980 (Phylaktis 1995). The Co-operative movement was assisted again in late 1980s by obtaining a support package of CY£67 million (or 3 % of Cyprus's GDP in 1989) which was repaid in 2006 (Argyridou-Dimitriou and Kanaris 2012). The Co-operative Societies' Supervision and Development Authority (CSSDA) was created in 1935 under the Ministry of Commerce, Industry and Tourism and, in July 2003 [Co-operative Societies Law of 1985–2011, Law 123(I)/2003], it became independent (Argyridou-Dimitriou and Kanaris 2012). Following the creation of CSSDA, the government decided for the Co-operative Societies Supervision and Development Authority (CSSDA) to supervise the Co-operative societies and, for the Central Bank of Cyprus to supervise the Co-operative Central Bank (Argyridou-Dimitriou and Kanaris 2012).

Since the Co-operatives Act of 1985(22/1985), Co-operative Credit Institutions enjoyed some privileges, i.e. exemptions from stamp duties and mortgage- registry fees, but these were abolished in 2003 [Co-operative Reform Law 124(I)/2003] (Co-operative Central Bank 2014d).

The first legal framework for Co-operatives was put in place, in 1914, with the Co-operative Companies' Law of 1914 "Law 13 regarding the Co-operative Credit Companies" (CSSDA 2014b). In 1985, the law was updated based on Law 22/1985 which subsequently changed several times to improve its effectiveness and to keep it updated (CSSDA 2014b). It is further noted that the Co-operative Special Institutions ("*Θεσμοί*") are prepared by the Council of Ministers and are approved by the Parliament (CSSDA 2014b).

Today, the Co-operative Credit Institutions are governed by the Co-operative Companies' Laws of 1985–2014, the Co-operative Companies' Special Institutions of 1985–2012, and the instructions, decrees and circulars of the Commissioner of the Co-operative Societies Supervision and Development Authority, which regulate all matters that relate to their registration and operation of Co-operative Societies (CSSDA 2014b). However, based on the "Business of Credit Institutions Law of 1997 to (No. 4) of 2013", Co-operative Credit Institutions are under the supervision of the Central Bank of Cyprus for issues such as their licensing, regulation and supervision (CSSDA 2014b).

2 The Current Model

Co-operative Credit Institutions in Cyprus offer the full range of banking products including loans (housing, student, consumer and commercial), deposits, current and overdraft accounts (with or without cheque book), debit and credit cards, internet banking, ATMs, foreign currency, wire transfers, insurance, etc. The operations of Co-operative Credit Institutions are limited within Cyprus and they have no presence abroad. Presently, there is no European Credit Institution (SCE) that operates in Cyprus.

The Co-operative Central Bank acts as the banker for all registered Co-operative companies and as the central banker for the Co-operative Credit Institutions and hence, as lender of the last resort for the Co-operative Credit Institutions, provides liquidity and general support (CSSDA 2010).

Following the accession of Cyprus in the EU in 2004, the Co-operative movement had to adopt a number of reforms in order to comply with the European acquis and be able to continue to function as Credit Institutions (Argyridou-Dimitriou and Kanaris 2012). Furthermore, in response to the EU Directive 2006/48/EC, Article 3, on 1 January 2008, all but one Co-operative Credit Institutions were permanently affiliated to the Central Body (role performed by the Co-operative Central Bank) (Argyridou-Dimitriou and Kanaris 2012). The role of the Central Body is to guarantee 100 % of the deposits and the other commitments of Co-operative Credit Institutions, to satisfy in a consolidated manner the operating requirements (liquidity and solvency ratios) in order to continue operating as Credit Institutions (CSSDA 2010) and to issue instructions to the institutions that are permanently affiliated to it.

In recent years, the adverse financial conditions that were created by the financial crisis of 2008 led the Cyprus government to apply to the *European Stability Mechanism* (*ESM*) (CSSDA 2014a). Based on the obligations that the Cyprus government undertook due to the Memorandum of Understanding, in December 2012 and April 2013, the restructuring of the Co-operative Financial Sector was necessary (CSSDA 2014a). This restructuring plan included the reduction of the number of Credit Unions to 18 (up to the 14th of March 2014), the recapitalization of the Co-operative Financial Sector by 1.5 billion euros through government bonds and further structural and other changes (CSSDA 2014a). The recapitalization of the Co-operative Financial Sector was done by transferring 99 % of the shares in the Co-operative Central Bank to the government (CSSDA 2014a). According to the restructuring plan, the Credit Unions, have the right to buy back their shares from the state by repaying the 1.5 billion euros plus 10 % interest per annum (CSSDA 2014a).

2.1 Minimum Capital Required for the Establishment and Function of a Cooperative Bank

In 2006, Cyprus aligned with the European Law regarding the creation of the European Co-operative Company (SCE) (1435/2003 of 22 July 2003) (CSSDA 2014b).

Following "The business of Credit Institutions Laws of 1997 to (No. 3) 2013", the Co-operative Special Institutions of 2000–2009 regarding the creation and operation of the "Fund for the Protection of Deposits" were abolished and the Fund itself was taken under the supervision of the "Deposit Protection and Resolution of Credit and Other Institutions Scheme"(CSSDA 2014b). It is now governed by a Committee comprised by employees of the Central Bank of Cyprus and the Ministry of Finance (CSSDA 2014b).

According to the unofficial consolidation and translation of "The business of Credit Institutions Laws of 1997 to (No. 3) 2013", the licensing, regulation and supervision of Co-operative Financial Institutions are exercised by the Central Bank of Cyprus and not by the CSSDA as was the case before 9 September 2013 (Central Bank of Cyprus 2013b). Additionally, since 2013 in order to be granted a license, the Credit Institution must have at least 5,000,000 € as its own funds (paid in share capital), in line with the "The business of Credit Institutions Laws of 1997 to (No. 3) 2013" and not only 1,000,000 € {#41.B.(1)(a)(i)} as was previously the case (based on "the Co-operative Companies' Laws of 1985–2012") (Central Bank of Cyprus 2013b).

Additionally, according to the Memorandum of Understanding, the Central Bank of Cyprus had to introduce a minimum of 4 % for the Core Tier 1 capital requirements ratio for the individual Co-operative Credit Institutions that will be affiliated to the Central Body, while on a consolidated level, the Co-operative sector has to have at least a 9 % Core Tier 1 capital requirements ratio (Ministry of Finance 2014).

2.2 State Tax Policy and Way Credit Cooperatives Distribute Surpluses

Types of Co-operative Institutions
According to the Law, the various types of Co-operative institutions are the following:

(a) First Level Co-operative company: members can only be physical persons (at least twelve people)
(b) Second Level Co-operative Company: its members could be (a) at least 12 physical persons and one first level Co-operative Company or (b) at least five First level Co-operative companies.
(c) Third Level Co-operative Company: its members should contain at least one Second level Co-operative Company (CSSDA 2014a).

For example, Co-operative Credit Institutions can only be first level Co-operative companies whereas, the Co-operative Central Bank is a third level Co-operative Company as at least one of its members is a second level Co-operative Company (Co-operative Central Bank 2014c). According to CSSDA (2010), the members of the Co-operative Central Bank are exclusively Co-operative Credit Institutions (286 at 31 December 2009) and each member has one vote.

Taxation
Co-operative Credit Institutions pay tax at the normal company rates on the profits that are attributable to their operations with their members (taxable profits are usually apportioned based on the value of members' activity in relation to the total activity for the year).

Maximum Percentage of Ownership
According to the Co-operative Companies' Special Institutions of 1987–2012 (#23), no physical person, can own more than 20 % of the shares of a registered Co-operative company.

Registration of Members
All physical persons can become members of any Co-operative company, as long as they fulfil the criteria of "common bond" (or "bond of association"), i.e. are older than 18 years old and are residents or are the owners of property in the area in which the specific Credit Union is operating (CSSDA 2014a).

Internal Structures
The Co-operative companies are independent organisations and are managed by the Board of Directors which is elected by the members every 3 years during the General Meeting (CSSDA 2014a). The members of the Board of Directors offer their services voluntarily, without any payment (CSSDA 2014a). The election of the members of the Board of Directors of the Credit Unions is governed by the corporate governance rules that were agreed upon during the Memorandum of Understanding between the Cypriot government and Troika (CSSDA 2014a).

Investment of Funds

According to the Co-operative Companies' Special Institutions of 1987–2012 (CSSDA 2012a), Co-operative Credit Institutions can:

(a) deposit their cash in the Co-operative Central Bank and, being granted permission by the Commissioner of CSSDA, to any other bank or registered company.
(b) to invest, being granted permission by the Commissioner of CSSDA, in shares of listed companies or any other company.
(c) to invest, being granted permission by the Commissioner of CSSDA, in Government Bonds,
(d) to buy, renovate or expand its immovable property or buy movable property

Distribution of Surpluses

According to "the Co-operative Companies' Laws of 1985–2012" [#41.(1)], at least 50 % of the surplus should be transferred to the capital reserves. Part of the surplus is returned/ distributed to the members in the form of dividends, based on the number of shares each member has or in the form of dividends according to the value of each member's transactions with the company (CSSDA 2014a). According to the Co-operative Companies' Special Institutions of 1987–2012 [#24(2)] (CSSDA 2012a), the maximum amount of dividend to be distributed is specified in the Special Articles, of the specific institution.

According to the Law, in the case of dissolution of a Co-operative institution, the members which are physical persons are not entitled to any part of the reserves (CSSDA 2014a). These reserves could be used only to create a new Co-operative institution, which will operate within the same area and which will have the same operations as the dissolved institution (CSSDA 2014a). Additionally, any remaining reserves could be used for philanthropic or public purposes (CSSDA 2014a).

In the case of dissolution of a secondary or third level company, the reserves could be distributed to the Co-operative companies that are members, in accordance to the Special Articles of the dissolved company (CSSDA 2014a). Furthermore, it is noted that, after the financial crisis of 2013, the distribution of the surplus of the Credit Unions is dealt by the Restructuring Plan of the Co-operative Financial Sector which was agreed on the Memorandum of Understanding between the Cyprus government and Troika (CSSDA 2014a).

3 The Importance of the Credit Co-operative System in the National Banking Market

The significance of the Co-operatives for the economy of Cyprus was identified even by Troika in the Memorandum of Understanding of 13 September 2013 where it is stated that: "*1.14. Cooperative credit institutions have played a significant role in the domestic economy and an important objective of the programme is to strengthen the regulation and supervision of the cooperative sector*" (Ministry of Finance 2014, p. 4).

Phylaktis (1995, p. 38) states that the Co-operative Credit Institutions were important for the Cyprus economy as they "*undoubtedly contributed to the economic and social improvements of the farmers on the island*" and that this was done because Co-operative Credit Institutions had good knowledge of their customers, which resulted from the "*very nature of their structure*". Additionally, Co-operative Credit Institutions encouraged farmers to save money no matter how poor they were and rendered them more self-determined to confront hardships without depending on anyone else's assistance (Phylaktis 1995, p. 38).

According to Rabobank (2008), Co-operative Credit Institutions in Cyprus play an important role in the local banking sector as they have a considerable share of local deposits and loans. Additionally, Co-operative Credit Institutions have presence almost in every town and village of the island and have a network of 500 branches and outlets (Rabobank 2008).

However, the number of Co-operative Credit Institutions has declined sharply since 2005 mainly because of the mergers among themselves following the accession of Cyprus in the EU and the need to comply with the minimum requirements imposed by the EU. More specifically, based on the common position of the European Union and Cyprus, Co-operative Credit Institutions in Cyprus needed to align with the European acquis, which meant changes in their structure and their way of operating as well as merging on a geographical or operational basis (CSSDA 2010). The mergers were necessary to bring Co-operative Credit Institutions up to date and to enable them to face the increased competition from the liberation of the financial system in Cyprus (CSSDA 2010). Additionally, the mergers would facilitate the restructuring and the strengthening of Co-operative Credit Institutions enabling them to operate more efficiently and compete more effectively (CSSDA 2010). Moreover, according to the Memorandum of Understanding, the number of Co-operative Credit Institutions had, by March 2014, to be reduced to the maximum of 18 entities (Ministry of Finance 2014) something that has been achieved. In case that recapitalized Co-operative Credit Institutions become unviable, then these would be merged even further with viable ones (Ministry of Finance 2014). Troika requested that the injection of the capital needed to recapitalize the Co-operative Credit Institutions will be done by the Co-operative Central Bank (using the 1.5 billion euros that obtained from the Cyprus government) only once the mergers are completed (Ministry of Finance 2014). Troika stated that the mergers of Co-operative Credit Institutions were designed to "*achieve viability, efficiency and profitability*" (Ministry of Finance 2014). The Independent Commission on the future of the Cyprus banking sector stated that the number of Co-operative Credit Institutions has indeed been reduced drastically from around 90 to just 18, in an attempt to consolidate the sector and to eliminate the non-viable ones (Central Bank of Cyprus 2013a). Additionally, the Independent Commission's opinion about the future of the Cyprus banking sector is that the remaining 18 remaining Co-operative Credit Institutions should be merged further, into a single entity creating a group of companies (Central Bank of Cyprus 2013a).

Table 2 Evolution of number of Co-operative Credit Institutions in period 1998–2013

	1998	1999	2000	2001	2002	2003	2004	2005	2006
Number of Co-op Credit Institutions	361 (1)	359 (1)	360 (1)	363 (1)	363 (1)	N/A	360 (2)	347 (2)	293 (2)
	2007	2008	2009	2010	2011	2012	2013		
Number of Co-op Credit Institutions	170 (3)	118 (2)	111 (2)	110 (3)	101 (4)		18 (5)		

The table was compiled by the author using data from the Annual Reports of the Commissioner of CSSDA and the final report of the Independent Commission on the future of the Cyprus banking sector

(1): CSSDA Annual Report for 2000- 2002 (page 8, 18)
(2) CSSDA Annual Report for 2003- 2009 (page 58)
(3) CSSDA Annual Report for 2010 (page 69)
(4) CSSDA Annual Report for 2011 (page 72)
(5) Central Bank of Cyprus, 2013a

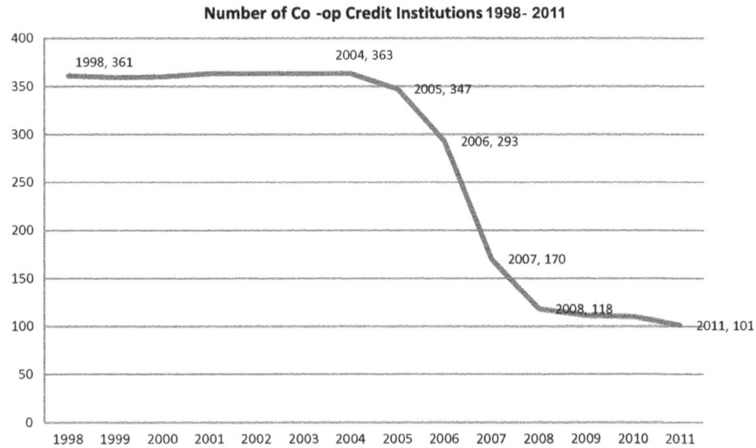

Fig. 1 Evolution of number of Co-operative Credit Institutions in period 1998–2013. *Source*: (1) CSSDA Annual Report for 2000–2002 (page 8, 18). (2) CSSDA Annual Report for 2003–2009 (page 58). (3) CSSDA Annual Report for 2010 (page 69). (4) CSSDA Annual Report for 2011 (page 72). (5) Central Bank of Cyprus (2013a)

The evolution of the number of Co-operative Credit Institutions in operation from 1998 to 2013 is shown in Table 2.

Additionally, the evolution of the number of Co-operative Credit Institutions for the period 1998–2011 is shown in Fig. 1.

Co-operative Credit Institutions are significant in the banking sector of Cyprus having about 20 % of the market share of deposits and 10 % of total assets: locally and overseas (Argyridou-Dimitriou and Kanaris 2012) (Note: Co-operatives have only local presence). Additionally, based on the Annual Reports of the

Table 3 Evolution of Co-operative Credit Institutions' market share regarding local deposits and loans for the period 2004–2012

	Deposits	Loans
	Local market share (%)	Local market share (%)
2004	26.27	26.06
2005	22.96	26.37
2006	22.81	21.70
2007	20.00	22.00
2008	19.00	16.00
2009	22.00	19.50
2010	19.34	20.35
2011	20.64	19.53
2012	21.60	19.20

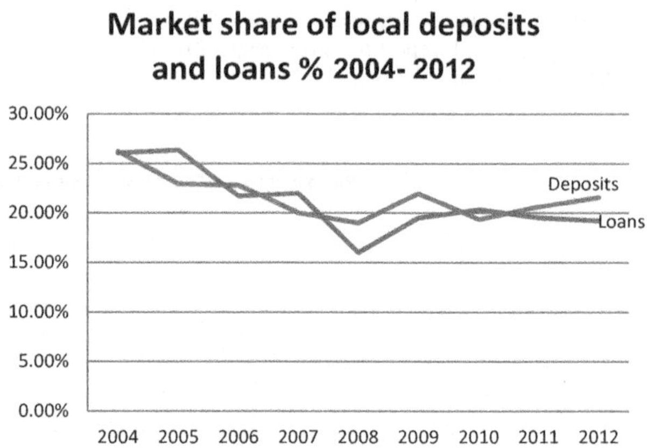

Fig. 2 Evolution of Co-operative Credit Institutions' market share regarding local deposits and loans for the period 2004–2012

Commissioner of CSSDA and the EACB, Co-operative Credit Institutions are very important for the Cyprus economy as they represent around 20 % of the deposits and the domestic loans.

Table 3 and Fig. 2 show the market share of Co-operative Credit Institutions for the years 2004–2012 (Note: data were compiled by the author using data from the EACB website and specifically "Key Figures on the Sector" tables).

The Co-operative Credit Institutions' Deposits, Loans and total assets evolution can be found in Table 4:

According to the Independent Commission on the Future of the Cyprus Banking Sector (Central Bank of Cyprus 2013a), Co-operative Credit Institutions amount to 18 % of the local market share with local commercial banks holding 72 % share and foreign banks that operate locally holding the remaining 10 % share (see Fig. 3). Currently, the banking sector in Cyprus is "*undergoing what is possibly the most severe banking crisis of any country in the EU*" (Central Bank of Cyprus 2013a). Following the collapse of the Cypriot banking sector in 2012, the local banks in Cyprus are undergoing restructuring and recapitalization with the support of the Cyprus government and "uninsured" deposits of customers, in line with a rescue plan agreed with Troika (IMF, ECB and EU) (Central Bank of Cyprus 2013a).

Table 4 Evolution of Co-operative Credit Institutions' deposits and loans in Euros and as market share for the period 1965–2012

Year	Deposits €'000	Deposits Cy market share (%)	Loans €'000	Loans Cy market share (%)	Total assets €'000
1965 (1)	19,859		18,096		
1970 (1)	48,029		41,502		
1975 (1)	84,953		63,275		
1980 (1)	212,878		164,311		
1985 (1)	573,976		492,696		
1990 (1)	1,542,630		1,346,293		
1991 (1)	1,803,955		1,600,903		
1992 (1)	2,102,118		1,893,170		2,355,649
1993 (1)	2,421,532		2,170,660		2,703,349
1994 (1)	2,748,144		2,481,439		3,034,818
1995 (1)	3,076,173		2,821,560		3,398,921
1996 (1)	3,377,796		3,137,618		3,896,466
1997 (1)	3,735,922		3,401,894		4,302,296
1998 (1)	4,128,676		3,643,951		4,500,424
1999 (1)	4,392,280		4,118,095		4,957,299
2000 (1)	4,820,921		4,244,052		5,464,998
2001 (1)	5,312,179		4,304,133		5,975,926
2002 (1)	6,002,937		4,562,393		6,665,821
2003 (2)	6,810,259		5,035,345		N/A
2004 (5)	7,231,000	26.27	5,591,000	26.06	7,849,000
2005 (6)	7,957,000	22.96	6,169,000	26.37	8,448,000
2006 (2)	9,048,075	22.81	6,755,736	21.70	9,739,000
2007 (7)	9,048,000	20.00	6,756,000	22.00	9,739,000
2008 (3)	10,699,113	19.00	10,319,125	16.00	14,773,571
2009 (3)	12,778,512	22.00	11,657,609	19.50	19,068,816
2010 (3)	13,489,794	19.34	13,045,208	20.35	19,936,298
2011 (4)	14,228,868	20.64	13,901,499	19.53	20,766,413
2012 (8)	15,165,000	21.60	13,923,000	19.20	21,169,000

(1) CSSDA Annual Report for 2000–2002 (excludes Co-op Central Bank) (page 22)
(2) CSSDA Annual Report for 2003–2009 (excludes Co-op Central Bank) (page 16)
(3) CSSDA Annual Report for 2010 (includes Co-op Central Bank and ST Lemesou) (page 12)
(4) CSSDA Annual Report for 2011 (includes Co-op Central Bank and ST Lemesou) (page 13)
(5) EACB, Accessed on 14.7.14; https://www.globalcube.net/clients/eacb/content/medias/key_figures/Key_Statistics_2004.pdf
(6) EACB, Accessed on 14.7.14; https://www.globalcube.net/clients/eacb/content/medias/key_figures/Key_Statistics_2005.pdf
(7) EACB, Accessed on 14.7.14; https://www.globalcube.net/clients/eacb/content/medias/key_figures/Financial_Key_statistics_2007.pdf
(8) EACB, Accessed on 14.7.14; https://www.globalcube.net/clients/eacb/content/medias/key_figures/FINAL_Key_stats_2012_UPDATED-_financial_indicators.pdf

Fig. 3 Market share of total assets March 2013, taken from Central Bank of Cyprus (2013a)

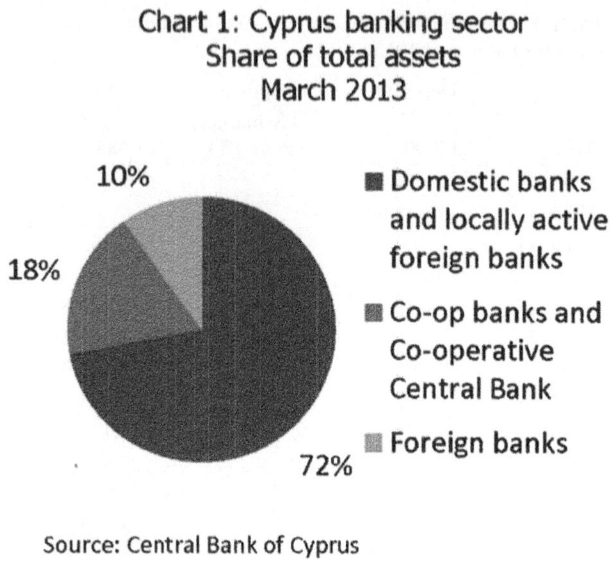

Fig. 4 Growth of domestic loans for period 2002–2012, taken from Central Bank of Cyprus (2013a)

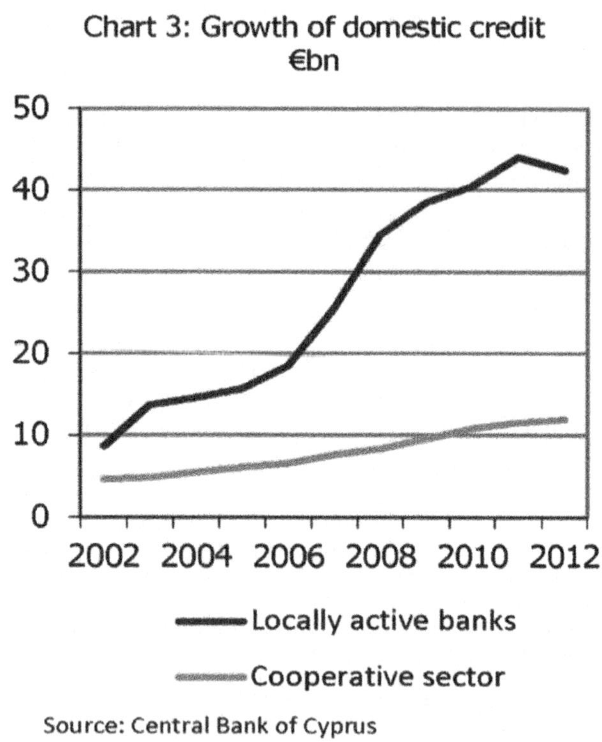

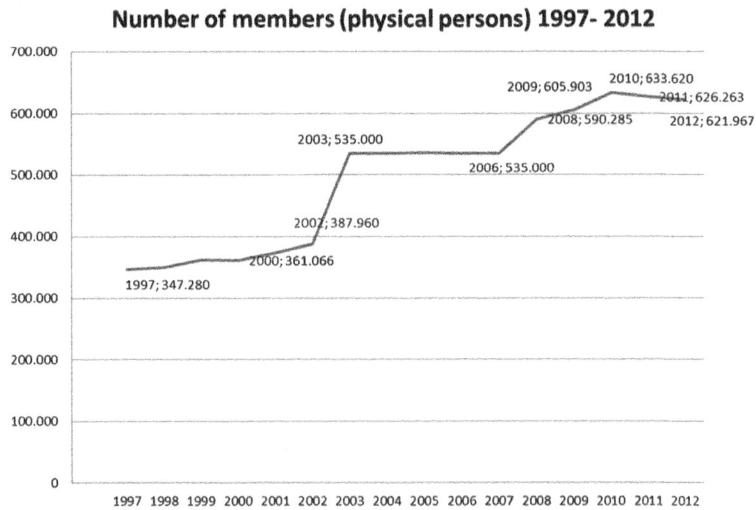

Fig. 5 Growth of membership numbers (physical persons) for the period 1997–2012, prepared by author

As can be seen in Fig. 4, Co-operative Credit Institutions, in contrast to the commercial banks, have not stopped lending even during the years 2010–2012.

The number of members (physical persons) in the Co-operative institutions, regardless of industry, in which they operate is shown (Table 4 and Fig. 5) as decreasing but this could also be due to the process of mergers through which the membership registers are verified and common members are left only once in the registry.

Table 5 shows the number of members (physical persons) in First Level Co-ops (all Co-ops not only Co-operative Credit Institutions), whereas Fig. 5 shows the growth of membership numbers (physical persons) for the period 1997–2012.

4 Crises Problems and Changes

In 2000, the Co-operative movement in Cyprus decided to align with the EU acquis and a transitional period was granted in order to comply fully with the regulatory provisions of the relevant European Union directives (Co-operative Central Bank 2014a). There were two options for the Co-operative movement: (a) each Co-operative Financial Institution would need to satisfy, on its own, the minimal criteria laid down by the relevant directives of the European Union or (b) to create a Central Body (a role that was undertaken by the Co-operative Central Bank) where all the Co-operative Financial Institutions and the Central Body together would have to meet the minimum requirements (Co-operative Central Bank 2014a). Cyprus chose the second option and thus, since 1 January 2008, all Co-operative

Table 5 Evolution of number of members for all first level co-operatives for the period 1990, 1997–2012

Year	1990	1997	1998	1999	2000
Number of members	302,330 (1)	347,280 (1)	350,500 (1)	362,000 (1)	361,066 (1)
Year	2001	2002	2003	2004	
Number of members	373,000 (1)	387,960 (1)	N/A	535 (2)	
Year	2005	2006	2007	2008	
Number of members	536 (3)	535,000 (4)	535,000 (5)	590,285 (6)	
Year	2009	2010	2011	2012	
Number of members	605,903 (7)	633,620 (8)	626,263 (9)	621,967 (10)	

The table was compiled by the author using data from the Annual Reports of the Commissioner of CSSDA (for years 1990–2002) and the EACB Key Figures on the sector tables (for years 2004–2012)

(1) CSSDA Annual Report for 2000–2002 (page 22)

(2) EACB, Accessed on 14.7.14; https://www.globalcube.net/clients/eacb/content/medias/key_figures/Key_Statistics_2004.pdf

(3) EACB, Accessed on 14.7.14; https://www.globalcube.net/clients/eacb/content/medias/key_figures/Key_Statistics_2005.pdf

(4) EACB, Accessed on 14.7.14; https://www.globalcube.net/clients/eacb/content/medias/key_figures/Key_Statistics_2006.pdf

(5) EACB, Accessed on 14.7.14; https://www.globalcube.net/clients/eacb/content/medias/key_figures/Financial_Key_statistics_2007.pdf

(6) EACB, Accessed on 14.7.14; https://www.globalcube.net/clients/eacb/content/medias/key_figures/Key_statistics_Financial_Indicators_2008.pdf

(7) EACB, Accessed on 14.7.14; https://www.globalcube.net/clients/eacb/content/medias/key_figures/Key_Financial_Statistics_2009.pdf

(8) EACB, Accessed on 14.7.14; https://www.globalcube.net/clients/eacb/content/medias/key_figures/Copy_of_Key_stats_2010_-_financ_indicator_revised_for_website_.pdf

(9) EACB, Accessed on 14.4.14); https://www.globalcube.net/clients/eacb/content/medias/key_figures/Key_stats_2011_-_financial_indicators_new.pdf

(10) EACB, Accessed on 14.7.14; https://www.globalcube.net/clients/eacb/content/medias/key_figures/FINAL_Key_stats_2012_UPDATED-_financial_indicators.pdf

Financial Institutions, apart from the Limassol Credit Union Ltd (which has chosen to comply independently), have joined the Central Body, signing the relevant Association and Warranty Agreement, and are now authorized Co-operative Financial Institutions by the Central Bank of Cyprus (Co-operative Central Bank 2014a).

It must be clarified that the permanent affiliation of Co-operative Credit Institutions to the Central Body does not create a parent-subsidiaries relationship or a group of companies, but merely creates a special relationship which enables the affiliated institutions to satisfy the European acquis and hence, be able to continue to provide banking services (Argyridou-Dimitriou and Kanaris 2012; Co-operative Central Bank 2014a). The affiliated Co-operative Credit Institutions continue to be autonomous and independent under their own administrative and governing bodies, as required by the cooperative societies Law administration (Argyridou-Dimitriou and Kanaris 2012; Co-operative Central Bank 2014a). In an effort to meet the EU Directives' requirements on Credit Institutions' minimum capital, Co-operatives in Cyprus have started undergoing significant consolidation (Argyridou-Dimitriou and Kanaris 2012). It is noted that Co-operative Credit Institutions are managed and owned by their members and they accept deposits (from their members and clients) and grant loans to their members only (Argyridou-Dimitriou and Kanaris 2012).

The rights and obligations of the Co-operative Central Bank as Central Body and of Co-operative Credit Institutions stem from the institutional framework which governs the operation of the Central Body (Article 3 of the EU Directive 2006/48/EC) (Co-operative Central Bank 2014b). Since 1 January 2008, when the affiliation agreement was put in place, the Central Body provides:

- coverage, through the guarantee in favour of the depositors, creditors, or other beneficiaries of Co-operative Financial Institutions and the repayment in full of all the obligations of the affiliated Co-operative Financial Institutions, including all off-balance-sheet obligations and commitments and;
- in cooperation with the Commissioner of CSSDA, the necessary technical and advisory support for affiliated Co-operative Financial Institutions is provided in order to improve their administrative and organisational structure to ensure their viability and solvency, the continuous updating, expansion and development of their activities and generally their smooth operation (Co-operative Central Bank 2014b).

The Central Body has also, certain rights which include:

- the issuance of instructions to the affiliated Co-operative Financial Institutions, regarding specific issues and sectors and, in accordance to the context of the overall regulatory framework;
- the effective monitoring of the financial situation and the operational adequacy of affiliated Co-operative Financial Institutions;
- the verification of the correctness and the full implementation of the directives issued by the affiliated Co-operative Financial Institutions;
- the obtaining of the necessary information and statements for an objective and comprehensive assessment of the organizational, economic and operational efficiency of affiliated Co-operative Financial Institutions and;
- to ensure and verify the correctness of the information submitted through carrying out visits to affiliated Co-operative Financial Institutions in collaboration with the Commissioner of CSSDA (Co-operative Central Bank 2014b).

Changes

The co-operative movement in Cyprus implemented a series of legal and structural changes in order to protect its members and the general public (CSSDA 2012b). These include the introduction of the "Deposit Protection Scheme for Cooperative Credit Institutions" in 2000 which is in line with the European Ordinance (CSSDA 2012b). Due to the transfer of the supervision of Co-operative Credit Institutions to the Central Bank of Cyprus, since 9 September 2013, the aforementioned deposit protection scheme was transferred also to the Central Bank of Cyprus and is under the "Deposit Protection and Resolution of Credit and Other Institutions Scheme (DP&RCOIS)", which is managed by a committee that comprises of representatives from the Central Bank of Cyprus and the Ministry of Finance (CSSDA 2014c). Moreover, the Co-operative movement created the "Fund for the cohesion, support and growth of the registered companies that operate as Co-operative Credit Institutions" (CSSDA 2012b).

The Independent Commission on the Future of the Cyprus Banking Sector stated that as a consequence of the support from the Cyprus government, Co-operative Credit Institutions are undergoing a fundamental restructuring in order to mitigate the effects of major losses from loans and ineffective management practice (Central Bank of Cyprus 2013a). Additionally, the Independent Commission on the Future of the Cyprus Banking Sector stated that a law was passed which demutualized Co-operative Credit Institutions by injecting new capital of 1.5 billion euros from the Cyprus state (Central Bank of Cyprus 2013a). Moreover, the supervision of Co-operative Credit Institutions was transferred from the Commissioner of Co-operative Societies' Supervision and Development Authority to the Central Bank of Cyprus (Central Bank of Cyprus 2013a). According to the Independent Commission on the Future of the Cyprus Banking Sector, all these changes were necessary because Co-operative Credit Institutions had deficiencies: the personal interests of management and the Boards, in many, cases were "*intertwined with those of their customers, particularly their borrowers*", they were influenced by political parties and were poorly supervised (Central Bank of Cyprus 2013a, p. 61). To correct these deficiencies, the Independent Commission on the Future of the Cyprus Banking Sector, suggests that the Co-operative movement must be restructured so that this culture is changed and to "*introduce governance that is strong and, above all, independent*" (Central Bank of Cyprus 2013a, p. 61).

Following the restructuring of the banking sector in Cyprus, there will be a huge commercial bank with 50 % of the market, followed by Co-operative Credit Institutions and thirdly by the second largest commercial bank and the remaining local and foreign banks (Central Bank of Cyprus 2013a). Under these conditions, the Independent Commission on the Future of the Cyprus Banking Sector believes that the Co-operative Credit Institutions could increase their market share, provided that they have a "*stronger commercial management*"(Central Bank of Cyprus 2013a, p. 46).

5 The Future of the System

With regards to the future, the author believes that many of the changes that will be imposed on the Co-operative Credit Institutions in Cyprus will be related to the findings and the recommendations contained in the final report of the Independent Commission on the Future of the Cyprus Banking Sector. To this effect, the major findings and recommendations of the aforementioned Commission will be discussed and then, counter arguments will be proposed.

Starting from the findings and recommendations, the Independent Commission on the Future of the Cyprus Banking Sector believes that even after these changes, the Co-operative sector is still fragmented, the inefficiencies of management have not yet been resolved and Co-operative Credit Institutions will still be open to outside influence through the local Board of Directors (Central Bank of Cyprus 2013a). Additionally, part of the new Co-operative Credit Institutions that will result from the mergers will be very small, averaging 1.5 % of the market (Central Bank of Cyprus 2013a), possibly rendering them unprofitable or even unviable. Furthermore, the state loan of 1.5 billion euros has "*an exceedingly high 10 per cent rate of interest*", which seems to be deliberately set at this height in order to facilitate the required changes (Central Bank of Cyprus 2013a, p. 45). The Independent Commission on the Future of the Cyprus Banking Sector suggests that the Co-operative Credit Institutions must undergo more reforms and that the crisis represents the right opportunity to implement them: the Co-operative Credit Institutions must merge into a "*single commercial entity with a joint stock structure*" enabling them to become a competitive and efficient group with an independent character and professional management at the group level (Central Bank of Cyprus 2013a, p. 45). The new Co-operative Credit entity could continue to engage in retail banking but it could also expand in business banking, where there will be shortage of funds over the next years (Central Bank of Cyprus 2013a).

Moreover, the Independent Commission on the Future of the Cyprus Banking Sector argues that the reform of the Co-operative sector is controversial and causes debate (Central Bank of Cyprus 2013a). According to the same report on the Future of the Cyprus Banking Sector the counter argument is that the Co-operative Credit Institutions offer unparalleled levels of personalized banking to consumers, something which will be lost if their anthropocentric character is altered (Central Bank of Cyprus 2013a). However, the Independent Commission does not agree with this and states that today's economy is totally different from the agrarian economy that Co-operatives used to serve and on which they grew so much (Central Bank of Cyprus 2013a). Additionally, the same Commission believes that this special character of Co-operatives is very expensive for the taxpayers (Central Bank of Cyprus 2013a) because of the 1.5 billion euros capital injected by the Cyprus Government. This argument is more or less the same with the argument that "*this will be the third time in living memories that the co-ops will have been bailed out*" by the government (Central Bank of Cyprus 2013a, p. 45). Finally, the Independent Commission believes that the present form of the Co-operatives' ownership is uncertain as, even though, the members have an option to buy it back by repaying the state loan of 1.5 billion euros plus 10 % interest per year, in reality, the cost of doing so will be so high that most probably Co-ops will be bought by another entity, e.g. a foreign bank "*8.12 We recommend that this opportunity be used to combine the co-operative credit institutions into a single entity with a joint stock structure and a commercial culture to make them a stronger competitive force on the banking market*" (Central Bank of Cyprus 2013a, p. 45).

On the other hand, the author believes that unfortunately, the present financial crisis has brought people back to the times when usurers were the only source of loans, at formidable rates, an area where Co-operatives are very effective. Additionally, Co-operative Credit Institutions have been, are and will continue to support the middle and lower classes of people offering good quality products at affordable costs (Alexopoulos and Goglio 2011). The Co-operative movement has been created by the people and for the people in response to the adverse market conditions (Spear 2000) and to combat the opportunistic behaviour of banks and usurers (Fonteyne 2007) hence, there is no match for the Co-operative financial model.

It may be true that supervision could improve even more as "*the interests of the boards and management of many of these {*Co-operative*} banks were closely intertwined with those of their customers, particularly their borrowers*" (Central Bank of Cyprus 2013a, p. 61). However, what is important is that Co-operative Credit Institutions have never taken "*the fatal step of acquiring 5.7 billion euros of Greek Government Bonds*" in an effort to increase their profits as banks have "*despite Greece's rapidly worsening economic plight and the downgrading of these bonds by the rating agencies*", which caused a "*devastating haircut*" and a huge loss of 4.5 billion euros (Central Bank of Cyprus 2013a, p. 86). Additionally, Co-operative Financial Institutions, have never spent millions of Euros in setting up subsidiaries in foreign countries and a "*surprisingly high number of branches... in the period leading up to Greece's crisis*" {from 135 branches in 2007 to 186 in 2010}, or acquiring them, e.g. "*the acquisition by Bank of Cyprus of Uniastrum Bank in Russia in 2008*" (Central Bank of Cyprus 2013a, p. 85, 86). Moreover, Co-operative Financial Institutions have never granted loans outside Cyprus which led "*to a heavy exposure to bad debts in Greece*" and the management has never faced the "*increasingly desperate need to generate income to finance their greatly expanded operations, and meet their bonus targets*" as has happened in the case of commercial banks (Central Bank of Cyprus 2013a, p. 25).

Co-operative Credit Institutions have always borrowed and invested locally, assisting the local economy and reducing unemployment. The consolidation of Co-operative Credit Institutions and especially the move from around 100 to just 18 Institutions is welcomed as is the creation of a Co-operative group (provided that this will be for the best of members and the greater society). However, the suggestions of the Independent Commission on the Future of the Cyprus Banking Sector may not seem as helpful as intended, as, on the one hand, they seem to acknowledge that it is the commercial banks that have caused the financial crisis, but, on the other hand, it seems that they would prefer that Co-operative Credit

Institutions are punished for this; by consolidating them, changing their supervisory authority and selling them as a group to a foreign bank. The Co-operative movement in Cyprus had, has and will have a role to play in the Cypriot economy and this role is not confined to the agrarian societies of the past. Due to the reasons that were mentioned by the Independent Commission on the Future of the Cyprus Banking Sector, it is the whole financial system (and not only Co-operatives) in Cyprus that needs to change with regards to its culture and adjust to the new economic conditions (through better supervision, better governance and a new culture):

> *A.18 Culture. We believe that the introduction of fresh people, new sources of advice, international experience and different attitudes are all essential if Cyprus is to give itself a fresh start. Changes of this kind would transform the banking system in all the necessary ways, by delivering better governance, better provision of financial services, better supervision and—importantly—greater confidence on the part of its international lenders. Cultural change will involve reducing political interference in the management and supervision of the banking system, putting in place objective decision-making processes and creating incentives and sanctions to strengthen personal accountability.*
>
> Central Bank of Cyprus (2013a, p. 6).

The author does not see the reason why the commercial banks, after being rescued and strengthened, using the uninsured deposits of their customers and state money, have to remain as they were; but Co-operative Credit Institutions which are the last to blame for what has happened in the Cypriot economy, must undergo such radical transformation that will render them something completely opposite to their true nature, i.e. transform them into for-profit institutions.

Concerning the argument that "*this will be the third time in living memories that the co-ops will have been bailed out*" by the government (Central Bank of Cyprus 2013a, p. 45), the Independent Commission on the Future of the Cyprus Banking Sector seems not to have mentioned that the reason behind the second rescue was the fact that the Co-operative movement created companies in order to assist with the housing of the relocated population caused by the Turkish invasion in 1974 and that for the same reason many of the loans that it granted during this period were not recovered: "*after the Turkish invasion of 1974…, the cooperative movement, … played a crucial role in addressing the housing and other problems, thereby supporting the government in its daunting task and at the same time fostering social cohesion. In the context of the restructuring and reconstruction …, as well as in an effort to create new jobs, new cooperative societies were founded in the construction and industrial sectors with financing from the Co-operative Central Bank. However, as lending to those societies was often not based on proper feasibility studies, many of the loans fell overdue and, as a result, co-operative societies went bankrupt*"(Argyridou-Dimitriou and Kanaris 2012, p. 282). Also, the report of the Independent Commission on the Future of the Cyprus Banking Sector does not seem to mention that the financial support to the Co-operatives was repaid in full in 2006: "*The government and commercial banks provided financial support of CY£17.8 million and CY£4.5 million, respectively (Phylaktis 1994), which in total corresponded to 3 % of GDP in 1980. In the late 1980s, an additional support package was granted, totalling CY£67 million or 3 % of GDP in 1989, and was eventually repaid in 2006*" (Argyridou-Dimitriou and Kanaris 2012, p. 282).

Another suggestion by the Independent Commission on the Future of the Cyprus Banking Sector, in order to attract new entrants and to strengthen the local economy, is the introduction of Islamic Finance and microfinance (*#9.8, #11.16, #A.37*). This seems surprising somehow, as the suggestion is for the introduction of two financial models that are unknown and "totally different" from the reality in Cyprus. Islamic finance is growing but for the moment it is mainly targeting people of a certain religion and has to overcome a number of obstacles (standardization of products offered, increase awareness of possible clients, sort remaining taxation and regulation issues and speed up the introduction of "Shariah law" compliant products), before it can cater for the needs of a wider clientele (HM Treasury 2008; Alexander von Pock 2006). On the other hand, microfinance targets the developing world and its 2.8 billion of people that live on less than $60 per month, with loans in India averaging $135 in 2009 (Khavul 2010); something that seems to render microfinance unable to cater for the needs of banking clients in Cyprus: it does not provide for current accounts, overdraft facilities, debit and credit cards and all other products that are considered as "basic" for banking customers in Cyprus. Additionally, since the late 1990s, when microfinance was founded, only a few microfinance institutions managed to remain profitable and these days a big part of microfinance is handled through Credit Unions and/or other types of banking institutions (Dichter 2010).

Another suggestion of the Independent Commission on the Future of the Cyprus Banking Sector is the transformation of Co-operative Credit Institutions into commercial banks. Again, this came as a surprise as it asks for the transformation of Co-operatives, which have 20 % market share in local deposits and loans and have undoubtedly assisted the local economy for over 100 years, into something opposite to their real nature. It seems that the suggestion could have been much more meaningful and socially acceptable if the proposed restructurings were such that the problems of the past were resolved, but at the same time the anthropocentric character of Co-operatives was safe guarded or even expanded. The suggestion of the Independent Commission on the Future of the Cyprus Banking Sector sounds as if the Co-operative movement is something of the past and that its time has come to be transformed into something else. This, however is far from true as Co-operative Credit Institutions, are not only important for the Cypriot economy, but also for the European economies. Co-operative Financial Institutions in Europe rank among the top 25 financial institutions with respect to amount of equity, having 40 % of the number of branches and 30 % of total assets; (Hesse and Čihák 2007; Fonteyne 2007; Brannen and Ibrahim 2010; Stolz and Wedow 2005; Talwar 2011; Goddard and Wilson 2005). Moreover, according to Birchall (2013), in 2010, i.e. 2 years after the financial crisis of 2008, in Europe, there were 3874 Co-operative banks, serving 181.1 million customers, having 50.4 million members and 21 % market share of deposits and 19 % of loans. In 2010, Cyprus (with 19.3 %) runs seventh in terms of deposits' market share after France with 44.8 %, Netherlands with 40 %, Austria with 36.5 %, Italy with 34.2 %, Finland with 32.5 % and Germany with

19.4 % (Birchall 2013). Co-operative Credit Institutions will continue to be important because they offer products and services aiming at the increase of their members' wealth. In the UK, the government and the commercial banks are assisting Credit Unions because Co-operatives can enhance financial inclusion much more effectively than banks (Cuevas and Fischer 2006). Moreover, in 2010, the Cabinet Office in the UK having realized the possibilities that non-for-profit organizations possess, has even published a Policy paper entitled: "Building the Big Society" stating its plans to support the setting up and expansion of Co-operatives and providing assistance to public sector employees to set up their own Co-operatives (UK government 2010).

Co-operative Credit Institutions in Cyprus need to be up to date with the technology advancements, to introduce new products and services, attract younger generations, become more efficient and engage in marketing activities in order to remind older people and to educate younger people about their ideological difference in relation to commercial banks, but they should never be transformed into a commercial bank. This is simply because their role is completely different from that of commercial banks and this has been proven by the market share that Co-operative Financial Institutions have especially these days. This different role is true all over the world, including the most progressive western (North American) societies, in which, in 2011, Co-operatives had 104.5 million members, in Europe Co-operatives had 8.1 million members, whilst worldwide there were 51,013 credit unions, with a total of 196.5 million members (Birchall 2013). Finally, it is stressed that the most important distinction between Co-operative Credit Institutions and commercial banks is the non for profit maximizing objective of the former as opposed to the latter. Co-operative Credit Institutions aim at increasing the wellbeing of their members (economic, educational, and societal) and not at maximizing the profits for their shareholders/ investors. At the same time, Co-operative financial institutions effectively create a "*competitive yardstick*", forcing the rest of the financial institutions to be honest (Hogeland 2006, p. 69). In Cyprus, a 634,000 people strong membership base (Birchall 2013) should leave no doubt as to the need for Co-operative Credit Institutions alongside commercial banks, each performing its own role in society.

References

Alexopoulos Y, Goglio S (2011) Financial cooperatives: problems and challenges in the post-crisis era. J Rural Coop 39(1):35–48

Argyridou-Dimitriou C, Kanaris E (2012) The financial system of Cyprus, Chapter 7. In: Orphanides A, Syrichas G (eds) The Cyprus economy. Historical review, prospects, challenges. Central Bank of Cyprus, Nicosia, pp 280–284, http://www.centralbank.gov.cy/media/pdf/CBC_book_EN.pdf. Accessed on 7 Jul 2014

Birchall J (2013) Resilience in a downturn: the power of financial cooperatives. International Labour Office, Geneva, http://www.ilo.org/wcmsp5/groups/public/---ed_emp/---emp_ent/---coop/documents/publication/wcms_207768.pdf. Site accessed on 23 Jul 2014

Brannen D, Ibrahim N (2010) The role and level of involvement of credit union directors in strategic management: a research agenda. Int J Manag 27(3):680–692, Part 2

Central Bank of Cyprus (2013a) Independent commission on the future of the Cyprus banking sector, final report and recommendations, October 2013. http://www.centralbank.gov.cy/media//pdf/LSE_ICFCBS_Final_Report_10_13.pdf. Accessed on 7 Jul 2014

Central Bank of Cyprus (2013b) Unofficial consolidation and translation of "The business of Credit Institutions Laws of 1997 to (no. 3) 2013". http://www.centralbank.gov.cy/media/pdf/EN_consol_BUSINESS_0F_CI_LAW_19 9 7_to_No3_2 013.pdf. Site accessed on 10 Jul 2014

Clerides N (1947) A historical note. In: Co-operation in Cyprus (each for all and all for each). Registrar of Co-operative Societies, no. 7

Co-operative Central Bank (2014a) http://www.coopbank.com.cy/index.php?option=com_content&view=article&id=103&Itemid=124. Site accessed on 11 Jul 2014

Co-operative Central Bank (2014b) http://www.coopbank.com.cy/index.php?option=com_content&view=article&id=110&Itemid=126. Site accessed on 11 Jul 2014

Co-operative Central Bank (2014c) http://www.coopbank.com.cy/index.php?option=com_content&view=article&id=85&Itemid=92. Accessed on 19 Jul 2014

Co-operative Central Bank (2014d) Co-operative law 1985 unofficial consolidation of modifications 1985–2014 "ΟπερίΣυνεργατικώνΕταιρειώνΝόμοςτου 1985 (22/1985)". http://www.cylaw.org/nomoi/enop/non-ind/1985_1_22/full.html. Site accessed on 3 Jul 2014

CSSDA (2010) Annual report 2003–2009. Authority for the supervision and development of co-operative societies. http://www.cssda.gov.cy/cssda/cssda02.nsf/All/9F37A3431417A51BC2257C1B00461E48/$file/Ετήσια%20Έκθεση%20ΥΕΑΣΕ%202010.pdf. Site accessed on 14 Jul 2014

CSSDA (2012a) Unofficial consolidation of the co-operative companies Thesmoi of 1987–2012. http://www.cssda.gov.cy/cssda/cssda02.nsf/All/6E3792FAA204B18EC2257C0500336F10/$file/Οι%20περί%20Συνεργατικών%20Εταιρειών%20Θεσμοί%20του%201987%20έως%202012.pdf. Site accessed on 3 Jul 2014

CSSDA (2012b) Annual report 2011. Authority for the supervision and development of co-operative societies. http://www.cssda.gov.cy/cssda/cssda02.nsf/All/AC4114BEC8A34F90C2257C1B0045EDB7/$file/Εκτυπομένη%20Έκθεση.pdf. Site accessed on 3 Jul 2014

CSSDA (2014a) http://www.cssda.gov.cy/cssda/cssda02.nsf/page11_gr/page11_gr?OpenDocument. Site accessed on 8 Jul 2014

CSSDA (2014b) http://www.cssda.gov.cy/cssda/cssda02.nsf/page05_gr/page05_gr?OpenDocument. Site accessed on 3 Jul 2014

CSSDA (2014c) http://www.cssda.gov.cy/cssda/cssda02.nsf/page06_gr/page06_gr?OpenDocument. Site accessed on 15 Jul 2014

Cuevas C, Fischer K (2006) Cooperative financial institutions issues in governance, regulation, and supervision. World Bank working paper no. 82, The World Bank

Dichter T (2010) Too good to be true: the remarkable resilience of microfinance. Harvard International Review Spring 2010

Fonteyne W (2007) Cooperative banks in Europe—policy issues. International Monetary Fund WP/07/159

Goddard J, Wilson J (2005) US Credit Unions: an empirical investigation of size, age and growth. Ann Public Coop Econ 76:3

UK Government (2010) Policy paper: building the big society. https://www.gov.uk/government/publications/building-the-big-society. Site accessed on 22 Jul 2014

Guinnane T (1994) A failed transplant: Raiffeisen's credit cooperatives in Ireland, 1894–1914. Explor Econ Hist 31:38–61, http://ac.els-cdn.com/S0014498384710023/1-s2.0-S0014498384710023-main.pdf?_tid=f867e4c4-0bf0-11e4-93b4-00000aab0f26&acdnat=1405409211_60fdd83b512d5a5bd100ceff238587ab. Site accessed on 15 July 2014

Hesse H, Čihák M (2007) Cooperative banks and financial stability. International Monetary Fund WP/07/2

Hogeland JA (2006) The economic culture of US agricultural cooperatives. Culture and Agriculture 28(2):67–79

Khavul S (2010) Microfinance: creating opportunities for the poor? Academy of Management Perspectives 24(3):58–72

Ministry of Finance (2014) Memorandum of understanding on specific economic policy conditionality. http://www.mof.gov.cy/mof/mof.nsf/MoU_Final_approved_13913.pdf. Site accessed on 22 July 2014

Phylaktis K (1995) The banking system of Cyprus: past, present and future. Palgrave Macmillan, Hampshire

Rabobank (2008) The European banking sector and the co-operative banks. Economic Research Department. Rabobank.https://economics.rabobank.com/PageFiles/5698/SP0806bvr%20overview%20European%20Co-operative%20banking%20sector.pdf. Site accessed on 23 July 2014

Spear R (2000) The co-operative advantage. Ann Public Coop Econ 71:4

Stolz S, Wedow M (2005) Banks' regulatory capital buffer and the business cycle: evidence for German savings and cooperative banks. Deutsche Bundesbank discussion paper series 2: banking and financial studies No 07/2005

Talwar S (2011) Jewell to rust: sleazy co-operative sector. SCMS J Indian Manag 8(3):29–46

HM Treasury (2008) The development of Islamic finance in the UK: the Government's perspective. http://www.hm-treasury.gov.uk

von Pock A (2006) Strategic management in Islamic finance. Gabler, Deutscher Universitätsverlag, Wiesbaden

Co-operative Banks in Finland

Panu Kalmi

Abstract Finnish cooperative banks originated in the early twentieth century as agricultural lenders. Initially they were small Raiffeisen—type credit cooperatives, that operated in limited geographical area only. Their importance grew after the Second World War due to their participation in the reconstruction efforts. In the postwar period, their management professionalized and they started to function as retail banks. In 1970, their legal status was converted to banks. Finnish cooperative banks emerged relatively unharmed from the Finnish banking crisis of the early 1990s. An important consequence of the crisis was that the group structure was changed into tightly integrated one, including joint liability of all banks. This change was controversial and as a consequence, the cooperative banks seceded into two groups, the OP Group and the POP Group. The OP Group purchased a leading insurance company in the 2000s. It steadily increased its market share and had become the market leader in lending and deposits by 2009. During the crisis, both cooperative banking groups have remained well capitalized and successful. However, largely because of regulatory pressures both of them have went through a number of structural changes in the recent years.

1 Evolution of Credit Co-operatives in Finland

Finnish co-operative banks originate from the turn of the twentieth century. A professor from Helsinki University, Hannes Gebhard, had become familiar with the concept of credit co-operatives in Germany. Gebhard promoted especially agricultural co-operatives and he was the leading figure in the establishment of Finnish confederation of agricultural co-operatives, Pellervo, in 1899. He was also active in the promotion and design of the law on co-operatives that was enacted in 1901 (see Kuisma et al. 2000).

P. Kalmi (✉)
University of Vaasa, Vaasa, Finland
e-mail: panu.kalmi@uva.fi

S. Karafolas (ed.), *Credit Cooperative Institutions in European Countries*, Contributions to Economics, DOI 10.1007/978-3-319-28784-3_3

Gebhard saw a need for credit co-operatives in agricultural finance. In the early twentieth century, Finland had many savings banks, but these did not typically finance agricultural loans, and especially not to poor landless crofters. Gebhard was especially concerned about the poorest agricultural population and saw that credit co-operatives could help them to emancipate (Kuusterä 2002). He was greatly helped in this by the political establishment. In the early twentieth century, Finland was part of the Russian empire, even though Finland had substantial autonomy: its own governing body (the senate) and even its own legislative assembly (the parliament) since 1906. Nevertheless, expressions of political nationalism were forbidden. In this situation economic organizations that were perceived to strengthen the nation, especially co-operatives, were popular among the Finns and tolerated by the Russian authorities.

Against this background, it is understandable that the Finnish state was very active in the establishment of Finnish credit co-operatives. The central unit of Finnish credit co-operatives, the OKO-Bank, was established to provide low-cost loans to farmers that were guaranteed by the state. The OKO-Bank itself was initially owned by wealthy individuals who were supportive of the co-operative movement. One of the notable features of Finnish credit co-operatives is that they were established top down; first the central unit was established and only afterwards the individual credit unions were formed. Later on the credit co-operatives bought out the individual owners of the OKO-Bank.

Finnish credit co-operatives were initially established according to the Raiffeisen concept (see Prinz 2002). The area of co-operatives was relatively small, often one parish. All members knew each other well and were jointly liable of each other's debts. In the first two decades, the emphasis was on the establishment of new credit co-operatives. OKO and Pellervo and their advisory work played a key role in this.

The biggest growth in credit co-operatives took place between 1920 and 1930; the number of co-operatives increased from 602 in 1920 to 1416 in 1930; the latter figure was the all-time record for credit co-operatives. In 1930, the market share of credit co-operatives was around 8 % in loans and 4 % in deposits (see Table 1). In the 1930s, the structure of credit co-operatives started slowly to change. The strict Raiffeisen principles were gradually abandoned. For instance, credit co-operatives started to serve larger areas and some credit co-operatives merged to achieve better economic viability. In the late 1920s, credit co-operatives also started to accept deposits from non-members, including companies.

There were also important changes in the group structure. In 1928 the Central Association for Credit Co-operatives (in Finnish *Osuuskassojen keskusliitto, OKL*) was established. OKL took into its responsibilities the supervision of credit co-operatives, collection of statistics on the movement, advisory services, promotion of new co-operatives, and external relations, whereas OKO focused more on its operations as central bank for the group. A guarantee fund, to which the co-operatives had to make mandatory contributions, was established in 1932. Credit co-operatives were granted the right to open checking accounts in 1932.

Table 1 The development of number of financial co-operatives, members, and market shares in loans and deposits between 1910 and 2013

Year	Number of financial co-operatives	Number of members	Market share in loans (%)	Market share in deposits (%)
1910	370	17,000	0.5	0.1
1920	602	31,000	0.3	0.2
1930	1416	144,000	8	4
1940	1079	156,000	10	8
1950	684	230,000	22	16
1960	537	302,000	20	18
1970	445	290,000	21	20
1980	372	362,000	25	24
1995	301	674,000	32	32
2013[a]	221	1,515,000	36	39

Sources: Kuusterä (2002); annual reports for OP-Pohjola and POP Groups and FFFS (for 2013)
[a]Combined for OP-Pohjola Group and POP-group

In the end of 1930s credit co-operatives had already a well-established position in the Finnish financial markets, even though they were much smaller than savings banks or commercial banks. Unexpectedly, the war with Soviet Union strengthened their competitive position. Finland had to cede significant territory from Eastern Finland to Soviet Union. This meant that 450,000 people had to be relocated (around 12 % of total Finnish population). In addition to that, during the war the government had promised that landless crofters could purchase land in favourable terms. The government gave loans to immigrants and crofters after the war, and most of these loans were handled through credit co-operatives. As a consequence of this programme, the market share of credit co-operatives of loans increased from 10 % in 1944 to 25 % in 1948 (though decreasing to 20 % by 1954); at the same time, the number of members grew from 164,000 in 1944 to 223,000 in 1949, after which the growth slowed down. Even though the influence of the land purchase programme was partly a temporary boost, it elevated co-operative bank to a level where they became significant competitors to savings and commercial banks.

The postwar period until the mid-1980s was a period of heavy regulation for the Finnish banking sector. Both the loan and deposit rates were regulated by the Bank of Finland. The access to capital markets was restricted, which allowed the central bank to control for the money supply. There was a constant shortage of loanable funds, and the role of price competition was eliminated. The main way to compete was by setting up new branches.

During the postwar period, credit co-operatives became more similar than commercial banks. The employees were no longer volunteers but professionals, and irregular opening hours were replaced by regular hours and own premises located in town centers. The legislation followed this development. While initially credit co-operatives had been regulated only through general co-operative legislation and model rules devised by Pellervo and OKO, the internal regulations became more formal since 1930s onwards. OKL was the body conducting supervision of credit co-operatives and it formulated the model rules for credit co-operatives. The first law on credit co-operatives came into effect only in 1970. In this law, credit co-operatives became under banking legislation and were thus recognized to be banks. However, de facto they had operated as banks already quite some time.

An important change that took place in the 1960s–1980s was the urbanization of the country. This was expected to disadvantage especially co-operative banks, because they were generally viewed as the bankers of the agricultural population. However, especially during the 1970s co-operative banks successfully transformed themselves into the banking group for "everyman", and they were no longer strictly confined to any social groups. Overall, the co-operative banks managed to increase their markets share during the 1970s even though the agricultural sector was rapidly losing its importance.

The era of high regulation ended abruptly in the mid-1980s when the central bank abandoned the interest rate regulation, and borrowing from foreign financial markets was liberalized. For a few years in the latter half of 1980s, this created an unforeseen economic boom, that in the early 1990s rapidly transformed into the Great Finnish Depression: the biggest post-war economic decline of any OECD country by that time (Kiander and Vartia 1996). GDP declined around 14 % in 2 years and unemployment increased to 17 %. The economic depression was accompanied by a banking crisis that decimated the savings bank group that used to be the main competitors of co-operative banks. Most savings banks were liquidated, and only 40 savings banks continued their operations. Although this was 50 % of the number of the savings banks around that time, they represented only 15 % of the assets. Co-operative banks had also their share of difficulties. Around 15 % of co-operative banks (around 50 in number) incurred significant losses during the crisis, and they had not survived the crisis without the help of other banks in the group. The troubled banks included some of the largest co-operative banks located in larger towns. However, co-operative banks managed to survive without any explicit subsidies from the government and actually emerged among the strongest banks from the crisis. In 1993, the assets of liquidated savings banks were sold to the remaining banking groups, co-operative banks being one of the buyers (Kalmi 2012).

After the crisis the group structure of Finnish co-operative banks was significantly changed. Even though the group had a mutual insurance fund, it had been insufficiently capitalized during the crisis. Economically solid banks in the group had to bail out some of the weaker banks. Furthermore, some banks had not followed the advice of the central units of credit co-operatives before the crisis and it turned out that the center did not have means to force the dissident banks to comply with their directions. Many of these banks inflicted large losses on other banks in the group. For these reasons, the joint liability between banks was made explicit. Also, the powers of the OKL vis-à-vis member banks were strengthened. These issues are further explored in the section discussing the governance structure of co-operative banks.

The changes in the co-operative groups were not universally accepted, however. A group of co-operative banks actively opposed these changes, and they thought that the joint liability rules would ultimately threaten the viability of the group as a whole. Ultimately, 44 banks separated from the OP-group and formed their own group called Local Co-operative Banks (in Finnish: *Paikallisosuuspankkiryhmä*), known by their Finnish acronym POP Group.

2 Current Model

It is important to realize that there are two groups of co-operative banks in Finland currently, even though most discussions on Finnish co-operative banks miss this point. Unlike in some other countries, where the existence of two groups is a historical phenomenon based on the division between the Raiffeisen banks and the Schultze-Delitzsch banks, in Finland both of these banks have their roots in rural (Raiffeisen) model and differed in their attitudes towards tighter integration and joint liability. In the following, more attention will be paid to the OP Group,[1] and POP Group will be discussed separately towards the end of this section.

OP Group is together with the Dutch Rabobank among the most integrated co-operative banking groups in Europe (Ayadi et al. 2010). According to Cuevas and Fischer (2006), two main cases of co-operative networks can be distinguished: consensual networks and strategic networks. In consensual networks there is significant pooling of resources, for instance in the fields of payment systems, IT systems, liquidity management, and employee training. Co-operative banks in consensual networks limit intra-network competition, and they have joint marketing and brand name. The center is engaged in strategic planning; however, there is no mandatory compliance on behalf of the member banks. The strategic networks share these features, but they have important additional features. These are: the center can give strategic direction to member banks; there is mandatory auditing performed within the group; and there is joint and unlimited liability of all debts of member banks (i.e. not just on deposits, and the liability is not limited to a predefined amount). Finnish co-operative banks within the OP Group share all of these characteristics. Even though cross-guarantees are very common among European banking groups, according to Ayadi et al. (2010) only Rabobank and the OP Group have full and explicit joint liability. The group structure of the OP Group is also codified in the Law on Co-operative Banks from 2001, where it is regulated that due to joint liability, the co-operative group can be regarded as one banking consortium.

Another peculiar feature of the OP Group is that there are two central organizations: Pohjola Bank (formerly OKO-Bank), and OP Financial Group Central Cooperative (formerly OKL, referred below as OP Group Central). In the recent decades, the position of Group Central has been strengthened at the expense of OKO/Pohjola. In the end of 2013, there were 187 co-operative banks in the

[1] In years 2008–2014, the OP Group was called OP-Pohjola Group.

group. In 2005 there were still around 240 co-operative banks, but their number has been reduced through mergers. The co-operative banks own fully the Group Central, which in turn is the largest owner of the Pohjola Bank.

The responsibilities of the two central units are divided so that OP Group Central is responsible for the general management issues, supervision and auditing of member banks, training of employees and member-directors, joint marketing, and payments systems. The role of OP Group Central is to provide services for member banks in issues that the member banks could not profitably provide themselves. Also, OP Group Central has a public mandate to supervise the banks. The national Financial Supervision Authority in turn conducts supervision at the group level. This system has been in place throughout the history of Finnish of co-operative banks.

Pohjola Bank (formerly OKO-Bank) has services directed both to the network members and to external customers. Of the services to network members, the most important are related to liquidity management. Pohjola Bank functions as a central bank among co-operative banks and it takes care that net saver co-operatives lend their funds to net borrower co-operatives. Pohjola Bank takes also care of interbank lending. Of its external functions, the most important ones are related to lending to corporate customers. Small co-operative banks are unable to lend to big corporate clients, because their borrowing needs would represent too important risk concentrations. Therefore this task has been delegated to Pohjola Bank that is more able to take care of these functions. Additionally, Pohjola Bank is involved in providing insurance and in wealth management. While OP Group used to be engaged in insurance to some extent already before 2005 (especially in life insurance), their involvement in insurance business increased dramatically after the purchase of Pohjola, one of the biggest insurance companies in Finland, in 2005. The name of OKO-Bank was changed into Pohjola Bank in 2008, and the name of the group was changed from OP-Group into OP-Pohjola Group at the same time.

OKO Bank and its successor Pohjola Bank was a listed subsidiary of the OP Group in the Helsinki Stock Exchange between 1989 and 2014, until it was delisted in April 2014 (see discussion below). The majority of voting shares were owned by the OP Group Central, but there used to be a significant minority ownership by institutional investors and individuals. The predecessor of Pohjola, OKO-Bank, was listed in 1989. The listed status of the subsidiary was especially important when organizing funding for the purchase of Pohjola Insurance Company through a targeted public offering.

Despite the pronounced role of central organizations within the OP Group, local banks retain substantial autonomy. For instance, they make the lending decisions independently, set lending and deposit interest rates, and make decisions concerning the personnel hires. Co-operative banks are governed by the one member, one vote principle. There are two main governing bodies within the co-operative banks: the supervisory board, which takes care of general guidelines and convenes 3–4 times a year, and the management board, that convenes monthly and works in close contact with the CEO. Both supervisory board and management board are elected by the members in the annual member meetings or members' representative assembly.

Co-operative banks serve both members and non-members, and there is no obligation for customers to become members. To become a member, an individual has to buy a member share. Typically the member share costs 100 euros. There is no interest paid on member share. If the member wishes to leave the co-operative, she receives back the nominal share in equity. Additionally, members can invest in additional equity, for which interest is paid. Each bank is free to set its own interest rates for additional equity. Typically the members are private individuals rather than companies or other co-operatives. Juridical persons (such as companies) are eligible to become members, but they do not have voting rights and do not receive bonuses.

The main incentives to become a member are financial. Co-operative banks use patronage dividends (called bonuses), where members are compensated on the basis of their financial transactions with the banks. Members receive dividends on the basis of their deposits, loans, investments in mutual funds, and insurance. In effect, this means that members get lower interest rates for loans and higher interest rates for deposits than non-members. Members can use bonuses to reduce their banking and insurance fees and receive the remaining bonuses in cash. The amount of bonuses that are used the offset the fees are tax-free, whereas cash bonuses are taxed. There are no specific tax advantages targeted to co-operative banks in Finland.

The remuneration rates do not depend on profitability. However, there may be a link through the interest rates paid on additional equity: the banks can use this to compensate for increased profitability. However, patronage dividends have been a much more important source for member remuneration than are interest on additional equity. The role of additional equity has become more important recent (see Sect. 4).

The local co-operative banks (the POP Group) share many features of the OP Pohjola Group, due to their long shared history. For instance, the local governance structure is roughly the same. However, the governance structure of the group used to differ. The POP Group has not been as tightly integrated and the local banks are more independent as in the OP-Pohjola Group. Until recently, the banks in this group did not have joint liability of each other's debts, although they had a more limited joint stability fund. Additionally, the POP Bank has outsourced many functions that in the OP-Pohjola group are produced internally; for instance, the liquidity management services were purchased from Aktia Bank (a joint stock bank formed by former savings banks). The POP Group also collaborated in payment systems with Aktia and it does not have own investment banking operations; rather it buys those services from its partners. For instance, it does not operate mutual investment funds on behalf of its customers by itself. Instead, it sells the funds operated by its partners. In 2011 the POP Group made a new initiative by establishing its own insurance company. In 2014, there were 34 co-operative banks in the POP Group. The more limited nature of the central unit of the POP Group can be illustrated by the fact that in 2013, the central unit of the POP Group included only around 20 employees, compared to over 2000 people in the central organization of the OP Pohjola Group, even though in other dimensions the size difference between these two banks are roughly 1:10. However, the internal structure of the POP Group is undergoing significant changes, which will be discussed in Sect. 4.

It could also be mentioned that there is another small bank, S-Bank, that is owned by Finnish consumer cooperatives. It is not a cooperative bank in a traditional sense, but its owners are (indirectly) the members of the consumer cooperatives, in a similar way than the Co-operative Bank in the UK. It started in 2006, and it had in 2013 a market share in deposits of around 3 % (and a much smaller market share in loans). In this presentation, it has not been included among cooperative banks.

3 The Importance of Co-operative Banks

As can be seen from Table 1, the economic importance of co-operative banks, measured in terms of market shares, in Finland has steadily increased throughout their existence, being clearly over one-third in 2013. The OP Group became the largest retail bank in Finland in 2009, when it surpassed Nordea in size. In 2013, the market share of the OP Group in loans was 34.2 % and in deposits it was 36.2 %. The market shares of its closest competitor Nordea were 29.0 % in loans and 29.5 % in deposits. In euros, the amount of loans was 68.1 billion euro and the amount of deposits was 46.3 billion euro for the OP Group. The market shares of the POP Group were 1.8 % in loans and 3.1 % in deposits in 2013. The POP Group had loans of 3.7 billion euro and deposits of 3.9 billion euro. The Tier 1 capital ratio for OP Pohjola Group was 14.3 % in 2013. Because the POP Group is not a consortium, the Tier 1 ratio is not calculated, but if it were, it would be even higher. The total capital ratio was 22 % for POP Group, making it the most capitalized banking group in Finland. An important difference between the OP Group and the POP Group is that the latter is very dependent on interest revenues, which formed 65 % of the revenues of the banking group in the year 2013. The POP Group has traditionally been among the most retail-oriented of Finnish banks. The ratio of interest revenues of all revenues for the OP Group was only 36 % making it actually less retail oriented than its biggest competitors. This is largely due to the large volumes of insurance-related income in the OP Group. Both groups are among the most profitable in Finland (FFFS 2014; material from Bank's websites and annual reports).

The OP Group employed around 12,000 employees at the end of 2013, which was almost 42.5 % of total personnel in banking services in Finland. It had 485 branches, which makes a market share in branches of 35.2 %. For POP Group, the share of personnel was 2.5 % (704 employees) but the share in branches was as high as 8.1 % (111 branches). This demonstrates that the banks and branches in the POP Group are fairly small, and their business strategy is to be close to the customers. In fact, the POP Group has repeatedly been selected as having the most satisfied customers of all banking groups. However, in both groups and similarly to other banks in Finland, there has been a clear downward trend in the number of branches. The OP Group has been one of the pioneers in internet banking in Finland and it has currently the leading position in the number of internet banking customers among the Finnish banks. The OP Group is also among the leading insurance companies in Finland. In 2013 its market share in life insurance was around 25 % and in non-life insurance around 30 %.

The most recent reported disaggregated data for the size of co-operative banks in terms of members and customers are from 2009. Then the average bank had around 14,300 customers and 5900 members, the average membership ratio being around 42 % (Jones and Kalmi 2015). However, the variation in size is quite large for the banks in the OP Group, some banks being regional and covering a large population, some covering only a few villages. For the POP Group, similar information is not available, but the general understanding is that they are smaller. In both groups, mergers among banks are increasing the average size.

Jones et al. (2012) studied the role of training in co-operative banks. They report that on average co-operative banks invested in employee training a sum of 3.0 % of personnel costs and the average duration of training per employee was 5 days. Both of these figures are substantially above the average of Finnish firms. The authors argue that co-operative banks have higher incentives to invest in human capital than profit-maximizing firms. They also find that training boosts wages but does not influence profitability or cost efficiency.

The role of co-operative banks is pronounced especially in rural towns and communities. Their largest competitors, the Pan-Scandinavian Nordea and Danske Bank are focusing on largest towns. The savings banks, that used to be very important in countryside, were much weakened due to the banking crisis of the early 1990s. Thus co-operative banks remain important providers of financial services in areas that might otherwise be underserved.

4 The Influence of the Crisis

The banks operating in Finland have not markedly suffered from the financial and economic crisis that started in 2007. Even though the Finnish real GDP dropped 8 % in 2009, and the growth figures after 2010 have been very modest so that the real GDP per capita at the time of the writing (May 2015) is at 2006 levels, increases in unemployment have been moderate and there have been no bankruptcy waves. Both the OP Group and the POP Group have performed fairly strongly in the crisis. Even though the OP Group incurred some losses after the bankruptcy of Lehman Brothers in 2008, it has been able to increase its market share especially in corporate finance during the crisis. It was the only Finnish banking group that was included in the stress tests of the European Banking Authority in 2010 and 2011 and the reports on it were very favorable in both times. It also passed the ECB/EBA stress tests in 2014 without problems.

Both cooperative banking groups have been able to increase their market shares during the crisis and they have also increased their membership significantly. Both of them have consistently had comfortable levels of profitability and they have increased their capitalization from already quite high levels. However, the crisis and declining interest and profit margins have influenced the levels of employment and number of branches, both of which have been in decline, especially after 2012. OP Group Central has announced several rounds of lay-offs and it has outsourced IT operations significantly. The lay-offs have been controversial, because they have not been caused by economic distress, but rather from the desire to increase economic efficiency. At the same time, the OP Group has reached record levels of profitability. The local banks have been less affected by layoffs. Until recently, the OP Group was considered not practicing lay-offs as means of improving efficiency and profitability.

Both bank groups are experiencing significant structural changes due to the ongoing reregulation of the banking sector. The POP Bank had a well-functioning cooperation in liquidity management with Aktia Bank. However, due to the new liquidity regulation introduced in Basel III, providing this service becomes prohibitively expensive to Aktia. In 2013, Aktia announced that it will discontinue this service in 2015. POP Bank has established its own central bank for interbank transactions within the group and for payment services. However, as a small banking group it was in danger of being in a comparative disadvantage in the interbank market. For this reason, it decided to strengthen its position to form a similar joint-liability structure than the OP Group has. There was a certain irony in this decision, because the reason for the secession in 1997 had been a dispute over the joint-liability structure. The decision was a difficult one and 6 banks out of 34 decided to return to the OP Group after the decision.

OP Group announced in February 2014 that they will buy all the shares of the publicly traded Pohjola bank which will be fully annexed to the group. This happened in April 2014. The funding for the transaction, which is the third largest voluntary banking sector transaction in Europe since 2008, will come partly from member banks, partly from individual members, and partly from the issuance of new debt. This move removes the outsider shareholders from the group and thus makes the group more cooperative than before. This interesting and unusual transaction was largely motivated by new regulatory requirements in the risk management of the group. In the process, the group launched a new financial instrument, investment shares, where members can invest against a fixed rate return. This is a hybrid equity instrument which is not covered by the deposit insurance. The subscription process lasted until the end of 2015, and there was a lot of demand for the shares.

5 Conclusion

Finnish co-operative banks have become from small village banks large universal banking groups, currently occupying more than one-third of the retail banking market share. The bigger of two groups, the OP Group, is even the largest retail banking group in Finland. Their performance and market share trajectory has been upwards throughout their existence. Both groups are currently very profitable, and the OP Group is considered as one of the most robust retail banks in Europe, as evidenced by the consistently high ratings it gets from Moody's and Fitch rating agencies.

The meaning of being a co-operative has changed throughout their existence. For instance, the OP Group stresses almost exclusively financial aspects when advertising membership. The average size of banks has increased through members. On the other hand, member recruitment in both groups has been much more active after the Finnish banking crisis in the early 1990s than before it, which is evidenced in considerable increases in membership in both groups. The POP Group has been somewhat more successful in retaining the proximity to members. The local banks in the POP Group used to be more independent than in the OP Group, but this may be changing.

Recently, there have been very important changes for both groups. This has not been so much as reactions to the crisis, as both banks have been very robust, but more as a response to the regulatory challenges. The OP Group bought out its listed subsidiary, which is now fully-owned by the group. The POP Group adopted the joint liability structure as a response to new demands regarding its interbank operations. Unintentionally, these changes have brought the two co-operative banking groups somewhat closer together.

There are no big risks for either group in immediate sight. Both of them are highly capitalized that should make them more resilient in the crisis. However, the high level of integration in the OP Group may increase their vulnerability to crisis that would spread from the centrally managed operations. Such risk taking incentives have been further reduced by the delisting of the central bank. For the POP Group, the small size has created certain problems of regulatory nature, but the strategy of the banking group is conservative and risk averse, and it fills a certain niche in the Finnish banking markets.

References

Ayadi R, Llewellyn DT, Schmidt RH, Arbak E, Pieter De Groen W (2010) Investigating diversity in the banking sector in Europe: key developments, performance and role of cooperative banks. Centre for European Policy Studies, Brussels

Cuevas CE, Fischer KP (2006) Cooperative financial institutions: issues in governance, regulation and supervision. The World Bank, Washington, DC

FFFS (2014) Pankit Suomessa 2013. Federation of Finnish Financial Services, Helsinki

Jones DC, Kalmi P (2015) Membership and performance in financial co-operatives: evidence from Finland. Rev Soc Econ 73(3):1–27

Jones DC, Kalmi P, Kauhanen A (2012) The effects of general and firm-specific training on wages and performance: evidence from banking. Oxf Econ Pap 64(1):151–175

Kalmi P (2012) Finnish co-operative banks and the crisis of the early 1990s. In: Boonstra W, Mooij J (eds) Co-operative banking in times of crisis. Amsterdam: VU Press.

Kiander J, Vartia P (1996) The great depression of the 1990s in Finland. Finn Econ Pap 9(1):72–88

Kuisma M, Henttinen A, Karhu S, Pohls M (2000) The pellervo story: a century of finnishcooperation, 1899–1999. Kirjayhtymä, Helsinki

Kuusterä A (2002) Lähellä ihmistä. Osuuspankkitoiminta 100 vuotta. Otava, Helsinki

Prinz M (2002) German Rural Cooperatives, Friedrich Wilhelm Raiffeisen and the Organization of Trust. 8th International Economic History Association Congress, Buenos Aires, Jul 2002

Cooperative Banks in France: Emergence, Mutations and Issues

Nadine Richez-Battesti and Gérard Leseul

Abstract The aim of this article is to present an overview of cooperative banks in France starting from their emergence, then provide the features of this model, their evolution in recent years, as well as the issues involved. Over the last 22 years, cooperative banks in France have displayed dynamism, especially in the face of listed commercial banks: they have gained market share, launched simple and easily understood products; they have been at the forefront of innovation (online banking services. . .), and have taken a greater role in recent reorganizations of the banking sector (emergence of cooperative groups), all the while, protecting their jobs and their networks. If cooperative banks have not been spared from the financial crisis, they were not the cause, and have been better able to resist due to the importance of retail banking activity, a diversification into other activities (insurance, electronic surveillance, real estate transactions, etc.) and less of a dependence on networks concerned with financial markets. They have thus maintained a good level of activities, especially in lending, resulting in deposit/lending ratios that are declining and the challenge of winning new deposits, which indicates a "resilience in the cooperative model in a time of crisis".

1 Introduction

The idea of a cooperative bank emerges in the first half of the nineteenth century. At the beginning, cooperatives banks were organizations that brought individuals in rather similar economic circumstances together. These organizations were either specialized in a certain sector, or non-specific. These cooperatives, which belonged to their members, could offer their financial intermediation services to economic

N. Richez-Battesti (✉)
Aix-Marseille University and Lest-Cnrs, Aix-en-Provence, France
e-mail: nadine.richez-battesti@univ-amu.fr

G. Leseul
Crédit Mutuel and University of Rouen, Rouen, France
e-mail: gerard.leseul@creditmutuel.fr

S. Karafolas (ed.), *Credit Cooperative Institutions in European Countries*, Contributions to Economics, DOI 10.1007/978-3-319-28784-3_4

agents that the large national banks did not wish to invest in and to people who were not provided for by large commercial banks. Originally, this cooperative credit system involved both depositing and borrowing and presupposed a strong "*affectio mutualis*". Today, they are universal banks included in the banking and financial system.

Cooperative banks play a fundamental role in financing the economy within the countries of the European Union and in France in particular. The uniqueness of French banks, compared to other European countries, can be seen in the number of cooperative banking groups and the significant share that they have taken in finance and in the economy. They represent nearly two thirds of retail banking activity and have 22 million members who participate directly in the governance of these establishments. Over the last 22 years, cooperative banks in France have displayed dynamism, especially in the face of listed commercial banks: they have gained market share, launched simple and easily understood products; they have been at the forefront of innovation (online banking services...), and have taken a greater role in recent reorganizations of the banking sector, all the while, protecting their jobs and their networks.

If cooperative banks have not been spared from the financial crisis, they were not the cause, and have been better able to resist due to the importance of retail banking activity, a diversification into other activities (insurance, electronic surveillance, real estate transactions, etc.) and less of a dependence on networks concerned with financial markets. They have thus maintained a good level of activities, especially in lending, resulting in deposit/lending ratios that are declining and the challenge of winning new deposits, which indicates a "resilience in the cooperative model in a time of crisis" (Birchall and Ketilson 2009).

The aim of this article is to present an overview of cooperative banks in France, with an outline of their history and evolution, then to characterize the current model and its importance on the French banking scene, and finally to describe a few of the challenges and issues confronting them.

2 French Cooperative Banks and Their Evolution

Most cooperative financial establishments appeared for the first time in France towards the end of the nineteenth century. They aimed to fight usury, promote access to banking services and lending for those who were excluded from it, and contribute to the development of their economic activities. Since their creation, cooperative banks have striven to put savings to work collectively in order to allow independent workers organized in cooperatives or not, then individuals, SMEs and non-profit organizations an access to lending. They trace their origins to two distinct *roots*. The Raiffeisen movement ("Social Christian" inclination) inspired the Crédit Agricole and the Crédit Mutuel, while the Schulze-Delitzch ("liberal" inclination) was the basis for the Banques Populaires. In France, unlike in Germany, there were no charismatic individuals who set the cooperative credit institution in motion, thus leaving a central role to a popular initiative (Toucas 2005, p. 42), especially in the two geographic birthplaces located in the borderline regions of the Northeast and eastern Mediterranean seaboard (p. 63).

From the emergence of these cooperative establishments, and over a long period, the French banking system was characterized by a dualism between the group of the French Banking Association (FBA) and that of public banks and cooperatives, the latter being highly involved in drawing on people's savings and financing artisans and SMEs. Today, the entire banking network is united within a single national federation: the French Banking Federation. However cultural differences subsist and the FBA is pursuing its consultancy activity, especially on social issues for a larger part of the banking sector (except for Crédit Agricole and Crédit Mutuel).

The period from the end of the nineteenth century up to today can be divided into three phases related to the evolution of the law in regards to credit institutions. We thus underline the important role of public policies to endorse the development of cooperative banks and the marks left by the French tradition of state interventionism in the banking sector.

2.1 The First Phase (from the Late Nineteenth Century to the Great Depression): Birth and Rapid but Regulated Development

During the second half of the nineteenth century, the banking system consisted mainly of merchant banks, private deposit banks whose activities focused on financing industrial capitalism and therefore large companies, as well as purchasing stock and national or foreign public debt. The system was completed with the development of savings banks (the first one founded in 1818) which developed thanks mainly to their savings accounts and whose funds were managed by the Caisse des Dépôts. This system excluded the financing of small farmers and craftsmen, giving rise to the emergence of several very fragile and rather unsustainable banking experiments such as small mutual credit unions as early as the 1860s: for example the establishment of the Crédit au Travail in 1863 aimed at cooperatives and the Société Crédit au travail, in 1865 the Caisse d'escompte des associations populaires. It wasn't until the end of the nineteenth century that these social economy banking initiatives born by grassroots organizations were institutionalized: Banques coopérative des associations ouvrières (Cooperative banks for workers' organizations) (1893), later becoming the Crédit cooperatif, the Crédit Agricole (1894); Banques Populaires (1878) the Crédit Mutuel (1899).

The state gradually granted them a legal framework which, nonetheless, was not codified into a single text for all cooperative banks. They formed a third category of banks, "organizations with a special legal status" which were more heavily regulated than commercial banks and private deposit banks. From a regulatory perspective, they were characterized by a limited area of activities; strict rules concerning the make-up of their membership, direct government support for part of their funding and their credit; tax liens especially regarding tax exemptions on profit, on the business license tax, on income securities, etc. They were increasingly endowed with central bodies, under state supervision, through which public funding was conveyed in the form of subsidized loans. The Law of 1917 standardized operating rules for the Banques Populaires, while the Law of 1920 set up a National Office of the Crédit Agricole (Toucas 2005, p. 79), a public institution to refinance the various banks originated from farmers' unions and to act as a financial network for diverse agricultural policies; the Crédit Cooperatif, organized as a central fund in 1937 also had to transfer state financial aid to cooperatives. A few were specialized: the Banques Populaires were involved with financing artisanal activities and SMEs, Crédit Agricole focused on farmers, Crédit Coopératif aimed more at cooperatives. Others had a general purpose: Crédit Mutuel or again Caisses d'Epargne (which were not yet cooperatives but promoted the acculturation of the French people in the use of savings accounts and expanded rapidly regionally) specifically targeted individuals in order to promote savings, access to banks, then to personal or consumer credit and to home loans. Thanks to their local presence, these banks also played an important role in financing small local associations in rural and urban areas.

2.2 *The Second Phase (1945 to the Beginning of the 1980s): Consolidation and Compartmentalization*

This second phase was characterized, first and foremost, by a consolidation of cooperative banks, largely encouraged by the government, through preserving advantageous conditions for access to resources and deposits. This was especially the case of Crédit Agricole which became the leading French bank.

Then, if in the beginning of this period, compartmentalization and specialization prevailed, the premises of a process of de-specialization were discerned. Thus, a first law in 1945 formalized compartmentalization, segmentation and the specialization of activities in the French banking system. It made provisions for the nationalization of the Bank of France and the large deposit banks and regulated the activity of "registered" banks (deposit banks, commercial banks and long- and medium-term loan banks). The specialization of "establishments with a special legal status" as well as within cooperative banks therefore spread to all credit organizations. But very quickly, contradictory trends appeared. In 1950, the Caisse Nationale du Crédit Agricole obtained the right to grant long-term loans; in 1959, it was entitled to develop the range of its activities beyond that of the rural world, a range which was thereafter steadily expanded. This de-specialization of cooperative banks was thus accompanied by an expansion of their clientele. In the same way, the savings and loan banks, Caisses d'Epargne, as of the Minjoz law of 1950, steadily achieved a virtual free use of their funds especially directed towards local government. In the middle of the 1960s, a series of reforms extended the de-compartmentalization and de-specialization of banking sector activities while continuing to disengage the state from financing channels. The scope of activity of cooperative banks was broadened once again (especially that of Crédit Agricole). This was seen as the first step in drawing closer to the activities of deposit banks and commercial banks.

Finally, the rapid expansion of cooperative banks and more widely of all financial intermediaries is attributable to the pace and nature of the economic growth rate during the "Trente Glorieuses", the Glorious Thirty (referring to the 30 years following WWII of dramatic economic growth in France) which was mainly founded on an economy of debt. In this unique context, cooperative banks were able to capitalize on advantages that their traditional focus on households and small entrepreneurs gave them. By developing the distribution of savings products or law taxes, cooperative banks were able to widen their product range and offer products and services to all middle and working class customers of a modernizing France.

2.3 *From 1980 to Nowadays: The Period of Mutations*

In a context of financial globalization on a European and international scale, the transformations which have affected cooperative banks are largely due to evolutions in the national or international environment (Pastré 2007). The French financial system reform, introduced by the banking law of 1984, supplemented by another law in 1996, was devoted to the de-specialization, de-compartmentalization, and de-intermediation ("the three D's) of banking activities in order to boost competition between financial intermediaries. The introduction of the term "credit institution" in view of European financial integration and harmonization, covers not only the former "registered" banks but also cooperative banks, Caisses d'Epargne (that the lawmaker legally transformed into cooperatives in June 1999 through an operation of "mutualization" designed to bestow an "owner" on all Caisses d'Epargne), financial companies and specialized financial institutions. The specialization of cooperative banks is being challenged as well as most of the advantages that they enjoy. Thus, these institutions have sought to form large competitive entities, not just in terms of the number of customers but also of the size of their workforce, resources or equity.

At the same time, lawmakers introduced a number of innovations and set up new markets and new products (MATIF, MONEP, a market for debt securities, etc.). These changes explain in part that cooperative banks, structures that up until then were in networks where the main activity remained *retail banking* (a legacy from their longstanding specialization) are restructured into larger entities (the *cooperative group*), which diversify the range of products offered to customers and enables the group to capture new markets. Capital increases and expansion of the area of activity, especially through internal growth, have contributed to the overlapping of the cooperative bank and conventional bank by trying to maintain financial control in the hands of cooperative banks. In fact increased competition has led to an intense restructuration of French and foreign financial sectors—activity reorganization, external growth operations (take-overs, acquisitions, mergers, etc.), market concentration, the search for productivity gains and critical size—where, with government support, cooperative banking networks are key players. Moreover, the efforts made on the part of cooperative networks to rationalize their IT systems, to pool small regional entities, develop inter-regional synergies in order to gain in efficiency and reduce operating coefficients are all very noteworthy.

Finally, the expansion of risk linked with the renewal of the characteristics of the lending market has required the development of common prudential regulations for all credit institutions and banking groups, regardless of their status (CCE 2010). Prompted by the continuous work achieved by the Committee of Basel and adapted to the European and national framework thanks to several directives, rules and regulations, this affiliation to strict prudential requirements through a process of standardization tends to obscure the uniqueness of cooperatives, both in the nature and remuneration terms of their equity capital which differ from that of conventional banks, and in the distinctive structure of the clientele making up their network.

Co-operative banks operate today in a competitive market where they are traditionally focused on retail financial business (Wyman 2008). Unfortunately, like the euro zone, the French economy had a difficult year, GDP growing by 0.4 % in 2014 as in 2013. The difficulties in international environment were aggravated by domestic issues. The fiscal consolidation weighed heavily on economic activity and the spending cuts decided in 2014 and tax increases of previous years depressed domestic demand. In this context, cooperative banks have more than demonstrated their ability to contribute to the financing of the economy.[1] Cooperative banks are a full model and not a substitute for joint-stock banks. They are competitive and resilient to the economic and financial crises. They are cost efficient and responsible because they retain the risks on their balance sheet. Consequently, the recent financial and economic crisis has reinforced the relevance of co-operative responses to today's needs.

3 The Current Model: Predominance of Retail Banking[2]

Retail Banking comprises the networks of regional cooperative banks and subsidiaries. This segment also includes some of the specialized activities whose products and services are marketed by the networks such as finance leasing, factoring, real estate businesses (investment, land development, real estate management, distribution and property development) and collective management of products distributed by networks.

[1] The Banker, FT Business, January 2013.

[2] Most of parts 2 and 3 were presented at the symposium of ACI in Lyon (France) in 2010.

All banking groups have attempted to extend their mesh by taking over companies with complementary networks. Thus, besides overseas achievements, BNP took over Banque de Bretagne in 1989, and Société Générale gained control of Crédit du Nord in 1997, then Paribas in 1999. Similarly, CCF acquired all of the capital of Banque de Savoie, Banque Dupuy de Parseval, Société Marseillaise de Crédit and Banque Hervet, before becoming HSBC France. For their part, cooperative banking groups have diversified their activities by taking over facilities specialized in financing large companies, in market activities or in certain types of loans. Thus, the Banques Populaires group acquired Natexis in 1998 (resulting from the merger of Crédit National with BFCE) which then became Natixis at the creation of BPCE, Crédit Agricole took control of Banque Indosuez in 1996, Sofinco in 1999 and Crédit Lyonnais in 2003, and Crédit Mutuel purchased CIC and Cofidis…

In a difficult economic environment, French bank earnings have confirmed their solidity thanks to rigorous risk management and a universal banking model which is based on a variety of activities noted the French Prudential Supervisory Authority in its annual reports.

After the year 2009 which continued to see some companies struggling with the financial crisis, the improvement of all intermediary balance sheets of the seven largest French groups in 2010 is an indication of the resilience of French banks in the face of the financial and economic crisis. Net earnings for the group (RNPG)[3] rose by 77 %, thus returning to its 2007 level (21.3 billion euros) before the financial crisis intensified/escalated.

The 2011 and 2012 figures showed sharp contrasts, with virtually constant increases for CM and BPCE and poor results for CA which had to manage its international development and its commitments related to Greek bank Emporicki. The 2013 performance showed CM and BPCE consolidated their growth and CA to restore its performance and thus recover its leadership. The 2014 figures below (Table 1) attest the predominance of cooperative banks in France.

Cooperative banks were created for a specific purpose: to supply banking services to their members and communities. Successfully they do not only provide benefits to their members and the local economy but also contribute to the diversity of the financial system and to offer better services to the clients. Even the most listed and world banks are (re)discovering retail banking.

Insofar as they are concerned, cooperative banks collectively account for 52 % of NBI (68.9 billion euros) of the main French companies. They have been particularly active in the renewal and resilience of the national banking scene maintaining the predominance of the retail bank in their portfolio of activities. Mergers between affiliates in the same group have often enabled companies to achieve economies of scale in administrative functions and to reinforce their sales teams. Companies authorized to deal with all banking and financial operations, French cooperative banks, still sometimes called "cooperative and mutual banks",

[3] Net income returning to group (or group share) does not take into account earnings returning to minority interests.

Table 1 Intermediary balance sheets for the five main French banks in 2014

In billions of euros	Total 2014	% Co-op	BNPP	SG	CA	BPCE	CM
Net banking income GNB	131.63	52	39.17	23.56	30.24	23.26	15.4
Operating costs	78.91	46	26.53	16.02	10.17	16.33	9.86
Gross operating income	46.71	56.8	12.64	7.54	11.06	9.92	5.55
Cost of risk	12.31	46	3.70	2.96	2.9	1.7	1.05
Operating ratio			67.7 %	67.7 %	63.4 %	70.2 %	64 %
Ratio common equity tier 1		<11.9	10.3 %	10.1 %	12.8 %	11.9 %	15.3 %
Leverage ratio		<4.5	3.6 %	3.8 %	5.2 %	4.5 %	6.4 %
Net profit	16.05	80[a]	0.5[b]	2.99	5.3	3.36	3.02
Net profit (group share)	13.61	80	0.16[c]	2.69	4.9	2.91	2.95

Source: data from banks (IFRS)
[a]Usely this ratio is about 66 %
[b]7.01 billion euros except US penalties
[c]7.01 billion euros except US penalties (six billions)

belong to networks endowed with central bodies governed by the provisions of articles L. 511-30 to L. 511-32 of the Monetary and Financial Code and whose powers must enable guaranteed respect of legal and regulatory measures, ensure liquidity and solvency for all the banks.

Though French cooperatives banks are each uniquely organised, they share a number of organizational traits directly related to their regional, philosophical, and rural or urban origins. Although there is a diversity of governance and development approaches, they all share a number of unifying characteristics and they all try to keep their own governance with a bottom-up structure. At French as international level their key values are: trust between the bank and its customers, democratic and prudent governance, resilience to adverse market developments, physical customer proximity, social commitment, solidarity, entrepreneurship and self-empowerment.

Therefore, the characteristics of the current cooperative banking model will now be presented.

3.1 From the Network to the Cooperative Group: Between Inverted Pyramid, Hybridization and Concentration

The term cooperative bank refers to the body consisting of different cooperative entities, organized geographically according to an inverted pyramid scheme, meaning that the local level holds the regional level which in turn controls the national level. Thus, a three-tier system is generally found: a local tier, and always both a regional and a national tier.

- On a local level, the local banks (Crédit Agricole, Crédit Mutuel), or local savings banks are cooperative entities, held in the form of shares by members. This "local" level does not exist in the Banque Populaire network. These local banks or local companies, organized on a local basis, then own the regional banks or credit unions.
- On a regional level, there are the regional savings and loan institutions (Crédit Agricole, Crédit Mutuel, Caisse d'Epargne) even inter-regional (Crédit Mutuel) or yet again regional banks (Banque populaire). In the Banque Populaire network, members, natural or legal persons, directly hold shares of the regional bank. These regional banks are all full-fledged credit institutions, and are cooperatives in the form of joint stock companies (as such, they have the legal and regulatory framework of joint stock companies apart from specific provisions applicable to cooperatives); they are cooperatives with fixed or variable capital, depending on the network. At Crédit Mutuel, there are also regional federations which serve as bodies for external representation and expression for local banks, and where regional strategies are discussed. In all these networks, regional entities hold joint control over the central body.
- The central body is the legal representative of the network for the government that must ensure affiliates of the cooperative group operate correctly and must also organize financial solidarity among the regional entities. Still called Central Fund, National Fund or Confederation initially, the central body's historic role has been to organize financial solidarity; in that capacity, it can centralize cash surpluses, temporarily refinance loss-making entities. Originally having the status of cooperative or association, this central organ has been transformed into a limited company, and even floated on the stock exchange. Apart from the special case of Crédit Mutuel whose official central body remains the political coordination entity for regional groups, namely the Confederation which has a status of association, Crédit Agricole and BPCE have made improvements to their organization. It is Crédit Agricole SA (a publicly listed corporation), which is the central body of regional banks that hold 54 % of the company, the rest spread around the market (shareholders, investors, employees, etc.). For Caisses d'épargne and Banques populaires, today, BPCE is the common central body equally owned by the network of 19 Banques Populaires and 17 Caisses d'épargne. In any case, when it is the financial body, the central body, is backed by a National Federation, a body for internal debate between the different regional entities in order to define strategic orientations for the group and sometimes serving as representative of the network before government. These organizations more or less are going to be harmonised in the next years, linked with the evolution of international (European Central Bank) and French banking supervision (ACPR). Thus, central bodies governing networks should be national financing structures, managing treasury for the regional groups and organizing the pooling of cooperative groups. The challenge is for cooperative movements to keep their specificities in a level playing-field. It means that cooperative organizations have to coordinate interactions with supervisors.

The term "cooperative group" characterizes all institutions and subsidiaries, whatever their legal status, controlled by the cooperative network. The vast majority of these subsidiaries are joint-stock banks, and are most often controlled either directly by the central body (e.g., Crédit Agricole, BPCE), or by a company which is itself a subsidiary of the central body (e.g., BPCE and Natixis) or by a regional entity (e.g., Crédit Mutuel). Cooperative groups are thus qualified as "hybrids", since they include a core of cooperative banks and are sometimes owners of a number of important joint-stock subsidiaries both within and outside national borders.

In the last 10 years, there has been a double movement of concentration. On the one hand, within each cooperative banking network, autonomy has been lost on the local level and a trend toward grouping on local levels and especially on the regional level has been seen. On the other hand, there has also been a consolidation among cooperative groups.

Since the consolidations of 2003 (after the participation of Crédit Coopératif in the membership of Groupe Banques Populaires) and of 2009 (creation of the BPCE group after the merger of two cooperative banks—Banques Populaires and Caisses d'Epargne), there are three cooperative banking groups left in France:

- The BPCE group resulting from the 2009 merger of Banques Populaires (consisting in regional Banques Populaires and two national Banques Populaires: Casden and Crédit Coopératif, since 2003, along with Crédit Maritime mutuel) and Caisses d'Epargne (formed since the Law of 25 June 1999, 275 Sociétés Locales d'Epargne, and Caisses d'Epargne et de Prévoyance), BPCE group has maintained its two brands, its two distribution networks and its two corresponding political federations;
- The Crédit Agricole Mutuel network, made up of local Crédit Agricole branches and regional banks affiliated with Crédit Agricole SA;
- The Crédit Mutuel network, consisting in general purpose local and federal Crédit Mutuel branches along with branches focused on agriculture, all affiliated with the Confédération Nationale du Crédit Mutuel.

Box 1: Overview of Cooperative Banks in France in 2014

The three cooperative groups Crédit Agricole, BPCE and Crédit Mutuel
(including Crédit coopératif)
Are among the five largest French banks
Together they amount to more than:
68.9 billion euros in combined turnover (GNP)
10.7 billion euros in net profit,
132 billion euros in equity
Leading banking network
Over 70 % of retail banks

(continued)

73 % of bank branches throughout France (excluding the Banque Postale network)
Over 90 % of the French population have a current or savings account
Over 22 million members
Leading lending institutions (more 60 % market share)
Leading financiers for SMEs and local development (74 % market share)
More than 330,000 employees (4/5 in France)
2/3 of employees and hirings in the banking sector
Sources: Annual reports Chiffres-clés 2014

3.2 Three Cooperative Banking Groups

After evoking the main data on the three French cooperative groups, we will describe them in three entries: their history, organization and corporate governance (Table 2).

Crédit Agricole Group
With 8,200,000 members, 2060 local banks, 11,300 branches and 150,000 employees, Crédit Agricole group is a decentralized mutual banking group, organized into three parts. It is the leading banking group in France and ranks second in Europe based on equity. The acquisition of Crédit Lyonnais in 2003 reinforced its position as leader in retail banking in France (with 28 % of retail deposits), brought a new dimension to its investment banking activities and allowed it to become the leader in asset management in France. Together, Crédit Agricole and LCL have over 50 million individual customers in France, as well as 1.4 million business customers, served by a network of over 9000 branches (11,300 windows). The first bank was created in 1894.

The central body of the Crédit Agricole network, CA S.A., is legally responsible for ensuring the liquidity and solvency of regional banks (however, not for Crédit Lyonnais), in accordance with L511-30 and L511-31 of the Monetary and Financial Code. 54 %-owned by the regional banks (with one exception) CA S.A. is listed on the Paris Bourse. The regional banks are required to retain a majority holding of CA S.A. and are not expected to raise their ownership stakes, in the immediate future. With no voting rights, CA S.A.'s 25 % stake in regional banks gives it only an economic interest. CA S.A. also acts as central bank for the group. Since 1988, the 39 regional banks and the central body have implemented a mechanism of pooling risk, under which regional banks have mutually pledged to honor their commitments, along with those of CA S.A. The economic and financial crisis over the past few years and a high exposure to certain risks for CA S.A. have been poorly coped with by a number of Crédit Agricole executives, bringing about a change of management. The 2012 performance was particularly poor, notably because of

Table 2 Main characteristics of banking groups in 2014

	N° cooperative structures and subsidiaries	N° members	N° clients[a]	N° employees[a]	GNB, balance sheet and income in billions of euros
Crédit Agricole Group	2489 local banks 39 regional banks 6990 branches in Fr. 2060 branches (around the world) 11,300 branches (total world)	8,200,000	50 millions	150,000 (1/3 out France)	GNB: 30.2 billion euros Balance sheet: 1.762 billion euros Net profit: 4.9 billion euros Shareholder's equity: 76.3 billion euros
BPCE Group	Two cooperative networks 8062 branches	8,900,000	36 millions	103,199	GNB: 23.257 billion euros Balance sheet: 1.223 billion euros Net profit: 2.907 billion euros Shareholder's equity: 55.3 billion euros
Includes: Caisse d'Epargne	245 local savings banks 17 Caisses d'Epargne 4.190 branches	5,000,000	25.5 millions	36,402	GNB: 7.1 billion euros
Includes: Banque Populaire Group[b]	19 Banques Populaires 3294 branches	3,900,000	9.1 millions	31,155	GNB: 6.3 billion euros
Crédit Mutuel Group	5790 branches (5298 in France) 18 regional Federations 2116 locals banks	7,600,000	30 millions	78,230	GNB: 15.4 billion euros Balance Sheet: 706 billion euros Net profit: 2.955 billion euros Shareholder's equity: 43.9 billion euros

Source: ACP 2011; ACPR 2014

[a]Including subsidiaries. Clients and employees (world)

[b]Including Crédit Coopératif group which has been a member of Banque Populaire group since January 2003

the disposal of Greek subsidiary Emporiki, which had an adverse impact on CASA's financial statements for a few months.

CA's poor internal performance finally had an impact on governance and the power balance between CASA, FNCA and the regional banks. The central body issue[4] and thus the question of ultimate power is raised within Crédit Agricole. Responses have been announced in 2014 in order to allow for a better combination and conciliation of the respective interests of the various members of the agricultural group, in order to protect their cooperative nature.

The latest renewal of statutory bodies provided the opportunity for fellow from the FNCA (national federation) and regional banks to regain control.

BPCE Group

The BPCE group has 8,600,000 members, 8000 branches and 115,000 employees. In November 2007, the Caisse d'Epargne and Banques populaires groups began to forge strong links between their banks by creating Natixis whose investments and stock market price tumbled over the course of the financial crisis causing a quasi-obligation to merge in June 2009 under government supervision.

The group, organized around a single central body since 31 July 2009, has sustained a strategy of co-existing networks while creating shared services that are increasingly integrated and under the responsibility of one authority. The appointment of its current president by the president of France has been protested against by labor unions who feel the group has suffered a loss of independence. A new network organization has arisen from this merger: the preservation of the national federation of Caisse d'Epargne savings banks and the creation of a federation of Banques Populaires allow the group to retain a political organization which conforms substantially to the historic structure and to the positioning of each of the cooperative networks. BPCE, the joint central body for Caisses d'Epargne and Banques Populaires, was set up on 31 July 2009. As central body, it is in charge of strategy, control, coordination, and management of the group, for which it ensures solvency. Replacing the Caisse Nationale des Caisses d'Epargne and Banque Fédérale des Banques Populaires, BPCE, which has the status of credit institution, has been organized as a limited company governed by an executive and advisory board. It is held equally by 17 Caisses d'Epargne and 19 Banques Populaires whose capital is respectively held 80 % by members and 20 % by the CCI mainly owned by Natixis which disposes of 27.7 in floating capital. The state holds preferred shares, with no voting rights. Today, BPCE ranks second in French cooperative banking groups.

- **including Caisse d'Epargne, 17 Caisses d'Epargne**
  5,000,000 members, 17 Caisses d'Epargne, 245 local savings banks, 37,240 employees, 4190 branches + 17 agencies *Monbanquierenligne*. The **Caisses d'Epargne** were not originally cooperative banks. They gradually diversified and expanded their activities becoming universal banks. After a process of intense concentration (the number of banks dropped from 600 to 35 between 1945 and 1991) the Caisses d'Epargne officially became cooperative banks with

[4] The central body carrying out the inspection, control and representation duties is determined by French law. Listed entities CASA and BPCE represent the Crédit Agricole group and the Banques Populaires and Caisses d'Epargne groups, respectively. In the case of Crédit Mutuel, the federation, which is a political body, represents the Group as a whole.

the law of 1999. The lawmaker and the government at the time hoped to bring an end to the formerly used status of *sui generis* and grant Caisses d'épargne a genuine status compatible with the evolution of the European banking world. In the mind of the lawmaker as it was for past directors, it was indeed the idea of granting Caisses d'épargne a status that would permit them to raise capital, participate in European banking restructuring, and eventually to consider a stock flotation which was impossible without a clear legal status. This choice, dictated by parameters of competition, was nevertheless consistent with the philosophy and practices of the Caisses d'Epargne and cooperative banks in France.

– **including Banques Populaires, 18 Banques Populaires**
  3,900,000 members, 9.1 millions customers, 31,535 employees, 3294 branches + 16 branches e-BanquePopulaires and Crédit Coopératif group, 2058 employees. The **Banques Populaires** provide a set of banking services to different customers: individual customers, small and medium-sized businesses and professionals. Through Natexis and its subsidiaries, they are also involved in factoring, leasing, private equity, employee savings, and insurance. Essentially with a domestic target, Banques Populaires are the sixth retail banking network in France.

The first Banque Populaire was founded in 1878 in Angers and after rapidly expanding; a status of Banques Populaires was adopted in 1917. Their aim was to promote business lending for small and medium-sized enterprises. The group was gradually structured and organized around the Caisse Centrale des Banques Populaires (1921) which centralized and invested the network's surplus funds. In this way the 74 Banques Populaires expressed their determination to be financially solidary. In 1929, the group set up a Chambre Syndicale des Banques Populaires, or trade association (association law 1901) which was in charge of inspections, coordination, collective management and representation. More recently, the Banque fédérale was transformed into a joint-stock bank and gradually superseded the Chambre Syndicale. It represented the Banque Populaire group and controlled its activities as well as defining its strategy. Several projects were carried out (a joint computing platform for the group, i-BP), an alliance with Crédit Coopératif and Crédit Maritime was organized and Banque Fédérale des Banques Populaires became their central body. In 2006, the group's managers decided to create Natixis with the Caisse d'Epargne group. This was followed by a policy of external growth: acquiring a majority stake in FONCIA (2007), acquiring the network of seven HSBC France regional banks. Then, with the 2009 recession, they sold off Société Marseillaise de Crédit to Société Générale in order to free up cash to reimburse a state loan which all French banks had underwritten.

Crédit Mutuel Group
7,600,000 members, 2131 local banks, 5790 outlets, 78,230 employees. Crédit Mutuel group is organized in three levels:

- Local: like the other mutual banking groups, the first level represents the members, who have 2131 local banks. The Crédit Mutuel local banks adhere to one of the 18 regional federations, which are affiliated to the Confédération Nationale du Crédit Mutuel (CNCM). CNCM is the central body of the network and the Caisse Centrale du Crédit Mutuel is the instrument used to organize national solidarity.

- Regional: strategic bodies, regional federations represent Crédit Mutuel in regions and control local banks and the federal bank that they adhere to. Federal or interfederal banks ensure banking operations (cash management, financial, technical and IT services).
- National: the Confédération Nationale du Crédit Mutuel (CNCM) which accounts for the third level does not carry on banking business. One of its main responsibilities is the cohesion and control of the whole group, representing the group vis-à-vis supervisory authorities and coordinating the mechanism of solidarity.

Crédit Mutuel is the least centralized cooperative group. It draws together the most members and manages the biggest network of directors (24,200). Its market share has steadily risen (15 % in deposits, 17 % in lending in 2010). The regional banks and federations, solidly entrenched in their territory, retain many prerogatives. Economic realities are very diverse: for instance, a large interfederal bank has developed around the historic Strasbourg Federation (Crédit Mutuel Centre Est Europe, the whole worth nearly 80 % of the total assets of the group) which will soon join 11 regional Federations in order to share the operations of deposits and financing and a second cluster (Arkéa) consisting in Brest, Bordeaux, and Clermont), while Crédit Mutuel du Nord continues its development independently.

Overall, the Crédit Mutuel-CIC group has the best ratio common equity, is the second network in market share for credit, the second retail banking network in number of branches, ranked third for equity (tier one), and is the third French cooperative banking group. In 2014, the quality and robustness of its assets was confirmed by the European Central Bank (ECB) and the European Banking Authority (EBA), which ranked it first among the largest French banks based on stress testing.

3.3 Characteristics in Common

True to their original mission, co-operative banks are committed to promoting the economic interests of their members/clients by supplying them with a comprehensive range of financial services and giving benefits such as local development, a general level of confidence in the market or better housing conditions.

Despite their specificities, cooperative banks have retained three shared characteristics:

- their activities cover all or almost all banking and financial operations and they target any customer whether they are members or not (possibility offered by the law of 1992.);

- their locations and development are generally linked to a territory which, depending on the networks, can cover one department (the case for a few regional banks for Crédit Agricole and Banques Populaires) or several (most Banques Populaires, Caisses d'Epargne, federal banks of Crédit Mutuel and regional Crédit Agricole banks);
- their cooperative or mutual mode of governance is characterized by a democratic involvement of members at every level of decision, a high level of decentralization and except for Crédit Coopératif, the existence of a hierarchical management structure.

Throughout the 2000s, the market share taken by cooperative banking networks remained substantial: they accounted for over 65 % of deposits and over 70 % of lending to small and medium-sized enterprises and industries. Their very large market share in mortgages and in business loans for small and medium-sized enterprises and industries, bears out how dug in cooperative banks, are in their territories as does their contribution to job creation. Furthermore, these banks appear to be over-represented in medium-sized towns and rural areas and targeted at families. Finally, their customers are on average wealthier than for other banks (Parpais 2004; Richez-Battesti, Gianfaldoni 2006). Their commitment to retailing gives them a competitive edge, linked to in-depth knowledge of the customer-members which facilitates the provision of loans, and enables them to manage risk well. Thanks to their strong position as retail banks, cooperative institutions handle a large proportion of payment flows: Crédit Mutuel and Crédit Agricole are the two main players in electronic banking.

Therefore, it is clear that cooperative groups retain a strong focus on retail banking: it is particularly true of Crédit Mutuel, the leading bancassurer,[5] which achieved nearly 90 % of its income and 87.2 % of its GNP in 2010 with retail bancassurance business (77 % retail banking and 10.2 % in insurance). As for Crédit agricole, if it is more invested in finance banking and investment business, since 2009, it has displayed a willingness to refocus on retail activities.

Mutual banks bring a strong contribution to the profitability of the retail banking sector. They are also effective in operational terms with a sound cost to income ratio (often lower than that of other players, i.e. 63 % as compared with 71 % in 2010 and 2011 and 63–64 % compared with 67–68 % in 2014). In general, mutual banks generate more than two thirds of French retail banking profits (Table 3).

[5] Bancassurance: the activities of banking and insurance as complementary was launched by Crédit Mutuel at the end of the 1970s and it allows banks to expand services to customer-members and the short cycles of banking complement the long cycles of insurance. Bancassurance is not a juxtaposition of two activities within a financial holding that are foreign to each other but rather an integrated model by which insurance products are sold almost exclusively by the banking network to its customers.

Table 3 Share of mutual players in the performance of retail banks in France

In billions of euros	% Co-op	BNPP (%)	SG (%)	CA (%)	BPCE (%)	CM (%)
Operating ratio		67.7	67.7	63.4	70.2	64
Ratio common equity tier 1	<11.9	10.3	10.1	12.8	11.9	15.3
Leverage ratio	<4.5	3.6	3.8	5.2	4.5	6.4

Source: Data from banks

4 Recent Trends and Issues

The French banking system remains characterized by a diversity of statuses but also by a trend toward homogenization (CECEI 2008; Pollin 2007). Indeed, the specificity and restriction in cooperative banking business have gradually disappeared since the Banking law of 1984 making them universal banks. Equally, the state's withdrawal from the banking system and waves of privatizations for formerly nationalized institutions have enabled cooperative banks to make acquisitions leading to a relative hybridization of the model (Ory et al. 2006; Guider and Roux 2010).

The relative standardization of banking products (range and rates), the disappearance of untapped profitable markets and the volatility of customers have contributed to the reinforcement of competition between banks, including between cooperative banks, and to a tightening of margins (Fonteyne 2007). Indeed, customers use multiple banks, are increasingly well informed, more mature about their banking needs, more demanding, and do not hesitate to call upon several banks and to pit them against each other. The penetration rate of banks in French households is close to 100 %: every French person has a bank account and half of them have opened two or more.[6] Distribution networks through call centers, Internet, cellphones, and so on have increased sharply. In this context, French co-operative banks build a high level of services.

After having failed for a long time to master the cooperative model and its governance, rating agencies are beginning to understand its relevance and authenticity (Fonteyne 2007; Kearney 2014). They even consider that it is a real asset which contributes to its economic success. Moreover, the local anchoring which is paramount to its business (cooperative banks are local players, but they are also important contributors at both county and regional level) makes them a pivotal player.

In an August 2013 study, Fitch ascertained that French cooperative banking groups, such as Crédit Agricole, BPCE and Crédit Mutuel, lead a risk-free strategy focused on volumes which, even if it exposes them to weaker margins, enables them to reinforce their balance sheets (Fitch 2013). Cooperative banks continue to consolidate the sources of financing by attracting more client deposits (Table 4).

[6] Gloukoviezoff (2010) reminds us however that nearly five millions people are excluded not from the French banking system but from credit. The themes of exclusion and over-indebtedness are being widely debated.

Table 4 Banks Image Ratio (Indice d'image des Banques)

	Index	Rank among the 30 French large companies
Crédit Mutuel	59	8th
Caisse d'Epargne	54	9th
Banque Populaire	52	10th
La Banque Postale	46	nc
Crédit Agricole	33	18th
BNP Paribas	30	23rd
LCL	29	22nd
Société générale	23	25th

Source: IPSOS/Posternak, May 2013
Note: The image Ratio is the difference between the % of persons having a good image and the % of persons not having a good image of the company
National sample composed of 968 persons, 18 years old or older

4.1 Regulatory Reforms

Successive regulatory reforms have gradually altered the French banking environment. The financial crises resulted in a regulatory strengthening aimed at a stricter supervision of the risks related to banking operations, a strengthening of consumer protection and the financial solidity of players on these markets. Such a move is observed world-wide, but also at European and national level (Banking Act of July 2013). More specifically, we may note since 2007 three regulatory waves concerning:

- the segregation of operations and the solution of crisis situations (bail-in debt, Liikanen proposal, taxes on financial transactions at EU level, Volcker rule, Barnier project, etc.);
- banks' financial solidity (Solvency II, Basle III, CRR-CRD IV, overhaul of the main risks, NSFR and LCR liquidity ratios, regulation on securitisation, IFRS 9 and 13, etc.);
- strengthened risk monitoring (Mifid 2, AML rules, heightened reporting of transactions and market instruments, etc.).

In general, these various regulations are designed for companies limited by shares and listed companies calling on institutional investors. These regulations too often neglect the specific features of cooperative groups in terms of governance or consolidation, and thus gradually alter the original model of cooperative banks. Such regulatory trivialization is accompanied with strategic impact related to compliance with the prudential ratios and growth objectives. Such regulatory changes thus tend to put the cooperative principles under pressure (Ory et al. 2012).

4.2 Mergers, Alliances and Internal Concentration

Since the bank law of 1984, the number of banking institutions has been falling continuously. The aims of these alliances and mergers are to reinforce synergies, to strive for economies of scale and to control costs. Between cooperative banks in the same group, the number of regional banks has dropped from 155 in 1999 to 101 in 2010, in other words a decline of one third in 10 years. Over the last 10 years, mutual banks have decreased from 54 to 39 in the Crédit Agricole network, from 24 to 18 in the Crédit Mutuel network, from 42 to 18 for the Banque Populaire network and from 34 to 17 within the Caisses d'Epargne network (CECEI 2008).

This phenomenon is not unique to cooperative banks. For 10 years, all lending institutions have experienced a decline in numbers. Commercial banks listed on the stock exchange have slid from 342 in 1999 to 290 in 2008 (−15 %) and specialized banks have plunged by 50 %. Thus a movement towards concentration and oligopolization of the banking market is being seen. At the end of 2009, the seven leading French banking groups were receiving around 90 % of deposits and granting 84 % of loans.

Thanks to setting aside a substantial portion of their profits and to a controlled evolution of weighted risks, the main banks have seen their solvency ratio reach historically high levels. During the first quarter of 2011, they were able to reimburse in full the last aid supplied by the state in 2009 (ACP).

Furthermore, banks are actively preparing for the move to new banking regulations (Basel 3). This new agreement will make provisions for strengthening the level of quality of equity in banking and cooperative banks are lobbying hard so that their mode of organization (shares…) will be taken into account in developing prudential standards. Increase in equity is mainly built up on core capital or Tier One which is made up of the "purest" elements. Cooperative banks have among the best ratios (11.5 % for Crédit Mutuel, 10.3 % for Crédit Agricole…).

Competition, however, continues to work; it has even intensified including among cooperative banks that have embarked on performance improvements.

But there has also been a movement toward creating banks (for example, a European passport for a foreign bank) and an expansion of retail banking services. While online banking is developing, the number of permanent branches and the total workforce, especially for cooperative banks, has risen by 10 % in 10 years.

Alliances have also concerned pooling and sharing services in the aim of cost control. With average operating ratios of roughly 60 %, weak earnings growth, banks have to focus all their efforts on banking fees. Electronic banking (means of payment) and information technology have been given priority. The IT system at CIC has been migrating towards Crédit Mutuel's system over the past several years. In early 2007, the Caisses d'Épargne began their migration towards a single system in order to gain 2 points on their operating ratio. Crédit Agricole initiated the migration of its five computer systems to a single system. This is now being followed by merging back-office services for sales staff (asset management, consumer credit). In this context, banks have developed several types of strategy: either intra-group pooling of services (Crédit Mutuel, Crédit Agricole or BPCE for means of payment, leasing, purchasing, etc.) or intra-group partnerships including with non-mutual institutions (BNP Paribas + BPCE or Société Générale + Crédit Agricole). But it doesn't seem foreshadow future hybrid alliances. . .

4.3 Diversification and External Growth: Hybrid Groups and European Banking Consolidation

The French cooperative banking groups have also begun operations of diversification and external growth. This has resulted in the creation of new institutions, licensed as banks, finance companies or investment businesses as well as in takeovers of existing institutions. The main takeover operations were those of Banque Indosuez, then Crédit Lyonnais by Crédit Agricole group, the Natexis takeover, and the affiliation of Crédit Coopératif and Crédit Maritime Mutuel to the Banque Populaire group, Crédit Industriel et Commercial's takeover by Crédit Mutuel via the Banque Fédérative of Crédit Mutuel—BFCM, Crédit foncier de France and Banque San Paolo's takeover by the Caisses d'Epargne. There was also an attempt at an alliance between the insurance division of Banques populaires and Caisses d'Epargne with two mutual insurers (Maif, Macif).

Trans-border operations are increasing. Uncommon until the early 2000s, trans-border mergers and acquisitions have been developing over the last 3 years, especially in markets where concentration levels are still low (Italy where a "France-Italy axis" is taking shape: BNP Paribas/BNL, Crédit Agricole/Cariparma, Caisse d'Epargne in alliance with Banca Carige, Crédit Mutuel in alliance with BPM in Italy or Banco popular in Spain, etc.; Germany where a wave of concentration is forecast), in Central and Eastern Europe (countries with strong growth potential, where consolidation is nearing completion), the Maghreb and as far away as Russia and Asia.

Cooperative banks are thus rather discrete but active players in bank consolidation in Europe:

- Trans-border retail banking (CMNE active in Belgium, CMCEE has 18,000 customers in Germany, Crédit Agricole Bankoa has about 50 branches in the Spanish Basque country, etc.);
- Trans-border external growth: the Austrian RZB pioneers in East-Central Europe (and today in Ukraine, in Bosnia. . .), CA in Italy, Greece, Portugal, Spain, etc.
- European partnerships: Unico (pooling of technical resources for several cooperative banks), and more recently Equens in SEPA payments (Rabobank + DZ Bank).

However, it should be noted that Crédit Mutuel group's European involvement remained weak, and is even being re-focused on France: roughly less than 10 % in the last 10 years but with a priority to a partnership with Caisses Desjardins in Québec for a joint development in North America, whereas Crédit Agricole's share in European business has risen from 13 to 33 % in the same period, the market accounting for, respectively 92 % of involvement for Crédit Mutuel and 47 % for Crédit Agricole SA).

4.4 A Cosmetic Reconquering of Membership?

All the cooperative banking networks have also built up strategies to win back their members, in particular through a better knowledge of their characteristics, an improvement in information intended for them, and an effort to rally them (Richez-Battesti 2007). Revitalizing *l'affectio mutualis* and promoting their cooperative distinction, they are reasserting their value system, especially with innovative partnership arrangements. Although the number of members actually did rise, the question of mobilizing them remains more complex, as is the issue of circulating information between administrators and members (Caire 2010). Can members play the role of regulating mechanism in a truly democratic process or are they forced to approve decisions taken by a technostructure within an official democracy? Without going as far as saying that the salaried top executives have taken all the power (Dubois and Abhervé 2008), it can nevertheless be underlined that members have been victims of complacency towards the proposals of their senior executives, of relative information asymmetry about the potential risks in future business, as well as insufficient cooperative training in order to understand and question managerial strategies, which are more often imposed than debated (Richez-Battesti 2009). Is there a third path between membership inefficiency and powerlessness, to ensure the sustainability of a democratic economic model, placing the issue of how to use money back to the core of its strategy? Will this model inevitably become trivialized? Can reconquering membership be done independently without strengthening the awareness of the cooperative specificity for employees?

A bill on the social economy and the cooperatives discussed at the end of 2013 and in 2014 in the French Parliament incidentally provides for several provisions in order to strengthen the transparency obligations vis-à-vis members. Such is, in particular, the case for the cooperative review process which will oblige all cooperative enterprises to regularly use a tool aimed at verifying the proper democratic and cooperative functioning of the bank. Moreover, the French Government wants to take special measures in order to better understand the sometimes hybrid nature of cooperative development (mix of cooperative companies and previously listed companies which were acquired by the cooperative through external growth).

In the same time French cooperative banks developed all their full membership while trying to put dynamism in their local and regional general meetings. The "membership" often is greeted in the various internal newspapers. The co-operative spirit is clearly asserted.

5 French Cooperative Banks During the Financial Crisis

While, in the nineteen nineties, French cooperative banks had stood out because they had proved more resilient than banks in the form of listed companies limited by shares, certain observers consider that such an assessment is not valid as regards the recent financial crisis (2007–2010). "The crisis did not really make a difference between cooperative banks and other banks" (Juvin 2013). This is due to many factors. "Mutual banks were recently converted to the management imperative, and they had the zeal of new converts: they wanted to do better than commercial banks! This led to indecent excesses, in particular in order to lower the cost to income ratio." While there may be some truth in this statement, may we consider that cooperative banks resisted less well the last financial crises or that they betrayed their principles?

On the contrary, in a study entitled "Resilience of the Cooperative Business Model in Times of Crisis", Johnston Birchall (2013) stated that, overall, during the recession, the banks owned by their customers had been more stable and more effective than major traditional banks.

Box 2: European Cooperative Banks During the Financial Crisis

- Between 2007 and 2010, cooperative banks' assets increased by 10 %.
- The customer base of cooperative banks increased by 14 %.
- 7 % of European cooperative banks recorded losses during the financial crisis.
- The lending banks' reserves increased by more than 14 %.
- The savings deposited with the lending banks increased by 1 % in 2008, 15 % in 2009 and 7.3 % in 2010.
- The loans granted by lending banks slightly decreased in 2008, and then increased by 7.6 % and 5.3 %, respectively, during the next 2 years.
- Almost all losses recorded by cooperative banks were covered in 1 or 2 years.
- Almost all indicators improved and became positive again.

Source: Birchall J., ILO March 2013

While listed banks were driven by the resolve to maximise profits for their shareholders, which led certain of these banks to assume increased risks when investing, cooperatives "made better use of their limited own funds and continued to register profits, because they were devoting their efforts to the recycling of savings into loans, rather than depending on the markets" (Birchall 2013).

During the years preceding the crisis, in Europe in general and in particular in France, cooperative banks were awarded a stability rating (capital ratio) higher on average than that of listed banks. They obtained a ratio equal to 9.2 % as compared with 8.4 % for listed banks. In France and in the Netherlands, nearly 50 % of the cooperative banks were more stable. "Financial co-ops may not have the same ups as other banks, but neither do they have the same downs. As such they are more sustainable businesses than other banks." (Birchall 2013)

Nevertheless, although financial cooperatives are more stable and risk-averse, they are not always immune to excess and their main risk consists in the loss of their specific nature. Is such a risk specifically French? In addition to the responsibilities of cooperatives themselves, which sometimes want to reach the same financial performance levels as listed companies, national supervisors and European authorities are not blameless. Their wish to have only one leadership leads them to promote conformance or even one single economic model, whilc the diversity of the various models is the key to resilience, whether in banking matters or society-wide (Juvin 2013). The transfer to the new European authority of the banking supervision and control function, as part of the Single Supervisory Mechanism (MSU), shall not simplify this situation, because, at European level, cooperative banks only account for a 20 % market share and are thus collectively less powerful than the dominant "listed company" model.

In January 2014 (position 3 dated 29/01) thus in June, the combination of the CRD IV and the reading that may be made of this provision by the French Prudential and Regulatory Authority (ACPR) challenged the characterisation of chairmen of the board of directors of cooperative banks as chief executive officers. The denial of such characterization is based on the segregation of duties and thus calls into question the patient dialogue and conservatism stemming from the "four eyes" rule dear to the cooperatives.

Nevertheless, the cooperative banking model moves forward in two directions: economic performance and cooperative spirit.

In one hand, recently, in an unprecedented year, the giant "audit" carried out in 2014 by the European Central Bank (ECB) and the European Banking Authority (EBA) on 130 eurozone banks showed the quality of the French cooperative banks' assets and its high level of resilience in the event of a crisis. The comprehensive assessment -which consisted of an asset quality review and forward stress tests- conducted by the European Central Bank (ECB) in 2014 highlighted cooperative banks' solidity in the face of unfavorable economic scenarios, with ratios reaching significantly much more than the 5.5 % hurdle rate set by the ECB (Crédit Mutuel: 12.91 %;...)

In the other end, in each annual report, French cooperative banks explain strategic plans including specific commitments to bring this cooperative banking model to life: a model it embodies, one that sets it apart from the competition and can be seen in practice each and every day. Three categories of program are usually conducting: "customers and regions, employees and cooperative shareholders.

With the aim of adding a cooperative dimension when measuring quality of service and relations, measuring the societal impact of banking activity, keeping track of how the regions use the deposited savings, preventing banking exclusion, ensuring the accessibility of energy transition investments, and involving cooperative shareholders in banking innovation."[7]

6 Conclusion

What clearly differentiates cooperative banks from incorporated joint-stock banks is their corporate governance structure characterized by the overlap between ownership and customers through the members, and the granting of a single vote to each member (Pflimlin 2009). Compared to the single mindset of "global" companies, cooperative banks counter with the network effect which allows them to combine retail banking in small units with the power of the union enabling them to share technical and financial tools. It is precisely this combination that must be preserved.

The financial crisis generated a crisis of confidence on the part of the general public toward the financial system (Deletré 2009). In this context where every bank is competing with marketing initiatives in order to attract and satisfy customers and to develop savings, the building of a new relationship between bankers and their customers, based on renewed confidence is the key to the future of these institutions. For cooperative banks, it is no longer enough to refer to historic values of ethics and solidarity and to recall their humanist basis (whether secular or religious) nor even to reassert the citizen's enterprise, other businesses do it and the current body of regulations (NRE, Grenelle II) push companies toward more transparency (Aglietta 2007; Juvin 2009). They must assert and live their difference. It is up to cooperatives to find the right balance between strong, rigorous and fully responsible management and boards of administration made up of elected officials who keep a close eye on how the company is managed and are attentive to the aspirations of society (Lamarque 2007). Without vigorous mutualism, cooperative banks would be like the others. Without good business performance, mutualism would only be another noble-minded idea, without resources or future. This implies that managers (elected or paid) know how to preserve the dialectic between sharing and autonomy, between individual responsibility and solidarity having the objective of satisfying the member and not the stock market price or achieving huge sizes.

A governance guide of cooperatives and mutual associations recently recalled such obvious principles (Pflimlin et al. 2014).[8] The guide contains several recommendations[9] aimed at organizing the board, making it more accountable and

[7] Annual report BPCE 2014.

[8] Published in January 2014 by the *Institut Français des Administrateurs* (IFA) and drafted under the aegis of Etienne Pflimlin, Honorary Chairman of Crédit Mutuel, this guide recalls the primary role of members and the role of elected officials/Directors representing the members.

[9] 33 recommendations form the substance of this governance guide.

increasing the effectiveness of its work. The sound governance of the cooperatives which is recalled in this guide relies on a sound combination between:

- first, the effective involvement of representative democracy in the determination of collective objectives and the supervision of their attainment, it being understood that, regardless of its composition, the board of directors[10] is a collegial body responsible for making decisions and supervising the operational management delegated to executive officers;
- second, the involvement of members within committees, commissions or working groups, in order to express the needs of users of cooperatives and mutual associations and prepare projects and decisions then submitted for approval to the authorities defined by the by-laws; i.e. participatory democracy;
- and finally, the initiative and responsibility of executive officers and their teams in keeping with the initial project, the entrusted mandates and the collective interests of the members.

Both on a European and national level, the fast " game of go" in banking alliances will continue (Pastré 2007) at the very moment when new arrivals such as insurers, large retailers, or telecom companies are intruding more and more in banking business, sometimes mounting alliances or subcontracting arrangements.[11] The model of the universal bank providing a wide range of products and services all over the world appears to be faltering but it remains well adapted on a supra-regional or continental level. Some banks might be tempted to form alliances in order to better specialize and hold strong global positions, thus, asset management activities at Crédit Agricole and Société Générale have been merged to create a new joint venture « Amundi ». A few opportunities may appear in domestic markets. Regulators are bound to recommend that certain weakened banks sell off companies acquired in the 2000s. Well-run cooperative banks, with stabilized equity will be able to seek buyouts and continue their external growth in the European market as did Crédit Mutuel recently in taking over Citibank Germany then Citibank Belgium...

Cooperative dynamism must most certainly seize a few opportunities, develop their expertise on a national and international level, but also enable the preservation of a strong regional culture and act locally. This will undoubtedly involve (depending on the networks) development and a better organization of shared resources (IT, cost control, etc.). This is particularly the case for a democratic cooperative organization through decentralizing responsibilities and through a participative operation that involves its members, both elected and employed. Recent mergers shouldn't change the strong presence of several French cooperative banks; this 'French exception" in the European banking sector should even be strengthened in the next years. Despite differences in governance, all the cooperative institutions are relatively centralized with a substantial degree of internal

[10] Or where applicable the supervisory board.

[11] Thus Crédit Mutuel has formed a partnership with Leclerc supermarkets for payment services.

cooperation, (especially for support operations and fund management...). One of the most daunting challenges for the sector remains the preservation of the cooperative identity in view of the development of integrated models (Richez-Battesti and Gianfaldoni 2008; CEPS 2010).

The hybrid model developed by certain cooperative banks (cooperative regional structures and central body partially listed on the stock exchange) offers the possibility of rapidly mobilizing capital and carrying out alliances without having to finance them with cash on hand. But it is similar to a veiled capitalism (Batac et al. 2008) which may gradually eat away at the cooperative foundations of these organizations: power can rapidly slip away from members to shareholders or their representatives. Overall, these risks have not escaped the attention of cooperative banks or their administrators and several groups have begun collective reflection on the issue. The financial crisis and a strong commitment to differentiation may quickly raise awareness about the need for renewing membership, and its involvement in the life and governance of local banks

Because its future is promising in the market economy, the cooperative bank should not reconcile its calling as a mutual organization with a capitalist evolution, but it should preserve the reconciliation of interests between the investor and the consumer who make up, at the heart of this organization, the one and only: member. The nerve centre of the cooperative agreement remains the membership (Richez-Battesti et al. 2006).

References

ACP (2011) Les chiffres du marché français de la banque et de l'assurance 2010

ACPR (2014) Les chiffres du marché français de la banque et de l'assurance. https://acpr.banquefrance.fr/publications/rapports-annuels/chiffres-du-marche-francais-de-la-banque-et-de-lassurance.html

Aglietta M (2007) In Pastré et al, 2007, La guerre mondiale des banques, coll. "Les cahiers - le cercle des économistes", PUF, Paris

Batac J, Maymo V, Pallas-Saltiel V (2008) "Entre mutualisme et capitalisme : le modèle de gouvernance hybride du groupe Crédit agricole". Recma 308:23–34

Birchall J (2013) Resilience in a downturn, the power of financial cooperative. International Labor Office, Geneva

Birchall J, Ketilson LH (2009) Resilience of the cooperative business model in times of crisis. BIT, Genève

Caire G (2010) De la démocratie dans certaines banques coopératives. RECMA, Paris 316: 41–57

CCE (2010) http://www.entreprises.coop/semaine/UPLOAD/media/file/209_GNCGouvernement%20dentreprises.pdf

CECEI (2008) Rapport annuel Du Comité des Etablissements de crédit et des entreprises d'investissement, Banque de France, Paris, www.cecei.org

CEPS (2010) Investigating Diversity in the Banking Sector in Europe: The Role of Cooperative Banks, Sept

Deletré B (2009) Le contrôle du respect des obligations professionnelles à l'égard de la clientèle dans le secteur financier. Rapport de l'Inspection Générale des Finances, Juillet

Dubois P, Abhervé M (2008) Les banques coopératives, du pire au meilleur pour le développement de l'Economie sociale. http://www.univ-mlv.fr/ecosoc
Fitch (2013) French cooperative banks peer review, Fitch France, Paris. https://www.fitchratings.com/gws/en/fitchwire/fitchwirearticle/french-bancassurers-may?pr_id=802951
Fonteyne W (2007) Cooperative Banks in Europe: Policy Issues. IMF Working Paper 07/159, July
Gloukoviezoff (2010) L'exclusion bancaire : le lien social à l'épreuve de la rentabilité, Coll. Le lien social, PUF
Guider H, Roux M (2010) L'essentiel de la banque coopérative en Europe : stratégies et défis, éd. Revue Banque, Paris
Juvin H (2009) "Les fantômes de la liberté", in Rapport moral sur l'Argent dans le monde, Revue d'Economie Financière, Paris
Juvin H (2013) L'avenir des banques mutualistes ou coopératives, éd. Revue Banque, Paris
Kearney AT (2014) Concilier democratie et efficacité économique; le modèle mutualiste. Institut Montaigne, Paris
Lamarque E (2007) Mutualisme et valeurs d'entreprise, Les cahiers pour l'histoire de l'épargne, n°11, Mars Paris
Ory J-N, Gurtner E, Jaeger M (2006) Les enjeux des mutations récentes des groupes bancaires coopératifs français. Recma 301:8–25
Ory J-N, De Serres A, Jaegger M (2012) Comment résister à l'effet de normalisation des banques coopératives ? La Revue des Sciences de Gestion 258:69–82
Parpais C (2004) Le rôle des banques coopératives et mutualistes, in Demoustier D.(dir.), Economie sociale et développement local, La mobilisation des financements et de la recherche. Les Cahiers de l'économie sociale, n°4, Lharmattan, , pp 115–173
Pastré O (2007) La guerre mondiale des banques, Coll. "les cahiers—le cercle des économistes", PUF
Pflimlin E (2009) Les atouts des coopératives. Revue européenne du droit bancaire et financier, avril, Paris
Pflimlin E, Lebègue D, Leseul G, Martel A (2014) Guide de la gouvernance des coopératives et des mutuelles. IFA, Paris
Pollin J-P (2007) In la guerre mondiale des banques, coll. Les cahiers—le cercle des économistes, PUF
Richez-Battesti N, Gianfaldoni P (dir) (2006) Les banques coopératives en France, le défi de la performance et de la solidarité. L'harmattan, Paris
Richez-Battesti N (2007) Les banques coopératives en France: entre banalisation et reconquête identitaire. In: Rapport moral sur l'argent dans le monde, Association d'Economie Financière, pp 103–115
Richez-Battesti N (2009) Les banques coopérative françaises dans la tourmente financière ? In: Draperi J-F (ed) L'année de l'économie sociale et solidaire. Dunod, pp 243–249
Richez-Battesti N, Gianfaldoni P (dir) (2008) La gouvernance des banques coopératives françaises. Rapport de recherche, DIIESES
Richez-Battesti N et al (2006) Banques coopératives et innovations sociales. Recma 301:26–41
Toucas P (2005) Les coopérateurs, deux siècles de pratiques coopératives. Ed. de l'Atelier, Paris
Wyman O (2008) Cooperative banks, customer champion. MMC. http://www.oliverwyman.com/insights/publications/archive/co-operative–bank--customer-champion.html#.VrS1c_GDvYU

The German Cooperative Banks. An Economic Overview

Massimo Biasin

Abstract Cooperative banking has a long and well established tradition in German speaking countries and in Germany in particular.

The cooperative financial network basis on the *Raiffeisenbanken* and *Volksbanken*, member owned financial intermediaries.

Although local banks in terms of operational territory at single level, the credit unions are able to offer their customers and members an extensive range of financial services due to the close cooperation with their specialized product institutes within the cooperative banking network, the so called *Finanzverbund*. In that sense the *Raiffeisenbanken* and *Volksbanken* might be viewed as *pocket* universal banks.

In this context, the present study—given a general background of the cooperative credit system within the overall German banking market—focuses on the institutional framework of the cooperative system, both on the entrepreneurship and associative level, considering its legal and economic relationship in order to highlight its specialness also in terms of potential replicability in other national experiences.

Summary: (1) Introduction; (2) The Background and Size of the German Cooperative Banking System; (3) The Institutional Framework: The Entrepreneurship and Associative Level; (4) Economic, Legal and Regulatory Relationships within the Cooperative Network; (5) Concluding Remarks;

1 Introduction

Cooperative banking has a long and well established tradition in German speaking countries and in Germany in particular.[1]

The cooperative financial network basis on the *Raiffeisenbanken* and *Volksbanken*, member owned financial intermediaries whose origins go back to the early promoters of the German cooperative banking concept, namely Friedrich

[1] The paper also relies on previous works of the author.

M. Biasin (✉)
Department of Economics and Law, University of Macerata, Macerata, Italy
e-mail: massimo.biasin@unimc.it

S. Karafolas (ed.), *Credit Cooperative Institutions in European Countries*,
Contributions to Economics, DOI 10.1007/978-3-319-28784-3_5

Willhelm Raiffeisen and Franz Hermann Schulze-Delitzsch, respectively. The *Raiffeisenbanken* were traditionally characterized by a rural context while the *Volksbanken* were typically established in towns and suburban areas.

The cooperative banks and their comprehensive financial institutions, linked together in the *Finanzverbund*, define the "third pillar" of the German banking system beside the so called *Grossbanken* and commercial banks (i.e. the large universal intermediaries) and the savings banks' network (namely *Sparkassen* and *Landesbanken*, the latter the central banks of the former). Each pillar has peculiar ownership structures and market characteristics.

The cooperative banking system controls roughly 14 % (2013) of the German banking market as measured by the total business volume, compared to a percentage of 57 % dominated by commercial banks (including the big banks and the Deutsche Postbank AG), while 29 % of the market is managed by the saving institutions (Table 1).

Despite the relatively limited business share, *Raiffeisenbanken* and *Volksbanken* play a relevant role in the German banking system from a substantial perspective because of their focus on the small and medium businesses that largely depend on banking services due to the limited market access capability of this enterprise segment. Although local banks in terms of operational territory at single level, the credit unions are able to offer their customers and members an extensive range of financial services due to the close cooperation with their specialized product institutes within the cooperative banking network. In that sense the *Raiffeisenbanken* and *Volksbanken* might be viewed as *pocket* universal banks.

In this context, the present study—given a general background of the cooperative credit system within the overall German banking market—focuses on the institutional framework of the cooperative system, both on the entrepreneurship and associative level, considering its legal and economic relationship in order to highlight its specialness also in terms of potential replicability in other national experiences. More in detail, the study addresses (i) the regulatory peculiarities governing the network of the German credit cooperatives in order to highlight if there are legal provisions able to positively influence the competitiveness of the credit unions; (ii) the financial and governance linkages, between the local banks and their central entities, induced by the institutional ruling of the *Finanzverbund*.

This in order to highlight from an economic point of view the capability of the German mutual banks to act as an universal banking group, by preserving the statutory independence of the individual first level entities, and not as a mere aggregation of local financial intermediaries.

The relative competitive advantage of the German cooperative network seems to result from the mandatory membership with the regional federations for the primary cooperative banks. This legal requirement has historically enabled a strong coordination of the cooperative system and the implementation of inherent network strategies. However, the regulatory constraint does not impair the legal and operational independence of the single *Raiffeisenkassen* and *Volksbanken* that are not legally required to convey the banking business towards the central business institutions. In turn the freedom degree at operational stage incentivizes the central

Table 1 Assets and liabilities of German banks

	Number of reporting institutions	Balance sheet total	Cash & equivalents[a]	Lending to banks	Lending to non-banks	Debt securities & treasury bills	Shares & participating interests	Other assets[b,c]	Amounts owed to banks	Amounts owed to non-banks	Securitised liabilities	Other liabilities[c]	Provisions & others[d]	Subordinated liabilities	Capital[e]
Assets and liabilities of German banks															
Million Euros															
	All banks														
2000	2740	6,148,318	67,083	1,497,307	2,942,901	973,254	340,352	327,421	1,769,439	2,226,911	1,432,138	314,836	74,983	77,406	252,605
2005	2089	6,903,169	63,262	1,956,772	3,020,110	1,222,491	376,687	263,847	1,943,192	2,554,049	1,616,781	325,322	81,739	93,260	288,826
2011	1903	8,466,239	110,378	2,138,873	3,229,751	1,257,035	298,783	1,431,419	1,859,802	3,218,400	1,376,504	1,445,467	99,367	102,073	364,626
2013	1846	7,604,225	104,430	1,935,483	3,097,419	1,187,144	309,265	970,484	1,651,794	3,260,992	1,143,945	955,558	127,807	86,725	377,404
	Commercial and other banks (including the so called "Big Banks")[f]														
2000	369	3,210,690	31,023	799,372	1,544,785	438,425	200,184	196,901	887,638	958,199	940,254	204,000	53,123	38,141	129,335
2005	318	3,708,581	25,076	1,110,954	1,588,297	619,956	187,665	176,633	1,054,184	1,141,032	1,064,616	210,427	53,602	49,219	135,501
2011	344	4,938,284	61,768	1,446,125	1,572,845	603,564	122,543	1,131,439	1,067,702	1,531,141	936,403	1,102,789	63,908	58,458	177,883
2013	336	4,366,192	68,550	1,397,547	1,450,066	552,678	131,199	766,152	947,234	1,567,868	803,120	742,625	93,371	49,047	162,927
	Savings banks (Sparkassen & Landesbanken)														
2000	575	2,176,624	23,373	543,152	1,021,177	383,427	103,956	101,539	671,790	863,460	415,502	89,698	15,506	33,593	87,075
2005	475	2,379,000	25,277	677,883	1,048,040	428,509	136,752	62,539	675,977	959,818	490,834	83,983	20,409	37,829	110,150
2011	437	2,512,085	30,960	484,304	1,200,585	447,190	108,731	240,315	547,726	1,130,137	367,277	275,200	26,346	36,473	128,926
2013	430	2,203,390	22,991	354,187	1,152,650	417,494	106,801	149,267	470,363	1,101,206	274,958	155,983	25,197	29,772	145,911
	Credit cooperatives and Regional institutions of credit cooperatives (Raiffeisen- und Volksbanken; Zentralbanken)[g]														
2000	1796	761,004	12,687	154,783	376,939	151,402	36,212	28,981	210,011	405,252	76,382	21,138	6,354	5,672	36,195
2005	1296	815,588	12,909	167,935	383,773	174,026	52,270	24,675	213,031	453,199	61,331	30,912	7,728	6,212	43,175
2011	1122	1,015,870	17,650	208,444	456,321	206,281	67,509	59,665	244,374	557,122	72,824	67,478	9,113	7,142	57,817
2013	1080	1,034,643	12,889	183,749	494,703	216,972	71,265	55,065	234,197	591,918	65,867	56,950	9,239	7,906	68,566
Percentage values															
	Commercial and other banks (including the so called "Big Banks")[f]														
2000	369	*52.2 %*	*46.2 %*	*53.4 %*	*52.5 %*	*45.0 %*	*58.8 %*	*60.1 %*	*50.2 %*	*43.0 %*	*65.7 %*	*64.8 %*	*70.8 %*	*49.3 %*	*51.2 %*
2005	318	*53.7 %*	*39.6 %*	*56.8 %*	*52.6 %*	*50.7 %*	*49.8 %*	*66.9 %*	*54.3 %*	*44.7 %*	*65.8 %*	*64.7 %*	*65.6 %*	*52.8 %*	*46.9 %*

(continued)

Table 1 (continued)

	Number of reporting institutions	Balance sheet total	Cash & equivalents[a]	Lending to banks	Lending to non-banks	Debt securities & treasury bills	Shares & participating interests	Other assets[b,c]	Amounts owed to banks	Amounts owed to non-banks	Securitised liabilities	Other liabilities[c]	Provisions & others[d]	Subordinated liabilities	Capital[e]
Assets and liabilities of German banks															
2011	344	*58.3 %*	*56.0 %*	*67.6 %*	*48.7 %*	*48.0 %*	*41.0 %*	*79.0 %*	*57.4 %*	*47.6 %*	*68.0 %*	*76.3 %*	*64.3 %*	*57.3 %*	*48.8 %*
2013	336	*57.4 %*	*65.6 %*	*72.2 %*	*46.8 %*	*46.6 %*	*42.4 %*	*78.9 %*	*57.3 %*	*48.1 %*	*70.2 %*	*77.7 %*	*73.1 %*	*56.6 %*	*43.2 %*
	Savings banks (Sparkassen & Landesbanken)														
2000	575	*35.4 %*	*34.8 %*	*36.3 %*	*34.7 %*	*39.4 %*	*30.5 %*	*31.0 %*	*38.0 %*	*38.8 %*	*29.0 %*	*28.5 %*	*20.7 %*	*43.4 %*	*34.5 %*
2005	475	*34.5 %*	*40.0 %*	*34.6 %*	*34,7 %*	*35.1 %*	*36.3 %*	*23.7 %*	*34.8 %*	*37.6 %*	*30.4 %*	*25.8 %*	*25.0 %*	*40.6 %*	*38.1 %*
2011	437	*29.7 %*	*28.0 %*	*22.6 %*	*37.2 %*	*35.6 %*	*36.4 %*	*16.8 %*	*29.5 %*	*35.1 %*	*26.7 %*	*19.0 %*	*26.5 %*	*35.7 %*	*35.4 %*
2013	430	*29.0 %*	*22.0 %*	*18.3 %*	*37.2 %*	*35.2 %*	*34.5 %*	*15.4 %*	*28.5 %*	*33.8 %*	*24.0 %*	*16.3 %*	*19.7 %*	*34.3 %*	*38.7 %*
	Credit cooperatives and Regional institutions of credit cooperatives (Raiffeisen- und Volksbanken; Zentralbanken)														
2000	1796	*12.4 %*	*18.9 %*	*10.3 %*	*12.8 %*	*15.6 %*	*10.6 %*	*8.9 %*	*11.9 %*	*18.2 %*	*5.3 %*	*6.7 %*	*8.5 %*	*7.3 %*	*14.3 %*
2005	1296	*11.8 %*	*20.4 %*	*8.6 %*	*12.7 %*	*14.2 %*	*13.9 %*	*9.4 %*	*11.0 %*	*17.7 %*	*3.8 %*	*9.5 %*	*9.5 %*	*6.7 %*	*14.9 %*
2011	1122	*12.0 %*	*16.0 %*	*9.7 %*	*14.1 %*	*16.4 %*	*22.6 %*	*4.2 %*	*13.1 %*	*17.3 %*	*5.3 %*	*4.7 %*	*9.2 %*	*7.0 %*	*15.9 %*
2013	1080	*13.6 %*	*12.3 %*	*9.5 %*	*16.0 %*	*18.3 %*	*23.0 %*	*5.7 %*	*14.2 %*	*18.2 %*	*5.8 %*	*6.0 %*	*7.2 %*	*9.1 %*	*18.2 %*
Asset & Liabilities as Proportion (%) of relative balance sheet total															
	Commercial banks (including the so called "Big Banks")[f]														
2000	369	100 %	1 %	25 %	48 %	14 %	6 %	6 %	28 %	30 %	29 %	6 %	2 %	1 %	4 %
2005	318	100 %	1 %	30 %	43 %	17 %	5 %	5 %	28 %	31 %	29 %	6 %	1 %	1 %	4 %
2011	344	100 %	1 %	29 %	32 %	12 %	2 %	23 %	22 %	31 %	19 %	22 %	1 %	1 %	4 %
2013	336	100 %	2 %	32 %	33 %	13 %	3 %	18 %	22 %	36 %	18 %	17 %	2 %	1 %	4 %
	Savings banks (Sparkassen & Landesbanken)														
2000	575	100 %	1 %	25 %	47 %	18 %	5 %	5 %	31 %	40 %	19 %	4 %	1 %	2 %	4 %
2005	475	100 %	1 %	28 %	44 %	18 %	6 %	3 %	28 %	40 %	21 %	4 %	1 %	2 %	5 %
2011	437	100 %	1 %	19 %	48 %	18 %	4 %	10 %	22 %	45 %	15 %	11 %	1 %	1 %	5 %
2013	430	100 %	1 %	16 %	52 %	19 %	5 %	7 %	21 %	50 %	12 %	7 %	1 %	1 %	7 %
	Credit cooperatives and Regional institutions of credit cooperatives (Raiffeisen- und Volksbanken; Zentralbanken)														
2000	1796	100 %	2 %	20 %	50 %	20 %	5 %	4 %	28 %	53 %	10 %	3 %	1 %	1 %	5 %
2005	1296	100 %	2 %	21 %	47 %	21 %	6 %	3 %	26 %	56 %	8 %	4 %	1 %	1 %	5 %

2011	1122	100 %	2 %	21 %	45 %	20 %	7 %	6 %	24 %	55 %	7 %	7 %	1 %	1 %	6 %
2013	1080	100 %	1 %	18 %	48 %	21 %	7 %	5 %	23 %	57 %	6 %	6 %	1 %	1 %	7 %

Source: processed by the author from "Deutsche Bundesbank, Bankenstatistik", Statistisches Beiheft zum Monatsbericht, February 2014, February 2012, February 2006, February 2001

[a]Including balances with Central Banks

[b]Fiduciary assets & equalisation claims, fixed assets, others

[c]Including derivatives of the trading portfolio starting from 2010 due to reporting changes (Act Modernising Accounting Law)

[d]Provisions for liabilities and charges & general and country risk allowances

[e]Including participation rights

[f]Including Deutsche Postbank AG (starting from 2004) and subsidiaries of foreign banks

[g]Please note that the reported values are not netted out at consolidated level (i.e. large parts of the liabilities to banks reported by the regional institutions of credit cooperatives are to primary Volksbanken and Raiffeisen)

business entities to offer their services at competitive market condition. This market capability is testified by the high percentage of captive business outsourced by the primary banks towards the network institutions.

The study is organized as follows. Section 2 provides a general overview of the role of the cooperative sector within the German banking system in terms of size, structure and taxonomy. Section 3 highlights the (Sect. 3.1) entrepreneurship and (Sect. 3.2) associative organization in order to portray the institutional framework. Section 4 depicts the economic and legal relationships between first (i.e. *Raiffeisenkassen* and *Volksbanken*) and second level entities (i.e. the central product institutions). The conclusions are drawn in Sect. 5.

2 The Background and Size of the German Cooperative Banking System

The overall taxonomy and size upon business volume composition by category of banks is depicted in Table 1 that summarizes the overall structure of the domestic financial sector.

The *Raiffeisenbanken* and *Volksbanken*, together with their parent companies and central intermediaries, define a peculiar institutional segment of the German banking market because of their governance structure as well as of the regionally oriented business model largely focused on traditional banking products and on local retail customers (over 30 million in 2012[2]), most of them at the same time also cooperatives' members (17.7 million[3]). In that sense they significantly differ in nature both from the large commercial banks and the saving institutions despite their ability to potentially cover the entire set of financial intermediation services.

The strong members' and customers' relationship represents a resilient entry barrier enabling the cooperative sector to successfully stand up against potential competitors interested in their local business model largely oriented towards traditional banking. In that way, differently from other regionally oriented banking institutions with a less focused business model and client target—like the saving banks that experienced a significant market decline over the last decade—the *Volksbanken* and *Raiffeisenbanken* have been able to preserve and implement their market share of circa 14 % of the overall German banking business amounting to over 1,034 billion euros (Table 1). This despite the intense competition in certain financial service areas (like in the asset management sector) and in larger metropolitan areas where cooperative banks suffer from competition with the large commercial banks and the saving banks, respectively.

---

[2] Bundesverband der Deutschen Volksbanken und Raiffeisenbanken (2013b), *Zahlen und Fakten 2012*.

[3] Bundesverband der Deutschen Volksbanken und Raiffeisenbanken (2014), *Entwicklung der Volksbanken und Raiffeisenbanken Ende 2013*.

In particular, credit cooperatives—consistently with their institutional nature described more in detail next—are largely devoted to traditional banking activities towards small and medium business as well as private retail clients located in rural areas and small towns. Their presence in large urban centers is generally weaker. Due to customary relationship activities, cooperative banks benefit from higher direct retail funding (57 % of the total liabilities—Table 1—equal to a market share of over 18 % of domestic deposits from non-banks) compared to commercial and savings banks (with 36 % and 50 % respectively [2013 data]) which rely more heavily on securitized liabilities (commercial banks 18 %; savings banks 12 % of total liabilities versus 6 % of market type debt of cooperative banks including their central institutions). At the same time interbank liabilities if netted out at consolidated level (i.e. large parts of the deposits from banks reported by the regional institutions of credit cooperatives are liabilities owed to primary *Volksbanken* and *Raiffeisenbanken*) amount to roughly 103 billion euros (2011),[4] making funding on the interbank market not strategically important to the sector.[5]

The strong direct funding capability at primary level enables the credit cooperatives to almost close the intermediation process. The lending activity, mainly towards non-banks [48 % of the total assets versus 33 % of the big banks and commercial banks (2013)], is therefore largely financed via retail deposits and—to a minor extent—interbank liabilities. The credit cooperatives' loan and (retail) funding activity is consequently more than proportional to the overall market share of the *Volksbanken* and *Raiffeisenbanken* as measured upon total assets and characterized by a relevant maturity transformation. Other things equal, the profit and loss accounts benefit from this conservative balance sheet in terms of net interest income and a lower exposure to the monetary market interests' volatility.

This evidence is depicted in Table 2 reporting the cost and income structure of the German banking industry. In the last decade, the significant business volumes with private retail clients and small and medium-sized firms of the cooperative banks lead to above average net interest margin. The net interests received ranged between 76.5 % (2000) and 78.2 % (2012) of the total operating income in respect to a contribution between 67.8 % (2005) and 71.50 % (2012) for the overall banking system.[6] More in detail, due to their business model and geographical focus—where financial competition is somehow lower—*Raiffeisenbanken* and *Volksbanken* enjoyed a higher interest income (2.21 % of the total assets in 2012; 2.46 % in 2005 and 2.45 % in 2000) than the commercial banks [0.85 % (2012); 1.27 % (2005); 1.17 (2000)], largely involved in wholesale activities, and, partly, in

---

[4] Bundesverband der Deutschen Volksbanken und Raiffeisenbanken (2012b), *Konsolidierter Jahresabschluss 2011* and Bundesverband der Deutschen Volksbanken und Raiffeisenbanken (2013c), *Konsolidierter Jahresabschluss 2012*.

[5] DZ Bank (2014), *2013 Annual Report, Group Management Report*, p. 57.

[6] Deutsche Bundesbank (2013b), *The Performance of German Credit Institutions in 2012*, Monthly Report.

Table 2 Cost and income items for major bank categories[a]

	Year	All banks	Big banks	(Primary) Savings banks	Credit cooperatives: Regional Institutions	Credit cooperatives: Primary credit cooperatives
Net interest margin (1)	2000	67.80 %	49.20 %	80.90 %	71.20 %	76.50 %
	2005	68.20 %	49.30 %	79.00 %	57.40 %	74.70 %
	2011	72.90 %	57.50 %	79.60 %	70.40 %	78.00 %
	2012	71.50 %	61.10 %	79.40 %	53.90 %	78.20 %
Net commission margin (2)	2000	24.80 %	35.40 %	19.00 %	19.50 %	21.40 %
	2005	21.50 %	25.60 %	19.40 %	19.90 %	20.40 %
	2011	23.00 %	31.90 %	20.70 %	20.00 %	19.50 %
	2012	21.70 %	28.30 %	20.90 %	14.00 %	19.60 %
Net results from trading portfolio/ financial operations	2000	5.70 %	16.50 %	0.60 %	8.60 %	0.10 %
	2005	8.80 %	27.30 %	0.60 %	22.40 %	0.30 %
	2011	3.70 %	13.80 %	−0.10 %	10.20 %	0.10 %
	2012	5.50 %	14.50 %	0.10 %	32.00 %	0.10 %
Other operating income and charges	2000	1.80 %	−1.10 %	−0.40 %	0.70 %	1.90 %
	2005	1.40 %	−2.10 %	1.00 %	0.40 %	4.70 %
	2011	0.40 %	−3.20 %	−0.20 %	−0.60 %	2.40 %
	2012	1.20 %	−3.90 %	−0.40 %	−0.10 %	2.10 %
Operating income		100.00 %	100.00 %	100.00 %	100.00 %	100.00 %
General administrative spending. *Of which:*	2000	−68.40 %	−79.00 %	−68.90 %	−51.80 %	−74.50 %
	2005	−61.00 %	−60.50 %	−66.00 %	−53.90 %	−70.00 %
	2011	−63.90 %	−72.50 %	−62.70 %	−57.70 %	−63.90 %
	2012	−64.20 %	−68.80 %	−65.70 %	−42.30 %	−65.80 %
Staff costs	2000	*−37.00 %*	*−42.30 %*	*−41.30 %*	*−24.30 %*	*−43.10 %*
	2005	*−33.60 %*	*−31.90 %*	*−40.80 %*	*−30.00 %*	*−42.00 %*
	2011	*−33.30 %*	*−33.40 %*	*−38.70 %*	*−30.10 %*	*−38.10 %*
	2012	*−34.00 %*	*−32.90 %*	*−41.20 %*	*−21.60 %*	*−39.20 %*
Other administrative spending	2000	*−31.40 %*	*−36.70 %*	*−27.60 %*	*−27.50 %*	*−31.50 %*
	2005	*−27.40 %*	*−28.60 %*	*−25.20 %*	*−23.80 %*	*−27.90 %*
	2011	*−30.60 %*	*−39.20 %*	*−24.00 %*	*−27.70 %*	*−25.80 %*
	2012	*−30.20 %*	*−35.90 %*	*−24.50 %*	*−20.60 %*	*−26.60 %*
Net income/ charges from asset valuation	2000	−14.00 %	−8.20 %	−15.90 %	−43.30 %	−14.50 %
	2005	−10.80 %	−4.30 %	−17.00 %	−10.00 %	−15.70 %
	2011	1.80 %	−5.70 %	24.80 %	63.80 %	−1.60 %
	2012	−3.30 %	−8.50 %	2.40 %	−5.30 %	1.20 %
Net other and extraordinary income/charges	2000	−0.50 %	−1.80 %	3.70 %	27.80 %	1.50 %
	2005	−2.50 %	2.50 %	0.00 %	−13.70 %	7.50 %
	2011	−13.60 %	−22.10 %	−6.10 %	−37.40 %	−1.20 %
	2012	−9.10 %	−8.50 %	−4.30 %	−29.10 %	0.00 %

(continued)

Table 2 (continued)

	Year	All banks	Big banks	(Primary) Savings banks	Credit cooperatives: Regional Institutions	Credit cooperatives: Primary credit cooperatives
Profit before taxes	2000	17.00 %	11.00 %	18.90 %	32.70 %	12.40 %
	2005	25.70 %	37.70 %	17.00 %	22.50 %	21.80 %
	2011	24.30 %	−0.30 %	56.10 %	68.60 %	33.30 %
	2012	23.40 %	14.30 %	32.30 %	23.30 %	35.50 %
Taxes on income and earnings	2000	−5.90 %	1.50 %	−10.40 %	−10.40 %	−6.50 %
	2005	−7.50 %	−10.20 %	−7.90 %	−0.60 %	−7.60 %
	2011	−5.50 %	−1.70 %	−9.20 %	−5.20 %	−9.20 %
	2012	−6.70 %	−8.00 %	−9.10 %	15.80 %	−9.50 %
Profit after taxes	2000	11.10 %	12.60 %	8.50 %	22.30 %	5.90 %
	2005	18.20 %	27.50 %	9.10 %	21.90 %	14.20 %
	2011	18.80 %	−2.00 %	46.90 %	63.50 %	24.10 %
	2012	16.70 %	6.30 %	23.30 %	39.20 %	25.90 %
Return on equity pre−tax	2000	9.32	6.34	13.39	12.95	8.59
	2005	13.00	31.72	10.45	5.25	13.79
	2011	8.36	−0.12	27.35	10.27	16.39
	2012	7.81	6.65	12.99	4.94	15.73
Return on equity (ROE)	2000	6.07	7.23	6.02	8.84	4.09
	2005	9.19	23.12	5.60	5.12	9.00
	2011	6.49	−0.83	22.88	9.50	11.87
	2012	5.59	2.91	9.34	8.30	11.51
General administrative spending as % of (1) Net interest margin and (2) Net commission margin	2011	66.70 %	81.10 %	62.50 %	63.90 %	65.50 %
	2012	68,90 %	76.90 %	65.50 %	62.20 %	67.30 %

Note: primary credit cooperatives do not include building and loan associations
Source: processed by the author from Deutsche Bundesbank, The performance of German credit institutions, September 2013, 2012
[a]All values as percentage of operating income. 2000–2005–2011–2012

respect to the competing savings institutions, serving a similar clientele (2.12 %; 2.30 %; 2.33 %).[7]

In turn, the net commission incidence on operating earnings is somehow lower for the *Raiffeisenbanken* and *Volksbanken* than for commercial banks due to the type of customers served and the contained offering of highly specialized financial and asset management services. In the reported time windows (Table 2), the primary credit

[7] Deutsche Bundesbank (September 2013a), *Die Ertragslage der deutschen Kreditinstitute im Jahr 2012*, Monatsbericht.

cooperatives achieved a net commission margin of 19.6 % (2012), 20.4 % (2005) and 21.4 % (2000) of the operating earnings (equivalent to 0.56 %; 0.67 % and 0.69 % of the total assets, respectively[8]) where the commissions' incidence for the (large) commercial banks was equal to 28.3 % (2012), 25.6 % (2005) and 35.4 % (2000).

At the same time, the contribution to the operating income of financial operations and own portfolio trading activity is very limited and of marginal relevance (2012: 0.10 %; 2005: 0.30 %; 2000: 0.10 %) for the primary credit cooperatives, similarly to the savings institutions.

The strong focusing on traditional lending activity necessarily turns out—similarly to the savings banks—in relatively higher net charges from asset valuation via bad loans provisions compared to commercial banks whose operating income is largely generated by financial services and security trading. As shown in Table 2, net charges from asset valuation are typically above average for credit cooperatives as it is also for the savings institutions.

The strong territorial presence of the German cooperative banks that follows their orientation towards traditional banking activities, is attested by the wide branch network (2012: 11,778 offices equal to 32.5 % of the whole banking industry) and the high number of primary institutions (2012: 1,104 units) (see Table 3), reflecting the local nature of the *Raiffeisenbanken* and *Volksbanken* that had been historically established at rural and municipality level.

These circumstances generate two important effects in terms of cost-income structure and related efficiency.

At first stage, the nature of independent, local banks of the credit unions drives down the company size of the single cooperative institution measured by total assets (see Table 4): in 2012 credit cooperatives had an average balance sheet total of 661 million euros compared to 298 million of 2000 (+121.8 % on nominal values). 41 % of the *Raiffeisenbanken* and *Volksbanken* had a company size below 250 million euros, while almost one quarter (23 %) was concentrated between 250 and 500 million; the remaining 36 % might be viewed as "larger" credit cooperatives totaling more than 500 million euros of assets. The increase in size follows the dramatic reduction of the number of cooperative banks (−38.5 % over the period) pursuing a precise strategy that aims to reduce the relative incidence of fixed costs and to improve efficiency of the first level banks of the *Finanzverbund* consistently with the findings of scale economies.[9] At the same time, the merger process should limit competition and overlaps between primary institutions serving the same geographical area following the "one market—one bank" principle, providing—all other things been equal—higher revenues.[10]

---

[8] Idem.

[9] Lang G., Welzel P. (1996), *Efficiency and technical progress in banking. Empirical Results for a panel of German cooperative banks*, Journal of Banking and Finance, 20, 1003–1023.

[10] Krüger M., *Gestaltung der Zukunft kommt voran*, Bankinformation und Genossenschaftsforum, 6/2002.

Table 3 Number of German banks and their branches. Credit Cooperatives' distribution and average size

	All banks	Commercial banks and other credit institutions [including the "Big Banks" (Grossbanken)][a]	Savings banks (Sparkassen & Landesbanken)	Credit cooperatives and regional institutions of credit cooperatives	Regional institutions (Zentralbanken)	Credit cooperatives (Raiffeisen und Volksbanken)[b]
	Number of banks[a]					
2000	2912	539	575	1798	*3*	*1795*
2005	2344	574	475	1295	*2*	*1293*
2010	2093	511	439	1143	*2*	*1141*
2012	2053	515	432	1106	*2*	*1104*
	Branches					
2000	56,936	24,049	17,530	15,357	*25*	*15,332*
2005	44,100	16,837	14,530	12,733	*11*	*12,722*
2010	38,183	12,630	13,496	12,057	*11*	*12,046*
2012	36,283	11,400	13,094	11,789	*11*	*11,778*
2000	100 %	42.2 %	30.8 %	27.0 %	*0.0 %*	*26.9 %*
2005	100 %	38.2 %	32.9 %	28.9 %	*0.0 %*	*28.8 %*
2010	100 %	33.1 %	35.3 %	31.6 %	*0.0 %*	*31.5 %*
2012	100 %	31.4 %	36.1 %	32.5 %	*0.0 %*	*32.5 %*

Source: processed by the author from "Deutsche Bundesbank, Bankenstatistik, Statistisches Beiheft", Dezember 2006, Februar 2002 and "Deutsche Bundesbank, Banking Statistics, Statistical Supplement to the Monthly Report", February 2014

[a]Including Deutsche Postbank AG

[b]Including 3 banks affiliated to the BVR but not established as credit cooperatives

Table 4 Credit cooperatives only—distribution and average size (balance sheet total)

Number of banks per size class	2000	%	2005	%	2010	%	2012	%
Balance sheet total < 25 million euros	67	3.7	–	0.0	–	0.0	–	0.0
Balance sheet total between 25 > 50 million euros	217	12.1	120	9.3	66	5.8	53	4.8
Balance sheet total between 50 > 100 million euros	368	20.5	199	15.4	127	11.2	121	11.0
Balance sheet total between 100 > 250 million euros	559	31.2	364	28.1	307	27.0	277	25.1
Balance sheet total between 250 > 500 million euros	346	19.3	313	24.2	261	22.9	251	22.8
Balance sheet total between 500 million > 1 billion euros	151	8.4	189	14.6	211	18.5	222	20.1
Balance sheet total between 1 billion > 5 billion euros	79	4.4	101	7.8	152	13.4	163	14.8
Balance sheet total between 5 billion > 10 billion euros	3	0.2	6	0.5	12	1.1	13	1.2
Balance sheet total > 10 billion euros	2	0.1	2	0.2	2	0.2	2	0.2
	1.792	100.0	1.294	100.0	1.138	100.0	1.102	100.0
Average Size (based on balance sheet total)								
Average balance sheet total (million euros)	*298*		*457*		*620*		*661*	

Note: Excluding Regional/Central institutions of credit cooperatives and (no. 2) banks not established as credit cooperatives but belonging to the BVR
Source: processed by the author from "Deutsche Bundesbank, Bankenstatistik, Statistisches Beiheft", Februar 2013, Dezember 2006, Februar 2001 and "Deutsche Bundesbank, Banking Statistics, Statistical Supplement to the Monthly Report", March 2013

At the second stage, as maintaining bank offices is cost intensive, the widespread branch network and the limited company size of the *Raiffeisenbanken* and *Volksbanken* generate high administrative spending which, in turn, leads to a relative high cost/income ratio. Excluding their central institutions, cooperative banks have a cost/income ratio of almost 65.8 % in 2012 (70.0 % in 2005; 74.5 % in 2000—see Table 2), which is generally higher than the average efficiency ratio of the German banking system. More in detail, contrary to the mean systemic values, the largest component of the administrative expenditures is represented by staff costs (39.2 % of the operating income in 2012, equal to 59.6 % of the general administrative spending) while the other executive costs are below average. In that respect it is however worth mentioning that the cooperative banking sector has been able to achieve an almost steady cost reduction over the reported time period consistent with the expense saving strategy mentioned above and pursued both at associative and at entrepreneurship level.

Contrary to other European fiscal legislations, credit cooperatives de facto do not enjoy any tax benefit. This leads to median return on equity of roughly 9.1 % for the reported time window (11.51 %; 11.87 %; 9 %; 4.09 % respectively) and of 13.6 % at pre-tax (mean) level.

Beside possible efficiency gaps in respect to commercial banks (the latter characterized by a higher volatility and implied risk), RoE analysis must consider the fact that due to the cooperative nature of the *Raiffeisen* and *Volksbanken*, profits are driven to their shareholders not only in form of dividends but also in terms of better economic conditions (lower costs or higher earnings), compared to non-member clients, as well.

3 The Institutional Framework: The Associative and Entrepreneurship Level

The German cooperative banking system is basically a two-stage network consisting of an associative and entrepreneurship platform largely organized at local and national level. Both levels and platforms are characterized by a strong and continuous networking based on regulatory and economic relationships.

3.1 The Entrepreneurship Level

The German credit cooperatives are basically a double-level financial grid constituted by (i) the primary *Volksbanken* and *Raiffeisenbanken*, on the one side, and (ii) by their central institutions, on the other side. First and second level cooperative entities form a highly interrelated financial network, however not a banking group from a legal point of view, the so called *Finanzverbund*.

(i) The first level *Volksbanken* and *Raiffeisenbanken* are independent cooperative banks established locally in form of registered associations with legal personality (so called "*Eingetragene Kreditgenossenschaften*"). Members—individuals as well as legal entities forming a broad ownership base—are united voluntarily to meet their common economic and social needs through the jointly-owned and democratically controlled cooperative institution. In that sense, *Volksbanken* and *Raiffeisenbanken* are by definition local banks because of their territorial membership-basis to which their banking activity is largely devoted. Members participate through the acquisition of capital units (i.e. shares) authorized by the governing board of the cooperative union. Ownership is characterized by co-determination. Shares are normally entitled to one vote per unit regardless of the participation held (upon the "one member, one vote"-principle) but the by-law may entitle multiple voting rights to particular members.[11] The statutes might also cap the overall participation

[11] § 43, *Gesetz betreffend die Erwerbs- und Wirtschaftsgenossenschaften* (Genossenschaftsgesetz—GenG), 1.5.1889, last amendment 15.7.2013 (BGBI. I S. 2379).

that can be held by each member in order to ensure a widespread shareholder basis.

In the general case, shareholders' liability is limited to the initial capital contribution but might be increased—as enforced by several cooperative banks—by an additional amount capped to a maximum volume (*Haftsumme*) defined upon articles of association,[12.13]

Although sharing the same legal and operational framework, credit unions are traditionally divided in *Raiffeisenbanken* and *Volksbanken* reflecting the different historical background.[14] *Raiffeisenbanken* were originally founded in rural areas by farmers, while *Volksbanken* were established in towns and urban centers by (retail) business men. Beside the nominal indication, both categories act nowadays as one single network sharing the same central institutions at entrepreneurship level as well as regional and federal organizations at associative stage.

From a legal point of view, the credit cooperatives' banking business is subject to the federal banking law (*Kreditwesengesetz*) ruling the German banking system upon the European Union's financial services sectorial regulation, while the cooperative federal law (*Genossenschaftsgesetz*)[15] rules the corporate governance of the primary banks. The by-laws, enacted by each single credit union in accordance to the general regulatory framework of the *Genossenschaftsgesetz*, detail the rules for conduct of the cooperative's operation and management.

The governance structure consists of a board of managing directors, which is directly responsible for all business activities of the cooperative, a supervisory board and a general shareholders (or members) meeting. All members of the board of directors as well as of the supervisory committee must be member of the cooperative union. The shareholders assembly elects the supervisory board members, who in turn appoints the board of the managing directors, carries out the annual closing of the accounts and is responsible for the supervision of both the executive and the supervisory board as well as for extraordinary decisions exceeding the normal operations.[16]

---

[12] § 6 and § 22a, idem.

[13] The additional capital contributions to which members are obliged (*Haftsummen*) are regarded as regulatory capital. This special regulation reflects the legal peculiarities of cooperative institutions [*Gesetzüber das Kreditwesen*] (Gesetz über das Kreditwesen (Kreditwesengesetz – KWG), 1961, Bek. v. 9. 9.1998, last amendment Art. 2 G v. 7.5.2013).

[14] Sparda-Banken (12 entities) and PSD-Banken (15) also belongtothecooperativecreditsector [Bundesverband der Deutschen Volksbanken und Raiffeisenbanken (2013), *Jahresbericht 2012*, p. 116]. They were established as credit unions of specific categories of workers (like for example railway or post employees). Due to their limited number and relevance they are not going to be considered separately.

[15] Lang J., Weidmüller L, *Genossenschaftsgesetz. Mit Erläuterungen zum Umwandlungsgesetz. Kommentar*, Gruyter, 2005.

[16] Kramer J. W., *Co-operative Development and Corporate Governance Structures in German Cooperatives—Problems and Perspectives*, paper presented at the XIV International Economic History Congress, Helsinki, 2006.

It should also be noted that the federal cooperative law forces primary credit union to apply for mandatory membership in a co-operative auditing association (the so called *Prüfungsverband*) which, in turn, is in charge for the annual audit of the financial statements and the overall management and operational conduct of the associate cooperative banks. As described in detail next (Sect. 3.2.), this provision—that might appear of secondary relevance—is in fact a grounding element of the German cooperative to act as a cohesive financial network.

At operational level, credit cooperatives act as full financial intermediaries with de facto no legal limitations or regulatory burdens different from the general rules applying to commercial banks. As such, *Volksbanken* and *Raiffeisenbanken* are therefore supervised by the Federal Financial Authority (*Bundesanstalt für Finanzdienstleistungsaufsicht*—BAFIN). Yet cooperative banks perform locally; competitions between credit unions is therefore constrained—even if not at legal stage—by the so called *Regionalprinzip*, largely followed at *Verbund*-level, limiting their activities to a specific regional area.

Due to the fact that the cooperative banks are considered ordinary financial intermediaries from a regulatory perspective, German credit unions do not enjoy particular tax benefits.

(ii) The regional or central entities form the second stage of the cooperative network.[17] The key central institution is represented by the *Deutsche Zentral-Genossenschaftsbank* (DZ-Bank), the fourth largest German bank, functioning primarily as financial service provider for the local credit cooperatives' business needs.[18] In doing that DZ-Bank serves as parent holding company of several product entities, joint in the DZ-Bank group, acting as specialized service units organized in the four major business areas of corporate and private banking, capital markets and transaction banking.[19]

The DZ-Bank plays a key role within the German cooperative banking system by supporting the local *Raiffeisenbanken* and *Volksbanken* as subsidiary partner and by acting as commercial bank being a relevant institutional player in the German wholesale banking market also as interface between the

---

[17] The entrepreneurship level of the cooperative sector is described more in detail in par. 2.2.

[18] At year end 2012 the total asset of the DZ Bank Gruppe amounted to 407 billion Euros [DZ Bank Gruppe (2013), *Zusammen geht mehr*, p. 8].

[19] The most important central units, among others, are: Union Investment Group (asset management); R + V Versicherung AG (insurances); Bausparkasse Schwäbisch Hall AG (building savings bank); DG HYP (commercial real estate finance); DZ Privatbank Gruppe (private banking); VR LEASING (leasing). Most affiliated companies of the DZ-Bank group hold leading market shares in the respective business areas: VR Leasing is considered the second largest leasing company in Germany. Union Investment and R + V Versicherung rank second in the respective business area while Bausparkasse Schwäbisch Hall is considered the largest German building society. The DZ-Bank as well as the majority of the parent companies are organized as joint-stock companies [DZ Bank Gruppe (2013), *Zusammen geht mehr*].

cooperative network and the (international) capital markets.[20] In that respect the interaction between the first and second entrepreneurship platform is twofold in the sense that DZ-Bank offers the primary banks access to the monetary markets and the broad range of *Allfinanz* products via the scale and scope economies achievable at aggregate level but at the same time the DZ-Bank group profits from the placing power of the local cooperative banks when offering investment services to her (larger) corporate or institutional clients.

In that sense it can be stated that the general responsibility for tapping the market in the respective market area lies with the individual cooperative banks. This means that the sales activities in the local market shall generally be performed under the direction of the single credit union while the central institutions and their parent companies are responsible, as product specialists, for offering services to cooperative banks at financially viable, competitive rates. The bidirectional relationship also implies that if the first level bank fails to work the market adequately, the financial network should be given the opportunity to work the corresponding market segments, subject to the prior consent of the respective local bank.[21]

The DZ-Bank serves as central institution for virtually all primary *Raiffeisenbanken* and *Volksbanken* (at present about 900 local banks, equal to more than four fifths of the total, are served by the summit institution[22]), with the only exception of the credit cooperatives of the federal districts (*Land*) of Rheinland and Westfalen operating under the umbrella of the *WGZ-Bank* (*Westdeutsche Genossenschafts-Zentralbank*), a regional second level cooperative institution owned by the same local banks served by the former.[23]

The lead cooperative institution emerged from the progressive merger of previous regional and supra-regional central banks (seven in 1985) originally established in almost every federal district (*Land*) which in turn controlled the cooperative central bank originally known as *Deutsche Genossenschaftsbank* (DG-Bank). The *Finazverbund* was therefore historically a three-tier platform replicating the political governance structure at federal level that interprets Germany as a union of *Länder*. Following the current debate, the merger process may in the near future be completed by involving also the WGZ-Bank in order to achieve better scale effects and remove potential operational overlaps and cost duplications, leading to a unique central bank.[24]

[20] DZ-Bank (2013), *DZ-Bank—Zusammen geht mehr*.

[21] Bundesverband der DeutschenVolksbanken und Raiffeisenbanken (2005), *By-Laws*, Preamble, Adopted by the BVR's Members' General Meeting on December 1, 2004.

[22] DZ Bank Gruppe (2014), *Zusammen geht mehr*.

[23] Even if incorporated in form of joint-stock corporations, the central institutions (DZ-Bank, WGZ-Bank) and their parent companies are considered as part of the cooperative sector due to their shareholders' structure and captive business volumes.

[24] *Genossenschaftsbanken, Ehre wem Ehre gebührt*, Zeitschrift für das gesamte Kreditwesen, 19/2004, p. 1034.

The DZ-Bank is controlled by the local credit unions. In that sense the governance structure of the German cooperative system may be viewed as a two-stage bottom up structure. The primary credit unions served by the central bank hold 82.3 % of the share capital either directly or indirectly through regional holding companies resulting from the above mentioned merger process of the previous existing regional central institutions which, in turn, participated in the share capital of the former *Deutsche Genossenschaftsbank* (DG-Bank).[25] For the same reason, WGZ-Bank holds—as the last remaining regional central institution serving a group of about 210 local cooperative banks not yet merged with the DZ-Bank—almost 7 % of the share capital of the latter superregional central bank, while the remaining capital is controlled by other non-credit cooperatives (6.9 %) and, for a minority stake, by the federal association of the German *Volksbanken and Raiffeisenbanken*, described next.

In respect to the governance structure it should be noted that the share capital composition does not directly reflect the shareholders' capability of addressing the DZ-Bank's governing bodies due to the fact that the bank's by-laws establish that nine members out of 20 constituting the so called supervisory board (which in turn appoints the board of managing directors) shall be elected by the shareholders, ten by the employees, while the *Bundesverband der Deutschen Volksbanken und Raiffeisenbanken* (BVR) is entitled to appoint a member of its executive committee as a member of the supervisory board of the bank. This regardless of the minority stake that the BVR holds of the DZ-Bank's share capital.

3.2 The Associative Level

The cooperative associations define the institutional representation and strategic organization of the cooperative financial network and of its members, acting as political and service centers for the cooperative banks and their affiliated companies. The associative organization is basically structured in five regional and one national (i.e. federal) federations denominated *Regionalverbände* and *Bundesverband deutscher Volksbanken und Raiffeisenbanken* (*BVR*), respectively.[26] In addition there are two superregional associations devoted to special

[25] The leading regional holding companies hold together about 76 % of the subscribed capital of the DZ-Bank [DZ-Bank, *Debt Issuance Programme Prospectus*, 15 May 2009].

[26] The geographic area of the *Regionalverbände* does not correspond to the one of the *Länder* due to historic reasons and repeated mergers that altered the original territorial distribution. At the same time, the BVR results from the merger in 1972 of the previous national associations of the *Raiffeisenbanken* and *Volksbanken* which were formerly independent federations of the two cooperative banking circuits (*Genossenschaftsverbände in der Bundesrepublik Deutschland*, in "Handwörterbuch des Genossenschaftswesens", 1980).

categories of credit unions, the Sparda-Banken and PSD-Bankengruppe, originally representing cooperative banks of specific categories of workers (i.e. the railway and post-office employees) and now partly evolved into specialized private- and direct-banking financial intermediaries, respectively.

The key point is given by the fact that first level *Raiffeisenbanken* and *Volksbanken* are obliged by law to become member of a co-operative auditing association (*Prüfungsverband* incorporated in the *Regionalverbände*) deputized to perform the annual audit of the financial statements as well as of the overall correctness of management of the associate cooperative banks,[27] [28]

The mandatory membership has relevant strategic and operational implications due to the fact that this constraint implicitly attributes to the associative organizations a governance capability of the cooperative systems that largely exceeds the mere ordinary audit task. In fact, profiting from the inspection services provided, the legal provision of the mandatory membership has de facto enabled the regional and national associative organizations to extend the range of services offered to the member banks in a captive context—but on a voluntary basis—and, in that way, to achieve a preeminent role in addressing and unifying the overall strategy and business activities of the cooperative banks enhancing the network's cohesion, at the same time.[29] In addition, as described above, the presence of national associations' representatives in the boards of the central business institutions enforces their coordination influence over the sector.[30]

Part of the services is provided to the affiliated primary banks for free, being their costs cross-subsidized by the audit services and membership-fees invoiced,

---

[27] §53, *Gesetz betreffend die Erwerbs- und Wirtschaftsgenossenschaften*, cit.

As mentioned, the *Volksbanken* and *Raiffeisenbanken* are also subject to the regulatory vigilance of the BAFIN. In 2011 the supervisory authority conducted 105 special audits of institutions belonging to the cooperative sector, equal to 8.9 % of the total number of cooperative banks. The percentages of audited commercial banks and savings institutions were of 17.8 % and 14.0 %, respectively (2011 data). Please note that the significantly higher overall percentage of audits at commercial banks and savings bank compared with the cooperative sector reflects the greater systemic importance of the former institutions in accordance with a risk-weighted approach of the supervisory authority [Bundesanstalt für Finanzdienstleistungsaufsicht (2012), *Annual Report 2011*, pp. 160–161]

[28] On the contrary, cooperative institutions are not obliged to become member of the national federation. Even if limited in numbers, there have been cases of primary banks refusing national membership but legally obliged to maintain regional association. Due to their legal form classification, these banks were entitled to carry the denomination of *Volksbanken* or *Raiffeisenbanken* but were restrained from using the credit cooperatives' logo belonging to the federal association.

[29] In accordance to audit regulation (*Bilanzrechtsreformgesetz*—BILREG), cooperative associations have to separate their audit activities from their remaining operations (Jessen U., *Regelungen zur Unabhängigkeit der genossenschaftlichen Prüfungsverbände nach dem Bilanzrechtsreformgesetz*, Zeitschrift für das gesamte Genossenschaftswesen, 2005, Band 55, p.45; Esser I., Hillebrand K.P., Wlater K.F., *Unabhängigkeit der genossenschaftlichen Prüfungsverbände*, Zeitschrift für das gesamte Genossenschaftswesen, 2006, Band 56, pp. 26–58).

[30] Backenköhler R., *Der moderne Genossenschaftsverband—Neue Wege für Dienstleistungen und Prüfung*, Newsletter des Instituts für Genossenschaftswesen der Universität Münster, n.2/2002.

while part of the services is billed separately on the basis of the effective facilities requested by the single bank.[31] In this respect, the legal tying therefore represents, on the one side, an extraordinary discipline for incentivizing the local banks to profit from the cooperative network's assistance due to the fact that buying the same services in the market from external suppliers would partly duplicate the costs (being the membership-fee invoiced anyway), and, on the other side, enables the regional associations to enhance the service quality due to the economies of scale and of specialization resulting from the captive business volume.

In that way the regional associations have been able to provide adequate services—like legal and tax support as well as counseling in general management issues (e.g. risk management and compliance) and staff training—to their members at viable rates.

The strong linkages between entrepreneurship and associative level especially at regional stage have also enabled a knowledge spillover within the cooperative banking sectors, allowing the primary banks to improve their competences both at commercial as well as at management stage by profiting from the know-how and professional competences of the regional associative service centers.[32] Evidence of this fact is the relative low performance volatility within the cooperative banking sector.[33]

In order to further strengthen and coordinate the assistance to the affiliated member banks and limit the competition of external service providers the *Finanzverbund* has implemented over the last years a market strategy, called *Bündelung der Kräfte*, involving both the associative and the entrepreneurship levels. The strategy requires a strengthening of the cooperation within the cooperative sector; in turn, given the autonomy of the single credit unions, this relies on the economic incentives and convenience of the local institutions to pursue the defined goals.[34]

The strategy defines a clear competence and job division between national and regional associations, where the BVR is in charge for the strategic action (considering the indications expressed by the local banks through their regional associations and the BVR's general meeting) while regional organizations assist the primary banks in the respective local area also via standardized information

[31] In addition to the ordinary membership-fees, *Volksbanken* and *Raiffeisenbanken* associated to the BVR are also levied contributions to a nationwide advertising fund operated by the federal association. The fund finances nationwide marketing campaigns for the cooperative brand as well as the development of marketing concepts and advertising tools for local, regional and nationwide use (BVR, *By-laws*, Section 12a).

[32] Göhlich T. (2012), *The Performance Effects of Mergers within the German Cooperative Banking Sector*, Grin Verlag.

[33] Kontalaimou A., Tsekouras K. (2010), *Are cooperatives the weakest link in European banking? A non-parametric metafrontier approach*, Journal of Banking and Finance, 34, 1946–1957.

[34] Bundesverband der Deutschen Volksbanken und Raiffeisenbanken, *Bündelung der Kräfte: Ein Verbund—eine Strategie*, 1999, Band 1,2; DG Bank, *Die deutschen Genossenschaften. Statistik*, 1999.

processes and platforms, mainly at entrepreneurial stage.[35] For these reasons the BVR has implemented at central stage the so called "competence committees", also foreseen in the by-law of the association, in the areas of: market and product development; information technology; staff; legal services; management; payment systems.[36] The competence committees are in charge for the development of the corresponding business areas whose implementation in terms of service facilities and procedures is performed locally by the regional cooperative associations interfacing the local credit banks.

Those competence centers pursue economies of scale in developing at central stage the necessary know-how—especially in the risk management control and compliance procedures—otherwise non obtainable at economic and efficient conditions at local level; representatives of the *Raiffeisenbanken* and *Volksbanken* participate in the working groups established within each competence center in order to bring in the operational needs of the category and act as interlink between the associative and entrepreneurship circuit.[37]

4 Economic, Legal and Regulatory Relationships Within the Cooperative Network

The main peculiarity of the German cooperative banking system is a twofold classification perspective. From a legal point of view, the cooperative banks describe a collection of single bank entities preserving their individual independence and autonomy of the governing bodies. However, from an economic perspective, the German credit unions and their parent central institutions may be interpreted as an integrated but decentralized economic network characterized by a high degree of mutual support and subsidiarity, largely based on voluntary relationships intended to strengthen the captive activity and, in that way, to enhance the network's competitiveness in the overall market. The regional and national associations represent the unifying element ensuring the overall coordination of the entrepreneurship level following a bottom-up governance approach.

In that sense the cooperative network might be viewed as an cohesive economic banking group (also called *Finanzgruppe*) with a common risk profile. This progressive integration is attested by the publication (starting from 2003) of consolidated accounts and by the fact that the *Finanzgruppe* is also formally rated by the major credit scoring agencies (Fitch and Standard & Poor's) where the rating also

[35] Kubista B., Ein unternehmerischer Verband. Der BVR—ein Verbundunternehmen sui generis, Bankinformation, Januar 2012.

[36] BVR, *By-laws*, Section 26.

[37] Krüger M., *Neue Ära*, Bankinformation und Genossenschaftsforum, 12/2004.

explicitly recognizes the major peculiarities of the German cooperative banking sector in terms of mutual support and subsidiarity.[38]

The critical key elements peculiar to the *Finanzverband* able to ensuring the high cohesion might be identified in: (i) the provision of an exclusive safety net; (ii) the strong infra-sectorial cooperation between first and second level cooperative institutions characterized by a relevant separation between distribution and production *momentum* at market stage; (iii) the mutual interest of a strong cooperation in a voluntary context.

(i) *Safety net*. The exclusive protection scheme adopted by the German *Volksbanken* and *Raiffeisenbanken* differs from the traditional deposit insurance in the sense that it is conceptually intended to safeguard the solvency of the associate members and not only of the customers' deposits. This by ensuring that each banking institution meets its entire payment obligations in order to prevent any negative impact on confidence in the cooperative banks. In that sense the protection scheme, managed by the national association (BVR), exceeds—although fully in line with and integrated into—the deposit insurance schemes at foreseen by the European Union prudential regulation and may be viewed as a guarantee fund linked to a guarantee network.[39] As such, the protection scheme also aims at preserving the customer relationship and informational know-how on the asset side of the balance sheet by avoiding that (entrepreneur) debtors need to swap their liability with other financial intermediaries and repeat the information costs of the credit process.

Yearly levy contributions constituting the guarantee fund are charged to the credit cooperatives upon a (credit) classification system (also considering the risk-weighted assets) which is intended to enable early identification and correction of critical situations. Member banks with a good credit rating are rewarded with reduced contributions while banks with poorer ratings, showing a significantly higher probability of failure according to the classification result, are motivated through differentiated surcharges to improve their credit rating.[40]

In addition to capital contributions and based on the subsidiarity rule, member banks are also obliged to guarantee collectively for the obligations

[38] In 2011 Fitch Ratings and Standard &Poor's awarded the cooperative banking sector long-term ratings of AA and A+ respectively [Bundesanstalt für Finanzdienstleistungsaufsicht—Bafin (2012), *Jahresbericht 2011*, p. 161].

[39] Bundesverband der Deutschen Volksbanken und Raiffeisenbanken, *Statute of the Protection Scheme*, § 1.

In future, starting from July, 2015, the deposit insurance scheme will be managed by the BVR Institutssicherung GmbH, a 100 %-owned subsidiary of the BVR, which meets the statutory deposit insurance scheme requirements harmonized across the European Union.

[40] Bundesverband der Deutschen Volksbanken und Raiffeisenbanken Banken, *Consolidated Accounts of the German Cooperative Banking Sector*, 2003, p. 4

of the protection scheme by providing guarantee bonds; these bonds form the so called guarantee volume.[41]

The BVR is also authorized to take preventive measures should it become convinced that the operating policy of an institute is not consistent with the solvency standard upon notification by the corresponding regional association in charge for the audit of the interested bank and might request ex ante restructuring plans in order to avoid the risk of potential crisis.

(ii) *Origination and distribution. Raiffeisenkassen* and *Volksbanken* are able to offer their customers (and their members in particular) the whole range of financial services following an *Allfinanz*-approach, typical of German intermediaries. However, in that respect it is necessary to distinguish between the (central) production and (local) distribution *momentum* of the banking services.

As already mentioned, "responsibility for tapping the market and revenue potential in the respective territorial area lies with the individual cooperative bank[42]", exploiting the distribution power of its branches. The relationship management is therefore generally always allotted locally; this because of the strong personal acquaintance of the client (often also a union's member) by the primary bank, consistently with the cooperative inception that relies on local needs.

However, the production chain differs in respect to the nature of the financial services, based on the macro-distinction between products of "asset broker" or "asset transformer"-type. When the primary bank acts as asset transformer (i.e. when offering loans, deposits and similar banking products implying a [credit and market] risk intermediation) the services are originated (and distributed) by the same institution. In the case of asset broker services (e.g. asset management and private banking products, insurances, security trading, etc.), but also for some specialized loan facilities like leasing and factoring, they are generally originated (i.e. produced) by the central cooperative institutions but distributed by the primary credit union preserving the customer relationship. In doing that, local banks might eventually be supported by product specialists of the second level entities (which, in turn, enhances the professional skills of the periphery). This because of the general limited average bank size of the local cooperatives that does not allow to provide the service directly due to the economies of scale and of specialization requested for those product range [Lang, Welzel (1996)]. At the same time, primary banks outsource other business services, like liquidity management, own security trading and data processing to the DZ-Bank or to cooperative service companies generally serving supra-regional areas.

---

[41] Bundesverband der Deutschen Volksbanken und Raiffeisenbanken, *Statute of the Protection Scheme*, § 5.

[42] Bundesverband der Deutschen Volksbanken und Raiffeisenbanken (2013a), *By-laws*, Preamble.

This job division between central production and local distribution is intended to segment the market and strengthen the territorial presence of the local credit institutions helping them to serve the market efficiently and to fully exploit their distribution power by meeting the specific client's needs through the wide product range of the *Finanzverbund* without having to produce the whole product assortment themselves.[43]

(iii) *Mutual cooperation incentives.* Given the above mentioned job division, what are the incentives for the primary banks to buy the financial services from the central institutions and not to profit from service providers external to the cooperative sector? In that respect, the key elements in explaining the inherent cohesion of the cooperative banking system lies, on the one side, in the voluntariness of the outsourcing mechanism and, on the other side, on the governance schemes that link primary and secondary sector institutions.

In obedience to their legal independence, primary banks are not required to convey the "outsourced" banking business towards the central institutions. So the central institutions, namely the DZ-Bank Group and related entities, are incentivized to supply the financial services at competitive market rates otherwise facing competition from non-cooperative financial intermediaries.[44] The DZ-Bank Group has therefore to seek constantly for the potential captive cooperative market. Given the comparable product pricing, the primary credit unions will prefer to buy the services within the *Finanzverbund* which, in turn, strengthens the competitive capability of the central institutions to work efficiently by achieving adequate business volumes. In doing that the shareholder and governance structure of the central institutions favor the infrasectorial outsourcing process, due to the fact that the local *Raiffeisenbanken* and *Volksbanken* are at the same time clients and owner of the DZ-Bank Group, so participating—via property rights—in her economic performance which is boosted by the same network participants. In that sense the relationship between first and second level institutions might be viewed as self-referring.

In that context a key role is played by the pricing mechanisms of the services provided, pursuing a correct alignment of interest. Generally speaking, pricing policy basically follows a cost approach in the sense that the products or services are invoiced separately; in addition prices tends to decrease in parallel to higher business volumes also via bonus and commission retrocession, representing implicit performance attribution.

Moreover, in order to steadily adapt the product range and service quality to the needs of the primary banks, the central bank has established at regional level joint consulting committees (so called *Beiräte*) formed by

[43] Kless M. (2012), *Benchmarking wirkt. Wie gute Banken permanent ein bisschen besser werden*, Bankinformation, 10.

[44] The DZ-Bank articles of association obliges the bank to serve reliably the cooperative banks.

representatives of the local *Raiffeisenbanken* and *Volksbanken* as well as of the DZ-Bank.[45] In addition, the DZ-Bank has recently established also the so called *Allfinanzbeirat*, which is in charge for new product developments based upon the financial and marketing needs manifested by the local banks.[46]

The central institutions seem to have historically been able to adequately serve the cooperative sector by capturing large shares of the business volumes generated by local banks. DZ-Bank estimates the amount of captive business volume (*Verbundquote*) in more than 90 %.[47]

The relevance of the governance structure is enhanced by the fact that the national association (BVR) is entitled to appoint one member (usually the chairman) of the supervisory board of the DZ-Bank which act as holding company of the central banking group. This enables a strong interlink between the associative and entrepreneurship level of the cooperative sector and facilitates the implementation of the *Verband*'s strategies; it also helps in mitigating possible frictions among shareholders, on the one side, and between local banks and the board of directors of the central bank itself, on the other side.

The above mentioned qualification of the *Finanzverbund* as banking group from a financial perspective but not in the formal sense might become a critical issue in the future considering the expected amendments in the overall prudential vigilance that might negatively impact on the regulatory burden.

In addition, below others, as indicated by the supervisory authorities, the so called *Haftssumme* (i.e. the additional capital contribution that might be requested to shareholders in addition to the initial capital payment) will no longer be regarded as regulatory capital. Moreover, credit cooperatives face the threat of a further negative effect on their own funds because they will be requested to deduct equity interests in their central institutions (mainly WGZ Bank and DZ Bank) from their liable capital.[48] In turn, this might limit the overall financing capacity of the central institutions by the primary credit cooperatives, leading potentially to a higher refinancing cost of the latter because recurring to market debt. These elements could potentially weaken the overall competitive capacity of the cooperative sector despite its past ability to recognize adequate capital provisions due to positive earnings trends.

In addition to the above mentioned critical issues, the cooperative sector might prospectively suffer from the new European (micro)vigilance framework (i.e. the Single Supervisory Mechanism). In this respect the BVR was in favor of a supra-national supervision provided that the central authority plays a subsidiary role in respect to the operational vigilance that should be maintained at national stage also

---

[45] DZ-Bank (2012a), *Jahresbericht2011*.

[46] DZ-Bank (2012b), *Nachhaltigskeitsbericht 2011*.

[47] DZ-Bank (2014), *Zusammen geht mehr*.

[48] Bundesanstalt für Finanzdienstleistungsaufsicht—Bafin (2012), *Jahresbericht 2011*.

in terms of inspections and interventions. This with the only exception of the so called systemically important financial institutions (banks and financial conglomerates) that will be supervised centrally due to their size and potential instability effects in the case of financial crisis.[49] In that respect the expectations of the BVR have been fulfilled only in part, due to the fact that the new system of vigilance clearly states that the European Central Bank (ECB) is responsible for the effective and consistent functioning of the supervisory mechanism, closely working with the domestic competent authorities that will be in charge of the execution of the banking supervision in the respective domestic market but under the overall oversight of the ECB. The ECB will directly supervise significant credit institutions (i.e. around 130 banking groups, representing almost 85 % of total banking assets in the euro area) but may decide at any time to take responsibility also for any less-significant credit institution. In that perspective, the German vigilance authority Bafin (*Bundesanstalt für Finanzdienstleistungsaufsicht*) will be responsible for the local credit cooperatives while the ECB will assume responsibility for the supervision of the DZ-Bank in consideration of its size and systemic importance. This inclusion imposes enhanced regulatory standards and comprehensive assessment in terms of risk assessments, asset quality review and stress tests that will request capital increases to be subscribed by the respective local banks.[50]

At the same time, the BVR used to be also strict against a pan-European safety net centralizing and mutualizing deposit insurance considering the German cooperative banks' guarantee scheme a better protection due to the supposed higher standards.[51] However, this indication seems defensive and does not consider the implied stabilization effects and positive externalities of a supranational mutual support able to better deal with local instabilities because of the implied size and inherent diversification effects.

5 Concluding Remarks

German credit unions are a cohesive financial network characterized by a strong interaction between associative and entrepreneurship stages and by intense economic transactions between local and central institutions.

In this respect the regional and central associations have been able to successfully address the strategic orientation of the cooperative banking sector also profiting from the legal provision of the mandatory membership of the primary

[49] Becker E., Baustelle Finanzarchitektur. 6. Europäische Bankenaufsichts- und Risikomanagementkonferenz beim BVR, Bankinformation, August 2012.

[50] DZ Bank (2014), *2013 Annual Report, Group Management Report*, p. 90.

[51] Bundesverband der Deutschen Volksbanken und Raiffeisenbanken (2012a), *Gemeinsames Positionspapier zu einem einheitlichen Aufsichtsmechanismus für Kreditinstitute im Sinne der Gipfelerklärung der Mitglieder des Euro-Währungsgebiets vom 29. Juni 2012.*

banks in order to fulfill audit requirements. This regulatory constraint is largely compensated by a bottom-up governance structure which confers to the local banks a strong incentive to engage in the *Verband* and strengthens the sector's cohesion and mutual support.

Due to these peculiarities and their cooperative nature (and implied local activity) the German cooperative system has been able to maintain a favorable earnings situation by adequately serving the market and their members. In that sense they represent a peculiar banking sector which significantly differs from other financial intermediaries and from commercial banks, in particular.

At business level, the *Finanzverbund* has implemented a largely successful job separation between the first level cooperative banks and the central bank(s),by separating the distribution and relationship management—mainly attributed to the local cooperative banks—and the production momentum which is largely delegated to the central institutions, namely the DZ-Bank and her parent product companies. This organizational structure helps levering the variable revenue and lowering the fixed cost component of primary banks in order to strengthen their profitability and allow to offer their clients the whole range of financial products regardless of their individual (limited) size.

However, in obedience to their legal independence, primary banks are not obliged to convey the outsourced banking business towards the central entities. This incentives the second level institutions to supply the financial services at competitive market rates otherwise facing competition from non-cooperative intermediaries.

The fact that local credit unions are at the same time the main clients as well as the controlling shareholders of the DZ-Bank Group implies that—given comparable economic market conditions—the primary banks will prefer to buy the services within the cooperative network because sharing the implied added-value and central earnings. In turn, this self-reference approach strengthens the competitive capability of the central institutions to work efficiently by achieving adequate business volumes.

This has historically proved to be the case. At present, beside legal considerations, the German cooperative sector may be viewed as an integrated banking group as testified by the consolidated financial statements and the rating attributions.

Prospective regulations at supranational stage might force the cooperative sector to further strengthen the economic and associative partnership in order to be recognized as a banking group also at regulatory level. The challenge will be to preserve the independence of the local banks by ensuring a uniform group orientation.

References

Backenköhler R (2002) Der moderne Genossenschaftsverband—Neue Wege für Dienstleistungen und Prüfung, Newsletter des Instituts für Genossenschaftswesen der Universität Münster, n.2

Becker E (2012) Baustelle Finanzarchitektur. 6. Europäische Bankenaufsichts- und Risikomanagementkonferenz beim BVR, Bankinformation 8

Bundesanstalt für Finanzdienstleistungsaufsicht (2012) Jahresbericht 2011

Bundesverband der Deutschen Volksbanken und Raiffeisenbanken (1999) Bündelung der Kräfte: Ein Verbund—eine Strategie, Band 1,2

Bundesverband der Deutschen Volksbanken und Raiffeisenbanken (2012a) Gemeinsames Positionspapier zu einem einheitlichen Aufsichtsmechanismus für Kreditinstitute im Sinne der Gipfelerklärung der Mitglieder des Euro-Währungsgebiets vom 29. Juni 2012

Bundesverband der Deutschen Volksbanken und Raiffeisenbanken (2012b) Konsolidierter Jahresabschluss 2011

Bundesverband der Deutschen Volksbanken und Raiffeisenbanken (2013a) By-Laws, Preamble, Adopted by the BVR's Members' General Meeting on 1 December 2004. Last amended by resolution passed at the BVR's Members' General Meeting on 21 June 2013

Bundesverband der Deutschen Volksbanken und Raiffeisenbanken (2013b) Zahlen und Fakten 2012

Bundesverband der Deutschen Volksbanken und Raiffeisenbanken (2013c) Konsolidierter Jahresabschluss 2012

Bundesverband der Deutschen Volksbanken und Raiffeisenbanken (2014) Entwicklung der Volksbanken und Raiffeisenbanken Ende 2013

Bundesverband der Deutschen Volksbanken und Raiffeisenbanken, Statute oftheProtectionScheme

DZ Bank (2014) 2013 Annual Report, Group Management Report

Deutsche Bundesbank (September 2013a), Die Ertragslage der deutschen Kreditinstitute im Jahr 2012, Monatsbericht

Deutsche Bundesbank (September 2013b), The Performance of German Credit Institutions in 2012, Monthly Report

Deutsche Bundesbank, Bankenstatistik, Statistisches Beiheft zum Monatsbericht, February 2014, February 2012, February 2006, February 2001

Deutsche Bundesbank, Banking Statistics, Statistical Supplement to the Monthly Report, March 2013

DZ Bank Gruppe (May 2014), Zusammen geht mehr

DZ-Bank (2012a) Jahresbericht2011

DZ-Bank (2012b) Nachhaltigskeitsbericht 2011

DZ-Bank, Debt Issuance Programme Prospectus, 15 May 2009

Genossenschaftsbanken, Ehre wem Ehre gebührt, Zeitschrift für das gesamte Kreditwesen, 19/2004

Gesetz betreffend die Erwerbs- und Wirtschaftsgenossenschaften (Genossenschaftsgesetz—GenG), 1.5.1889, last amendment 15.7.2013 (BGBI. I S. 2379)

Gesetz über das Kreditwesen (Kreditwesengesetz—KWG), 1961, Bek. v. 9. 9.1998, last amendment Art. 2 G v. 7.5.2013

Göhlich T (2012) The performance effects of mergers within the German cooperative banking sector. Grin Verlag, Munich

Genossenschaftsverbände in der Bundesrepublik Deutschland, in Handwörterbuch des Genossenschaftswesens, 1980

Kless M (2012) Benchmarking wirkt. Wie gute Banken permanent ein bisschen besser werden, Bankinformation 10

Kontalaimou A, Tsekouras K (2010) Are cooperatives the weakest link in European banking? A non-parametric metafrontier approach. J Bank Finance 34:1946–1957

Kramer JW (2006) co-operative development and corporate governance structures in German cooperatives—Problems and Perspectives. Paper presented at the XIV International Economic History Congress, Helsinki, 2006

Kubista B (2012) Ein unternehmerischer Verband. Der BVR—ein Verbundunternehmen sui generis. Bankinformation 1:22–27

Lang J, Weidmüller L (2005) Genossenschaftsgesetz. Mit Erläuterungen zum Umwandlungsgesetz. Kommentar. Gruyter, Berlin

Lang G, Welzel P (1996) Efficiency and technical progress in banking. Empirical Results for a panel of German cooperative banks. J Bank Finance 20:1003–1023

The Greek Cooperative Credit System

Simeon Karafolas

Abstract The credit cooperative system was introduced into the Greek banking system at the beginning of the 1990s. According to Greek Law, the credit cooperative system is distinguished between cooperative banks and credit cooperatives. Cooperative banks are banking institutions, while credit cooperatives are not banking institutions and cannot offer banking services. Since its establishment, the credit cooperative system has developed remarkably with regards to the number of cooperative banks, geographic regions and banking operations. Some cooperative banks exhibit much higher development in comparison to others. On a national level, cooperative banks have a limited position in the Greek banking sector concerning assets and branches. This is primarily due to the restrictions imposed on the credit cooperative system by the Greek legislative framework and the absence of cooperative banks in Greece's two main urban centers. The Greek credit cooperative system is characterized by its autonomy based on independent local cooperative banks. These banks undertook efforts to create a nationwide non-cooperative bank.

The international financial crisis resulted to economic crisis in Greece that created a significant recession during the period of 2009–2014. As a consequence significant problems have been created in the banking sector. Cooperative banks suffered from the economic recession at a different level. They mainly suffered the consequences of non-repayment of loans. This new banking environment set further limits on the growth of the Greek credit cooperative system. Consequences were very serious for six cooperative banks because the Bank of Greece recalled their licenses, while, for others, consequences were more limited, even in comparison to commercial banks.

S. Karafolas (✉)
Department of Accounting and Finance, Western Macedonia University of Applied Sciences, Kozani, Greece
e-mail: skarafolas@yahoo.gr

S. Karafolas (ed.), *Credit Cooperative Institutions in European Countries*,
Contributions to Economics, DOI 10.1007/978-3-319-28784-3_6

1 The Establishment and Evolution of the Greek Cooperative Credit System

Despite the long tradition of co-operative credit in Europe, in Greece the establishment of the credit cooperative system was only permitted in 1992. Since 1992, by the Law 2076/1992, and thereafter followed by the Act 2258/1993 of the Governor of the Bank of Greece, a credit cooperative can be established and function as a financial institution. Before 1992, a vague legislative framework on credit cooperatives existed that did not consider a credit cooperative as a financial institution. Therefore, the evolution may be distinguished by two periods, the first before 1992 and the second after this date.

1.1 The Status Before 1992

Two laws refer to the possibility of the establishment and function of a credit cooperative, the Law 602/31.12.1914 "For Cooperatives", (General Codification 1933) and the Law 1667/1986 "For Civil Cooperatives" (Journal of the Government 1986). The Law 602/1914 "For Cooperatives", in article 1 provides that a cooperative can be a credit, purchase, sale, consumer, producer or building cooperative. The reference to the credit cooperative permitted the establishment of the first credit cooperative in Greece. No detailed description of credit cooperative operation as a credit institution was provided for in this law. The law provides that the cooperative that receives deposits or securities from their members is obliged to publish biannual balance sheets and invest half of these deposits in public securities. Special reference was made to agricultural credit cooperatives, whose operations were described more in detail, in conjunction with the Royal Decree 157-24/7/1915 "For the accounting books of the agricultural cooperatives". Despite the existence of this law, the agricultural credit in Greece was exercised essentially by the Agricultural Bank of Greece (ATE). This bank was founded in 1929 after an agreement between the Greek government and the National Bank of Greece in order to finance agriculture (Tragakis 1980). The role of ATE was that of a Raiffeisen cooperative bank in a rural area [for details of Raiffeisen and Schulze-Delitzsch credit cooperatives see Aschhoff and Henningsen (1996)]. In a country long characterized by the importance of the rural economy, we can assume that the existence of ATE prevented the development of credit cooperatives in Greece. The Law 1667/1986 for Civil Cooperatives replaced the previous 602/1914 with regard to credit cooperatives. Since the passing of the new law, credit cooperatives have converted their statute under it. This Law provided that a civil cooperative may offer credit and other economic facilities to its members. This is the only reference made by Law 1667/86 to the financial character of a civil cooperative; furthermore, no other financial services are authorized by this law. The establishment of a civil cooperative requires a statute signed by 15 persons at least; this statute is entered into the register of cooperatives of the county court of the prefecture within which the cooperative is located. Each partner joins the cooperative obtaining a compulsory share which is undivided and equal for each partner. The statute of each cooperative may permit a partner to acquire up to five optional shares in addition to the compulsory one. A partner participates in the General Assembly, having the right for one vote regardless of the number of cooperative shares owned. Thus, control of the credit cooperative by one or a few persons is prevented, as opposed to the case of a stock company. The transfer of a share to a third person can only take place in agreement with the Board of Directors and said cooperative share is not subject to confiscation due to debts of the partners towards third persons. When a partner leaves or is expelled from the cooperative, the cooperative refunds him for the shares he owns in real time. The General Assembly consists of all the members who assemble in a regular or extraordinary assembly according to the law. Decisions to be taken require absolute majority of the voting members. Under this legislative framework three credit cooperatives were created. The first was created at the beginning of the twentieth century, the Credit Cooperative of Workers and Technicians of Lamia, which became the Credit Cooperative of Lamia and is one of the oldest institutions in Greece offering credit services in the town of Lamia in Central Greece. On 1979, the Credit Cooperative of Ioannina was created in the town of Ioannina in Epirus and on 1984 the Credit Cooperative of Xylokastro was created in the small town of Xylokastro in North Peloponnesus. They offered credit and deposit services to their members without being financial institutions under the inspection of the Greek central bank, the Bank of Greece, as is the case for other financial institutions in Greece.

1.2 The Status After 1992: The New Legal Framework

In 1992, in order to harmonize the Greek legislation with the relative European Commission decision, the Greek government passed the Law 2076/1992 for credit institutions (Journal of Government 1992). With reference to credit cooperatives, this law acknowledged the possibility of establishment and function of banking institutions in the form of a cooperative for the first time. The Act 2258/1993 of the Governor of the Bank of Greece regulated the function and services a credit cooperative can provide (Bank of Greece 1993). In addition, the Law 2076/1992 and the Act 2258/1993 draw a distinction between a credit cooperative and a cooperative bank for the first time.

According to the new legislation, cooperative credit institutions are divided into two categories:

Credit cooperatives which are not banking institutions and cannot offer banking services (only limited financial help to their members). Their aim is to collect the requested capital in order to become cooperative banks. They are subject to the supervision of the Ministry of National Economy and Finance.

Cooperative banks, as a credit institution, can offer all banking services, except for underwriting. Their establishment results from the accomplishment of the principal request, the collection of a minimum capital. Until September 2006, it could do business exclusively with its members, other credit institutions and the Greek State. Since, according to the authorization of the Bank of Greece, the cooperative bank can offer services to non-members up to the amount of 50 % of its loans or its deposits (Journal of the Government 2006). Cooperative banks are subject to the same supervision and regulation imposed by the Bank of Greece on any other bank. The share capital required for the creation of a cooperative bank depends on the bank's geographical expansion which is determined by three levels: prefecture, regional and national. Greece is divided administratively into 13 regions and 52 prefectures. The Act 2258/1993 determined that the minimum capital required for the three levels to be 2 million euros, 6.6 million euros and 13 million euros respectively. It was revised twice by Acts of the Governor of the Bank of Greece. The Act 2471/2001 of the Governor of the Bank of Greece determines the actual minimum capital requirement to be as follows (Bank of Greece 2001):

- 6 million euros for a cooperative bank having members and branches in only one prefecture except for the prefectures of Attica (where the capital, Athens, belongs) and Thessalonica (the second most populated Greek town).
- 10 million euros for a cooperative bank with members and branches in the prefectures on the frontier as well as in their administrative region.
- 18 million euros for a co-operative bank expanded all over Greece or whose head office is in the prefecture of Attica or Thessalonica. This capital amount is required for the establishment of any other bank in Greece.

The creation of the legislative framework has resulted in the establishment of numerous credit cooperatives, most of them converted to cooperative banks. The majority were created during the years 1994 and 1995 following the initiatives undertaken mainly in 1993. They were created principally in the provinces of Greece and not the main urban centers of Athens or Thessalonica. The minimum capital required for the creation of a cooperative bank in these two areas is the principal reason for the absence of a cooperative bank in Athens and Thessalonica. The Greek state using funds of the European Union facilitated the creation of cooperative banks by financing initiatives for the conversion of credit cooperatives to cooperative banks (Karafolas 2002).

2 An Autonomous and Non-homogenous Development

2.1 An Autonomous Development

The Greek credit cooperative system is characterized by the autonomy based on local credit institutions. Initially, the system constituted only of credit cooperatives.

Since 1993, due to strong interest, 31 credit cooperatives have been created in 30 towns. During the period that followed, 16 credit cooperatives succeeded in their transformation into a cooperative bank, gathering the respective required capital for a co-operative bank, while 11 continued to function as credit cooperatives. By the end of 2014, there were ten cooperative banks and five credit cooperatives.

The Greek system did not recognize the existence of regional cooperative banks, as in the case of France (Ory et al. 2006; Palomo Zurdo 1997), Germany (Aschhoff and Henningsen 1996; Palomo Zurdo 1997) or Italy (Di Trapano 2004). The legislation does not presuppose the existence of a central cooperative bank as is the case of numerous credit co-operative systems in Europe (Palomo Zurdo 1997; Cote et al. 1998). The idea of a central co-operative bank has been discussed because of the weaknesses in the development of the system, and especially for most of the participant institutions (Association of Greek Co-operative Banks 2001). The creation of this bank targeted the development of those services which cannot be offered or are very costly for the bank's clients. Its intervention could be on several levels with the offer of a network spreading nationally and even internationally, in addition to the offer of central services with an acceptable cost and transfer of technology. A response to this necessity was given in 2001 with the creation of the Panellinia Bank as a stock company and not a cooperative bank. Its creation was due to some cooperative banks, particularly to Pagritia Cooperative Bank, which participated with 49 % of the stock capital of Panellinia Bank. Three other main stock holders have been the Cooperative Bank of Chania (15.9 % of the capital), the Ahaiki Cooperative Bank and the Cooperative Bank of Dodecanese having each 8 % of the capital respectively. The rest of the stock capital was covered by 11 other cooperative banks and 14 credit cooperatives (Panellinia 2003).

The strategic role of Panellinia Bank has been supported by the involvement of the German cooperative bank, DZ Bank, which participated, from 2005, in 10 % of the stock capital of Panellinia Bank. DZ Bank's involvement could result to the support of the stock capital for Panellinia Bank and the offer of an international network and new banking and financial services from which Greek cooperative banks could benefit (Panellinia 2006). Results were not the expected due to the formation of the cooperative credit system and the changes that took place in the Greek banking system and the Greek economy because of the debt crisis in Greece.

2.2 *Concentration of Development*

The development of the Greek credit cooperative system is notable if we consider total assets, number of branches and members. During the period 2000–2013 assets had a growth of 486 %; branches and members of cooperative banks grew by 180 % and 78 % respectively during the same time period (Table 1). This evolution is the consequence of the huge growth until 2009; from 2010 to 2013 all aggregates decreased as a consequence of the measures undertaken through the Memorandum of Understanding (MoU) agreed between the Greek state and its lenders,

Table 1 Consolidated assets, branches and members of the Greek cooperative banks, 2000–2013[a]

	2000	2001	2002	2003	2004	2005	2006	2007	2008	2009	2010	2011	2012	2013
Assets[b]	548	735	926	1.254	1.573	2.042	2.568	3.291	3.752	4.544	4.447	3.610	3.610	3.216
Branches	46	59	72	96	112	128	145	157	177	183	191	165	162	129
Members	88,475	101,370	114,670	129,577	144,176	160,136	175,541	187,347	196,179	205,495	212,488	184,614	189,232	157,835

Source: Author's calculations on "Association of Greek cooperative Banks (2015), Financial data", years: 2000–2013
[a]Data is of 16 cooperative banks from 2000 to 2012 and 10 the year 2013
[b]In million euros

International Monetary Fund (IMF), European Commission and European Central Bank (ECB) (Bank of Greece 2014).

This development has not been homogeneous within cooperative banks. Furthermore, it presented a strong local character since only two cooperative banks have branches outside their region, Pagritia and Chania Cooperative banks. The concentration on assets became even stronger after the liquidation of six cooperative banks in 2012 and 2013. Table 2 presents the assets and branches of the 16 cooperative banks in 2010 and the 10 cooperative banks in 2013, not including the 6 liquidated banks. Pagritia Cooperative bank had by the end of 2010, 46 % of consolidated assets and 37 % of members of cooperative banks in Greece. By the end of 2013, after the liquidation of six cooperative banks, Pagritia concentrates 52 % of consolidated assets and 51 % of members (Table 2). The second most important bank, Cooperative Bank of Chania, had 11 % of assets and 12 % of cooperatives' members on 2010. On 2013, its part grew up to 17 % and 15 % respectively. Both banks had 57 % and 47 % respectively of assets and cooperatives' members on 2010; in 2013 these increase to 69 % and 66 % respectively. The predominance of Pagritia Cooperative Bank and Cooperative Bank of Chania can be explained by several reasons:

1. A strong spirit of cooperation due to a healthy cooperative development, on the islands of Crete. Pagritia Cooperative Bank and Cooperative Bank of Chania have their head offices in Iraklion and Chania, respectively, both towns of the island of Crete. The Greek cooperative movement, related to agricultural sector mainly, was often criticized for inefficiency because of political interventions (Kamenidis 1991; Klimis 1991). These problems provoked a loss of confidence on the part of the population towards the cooperative movement. In the cases of Crete, a healthy cooperative organization in navigation, along with the creation of shipment cooperatives, led to the success of cooperative banks as well.
2. The confidence of the pioneers encouraged the participation of the local population to become members of the credit cooperative in order to transform it into a cooperative bank.
3. The expansion policy followed, especially by the Pagritia Cooperative Bank and to a lesser extent by the Cooperative Bank of Chania, while other cooperatives had a conservative expansion policy. In the case of Pagritia Cooperative Bank, the expansion policy was related to the creation of peripheral councils which had the role of motivating the local population; the council could suggest the creation of a branch as well.

Table 2 Concentration of cooperative banks market for 2010 and 2013

End of 2010					End of 2013			
Cooperative bank	Assets[a]	Part of total (%)	Members	Part of total (%)	Assets[a]	Part of total	Members	Part of total (%)
Pagritia Bank	2063	46	79,585	37	1668	52	81,002	51
Bank of Chania	508	11	21,865	10	537	17	23,860	15
Bank of Dodecanese[b]	311	7	21,393	10				
Ahaïki Bank[b]	300	7	14,968	7				
Bank of Epirus	218	5	8633	4	256	8	12,601	8
Bank of Thessaly	213	5	8934	4	238	7	10,946	7
Bank of Peloponnesus	137	3	3439	2	176	5	5131	3
Bank of Evia[b]	131	3	8189	4				
Bank of Lamia[b]	89	2	12,333	6				
Bank of West Macedonia[b]	85	2	5580	3				
Bank of Lesvos-Limnos[b]	80	2	6100	3				
Bank of Serres	73	2	3847	2	81	3	4644	3
Bank of Karditsa	67	2	4251	2	100	3	5361	3
Bank of Evros	61	1	5362	3	70	2	5927	4
Bank of Drama	57	1	4627	2	40	1	4715	3
Bank of Pieria	54	1	3382	2	49	2	3648	2
Total	4447	100	212,488	100	3215	100	157,835	100

Source: Idem Table 1
[a]Assets in million euros
[b]Bank not in operation for 2013

3 Part of Cooperative Banks in the Greek Market

Two years were chosen, 2010 and 2013; that is the beginning, and during, the period when MoU's measures were undertaken in Greece. For this period, the whole Greek banking system was influenced not only by mergers and acquisitions, but also the liquidation of banks.

In 2010, despite the big number of cooperative banks, 16 cooperative banks against 19 nationwide Greek commercial banks, cooperative banks had a limited part in the Greek banking market (Table 3). The same year cooperative banks had a network of 191 branches while Greek non-cooperative credit institutions had a total of 3733 branches, which is about 196 branches per bank against 12 branches per cooperative bank. Assets of cooperative banks are very limited, representing only 1 % of consolidated assets. The absence of cooperative banks in all Greek areas,

Table 3 Credit institutions in Greece: assets and branches at 2010 and 2013

	2010				2013			
Institutions	Number	Branches	Assets[a]	Assets: part in total (%)	Number	Branches	Assets[a]	Assets: part in total
Nationwide Greek Banks	19	3733	447,151	99.0	9	2884	315,485	99.0
Cooperative banks	16	191	4544	1.0	10	129	3216	1.0
	35	3924	451,695		19	3013	318,701	

Source: Hellenic Bank Association (2015) and Association of Greek cooperative Banks (2015), author's calculations
[a]In million Euros

especially in the two main Greek towns, Athens and Thessalonica, influenced the limited participation of cooperative banks in the Greek banking market.

In 2013, mainly because of mergers and acquisitions, only nine non cooperative banks continued to function; with regard to cooperative banks, only ten of them continue operations since the Bank of Greece recalled the licenses of six other cooperative banks. Consolidated assets and branches are reduced for both groups of banks, while part of cooperatives in the total assets remained unchanged at 1 % (Table 3).

If we now take into consideration, the part the cooperative banks play and the local market in which they are established, the image we have is radically different showing an important involvement of these banks within the local economy. We identify two aggregates:

- the deposits in the cooperative bank and the deposits in all banking branches in the prefecture; that reflects the involvement of the cooperative bank in the savings of its local market;
- the number of members (and main clientele of cooperative banks), in comparison to the total local population. By this aggregate we can see how much the cooperative bank is involved in the local population. Someone can have one or more accounts at one or more banks, cooperative or not.

As stated previously, 2 years were incorporated, 2010, being the beginning of the MoU and 2013, where the measures undertaken by the MoU had serious consequences on the Greek economy and the banking system.

The data on cooperatives is provided by banks and data on deposits by prefecture is provided by the Bank of Greece; it covers all forms of deposits placed into all banks in the prefecture. The prefecture's population was incorporated as the Census of the population 2011. Samples focus on prefectural level, presenting the local banking market. Exceptionally, for two cooperative banks on the Island of Crete, Pagritia Cooperative Bank and the Chania Cooperative Bank, data on population and deposits concern the four prefectures of the Island; that is because the two banks are highly operational across the whole Island of Crete. For 2010, the data of 16 cooperative banks was incorporated.

Market share of local deposits differs between cooperative banks (Table 4). It is very significant, especially for the Pagritia Bank (18.4 % of prefecture's deposits) and significant for some others as the Cooperative Bank of Thessalia (10.2 %) the Cooperative Bank of Dodecanese (9.2 %) and the Cooperative Bank of Epirus (7.1 %).

The involvement of local population differs as well, between cooperative banks. On average it represents 6.5 % of the examined population. Cooperative Bank of Dodecanese has the highest involvement at 21.2 % of the local population, followed by the Pagritia cooperative Bank (12.8 %), the Cooperative Bank of Evros (7.8 %), the Cooperative Bank of Thessalia (6.9 %) and the Cooperative Bank of Epirus (6.3 %) (Table 4). The interest of the local population may be higher than indicated since population data utilized is of total population, while data on members are limited mainly in the adult population.

Table 4 Market share of the cooperative bank in local market through deposits and local population, end 2010

Cooperative bank	Bank's deposits	Deposits at the prefecture	Bank's share (%)	Bank's members	Prefecture's population[a]	Part on prefecture's population (%)
Pagritia Cooperative Bank[b]	1518	8250	18.4	79,585	621,340	12.8
Cooperative Bank of Chania[b]	388	8250	4.7	21,865	621,340	3.5
Cooperative Bank of Dodecanese	268	2907	9.2	25,393	119,640	21.2
Ahaïki Cooperative Bank	238	4077	5.8	14,968	310,580	4.8
Cooperative Bank of Epirus	186	2622	7.1	10,610	167,400	6.3
Cooperative Bank of Thessalia	172	1689	10.2	8934	129,700	6.9
Cooperative Bank of Peloponnesus	108	1978	5.5	3439	145,360	2.4
Cooperative Bank of Evia	105	2597	4.0	10,643	210,210	5.1
Cooperative Bank of Lamia	68	1966	3.5	12,333	158,220	7.8
Cooperative Bank of West Macedonia	61	2005	3.0	5980	149,270	4.0
Cooperative Bank of Lesvos-Limnos	65	1616	4.0	6100	102,600	5.9
Cooperative Bank of Serres	54	2123	2.5	3847	176,050	2.2
Cooperative Bank of Karditsa	48	1172	4.1	4251	113,070	3.8
Cooperative Bank of Evros	49	1959	2.5	10,863	147,530	7.4
Cooperative Bank of Drama	45	1428	3.2	4123	98,540	4.2
Cooperative Bank of Pieria	39	1418	2.8	3382	127,400	2.7

Source: Association of Greek cooperative Banks (2015), Bank of Greece (2015a, b, c) and ELSTAT (2012)

[a]Census of 2011

[b]Four prefectures of the Island of Crete are included

Results show that some banks are more active in the local market than others. A distinguished case of this is the Pagritia Cooperative Bank which followed an aggressive policy to attract members from the local population of the Island of Crete but also within immigrant population of Cretans within Greece, especially in Athens. A similar policy has been followed by some other banks, as the Chania Cooperative Bank and Dodecanese (see also Karafolas and Konteos 2010).

For 2013, the sample is limited to ten cooperative banks, since the licenses of six of them were recalled, data is not available. In the remaining banks, we can observe a penetration into the local market appearing in aggregates, local deposits and local population. Amounts deposited to cooperative banks had a minor decrease compared to those towards the non-cooperative banks. During the same year, cooperative banks increased their members compared to 2010. The banks with higher involvement in the local market shown in the table are Pagritia (19.5 % of deposits and 13 % of the local population), Cooperative Bank of Thessalia (14.8 % and 8.4 % respectively) and Cooperative Bank of Epirus (10.4 % and 7.5 % respectively) (Table 5).

4 The Crisis' Consequences on Greek Cooperative Banks

The debt crisis in Greece and the measures undertaken from 2010 provoked the recession of the Greek economy. A main consequence regarding the banking market has been the huge increase of unpaid loans of nonbanking customers. By the end of 2013, the unpaid loans were estimated to be on average 31.9 % of total loans, while by the end of 2014 they were 33.8 % (Bank of Greece 2015c). Furthermore, Greek banks, especially systemic commercial banks, suffered from the 'haircut' of Greek bonds through the PSI (Private Sector Involvement) agreement passed in 2012 (Bank of Greece 2014). Through this agreement, banks lost almost half the value corresponding to the Greek bonds they held before the agreement.

Contrary to systemic banks that have been involved in Greek debt, the involvement of cooperative banks had been very limited. For example, in 2010 Alpha Bank and Eurobank, two systemic banks, had Greek bonds corresponding to 13 % and 11 % of bank loans respectively; within cooperative banks, Pagritia bank had Greek bonds corresponding only to 2.5 % of its loans (Karafolas 2013). The 'haircut' of bonds, impaired loans and the general recession of the economy influenced banks' assets and results; banks were obliged to register important provisions which provoked negative results. These negative consequences appeared in banks' capital adequacy, according to Basel II requests; Greek banks had to face important growth of capital. In order to solve the capital problem, systemic banks (Alpha Bank, Eurobank, National Bank of Greece and Piraeus Bank), profited the financing of the Financial Stability Fund (FSF) created through the MoU agreement. Contrary to systemic banks, cooperative banks did not have this option available. Cooperative banks had to find, without assistance, old and new members in addition to the

Table 5 Part of the cooperative bank in local market through deposits and local population, end 2013

Cooperative bank	Bank's deposits	Deposits at the prefecture	Bank's part (%)	Bank's members	Part on prefecture's population[b] (%)
Pagritia Cooperative bank[a]	1336	6834	19.5	81,002	13.0
Cooperative Bank of Chania[a]	452	6834	6.6	23,860	3.8
Cooperative Bank of Epirus	226	2183	10.4	12,601	7.5
Cooperative Bank of Thessalia	203	1371	14.8	10,946	8.4
Cooperative Bank of Peloponnesus	134	1638	8.2	5131	3.5
Cooperative Bank of Serres	58	1723	3.4	4644	2.6
Cooperative Bank of Karditsa	74	969	7.6	5361	4.7
Cooperative Bank of Evros	52	1565	3.3	5927	4.0
Cooperative Bank of Drama	32	1127	2.8	4715	4.8
Cooperative Bank of Pieria	39	1120	3.5	3648	2.9

Source: Association of Greek cooperative Banks (2015) and Bank of Greece (2015a, b, c)
[a]Four prefectures of the Island of Crete are included
[b]Census of 2011

necessary funds to fulfill the capital demands according to Basel II requirements. Most cooperative banks succeed in this respect; however, six of them did not. A situation which was not without criticism, as cooperative banks did not have the same favorable treatment with the systemic banks, Bank of Greece decided to recall the licenses of six cooperative banks in 2012 and 2013. In 2012, by the Decision of the Commission on Credit and Insurance Issues of the Bank of Greece the license was recalled for the cooperative banks Ahaïki Cooperative Bank, Cooperative Bank of Lamia and Cooperative Bank of Lesvos-Limnos (Bank of Greece 2012). On December 2013, the same Commission of the Bank of Greece decided to recall the license of the Cooperative Bank of Dodecanese, Cooperative Bank of Evia, and the Cooperative Bank of West Macedonia (Bank of Greece 2013). A portion of the assets and liabilities of the cooperative banks were transferred to other systemic banks. Thus, assets and liabilities of the Cooperative Bank of Dodecanese, Cooperative Bank of Evia, and Cooperative Bank of West Macedonia were transferred to Alpha Bank. Assets and liabilities of the Cooperative Bank of Lamia, Ahaiki Cooperative Bank, and the Cooperative Bank of Lesvos-Limnos were transferred to the National Bank of Greece. Greek cooperative banks faced a further consequence since on 2015 the license of the Panellinia Bank was recalled by the

Decision of the Central European Bank on April 2015 (Bank of Greece 2015a), and assets and loans were transferred to Piraeus Bank.

5 Conclusions

The Greek cooperative credit system is one of the new established in Europe under a form of financial institution. The Greek system distinguishes two forms of cooperative credit institutions, the credit cooperative that is not a financial institution and the cooperative bank that is a financial institution. For a cooperative bank, while not a stock institution, legislation demands a minimum cooperative capital relevant to the prefecture in which it is established and operates. This request distinguishes the Greek system from other, old or new, established systems. The financial crisis seems to generalize this requirement by the European authorities. The Greek system represents the originality of a system which is based on independent cooperative banks located in their local markets. It is not characterized by a pyramid structure with local, regional and a central cooperative bank, contrary to both examples of other countries, and the agriculture cooperative system in Greece. Cooperative banks have a limited part of the banking market on a national level, mainly because of their absence in the two main urban centers, the Greek capital of Athens and Thessalonica, due to the high minimum initial capital which is a requirement of forming a cooperative bank in these locations. On the contrary, a lot of them have a notable penetration into the local banking market and local economy within their respective regions and prefectures. Cooperative banks experienced very strong development from the decade of the 1990s, when they were created. This development profited some of them more, in particular the Pagritia Cooperative Bank and the Cooperative Bank of Chania, both of which were established on the island of Crete. Due to this, it then appears that these banks have a concentration of assets. Financial and especially debt crisis in Greece had severe consequences on the country's banking system, and in particular, the credit cooperative system. Six cooperative banks, and the stock bank created by cooperative banks, had their licenses recalled by the Bank of Greece. The reason was the failure to collect the requested capital in order to respond to capital adequacy in accordance with the regulatory framework of Basel II. The other cooperative banks faced the crisis more effectively, even compared to nationwide non-cooperative banks. This crisis created a new banking environment in Greece, characterized by mergers and acquisitions, but also by a strong participation of the financial stability fund in the recapitalization of banks, excluding cooperative banks.

References

Aschhoff G, Henningsen E (1996) The German co-operative system. Fritz Knapp Verlag, Frankfurt

Association of Greek Co-operative Banks (2001) Annual report for 2000 (in Greek)

Association of Greek Co-operative Banks (2015) Financial data. http://www.este.gr/index.asp. Received on Jun 2015

Bank of Greece (1993) Act 2258/1993 of the Governor of the Bank of Greece. Definition of the framework of operation and supervision of credit institution under the form of credit cooperative of the Law 1667/1986, pp 1–6 (in Greek)

Bank of Greece (2001) Act 2471/2001 of the Governor of the Bank of Greece. Definition of minimum initial capital of credit institutions, pp 1–3 (in Greek)

Bank of Greece (2012) 34/ 18/3/2012, Decision of credit and insurance issues, of the bank of Greece

Bank of Greece (2013) 97-1, 2, 3 / 8/12/2013, Decision of credit and insurance issues, of the bank of Greece

Bank of Greece (2014) The chronicle of the big crisis. Bank of Greece, Athens (in Greek)

Bank of Greece (2015a) Deposits per prefecture. http://www.bankofgreece.gr/Pages/el/Statistics/monetary/deposits.aspx

Bank of Greece (2015b) Report for the monetary policy, 2014–2015. Bank of Greece, Athens (in Greek)

Bank of Greece (2015c) 136/17/4/2015, Position of the credit institution 'Hellenic Bank SA' in special liquidation and appointment of the special liquidator Credit and Insurance Issues, of the Bank of Greece

Cote D, Vezina M, Tetrault M (1998) Profil des institutions bancaires coopératives dans le monde. Centre de gestion des coopératives, Ecole des HEC, Montréal

Di Trapano A (2004) Italia (I). Los bancos de credito cooperative y la economia social. In: Palomo Jurdo R (coord) Banca Cooperativa y Economia Social en Europa. Union Nacional de Cooperativas de Credito, Madrid

ELSTAT (2012) Publication of provisional results of the 2011 population census. Hellenic Statistical Authority, Piraeus, www.statistics.gr

General Codification on the Greek Legislation (1933) Law 602/1914 on cooperatives, vol H. Edition Zaharopoulou, Athens, pp 960–1016 (in Greek)

Hellenic Bank Association (2015) Greek banking system data. http://www.hba.gr/English/Index_en.asp?Menu=5. Receive on Jun 2015

Journal of Government of Hellenic Republic (1992) Law 2076/1992, On the establishment and the exercise of activities of credit institutions. Issue A, 130: 2443–2456 (in Greek)

Journal of the Government of Hellenic Republic (1986) Law 1667/1986, "Civil Cooperatives", Issue A, no 196, 06.12.1986, pp 3553–3560 (in Greek)

Journal of the Government of Hellenic Republic (2006) Law 3483/2006 "On Leasing and other decisions", Issue A, no 169, pp 1981–1983 (in Greek)

Kamenidis H (1991) Competitive problems of Greek agricultural cooperatives. In Cooperatives and Common European Market. Institute of Cooperatives Research and Studies, Athens (in Greek)

Karafolas S (2002) Aide Financière Publique pour le Développement des coopératives, le cas des coopératives de Crédit en Grèce. Revue Internationale de l' Economie Sociale 284:45–59

Karafolas S (2013) Greek cooperative banks in the financial and economic crisis: a balance sheet analysis. Cooperatives during crisis and post-crisis period. ICA Global Research Conference 2013, European University of Cyprus, Nicosia, June

Karafolas S, Konteos G (2010) Local financial factors influencing activities of Greek cooperative banks. REVESCO 108:59–74

Klimis A (1991) Some remarks from the history of cooperatives in Greece, useful for today and the future. In: Cooperatives and Common European Market. Institute of Cooperatives Research and Studies, Athens (in Greek)
Ory J-N, Gurtner E, Jaeger M (2006) The challenges of recent changes in french cooperative banking groups. Revue Internationale de l' Economie Sociale, Hors-Serie, Octobre, pp 43–59
Palomo Zurdo R (1997) The main European cooperative banking systems. Union Nacional de Cooperativas de Crédito, Asociacion Espanôla de Cajas Rurales, Madrid
Panellinia Bank (2003) Annual report for 2002 (in Greek)
Panellinia Bank (2006) Annual report for 2005 (in Greek)
Tragakis G (1980) Greek legislation and practice. Edition Legislative Library, Athens (in Greek)

The Financial Co-operative System in Ireland

Olive McCarthy, Sharon Farrell, and David Hewson

Abstract The financial co-operative system in Ireland is comprised mainly of credit unions. The Irish credit union movement includes over 520 individual credit unions with a combined asset base of over 16 billion euros, total membership of over 3.6 million people, total savings of over 13 billion euros and total lending of over 4.5 billion euros. This chapter explores the current size, structure, operations and challenges of the movement across two jurisdictions: Northern Ireland and the Republic of Ireland. This is a particularly difficult and complex time for credit unions in both jurisdictions as they face significant regulatory, legislative and structural changes.

1 Introduction

This chapter examines the financial co-operative system on the island of Ireland. The focus of the chapter is on the Irish credit union movement as this is the main form of financial co-operative in existence. Until recently there were two building societies in operation in the Republic of Ireland but these have since been nationalised following the restructuring of the banking sector. A small number of building societies continue to operate in Northern Ireland.

While the Irish credit union movement differs between Northern Ireland (NI) and the Republic of Ireland (RoI) in terms of legal and regulatory jurisdiction,

O. McCarthy (✉)
Centre for Co-operative Studies and Department of Food Business & Development, University College Cork, O'Rahilly Building, Cork, Ireland
e-mail: o.mccarthy@ucc.ie

S. Farrell
Credit Union Compliance Centre, Irish League of Credit Unions, Dublin, Ireland
e-mail: sfarrell@creditunion.ie

D. Hewson
Monitoring Department, Irish League of Credit Unions, Dublin, Ireland
e-mail: dhewson@creditunion.ie

S. Karafolas (ed.), *Credit Cooperative Institutions in European Countries*, Contributions to Economics, DOI 10.1007/978-3-319-28784-3_7

the majority of credit unions across the island have been united since their establishment through a common umbrella body and have acted largely as a united movement. The credit union movements in both NI and the RoI are undergoing significant changes at present, some of which are discussed later.

2 Establishment and Evolution

Nearly every town and city in Ireland has a credit union office serving many of the financial needs of its members. The Irish credit union movement has one of the highest membership penetrations of all credit union movements throughout the world with about one in every two citizens holding credit union membership. Most Irish credit unions are community based and offer services, such as savings and loans, to meet the needs of their members.

Credit unions first emerged in Ireland in the late 1950s primarily as a response to a lack of adequate banking facilities for ordinary people.[1] At that time, Ireland was characterised by high levels of poverty and unemployment. Access to savings and loans services was difficult for those with little or no income as conventional banks chose to confine their dealings to more wealthy customers. This led many to resort to moneylenders and pawn brokers for credit, who usually charged usurious rates of interest. The foundations of the Irish credit union movement are mostly attributed to the pioneering efforts of Nora Herlihy, a school teacher, who witnessed daily the effects of poverty and unemployment on families, and on children in particular. In 1957, together with two other social activists, Sean Forde and Seamus MacEoin, she set up the Credit Union Extension Service, the role of which was to promote the credit union idea in Ireland. They were not alone in their quest, as other individuals and organisations in other parts of the country were also familiar with and were promoting the concept. Their efforts culminated in the foundation of the first credit union in Dublin in 1957. A momentum began to build as the strong support for credit unions from the deeply influential Catholic Church led to a rapid growth in the numbers of credit unions being established. The foundation of the Credit Union League of Ireland (now the Irish League of Credit Unions) in 1960 as an umbrella body for Irish credit unions, together with the enactment of credit union specific legislation in the RoI in 1966, contributed to the early and rapid growth of the sector.

Within 8 years of the first credit union being formed in Ireland, over 28,000 people had joined 100 credit unions. In 2015, 3.6 million people are members of over 525 credit unions throughout the island of Ireland.

There are three main credit union umbrella bodies in Ireland: the Irish League of Credit Unions (ILCU), representing 455 member credit unions in the Republic

---

[1] For detailed accounts of the origins and evolution of the co-operative credit and credit union movements in Ireland, see Power et al. (2011)

Table 1 Breakdown of main statistics of Irish credit unions

	Number of credit unions	Total assets	Total savings	Total lending	Total membership
Northern Ireland[a]	161	1.39 billion pounds	1.191 billion pounds	0.517 billion pounds	0.519 million
		1.96 billion euros	1.68 billion euros	0.73 billion euros	
Republic of Ireland[b]	367	14.5 billion euros	12.2 billion euros	3.9 billion euros	3.1 million
Total	528	16.46 billion euros	13.28 billion euros	4.63 billion euros	3.619 million

[a]Bank of England Prudential Regulation Authority, as at December 2014, based on prudential returns made. Sterling figures are also shown in Euro using an exchange rate of £1/1.41 €
[b]Communication from the Registry of Credit Unions, June 2015, giving statistics as at March 2015 and based on prudential returns made

(359) and North of Ireland (96), the Credit Union Development Association (CUDA), representing ten member credit unions in the Republic (and with some overlapping membership with the ILCU) and the Ulster Federation of Credit Unions (UFCU), representing 46 credit unions in the North. In NI, there is also a small number of credit unions affiliated to the Tyrone Federation and others which remain independent. There are five additional independent credit unions in the RoI. Table 1 gives a breakdown of total assets, total savings, total lending and total membership of credit unions on the island of Ireland broken down by jurisdiction.

The ILCU is a credit union trade and representative body for credit unions, providing various business and support services for its members, including monitoring and supervision, training, marketing and advice on day to day operations. As already noted, its membership comprises credit unions throughout the island of Ireland. The seeds of the UFCU developed in the mid 1980s to support the development of credit unions in NI with 'a British identity',[2] with assistance from the National Federation of Credit Unions (NFCU) in England. The UFCU was formed in 1995 when these credit unions in NI broke away from the NFCU to form their own representative body. The UFCU provides various support services to its member credit unions and lobbies on their behalf. The CUDA represents a small number of large credit unions in the RoI, most of which broke away from the ILCU as a result of frustrations with the handling of a major IT project (ISIS[3]), representation of larger credit unions within the ILCU and the structuring of the Savings Protection Scheme (SPS[4]). The CUDA is a representative and development association for its member credit unions.

[2] *Source*: www.ufcu.co.uk

[3] Discussed later.

[4] Discussed later.

3 The Current Model

Credit unions in the RoI are primarily legislated for by the Credit Union Act, 1997 (as amended[5]) although provisions in other legislation, such as the Central Bank Reform Act 2010, the Central Bank and Credit Institutions (Resolution) Act 2011, and EU directives also apply to credit unions. They are regulated by the Registry of Credit Unions (RCU) within the Central Bank of Ireland. This position was effectively created in 2003 under the then Irish Financial Services Regulatory Authority (IFSRA) which itself was subsumed into the Central Bank in 2010. The functions of the RCU are to regulate, register and supervise credit unions with a view to ensuring the protection by each credit union of its members' funds and to maintain the financial stability and well-being of credit unions more generally.[6] In addition, the Credit Union Advisory Committee (CUAC) has a statutory role in advising the Minister for Finance on matters relating to credit union legislation. Significantly, the government established a Commission on Credit Unions on 31st May 2011 to conduct an in-depth review of the credit union movement in the RoI and to make recommendations on the structure, regulation and legislation of credit unions.[7]

NI credit unions are legislated for under the Credit Unions (Northern Ireland) Order 1985 (as amended) and by subordinate legislation. The Department of Enterprise, Trade and Investment (DETI) is responsible for the registration of credit unions. In August 2011, the Financial Services Authority (FSA) and HM Treasury published a joint consultation paper setting out proposals for the transfer of the regulation of NI credit unions from the DETI to the FSA. The stated aim was to enable credit unions in NI to offer a wider range of services than they were at the time permitted to do, and to extend the Financial Services Compensation Scheme and the Financial Ombudsman Service to NI credit unions, thereby protecting credit union members more fully. Since 31st March 2012 the responsibility for the regulation of credit unions is the responsibility of the Prudential Regulatory Authority (PRA) of the Bank of England and the Financial Conduct Authority (FCA).

3.1 Services

The core services provided by credit unions are shares, deposits and loans. The rules governing the provision of these services differ between NI and the RoI. In NI, a member cannot have shares greater than STG£15,000 or 1.5 % of the total

[5] By the Credit Union and Co-operation with Overseas Regulators Act 2012 and various statutory instruments.

[6] *Source*: www.centralbank.ie

[7] Some of the Commission's findings and recommendations are discussed later in this chapter.

non-deferred shares in the credit union. In the RoI, these limits are greater and deposits are also permitted. Members can hold a maximum of 100,000 € in deposits. Total savings, including deposits and shares, must not exceed 200,000 € or 1 % of the total assets of the credit union, whichever is the greater. It should be noted that shares are non-tradable, meaning they are not quoted on the stock exchange.

Interest is paid on deposits, subject to the rate not exceeding the rate of return received by the credit union from employing the funds received. Dividends are paid on shares annually, where there is sufficient income to do so. In NI, the maximum dividend allowed is 8 % and in the RoI, this maximum is 10 % of the nominal value of shares. The average dividend paid by ILCU member credit unions in ROI in 2014 was 0.77 %. In NI, the average dividend paid in 2014 was 1.25 %. These figures have dropped considerably even since 2008, when the average dividend was 2.02 %. 14 % of credit unions did not pay a dividend in 2013 (ILCU 2014).

Lending in credit unions is also subject to various limits. In NI, the board of directors decides on the maximum loan that can be made to a member subject to the limits prescribed by the FSA. A Version 1 credit union[8] must not lend for a period of more than 5 years where unsecured and 10 years where secured. A Version 2 credit union must not lend for a period of more than 10 years where unsecured and 25 years where secured. In the RoI, the maximum loan that can be given is such that the total debt of the member to the credit union cannot exceed 39,000 € or 1.5 % of the total assets of the credit union. This is due to change by the enactment of regulation (expected by the end of 2015) to enable the Central Bank to stipulate the limits on the total, including percentage, amount of loans generally, or unsecured loans or class or classes of loans, that may be lent by credit unions. Currently, credit unions are permitted to give loans for periods in excess of 5 years to a total of 30 % of total gross loans outstanding if they meet certain regulatory liquidity[9] requirements (Central Bank 2010a). For example, a credit union, where between 20 and 25 % of lending exceeds 5 years, must have at least a 25 % liquidity ratio. A credit union where between 25 and 29 % of lending exceeds 5 years, must have a liquidity ratio above 25 %. If a credit union does not meet the liquidity requirements, lending in excess of 5 years cannot exceed 20 % of total gross loans outstanding. Credit unions must maintain a minimum liquidity ratio of not less than 20 %. Credit unions in Ireland are highly liquid with average liquidity levels of almost 42 %.

All credit unions have lending policies but there is a clear indication now that, due to increasing loan defaults, these policies are becoming stricter and greater evidence of members' income and expenditure (bank statements, credit card statements and so on) is being required to assess creditworthiness. Two thirds of credit unions in the ROI are members of the Irish Credit Bureau (ICB), a credit reference agency. The ILCU reported that loan write-offs in member credit unions in the ROI

[8] NI credit unions are considered to be Version 1 or Version 2 credit unions. Version 1 credit unions generally operate on a smaller scale and are more limited in their activities than Version 2 credit unions.

[9] Measured by liquid investments/uncommitted savings.

fell by 28 % in 2014 to 90 million euros which meant that loan write offs were lower than 100 million euros for the first time since 2009. Average loan arrears[10] were 16.1 % at December 2014, a figure which has fallen significantly in recent years as the economic recovery gains ground. Loan arrears peaked at 925 million euros in ILCU credit unions in the ROI in 2011, but loan arrears have fallen for 12 consecutive quarters since then. Total gross loan arrears stood at 573 million euros at December 2014. Provisions for bad and doubtful debts stood at 18.7 % at December 2014.[11] It should be noted that loan provisions in ILCU credit unions in the ROI now exceed total gross loan arrears (total gross arrears were 573 million euros by December 2014 with total loan provisions of 666 million euros, giving a buffer of 93 million euros). Credit unions may re-schedule loans, but regulatory requirements regarding re-scheduling were tightened in 2010 to prevent large scale re-scheduling during economic crisis. Re-scheduling is often viewed as a 'quick fix' which may hide an underlying problem with a loan or allow a credit union to mask its debt problems, potentially leading to much more substantial difficulties in the future. The level of rescheduling has dropped substantially since these regulatory requirements were introduced. In 2011, 2.39 % of loans were re-scheduled and this had dropped to 1.5 % by year end September 2014.

As a result of increasing bad debts, a majority of credit unions in the RoI face additional restrictions in their lending at present, restrictions which have been placed upon them by the RCU and the Central Bank. Four main restrictions are in operation: a limit on the total amount that can be loaned per month; or a limit on the total lending per member—some credit unions have a limit of 25,000 € in total that can be on loan to any one member (including any members who depend on the same source of income) while for others this figure is 10,000 €; or a limit on the loan duration; or finally, a limit based on the total loan repayments or a percentage of the total loan repayments received in that month. Credit unions have sharply criticised the imposition of these additional restrictions for several reasons. Firstly, the restrictions can inhibit the ability of credit unions to trade their way out of financial difficulty. Loan interest is the main source of income for most credit unions and a restriction on their ability to earn is seen as hindering their financial recovery. Secondly, for some credit unions, it results in rejecting loan applications from creditworthy members and for some members, may result in their resorting to other sources of credit. The concern here is that members will turn to moneylenders whose interest rates far exceed those of credit unions. Credit union managers and the media are reporting increasing resentment among members who have had reasonable loan applications rejected due to these restrictions. Thirdly, credit unions are frustrated by what they see as the lack of transparency in the decisions by the RCU and Central Bank to impose lending restrictions. However, since August 2013, credit unions may now appeal a regulatory direction to the Irish

[10] Calculated as gross loans which had not had a repayment for 10 weeks or more.

[11] There is further discussion of these figures later.

Financial Services Appeals Tribunal (IFSAT). There have been no known such appeals to date.

When compared to the banking sector as a whole in the RoI, credit union market share of household savings is in the region of 12.9 %[12] and about 34.5 % of consumer lending (excluding mortgages[13]). Between 2011 and 2013, savings in credit unions[14] decreased by 3 % and lending decreased by 27 %. Comparative figures for the banking sector (Central Bank 2011c, 2014a) show a decrease of 5 % and 37 % respectively, showing that credit unions are performing better than their banking counterparts. In 2014, the total assets of credit unions in the RoI represented approximately 2.7 % of the total assets of all domestic credit institutions.

The maximum rate of interest which can be charged on loans in both jurisdictions is 1 % per month on the reducing balance of the loan. This equates with an APR (annual percentage rate) of 12.67 %. In the RoI, credit unions are the only regulated financial institution for which there is cap on the interest rate that can be charged on loans.[15] The average rate of interest charged by ILCU-affiliated credit unions is 8.8 % APR (ILCU 2015). Some categories of loan have lower rates. For example, the average 'home improvement' loan interest rate is 7.25 % APR.

According to the ILCU (2010), among its member credit unions, 96 % of total lending is personal lending. Some credit unions also pay a loan interest refund (known as a rebate) to borrowing members from the operating surplus of the credit union. A refund of a percentage of loan interest can be given to borrowing members where a dividend has been paid to shareholders. The average loan interest refund paid in the ROI in 2014 was 9.55 % and in NI was 17.24 % (ILCU 2015). Some credit unions prefer to charge the full rate of loan interest allowable and to give a generous loan interest refund at the end of the financial year, as this is seen to reward members for making loan repayments. In an effort to encourage lending, more credit unions opt to pay a higher loan interest rebate rather than pay a higher dividend. Some 100 ILCU credit unions paid a higher loan interest rebate in 2014 than in 2013 (ILCU 2015).

Credit unions also give business loans, mostly to individuals. Some credit unions offer special interest rates on such loans. Given wide variations in practice and expertise among credit unions in the granting of business loans, the RCU in 2007 advised greater caution by credit unions in the RoI in the granting and monitoring of business loans (Financial Financial Regulator 2007). About 40 % of credit unions are now prohibited by the RCU from making any business loans as part of the additional restrictions discussed earlier.

Credit unions have in-built life savings and loan protection insurance. This means that in the event of a member's death, and subject to certain terms and

[12] Measured against total household savings taken from Central Bank (2014a).

[13] Mortgages are excluded because credit unions generally do not offer mortgages.

[14] ILCU affiliates.

[15] In fact, regulated moneylenders must charge a *minimum* of 23 %, and have no maximum limit.

conditions, members can have their outstanding loans cleared and next-of-kin can receive up to 100 % of their savings in a life insurance payment. Premiums for these insurances are paid as an operating expense of the credit union. Some credit unions also provide Death Benefit Insurance (DBI) as an extra service, whereby, in the event of a member's death, next-of-kin receive a payment to help pay for funeral expenses. Some credit unions pay the cost of the premium for this insurance as an operating expense, while others offer it as an optional service for which members pay directly.

Other services available from typical credit unions include money transfer, foreign currency exchange, home and car insurance and loan repayment protection insurance, all of which are offered by credit unions as agents of other companies. Credit unions also provide free debt counselling and financial advice, and work closely in association with the Money Advice and Budgeting Service (MABS), which is a publicly funded, free advice service for those experiencing problems with debt. Prior to the economic downturn, a very small number of credit unions offered mortgage facilities to members either directly or as a bank agent. Since the downturn in the economy, few, if any, credit unions continue to offer mortgage services.

Unlike the wider banking sector, a very limited number of credit unions offer debit card and prepaid card services and ATMs (cash dispensers). In fact, one of the main drawbacks which has been facing Irish credit unions in developing their range of services has been their limited technological capability. Because credit unions are autonomous, there has been limited co-ordination between them in respect of many aspects of their operations. This is due primarily to the fact that credit unions are not linked together through IT systems. Each credit union operates its own system. While this is beneficial in some respects, it also causes unnecessary duplication in function and expense. In the late 1990s, there were as many as 33 different IT operating systems in the credit union movement, each carrying its own maintenance and development costs. Few, if any, of the IT systems could integrate with one another in whole or in part. The ILCU initiated the 'ISIS project' to create a centralised banking system for all credit unions and which would be owned and managed by them. Following enormous overruns in the estimated costs of the system and weak project management, the project was abandoned. Untold damage was done to the confidence of credit unions and of the RCU in the ability of credit unions to introduce a central IT system. Another consequence was a split in the movement as the larger credit unions moved away from the ILCU and formed CUDA, as discussed above. There are now a reported 11 IT providers servicing the credit union movement.

3.2 Membership

Credit unions in Ireland operate under a common bond system. The common bond is normally defined in three ways: by residence, that is, members working or living in a certain geographical area; by occupation, that is, members who are police officers, teachers, civil servants; and by employer, such as members employed by the postal services, telephone company etc. In very broad terms, credit unions defined by geographical area are referred to as 'community credit unions' and those defined by occupation or employer are referred to as 'industrial' credit unions. About 10 % of Irish credit unions fit the 'industrial' description while the remaining 90 % are organised as 'community' credit unions.

The common bond is the sense of shared belonging and collective interest (FSA 2003) intended to help credit unions to "*circumvent the problems of imperfect information*" (Interim Report of the Credit Union Commission 2011: 17). In other words, it is designed to help credit unions to know who their members are, thereby reducing lending risk and increasing the incentive to save.

Credit unions are permitted to recruit members who hold the common bond of the credit union and can only provide services to existing members. Where a member ceases to hold the common bond of the credit union of which they are a member, the member can retain membership and voting rights. In the RoI, loans outstanding to members who cease to hold the common bond cannot exceed 10 % of total outstanding loans. There is no such stipulation for NI credit unions but members who no longer hold the common bond, referred to as non-qualifying members, cannot exceed 10 % of the total membership.

For some credit unions, the existence of a common bond restricts further growth, particularly where the potential membership of the existing common bond has been saturated. And because Ireland has so many credit unions geographically speaking, there are scarcely any members of the population who are not served or potentially served. Credit unions have adopted a number of approaches in revising and redefining their common bonds in order to sustain membership growth. For example, some industrial credit unions, where recruitment of employees by the companies being served under the common bond has ceased or been restricted, have widened their common bonds to include membership by employees of additional companies providing similar products or services, and to family members. Some community credit unions have taken the approach of extending their common bond to include all 'non-qualifying' members at a certain point in time or to include new housing estates on the margins of the existing common bond. Clearly, this approach to redefining common bonds is not sustainable in the medium to long term in preserving growth in membership where common bonds are already saturated. If credit unions wish to continue to grow in membership size, they must, where possible, identify and target non-members who hold the common bond. About one half of the population have yet to join a credit union, so enormous potential remains to grow the membership of the movement. This most certainly will mean targeting younger generations of members. Because of the limitations of the common bond, credit unions can focus their member recruitment efforts on their potential membership with relative ease. However, given that each credit union has to do its own recruitment, within its own individual budget constraints, this can be expensive. For the past 6 years, the ILCU has run a national advertising campaign, funded collectively by contributions from individual credit unions, to attract new members. The emphasis of the advertising is on the safety, security and flexibility of credit unions and their local, friendly approach to providing financial services.

The only other realistic option for credit unions to grow their membership is to merge with neighbouring credit unions, an issue discussed later in this chapter. There are some who would state that the common bond concept is outdated and, apart from restricting growth, also discourages competition between credit unions and should be relaxed as it has been in other countries, such as the US and UK. The Commission on Credit Unions, in its terms of reference, was asked to consider the "*function of the common bond in the context of modern financial services systems*" which suggested that the current common bond model needed to be modernised in some way. The Commission recommended that no change be made, stating that, "*the common bond is a fundamental characteristic of credit unions and the Commission envisages that credit union members will continue to have a strong sense of belonging to their credit union*" (2012: 87). However, it did note that there is scope for closer co-operation and co-ordination among credit unions towards shared services.

3.3 Organisational Structure and Governance

Each credit union is entirely autonomous. This means that each credit union's finances and operations are completely independent of any other credit union or other body. There are inherent advantages and disadvantages in this organisational approach. The advantages include a clear sense of ownership and control of local entities by local members and protection of individual credit unions from any potential poor financial management in other credit unions. The disadvantages can include an inability to achieve efficiencies due to the often unnecessary replication of functions and processes across a large number of similar entities. These are issues to which we will return in the discussion of rationalisation later.

Figure 1 demonstrates the structure of a typical credit union. As with other co-operatives, credit unions are owned and controlled by their members. The members elect a board of directors to represent them. Boards must be comprised of an uneven number of members between 7 and 11 (RoI) and between 5 and 15 (NI). Boards have responsibility for the general control, direction and management of the affairs, funds and records of the credit union. Board members are elected at the annual general meeting of the credit union and receive no remuneration for fulfilling their duties. The members also elect, from among themselves, a supervisory (NI)/board oversight (RoI) committee, comprising of three or five members (RoI) or not less than three and not more than seven members (NI), whose role it is to oversee the performance of their functions by the board. This is much like what is termed an 'audit committee' in more conventional organisations, but the key difference is seen in the total independence in credit unions of the supervisory/board oversight committee from the board. The committee members receive no remuneration for their duties. The Commission recommended the

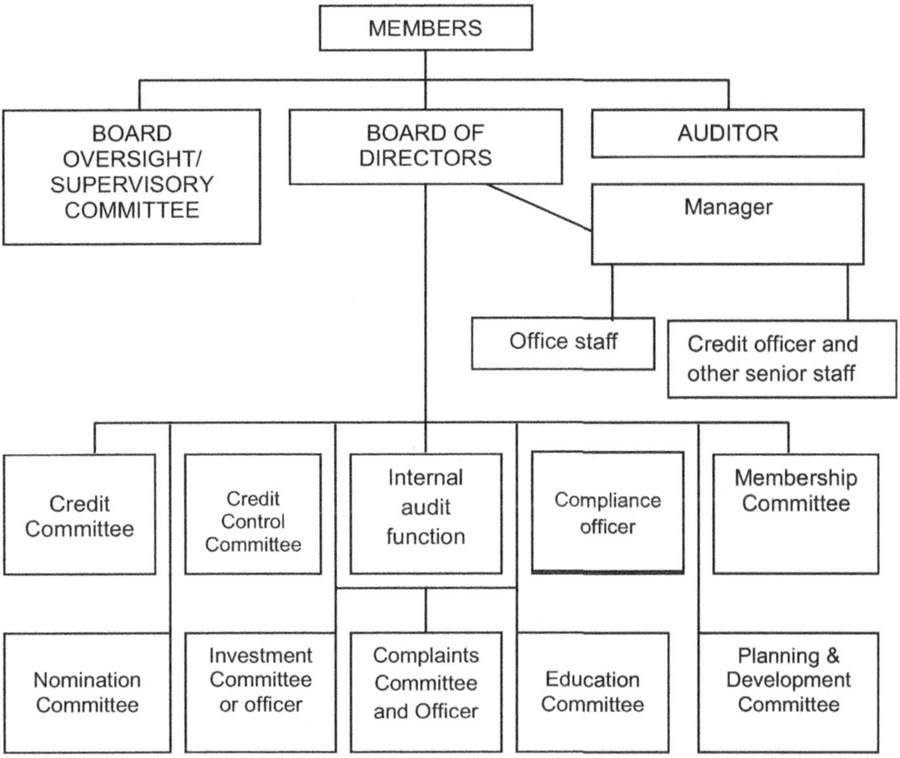

Fig. 1 Structure of a typical credit union

establishment of an additional internal audit function to provide for the evaluation of the effectiveness of the credit union's risk management, internal controls and governance processes (2012: 158) "*in light of the ever-growing complexity and technical detail facing credit unions in their day to day operations*" (2011: 58). The members also elect an external financial auditor to audit the annual accounts. The board of directors appoints a CEO or manager to oversee the day to day operations of the credit union who, in turn, may appoint other office staff members.

There is also a sub-committee structure in credit unions which fulfils various functions, including the approval of loans (credit committee), pursuing members in debt (credit control committee), approval of new members (membership committee), nomination of members to serve on the board and committees (nominating (NI)/nomination (RoI) committee), and so on.

Various problems with the organisational and governance structure of Irish credit unions have been apparent, such as dominant individuals, gender imbalances, lack of youth involvement, very poor attendance at AGMs, lack of relevant training and education of the board and supervisors, volunteer burnout, unrepresentative boards, failure to hold proper elections, and so on [see for example, Byrne (2006), McKillop et al. (2002, 2006), McCarthy (2005), Byrne et al. (2002, 2004)]. Many of these relate to difficulties around the participation of members in the governance of the organisation. Credit union ethos strongly urges members to become actively involved in what Briscoe and Ward (2005) refer to as the *design for use* of their credit union—giving feedback, participating in the AGM, volunteering their services for positions on the board and sub-committees and so on. Education is also seen as fundamental in giving members the skills and knowledge they need to be effective and informed participants in their organisation.

Governance weaknesses have not gone unnoticed within the sector. Indeed, the RCU in the RoI issued a guidance note to credit unions in May 2005 on the control, direction and management of credit unions, reminding boards and key committees of their duties and highlighting good practice regarding elections (Financial Financial Regulator 2005). Various educational and training courses have been put in place through the representative bodies and universities in particular. Indeed, the Central Bank (2014b :5–6) stated it was "*concerned about the fundamental weaknesses [it] identified in governance, lending, operations and risk management*", highlighting that credit unions had not addressed "*the scale and scope of governance, risk and operational management changes required under the strengthened regulatory framework*". With the near collapse of the banking system in Ireland, new fitness and probity requirements have been introduced by the Central Bank of Ireland under the Central Bank Reform Act 2010. Under a new Fitness and Probity Standards Code (Central Bank 2011a: 7), persons are required to be "*competent and capable; honest, ethical and to act with integrity; and financially sound*". The new Fitness and Probity regime for credit unions came into effect on 1st August 2013 and is expected to be fully implemented by 1st August 2016. The Central Bank (2011b) has also set out revised minimum competency requirements for all those providing retail financial products. While this also applies to credit unions, The Commission recommended that consideration be given to developing a wider minimum competency code for credit unions following implementation of the governance requirements and fitness and probity regime (2012: 165).

As mentioned above, all credit unions in Ireland are autonomous units and most affiliate to a central umbrella body. By and large, the umbrella bodies act as representative organisations. They do not provide central banking services for credit unions, although the development of some central services for credit unions has been ongoing, as discussed earlier. The ILCU has also put a regional structure in place. This takes the form of 25 'Chapters' organised on a geographic basis, comprising what are essentially clusters of credit unions. Chapters have no powers and are designed as a means to share information between credit unions in similar geographic areas. Chapters are supported by credit unions to varying degrees and there have been numerous failed attempts to re-structure the Chapter system. Credit unions normally meet as a body once a year at the annual general meeting (AGM) of their representative body. The AGM is a forum to discuss issues affecting credit unions and to decide on major policies, vote on various motions and elect a representative board. Each credit union carries two votes at the AGM of the ILCU, regardless of the size of the credit union.

There is also a number of 'interest' groups among credit unions. The Credit Union Managers' Association (CUMA) was set up by credit union managers as a professional resource organisation. It has no powers per se and acts to represent the interests of managers and of credit unions in general. The National Supervisors' Forum (NSF) was established by supervisory committee members in credit unions to provide support and information for supervisors. IT users' groups have also been established among credit unions using the same IT platforms.

Despite the existence of various groupings within the credit union movement, there has been very little rationalisation among credit unions through the establishment of shared services, networks or collaboration. Later, this chapter examines more recent moves towards greater rationalisation in the movement.

3.4 *Financial Structure and Performance*[16]

Credit unions' main sources of income are loan interest and returns on investments. In general terms, credit unions have traditionally invested surplus funds, that is, funds which are not lent to members, in deposit accounts, government bonds, bank bonds, equities and collective investment schemes. Loan interest, giving an average return in the RoI in 2013 of 8.8 %, is considerably higher than investment income, which gave an average return of 3.1 % in the ROI in 2013. It is clear that investment returns are falling and that this average return of 3.1 % recorded in 2013 will not be maintained as most credit union investments are in bank deposits and banks are cutting margins. Therefore, at least in theory, credit unions need to maximise lending in order to maximise income. This, of course, assumes that borrowers repay their loans in full and on time. Credit union surplus (profit) is defined as the excess of income over expenditure. Expenditure includes insurance, salaries, office expenses, bad debts and investment write-downs. Unlike the profits of banks in Ireland, credit union surpluses are not subject to corporation tax. Investment write-downs, caused by the collapse in the financial markets, reached a high of 73 million euros in 2008. This impacted heavily on the operating surpluses of credit unions and hindered their ability to pay dividends on shares. Credit unions allocate their surplus as a dividend on shares, and in some cases as a loan interest rebate, only after reserves are set aside. They are required to ensure that the statutory reserve is at least 10 % of total savings. In addition, under the Regulatory Reserve Ratio (RRR), credit unions in the RoI must ensure that total reserves as a percentage of total assets are at least 10 %. Finally, credit unions in the RoI must also maintain a Minimum Reserve Requirement of 1 % of savings with the Central Bank. Most credit unions also allocate to a general reserve or to a specific reserve for future use.

[16] For a comprehensive analysis of the financial performance of Irish credit unions, see McKillop et al. (2006) and the Report of the Commission on Credit Unions (2012). The data presented in this section is taken from the ILCU Annual Report (2014).

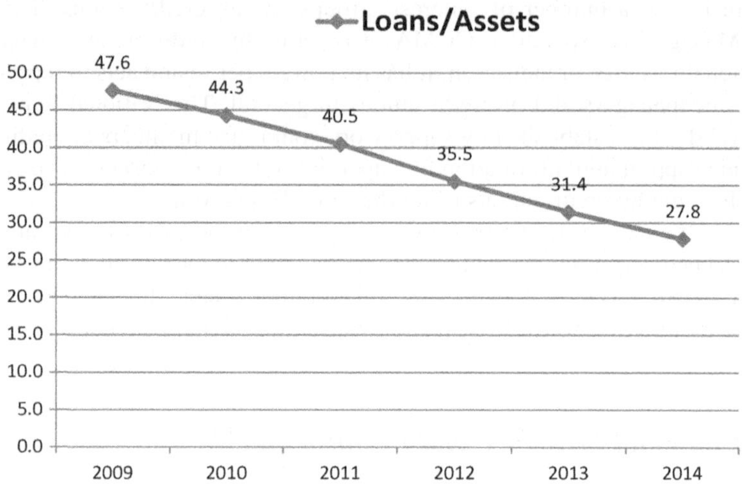

Fig. 2 Loan/assets

Each credit union is required to make a prudential return of key financial information. This section presents some of the key financial ratios of Irish credit unions for 2009–2014 based on the returns made to the ILCU. Detailed figures are not available for non-ILCU credit unions but given that the ILCU represents over 85 % of all credit unions, these figures can be taken as indicative of the overall financial situation in Irish credit unions. An analysis of the prudential returns is conducted by the ILCU using the 'PEARLS[17] ratios'. These are a set of ratios used to monitor the financial performance of and financial trends in credit unions. An analysis of the ratios shows increasing pressure on credit union finances, as lending and investment income are declining, and operating costs and loan arrears are increasing. On the other hand, reserves, liquidity and solvency are strong so the longer term outlook is reasonably positive. A selection of these ratios is presented here.

Figure 2 shows lending as a percentage of total assets. Total lending is in decline and, at December 2014, stood at 27.8 % of total assets. The PEARLS ratios norms recommend that credit union lending should exceed 70 % of total assets. At December 2014, total investments as a percentage of total assets were 71.4 %, while PEARLS ratios recommend that investments should not exceed 30 %. Given that loan interest is far higher than the return on investments, this is impacting negatively on credit union income. On the other hand, decreased lending may also protect credit unions from increasing bad debts, although it raises questions about the core business of credit unions.

[17] The PEARLS monitoring system was devised by the World Council of Credit Unions. The ratios are Protection, Effective financial structure, Asset quality, Rates of return, Liquidity, and Signs of growth.

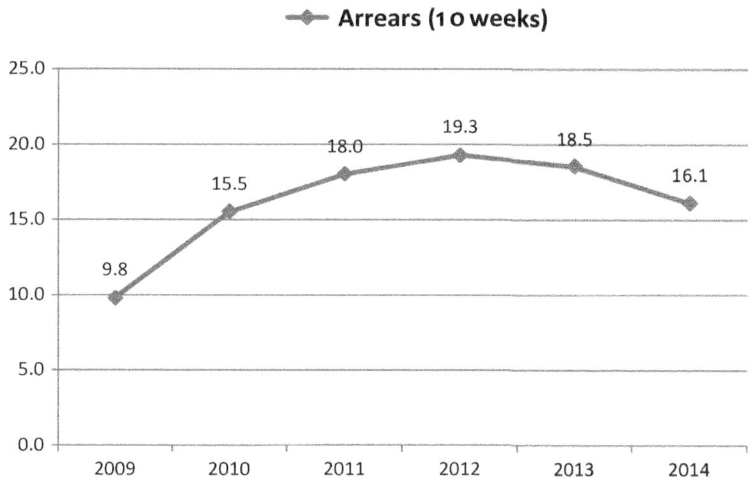

Fig. 3 Loan arrears (10 weeks or more)

Figure 3 demonstrates that loan arrears doubled between 2009 and 2013, from 9.8 to 18.5 %, but this figure is now in decline. Loans written-off for the full year to September 2014 stood at 2.5 % of total loans, while 1.5 % of total loans were re-scheduled.

Figure 4 shows that the capital of credit unions as a percentage of total assets is growing. This reflects the increased reserve requirements of the RCU and shows credit unions to be in a healthy condition from a capital point of view. ILCU credit unions in the RoI have 709 million euros in surplus capital (reserves).

Figure 5 shows the average solvency ratios. These have remained reasonably stable, currently standing at 121 %, well in excess of the recommended 109 %.

Liquidity in credit unions, as shown in Fig. 6, has grown considerably since 2009. Credit unions have put an emphasis on increasing their liquidity and given that short-term deposits now offer relatively high rates of return, credit unions have grown their liquid investments.

3.5 Stabilisation and Compensation[18]

In 1989, the ILCU put a Savings Protection Scheme (SPS) in place to protect the savings of its members in the event of credit union insolvency. All ILCU-affiliated credit unions must contribute to the scheme as a condition of affiliation. The SPS is

[18] For a more detailed discussion of existing and suggested stabilisation arrangements in Irish credit unions, see for example, Central Bank and Financial Services Authority of Ireland (2010b), Spotlight (2011) and the Commission on Credit Unions (2011).

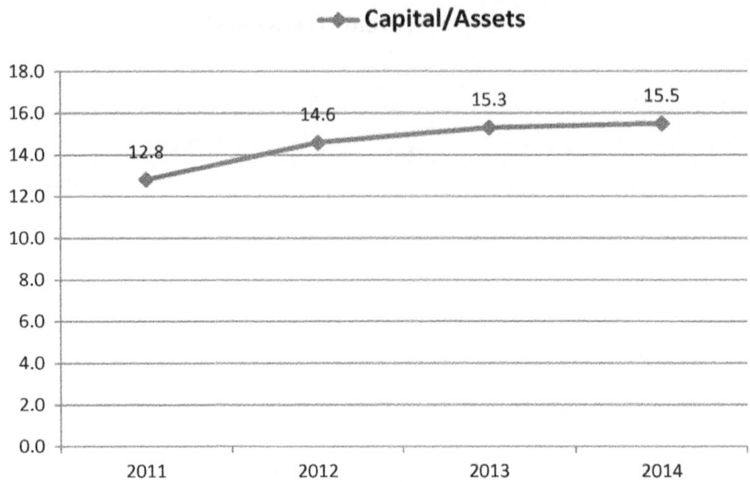

Fig. 4 Capital/total assets

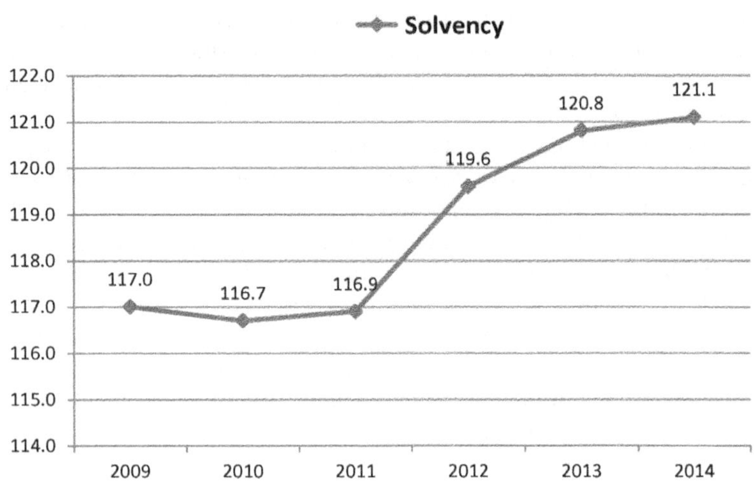

Fig. 5 Solvency

a non-statutory fund controlled by the ILCU. The SPS can help credit unions to trade out of difficulty (stabilisation). It can also compensate individual credit union members up to a maximum of 12,700 €/STG£10,000 (compensation), although this has never been necessary. In more recent years, the SPS has been the subject of much controversy for a range of reasons. These are summarised by the Central Bank (2010b: 2): "*there are questions about governance and accountability arrangements, which reflect the fact that it is a discretionary arrangement operated by the board of the ILCU, and is not a scheme open to all credit unions. This*

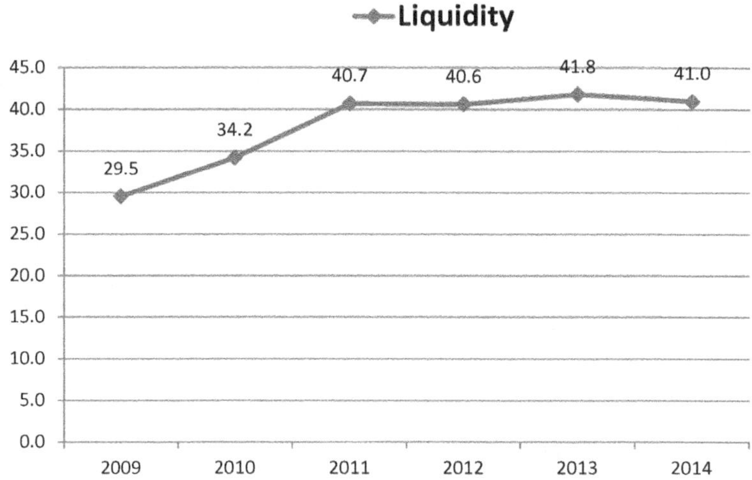

Fig. 6 Liquidity

discretion inevitably introduces uncertainty about the circumstances when the SPS could be utilised." As the number of credit unions facing difficulty increases, the value of the fund has been reducing.[19] If there were larger scale problems in credit unions, there is a fear that the SPS would not be sufficient to assist credit unions and their members. The Central Bank in the RoI does not approve of the SPS due to "*its operational platform, governance issues and lack of consensus within the movement about the scheme*" (Central Bank 2010b: 6). Addressing this issue is quite complex, not least because the fund is owned by credit unions in two different jurisdictions. Furthermore, in September 2008, credit unions in the RoI were included in the Statutory Deposit Guarantee Scheme (DGS) under which 100 % of individual members' savings have guaranteed protection up to a maximum of 100,000 €. Since then, "*the purpose and relevance of the current SPS is in doubt*" (Central Bank 2010b: 2). In 2010, the Central Bank issued a consultation paper on stabilisation support for credit unions, presenting a number of possible stabilisation models. It would appear that the Central Bank favours an external stabilisation solvency support mechanism to give short term, time limited support to credit unions in difficulty. This presumably means that credit unions facing longer term difficulties would be wound up by the Central Bank. The Commission recommended the establishment of a statutory stabilisation scheme to be funded by mandatory contributions by credit unions. The legislative basis for stabilisation is now contained in the Credit Union and Co-operation with Overseas Regulators Act 2012 (the 2012 Act). The Act enables the Minister for Finance to provide stabilisation support from what has been termed 'the Credit Union Fund'.

[19] It decreased from 119 million euros in 2009 to 96 million euros by the end of 2014.

The Central Bank and Credit Institutions (Resolution) Act 2011 enables the Central Bank to intervene swiftly where a credit union is experiencing difficulties with stability. It gives the Central Bank powers to order a transfer of engagements by one credit union to a willing transferee and to appoint a special manager to a credit union in distress for a period of up to 6 months. The government transferred 250 million euros to a 'Credit Institutions Resolution Fund' to fund resolution of credit unions in difficulty. There have been four cases of credit unions in difficulty since 2012 where the Central Bank has intervened. The first of these credit unions, following the appointment of a special manager, had its assets and operations transferred to a bank. Two cases involved credit unions which were forced to merge with another, while the fourth was liquidated.

3.6 *Moves Towards Rationalisation*

In 2002, the ILCU began to discuss the need for rationalisation in the credit union movement. A range of driving forces for rationalisation were beginning to appear (Byrne 2006): tightening margins, increasing loan defaults, decreasing market share for loans, declining growth rates, very weak liquidity some credit unions; limited technological capacity and fragmented IT systems, limited product range, restrictive legislation, weak governance, and ultimately a potential for credit union failure. All of these issues were seen as key driving forces for credit union rationalisation in other countries, including the US, Canada, Australia and New Zealand. In 2004, the ILCU set up a Rationalisation Committee to explore the options available to credit unions to strengthen their business model through rationalisation. Three options were presented to credit unions in the final report: do nothing, which was seen as not sustainable; amalgamations/mergers (legislated for as 'transfers of engagement'), which was seen as not always being desirable; or the development of strategic alliances, networks, credit unions service organisations and federated models, complemented by some amalgamations where necessary, which was seen as the most viable approach (Byrne 2006).

While there was much discussion within the credit union movement on the options available, little systematic progress on rationalising the movement occurred. Since 2006, many of the conditions which were seen to be driving rationalisation have deteriorated, not least because of the economic recession in Ireland. Detailed analysis of the financial situation of credit unions in the RoI is presented in the Commission on Credit Unions (2011) showing credit union income to be in decline, having decreased by 2 % since 2006 overall, but with a very sharp decline of 9 % between 2009 and 2010. The decline in income is being experienced by credit unions of all sizes. Operating costs have doubled since 2006. The dramatic increase in costs is a result of increasing bad debts provisions, loans written off and investment losses, already discussed above. There have been 60 transfers of engagements of ILCU-affiliated credit unions since 2006 (55 in the RoI and 5 in NI). All of these involved the transfer of a relatively weak credit union to a relatively strong credit union. More strategic transfers, where relatively strong credit unions merge with similarly strong credit unions, have not occurred to date. This reflects experience in other countries where the elimination of the weakest credit unions took place first before strategic mergers began. Since 2009, the RCU has been actively encouraging credit unions to consider merging, particularly where significant financial or governance problems exist. Under the EU/IMF Programme of Financial Support for Ireland (2011: 9–10), the Irish government has committed to obtaining "*the necessary powers to promote a higher degree of consolidation in the sector through mergers, where appropriate, with government financial support if warranted*". The ILCU provides information and assistance to member credit unions seeking to merge. Following a recommendation of the Commission on Credit Unions, a Credit Union Restructuring Board, known as 'ReBo' was established on 1st January 2013 in accordance with the 2012 Actas the "statutory body responsible for facilitating and overseeing the restructuring of credit unions to support their financial stability and long term sustainability".[20] To date, approximately 110 credit unions are said to be engaging with the ReBo.

Apart from the work of the ReBo, a number of credit unions have been forming strategic alliances. One formal strategic alliance of credit unions has been formed in the south west of Ireland, comprising seven credit unions. It is a registered co-operative and, while it is in its early stages, it employs a project manager, a solicitor and a credit control officer. Another is the Unity Co-operative Society Limited, a shared services company run by and for seven credit unions in the South West Dublin area. In 2010, the ILCU also formed a Credit Union Services Organisation known as 'CUSOP'. CUSOP (Payments) Limited is a payment institution authorised and regulated by the Central Bank. It provides a single payment platform for participating credit unions enabling them to provide electronic payment services to their members. This is now live with 68 credit unions processing payments. CUDA has also established a shared IT platform for its member credit unions.

4 Future Outlook for the Irish Credit Union Movement

The credit union sector in Ireland has been under intense scrutiny since 2010 and the way in which credit unions operate and the extent to which they are regulated has changed dramatically since then. In NI, regulation of credit unions has transferred to the PRA and the FCA in the UK. This effectively creates a two-tiered credit union movement. 'Version 1' credit unions will still be quite restricted in the services they offer, including a limit on lending to any individual of a maximum of STG£15,000 in excess of the attached shares held by that member. 'Version 2' credit unions will have far greater scope than heretofore, albeit operating with higher minimum prudential requirements and more detailed procedures and

[20] www.rebo.ie

controls (FSA 2012). Potentially, it will mean that some credit unions in NI will be able to expand their services significantly.

In the RoI, the focus is on greater consolidation of the sector. An independent strategic review of the sector was conducted at the request of the Irish government's Minister for Finance in 2010, followed by regulatory stress testing in early 2011. Following a change in government in March 2011, a Commission on Credit Unions, inclusive of key representatives of the credit union sector, was appointed to make recommendations to strengthen the regulatory framework and to provide for more effective governance of the sector. The government has commitments under the EU/IMF programme of support to consolidate the sector and has committed funds of up to 1 billion euros aside to re-capitalise credit unions if necessary. The recommendations of the Commission on Credit Unions informed the preparation of credit union legislation which was published in July 2012 and made various recommendations regarding the strengthening of the regulatory framework for credit unions including more effective governance and regulatory requirements.

According to the Commission, significant financial problems were apparent in up to 50 or so credit unions. Collectively, credit unions are facing increased bad debts and arrears, decreased lending and tight cost/income margins. At the same time, they have been increasing their reserves and the majority of credit unions remain solvent. It is clear that there will be more mergers, particularly of weaker credit unions with stronger credit unions. What is not so clear is how credit unions will protect and build upon their unique voluntary, not-for-profit, member orientation. Increasing regulation needs to be balanced with enabling credit unions to continue to serve the borrowing and saving needs of the members. The member is at the heart of the co-operative idea and a co-operative that does not or is unable to meet the needs of its members does not survive for long. Credit unions are seen as critical in their local areas and they enjoy widespread political and community support. It is hoped that the results of consolidation in the sector will be a stronger, more resilient credit union movement that can survive to serve its local member needs in the long-run.

Acknowledgement The authors would like to acknowledge the input and advice of John Knox, Kevin Loughnane and David Matthews of the Irish League of Credit Unions in compiling this chapter.

References

Briscoe R, Ward M (2005) Helping ourselves: success stories in co-operative business and social enterprise. Oak Tree Press, Cork

Byrne N (2006) Rationalisation committee report. Irish League of Credit Unions, Dublin

Byrne N, McCarthy O, Ward M (2002) Training and education in Irish credit unions. Centre for Co-operative Studies, Cork

Byrne N, McCarthy O, O'Shaughnessy M (2004) A study of volunteerism in Irish credit unions and social enterprises. Centre for Co-operative Studies, Cork

Central Bank and Financial Services Authority of Ireland (2010a) Section 35: regulatory requirements for credit unions. Registry of Credit Unions, Dublin

Central Bank and Financial Services Authority of Ireland (2010b) Consultation paper CP44 Stabilisation support for credit unions. Registry of Credit Unions, Dublin

Central Bank of Ireland (2011a) Fitness and probity standards (Code issued under section 50 of the Central Bank of Ireland Reform Act 2010). Registry of Credit Unions, Dublin

Central Bank of Ireland (2011b) Minimum competency code 2011. Registry of Credit Unions, Dublin

Central Bank of Ireland (2011c) Quarterly Bulletin Number 4 for the Central Bank of Ireland 2011. Registry of Credit Unions, Dublin

Central Bank of Ireland (2014a) Quarterly Bulletin Number 3 for the Central Bank of Ireland 2014. Registry of Credit Unions, Dublin

Central Bank of Ireland (2014b) Credit union PRISM risk assessments supervisory commentary, May 2014. Registry of Credit Unions, Dublin

Commission on Credit Unions (2011) Interim report of the Commission on Credit Unions. Department of Finance, Dublin

Commission on Credit Unions (2012) Report of the Commission on Credit Unions. Department of Finance, Dublin

EU/IMF Programme of Financial Support for Ireland (2011) http://www.finance.gov.ie/documents/publications/other/2011/draftmoumay2011.pdf

Financial Regulator (2005) The control, direction and management of credit unions. Office of the Registrar of Credit Unions, Dublin

Financial Regulator (2007) Guidance note on credit and credit control for credit unions. Office of the Registrar of Credit Unions, Dublin

FSA (2003) The credit union common bond. Guidance note no. 8. Financial Services Authority, London

FSA (2012) Information for credit unions in Northern Ireland: becoming a version 2 credit union. FSA Factsheet for Credit Unions SFDFS090 12/11. Financial Services Authority, London

ILCU (2010) Annual report. Irish League of Credit Unions, Dublin

ILCU (2015) Annual report. Irish League of Credit Unions, Dublin

ILCU (2014) ILCU Credit Union statistics. Irish League of Credit Unions, Dublin

McCarthy O (2005) The Irish credit union movement: member participation and organisational effectiveness. Unpublished PhD thesis to the Department of Food Business and Development, University College Cork

McKillop D, McCarthy O, Ward M, Briscoe R, Ferguson C (2002) Women in the Irish credit union movement: north and south. Oak Tree Press, Cork

McKillop D, Goth P, Hyndman N (2006) Credit Unions in Ireland: structure, performance and governance. Institute of Chartered Accountants in Ireland, Dublin

Power C, O'Connor R, McCarthy O, Ward M (2011) The origins, ethos and evolution of co-operative credit in Ireland: celebrating the centenary of the birth of Nora Herlihy. Centre for Co-operative Studies and Duhallow Women's Forum, Cork

Spotlight (2011) Credit union regulation. Oireachtas Library & Research Service, Dublin

Italian Credit Cooperative Banks

Ivana Catturani and Maria Lucia Stefani

Abstract Italian Credit Cooperative Banks (*Banche di credito cooperativo,* from here after CCBs) represent a significant part of the Italian banking system. Born in the second half of the nineteenth century, they have been able to grow and to adapt to new social, economic and legal environment. The Banking Law, which entered into force in 1993, has weakened the differences between CCBs and commercial banks with respect to the previous legislation, while preserving mutualism, democracy, localism and not-for profit goals. In this context CCBs, from being banks aimed at lending small credits to local farmers and handcrafts in rural areas where they were in most case the only banking institution, have become able to compete with commercial banks on wider areas. One of the main contribution to this evolution has been given by the second level networks—i.e. the banking and the association networks that help single cooperative banks to increase efficiency and to be competitive on the banking market. With respect to other European cooperative banks, however, the Italian system is at present among the least integrated. During the financial turmoil started in 2007, Italian CCBs kept on financing local economies, not without relevant costs, particularly in terms of non-performing loans; the number of CCBs under default procedure has increased. Today a debate is in place for a reform of the network, to give rise to a more integrated system, based on membership of banking groups.

1 Introductory Note

In Italy there are two categories of cooperative banks: *Banche di credito cooperativo* (Credit Cooperative Banks or Mutual Banks, hereafter CCBs) and *Banche popolari*. While closing this chapter (June 2015), they are both under reform. A recent law, entered into force in March 2015, has stated that *Banche*

I. Catturani (✉)
University of Trento and Euricse, Trento, Italy
e-mail: ivana.catturani@unitn.it

M.L. Stefani
Bank of Italy, Rome, Italy
e-mail: marialucia.stefani@bancaditalia.it

S. Karafolas (ed.), *Credit Cooperative Institutions in European Countries*, Contributions to Economics, DOI 10.1007/978-3-319-28784-3_8

popolari with more than 8 billion euros of assets must be converted into limited companies. The cooperative governance, with the "one member—one vote" regime, is therefore maintained only by smaller ones. For CCBs a reform of the network is currently under debate. In what follows we concentrate on CCBs since *Banche popolari* cannot be considered mutualistic companies (*Banche popolari* will be briefly introduced and discussed at the end of Sect. 3).

2 The Establishment and Evolution of the Credit Cooperative System[1]

The first cooperative wave in Italy took place in the second half of the nineteenth century and was mainly inspired by the liberal thought. The cooperative form was implemented in order to organize both consumers' and producers' enterprises, especially in reaction to the agrarian crisis of 1882–1883. Following the model introduced by Friedrich W. Raiffeisen in Rhineland, the first "Cassa Rurale" (Rural Bank, hereafter RB) was established by Leone Wollemborg, together with 32 members, in a rural area close to Padua (Loreggia) in 1883. The RBs were closely linked to the local community since they hinged on ethical and solidarity principles. The number of RBs started rapidly to grow. In 1888, 51 RBs joined the "Federation of Rural Banks and Similar Enterprises" (FRBs).

An important input for the development of the movement came from the Catholic church. With his Encyclical "Rerum Novarum" (1892), Pope Leo XIII underlined the need to fight against what he called the *usura vorax* (the "devouring usury"), through social action and solidarity. After the encyclical the involvement of the clergy in the process of development of RBs resulted in a considerable expansion of RBs all over Italy (Zamagni 2006).

At the end of the nineteenth century, there were almost 900 RBs, 775 of which were of Catholic inspiration established especially in the North East, in Lombardy, in Piedmont and in Rome. In the South of Italy only the Sicilian provinces of Agrigento and Catania could be compared with the North in terms of RBs diffusion and this was largely due to the efforts of a priest, Don Luigi Sturzo. Even though those banks were spread over in the country, their development was affected both by their poor assets and by the small volume of their business. In 1917 the "National Federation of Rural Banks" (NFRB), established in 1909 as an evolution of the

[1] We are grateful to Carlo Borzaga, Giorgio Gobbi, Panu Kalmi, Nicoletta Mascher, Valerio Vacca and Ragupathy Venkatachalam for very helpful comments on a previous version. We are the sole responsible for the opinions expressed in this paper, which do not involve the responsibility of the Bank of Italy.

This article is a version revised and updated for the aim of this book of the chapter written by the same authors "Le banche di credito cooperativo: cenni storici, istituzionali e dinamiche recenti" (2014), in Carlo Borzaga (editor), *La cooperazione italiana negli anni della crisi*, Trento, Euricse.

FRBs at the national level and supported by the Catholic movement, emerged as the promoter and supporter of the movement of RBs. In order to be more effective, it structured RBs into local federations. The NFRB can be seen as the predecessor of the present national Federation (Federcasse, see Sect. 3).

After the First World War, RBs were challenged by the liquidity shortage of both peasantries and Federation bodies. The structural limits of the cooperative financial industry surfaced when Italy had to face both economic and social problems, such as high inflation, unemployment, weakening of the liberal government, and internal divisions (Zamagni 2006).

The rise of fascism in 1922 had a strong impact on RBs, too. Fascism used the cooperative influence as a tool of control and propaganda by appointing representatives of the Fascist Party as cooperative managers. The violent actions of the fascists against people and against banks' officers prompted depositors to withdraw money from RBs. The decline in the number of the RBs could not be prevented by the introduction of the "Banking Law for Rural and Handcraft Banks" passed in 1937. From 1922 to 1947 RBs decreased, on average, by 3 % yearly. Meanwhile, the Banking Law passed in 1936 put all banks under the supervision of the Bank of Italy and, in the same year, the "National Board of the Rural Agrarian Banks" was established with the aim of supervising the technical coordination and of promoting the formation of new RBs. Moreover, before the end of the Second World War, the second level network of the RBs was dismantled.

After the Second World War, RBs faced a period of re-organization. In 1946 the Catholic movement re-established the "Confederation of Italian Cooperatives" and in 1950 the NFRB was rebuilt. Between the 1960s and the 1980s, the RBs movement garnered a growing role in the Italian credit market due to an effort to reaffirm the inspiring principles of the cooperation and to strengthen the internal linkages. The local Federations were also re-founded and empowered with the role of representation, protection and technical assistance, both at regional and interregional level. The structuring of the Federation on local basis was completed in the period 1964–1975 (Cafaro 2001). In 1963 Badioli, the president of Federcasse, was authorized to create a central institute for the credit cooperative system (*Istituto di credito delle casse rurali e artigiane*, nowadays ICCREA), that is a reference institute for the provision of financial services to RBs. In the same period, the process of democratization and of managerial integration had started, involving the second level network. Moreover, the "Central Guarantee Fund" was established as the main safeguard tool for the RBs.

In the second half of the 1970s and during the 1980s, RBs faced a period of slow decline, mainly due to the fading role of farmers (the main owners of rural banks) and to the public subsidies to farming, which transformed farmers from being net depositors to net borrowers.

In 1980 the Federation together with numerous RBs joined the Italian Banking Association.

The new Banking Law passed in 1993 represented a turning point for RBs, since, among other things, it relaxed their previous limits to credit specialization and extended the geographical area of business. *Banche di credito cooperativo* (Credit

Cooperative Banks, this is the new name established by the law[2]) were basically allowed to offer all types of financial services and products. After this law CCBs underwent a profound restructuring, whereby some of them were liquidated, others were converted into commercials banks, and others merged or got acquired. CCBs improved their general performance and started growing in size mostly thanks to M&A that reduced them in number.

In 1997 the Deposits Guarantee Fund of Cooperative Banks substituted the Central Guarantee Fund (see Sect. 3). In 1999 the CCBs' movement signed the "Charter of Values of the Cooperative Credit" during the XII National Congress. 6 years later, during the XIII Congress, the movement approved the "network system" project for CCBs, together with the "Charter of cohesion", which involved creating a form of cross-safeguard to protect the customers of CCBs (the "Institutional Guarantee Fund"), that has not been implemented.

3 The Current Model

Italian CCBs are subject to the same banking legislation and supervisory regulation as other banks, with some additional restrictions. The Civil Code provisions on cooperatives apply to CCBs only when they complement the banking legislation or are not in conflict with it. In other words, at least from a legislative point of view, CCBs are firstly banks, and secondly cooperatives. Differently from other banks, their Statute plays a crucial role, since it translates into internal rules the supervisory regulation of the Bank of Italy.

The Banking Law of 1993 (D.Lgs. 385/1993, "Testo Unico delle Leggi in materia bancaria e creditizia", hereafter BL) weakened the differences between CCBs and commercial banks compared to the 1937 legislation, by imposing, among other things, limited liability, by allowing product diversification, and by deregulating the establishment of branches.[3] The BL has, however, preserved mutualism, localism, democracy and the non-profit aim.

---

[2] By changing the name, the legislator wanted to put the accent on the "cooperative" character of this type of banks, instead of stressing the sectors with which they were allowed to work, as it was with the previous name ("Casse rurali e artigiane"—Rural and Handcrafts Banks). According to the 1937 legislation, 80 % of members had to be farmers or craftsmen. Moreover, body corporates could not become members.

[3] The establishment of a new branch is liberalised in the sense that, like for the other categories of banks, it no longer requires a Bank of Italy's authorization. The intention to open a new branch must be communicated to the Supervisory Authority and the branch can be opened unless the Bank of Italy prevents it within 60 days from the communication. The opening of a new branch can be stopped when the Bank of Italy considers the organization of the bank not adequate, or because of its economic, capital o financial situation. The local character of CCBs implies however that a new branch can be opened only in municipalities that are included in the "competence area" (see below in this Section). An exception to this rule is the case of a "secondary headquarter", which can be opened under stricter conditions (see, "Istruzioni di Vigilanza per le Banche", Title VII, Chap. I).

CCBs are mutual in the sense that they have to lend mainly to members (art. 35 BL).[4] The Statute establishes the exact percentage, but, according to the Bank of Italy's regulation,[5] the legal requirement is fulfilled if at least 50 % of total risky assets are devoted to members or invested in government bonds (or in other assets with a zero-weighting coefficient according to Basel rules).[6] In practise, the actual amount of loans to members (over total loans) differs among CCBs.[7] Moreover credit conditions tend to be generally more favourable for members with respect to non-members (Piersante and Stefani 2012).

Italian CCBs are local since they can operate only in municipalities where they have branches and in neighbouring ones, with geographical continuity[8] (the "competence area").[9] Moreover members must live or operate on a continuous basis in that area. Finally, the name of the bank must explicitly mention the competence area.

CCBs' democratic structure is mainly based on three elements. First, the social basis must be widespread in order to have local interests sufficiently represented (the minimum number of members is 200; art. 34 BL; see Table 1). Second, the company capital consists of nominative shares and the law sets the maximum capital share that each member can hold.[10] As for cooperative in general, shares are not freely tradable on the market, since new subscribers are subject to the approval by old cooperative members. Third, regardless of the number of shares, each member has only one vote in meetings, that is the "one member—one vote" principle applies. This principle implies that "ownership rights" only stem from membership, while they are unrelated with the amount of shares. Therefore, besides the provision of a maximum threshold for the acquisition of shares, members do not have any incentive in buying more than one share, since they would not acquire

[4] The 2003 Company Law Reform (Law 6/2003) introduced the distinction between "mutualism prevailing cooperatives" and "non-mutualism prevailing cooperatives" and allowed, among other things, a favourable tax treatment only to the former. Because of the compulsory "mutuality" requirement, all CCBs are by law "mutualism prevailing cooperatives". As the other cooperatives of the same kind, they are under the supervision of a special authority for cooperatives, whose aims are different from the ones of the Bank of Italy and cannot be in contrast with them.

[5] The Bank of Italy's supervisory regulation concerning CCBs is contained in the *Circolare* n. 229 "Istruzioni di Vigilanza per le Banche", Title VII, Chap. I.

[6] No mutual requirement is set for the funding activity or the provision of financial services.

[7] Considering the 15 areas which coincide with the competence of local Federations, over the 2004–2011 period, loans to members have been on average over the 50 % requirement only in Alto Adige, Abruzzo-Molise, Tuscany, Piedmont-Valle d'Aosta-Liguria and Trentino, while in the other areas the supervisory requirement have been on average fulfilled thanks to investments in government bonds.

[8] A "discontinuous" competence area is allowed when CCBs merge with other CCBs whose reference area is not contiguous and in the case of a "secondary headquarter" (see footnote 3).

[9] The amount of business activity referring to outside the competence area cannot exceed 5 % of total.

[10] The present maximum value is 50,000 of euros, according to Bank of Italy's regulation.

more voting power[11] and residual rights to control. The "one member—one vote" principle separates proprietorship from control and makes takeover not possible. An external investor who, for instance, thinks a given cooperative is poorly managed cannot make a tender offer and get the control of it. This "separation problem" is somewhat softened since directors in the boards must be members themselves, and because the *peer monitoring* mechanism, besides reducing information asymmetries in screening and monitoring customers, could also prevent directors from behaving against members' interests.

The non-profit aim is assured by two conditions: first, banks reserves (both compulsory and statutory-based and those decided by the general meeting) can never be distributed to members and, second, there are legal constraints on profit distribution. As regards the former provision, in case of withdrawal or exclusion of a member and in case of bank liquidation, members cannot be reimbursed more than the share price. Moreover, upon liquidation of the CCB, its capital (net of the share price paid back to members according to the above mentioned rule) must be devoted to "Mutual Funds for the Promotion and Development of Cooperation". The obligation not to distribute reserves is the crucial difference between CCBs and other categories of banks. In order to avoid infringements to this rule, mergers involving the transformation of a CCB into a bank of a different institutional nature (that is a limited company or a *Banca popolare*) must be authorized by the Bank of Italy. This authorization is possible only when the merger is required in order either to preserve the "creditors' interests" or to guarantee the "bank stability". These two conditions imply a situation of crisis and are stricter than the general "healthy and cautious management" principle that applies to other bank mergers.

As regards the second provision, the non-profit aim is also ensured by the compulsory destination of 70 % of net annual profits to legal reserve and an additional 3 % to Mutual funds[12] (art. 37 BL). In exchange for that, due to their social role, CCBs benefit from a favourable tax treatment.

CCBs are fully independent banks, and they are connected to each other, on a voluntary basis, through a network made up of two components: an association network (namely, the national and the local Federations) for the provision of non-financial services, and a second level banking structure for the provision of financial products and services (see Fig. 1). The aim of the network is to develop and exploit scale- and scope- economies so to improve the strength of the cooperative movement to enhance product differentiation, economic efficiency and thus

[11] Moreover, as members do not receive any dividend (see below in this Section), the only plausible reason to hold more than one share is to support the existence of the cooperative bank.

[12] In case of distribution to members of remaining profits, according to art. 2514 of the Italian Civil Code, CCBs cannot distribute dividends superior to the maximum interest on postal bonds increased by 2.5 %. In practice, CCB profit distribution policies, beyond mandatory reserves, devote an additional fraction of profits to charity so that in most cases members do not receive any profit. Membership is therefore not motivated by profit earning, but rather by expectation of better credit conditions, less costly financial services and higher credit availability (Di Salvo and Schena 1998).

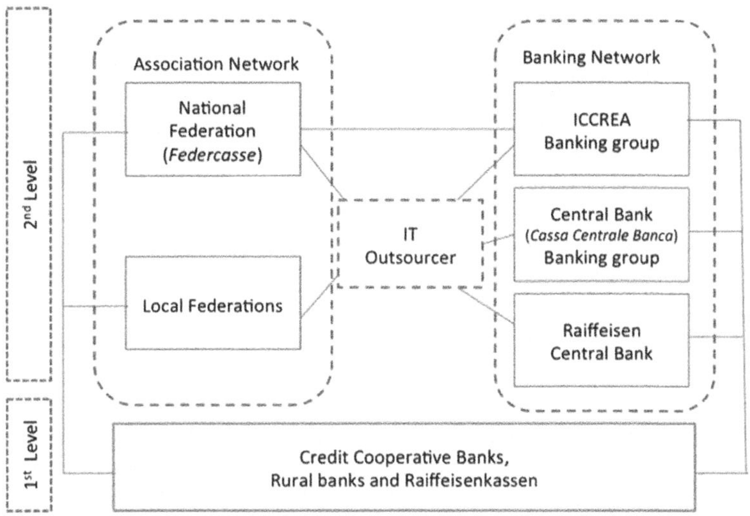

Fig. 1 The Italian Credit Cooperative System

competitiveness. More precisely, from an association point of view, CCBs are organised into 15 local Federations that are, in turn, affiliated to the national Federation ("Federcasse"). The Federations provide non-financial services. The extent of these services varies amongst them, with almost all Federations provide internal audit, compliance and anti-money laundering services, while only a few have extended their offer to governance and strategy (Tarantola 2011). Moreover they provide information technology systems that are however not homogenous over the territory. From a banking point of view, the second level structure consists of three Central Cooperative Banks,[13] which provide single CCBs with a range of financial services that CCBs (that is the first level of the network) cannot economically produce by their own, given their small scale. These services include payment system services, financial and insurance product provision, portfolio management, securization, in-pool operations, leasing and factoring.

CCBs adhere on a compulsory basis to the "Fondo di garanzia dei depositanti del credito cooperativo" (Deposit Guarantee for Cooperative Banks), set in 1997, following the European directive n. 19/1994.[14] Moreover, the credit cooperative system

[13] The three Central Cooperative Banks are ICCREA (whose headquarter is in Rome), Cassa Centrale Banca—Credito Cooperativo del Nord Est (whose headquarter is in Trento) and Cassa Centrale Raiffeisen dell'Alto Adige (established in Bolzano). All three banks are limited companies which offer financial services to CCBs, directly or through companies of their groups. ICCREA, in particular, is a holding company—owned by the cooperative banks, the national Federation (Federcasse), the regional Federations, the Central Banks of Trento and of Bolzano—which operates through its members' companies: ICCREA Bank spa (the central Institute built in 1963 with its six branches), Agrileasing created in 1977, Aureo Gestioni spa, IMMICRA spa, Simcasse spa, Assimoco spa and Assimoco Vita spa, Ciscra spa, and SEF srl.

[14] An analogous fund therefore exists for the other Italian banks.

has established its own "Fondo di garanzia degli obbligazionisti" (Bondholder Guarantee Fund for the Credit Cooperative Banks) that intervenes in case of default by a bond issuer; the participation to the Fund is voluntary. In December 2011 the Bank of Italy approved the Statute of a "Fondo di garanzia istituzionale" (Institutional Guarantee Fund) of CCBs, a cross-guarantee system that has not been implemented.

Compared to other European cooperative banks, Italian CCBs, as single banks, share the basic characteristics and remain under several aspects more loyal to the original roots. As a system, they are less integrated: by measuring integration through the extent of mutual support, the cross-guarantee schemes is based on the coverage provided by the compulsory and supplementary deposit insurance schemes and bond insurance mechanisms that are in place; the support is limited to paid-up funds (Ayadi et al. 2010).

While closing this chapter, a debate is in place in Italy on a reform of CCBs to enhance efficiency and balance sheet equilibria through a higher integration, based on membership of banking groups, in order to be able continue to support local markets and preserving their mutualistic nature (Banca d'Italia 2015).

CCBs are not the only kind of cooperative banks in Italy, the second type being *Banche popolari*, which however have not a prevailing mutual character according to the Banking law.[15] As a matter of fact, before the recent reform,[16] they could be divided into two categories (Rossi 2015). The first group is composed by little banks which operate in a limited geographical area; the second is formed by big banking groups, which result in general from merging processes, whose parent company is in most cases listed. Their legal discipline has recently been reformed, by restricting the bunch of *Banche popolari* which can maintain the cooperative nature to the ones with not more than 8 billion euros of assets (in case of banking groups, assets are calculated in consolidated terms). *Banche popolari* above this threshold must transform into limited companies within 18 months.[17] The law has introduced some new rules also for *Banche popolari* that do not need to transform,[18] which, according to the Banking law, share with CCBs the "one member—one vote" principle, a constraint on the maximum amount of shares that each member can hold, a compulsory

[15] Italian *Banche popolari* are the only case of cooperative banks in Europe that does not have cross-guarantee schemes beyond the compulsory deposit insurance schemes (Ayadi et al. 2010).

[16] See the Law 24.3.2015, n. 33.

[17] This term is valid for *Banche popolari* having more than 8 billion euros of assets at the moment when the law entered into force; for future cases of *Banche popolari* overpassing the threshold term for transformation is 12 months. Majorities for the decision are the ones described in the following footnote.

[18] The maximum number of proxies in meetings that Statutes have to fix must be increased: it must be a number in between 10 and 20. Moreover, according to the new discipline, Statutes have to be revised also as for the number of members required for the validity of meetings deciding on the transformation of a *Banca popolare* into a limited company: more precisely the new law requires that meetings are legally valid if one tenth of members are present at the first call (instead of one third). For the second call no quorum has to be achieved. In both calls a decision is reached with the majority of two thirds of the members who are present.

net profit destination to legal reserves higher than the ordinary one (but much lower than the one of CCBs; see Table 2), the variable capital.

However, differently from CCBs, *Banche popolari* are in any case not subject to any constraints concerning the "prevailing mutualism" principle. Moreover, they do not have to devote part of their profits to mutual funds. Their capital can be distributed and *Banche popolari* are not subject to any restrictions when they intend to transform into limited companies (see Table 1).[19] Given this possibility, they cannot be considered "mutualistic" from a substantial point of view.

4 The Importance of the Credit Cooperative System in the National Banking Market

In terms of number of intermediaries, Credit Cooperative Banks are the largest category among Italian banks.[20] At the end of 2014 they accounted for 376 banks throughout the country (56.6 % of total banks) with a network of 4,432 branches (the 14.4 % of total branches; see Table 2). CCBs exist in one third of Italian municipalities and in more than 500 municipalities they represent the only financial institution. Their presence is heterogeneous: most of the CCBs have their headquarter and their branches established in the North Eastern regions (39.8 % of the total number), with a 15 branches per 10,000 inhabitants and also the highest incidence of branches over total branches (see Fig. 2).

From the nineties the number of CCBs has gradually decreased, mostly due to mergers, and their reduction has been higher than the one registered by total banks[21] (see Fig. 3). The consolidation process has been particularly marked in the period 1995–2005, when CCBs reduced by about one third. Even though mergers has risen the market concentration, so that 20 BCCs hold one quarter of the overall BCCs' assets, the presence of small size CCBs remains very high (Visco 2012). Despite of a declining number of banks, the network of CCBs branches has increased more than the one of the total banking industry.[22] This expansion has led to a wider

[19] Actually, as mentioned, this transformation has been made easier by the recent law that has reduced the quorum required for this decision by the general assembly.

[20] According to the BL, Italian banks can be divided into four legal forms: (1) *Banche spa* (Limited Company Banks); (2) *Banche popolari*; (3) *Banche di credito cooperativo* (Credit Cooperative Banks, also called Mutual Banks); and (4) *Filiali di banche estere* (Branches of Foreign Banks). At the end of 2014 the Italian banking industry accounted for 171 Limited Company Banks, 37 *Banche popolari*, 376 Credit Cooperative Banks and 80 Branches of Foreign Banks (Banca d'Italia, *online statistics*, 2015).

[21] From 1999 to 2014 the number of CCBs decreased by 29.2 %, while the total number of banks decreased by 24.1 %.

[22] In particular, from 1999 to 2014 the number of CCBs branches has increased by 54.8 %, against a rise by 13.2 % of total banks. The number of CCBs' branches increased also during the crisis (13 %) while the total number of bank branch decreased (−7.5%).

presence of CCBs outside the rural area, namely in towns and urban areas. In the same period the number of members significantly increased, more than doubling from 1999 to 2014 when it reached 1.2 million.

While the number of employees for CCBs has increased by 42 %, it has decreased by about 13 % for the whole banking system from 1999 to 2014.[23] Consequently, the structure of CCBs has deeply changed: in 1999 the average CCB had five branches and 42 employees; in 2014 these figures have increased to about 12 branches (the mode is 5; it was 3 in 1999) and 84 employees.

As for the market share on loans, at the end of 2014 CCBs accounted for about 10 % of the lending to Italian households and firms.[24] This proportion has steadily increased from the end of the nineties (when it was around 6 %) until the first wave of the financial crisis (2008–2009; see Fig. 4). The market share of CCBs is higher towards small and medium enterprises[25] (SMEs) which represent their traditional customers (this market share was 19.7 % at the end of 2014; 13 % at the end of 1999). The CCBs have also increased their market share on loans to larger firms from 3.1 in 1999 to 7.6 % (see Fig. 5).

The increase in the market share between the end of the nineties and the first half of the following decade has been affected by the process of formation and re-organization of Italian large banking groups. Large banks might have focused less on certain categories of clients, such as small borrowers (households and small firms), leaving room for CCBs to intervene. According to Bonaccorsi di Patti et al. (2005), the consolidation of the banking system would help explaining the growing market share of CCBs (and of small banks in general) more than other possible causes, such as sector and geographical specialisation, better liquidity and capitalisation indexes, and the price policies. These findings do not exclude that the positive performance of small banks could have been the result of a transitory phenomenon that should have ceased after the restructuring process of large banks. A further study by Bongini et al. (2007), covering the period from 1998 to 2004, has stressed the role of CCBs' comparative advantages due to localism and relationship lending that is to the peculiarities of their lending technology.

5 The Recent Trends

As mentioned, CCBs' market share increased also during the international financial crisis (2008–2009), when they continued to accommodate the financial needs of their traditional customers and gained further market shares in financing local

[23] The number of CCBs' employees increased also during the crisis, by 8.2 % between the end of 2007 and the end of 2014 while in the same period the number of employees of the banking system decreased.

[24] Data on market shares on loans include the three Central Banks of the credit cooperative system.

[25] In this paper the expression SMEs refers to either sole-proprietorships or firms (different from limited companies) with less than 20 employees, according to the definition followed in the Bank of Italy's Supervisory Reports.

economies, at the expenses of large banks, that faced more severe constrains in funding (Draghi 2009; Tarantola 2011; see Fig. 4). CCBs are in fact less internationalised and their funding structure is mainly based on direct funding, that is on deposits and bonds subscribed by customers, while the inter-banking funding provision is less relevant than for other types of banks.[26]

During the following debt sovereign crisis, and particularly in 2011, CCBs adopted tighter lending policies, mostly due to the liquidity shortage that they experienced in that period.

During the two crises, however, CCBs maintained in general higher rate of growth of loans to firms and households with respect to other banks (Banca d'Italia 2014; Stefani, Vacca et al. 2016; see Figs. 6 and 7). In the second half of 2012 the rate of growth of CCBs' loans to firms stopped its positive trends, following the low credit demand in a context of long-lasting crisis and tighter supply conditions also induced by the deep credit quality deterioration. The net flow of new defaulted (bad) loans to total outstanding loans has grown from 1.5 % at the end of 2008 to 2.8 at the end of 2012 (see Fig. 8). Since the second half of 2012 the rate of variation of CCBs' loans to firms has been negative, while that to households remained slightly positive. In the meantime the flow of new bad loans continued to worsen: from the end of 2013 to the end of 2014 it raised from 3.6 to 3.9 %, while the same indicator for the rest of the banking industry was slightly improving.

Various causes may have played a role in this credit worsening: this is partly connected with the expansion of credit during the crisis that, to some extent, led to an increase in the financing of non traditional customers, namely larger firms. Moreover loans to construction and real estate sectors (two industries that have been particularly hit by the crisis) represent more than one third of the credit portfolio of CCBs, a higher share than the average banking system (around 35 % and 30 % respectively in 2014).

During the crisis CCBs' profitability margins have shrunk, mainly as a consequence of credit devaluations and lower growth of assets in a context of a rigid cost structure and a high dependence on the interest rate margin. The latter are the two main fragilities of the CCBs structure that the crisis has exacerbated (Visco 2012). From December 2011 to June 2014 operating costs have risen by 2.6 % while they have decreased for the rest of the banking system (Barbagallo 2015).

Due to the legal restriction on profit distribution, namely the compulsory destination of 70 % to legal reserve, CCBs have been traditionally better capitalised than other categories of banks. This advantage on average remains: at the end of 2014 their CET1 (Common equity tier1 ratio) was 16.1 % compared to 11.8 % of the remaining banking industry (Banca d'Italia 2015). There is however a large heterogeneity among CCBs: in June 2014 about 70 CCBs presented capital ratios below the first quartile of the distribution of banks according to the CET1 ratio (Barbagallo 2015). Profit and credit worsening may significantly erode average capital ratios in the future, especially in a scenario of persisting unfavourable economic conditions.

[26] Banca d'Italia, *Annual Report*, *Statistical Appendix*, various years.

From 2007 the number of bank crisis situations involving CCBs has dramatically risen: about 30 CCBs were under default procedures from the outbreak of the financial turmoil to end 2014 (Stefani, Vacca et al. 2016). Two main causes derive from the crises: a negative conditioning of the territory (bank capture) on the decision to finance a firm; the expansion of their business towards customers different from the traditional ones, namely bigger firms or firms located in less known areas (Barbagallo 2015).

The current context puts CCBs in front of important challenges in terms of risk control, efficiency and corporate governance. In many cases the growth in scale has not been followed by an organizational adjustment, so that CCBs appear, on average, more fragile in a context where the risk is increasing. In comparison with European cooperative banks, the Italian credit cooperative system is weakly integrated: the enhancement of the network dimension, based on membership of banking groups, can represent the way to better tackle the new challenges and to gain efficiency.

Appendix: Tables and Figures

Table 1 Comparison between Credit Cooperative Banks and *Banche popolari*

		Credit Cooperative Banks	*Banche popolari*
Minimum required capital		5 million of euros	10 million of euros
Maximum assets		–	8 billion
Nominal shares value		From 25 to 500 €	2 €
Members	Requirements	To reside, to have the headquarter or to operate with continuity in the competence area of the CCB.	–
	Minimum number	200	200
Limits to the ownership		50,000 € (nominal value)	0.5 %[a]
Profits' allocation		70 % to legal reserve 3 % to Mutual funds for the promotion and development of the cooperation Remainder – Shares' revaluation – Other reserves or funds – Dividends to shareholders – Charity/mutuality	10 % to legal reserve Remainder – Legal reserve – Other reserves – Other allocations either Statutory-based or not – Charity or assistance's purposes – Dividends to shareholders
Voting mechanism		One member—one vote	One member—one vote
Geographical limits		Competence area: it includes the municipalities in which the CCB has either its head office or its branches and neighboring ones in order to guarantee territorial contiguity	–
Mutualistic requirement		At least 50 % of total risky assets must be addressed to either loans to members or to Treasury Bonds (or other assets with a weighted coefficient equal to zero according to Basel rules)	–
Mergers implying a transformation of the bank's nature		Mergers implying the transformation of a CCB into an other type of bank must be authorized by the Bank of Italy and have to be justified only by "creditors' interests" or "stability reasons"	Mergers implying transformation into limited companies are approved by the Assembly with quorum that are recently reduced (march 2015)

[a]The limit does not apply to undertakings by Institutional investors

Table 2 The Credit Cooperative System in Italy (1999–2014)[a]

Year	CCBs	Branches	Members (thousands)	Employees (thousands)	Total assets (billion)
1999	531	2,863	558	22.1	77,084
2000	499	2,954	586	22.7	82,327
2001	474	3,044	616	23.6	93,712
2002	461	3,191	649	24.6	104,904
2003	445	3,323	686	25.3	116,404
2004	439	3,465	729	26.3	127,873
2005	439	3,605	776	26.9	139,691
2006	436	3,752	823	27.8	152,568
2007	440	3,922	885	29.1	167,207
2008	432	4,109	939	30.4	164,577
2009	421	4,243	995	31.1	177,616
2010	415	4,373	1,052	31.5	185,620
2011	411	4,427	1,097	31.7	194,507
2012	394	4,445	1,135	31.7	215,976
2013	385	4,449	1,173	31.7	227,426
2014	376	4,432	1,200	31.5	240,296

Source: Bank of Italy, Supervisory reports
[a]Data refers to the end of the year

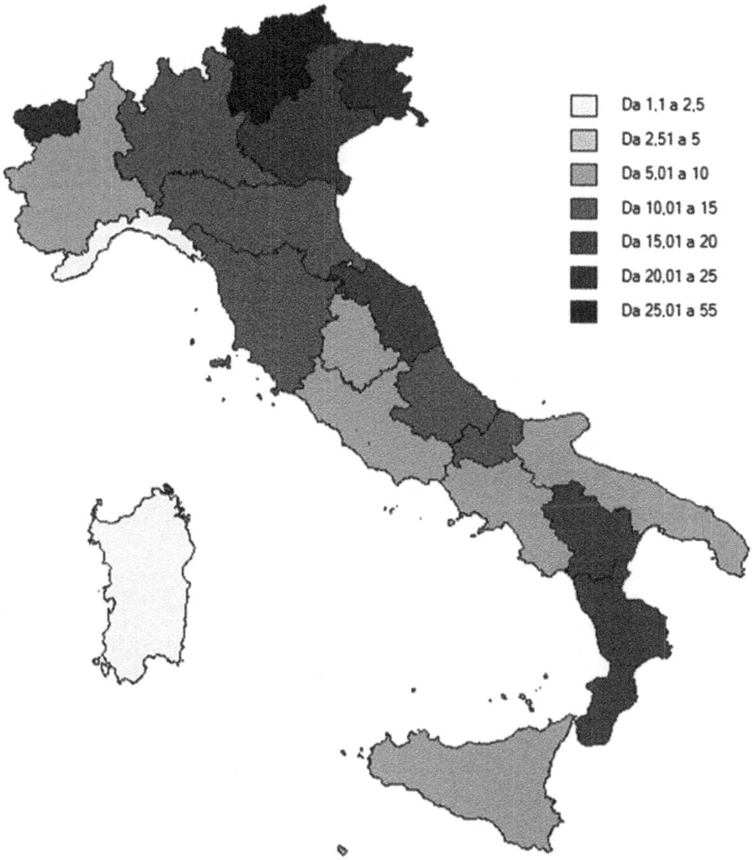

Fig. 2 Credit Cooperative Banks' branches by region (Ratio between the number of branches of Credit Cooperative Banks in the region and total bank branches) (percentage values). *Source*: Bank of Italy, online statistics

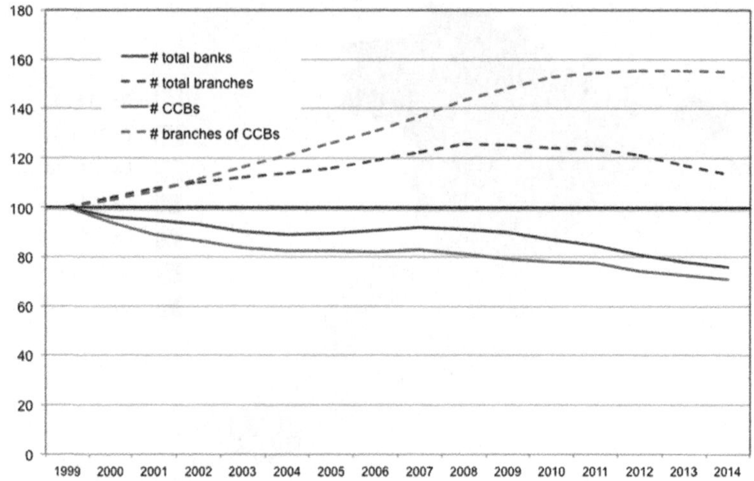

Fig. 3 Banks and branches (1999–2014) (index numbers; 1999 = 100). *Source*: Bank of Italy

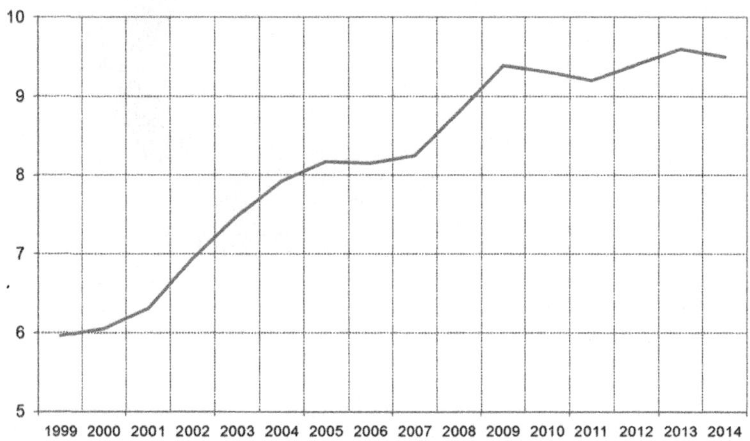

Fig. 4 Credit Cooperative Banks' market share on loans to households and firms (1999–2014) (The market share is computed on loans including non-performing loans) (percentage values). *Source*: Bank of Italy, Supervisory reports

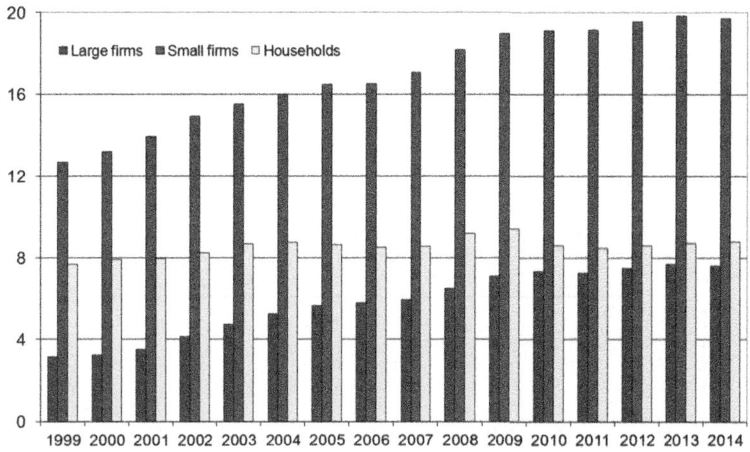

Fig. 5 Credit cooperative banks' market shares by sectors (1999–2014) (The market share is computed on loans including non-performing loans) (percentage values). *Source*: Bank of Italy, Supervisory reports

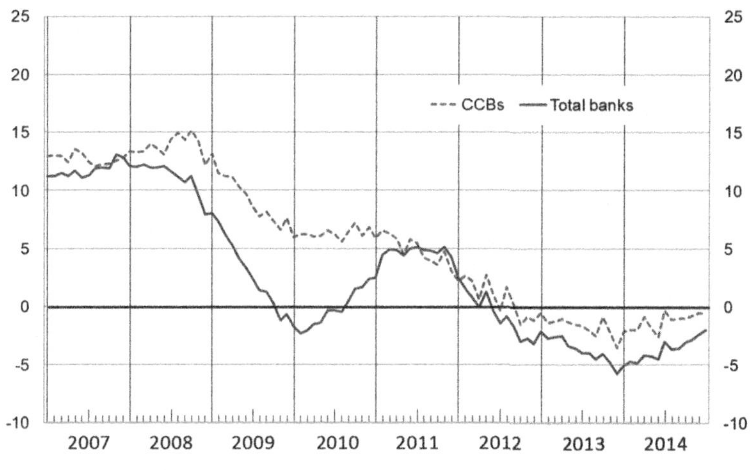

Fig. 6 Loans to firms (Loans include non-performing loans) (monthly rate of growth on yearly basis; percentage values). *Source*: Bank of Italy, Supervisory reports

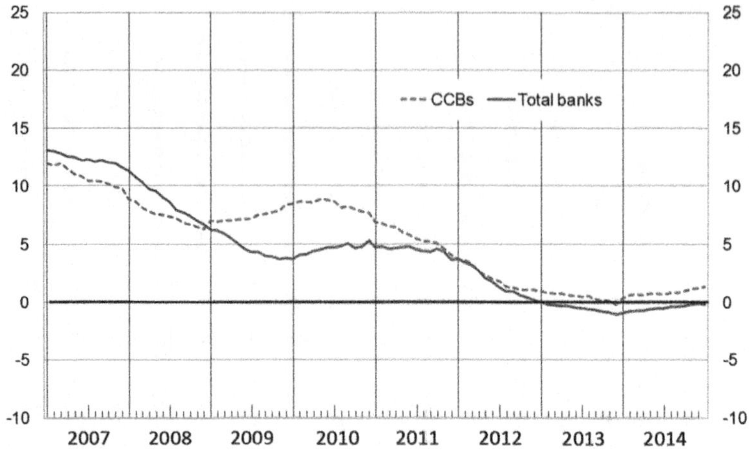

Fig. 7 Loans to households (Loans include non-performing loans) (monthly rate of growth on yearly basis; percentage values). *Source*: Bank of Italy, Supervisory reports

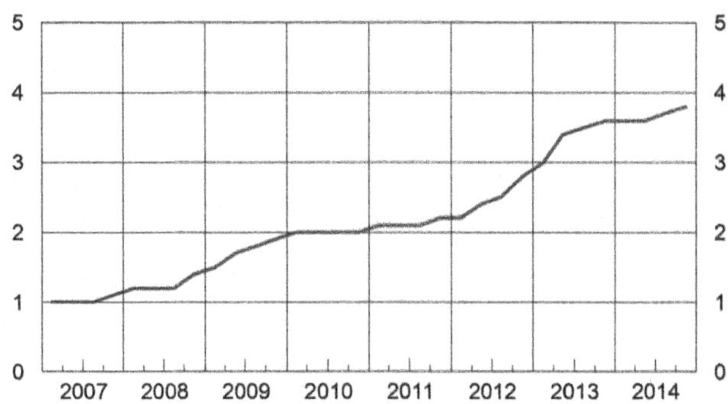

Fig. 8 Credit cooperative banks: new defaulted loans (Ratio between the flow of new defaulted (bad) total loans over outstanding loans) (monthly data; percentage values). *Source*: Bank of Italy, Supervisory reports

References

Ayadi R, Llewellyn DT, Schmidt RH, Arbak E, De Groen WP (2010) Investigating diversity in the banking sector in Europe: key development, performance and role of cooperative banks. Centre for European policy Studies, Brussels

Banca d'Italia (2014) L'economia delle regioni italiane: dinamiche recenti e aspetti strutturali, Economie regionali, n. 43, December

Banca d'Italia (2015) The Governor's Concluding Remarks, Ordinary Meeting of Shareholder, 26 May, Rome

Banca d'Italia, Annual Report, years from 2003 to 2012, Rome

Barbagallo C (2015) Le banche locali e di credito cooperativo in prospettiva: vigilanza europea ed evoluzione normativa. Federazione delle cooperative Raiffeisen, Bolzano

Bonaccorsi di Patti E, Eramo G, Gobbi G (2005) Piccole e Grandi Banche nel Mercato del Credito in Italia. Banca Impresa Società, XXIV (1): 3–34

Bongini P, Di Battista ML, Zavarrone E (2007) The Value of Relationship Lending: Small Banks in an Era of Consolidation. Rev Bank Finance Monet Econ 36(3):209–230

Cafaro P (2001) La Solidarietà Efficiente. Storia e Prospettive del Credito Cooperativo in Italia. Roma-Bari, Laterza

Di Salvo R, Schena C (1998) Assetti societari e di governo delle MCB. Quali effetti sulle performance? Cooperazione di credito 160–161:147–62

Draghi A (2009) Credito Cooperativo nelle Economie Locali. Speech at the workshop on "Solidarietà nella crisi. Il Credito Cooperativo nelle Economie Locali" organised by CrediUmbria, December 10, Città della Pieve, Perugia

Federcasse, Official Web Side of the Co-operative credit, www.creditocooperativo.it

Piersante F, Stefani ML (2012) Mutualismo e peer monitoring nelle BCC italiane. WP Euricse n. 38

Rossi S (2015) Audizione nell'ambito dell'istruttoria legislativa sul disegno di legge C. 2844, di conversione in legge del decreto-legge n. 3 del 2015, recante misure urgenti per il sistema bancario e gli investimenti. Testimonianza del Direttore Generale della Banca d'Italia, Camera dei Deputati, 17 febbraio

Stefani ML, Vacca V et al. (2016) Le banche locali e il finanziamento dei territori: evidenze per l'Italia (2007–2014), Banca d'Italia, Occasional Papers, n. 324

Tarantola AM (2011) Il Credito Cooperativo del domani: sviluppo, efficienza e solidarietà. Speech at the XIV Congresso Nazionale del Credito Cooperativo, Rome

Visco I (2012) Borghi, distretti e banche locali. Speech at the presentation of the book "Civiltà dei borghi: culla di cooperazione", Rome

Zamagni V (2006) L'Impresa Cooperativa Italiana: dalla Marginalità alla Fioritura. XIV International Workshop of Economic History "Imprese cooperative e consorzi di cooperative: successi e fallimenti", Section 72, Helsinki

Rabobank Before, During and After the Credit Crisis: From Modesty via Complacency to Fundamental Steps

Hans Groeneveld

Abstract Rabobank survived the financial turbulences of 2007–2010 well and without governmental support. In 2010, Rabobank even booked the highest net profit in its history. However, Rabobank could not escape from the fall-out of the credit crisis and the break-out of the sovereign debt crisis in Europe a few years later. For instance, the credit crisis triggered economic recessions and changed the business and regulatory environment of banking drastically. Moreover, structural imbalances in the Eurozone came to the fore and the ECB took unprecedented monetary steps which resulted in a very low interest rate environment. In its home market, the whole banking sector lost the lustre of reliability and Rabobank incurred reputational damage due to its involvement in the Libor affair at the end of 2013. The bank took fundamental measures to cope with all these challenges: a further virtualisation of its products and services, actions to increase the reservation capacity and initiatives to reinforce its participation in society to address social-economic issues together with members and customers. In May 2015, member representatives and banking executives decided to reshape the cooperative governance, while preserving the core principles and the cooperative profile.

1 Introduction

This article focuses on Rabobank, the Dutch cooperative banking group, in the wake of, during and after the credit crisis of 2007–2010 within the context of its historical evolution. Like all other banks, Rabobank has faced many social, economic, technological and regulatory challenges since its establishment some 120 years ago. These include, for example, the World Wars, the Great Depression of the 1930s, the reconstruction of the Dutch economy, the IT revolution and the

---

The views expressed in this paper are personal and do not necessarily reflect those of Rabobank. The article was finished in June 2015.

H. Groeneveld (✉)
TIAS School for Business and Society, Tilburg University, Tilburg, The Netherlands

Cooperative and Governance Affairs, Rabobank, Utrecht, The Netherlands
e-mail: j.m.groeneveld@tias.edu

S. Karafolas (ed.), *Credit Cooperative Institutions in European Countries*, Contributions to Economics, DOI 10.1007/978-3-319-28784-3_9

liberalisation and globalisation of the economy. More recently, the collateral effects of the credit crisis and following economic crises, the formation of the Banking Union and the transfer from prudential supervision from the national to the European level resulted in many short-term as well as longer-term challenges for the banking sector as a whole.

These introductory remarks illustrate the indispensability of a short retrospective to understand why Rabobank weathered the credit crisis of 2007–2010 well[1] and which factors provoked strategic reconsiderations and operational actions afterwards. Hence, this chapter does not provide a comprehensive overview of its history nor an in-depth discussion of the—legal and statutory—technicalities of its governance and capital structure. Only those elements are mentioned which are particularly relevant for answering both questions.

Section 2 highlights the organisational evolution up to the most recent developments. Section 3 discusses milestones in the development of its governance since the 1970s in three parts. The third subsection lifts a corner of the veil regarding the most fundamental governance revision in its history: the move to one cooperative bank with one banking license in 2016. Section 4 presents a general picture of its current market position and recent performance. Finally Sect. 5 summarizes and concludes.

2 Organisational Transformation

2.1 The Origins

As in many other Western European countries, the first local cooperative banks (henceforth LCBs) in the Netherlands had their roots in the local agricultural sector.[2] Misery and lack of access to affordable loans among farmers prevailed. Social abuse such as buying by instalments and the provision of loans at exorbitant rates were widespread (Van Diepenbeek 2007). In light of this, an advisory committee appointed by the Dutch government in 1888 emphasised the need for an agricultural credit system based on sound and fair principles. Moreover, this was to be set up by the concerned farmers themselves. The committee recommended the establishment of credit cooperatives based on the principles of the German Raiffeisenbanks. Around 1896, the first LCBs were set up in the Netherlands. Soon after, many other banks were launched throughout the country.

Although every LCB had its own unique historical background, there were also large similarities. For instance, farmers and dignities of the local community were often the bank's founding fathers. In the beginning, each LCB was run by a cashier

[1] Most European cooperative banks have weathered current and previous periods of financial distress relatively well (EACB 2010; Ayadi et al. 2010).

[2] A detailed description of Rabobank's history and development can be found in Mooij (2009).

in his home office, who only received a small salary (according to Raiffeisen's principle of 'sober management'). Moreover, each LCB applied the principle of solidarity. There was unlimited liability for all debts to be borne by all members. It was not necessary to become a member if you wanted to place your deposits at a LCB. Members did not have to capitalise their LCB by buying member shares, which was common practice at almost all other cooperative banks in Europe at that time. Instead, the financial policy consisted of full reservation of realised annual surpluses, and no-redistribution of any surpluses to individual members. Nevertheless, an appropriation of a responsible part of surplus for social and charitable purposes in order to improve local living conditions existed.[3]

As early as 1898, the LCBs started to work together by setting up two central—cooperative—organisations, one in the northern and the other in the southern part of the country. These central banks were not only helpful to overcome the disadvantages of the local banks' limited scale and to foster their development by performing the co-ordinating role of a "banker's bank". They also served as control or audit institutions as well as knowledge centres. These activities on behalf of member banks were executed out of self-interest. Since all member banks operated under the same brand, problems at one LCB could damage the reputation of all other LCBs.[4] In the following years, LCBs flourished due to their strong roots in local communities, their appealing democratic structure and their attractive loan and saving rates as compared to private banks. Since the first LCB in the Netherlands was founded, the number of LCBs and their members increased sharply to more than 1300 LCBs and 500,000 members around 1960.

2.2 *The Evolution of Rabobank: Local-National-International*

In the 1950s and 1960s, LCBs gradually transformed into retail banks and began to serve non-members. The latter development was chiefly related to technological developments in payment services and the increasing demand for mortgages due to the rising popularity of home ownership. Obviously, the homogeneity of the customer base of LCBs decreased accordingly. The central organisations became more and more important for the development of the LCBs. To reach economies of scale and to avoid inefficiencies from growing competition between LCBs of the two organisations, the two central organisations decided to merge in 1972 to form

---

[3] Rabobank still applies this principle today. Around 3 % of net profits is re-invested in society via local cooperative funds in The Netherlands and via Rabobank Foundation, which helps to establish and further develop agricultural cooperatives in emerging and developing countries (Rabobank 2012).

[4] As will be illustrated later on, the reputational risks for LCBs nowadays also depend on the reliability, uprightness and quality of the operations of national and international subsidiaries, especially if they are performed under the Rabobank brand.

Coöperatieve Centrale Raiffeisen-Boerenleenbank, known as Rabobank. In this way, the cooperative bank group was also able to improve its competitive position in a further consolidating Dutch banking landscape. This led to a national network organisation with a two tier governance structure: cooperative local Rabobanks (LCBs) and their central cooperative Rabobank Nederland (RN).

The merger of both centrals eventually resulted in cost reductions and a favourable scale for large investments to acquire market share and to serve the emerging mass markets and new economic sectors efficiently. Facilitated by the deregulation of financial services in the 1980s, this centralisation of activities and the creation of scale advantages made it possible to diversify and expand financial activities in other areas. Domestically, Rabobank Group entered into the fields of private banking, asset management, and life insurance via organic growth, joint ventures or acquisitions in the 1990s. All these developments dovetailed with the trend towards individualisation and the need for more customised solutions, stimulated by revolutionary developments in information and communications technology. The centralised support function was conducive to launch virtual distribution concepts, such as internet and mobile banking.

In the course of the 1970s, the first international ambitions were formulated. Initially, the leading motive for starting cross-border activities was the desire to serve domestic customers with international activities and aspirations, especially from the Dutch agricultural sector. In the early 1970s, this was done through collaboration agreements with banks in the United Kingdom (Continental Bankers) and the USA (Bank of America). In order to improve the level of commercial cooperation between European sister organisations, the Unico Banking Group (1977) was established by Rabobank and five other cooperative banks. The aim was to support the expansion of the partners' international operations. Thereafter, Rabobank pursued different international strategies, with varying degrees of success: takeovers, cooperation agreements and alliances with other partners, as well as setting up its own representative offices across the world.[5]

An important step was the concentration of all foreign business of Rabobank Group into a new entity named 'Rabobank International' (RI) in 1996. This was more than just a re-labelling action. Within RI all international activities were united in an organisational entity with a large degree of autonomy from the cooperative domestic banking part. The strategic responsibility for the development of international business was transferred from the Executive Board of RN to the newly established Managing Board of RI. The ambitions were high, e.g. RI soon attempted to develop a large investment banking division in London (Vogelaar 2012). After only a few years, the investment banking division was cut down substantially. The ambitions of the investment bankers brought on board were not in line with the moderate risk profile and the culture of Rabobank, and LCBs in particular. Besides, the associated remuneration structure in investment banking with substantial bonuses, was at odds with the Rabobank culture. Contrary to the

[5] The most salient steps and evolutions are presented in Groeneveld and Sjauw-Koen-Fa (2009).

general belief, the escapade into investment banking in the 1990s has on balance generated net profits. However, significant losses did occur in the area of corporate banking of RI at that time. Rabobank did not completely abandon investment banking, though. These activities had increased the knowledge and competences of Rabobank and hence a number of investment banking activities has been retained within acceptable cost and risk limits.

More recently, the division 'Global Financial Markets' within RI was involved in the so-called Libor affair. With regards to the latter issue, Rabobank Group agreed on financial settlements of EUR 774 million (US$ 1 billion) with various authorities in connection with their investigations into Rabobank's historical Libor submission processes in October 2013. The supervisory authorities concluded that the internal control mechanisms failed to ensure a correct procedure. It was also concluded that various responsible executives had not reacted decisively in response to letters from regulators about serious misconduct of a few traders some years before.

This affair caused great commotion outside and inside the organisation and triggered large organisational changes. Although LCBs had nothing to do with this affair, their reputation was severely impaired and many member councils[6] and local supervisory board expressed their anger and disappointment. Mainly due to their loud discontent, the executive board member who was responsible for this part of the international business had to resign eventually, though the Dutch banking supervisors and supervisory board of RN had initially allowed him to stay. The chief executive officer resigned when the settlement was made public. In effect, LCBs were associated with this scandal, since the name of 'Rabobank' was contaminated in the eyes of the public. These reputational contagion effects underscored the necessity to operate as one Rabobank with one common culture and adherence to identical behavioural standards in The Netherlands and abroad. By the end of 2013, it was decided to manage Rabobank Nederland and Rabobank International in an integrated manner again. The trade names Rabobank Nederland and Rabobank International were abolished and replaced by 'Rabobank'.[7] The staff directorates and departments of RN and RI were merged and a company-wide culture program was launched.

Libor

Libor is an interest rate benchmark. Libor rates are published daily on behalf of the British Bankers' Association (BBA) for five currencies in seven maturities ranging from overnight to 12 months (although, during the period covered by the investigation, it was published for ten currencies and

(continued)

[6] These councils form the basis of Rabobank's member-governed organisational structure.

[7] I shall continue to use the abbreviation RN in the remainder of this chapter to avoid confusion.

15 maturities). Libor rates are calculated based on submissions made by banks who sit on panels for each of these currencies. The BBA asks each panel bank to make its Libor submission at: '[t]he rate at which [it] could borrow funds, were it to do so by asking for and then accepting interbank offers in reasonable market size, just prior to 11.00 London time.' Each day, the members of each Libor panel submit their rates to Thomson Reuters, which uses a trimmed averaging process to determine the published Libor rates.

Evidently, the evolution of Rabobank Group was no linear process. Around 1985, the expansion accelerated with the adoption of the Allfinance strategy in the Netherlands and the growing international ambitions. Since then, the composition of Rabobank Group has been adjusted regularly to changing external circumstances and/or 'strategic reconsiderations'. Group subsidiaries have been acquired/set-up and some of them have been sold or dismantled again after a while. Step by step, Rabobank has discovered the international strategy that suits it best. To date, following local customers, taking small, well-considered steps and linking up with existing activities and core competences are the basic principles driving international activities. During its evolution, the tasks and responsibilities of RN as central service provider for LCBs and as holding company have expanded. The same holds for its supervisory responsibility vis-à-vis LCBs. In June 2015, Rabobank Group consisted of independent LCBs, their central cooperative RN and group subsidiaries (i.e. a number of specialised entities).

3 Salient Governance Developments

3.1 The Causes and Outcomes of the Great Cooperative Debate (1995–1998)

In the period after the merger of the two central cooperatives in 1972, the Rabobank organisation expanded steadily both domestically and internationally. The bank developed into an all-round banking organisation, offering its customers and members the complete spectrum of financial services. Simultaneously, the number of LCBs declined continuously due to mergers (Chart 1).

This expansion and mergers between LCBs as well as the emergence of large domestic competitors via consolidation provoked a fundamental self-assessment, culminating in the Great Cooperative Debate in the years 1995 through 1997. Since the merger of the two central organisations, the perception was that the cooperative philosophy had been subject to considerable erosion. Local member banks were fairly passive in engaging or attracting members. The number of members fell from 950,000 in 1979 to 510,000 in 1999. A local member bank acted and operated more

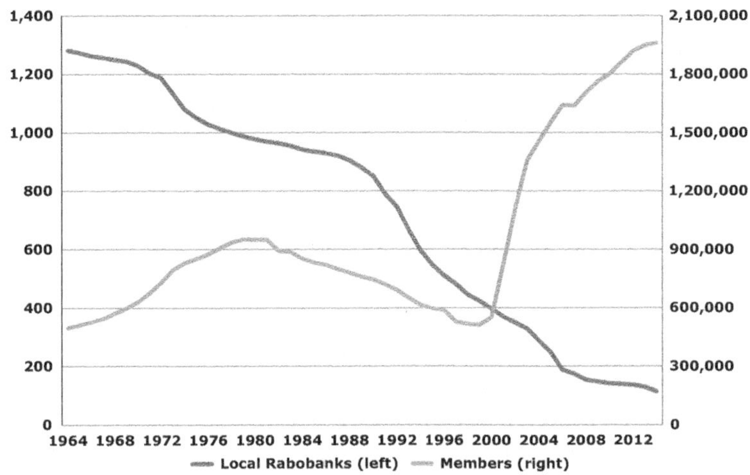

Chart 1 Number of members and local banks. *Source:* Rabobank

and more like a 'privately owned bank'. In this context, some felt that Rabobank could equally well become a listed bank. This would offer Rabobank better growth prospects and access to more funding sources to counter the increasing competition. Additional arguments were the rapidly growing costs and the required large investments in new banking technologies.

Though internal sceptics of the continuation of the cooperative banking model remained a minority, they actually pointed out highly relevant questions about the meaning of membership in the context of economic globalisation and the added value of the cooperative model in mature financial systems. After intense discussions, it was decided to retain the cooperative identity. This decision was mainly based on the consideration that Rabobank has always been and had to remain an organisation of and for the people. A different legal format with fairly uncertain effects would diminish the countervailing power of members' influence on the day-to-day business decisions of professionals managing the cooperative banking group. The conviction was that there were great opportunities for a viable and strong cooperative bank with a critical mass amidst private banks. The bank would enrich the banking landscape with a distinctive business model and philosophy, thereby contributing to diversity in banking. For a firm anchoring in society and for the justification of its existence, it was deemed highly desirable to obtain more and engaged members[8] and to enlarge the autonomy of LCBs. The new governance model reconfirmed the core principles of delivering customer value, contributing to societal development, realising employee value and revitalising the membership

[8] Every customer of a local member bank is free to become a member, but the Board of Directors of the bank decides whether or not a customer becomes a member of the bank. Members are engaged in the policy of the bank regarding activities and investments in the local community via cooperative funds. The Member Council appoints the local supervisory Board.

policy. It was acknowledged that only a financially sound organisation could meet these ambitions.

Another outcome of the Great Cooperative Debate was the complete abolishment of member liability. The argument was that this liability was only virtual; members have actually never been asked to fulfil their liability obligation, as no LCB has ever gone bankrupt. This step officially sealed the transformation of Rabobank from a member credit cooperative to a customer cooperative. The cooperative principle of 'economic member participation' or of 'mutual solidarity' according to Raiffeisen was completely abandoned.

Decisive Strategic Ambitions Since 1998

Following the cooperative Debate, Rabobank formalised its strategic ambition to be an Allfinance services provider in the Netherlands. Since then, new challenges have emerged. In order to maintain its position as Allfinance market leader, strategic adjustments were necessary. To this end, the Rabobank Group formulated so-called Strategic Frameworks that outlined the future course of action for the upcoming 3–5 years. Various Strategic Frameworks were formulated since 2000. However, the overall ambitions did not change:

1. Strengthening Allfinance market leadership in the Netherlands;
2. Strengthening the bank's position as a leading international Food & Agri bank.

The underlying business principles remained largely unaltered as well. The cooperative profile and concept will be treasured. Rabobank Group's aim is to obtain a high rating (which mirrors the solidity of the bank). Lastly, the Group wants to be among the best performing banks in terms of CSR and sustainability.

To achieve these ambitions, the executive board has formulated four directional themes in 2014. The first theme is customer focus by providing high-quality advice combined with continued virtualisation of services and participation in local communities. The second theme is Rabobank as a rock solid bank. The third theme is the strength of a meaningful cooperative. The fourth theme concerns the empowerment of employees.

3.2 *Legally Independent LCBs in a Highly Integrated Group (1896–2015)*

Among all group-level entities of European cooperative banking groups, RN has been mandated by LCBs with the most extensive responsibilities in the course of many decades. In June 2015, RN performed the following interrelated tasks:

1. Banker's bank for the group;
2. Supporting LCBs (i.e. product development, ICT, marketing HR, etc.);
3. Mandate for the preparation and execution of the Group strategy;
4. Holding company for (inter)national subsidiaries;
5. Delegated supervision over local cooperative banks on behalf of the European Central Bank as from November 2014 (and De Nederlandsche Bank from 1953-October 2014).

Traditionally, RN functions as bankers' bank for LCBs. LCBs are permitted to have accounts only at RN, which is the only place where LCBs can bring their excess liquidity and which acts as treasurer for LCBs. As is the case at most other European cooperative banking groups, the tasks and responsibilities of RN have increased over time. Nowadays, RN provides a wide array of services to LCBs in the form of support, advice and guidance. RN also functions as holding company for the Group and operates its own banking business, which is both complementary to and independent of the business of LCBs. These activities are partly needed for risk diversification, access to public capital markets for funding and for competitive reasons. In this respect, RN has issued (hybrid) capital instruments to acquire additional funding and/or equity for LCBs and/or other group subsidiaries. Since the 1990s, LCBs are confronted with a so-called deposit shortfall, i.e. the local deposit growth was too low to accommodate local credit demand.[9] At the same time, the retained earnings were too small to increase the capital base in line with domestic and international expansion. To bridge the deposit and equity gap, RN began to issue hybrid capital market instruments. Consequently, LCBs remained able to meet credit demand of the private sector. The flipside was that Rabobank Group became more dependent on wholesale funding and had to comply with the requirements of the financial markets, i.e. to get a credit rating and fulfil stringent reporting conditions. This has consequences for the functioning of the internal governance.

Moreover, RN issued Member Certificates in 2000, 2001, 2002 and 2005, which also classified as hybrid capital instruments. These certificates served a double purpose. They strengthened the capital position—and qualified as core tier 1 capital—and were an exclusive member product. Around 150,000 members bought these certificates, which were not publicly listed but traded on an internal market. By the end of 2013, the outstanding volume of these certificates was 5.8 billion

---

[9] Historical data show that LCBs have operated with sizeable surpluses of deposits in the period 1900–1972. During this time span, the average loan to deposit ratio was around 50 %.

euros. In December 2013, Rabobank expressed its intention to enhance the tradability of these certificates. By making these certificates available to external investors, institutional investors could buy these certificates as well. This step was partially motivated by the fact that the supply on the internal market had increased significantly in the last quarter of 2013. An important cause was the requirement of the Dutch behavioural supervisor (Autoriteit Financiële Markten; AFM) that LCBs had to draw the attention of all certificate holders to the fact that a member certificate was no risk free savings product, but should be considered as an investment product. LCBs were also demanded by the AFM to advice each certificate holder to limit the share of member certificates in its total investment portfolio to 20 %.

Since January 2014, these certificates are listed as Rabobank Certificates on Euronext Amsterdam and still count as core tier 1 capital without voting rights. This conversion could have impacted the functioning of the 'bottom-up' governance: the legal question arose to what extent the strategy of the group could be freely discussed in local and central governance bodies, because of the potential sensitivity of these discussions on the price of the listed certificates. If members would be for this reason constrained from freely discussing the policy and strategy of the group, it is obvious that the internal working of the democracy and governance would be obstructed. After some months, it turned out that this fear was largely unfounded.

According to the Dutch Financial Supervision Act, RN is also responsible for the supervision of LCBs.[10] From 1953 up to November 2014, RN has performed this so-called delegated supervision on behalf of the Dutch banking supervisors.[11] Economically and organisationally, LCBs and RN form one group, but LCBs have their own banking license. This special supervisory regime is also incorporated in European rules of Article 10 of the Capital Requirements Regulation and article 21 of the Capital Requirements Directive IV. According to this regime, individual LCBs are exempted from the application of a number of prudential requirements, but these demands have to be met at the consolidated level. The application of this article is linked to several conditions: LCBs are permanently affiliated to RN which supervises them, the management of RN is empowered to issue instructions to the management of LCBs, a cross-guarantee system exists, which means that the commitments of RN and affiliated institutions (LCBs) are joint and several liabilities, or the affiliated institutions are guaranteed by RN. This mechanism stipulates that if a participating entity has insufficient means to meet its obligations towards its creditors, all other participants must supplement that entity's

[10] The APEX organisations of the Finnish OP Group and the Portugese Credito Agricola Group also exercise 'delegated' supervision over the local cooperative banks.

[11] In fact, this is a continuation of the situation before the Dutch Central Bank started to supervise the banking sector. The predecessors of RN already executed this role since the establishment of the initial credit cooperatives in the late nineteenth century.

funds in order to enable it to fulfil those obligations. All participants are policyholders in a separate legal entity entitled 'Mutual Insurance Rabobank'.

In practice, the cross guarantee scheme has never been activated. Long before an LCB is about to fail, internal compensation arrangements are 'automatically' triggered. Since RN operates these schemes, it will immediately use them to mitigate identified shortfalls at LCBs with respect to equity, profitability, loan loss reserves and operational and financing losses. This internal financial support system is financed by charging all other LCBs. Hence, RN plays an active role in directing financial support to individual LCBs.

The shared ambitions of LCBs and their central institution RN have resulted in a highly integrated group with mutual risk sharing and necessitated internal supervisory and regulatory rules. In a sense, Rabobank is some kind of cohabitation agreement, where the total of the Group is more than the sum of the individual parts as a result of internal arrangements and close interlinkages between group entities. All kinds of internal financial agreements and settlement procedures were established to ensure smooth capital and liquidity flows within the Group. These factors reduced the scope for local deviations in banking practices and pricing and led to a higher level of alignment of local strategies with the overall group strategy. The freedom to choose how to express cooperative identity, to organise local relationship banking and to participate in local communities has remained predominantly local, though. Due to the tight financial relationships and internal arrangements, Rabobank Group has been awarded with high credit ratings, which secured access to international capital markets in recent turbulent times.

3.3 The Switch to One Banking License and One Consolidated Balance Sheet in 2016

Like the composition of the Group, the governance has evolved over time in response to or in anticipation of all kinds of developments. These modifications in the governance were and still are path and time dependent. Regular adjustments are necessary because the economic, technological social, institutional and regulatory environment and the business model change constantly. When this article was finalised in June 2015, Rabobank was engaged in a fundamental discussion about a new governance structure to be well positioned as a cooperative bank for the future. The transfer of the external supervision from the Dutch Central Bank to the European Central Bank in November 2014 and the installation of a European Resolution Authority as from 2016 were external catalysts for this reconsideration. Internal reasons for exploring possible governance adjustments were various supervisory issues and increasingly complex and burdensome internal rules and financial settlement procedures, which had resulted in a strong rise in audit and compliance costs at LCBs and RN and an excessive internal focus after 2011. One of the reasons was that RN was unable to convey to LCBs whether it acted in its capacity of central service provider or delegated supervisor. Obscurities in the governance were further amplified by the fact that the elected local supervisory boards also perform a 'local internal supervision' in a much stricter regulated banking industry. Local supervisors of some LCBs were confronted with internal administrative problems which they could not prevent nor cure; these issues were partly caused by the confusion regarding the different roles of RN. Anyway, some LCBs had difficulties to comply with regulatory requirements concerning customer due diligence on time.[12]

The governance revision intends to fix many of the issues mentioned above simultaneously. In short, the intertwined objective is to strengthen both the cooperative and the banking business. The core feature of the proposal is that all LCBs and RN will merge into one cooperative which operates with one banking license. If approved by the Member Councils of all LCBs in December 2015, LCBs will no longer operate as independent legal entities with an own banking license and own financial statements as from 2016, but will keep their own accounts. Delegated supervision of LCBs by RN as well as internal compensation rules will then cease to exist too. Since the proposed changes constitute the most fundamental adjustment in the organisation since the establishment of LCBs, it is obvious that this proposal was the result of long and intense discussions. Initially, some feared that the cooperative identity and local orientation would be ruined by an attempt to centralise all activities. Others argued that the cooperative heritage would be wasted by this proposal.

In May 2015, member representatives in Regional Assemblies and the Central Delegates Assembly felt comfortable with the suggested new structure and were convinced that the advantages would outweigh the disadvantages. Compared to the 'old' governance system, the consultative structure will be simplified and less hybrid. The countervailing power of members both at the local and collective level will be strengthened in the proposals. In The Netherlands, Rabobank will continue to operate as a decentralised organisation of LCBs based on cooperative principles, which are firmly embedded in local communities. Every LCB will be directly represented in the highest governance body of the cooperative, the new General Member Council, by the chairman of its local supervisory board. The new governance model enables Rabobank to comply with future requirements of financial markets and supervisors (bail-in requirements in particular). Furthermore, an enhancement of the (cost) efficiency of the Group is expected, because internal regulatory and compliance costs can be curbed. The new governance structure will require a complete redrafting of all statutes and by-laws. Since the proof of pudding is in eating, the functioning of the new structure will be evaluated by external governance experts in the next few years.

[12] Documented information about customers aim at ruling out money laundering and criminal activities. In combination with the requirements of the new European Resolution Authority, the longer term tenability of delegated supervision was internally doubted.

4 Present Market Position and Recent Performance

It must be emphasised that the performance of any cooperative bank cannot only be assessed by looking at financial indicators or hard data. Due to its 'dual bottom line' approach, it is also inappropriate to use only financial variables to compare cooperative banks with other banks. Indeed, financial data mask the realisation of societal goals. Apart from these qualifications, the concept of 'performance' has many dimensions: the degree of customer satisfaction, customers' perception that the bank acts in their interests, the access offered to networks and knowledge of the bank, the stability/duration of relationships, the perceived attention/concern for the environment and local communities, et cetera. Having said all this, the development of a number of key performance indicators will be discussed in the following subsections. Given the wide range of potential indicators, we had to make a selection. This section starts with an important cooperative indicator: the number of members. Then, developments in domestic market shares will be presented. Subsequently, profitability, capitalisation, efficiency and the share of international activities in total activities will be reviewed.

4.1 Members

After the Great Cooperative Debate, the revitalisation of the cooperative ideal reaffirmed that member influence is the core element of the organisation. Members keep the bank on track by exercising influence and having a say in policy on behalf of customers. Having a large membership is essentially the best legitimacy for the continued existence of the cooperative and for local autonomy. The bank subsequently developed and implemented a new membership policy, including member recruitment campaigns. These programmes were very successful. Over the past 15 years, the total number of members grew from 510,000 in 1999 to around two million in 2014 (Chart 1). The member to population ratio increased from slightly more than 3 % in 1999 to more than 11 % in 2014. Apart from the renewed focus on acquiring and binding members and the issuance of Member Certificates in 2000, this surge was the result of a combination of factors. For instance, customers would not be inclined to become members if they are dissatisfied with the—pricing of—products and services or attitude of employees. Hence, the rise in member to population ratio can be viewed as a rough indication of clients' appreciation of the cooperative banking model. It should be stressed that members do not receive individual financial.

The continuous decline in the number of banks deserves some elaboration. After a peak of 1324 LCBs in 1955, the number of LCBs is expected to drop to 100 in 2016. One may wonder whether this is a positive or negative development from a banking and cooperative perspective. For a long time, mergers were considered to have predominantly positive effects. The resulting larger LCBs were able to serve ever growing firms in their working areas themselves, because risk concentration became less of an issue. Initially, these mergers could also be largely justified by an increasing social-economic homogeneity of adjacent working areas of neighbouring individual LCBs.

On the other hand, consolidation has undoubtedly complicated member participation and engagement. Hence, mergers have clear trade-offs in terms of—proclaimed—efficiency gains on the one hand and a potential loss of member commitment/stewardship due to larger working areas on the other. Rabobank needs to look for ways to continue operating in proximity to and as relational organisation for customers and members, thus enhancing social-economic relationships with their territories and a sustainable development of these areas. Aiming at social goals simply asks for physical presence and close relationships with local authorities and economic actors. In this respect, it seems important that the territories of LCBs largely coincide with the local areas with which members feel connected. With less LCBs, more efforts are needed to stimulate member involvement and to remain informed about important local issues for members. New ways of communicating and making connections with the member base are required. For instance, members can be tremendously valuable to prioritise local activities which deliver mutual benefits for a large group of members and the LCB in question. In the new governance structure, risk management and/or efficiency motives for further consolidation between LCBs have lost their relevance.

4.2 *Domestic Market Shares*

With a market share of 85 %, the originally strong position in the Food and Agri sector has been retained.[13] In almost all other areas of retail banking, market positions ameliorated up to 2011 (Chart 2). In 2008 and 2009, the market share for deposits peaked at an all-time high (42), mirroring the perceived strong position of Rabobank amidst great turbulences in Dutch banking.

The market share for branches declined from a peak of 35 in 2006 to around 30 in 2014. Rabobank still has the most dense branch network in The Netherlands, which reflects the specific business and distribution model of Rabobank. For the banking business, branch networks provide an important, albeit declining, comparative advantage in the Dutch retail markets. They facilitate mobilising and retaining a stable funding source, though it should be noted that savings became a relatively expensive funding source as a result of the low interest rate policy of the ECB in recent years. From a cooperative perspective, the importance of spatial 'proximity' to members and customers should not be underestimated. Visibility and presence in local communities bolster physical participation of employees in local networks

[13] The size of this sector in the Dutch economy has shrunk over time and currently accounts for roughly 20 % of Rabobank's total loan portfolio.

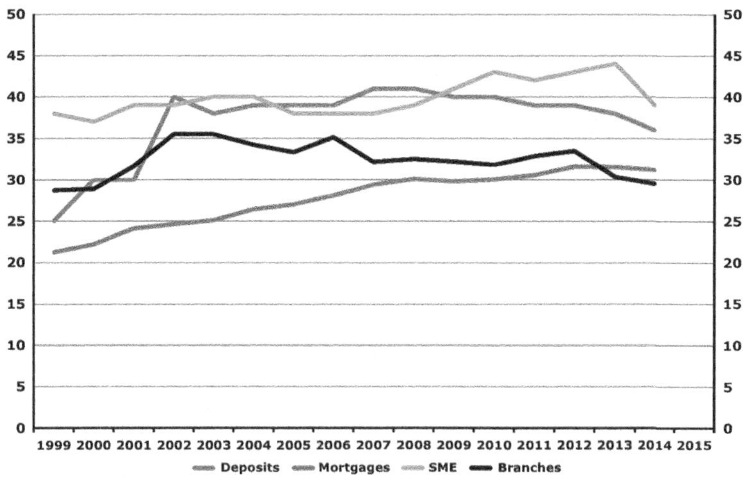

Source: Rabobank
Note: the market shares for deposits and mortgages denote the outstanding volume of deposits and mortgages of Rabobank as a percentage of total banking deposits and all outstanding mortgages (i.e. granted by banks, insurers, and all other parties) in the Netherlands, respectively. The SME market share reflects the percentage of Dutch SMEs which indicate that Rabobank is their primary bank.

Chart 2 Domestic market shares of Rabobank

and are conducive for a well-directed sustainable development of local regions in kind and with money via the local cooperative funds. Nonetheless, Rabobank has scaled down the number of branches as a result of changing customer preferences for virtual distribution channels and to lower costs.

4.3 Profitability

The business model of all cooperative banks is predominantly geared at retail banking. This type of banking generally generates more stable revenues and profits than wholesale or investment banking (see Groeneveld 2015). It appears that the return on equity or assets of European cooperative banking groups is much less volatile than that of shareholder value banks (Oliver Wyman, 2008). This statement is also true for Rabobank, though the variability of its net profits has increased in recent years (Chart 3).

Since 1967, net profits have always been positive and increased at an average growth rate of more than 11 % per year. Rabobank had a tradition of achieving virtually each year a net profit higher than the year before. In 2009, this tradition was broken; not because of write-offs due to the credit crisis, but as a result of the poor economic conditions during the ensuing recession in the Netherlands. This economic downturn caused a rise in bad debt costs to 48 basis points of the loan portfolio, whereas the long term average is about 25 basis points. Moreover, the

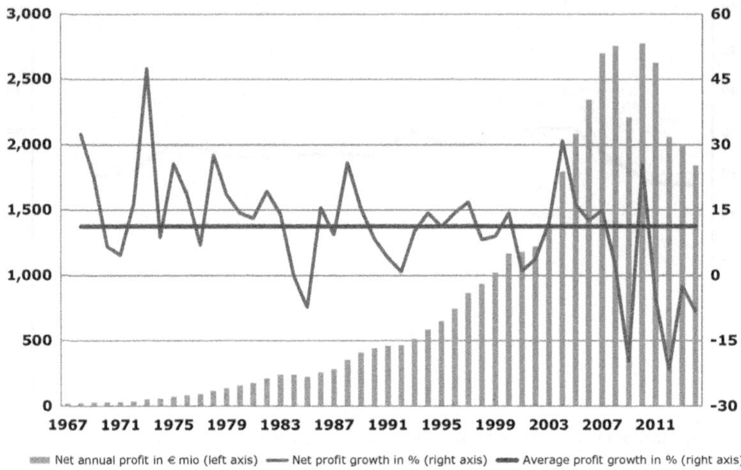

Chart 3 Size and growth of annual net profits of Rabobank Group. *Source*: Rabobank

bank was faced with very low margins on savings, caused by strong competition in this field.

Just after the climax of the crisis, net profits surprisingly bounced back to an all-time high in 2010. Underlying figures indicate that this was caused by—at that time still—low credit losses, international interest rate developments which turned out positively for Rabobank and high revenues from activities on global financial markets. However, this profit level could not be maintained in the following years. Net profits have decreased every year since then, which reflects (i) structural changes in banking, (ii) the effects of subsequent financial and economic crises (e.g. low credit demand) and, (iii) specific losses and write downs in Rabobank's own operations. It is expected that banking profitability will remain subdued in the years to come. The situation in banking has changed radically, with more banks returning to retail banking in a low interest rate environment. Regulatory and compliance costs have surged as well, apart from rising Dutch banking taxes.[14] As a result of changed consumer preferences and the need to maintain an economically sustainable business model with a healthy reservation capacity, Rabobank has embarked on a large virtualisation program of services and products, which entails many job losses in the next years.

4.4 *Capitalisation and Ratings*

The cooperative banking model guarantees solid capital buffers, because profits are not distributed but for the greater part added to their reserves. There is no one

[14] The Banking Tax equalled EUR 500 million in 2014 for Rabobank.

calling for profit to be maximised from the equity 'in the dead hand' of Rabobank Group. The equity 'belongs to no one' and has to a significant extent been accrued by adding profit to reserves year in, year out, for more than a century. According to Fonteyne (2007), the knowledge that this carefully built-up capital cannot be easily replaced by external sources after considerable losses, stimulates executive managers of cooperative banks to apply a relatively low risk appetite. This disciplining factor partly explained the relatively good performance of all cooperative banks during and right after the initial credit crisis (Birchall 2013). Up to the crisis, commercial or listed banks had distributed around half of their net profit to their shareholders.

Since the 1990s, Rabobank has always deliberately operated with a higher Tier 1 ratio (the ratio of equity versus risk-weighted lending) than the entire Dutch banking sector. Based on the risk profile, capital buffer, stability of income flows, market shares, strategy and diversification of activities, Rabobank was awarded with the highest rating among private banks from rating agencies Standard & Poor's and Moody's for many years. In 2012, Rabobank has lost its Triple A-rating from Standard & Poor's owing to the application of a new method of calculation or the ratings. However, what really matters is that its creditworthiness has remained unequalled. In 2015, Rabobank still belonged to the best-rated privately owned banks in the world according to all rating agencies.

It can be said that the high capitalisation and the associated high credit ratings have proven extremely important in the recent turbulent times. Due to this status, continued access to the financial markets was assured even during the crisis and hence, the independent position could be preserved. In 2008, the Tier 1 ratio stood at 12.7 % and even went up towards 17 % in 2011. Since then, this ratio has decreased to some extent, but stayed above the average ratio of all Dutch banks (Chart 4).

As stated before, Rabobank Group has found ways to finance its expansion throughout 1990–2010 via the issuance of hybrid capital instruments and Member Certificates without compromising its solvency position. A disadvantage of this kind of capital strengthening is that annual compensations to investors logically have to be paid, which in turn squeezes the reservation capacity. For this reason, Rabobank aims at a gradual reduction of the relative share of hybrid capital instruments and Rabobank Certificates in its capital base. Simultaneously, Rabobank has formulated a growth path that rests on both improving the reservation capacity and a moderate asset growth. Against this background, Rabobank has sold its subsidiaries Sarasin (Swiss private bank) in 2012 and Robeco (asset manager) in 2013.

4.5 Cost to Income Ratio

An often used measure for the efficiency of banks is the cost to income ratio (i.e. operational expenses divided by operational revenues). Up to 2009, Rabobank

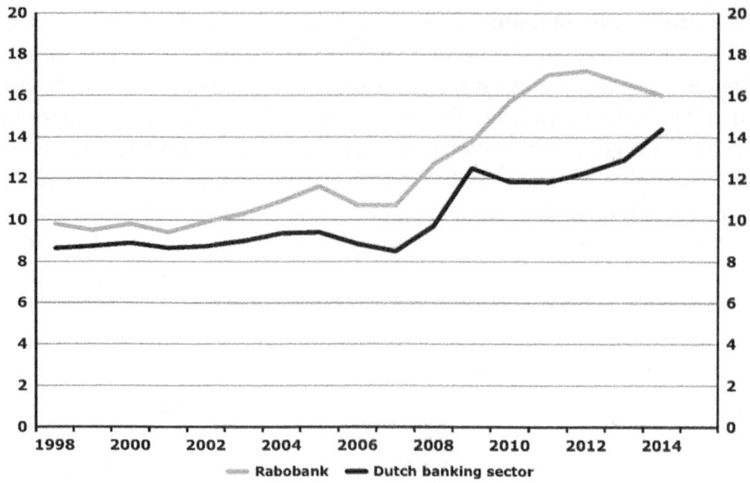

Chart 4 Tier 1 ratio of Rabobank Group and entire Dutch banking sector. *Source*: Rabobank and European Central Bank

has operated with a—somewhat—lower cost to income ratio than the entire Dutch banking sector. The relatively high costs of the dense branch network were thus compensated by higher returns in other areas. The large hike in this ratio for all other banks in 2008 catches the eye. This was obviously related to well-known large shocks in Dutch banking, i.e. the nationalisation of the Dutch part of Fortis/ABN Amro, and government support for ING and SNS (which was nationalised in 2013 as well). All in all, 60 % of the Dutch banking sector needed some form of government support. This massive government intervention has long lasting consequences for the competitive environment and trends in the Dutch banking sector.

Since then, ING and ABN Amro took major steps to slim down their organisations and to improve efficiency and profitability. Rabobank seemed to have been somewhat paralysed by its good performance before and just after the credit crisis. In 2012, newspapers wrote that the bank was acting with a slight arrogance, though it had always been characterised by a degree of modesty. With hindsight, it seems as if the media had a premonition of the issues Rabobank would encounter a few years later. As described above, Rabobank was confronted with internal issues and economic headwinds since 2010. With some delay, it responded to structural changes in external circumstances and internal problems with major adjustments in its governance and operations.

Whereas the efficiency in Dutch banking improved considerably after 2009, the cost to income ratio of Rabobank peaked at 78 in 2013 as a result of increasing loan losses and one-off effects like the Libor settlement, reorganisation costs, and high write offs on real estate and ground positions. The coming years will be dominated by an ongoing virtualisation and simplification of products and services and employment reductions. These programmes are assumed to generate cost savings and a structural improvement in the efficiency ratio in due time (Chart 5).

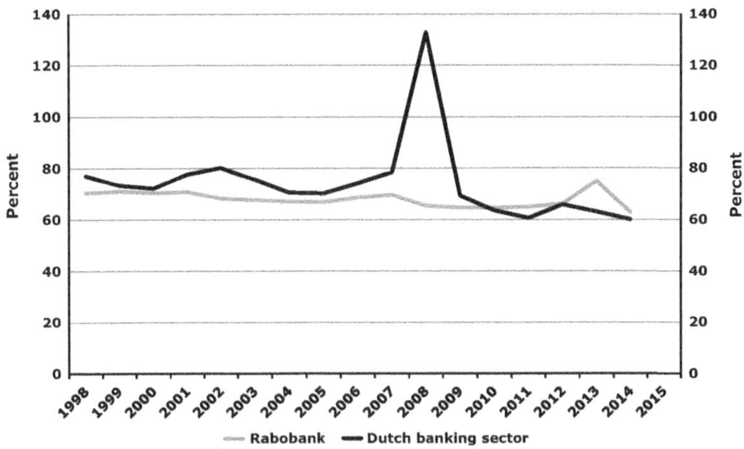

Chart 5 Cost income ratio of Rabobank Group and entire Dutch banking sector. *Source*: Rabobank and European Central Bank

4.6 International Activities

Chart 6 illustrates that the share of Rabobank's international activities has grown continuously since 1980 until the break-out of the credit crisis. In 1980, international activities were still virtually absent, but increased considerably in the subsequent 10 years as measured by international assets and foreign revenues as a percentage of total assets and revenues respectively. After a while, it became apparent that international investment, wholesale and corporate banking activities can be riskier and more volatile than the activities of LCBs in The Netherlands, with the latter focusing primarily on retail banking. The higher revenues that can be expected from the international wholesale business are sometimes counterbalanced by a greater volatility in returns caused by the deterioration of particular international markets or a rise in the level of credit or country risks. In the remote and recent past, substantial net losses and write-downs of Rabobank Group were mostly concentrated in the international activities (and/or at group subsidiaries). For instance, the share of foreign revenues in total revenues displayed a large drop in 2008. The reason is that in the period of 2007–2009 around 2.5 billion after tax has been written off through the profit and loss account on positions in the banking operations that had been impacted by the financial crisis (Vogelaar 2012, p. 207). However, these losses were more than offset by strong results of LCBs in particular.

The chart shows the drop in the share of all international assets from around 40 % in 2006 to 25 % in 2014. This is the consequence of a deliberate policy to cut back foreign credits to free capital for domestic retail activities. The international wholesale business was refocused towards customer-oriented activities. For its international business, Rabobank has the ambition to be a globally recognised food and agri bank.

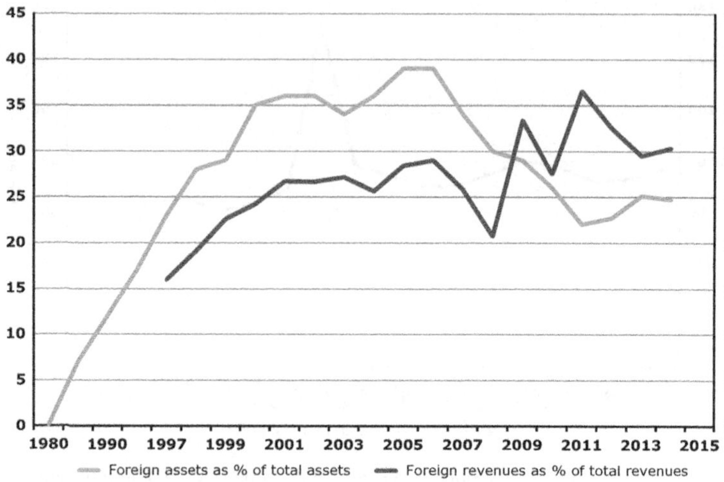

Chart 6 Development of international business as percentage of total business. *Source*: Rabobank

5 Concluding Remarks

Like other European cooperative banks, Rabobank survived the credit crisis 2007–2010 relatively well (Goglio and Alexopoulus 2014). Rabobank incurred losses and write-downs of around six percent of its total equity, but it did not need any form of state aid. Though it is difficult to pinpoint one specific cause for this achievement, it is safe to say that its solid and balanced corporate governance structure with member influence, a low risk profile and long-standing business model are important explanations. The former feature fosters a predominant focus on retail banking, i.e. financing the real economy. The conscious choice to remain a cooperative made in 1998 has surely paid off very well 10 years later. Furthermore, the resulting high capitalisation and credit ratings have proven to be powerful assets in the recent financial turmoil; Rabobank entered the crisis with solid liquidity and capital buffers, which largely explains why it retained good access to professional funding.

After 2010, Rabobank was obviously affected by the weak economic situation given its focus on the real economy. In addition, Rabobank was negatively impacted by the low interest rate environment and the general loss of confidence in the Dutch banking sector, which was exacerbated by its own role in the Libor fixing scandal. Regarding the reputational damage, the sector has taken various initiatives to restore its image, but that will not happen overnight. Recommendations and requirements for good governance and solid risk management were formulated, since banks can only adequately perform crucial public functions—which are vital for a well-functioning economic system—if trust and confidence in and among banks exist. In 2014, a banking oath was introduced in Dutch banking.

This oath is not something without obligation, since this oath is backed by a newly designated disciplinary law.

Though Rabobank is facing difficulties after the credit crisis, its financial solidity has never been put into question. In 2014, Rabobank comfortably passed the stress test carried out by the European Central Bank in order to be admitted to the Single Supervisory Mechanism, i.e. the Asset Quality Review. For the future, Rabobank has identified the following major challenges in banking:

- Tougher competition due to remarkable shifts in the business models and strategic focus of existing and new competitors;
- Great urge for cost reductions and efficiency improvements to increase the reservation capacity for the necessary capital expansion;
- Fundamental regulatory and supervisory changes.

Therefore, the key objectives for Rabobank are to strengthen its distinctive cooperative nature and to secure its solid financial profile simultaneously. The envisaged new governance structure is aimed at maintaining trust and confidence of internal and external stakeholders in Rabobank. Indeed, how Rabobank tackles all challenges is largely determined by the set-up and functioning of the representative democracy, i.e. how and to what extent members participate in strategy, control, supervision, policy and decision-making. Sound profitability is required for solid capital ratios, continuity and growth and for the realisation of social objectives like contributing to a sustainable development of society and boosting the vitality of communities. All these ambitions can only be realised with innovativeness, good products at fair prices, operational excellence and last but not least well-motivated and highly qualified employees, who participate actively in society.

References

Ayadi R, Llewellyn D, Schmidt RH, Arbak E, de Groen WP (2010) Investigating diversity in the banking sector in Europe: key developments, performance and role of cooperative banks. Centre for European Policy Studies, Brussels

Birchall J (2013) Resilience in a downturn: the power of financial co-operatives. International Labour Office, International Labour Organization, Geneva

EACB (2010) European cooperative banks in the financial and economic turmoil: first assessments. Research paper. European Association of cooperative Banks, Brussels

Fonteyne W (2007) Cooperative banks in Europe—policy issues. IMF working paper

Goglio S, Alexopoulus Y (eds) (2014) Special issue on co-operative banks. J Entrep Organ Divers 3(1), Trento, Italy

Groeneveld JM (2015) Member-based enterprises: the spotlight on financial Services cooperatives. Inaugural Publication, TIAS School for Business and Society, Tilburg University, 13 Feb 2015

Groeneveld JM, Sjauw-Koen-Fa A (2009) Co-operative banks in the new financial system. Report prepared by Rabobank for the IMF/World Bank meeting in Istanbul, Turkey, Oct 2009

Mooij J (ed) (2009) Rabobank matters. Rabobank, Utrecht

Oliver Wyman (2008) Cooperative bank: customer champion. Oliver Wyman Financial Services, London

Rabobank (2012) Cooperatives and rural financial development: great opportunities and surmountable difficulties. Rabobank, Utrecht

Van Diepenbeek WJJ (2007) Cooperatives as a business organization, lessons from cooperative organization history. University of Maastricht, Maastricht

Vogelaar N (2012) Rabobank and the credit crisis. In: Mooij J, Boonstra WW (eds) Raiffeisen's footprint. VU University Press, Amsterdam, pp 198–216

The Portuguese Cooperative Credit System

Paula Cabo and João Rebelo

Abstract This paper presents a literature review on the regulatory framework of the Portuguese cooperative credit system and some historic data. The aim is to understand their role in the Portuguese banking industry and how the regulatory framework affects cooperative banking activity. The cooperative credit system in Portugal comprises only agricultural credit cooperatives (Caixas de Crédito Agrícola Mutuo—CCAM). Its present corporate format was created in 1911, but the genesis of Portuguese agricultural credit cooperatives dates back to the sixteenth century and can be regarded as a typical example of how public policy can influence the development of cooperative credit institutions. The Caixa Central de Crédito Agrícola Mutuo is the pivotal institution in the Crédito Agrícola Group, with a remit that is the mainstay of the group, namely the strategic global coordination, supervision and guidance of its associates. The CCAM's strong customer deposit base and prudential credit management policy have proved to be crucial in confronting current hard times. Indeed Crédito Agrícola is the only one of the major Portuguese banks that has not experienced negative profits since the beginning of the present economic and financial crisis.

1 Introduction

Cooperation, as an economic and business model, was born in England in response to the abuses of market power and asymmetric information generated by the Industrial Revolution and subsequently spread to other countries. Almost two centuries later, the economic analysis of cooperatives has vanished from most

P. Cabo (✉)
School of Agriculture and CIMO, Polytechnic Institute of Bragança, Bragança, Portugal
e-mail: paulacabo@ipb.pt

J. Rebelo
Department of Economics, Sociology and Management and CETRAD, University of Trás-os-Montes and Alto Douro, Vila Real, Portugal
e-mail: jrebelo@utad.pt

S. Karafolas (ed.), *Credit Cooperative Institutions in European Countries*,
Contributions to Economics, DOI 10.1007/978-3-319-28784-3_10

economic textbooks, enjoying relatively little publicity (Shaw 2007; Cuevas and Fisher 2006). As a governance model, the cooperative has also been neglected by policymakers in most European countries (Groeneveld and Sjauw-Koen-Fa 2009). However, surprisingly, in the financial sector of some European countries, such as Germany, Finland, the Netherlands and France, cooperatives are among the largest and fastest growing groups.

Regarded by many people as an obsolete business model, the recent financial and ensuing economic crisis has proved that they are (still) a valid alternative way of doing business. Indeed, in the aftermath of the 2008 financial crisis, the dominant banking model based on investor-owned firms is being questioned while other models, such as cooperatives, regarded in the past as a lower level have weathered the crisis better. Worldwide, cooperative banks have remained financially sound because their inherent characteristics allow them to persevere and in some cases to outperform their peers (Ayadi et al. 2010; EACB 2010).

The current economic crisis and the mistrust in financial institutions have encouraged debate on the role of cooperative banks within a fairer society and their responsibility as key economic and social players in the challenges of economic development. Their historical background and important role in boosting local development give them a key role in economic recovery. Moreover, given the present lack of confidence in the shareholder model as an overriding paradigm, co-operation can be the foundation of a more sustainable, fair and transparent way of doing business (Cabo 2012).

The main aim of this paper is to provide some insights into the Portuguese regulatory framework for cooperative banks to understand how a particular regulatory framework affects cooperative banking activity. To achieve this goal, the remainder of this paper consists of the following sections: Sect. 2 describes the evolution of the agricultural credit cooperative system; Sect. 3 illustrates the positioning of Crédito Agrícola in Portuguese banking; Sect. 4 includes a description of the Portuguese regulatory framework for agricultural credit cooperatives and its governance model; finally, Sect. 5 presents the conclusions.

2 The Genesis

The cooperative credit system in Portugal comprises only agricultural credit cooperatives. Its present corporate format was created in 1911, but the genesis of Portuguese agricultural credit cooperatives (Caixas de Crédito Agrícola Mutuo—CCAM[1]) goes back to the sixteenth century, to an institution called Common Barns, allowing farmers to keep stock and seek financing. The early CCAM were very small units and membership consisted of small farmers with low incomes. The

[1] The abbreviation CCAM denotes both the singular 'Caixa de Crédito Agrícola Mutuo' and the plural 'Caixas de Crédito Agrícola Mutuo'.

Table 1 Creation and evolution of the CCAM in the twentieth century

New CCAM		Existing CCAM	
Before 1920	95		
(1920–1929)	67		
(1930–1939)	48		
(1940–1949)	18	In 1950	132
(1950–1959)	17	In 1960	149
(1960–1969)	4	In 1970	144
(1970–1979)	21[a]	In 1980	157
(1980–1989)	57	In 1990	222
(1990–1999)	6[b]	In 2000	145

Source: Cabo (2012)
[a]19: (1974–1979)
[b]Resulting from the merging of the existing CCAM

beginning of the system was an absolute failure: the capital provided by the state was insufficient to accomplish the objectives, the cooperatives were used to pursue managers' personal goals and management errors and even fraud were commonly found during auditing (Cabo 2003). Despite these setbacks, the number of CCAM grew significantly until the 1929 financial crisis (see Table 1). Subsequently, CCAM were placed under the umbrella of the Caixa Geral de Depósitos, a public institution and also the largest Portuguese bank. During the dictatorial and fascist regime 'Estado Novo' (1931–1974), the CCAM were used to restrict the expansion of communist ideology and for political control of the rural population. It was a lifeless period for the CCAM. Thus, until 1976 CCAM played a minor role in the banking system, with a share of only 1 % of total deposits and credit.

Following the political changes in 1974, all private financial institutions were nationalized, except for the CCAM and foreign financial institutions. Moreover, the CCAM started a lobby movement for autonomy, expanding their implantation and broadening their activity, and in 1978 the National Federation of Agricultural Cooperative Credit Institutions (FENACAM) was created to support and represent the interests of its members, both nationally and internationally. In 1982, the 60-year-old Agricultural Cooperative Credit law underwent profound alterations with the publication of a specific Legal Regime for Agricultural Cooperative Credit (RJCAM). Subsequently, the CCAM threw off the guardianship of the Caixa Geral de Depósitos and the Caixa Central was founded in 1984 with the purpose of regulating the credit activity of CCAM members. In 1986, Portugal joined the European Union (EU), and the following 10 years were a period of profound changes in the Portuguese economy. The CCAM were considered important players in the framework of a financing strategy for the development of the agricultural sector. Thus, during the 1980s CCAM activity experienced spectacular growth as reflected in annual rates greater than 40 % for deposits and approximately 35 % for loans and net assets on average (Cabo 2003). However, it was a decade of wild growth and mismanagement, negatively influencing the performance of CCAM and jeopardising their survival.

In 1991, the Integrated System of Agricultural Cooperative Credit (SICAM) was created through an association of the Caixa Central and the CCAM. The Caixa Central was empowered to supervise, intervene in, guide and represent the SICAM. The SICAM established a regime of co-responsibility between the Caixa Central and its members, so solvency and liquidity supervision was accountable on a consolidated basis. A more demanding framework for the creation and functioning of the CCAM, together with the reinforcement of their funds, ended the joint liability of CCAM members. The '*agency agreement*' allowed the CCAM to broker operations forbidden in their normal scope of activity by acting as agents of the Caixa Central. Four years later, in 1995, the RJCAM was modified, widening the scope of CCAM operations to other activities connected with the rural world, such as hunting, fishing, agro-tourism and handicrafts, and allowing the CCAM to share with their members part of the net benefits (limited to 30 % of net profits and in accordance with legal and prudential equity requirements) and convert reserves into capital shares transferable to members. These modifications were crucial for boosting the ability of the CCAM to attract new (and more heavily investing) members, improving their capitalization. In addition, the new diploma expanded the Caixa Central's activities, converting it into a truly universal bank.

In 2009, new changes were introduced to the RJCAM, adopting a governance model closer to that adopted by investors' own firms and extending the activities and membership of CCAM, widening the members' scope as well as enabling CCAM to extend credit operations to non-members or for purposes not agriculturally related. Furthermore, once CCAM complied with the prudential requirements applied to banks, they were authorized to perform the majority of commercial activities carried out by other financial institutions. Table 1 summarizes the dynamic of the creation and evolution of CCAM during the last century.

An analysis of Table 1 shows that in the early days, the creation and demise of CCAM were accentuated. Until 1950, for each five CCAM created two failed. During the Estado Novo the number of CCAM was relatively stable. After the April revolution in 1974, CCAM gained a new lease of life and proliferated, especially in the 1980s. In the last two decades no genuinely 'new' CCAM were born, the only ones created resulting from a process of merger.

Figure 1 illustrates the age of existing CCAM in 1990. We can see that more than 40 % of the existing CCAM were still juvenile, created in the 1970s and 1980s. With the exception of the island of Madeira, the entire continental (mainland) territory was already covered by CCAM, which, allied to regional restrictions on their activity, made it economically and legally impossible to establish new CCAM.

With the formation of the SICAM in 1991, the CCAM entered into an era of consolidation and the creation of new CCAM was a rare event. Thus, during the last two decades, together with the organic growth of the CCAM, a regional merger process occurred and consequently the number of CCAM cooperatives fell from 220 in the 1990s to 85 in 2010. Mergers between local CCAM have considerably increased their size, both in terms of assets and number of branches per CCAM. Profitability (return on assets—ROA) has also improved. Indeed, at the time the

Fig. 1 Year of creation of CCAM. *Source*: Cabo (2012)

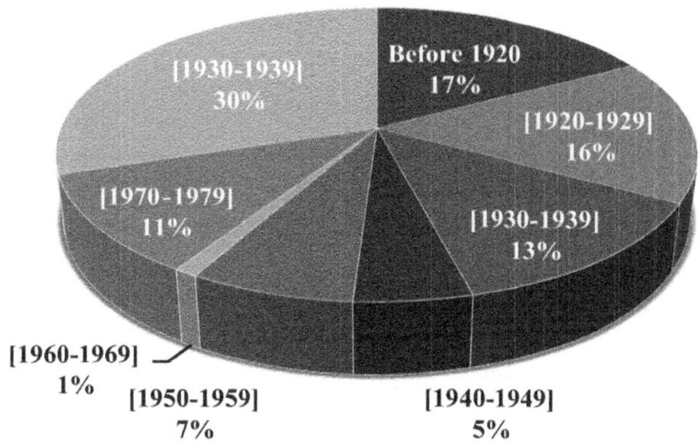

Table 2 Evolution of the SICAM 1995–2010

	Number of CCAM	Number of branches	Average assets per CCAM (million euros)	Average number of branches per CCAM	ROA[a] (%)
1995	186	465	22.28	2.5	−0.3
2000	140	–	47.56	–	0.7
2001	132	568	54.88	4.3	1.0
2002	126	580	61.50	4.6	0.4
2003	120	598	67.00	5.0	1.0
2004	118	616	71.80	5.2	1.0
2005	111	628	82.00	5.7	0.9
2006	105	632	91.60	6.0	1.0
2007	100	647	102.50	6.5	1.1
2008	92	670	116.90	7.3	1.1
2009	88	680	127.60	7.7	0.3
2010	85	689	132.40	8.1	0.3
2011	84	686	133.16	8.2	0.4
2012	84	686	140.70	8.2	0.3
2013	83	683	144.70	8.1	0.0

Source: Adapted from Cabo (2012)
[a]Ratios for 1995–2006 calculated in accordance with Portuguese rules (PCSB), transitional rules in 2007 (NCA) and IAS for 2008–2010

SICAM was created, the CCAM presented overall negative net results,[2] but the ongoing restructuring process allowed the CCAM to improve their performance (see Table 2) and experience profitability levels similar to those of the Portuguese banking system in general.

[2] The 1992–1993 Portuguese agricultural crisis together with the difficulty of CCAM in attracting new members resulted in the continuous degradation of CCAM results, which became negative from 1992 to 1995 (Cabo 2003).

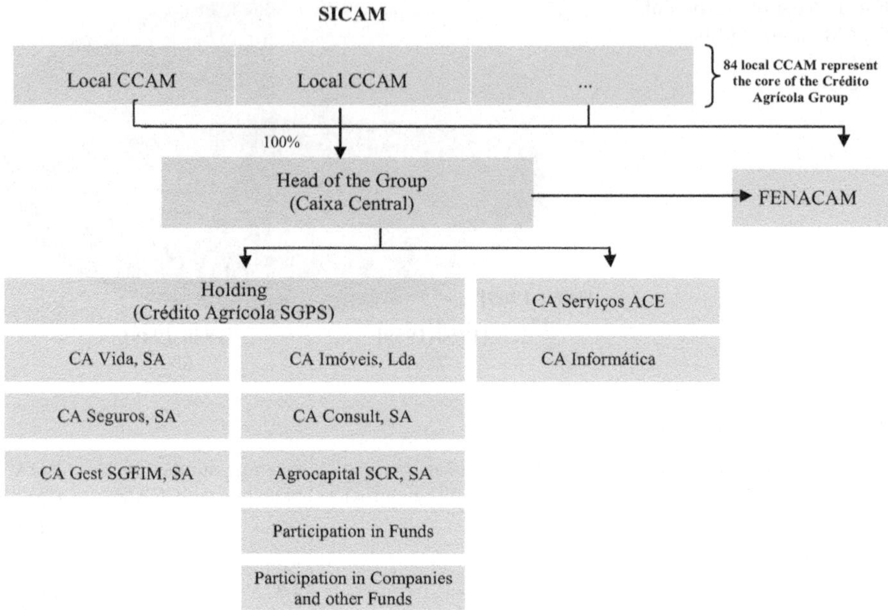

Fig. 2 Crédito Agrícola Group. *Source*: Adapted from Crédito Agrícola (2015)

Simultaneously, in the 1990s the Crédito Agrícola Group was founded. Nowadays, the Crédito Agrícola group is one of the leading financial groups in Portugal, composed of a large number of small- to medium-sized cooperative banks (CCAM) and some specialized companies, such as the shared services centre CA Serviços, under the supervision of the Caixa Central de Crédito Agrícola Mutúo, resulting in the group represented in Fig. 2.

3 Crédito Agrícola in Portuguese Banking

Today, Crédito Agrícola is a financial group that spans the country. In 2014, it comprised the following: approximately 400,000 members; 1.2 million customers, mainly small- and medium-scale savers, farmers, small- and medium-sized enterprises and traders; 84 local banks—the CCAM—with a network of 700 branches, scattered across the mainland and in the autonomous region of the Azores; a balance sheet of 14,000 million euros; equity totalling 1,100 million euros; a solvency ratio—Core Tier 1—of 11.9 %; a transformation ratio less than 90 % (Crédito Agrícola 2014, 2015).

These figures rank Crédito Agrícola as the fifth Portuguese financial group. Based on the 2013 balance sheet, Crédito Agrícola is ranked by The Banker

(2014), in relation to Portugal alone, as second in terms of soundness of capital/assets ratio, fourth for ROA and profits on capital, seventh according to Tier 1 capital size and eighth by assets. Table 3 presents the main indicators of the eight major retail banks operating in the Portuguese banking system for 2013. Together, these banking institutions have a market share of over 85 % of employment, the retail network and assets and a share of 90 % of customers' loans and deposits.

Considering the leading Portuguese retail banks, almost all of them suffered losses during the 2013 financial year and for some of them these were the equivalent to the losses they suffered during the 2 preceding years. The exception was Santander Totta, a subsidiary of Spanish Grupo Santander, and the CCAM integrated system. Looking at the banking industry results in these 7 years since the beginning of the financial crisis, among the eight major retail banks operating in Portugal, Crédito Agrícola is the only one that has not experienced negative profits.

In the words of a Crédito Agrícola leader: '*Profit is not an obsession, it's a consequence*' (Crédito Agrícola 2015: 17). This business approach has proved to be the source of Crédito Agrícola's strength and resilience. Indeed, the conservative management adopted by Crédito Agrícola has meant comfortable solvency levels and solid capital ratios, giving Crédito Agrícola a solid security buffer crucial in the context of the current economic and financial crisis. This fact, together with other particularities of Crédito Agrícola, has meant that the quantitative impact of the current negative business environment has not affected Crédito Agrícola to the same extent as other banking groups. The cooperative business model upon which Crédito Agrícola is founded has proved to be resilient during hard times, with its robust capitalization and ample liquidity. Low but steady results have allowed Crédito Agrícola to bolster its asset situation, which is still very robust even today. Given the cooperative nature of Crédito Agrícola, profits are mostly directed to the reinforcement of equity. This continuous capital reinforcement is reflected in robust solvency ratios. Over time Crédito Agrícola has shown a Core Tier 1 solvency ratio comfortably above the minimum level of 10 %. The 11.9 % ratio, obtained in December 2013 (against 11.6 % in December 2012), reflects the stability and robustness of Crédito Agrícola's equity. Also, the global solvency ratio of 11 % recorded in December 2013 is above the minimum level of 8 % set by the Bank of Portugal.

Indeed, Crédito Agrícola is one of the few Portuguese banking groups that did not resort to the banking recapitalization line of credit created within the scope of the Portuguese financial assistance programme. Furthermore, at present, after some 7 years of global and European financial crisis, Crédito Agrícola still shows a very comfortable liquidity position and very ample capital ratios, even with the new concepts and levels established in the new European regulations, e.g. Common Equity Tier 1 capital, a key element in the new regulations, the minimum level of which is set at 7 %; Crédito Agrícola's Common Equity Tier 1 capital stood at 13 % in the first semester of 2014. Structural analysis shows the robustness of Crédito Agrícola (see Table 4).

Table 3 Top eight Portuguese retail banks as at December 2013

	BES	CCAM	Montepio	CGD	Millennium BCP	Banco BPI	Santander Totta	Banif
Employment [a]	5.908	3.765	3.881	9.049	8.323	6.151	5.481	2.258
Market share[b]	11.2 %	7.2 %	7.4 %	17.2 %	15.8 %	11.7 %	10.4 %	4.3 %
Branches [a]	612	683	456	804	758	631	610	276
Market share[b]	11.0 %	12.3 %	8.2 %	14.4 %	13.6 %	11.3 %	11.0 %	5.0 %
Net assets[c]	66,167,561	12,968,918	26,466,936	93,835,993	76,792,289	41,173,146	40,260,304	14,689,832
Market share	15.3 %	3.0 %	6.1 %	21.7 %	17.8 %	9.5 %	9.3 %	3.4 %
Net loans[c]	35,872,194	7,491,909	15,139,969	59,557,428	40,298,300	23,199,771	26,216,988	7,205,286
Market share	14.8 %	3.1 %	6.2 %	24.6 %	16.6 %	9.6 %	10.8 %	3.0 %
Total deposits[c]	33,446,504	10,209,731	13,620,187	58,132,643	34,851,314	18,657,772	20,690,967	6,303,216
Market share	15.6 %	4.8 %	6.4 %	27.2 %	16.3 %	8.7 %	9.7 %	2.9 %
Equity[c]	5,701,684	1,105,873	1,700,006	4,922,234	1,774,286	1,304,962	1,471,116	834,577
Net profit[c]	−462,568	1,506	−262,513	−1,090,515	−1,958,730	−27,431	2,449	−494,341

Source: Authors' calculation based on company annual reports; Bank of Portugal and Portuguese Banking Association statistics (Associação Portuguesa de Bancos 2015; Banco de Portugal 2015)

[a]For domestic activiy only (#)

[b]Market share for the universe of Portuguese Banking Association affiliates

[c]Values in thousands of euros and for separate balance sheets

Table 4 Credit Agrícola's performance as at December 2013

Performance indicators	SICAM	Portuguese banking system[a]
Transformation ratio[b]	80.3 %	116.9 %
Efficiency ratio[c]	68.2 %	72.0 %
Return on Assets (ROA)[d]	0.01 %	−0.8 %
Return on Equity (ROE)[e]	0.3 %	−11.6 %
Core Tier 1 Ratio (Basileia II)[f]	11.9 %	12.3 %
Customer claims		
Deposits: claims per 1000 accounts	0.08	0.21
Mortgage credit: claims per 1000 contracts	0.72	1.01
Consumer credit: claims per 1000 contracts	0.17	0.48

Source: Crédito Agrícola (2014), Associação Portuguesa de Bancos (2015) and Banco de Portugal (2014a, b)

[a]Data for domestic banking groups and stand-alone banks, on a consolidated basis excluding insurance companies

[b]Gross loans/deposits for SICAM and Net loans/deposits for Portuguese banking system

[c]Structural costs/net worth [structural costs include amortization + general administrative expenses + staff costs; net worth includes financial margin + net commissions + other income (including results from financial operations)]

[d]Net profit/average net assets

[e]Net profit/equity

[f]Basic own funds/weighted risks (assets + off-balance sheet items) (Data for Crédito Agrícola Group)

As Table 4 shows, Crédito Agrícola presents a lower transformation ratio of 80.3 %, this indicator remaining at a clearly conservative level. Historically, it has never presented a value higher than 90 %, a percentage much lower than the general position of other financial institutions, which exceed 100 %. This has a positive influence in terms of the liquidity and solvency of CCAM. As mentioned, this is an important strategic advantage for Crédito Agrícola as it provides an ample margin for expanding its portfolio. The value of deposits continues to far surpass loans granted, keeping the SICAM in a strong position in terms of balance sheet liquidity. However, this does put pressure on the profitability of CCAM as the remuneration of excess liquidity by the financial markets is currently extremely unfavourable. Indeed, the worsening operating conditions, in which compression on the financial margin was compounded by the need to set aside higher provisions, resulted in the CCAM results being downsized. Thus, in 2013 Crédito Agrícola's financial results decreased considerably compared to 2012, which in turn were lower than in 2011. With regard to the individual CCAM, the financial results can be explained essentially by the rather considerable losses that occurred in a small number of associates, offsetting the profits obtained by the others, for which reason it should be noted that several CCAM, even against this difficult economic backdrop, managed to increase their earnings compared to recent years (Crédito Agrícola 2014).

Table 5 presents the evolution of the SICAM's performance prior to and after the 2008 financial crisis. The results show that despite the worsening operating conditions for banking activity, the SICAM proved able to endure with relative success, keeping above the waterline and not experiencing negative profits.

Table 5 Evolution of SICAM performance 2005–2013

	2004	2005	2006	2007	2008	2009	2010	2011	2012	2013
Transformation ratio	91.4 %	89.2 %	86.1 %	81.5 %	87.1 %	88.0 %	86.2 %	86.9 %	82.2 %	80.3 %
Efficiency ratio	52.5 %	55.2 %	58.4 %	54.1 %	55.5 %	69.4 %	67.1 %	64.7 %	65.3 %	64.0 %
Core Tier 1 ratio	10.4 %	10.5 %	11.6 %	11.6 %	12.2 %	12.1 %	12.7 %	12.5 %	11.6 %	11.9 %
ROE	13.7 %	11.8 %	11.5 %	13.0 %	12.4 %	4.2 %	3.5 %	4.5 %	3.8 %	0.1 %
ROA	1.0 %	0.9 %	1.0 %	1.1 %	1.1 %	0.3 %	0.3 %	0.4 %	0.3 %	0.0 %
Net profits (millions euros)	90	87	96	113	121	42	36	47	41	1.5

Source: Crédito Agrícola (2014)

As shown in Table 5, as a consequence of the 2008 financial crash and subsequent economic and sovereign debt crisis, the SICAM's efforts to control the increase in structural costs below net worth in recent years have been quashed by the harsher operating conditions. The deep economic crisis that has repressed the Portuguese economy for several years has affected the performance of the Portuguese banks in an extremely negative manner. The Portuguese banking industry has experienced a considerable increase in overdue debts, which has resulted in the need to increase provisions significantly. On the other hand, the recession has led to a fall in the value of real estate assets, reducing the value of collateral and forcing the recognition of impairments, sometimes of considerable value, with regard to the properties acquired by means of debt recovery processes. In a context in which the financial margins of institutions have also evolved negatively and in which, as far as debt is concerned, opportunities to generate new business have become scarcer, the pressure on provisions and the value of impairments, as well as the declines in assets, have led to appreciable losses in practically every banking group of relevance within the Portuguese banking industry. Consequently, the SICAM experienced a continuous drop in earnings from banking after 2008 and in 2013 banking activities obtained net earnings of only 1.5 million euros, corresponding to a decline of more than 98 % compared to results obtained in the years prior to the 2008 crisis, essentially due to the fall in the financial margin and the need to increase provisions both with regard to non-performing debt and direct or indirect devaluation of collateral. Thus, return on operations overall was poor, with ROE at 0.1 %, well below the figure of 12.4 % for 2008.

3.1 Regional Development

The real importance of Crédito Agrícola in the Portuguese banking industry lies in its business approach. Notable for their unique proximity to their communities, the CCAM are a powerhouse for local and regional development, fulfilling Crédito Agrícola's corporate mission '*... contributing to the development of Local Communities*' (Crédito Agrícola 2009). The CCAM meet this goal by virtue of being spread across the entire domestic territory, with the exception of the island of Madeira.

Despite their roots in rural communities, the actual mission of the CCAM is not restricted to such communities and Crédito Agrícola is currently positioned as a local universal bank: '*The perception in urban centers is that the Crédito Agrícola is a rural bank, which is a farmers' bank. Its genesis is agriculture but we are present and engaged in the development of all regions, whether rural or urban. We are a universal bank for sustainable development of all the communities where we operate*' (Crédito Agrícola 2015: 33). Figure 3 illustrates Crédito Agrícola's local market share per district.

Apart from the two metropolitan areas, Crédito Agrícola has a solid presence, as shown in Fig. 3, with a market share of more than 15 % in some regions—the north,

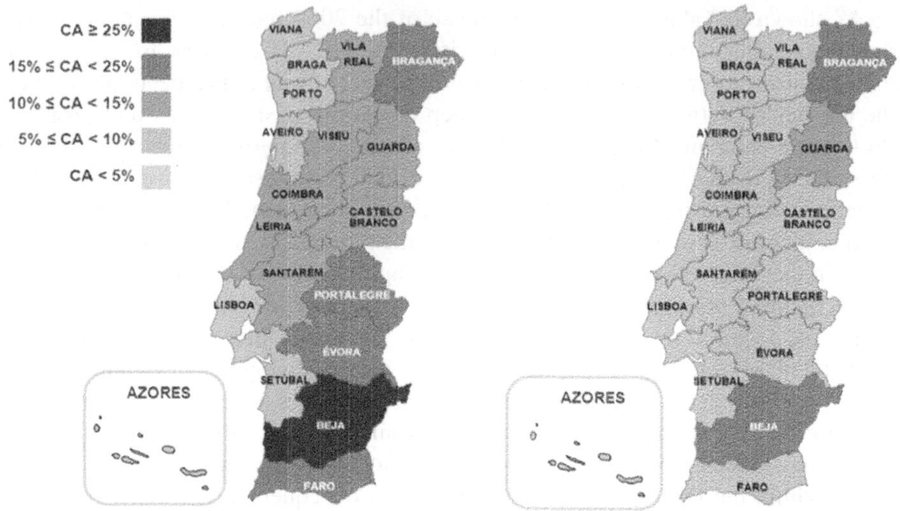

Market Share: Deposits **Market Share: Loans**

Fig. 3 Crédito Agrícola's local market share per district. *Source*: Crédito Agrícola (2013)

centre and south of the country. In some parts, this figure rises to over 30 %. However, there is another, more important point: in hundreds of places across the countryside, the only link to the financial system available for the local economy is the Crédito Agrícola network or its facilities—the ATMs, automatic banking counters or POSs—installed by the local CCAM (Crédito Agrícola 2011). In the words of a Crédito Agrícola leader: '*There are about 250 branches of Crédito Agrícola where no other bank wants to be. There are 400 ATMs in isolated places, inserted in parish councils. There are branches with 1 or 2 people, which do not give a profit, do not lose money, the spirit is to serve the community*' (Crédito Agrícola 2015: 31).

Figure 4 shows the geographic and income customer profile of the major retail banks operating in Portugal. In terms of geographic distribution, CCAM are very different from the other banks, given that over half of their customers (53.3 %) live in the country's inland regions. Crédito Agrícola has a special responsibility in these circumstances. Its distribution across regions means it is present in many places where economic strength has been sapped. Thus, a very high proportion of the customers (more than 90 %) have low or moderate incomes (Crédito Agrícola 2009).

3.2 Internationalization

Although 1992 marked the beginning of international business activity, it was still a new area for Crédito Agrícola. In 2013, the overall value of foreign operations

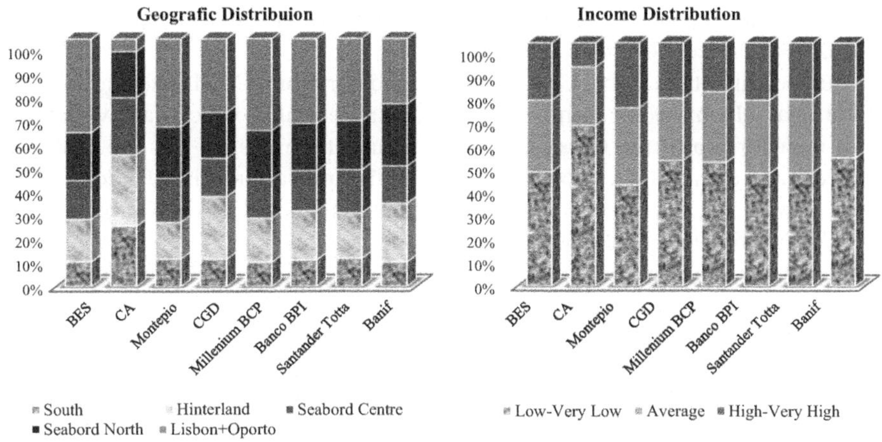

Fig. 4 Customer profile of the largest Portuguese banks. *Source*: Adapted from Crédito Agrícola (2009)

performed via Crédito Agrícola surpassed the 3000 million euros mark for the first time. Market share stands at 2.85 %. The overall amount of foreign operations for Crédito Agrícola developed positively, growing 20.7 %, compared to domestic growth during the same period of 2.4 % (Crédito Agrícola 2014).

This business area, especially emigration, is a specific segment with a role in the group which has been growing consistently over recent years, thanks to the excellent geographical distribution of Crédito Agrícola throughout the country and the dynamic approach of the group's branches abroad. Throughout 2013, Crédito Agrícola continued its efforts towards internationalization by investing in a presence in some of the markets in which Portuguese immigration is prevalent, such as France, Switzerland, Luxembourg and Venezuela. The sustained increase in emigrant remittances is symptomatic of this and in 2013 Crédito Agrícola's market share was 4 % in emigrant remittances and 4 % in emigrant deposits, to a certain extent reflecting the results obtained from this strategy.

4 Structure and Governance

Essentially, the agricultural cooperative credit system in Portugal is made up of an integrated system (SICAM) of two types of cooperatives: central and individual (associated or member), i.e. the SICAM = Caixa Central + Associated CCAM, including 84 CCAM. Together they own several specialized companies forming the Crédito Agrícola Group. The central structures of the group are the Caixa Central de Crédito Agrícola Mútuo and FENACAM. The former is a cooperative banking institution empowered to oversee, orientate and monitor operations in the local associated banks. The latter is a cooperative institution which provides specialized services for the group.

Membership of the Caixa Central is not mandatory for CCAM. There are CCAM in Portugal which are not members of the Caixa Central or which have withdrawn from membership of the Caixa Central, although the rules for this are relatively stringent and approximate more closely those that prevail in private credit institutions. Services are not offered by the Caixa Central to these CCAM. Currently, only five CCAM remain outside the SICAM.

Except for banking operations, the CCAM follow traditional cooperative principles, namely, open membership, democratic control and restricted residual claims. The dual nature of credit cooperatives is reflected in their formal and institutional solutions. According to the RJCAM,[3] the CCAM are credit institutions of a cooperative nature, the goal of which is to undertake agricultural credit operations in favour of their members, as well as the other banking functions inherent to banking activity. Thus, the CCAM are under a special regime, essentially because of their cooperative form and their priority goal of undertaking agricultural credit operations in favour of their members.

The RJCAM specifies that CCAM be created in a cooperative form, with limited liability, and should seek, without the aim of profit, the satisfaction of their members' economic, social and cultural needs and aspirations. The CCAM thus have structural and intrinsic differences from banks as, according to the law, banks must be in the form of public limited companies (corporations) and therefore aim for profit. The RJCAM imposes several limitations resulting from its social objectives, territorial area and members' attributes. In addition, it is difficult for CCAM to increase their issued share capital as they cannot publicly do so. These limitations have their counterpart in minor issued share capital, organizational structure, technical and human resources available, solvency, control and accountability requirements (on an individual but not a consolidated basis).

The 2009 alterations to the RJCAM basically aimed to adjust the governance model of CCAM to be in line with that established for corporations in the Portuguese Commercial Companies Code (CCC) and simultaneously to widen the CCAM membership base, bringing it more in line with other financial institutions and boosting an increase in issued share capital in view of the recession felt in the agricultural sector. Table 6 summarizes the main features of cooperative credit according to Portuguese legislation.

As mentioned, Crédito Agrícola takes a specialized approach to financial services. Most of the people who use the services of the local CCAM are non-members. However any person may open an account, make deposits, obtain loans and use the services of the CCAM, complying with the limits imposed by the

[3] Approved by Decree of Law n° 24/91, with the following alterations and republished in the appendix to the Decree of Law n° 142/2009.

Table 6 Overview of Portuguese credit cooperatives

Topic	Policy
Creation	Bank of Portugal approval, following the agreement of Caixa Central and FENACAM
Legal form and nature	Credit Institution, cooperative form RJCAM (and subsidiary: RG for banking activity and Cooperative Code and other cooperative legislation) applies
Operations	Granting credit primarily to members and for financing primary sector activities. CCAM complying, on individual basis, with prudential rules established in the RG, can perform operations with non-members or financing activities outside primary sector up to 35 % of net assets. Exceptionally, this limit can be raised to 50 % by the Bank of Portugal for SICAM associates at the suggestion of the Caixa Central In addition, CCAM that have adequate structural conditions and sufficient funds could be authorized by the Bank of Portugal to perform most other activities allowed to banks, with a few exceptions
Membership	Singular or collective persons who carry out any activity linked to the primary sector (production, transformation or services) in the CCAM territory (or adjacent). Membership outside primary sector activities is permitted but limited to 35 % of the CCAM members. Exceptionally, this limit can be raised to 50 % by the Bank of Portugal Minimum shareholding: 500 €; minimum of 50 members
Territorial activity	CCAM activity is restricted to their headquarter municipality. CCAM can expand to an adjacent region if there is no other CCAM operating there, or as a result of a CCAM merger
Opening of branches	Branch opening is subject to the authorization of the Caixa Central for associated CCAM and of the Bank of Portugal for independent CCAM
Shareholders' capital	Capital is variable; it can be increased by the admission of new members or higher shareholdings or by the incorporation of reserves; or it can be reduced by the exit of members or lower shareholdings or by covering losses Capital reduction is constrained by prudential rules. The maximum reimbursement value is defined by the accounting value net of compulsory reserves Capital minimum fixed by the Ministry of Finance: 7.5 million euros; SICAM associates: 5 million euros[a]
Resources	Deposits and other reimbursed funds from their members and/or customers. Access to other financing resources, namely the interbank market, requires Bank of Portugal (and Caixa Central for associated CCAM) approval General financing means are stipulated in the Cooperative Code, namely, issuing investment securities or debt
Financial applications	Besides deposits, CCAM can make applications concerning public debt under conditions established by the Bank of Portugal CCAM can only hold participations: (a) in regional unions, Caixa Central and FENACAM; (b) in enterprises the object of which is of regional interest (up to 20 % of equity); (c) to assure the reimbursement of credits; (d) when especially authorized by Bank of Portugal[b]
Governance bodies	The management and supervisory bodies (composition and competences) stipulated for corporations apply, preserving the importance and competences of the General Assembly characteristic of the cooperative model
Shares	No tradability of shares
Voting rules	Principle of democracy, voting right independent of shareholding position: one member, one vote

(continued)

Table 6 (continued)

Topic	Policy
Creation	Bank of Portugal approval, following the agreement of Caixa Central and FENACAM
Reserves	CCAM must allocate up to 50 % of net profits to reserves: (a) at least 20 % to the legal reserve until it reaches the value of issued share capital; (b) at least 20 % to the special reserve for reinforcement of equity in the case of CCAM under a financial restructuring process, until it reaches the value of the amount of the benefits obtained with the process; (c) 1–5 % to members' education; (d) a maximum of 5 % to the mutual reserve CCAM statutes can design other reserves
Profit allocation	After covering eventual losses of previous exercises, profits not allocated to the reserves can be distributed among members. The remuneration of capital shares is limited to 30 % of the results[c] Profits cannot be distributed if the CCAM do not comply with prudential rules, or if the member shareholding is lower than the minimum required, in which case that portion of the profit will revert to them
Supervision	Bank of Portugal. Caixa Central for SICAM members
Tax policy	Profits are subjected to a rate (IRC) of 20 %, excepting the results of no member operations or activities outside cooperative purposes and the taxation on a consolidated basis in which the IRC general rules apply[d]
Deposits insurance	Insurance Fund of Agricultural Cooperative Credit. This fund, as well as securing CCAM customer deposits, performs an active role in the SICAM's economic and financial restructuring process as part of its task to promote the SICAM's solvency and liquidity

Source: Cabo (2012)

[a]By 30th June 2015, CCAM capital should reach at least 5 million euros, beginning with 2.5 million euros by 30th June 2011 followed by an annual increase of 0.5 million euros

[b]CCAM have direct participation in Crédito Agrícola's specialized companies under this special authorization

[c]CCAM do not usually give out profit to members. Members' remuneration usually takes the form of capital share allocation resulting from the incorporation of reserves

[d]According to the Cooperative Tax Statute, Law n° 85/98, although, according to FENACAM (2009), the cooperative credit system is, within the Portuguese financial system, the greater contributor in percentile terms. In many cases, cooperative credit system taxation is triple that of other banking companies

RJCAM (Table 6). Of the approximately 1.2 million customers of the Crédito Agrícola Group, only around 400,000 are members. With certain incentives for membership having been removed in recent tax reforms, Crédito Agrícola is attempting to encourage membership to enhance the grass roots of the movement by offering special conditions attaching to financial products and services, such as the 'Clube A' card for members. This is a hard task in a country struggling with the definition of rural regions and the agro-business industry. Entering the new millennium, the number of Crédito Agrícola members has stagnated; new entries are scarce and diluted by the exit of members. Simultaneously, the number of CCAM customers has declined by almost 25 % in one decade. Crédito Agrícola is attempting to diversify its customer portfolio, targeting a new type of customer not linked to the primary sector activities, but it is up against the traditional Crédito Agrícola brand image and banking customers' perceptions.

Within the general prudential guidelines provided by Caixa Central, the local CCAM have control over their pricing and personal services. In general, CCAM sell products and services developed by Crédito Agrícola and pursuant to formal policies and procedures issued by Caixa Central to which the local CCAM must adhere. The CCAM operate from a common technology platform. The operations of the CCAM are restricted and limited to their headquarters region. Whenever competitive friction between local CCAM arises, any dispute is arbitrated by Caixa Central. The local CCAM consistently honour the principle of non-competition. Any new CCAM branch must be approved by the Caixa Central.

The role of the Caixa Central has no parallel in other financial institutions. The Caixa Central is a financial institution in cooperative form, offering a full banking service and competing on equal terms with the largest banks operating in Portugal˙ The Caixa Central aims at the concession of credit and other practices inherent to banking activity on the same terms as commercial banks. However, it should not compete with its own members. For example, the Caixa Central is authorized to open branches on the same terms as banks, but must first consult the local CCAM member.

Caixa Central acts as central bank for the group, creating and developing a joint banking strategy. For instance, individual excess of liquidity is transferred to the Caixa Central, which can lend to non-primary economic sectors or carry out transactions in the money, foreign exchange or capital markets. It pays the market rate on liquidity deposits and following the principle of 'user payer', charges fees to the CCAM for consultative and advisory services. The Caixa Central does not attempt to generate a profit from its transactions with its member CCAM. It sets prices to recover costs. The CCAM are its only members and have capitalized on this through share investments. As in the case of local CCAM, the capital of Caixa Central is variable and can be increased by the admission of new members or higher shareholdings, or by the incorporation of reserves; shareholding reimbursement is restrained by prudential rules and requires General Assembly approval. The minimum capital of the Caixa Central, as fixed by the Ministry of Finance, is 17.5 million euros; with a minimum shareholding of 5000 € and a maximum of 10 % of capital, except in the case of extraordinary supplies.

Although the Bank of Portugal is responsible for banking sector supervision (i.e. the financial regulator), with regard to SICAM associates, the law delegates a great part of these functions to the Caixa Central which, in turn, is under Bank of Portugal supervision. The Bank of Portugal defines the relations and prudential limits applicable to the SICAM and supervises the system's accounts on a consolidated basis. Caixa Central assures the fulfilment of the SICAM and associated CCAM solvency and liquidity rules, controlling and guiding them. The accounts consolidation of associated CCAM is a Caixa Central responsibility, in compliance with the terms defined by the Bank of Portugal. Specifically, the Caixa Central orientation powers include the definition of general rules: (a) necessary to assure the fulfilment of the solvency and liquidity rules of the SICAM and associated CCAM; (b) for commercial and credit granting policies, including the setting up of guarantees; (c) regarding engagement, remuneration, formation and qualification of staff; (d) regarding the creation of new branches; (e) to define general rules of office operation and security.

In addition, without prejudicing the Bank of Portugal's authority, the Caixa Central is empowered to control administrative, technical and financing aspects of associated CCAM and their organization[4] and management. Moreover, the Caixa Central can intervene by the assigning a representative to monitor CCAM management or the nomination of provisional directors when it encounters an unbalanced situation which could jeopardize the daily functioning of the CCAM, its solvency is at risk, or serious irregularities occur. In addition, when the member is in (or at risk of) financial imbalance and not following the Caixa Central's guidelines, the Caixa Central can dismiss all or part of the associated management and supervision boards and assign provisional directors.

Finally, the Caixa Central guarantees its associates without limitations and is also guaranteed by them. Indeed, the Caixa Central guarantees the obligations assumed by the associated CCAM even if these originate prior to the association, in the same way as a bailer guarantees the obligations of the warrantee, without enjoying the right of exclusion. The SICAM is, in this way, subordinated to a double guardianship; the Caixa Central is directly responsible not only for the organization, but also for the economic and financial management of its associates.

The autonomy of the local CCAM, combined with the assistance received from the Caixa Central, creates a decentralized, but strongly orchestrated, bottom-to-top decision-making process.[5] Figure 5 includes a summary of the skeleton of the SICAM structure governance, i.e. the different governance bodies and linkages between them.

---

[4] To exemplify, if the Caixa Central does not favour the registration of a member of governance bodies, the Bank of Portugal rejects the registration.

[5] Decision-making in General Assembly of Members of individual CCAM obey to the principle of democracy. This is also true for decision-making in General Assembly of Members of Caixa Central, except for some specific decisions (election of the Caixa Central board of directors, budget approval and profits allocation) in which the voting rights can differ according to the shareholding and CCAM average deposits and the solvency ratio.

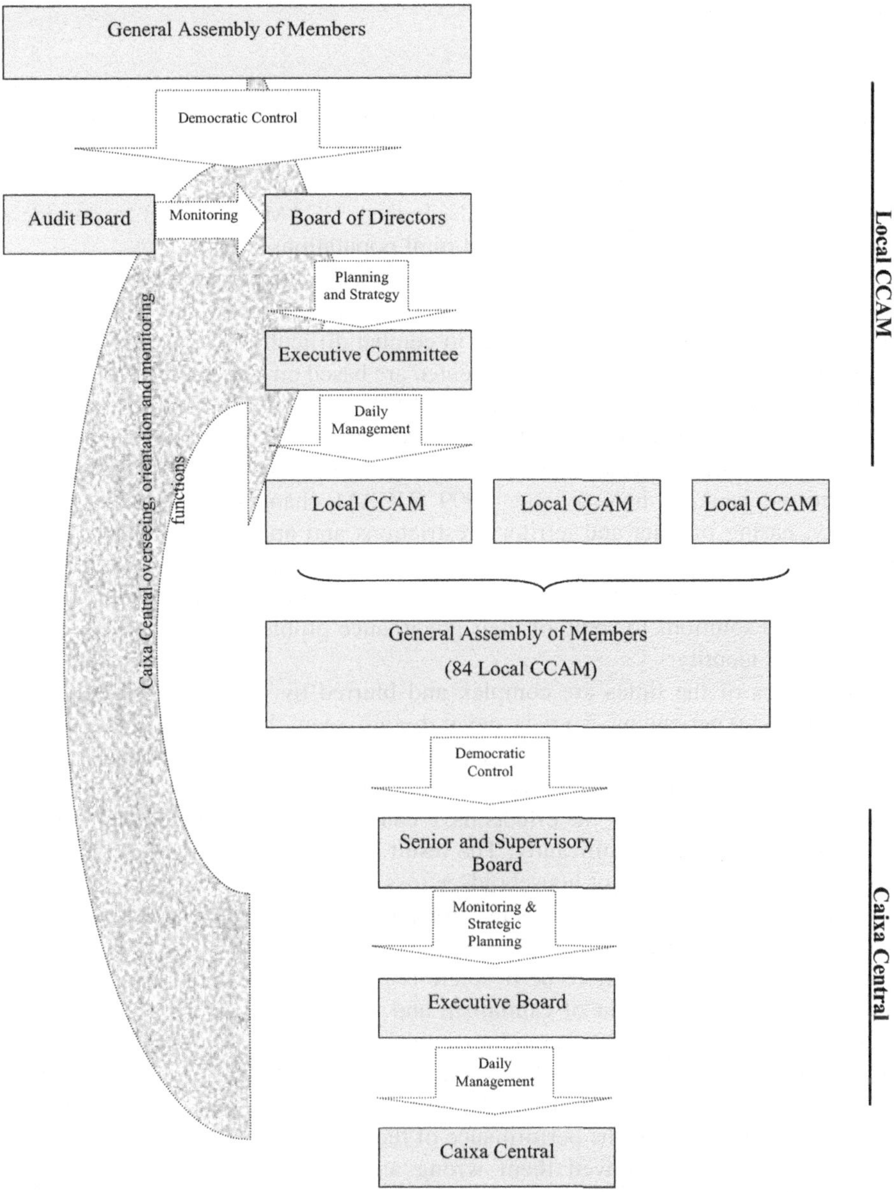

Fig. 5 Governance Structure of the SICAM. *Source*: Cabo (2012)

5 Conclusions

The Portuguese cooperative credit system is a typical example of how public policy can influence the development of cooperative credit institutions. Until the 1990s, CCAM had no control over their existence. Having been developed in a top-down process, the CCAM depended on public funds to carry out their mission and were often used to accomplish political goals. Indeed, CCAM were used to provide a public benefit to the rural economy and rural populations.

Like cooperatives in other sectors, the CCAM increasingly faced survival challenges, partly as a consequence of their cooperative nature. Worldwide cooperatives have adopted varied strategies to combat difficulties inherent to the cooperative form. Most of the solutions presented are based on some degree of deviation from traditional cooperative principles. CCAM implemented a very different strategy. They opted to focus their efforts on cooperative activity and performance, rather than on the cooperative rules themselves. Still, in the face of an increasingly competitive banking industry, the 2009 RJCAM changes ameliorated CCAM activity, easing product and territory restrictions and approximating their governance model to that of corporations. It was a change which distanced the RJCAM from the Cooperative Code. Nevertheless, it is in the Cooperative Code that CCAM can find the solutions to some of their governance problems, without losing their cooperative identity.

The signs of the times are complex and blurred by uncertainties. The world economy is experiencing a crisis never before seen. In Europe, the eurozone countries, above all the most vulnerable, have been caught up in shockwaves that have revealed structural weaknesses and triggered a sovereign debt crisis. With financial resources scarce, the effects have caused economic activity to falter and unemployment to rise significantly. The result has been a plummeting standard of living in many thousands of households across the country.

But 'what doesn't kill us makes us stronger'. This is perhaps the lesson to draw from this crisis. Worldwide, people are rediscovering cooperatives. A governance model considered by many to be obsolete is proving its strengths. Despite being crucial to the development of capitalism and a democratic society, cooperatives have vanished from most economic textbooks, considered a governance type that has outlived its *raison d'être* and neglected by policymakers. Considered by many an obsolete sector, remote from profit maximization and unable to offer sophisticated financial products, the performance of the cooperative banking sector during the recent crisis has proved them wrong and cooperatives have gained new supporters.

Today, more than ever, there is an urgent need to revive the concept of cooperation and investment in the social economy. The focus must be on fostering growth, employment and social cohesion. CCAM in particular have a crucial role to play in the economic recovery of local economies, not only providing finance for economic activity in their local area, but also supporting local social causes, giving their backing to cultural and social initiatives.

The futures of both CCAM and their communities are intrinsically connected. Walking on their own feet for first time in the last four decades, CCAM constantly take decisions to survive and improve their economic and financial health.

References

Associação Portuguesa de Bancos (2015) Statistics. http://www.apb.pt/studies_and_publications/statistics. Accessed 7/5/2015.

Ayadi R, Llewelyn D, Schmidt R, Arbak E, de Groen W (2010) Investigating diversity in the banking sector in Europe: key developments, performance and role of cooperative banks. Centre for European Policy Studies (CEPS), Brussels

Banco de Portugal (2014a) Relatório de Supervisão Comportamental 2013. Portugal de Banco, Lisboa

Banco de Portugal (2014b) Relatório de Estabilidade Financeira 2013. Portugal de Banco, Lisboa

Banco de Portugal (2015) BPstat—statistics online. https://www.bportugal.pt/en-US/Estatisticas/Pages/BPStat%E2%80%93Estatisticasonline.aspx. Accessed 7/5/2015

Cabo P (2003) As Fusões no Sistema Integrado de Crédito Agrícola Mútuo. Master dissertation, University of Minho, Portugal

Cabo P (2012) Essays on governance and failure of co-operative banks: the Portuguese agricultural credit co-operatives. PhD thesis, University of Trás-os-Montes and Alto Douro, Portugal

Crédito Agrícola (2009) Sustainability. Preliminary report. Crédito Agrícola Report and Consolidated Accounts 2008. Crédito Agrícola

Crédito Agrícola (2011) Sustainability. Preliminary report. Crédito Agrícola Report and Consolidated Accounts 2010. Crédito Agrícola

Crédito Agrícola (2013) Crédito Agrícola and its Customer Base. Crédito Agrícola

Crédito Agrícola (2014) Crédito Agrícola Report and Consolidated Accounts 2013. Crédito Agrícola

Crédito Agrícola (2015) Crédito Agrícola Relatório de Sustentabilidade 2013. Crédito Agrícola.

Cuevas C, Fisher K (2006) Cooperative Financial Institutions. World Bank working paper no. 82

EACB (2010) European co-operative banks in the financial and economic turmoil. European Association of Co-operative Banks

FENACAM (2009) Relatório e Contas 2008. Federação Nacional das Caixas de Credito Agrícola Mutuo

Groeneveld H, Sjauw-Koen-Fa A (2009). Co-operative banks in the new financial system. Economic Research Department of the Rabobank Group. Report prepared for the 'Duisenberg Lecture' at the annual meeting of the IMF and World Bank, Istanbul, Turkey, October

Shaw L (2007) Overview of corporate governance issues for co-operatives. Global Corporate Governance Forum, working meeting on corporate governance and co-operatives, London, 8 Feb

The Banker (2014) The Banker top 1000 world banks 2014. The Banker. Special issue, Jul 2014

The Credit Cooperative System in Spain

Gemma Fajardo-García and Francisco Soler-Tormo

Abstract Like other European countries, Spain has a long tradition of cooperative banks. Although some credit unions existed previously, essentially they date from the early twentieth century, originating as institutions founded by medium and small-sized farmers to improve their access to banking services. However, they occupied a marginal position in the financial system until the legislative reforms of the 1970s. During the two last decades of the twentieth century, Spanish cooperative banks suffered a deep crisis, two changes in their organizational model and the shock of transformation and innovation in the financial system. Currently, the sector is made up of 65 small institutions with a relatively small market share: slightly over 4.4 % of total assets. Their model of organization has been threatened by weak cohesion and by not behaving as a true group. The financial crisis that started in 2007 affected Spanish cooperative banks less than other institutions, especially saving banks, because they held higher levels of capital and their business was retail-oriented. The more competitive environment nowadays could jeopardize the valuable principals which inspire the cooperative movement. Economic viability can and must be compatible with the democratic principle of 'one member, one vote', with enhancing ownership participation, with neighbourhood and community, with transparency and with their combination of social and financial objectives.

1 The Establishment and Evolution of the Credit Cooperative System in Spain

Although some credit unions were set up at the end of the nineteenth century, the Spanish credit co-operative movement can be considered to date from the early twentieth century. It followed the French agricultural credit bank model and the basic ideas of Friedrich Wilhelm Raiffeisen, which spread thanks to the social

G. Fajardo-García (✉) • F. Soler-Tormo
University of Valencia, Valencia, Spain
e-mail: Isabel.Fajardo@uv.es; Francisco.Soler@uv.es

S. Karafolas (ed.), *Credit Cooperative Institutions in European Countries*,
Contributions to Economics, DOI 10.1007/978-3-319-28784-3_11

doctrine of the Catholic Church. As in the rest of Europe, it was a collective response by small and medium-sized farmers to being sidelined by the big banks. The nascent cooperativism was given strong institutional backing by the 1906 Farmers Union Law (*Ley de Sindicatos Agrícolas*), which gave professional farming organisations important privileges in the form of tax exemptions and other advantages for rural credit cooperatives. This was the first law in Spain to regulate the mutualist principles and cooperative institutions.

The 1906 law encouraged the spread of farmers' unions and a large number of rural cooperative banks (*cajas rurales*): at the beginning of the 1920s there were around 5000. The model was based on setting up small local cooperative banks linked to the Catholic farmers' unions. Nevertheless, their poor ability to organise themselves as a group and develop a farm credit market condemned them to a marginal position within the Spanish financial system, dominated by the big banking status quo.

However, during the 1960s and 1970s a number of factors roused the cooperative banks from their lethargy and triggered a stage of considerable growth. These factors included:

(a) The beginning of reform in the Spanish financial system, which brought recognition of the rural cooperative banks as credit institutions and a start to harmonising the different monetary financial institutions. The Banking Regulation Law (*Ley de Ordenación Bancaria*) of 1962 expressly stated that *all grades of rural cooperative banks shall be reorganised to strengthen their purposes at the service of agricultural credit. Without prejudice to the discipline to which they are subject at present, the Treasury Ministry shall exercise the inspection and control of the rural cooperative banks to ensure their compliance with their exclusive purposes and coordination with general credit policy.* In 1971 they came under the regulatory control of the Bank of Spain and their credit activities were regulated by the 1978 regulations.

(b) A period of great economic growth and modernisation in agriculture increased the demand for farm credit. It was met in part by institutions such as the rural cooperative banks that were part of the fabric of the farming world and were particularly well-adapted to the peculiarities of agricultural loans. The slogan *el dinero del campo para el campo* (the countryside's money for the countryside) was a call to place available funds on deposit in the rural cooperative banks, where in part they would be returned to the sector in the form of credit and loans.

(c) The development of farming was accompanied by the spread of associationism as a way to generate greater value added for the farmers. This led to a proliferation of farming cooperatives, particularly for marketing and processing agricultural products.

As a result of the spread of credit cooperatives, the sector as a whole organised itself around a central body, Caja Rural Nacional. This was set up in 1957 and acted as the interlocutor between government and the rural cooperative banks with more limited geographical scope. In turn, provincial rural cooperative banks formed through the conglomeration of smaller-scale ones became consolidated as the model throughout most of Spain. In this way, local- or district-level cooperatives disappeared from most of the country except in the East and South, where, in response to their marginalisation by the central body, they created a separate, independent organisation of their own.

The 1970s also saw a proliferation of non-farming credit cooperatives in urban areas. As a result of the advantages offered for setting up cooperatives and the difficulties in establishing private banks, around 40 'urban' credit cooperatives were born during this period, linked to professional bodies or to cooperative company groups. Nevertheless, bad management in many cases and the deregulation of the banking sector led to the disappearance of practically half of these. The Mondragón group's *Caja Laboral Popular*, set up in 1959, deserves a special mention as an example of the dynamic role that a credit cooperative can play in the leadership of a group of industrial and commercial cooperative companies in the Basque country.

In response to the greater presence of credit cooperatives, specific regulations were drawn up to govern them. Three major provisions of Royal Decree 2860/78 aimed to make these institutions take part in the transformation of the Spanish financial system: making the organic and functional characteristics of the different credit and savings institutions at the same time more homogenous and more flexible; establishing disciplinary rules to ensure their financial solidity; and making the governing bodies of financial institutions more democratic.

All these measures helped to increase the presence of the credit cooperatives in the financial system. Nevertheless, strong growth without the consolidation of sufficient reserves, the lack of professionalism in their management and the effects of an agricultural crisis halted their expansion and led to a number of serious problems that hindered their consolidation and cast the rural cooperative banks into deep crisis in the 1980s. As a result, around forty rural cooperative banks disappeared between 1984 and 1990, the disarray of their existing organisation led to the liquidation of *Caja Rural Nacional* and a new structure had to be created for this sector.

The crisis of the 1980s was influenced by the difficulties that the farming sector was going through and, above all, by managers who ignored the rules of prudence, concentrated risks without due control and operated in sectors where they did not have sufficient information or experience. This slack management was compounded by scanty observance of the cooperative principles as regards the openness of their relations with the members. The absence of external checks on the central organisations and poor group cohesion are further factors that made it difficult to prevent the crisis and to adopt appropriate measures to tackle it.

The resulting situation made it necessary for the authorities to intervene to re-establish confidence in these cooperative institutions and in the reorganisation of the sector. The reorganisation plans that were drawn up in 1984 provided for a series of measures to restructure the assets of the crisis-hit cooperative banks. At the same time, the coordination needs of the credit cooperatives were met by the creation of *Grupo Asociado BCA-CRA*, following the model of the French *Credit*

Agricole. Although this Associated Group did not last long, it deserves at least some attention. On the one hand, *Banco de Crédito Agrícola* (BCA), a state-owned bank entrusted with channelling official credit to farming, assumed the leadership of the group and acted as its controller. On the other hand, the associated rural cooperative banks (*cajas rurales asociadas*—CRA) placed at its disposal a dense network of branches throughout Spain, channelled a large part of their cash to the public bank and submitted to certain directives from it. The new logotype created at that time to relaunch the group, the yellow ears of wheat on a green background, have remained as the symbol of the rural cooperative banks.

However, later developments showed up major cracks that led to the breakdown of the Associated Group in 1988, only 4 years after the agreement had been signed, as a result of the imbalance of power in the governing bodies and the attitude of the authorities towards the disappearance of some rural cooperative banks. For instance, officials encouraged the absorption of rural cooperative banks by savings banks while *Banco de Crédito Agrícola* stood by and did nothing.

In view of this situation, the Spanish cooperative credit institutions looked for an alternative form of organisation. In 1990, they set up *Banco Cooperativo Español, S.A.* Its shareholders were the rural cooperative banks that voluntarily joined it and the German cooperative group *Deutsche Genossenschaftsbank (DG Bank). Banco Cooperativo Español* tries to provide banking services to its members which they would be unable to access individually, owing to their small size, and to take on the role of the central body of the rural cooperative banks group, using the rural cooperative banks' association (*Asociación Española de Cajas Rurales—AECR*) and specialist companies such as its IT and insurance arms (*Rural Informática* and *Rural Grupo Asegurador—RGA*). The result is a decentralised system with voluntary integration.

Since then, the consolidation of this model of organisation has been threatened by weak cohesion and by not behaving as a true group, leading to significant pull-outs by some rural cooperative banks. This was the situation when the international financial crisis struck in 2007, although its effects on the Spanish credit cooperatives were relatively minor. Because of their smaller size, they were not as badly affected by the liquidity strains on the international markets, they had not taken extraordinary risks in large property developments and they kept their business close to what has been being called for since then: *back to basics*. As a result, they have not suffered major solvency problems, although the low general efficiency of the sector still needs to be remedied.

Consequently, strong sector concentration is being encouraged, both by conventional mergers or through what are known as Institutional Protection Systems (SIP), in which the associated institutions retain a certain degree of management independence.

Although in general the crisis did not damage the solvency of cooperatives as much as that of other institutions, the government proposed strict regulations for them, similar to Law 26/2013 for saving banks and banking foundations. Finally it was put off because of the cooperatives' opposition and the proximity of elections in 2015 (Table 1).

Table 1 Historical data on number of banks, branches, employees and total assets of credit cooperatives in Spain

	Number of institutions	% of banking system	Number of operative branches	% of banking system	Number of employees	% of banking system	Total Assets (10^6 €)	% of banking system
1945	29							
1950	41							
1960	58							
1970	169							
1980	155	42.8	2668	10.3	9731	4.0	3371	3.5
1981	147	41.2	2841	10.3	10,347	4.1	4241	3.6
1982	154	40.7	3048	10.3	10,866	4.3	5060	3.7
1983	153	40.7	3197	10.3	10,880	4.4	5801	3.7
1984	149	40.4	3315	10.4	10,896	4.5	6091	3.3
1985	146	40.1	3350	10.3	10,823	4.4	7352	3.6
1986	138	38.9	3388	10.4	10,225	4.2	8406	3.2
1987	129	37.3	3248	9.8	10,153	4.2	9439	3.2
1988	117	35.0	3029	9.0	9674	4.0	10,072	3.1
1989	110	33.0	2890	8.4	9592	3.9	10,839	2.8
1990	107	32.7	2919	8.3	9968	4.0	12,321	2.9
1991	106	32.8	3018	8.7	10,643	4.2	14,154	3.0
1992	101	31.7	3080	8.7	11,016	4.4	15,548	3.0
1993	100	31.6	3072	8.7	11,225	4.5	17,938	2.9
1994	99	31.3	3107	8.7	11,195	4.5	20,151	3.0
1995	97	30.5	3195	8.8	11,626	4.7	23,399	3.2
1996	97	31.0	3311	8.9	12,024	5.0	25,983	3.4
1997	97	31.6	3468	9.2	12,804	5.3	28,551	3.5
1998	97	32.3	3607	9.3	13,292	5.5	31,721	3.6
1999	94	32.4	3744	9.6	13,855	5.8	34,811	3.6

(continued)

Table 1 (continued)

	Number of institutions	% of banking system	Number of operative branches	% of banking system	Number of employees	% of banking system	Total Assets (10^6 €)	% of banking system
2000	92	32.7	3888	10.0	14,495	6.1	39,601	3.7
2001	89	31.7	4091	10.6	15,580	6.5	46,069	3.9
2002	85	30.9	4275	11.1	16,414	6.9	50,485	3.9
2003	84	31.2	4460	11.3	17,067	7.1	56,162	3.9
2004	83	31.2	4563	11.3	17,650	7.3	65,132	3.9
2005	83	30.9	4657	11.2	18,395	7.4	82,180	4.0
2006	83	30.5	4771	11.0	19,382	7.6	98,123	4.1
2007	83	29.6	4953	11.0	20,429	7.6	110,765	3.9
2008	81	28.3	5097	11.2	20,940	7.7	115,846	3.7
2009	81	28.9	5043	11.4	20,757	7.9	122,933	3.9
2010	80	29.0	5018	11.7	20,545	8.0	125,702	4.0
2011	74	30.2	4928	12.4	20,036	8.2	126,891	4.0
2012	68	29.6	4832	12.4	19,674	8.4	131,649	4.2
2013	65	27.0	4651	13.9	18,910	8.9	125,593	4.4

Source: Up to 1980, Martín Mesa (1988). From 1980, Bank of Spain and UNACC

2 The Current Model

Credit cooperatives are governed by Law 13/1989[1] (LCC), by the Regulations pursuant thereto (adopted by Royal Decree 84/1993[2] (RLCC) and, secondarily, by the national Cooperatives Act, Law 27/1999[3] (LC). The Spanish Constitution (CE) orders the authorities to encourage cooperatives through appropriate legislation (CE art. 129.2). Additionally, cooperatives are subject to special fiscal legislation (LRFC, Law 20/1990[4]) and to accounting rules adapted to their peculiarities (Order EHA/3360/2010[5]).

2.1 *Governance and the Mutual Spirit: The Reasons for the Creation of Cooperative Banks*

The Spanish credit cooperatives were set up to meet the financial needs of their members, who were united by a common bond. The rural cooperative banks were created to address the financial needs of farmers and farm cooperatives, essentially, and the professional credit cooperatives, which arose at a later date, were associated with professional bodies such as the official colleges of engineers, architects, pharmacists or lawyers.

Apart from these cases, most credit cooperatives have resulted from mergers or reorganisation processes among other cooperatives.

Depending on how they were formed, the credit cooperatives can be classified into:

(a) Rural cooperative banks set up by farmers and farmers' cooperatives to meet their financial needs
(b) Local rural cooperative banks formed by splitting off the credit section of a farmers' cooperative
(c) District, provincial or regional level rural cooperative banks, formed by the amalgamation of farmers' cooperative credit sections and/or local rural cooperative banks or set up on the initiative of federations of farmers' cooperatives at these levels.
(d) Credit cooperatives founded by professional bodies such as the official colleges of engineers, architects, pharmacists or lawyers. The only remaining ones of this type are those of the engineers and architects, as the others have changed their form or been absorbed by other credit institutions.

[1] http://www.boe.es/buscar/act.php?id=BOE-A-1989-12296
[2] http://www.boe.es/buscar/act.php?id=BOE-A-1993-4684
[3] http://www.boe.es/buscar/act.php?id=BOE-A-1999-15681
[4] http://www.boe.es/buscar/act.php?id=BOE-A-1990-30735
[5] http://www.boe.es/buscar/act.php?id=BOE-A-2010-20034

(e) Credit cooperatives set up as the financial instrument of a cooperative company group in the industrial, commercial or service sector. This is the case of Mondragón's *Caja Laboral Popular* and of *Caixa Popular*.

In every case, initially the founders and members of the credit cooperatives shared much the same background, but over time, as the cooperatives have grown and extended their membership to other more heterogeneous and urban groups, the common bond has weakened. Nevertheless, permission to establish a new credit cooperative can be refused if the members have no shared interests or financial needs (RLCC art. 5.2).

The governance of credit cooperatives is shared between the membership (general meeting and board of directors) and the management.

The cooperative principle of participatory democracy is reflected in the voting rights that every member possesses; in the principle of 'one member, one vote' in most credit cooperatives; and in the legal limits on the number of votes that may be cast by any one member (not more than 2.5 % for an individual and 20 % for a legal person) and by legal persons that are not cooperatives (not more than 50 % in total). However, multiple voting rights, and even rights proportionate to capital, are possible in first and second tier cooperatives, and member participation in general assemblies is more restricted than in the case of bank shareholders (LCC arts. 9.2 and 7.3).

Firstly, the General Meeting need only be convened 15 days before it is held, compared to month for a bank. Secondly, if it is the Annual General Meeting it is advertised on the a notice boards in the headquarters and branches, though if the cooperative has over 500 members it must also be advertised in one of the highest-circulation newspapers in the province (LC art. 24.1), whereas notices of bank general meetings have to be published in the Official Gazette of the Company Register and the bank's web page or, if it does not have one, in a newspaper with a province-wide circulation.

In the larger cooperatives, preparatory meetings are often held locally in order to facilitate participation by their geographically scattered membership. However, it is not necessary to have held all the preparatory meetings before the meeting of delegates can take place, as 75 % is sufficient, nor do all the delegates elected at the preparatory meetings need to be present, as the quorum for holding the meeting of delegates and for the agreements it adopts to be valid is 40 %. Holding preparatory assemblies does not really make it easier for cooperative members to take part. Cooperative law has not yet provided for telematic attendance at meetings, as is allowed for commercial companies. Using the new information and communication technologies would undoubtedly facilitate democratic participation by credit cooperative members.

The data on member attendance and participation in the cooperatives' meetings could lead to the conclusion that there is a democratic deficit. However, it has been shown that when the members internalise the decisions as being important they mobilise, and they can even reject decisions that had been taken by the management and the board of directors, as has been seen recently on various occasions.

The general meeting elects the board of directors, which is normally made up of 12 members, mostly prominent members of the cooperative (68 %) or directors of other associated cooperatives (20 %); independent directors are infrequent (1.7 %). The system by which the credit cooperative directors are elected makes it difficult for the members to take part democratically. Firstly, the directors are elected through closed lists. Secondly, candidacies can be presented by members of the board of directors or by members with high percentages of representation (5 % of the members, 250 members or 25 % of the share capital). Removal of credit cooperative directors is subject to more conditions than in the case of a bank director, and two-thirds of the votes are required to hold them to account, compared to the simple majority that is required in a bank.

Although the general manager of a credit cooperative is not an organ of the cooperative but an employee, he or she is subject to conditions as regards incompatibilities, prohibitions and limitations in the performance of his or her functions that are similar to those for the directors. The general manager's powers are essentially concerned with the management and administration of the business, but include convening the board of directors and deciding on transactions with third parties, a decision which in other types of cooperatives lies with the members and must be allowed by the cooperative's statutes.

In recent years the credit cooperatives have made great efforts to improve the qualifications and professionalism of their managers, but some shortcomings are still apparent. The long service of the managers, around 20 years, gives an indication of their considerable independence from the governing bodies.

The European rules on assessing the suitability of members of the management bodies and those responsible for key functions were transposed to the RLCC by Royal Decree 256/2013. One of the requirements for obtaining and conserving authorisation as a credit cooperative is that the directors must be persons of recognised commercial and professional probity who have the adequate knowledge and experience to fulfil their functions and are in a position to exercise good governance of the institution. These requirements also apply to the general manager or similar positions and to those responsible for internal control functions and other key posts for the daily conduct of the institution's business. Information on all the above must be recorded in the Bank of Spain's Register of Senior Officers (*Registro de Altos Cargos*).

A natural or legal person may become a member by requesting membership and meeting the conditions laid down in the cooperative's statutes, which usually require ownership of at least one registered share documenting a contribution to capital of no less than 60 Euro (LCC art. 7). This contribution may be remunerated within the limits provided in law in the event of there being sufficient net income or freely-distributable reserves (RLCC art. 10).

Reimbursement of capital when a member leaves the cooperative has been limited since 2004, when Spain extended the obligation to draw up annual accounts in accordance with International Accounting Standards (IAS) to all credit institutions. Contributions to capital are reimbursed in the conditions set out in RLCC art. 10, and only if authorised by the board of directors. In no case may reimbursement be authorised if this would lead to shortfalls in the mandatory capital requirement, reserve or solvency ratio cover (LCC art. 7.4).

2.2 The Bank's Activities with Members and Non-members

The corporate object of Spanish credit cooperatives is to serve the financial needs of their members and others by pursuing the activities proper to credit institutions (LCC art. 1). Consequently, they operate with their members for preference but can engage in credit operations with non-members with up to 50 % of their total assets (not including operations with members of member cooperatives, the investment of spare cash or the purchase of shares).

In practice, the credit cooperatives have universalised their clientele far beyond their agricultural origins by accepting new customers in two main ways: accepting them directly as members through a small contribution to the share capital (normally 60 €) or accepting members of an associated cooperative (agricultural, industrial or, less frequently, service or retail, in which case the initial contribution tends to be even smaller). In this way, the membership of Spanish credit cooperatives, around 2.5 million, approximately matches the number of customers involved in loan operations. This is because the credit cooperatives usually make membership one of the conditions for granting a credit or loan. However, the clientele of the cooperative banks as deposit takers is over ten million, as their customers include their members' families, among others.

Lastly, it should be pointed out that in their business activities, the credit cooperatives do not normally make a distinction in the treatment of their member and non-member customers.

2.3 Other Services: Insurance, Stockbroking, Etc.

Credit cooperatives are considered credit establishments (Royal Decree 1298/1986) and may engage in all the types of lending, borrowing and service operations that other credit institutions are permitted to undertake, laid out in Directive 2006/48/EC (article 3 of the credit cooperatives law). Those that require a certain scale are normally provided by the central organisations (*Banco Cooperativo Español* or its specialist companies).

Credit institutions are also allowed to compete with stockbroking companies, so the credit cooperatives can operate directly on the stock exchange. Grupo Caja Rural has an on-line stockbroking service, RuralBols@, which can undertake all types of stock market operations and also provides information to help its customers to optimise their stock market investments.

However, the cooperative credit institutions account for a relatively small proportion of stock or securities market issues, both because of their relatively small individual size and because they have less need of wholesale capital market funding. The members' contributions to the share capital of the cooperatives cannot be traded on the Spanish stock market and their issues of quoted securities are very small: between subordinate bonds, securitised assets and mortgage debentures, they make up no more than 1 % of the total securities issued by credit institutions.

Other products and services that the credit cooperatives normally offer in addition to traditional banking and stock broking include on-line banking, credit and debit cards, mutual funds, the *Telepeaje* toll tag system, renting, insurance, pension plans, a property portal or ticket sales for shows, exhibitions, sporting events, etc.

2.4 The Relation Between Local, Regional and Central Banks

The Spanish financial system is currently undergoing an extraordinary transformation and the credit cooperatives are no exception in this respect. All the credit cooperatives belong to the National Union of Credit Cooperatives (*Unión Nacional de Cooperativas de Crédito*), which advises its members and publishes the most important information on its sector. Most of them also belong to the Spanish Association of Rural Cooperative Banks (*Asociación Española de Cajas Rurales*) and form the *Grupo Caja Rural*, which is headed by *Banco Cooperativo Español, S. A*. This bank provides financial services to its associates and is complemented by other companies in the group such as the IT company *Rural Servicios Informáticos*, the fund manager *GesCooperativo*, the insurance company *Seguros RGA*, or the property company *Rural Inmobiliaria*. The German cooperative groups *DZ Bank* (formed by the acquisition of GZ Bank by DG Bank in 2001) and *R + V Insurance* have holdings in all of these. This setup follows a federated bank model inspired by decentralisation, subsidiaries, solidarity, cooperation and territoriality.

Despite having been set up in the 1990s, the *Grupo Caja Rural* structure is not completely consolidated. *Caja Laboral Popular*, associated with the Mondragón cooperative group, has always remained aloof, while *Cajamar*, the largest of the originally rural cooperative banks, split off because of management disagreements and created an alternative group called *Banco Social y Cooperativo* (Social and Co-operative Bank), which accounts for over the 44 % of the total assets of credit cooperatives in Spain.

The Bank of Spain's aim to set up a single Institutional Protection System under the umbrella of *Banco Cooperativo Español* has not so far come into being and the direction that the group is taking at the moment is to consolidate a number of regional cooperative groups with relatively weak links to the central organisation.

As a result, totally independent local, district and regional institutions currently coexist, although the smaller ones are likely to join higher-tier cooperatives, whether by being absorbed or with a certain degree of autonomy, constituting a hybrid system.

2.5 The Minimum Capital for the Establishment and Functioning of a Cooperative Bank

Spanish law, in application of European directives, requires certain minimum levels of capital, fully subscribed and paid up, in order to engage in banking activities. The general level of 5 million euros can be lower when the institution only operates in a limited sphere. For instance, the minimum for credit cooperatives that operate in municipalities with 100,000 or fewer inhabitants is 1.05 million euros of equity, while for a sphere not exceeding the autonomous region it is 3.6 million euros and 4.8 million euros if it exceeds this sphere.

The credit cooperatives are also subject to the latest financial regulations adopted after the crisis in Spain, following the criteria of the European Union and the Basle III accords. The most important achievement has been the implementation of the framework for cooperation in the control of supervision and solvency within the Single Supervisory Mechanism (SSM) [*Regulation (EU) No 468/2014 (ECB/2014/17) of 16 April 2014*]. This includes setting minimum reserves, updating the deposit guarantee systems, uniform rules and procedures for the restructuring and resolution of credit institutions with problems, measures against market abuse, fiscal considerations and strengthening investor protection. The institutions supervised, which can receive assistance under the European Stability Mechanism, are classed as 'significant' or 'less significant' institutions. The second group, the 'less significant' institutions, are almost all Spanish credit cooperatives and are supervised directly by the Bank of Spain. Only one credit cooperative, *Cajamar,* is considerate 'significant' and is therefore supervised by the European Central Bank (ECB). This new legal framework for credit institutions is reflected in Law 10/2014 of 26 June 2014 and Royal Decree 84/2015, which completed the transposition of Directive 2013/36/EU of the European Parliament and of the Council of 26 June 2013 on access to the activity of credit institutions and the prudential supervision of credit institutions and investment firms, and other European regulations.

Since the financial crisis, increased emphasis has been placed on monitoring compliance with the equity requirements in relation to risky assets. In general, the Spanish credit cooperatives show greater ease in meeting the 9 % minimum requirement (increased in January 2013) and the instruments that make up their equity are also of better quality. In fact, Spanish cooperative banks typically hold around 2–2.5 % more capital than commercial or savings banks. Moreover, tier 1 common equity or core capital (common equity and reserves) make up 88 % of the total equity of the credit cooperatives, compared to 73 % for the banks and savings banks. The excess solvency of the Spanish credit cooperatives is largely due to their policy of retaining between 65 and 80 % of their annual profits.

2.6 The Guarantees System in Cooperative Banks

The credit cooperatives, like other credit establishments, are subject to a complex system of guarantees to ensure their liquidity and solvency, over and above the capital requirements referred to in the previous section.

On the one hand, they are governed by a special administrative supervision system (Law 26/1988 for individual institutions and Law 5/2005 for financial conglomerates). On the other hand, like the banks and savings banks before them, the credit cooperatives have had to set up a specific deposit guarantee fund (required by Royal Decree Law 18/1982) to guarantee the deposits placed with them and the restructuring and refloating of credit institutions in difficulties. If a credit cooperative or any other credit institution became insolvent, the respective fund could offer financial assistance such as non-refundable grants, guarantees, loans on favourable terms, subordinate financing, or the acquisition of damaged or unprofitable assets; it could also help to restructure the institution's capital by subscribing capital increases.

Royal Decree-Law 16/2011 of 14 October 2011 created the new Credit Institution Deposit Guarantee Fund through fusion of the three above-mentioned specific funds. Its purpose and function is limited to guaranteeing deposits held by credit institutions and its old function of strengthening their solvency has been taken over by the Fund for Orderly Bank Restructuring (FROB, the abbreviation of its Spanish name). The Guarantee Fund is made up of contributions from the credit institutions. It is governed by the rules of Directive 2009/14/EC, Directive 2014/49/EU and Law 10/2014 (mentioned in Sect. 2.5).

In addition, *Grupo Caja Rural* has voluntarily set up a Solidarity Fund to forestall and, if necessary, solve insolvency or mandatory equity cover requirement situations among its members.

To address the 2008 crisis, following the programme of assistance to Spain for recapitalising its financial system agreed in the Memorandum of Understanding of 20 July 2012, the Spanish government took extraordinary measures which included setting up the above-mentioned Fund for Orderly Bank Restructuring (FROB—*Fondo de Reestructuración Ordenada Bancaria*) through Royal Decree Law 9/2009. The purpose of this fund is to manage credit institution reorganization processes and help to reinforce their equity. The fund can be employed to restructure institutions with weaknesses in their economic and financial situation, and also to reinforce the equity of institutions without any weaknesses or solvency problems.

Should a credit cooperative undergo a banking reorganization process, the FROB could contribute to its funds by subscribing or acquiring contributions to its capital. Furthermore, Law 9/2012 also created the Company for the Management of Assets Resulting from Bank Restructuring (SAREB, the abbreviation of its

Spanish name, *Sociedad de gestión de activos procedentes de la reestructuración bancaria,* also known as the 'bad bank'). This company can receive the assets and liabilities arising from the restructuring process. However, as already mentioned, so far the credit cooperatives have not presented solvency problems and have not been involved in restructuring processes for this reason.

What they are engaged in, however, are integration processes to increase their size. This integration can take place through mergers, general assignment of assets and liabilities, the creation of second-tier cooperatives or cooperative groups, or Institutional Protection Systems (SIP). At all events, the measures introduced by the government to confront this crisis are available to the credit cooperatives just as they are to the other credit institutions.

A peculiarity of the Spanish system is that while the supervision of the credit institutions' solvency falls to the Bank of Spain, the Autonomous Communities (regions) also possess prudential supervision powers, cooperating with the Bank of Spain in this respect.

2.7 Profit Distribution in Credit Cooperatives

Spanish credit cooperatives differ widely in their distribution of surpluses. Once the balance has been determined, including the proceeds of lending to non-members and capital gains or extraordinary income of all kinds, the losses from previous years, tax liabilities and interest on paid-up capital are deducted.

Interest may be paid on the capital contributed by members if this is allowed by the cooperative's statutes. Such returns are limited to a rate no higher than six points above the statutory rate of interest and conditional on the cooperative's meeting the solvency ratios and minimum equity requirements and on there being no losses carried over. They may not be counted as operating costs or expenses.

Out of any available surplus, at least 20 % must be assigned to provisioning the mandatory reserve fund and at least 10 % to the education and promotion fund (this provision is tax-deductible up to a maximum of 30 %). Both of these funds are non-distributable except in the event of the cooperative's changing its form and the latter is also not attachable (with the exception of the immovable property of the cooperative).

The data from the years previous to the financial crisis give a general picture of the accounting profit's being distributed to taxes (around 15 %), interest on capital contributions (10 %) when allowed, and the remaining 75 % constituting the available surplus. The available surplus is mainly assigned to mandatory and voluntary reserves (80 %), the education and promotion fund (12 %) and dividends to cooperative members and other purposes (8 %).

2.8 *Tax Policy for the Credit Cooperative System*

Like other cooperatives, credit cooperatives are subject to a special tax system under the Cooperative Tax Regime Law (Law 20/1990) and, in the Basque Country, the region's autonomous rules (*normas forales*), and by Decree 1345/1992 which regulates the tax on the consolidated profits of cooperative society groups.

Under Law 20/1990, the credit cooperatives' profits are liable to company tax. Those obtained in the course of their ordinary activities are taxed at 25 % and their extraordinary profits at the general rate of 30 %. The Basque country's tax legislation generally applies lower company tax rates. As a result, credit cooperatives pay company tax on all their profits at 28 %.

Credit cooperatives enjoy other tax benefits under Spanish and Basque law, such as in the capital transfer tax and stamp duty on acts of establishment, capital increase, merger, split, award and cancellation of loans, in the acquisition of goods and rights for the education and promotion fund and in the economic activities tax (95 % tax relief).

2.9 *Credit Cooperatives Mainly Act as Deposit-Takers*

Because of their size and operative limitations, the credit cooperatives have traditionally behaved mainly as deposit-takers in a system in which the private commercial banks have obtained inter-bank funding from saving banks and credit cooperatives.

This situation changed considerably with the extraordinary expansion of credit between 2001 and 2007, when the credit extended to resident sectors of the Spanish economy grew far more than deposits. The resident private sector deposit-to-loan ratio of the cooperative banks fell from 119 % in the year 2000 to 94 % in 2010, while the ratios for the banking system as a whole were respectively 93 % and 80 %. As a result, credit cooperatives have been relatively well-insulated from the liquidity problems that the Spanish banking system has experienced during the financial crisis.

2.10 *Margins and Interest Rate Policy*

Because of their retail banking orientation and dense network of branches, particularly in places that other credit institutions do not reach, the profit and loss accounts of Spanish credit cooperatives present certain peculiarities. On the one hand, credit cooperatives obtain higher interest margins than banks and savings bank, but on the other hand, their operating costs are higher. As a result, their pre-tax profits (measured as a percentage of average total assets) are slightly lower

Table 2 Interest margin and pre-tax profits as a percentage of average total assets

	2005	2007	2010	2013
Interest margin				
– Private banks	1.04	0.98	1.10	1.98
– Savings banks	1.64	1.51	1.12	
– Credit co-operatives	2.31	2.30	1.56	1.58
Pre-tax profits				
– Private banks	0.91	1.13	0.50	0.42
– Savings banks	0.80	1.15	0.13	
– Credit co-operatives	1.07	0.97	0.28	0.30

Source: Bank of Spain, AEB, UNACC

than the average for the financial system as a whole. These high operating costs and consequently lower efficiency are one of the main weaknesses of the Spanish credit cooperatives in view of the likelihood of a more competitive future (Table 2).

3 The Importance of Credit Cooperatives in the National Banking Market

The cooperative credit system in Spain has a relatively low market share: around 4.4 % of the total assets of the banking system at the end of 2013. Nevertheless, in recent years its relative weight has increased, although moderately, following a slight decline during the years when the property boom was at its height (Table 3).

The growth of credit cooperative branches has been greater than in the banking system overall, reaching 11.7 % of the total. This share is considerably higher in rural areas, where the credit cooperatives play an important role in the financial integration of districts that are neglected by other intermediaries. Thanks to this network, they take around 6.5 % of resident private sector deposits, although this percentage varies widely in different parts of Spain. The cooperatives take more than 15 % of the deposits in Navarre, the Basque Country, Castile-La Mancha, Andalusia and Murcia, but under 2 % in Madrid, Catalonia and Galicia. In spite of the progress that has been made, the branch network of most cooperative banks in Spain is weak in the main cities and in tourist and commercial areas.

The proportion of deposits in the private sector is higher in relative terms than those of loans and total assets. This is the result of the retail banking character of the credit cooperatives, close to the customer and possessing a dense network of branches. Their lower unit size and links with the geographical areas in which they operate lead to a relatively greater weighting of funding to agriculture and to families. In spite of having diversified their credit operations in recent decades, because their origins lie in rural areas the Spanish credit cooperatives assign a significantly higher proportion of their loans to funding farmers. Around 12 % of the cooperative banks' loans for productive activities goes to the primary sector, compared to 2 % for the banking system as a whole. Equally, the credit

Table 3 Share of the credit cooperative system in the Spanish banking market

	2000	2010
Branches	10.0	11.7
Employees	6.1	8.0
Total assets	3.7	4.0
Liabilities. Resident private sector	7.3	6.4
Lending. Resident private sector	4.9	5.4
Lending. Agriculture	26.7	21.5
Lending. Industry	3.4	4.6
Lending. Construction	2.8	3.6
Lending. Households	5.4	6.6

Source: Bank of Spain

cooperatives' presence in the retail banking sector leads to greater specialisation in funding housing purchases by families, which make up 43 % of their total loans compared to 35 % for the banking system in general.

The changes in the business model have affected their financial performance. Spanish credit cooperatives base their resources on traditional deposit-taking. As mentioned above, their strong local orientation and neighbourhood bank character has allowed them to obtain higher financial margins than the rest of the banking system. Because of this, despite their efficiency problems they have presented higher return on assets (ROA) rates than the banks and savings banks. Nevertheless, because their equity is significantly greater, their return on equity (ROE) ratios have been slightly lower.

The current international financial crisis has affected the Spanish credit cooperatives to a significant degree, as the squeeze on their profit margins has increased and so have bad debts. However, Spanish credit cooperatives are generally encountering fewer problems than other banking institutions, owing to a series of circumstances.

Firstly, while they did take part in the excessive growth of credit in the years running up to the crisis, their expansion slowed during the years of maximum euphoria, when they lost market share (Table 1) to larger institutions that inflated the bubble by resorting to wholesale funding markets. Consequently, the barrier of their smaller size urged them to greater prudence and their comparative disadvantage in accessing international financial markets provided relative isolation from the credit euphoria.

Secondly, the initial impact of the crisis, between 2007 and 2009, was essentially financial and essentially affected international liquidity, so its impact on Spanish institutions, particularly cooperatives, was not very strong. However, from 2009 onwards the crisis affected the real economy badly, severely accentuating the basic imbalances. It was at that point that it hit the Spanish banks' balance sheets hard, through a combination of greater bad debt levels and an accumulation of devalued assets in Spain's heavily indebted economy. As a result, equity was eroded and confidence was lost.

To avoid insolvencies, in June 2009 the Bank of Spain set up the Fund for Orderly Bank Restructuring (FROB), as mentioned in Sect. 2.6, to help any bank in difficulties, encourage their integration, adjust oversized branch networks and ensure healthy balance sheets. The assessments and stress tests that have been carried out have proved satisfactory for the credit cooperatives: unlike some other institutions, no Spanish credit cooperative has needed recapitalisation and their solvency levels are more than adequate (only one small local cooperative, the *Caja Rural de Mota del Cuervo*, needed an 'early intervention' in January 2014, and its problems were solved by its merger with the regional credit cooperative, without any public-sector support). Despite this, the Bank of Spain is persistently calling for sector concentration, not so much on the grounds of solvency problems as of reasons of size and efficiency. In fact, the efficiency ratio of the credit cooperatives, defined as operating costs in relation to financial products, was 43.5 % in 2010 compared to 38 % for the system as a whole.

Nonetheless, strong concentration is indeed taking place among credit cooperatives, both through conventional mergers, splits and assignment of assets and liabilities (RLCC art. 20) and through Institutional Protection Systems (SIPs), as defined by European directives.

4 The Future of the System

In these times of change it is difficult to forecast the definitive future shape of the cooperative credit system in Spain, although a few possibilities may be ventured:

- The number of institutions will be considerably smaller, as they will unite with other cooperatives or join institutional groups. As a result, the major references in credit cooperatives will be *Laboral Kutxa*, which has a strong base in the North, *Cajamar*, which will be joined by other smaller institutions and consolidate into the largest Spanish rural cooperative bank, and all the other cooperatives, which will organise more or less cohesively in a two- or three-tier pyramid structure.
- If the savings banks (which have suffered the crisis more intensely) lose part of their social and local/regional character, as seems likely, the credit cooperatives can reinforce their neighbourhood bank philosophy, based on the cooperative identity, identified with the area where they operate, and on supporting the social economy of which they are a part. The credit cooperatives' role in financial integration in Spain, especially in the rural areas, has grown with the disappearance of the savings banks.
- Their greater solvency and moderation during the 'bubble' has made the Spanish credit cooperatives more crisis-resistant. In principle, this could encourage greater growth than among other financial institutions. However, the predicted lengthy period of sluggish banking credit operations and adjustment in the real

economy would indicate that any progress is likely to be modest and limited by branch network and staffing level resizing to improve efficiency.

- Credit cooperatives are social institutions that have won a significant share of financial activity. The financial crisis has generated a dangerous concentration in a small number of institutions and an excessive homogeneity within the bank system. This combination is the main threat to competition and financial stability. Consequently, one of the cooperatives' challenges is to enhance competiveness and biodiversity in the financial sector and avoid oligopolies. To live up to their potential, credit cooperatives must strengthen their transparency, their ethical behaviour and their governance values.
- The main weaknesses of the Spanish credit cooperatives are their high operating costs and their efficiency ratios. Greater integration could help to overcome these drawbacks and provide economies of scale that would allow them to undertake all types of banking business.
- At all events, the search for solutions in a changing climate could lead to redefining the structure of the cooperative credit system. Progress in the direction of greater integration and global cohesion would be desirable even if a two- or three-tier structure were retained.

Bibliography

Alguacil P (2001) Tratamiento fiscal de las cooperativas de crédito. Revista Jurídica del CIRIEC 12:51–84

Anguren R, Marqués JM (2011) Cooperative and saving banks in Europe: challenges and perspectives. Estabilidad Financiera 20:25–44

Ayadi R, Llewellyn DT, Schmidt RH, Arbak E, De Groen WP (2010) Investigating diversity in the banking sector in Europe: key development. Performance and role of cooperative banks. Centre for European Policy Studies (CEPS), Brussels

Belmonte LJ (2011) El nuevo modelo de negocio de las cooperativas de crédito españolas. Perspectivas futuras. Papeles de Economía Española 130:54–67

Belmonte LJ, Cortés FJ (2010) La concentración del sector de cooperativas de crédito en España. CIRIEC-Revista de Economía Pública, Social y Cooperativa 68:223–246

Belmonte LJ, Cortés FJ, Molina V (2013) Las cooperativas de crédito españolas y la lucha contra la exclusión financiera. Cooperativismo & Desarrollo 21(103):49–55

Boscia V (ed) (2010) Cooperative banking in Europe. Case studies. Palgrave MacMillan, Basingstoke

Chaves R, Soler Tormo F (2004) El gobierno de las cooperativas de crédito en España. CIRIEC-España, Valencia

Fajardo IG (2010) Aspectos de la transformación de las cooperativas de crédito tras la ley de modificaciones estructurales de 2009. Estudios de Derecho del Mercado Financiero. Homenaje al Profesor Vicente Cuñat. Ed. Universitat de Valencia, pp 67–91

Fajardo IG (2012) Medidas Legales de Recuperación del Sector Bancario Español tras la Crisis de 2008. In: (Coord) Newton de Lucca Ed. Direito Recuperacional, Vol 2. Quartier Latin, São Paulo, pp 107–129

Fonteyne W (2007) Cooperative banks in Europe—policy issues. IMF Working Paper WP/07/159

Ibarrondo Dávila P (2002) Cálculo, análisis y control de costes en las cajas rurales. Universidad de Granada-Ciriec España, Granada

Martín Mesa A (1988) La crisis de las cajas rurales españolas y el nuevo modelo del cooperativismo de crédito agrario. Universidad de Granada-Banco de Crédito Agrícola, Granada

Melián A, Palomo RJ, Sanchis JR, Soler F (2006) La investigación en materia de cooperativas de crédito y de grupos cooperativos. CIRIEC-Revista de Economía Pública, Social y Cooperativa 56:25–64

Oliver Wyman (2008) Cooperative bank: customer champion. Oliver Wyman, London

Palomo Zurdo RJ (2000) Pasado, presente y futuro de la Banca Cooperativa en España. CIRIEC-España, Valencia

Sanchis Palacio JR, Palomo Zurdo R (1997) El crédito cooperativo en España. CIRIEC-España, Valencia

Valenzuela F, Valenzuela J (2007) Las cooperativas de crédito en el vigente ordenamiento jurídico español (una visión sintética). En: Estudios de derecho de sociedades y derecho concursal: libro homenaje al Profesor Rafael García Villaverde Vol 3. Marcial Pons, Madrid, pp 1609–1632

Valenzuela F, Valenzuela J (2013) Cooperativas de crédito. En: Vázquez Ruano T (coord) Tratado de derecho de cooperativas. Tirant lo Blanch, Valencia, pp 1175–1202

http://cajarural.com. Visited on Jun 2011

http://www.unacc.com/documentos/Anuario/anuario2013.pdf. Visited on May 2015

www.eurocoopbanks.coop. Visited on Jun 2011

British Credit Unions: Transformation and Challenge

Paul A. Jones

Abstract This paper gives an overview and analysis of the development of the British credit union movement, and highlights current major challenges facing the sector. In 2013, the British Government announced a 35.6 million pounds investment into the sector through the Association of British Credit Unions to support its expansion within British society, particularly within low- and moderate-income communities. The paper will explore the background to this government investment as well as the dynamics of the strengthening and expansion programme it will support. A key element of the expansion programme is the migration of a group of lead credit unions onto a collaborative and shared electronic operating system.

1 Introduction

Credit unions in Great Britain are not-for-profit financial co-operatives that are owned and controlled by their members. By philosophy and legislation, they are limited to serving their members and unlike banks, are not open to the general public. Eligibility for membership is defined by a 'common bond' or field of membership, which may be living or working in the same locality, being a member of an association or organisation, or being employed in a particular sector, profession or company. Unlike banks, credit unions do not seek wholesale funds to finance operations and to build capital; they depend mostly on attracting savings deposits from members to finance lending to members.[1]

[1] Credit unions do sometimes receive grants or capital investments from Government, local municipalities, private or voluntary organisations to support lending particularly to low-income groups. The Government Financial Inclusion Growth Fund, for example, is referred to later in this article.

P.A. Jones, Ph.D. (✉)
Faculty of Education, Health and Community, Research Unit for Financial Inclusion, Liverpool John Moores University, 79 Tithebarn Street, Liverpool L2 2ER, UK
e-mail: P.A.Jones@ljmu.ac.uk

S. Karafolas (ed.), *Credit Cooperative Institutions in European Countries*, Contributions to Economics, DOI 10.1007/978-3-319-28784-3_12

Credit unions were first established in Great Britain in the 1960s, but have only begun to make any significant headway since the late 1990s. At year end 2014, there were 371 British credit unions serving 1,046,623 adult members and around 115,000 junior savers. Total savings on deposit amounted to 1.05 billion pounds; 688 million pounds was out on loan to members and credit union assets totalled 1.24 billion pounds.[2] About 2 % of the British adult population are members of credit unions.

However, credit unions have made making significant progress within certain segments of the financial market. They have grown particularly well in low-income communities, in certain regions of the country and among particular employee and professional groups. In the 10 year period 2003–2013, overall credit union membership increased by 110 %, savings by 169 %, loans by 125 % and assets by 179 % (see Table 1). In many cities and towns around the country, credit unions are establishing themselves as professional and visible co-operative financial institutions. Many of these modernised credit unions typically have between 5000 and 12,000 members with assets in the region of 3 million pounds to 10 million pounds (cf. Jones and Ellison 2011). There are now several credit unions in Britain each with over 30,000 members and with assets around 70–100 million pounds.[3]

2 Establishment and Evolution

2.1 Origins of the British Credit Union Movement

The first credit unions in Britain were established in the 1960s by immigrants to London who, once settled in Britain, found it difficult if not impossible to obtain credit from banks and mainstream financial providers. Often disadvantaged by loan companies charging excessive interest rates[4] (O'Connell 2005), yet familiar with credit unions in their home countries, they came together to create self-help financial co-operatives to serve the needs of their local communities (Jones and Ellison 2011).

The credit union concept spread to other communities in London and to other British cities. These early credit unions were small, local, self-help savings and loans organisations established and run by volunteers inspired by a sense of social purpose. There was a strong focus on serving people on lower incomes through the

[2] Financial Service Authority figures as of September 2012 as reported by ABCUL.

[3] In June 2012, Glasgow Credit Union was the first credit union in Britain to reach £100 million in assets. Glasgow Credit Union has 30,000 members cf. http://www.abcul.org/media-and-research/news/view/251, accessed July 2012.

[4] In the UK there is no interest rate cap on loans. In 2015, home credit companies that target low-income families can typically charge 272 % APR on a £200 loan over a 52 week period. Overall representative rate on loans is 399.7 % APR. Cf http://www.providentpersonalcredit.com (accessed 23/03/2015).

Table 1 British credit union statistics 1994–2014[a]

Year	Number of credit unions	Total assets (£000s)	Savings (£000s)	Loans (£000s)	Members
1994	475	60,742	53,706	49,590	138,582
1995	530	79,945	70,012	64,710	161,502
1996	550	100,348	87,686	81,242	190,825
1997	596	123,979	107,394	98,811	224,674
1998	630	147,940	126,721	121,813	255,596
1999	666	180,633	153,850	147,781	295,826
2000	687	214,977	182,771	174,667	325,058
2001	698	263,404	223,847	205,046	365,934
2002	686	318,877	272,491	246,138	406,564
2003	665	388,872	338,006	284,905	451,819
2004	594	432,031	381,495	314,418	496,254
2005	569	466,728	410,248	341,152	529,521
2006	554	505,034	438,680	363,335	553,892
2007	532	548,034	456,326	403,671	604,945
2008	508	595,142	489,537	441,694	659,281
2009	454	674,152	581,729	464,186	718,322
2010	436	751,483	648,606	506,364	777,454
2011	412	857,918	717,129	575,990	842,209
2012	389	956,614	807,377	605,787	917,544
2013	382	1,086,361	909,633	639,939	948,330
2014	371	1,237,979	1,048,532	687,783	1,046,623

With the exception of number of credit unions and membership, all figures are rounded to the nearest £'000

[a]Statistics supplied by ABCUL (March 2015) based on figures obtained from the regulator

provision of low-cost loans to small savers who had little or no access to other financial institutions. Most credit unions were run from community or church halls, or even from members' own homes, and high priority was given to community involvement, democratic member participation and the personal development of volunteers. These credit unions served often small local neighbourhoods where volunteer staff knew and understood the members (Jones 1999).

Through the 1980s and 1990s, the social and economic deprivation faced by many communities in Britain encouraged the continued development of community-based credit unions, often supported by local authorities as part of their strategic response to the fight against poverty and the regeneration of deprived local communities. Similarly, employee credit unions were also supported by employers as vehicles to assist their staff in achieving financial stability particularly through difficult economic times. With the support of publicly funded grants and resources, and the intervention of local authority development staff, the number of credit unions started to expand rapidly (Jones 1999; Goth et al. 2006). In 1986, there were just 94 British credit unions, but by 2001, there were almost 700, the majority of which were community credit unions serving low-income neighbourhoods.

By the end of the 1990s however, despite the rapid growth in the numbers of credit unions, it was clear that individual British credit unions were not developing at a rate seen in other parts of the world. Most community credit unions serving low income communities remained financially weak, vulnerable and serving less than 200 members (Jones 1999; Ward and McKillop 2005; Goth et al. 2006). The development of credit unions serving employee groups was stronger but still relatively modest, most recruiting less than 1000 members (Jones 1999).

2.2 *Change and Transformation: 1999–2011*

Taking into account the challenge of poor growth, research published in 1999 recognised that credit unions had to adopt a more professional and business-like approach if they were to succeed in the financial market-place (Jones 1999): even in low income communities, credit unions were not reaching many of those whom they were designed to serve. Credit unions began to question the traditional approach to development based on small, tight-knit common bonds, volunteerism and informal collective action.

Instead, credit unions began to promote a more business-focused approach to development based on robust business planning, suitable premises, the introduction of computerised accounting systems and the retention of staff to eliminate dependence upon volunteer labour. This resulted in the strengthening of a number of credit unions and in an increase in the number of mergers as credit unions endeavoured to benefit from economies of scale. From 2001 onwards, despite the registrations of new credit unions, increasing mergers resulted in the overall number of credit unions starting to decline (see Table 1). Over the period 2013–2013, the number of credit unions declined by 42 %, whilst overall membership increased by 110 %.

Around the same time, international research undertaken by the World Council of Credit Unions convinced many British credit unions that if they were to build the capacity to make a lasting impact within low-income communities, a much greater reform would be required than the adoption of basic business practices (Richardson 2000a, b; Branch and Cifuentes 2001; Jones 2004a, b). The transformation of credit unions, as argued for in international studies, demanded a more radical financial, organisational and operational restructuring, known as the ‘new model’ of credit union development (Richardson 2000b; Jones 2004b, 2008).

New model reform was based on seven key elements, regarded by Richardson (2000a) as “doctrines of success”, all of which would present significant challenges to the operation of traditional model British credit unions. The first element is to serve the financial needs of a wider population, rather than focusing entirely on low-income and financially-excluded communities. The second element was the maximisation of savings: traditional credit unions had often concentrated primarily on offering low-cost loans, and only marginally promoted member saving. Without generating the savings of members however, funds for on-lending would remain limited as would the income necessary to build credit union strength.

The third element of new model reform was product diversification, or offering a range of financial products and services in response to people's needs and wants. This was a major challenge for many credit unions, as most had offered a single identical savings and loan product to all. The next three elements of success were operating efficiency, financial discipline and effective self-governance, all of which would demand major reviews of operating practices in credit unions.

The seventh and final element was assimilation. By this was meant the process of bringing the poor into the mainstream economy by providing them with access to comparable financial products and services to those found in conventional financial institutions (Richardson 2000a). It was this final element that challenged many credit unions to rethink their role in low-income communities and the way in which they could offer members pathways to long-term financial inclusion. It was this concern that would result in some credit unions developing into full-service modern financial co-operatives, offering current accounts, insurance, money transmission services and a range of savings and loan products.

3 Legislation and Regulation

Since the turn of the century, the credit union movement, supported by the Association of British Credit Unions Ltd. (ABCUL), has prioritised sound governance and management, the development of sustainable business models and the diversification of products and services in order to strengthen individual credit unions and to expand their membership. However, it also recognised that the slow growth of credit unions was the result of restrictive British credit union legislation and regulation. In fact, by the early 1970s, appropriate credit union legislation and regulation was seen as central to credit union development. The Credit Unions Act, passed in 1979 gave credit unions, for the first time, a legal identity and the means to become secure and safer financial institutions. Under the 1979 Act, all credit unions were regulated by the Registry of Friendly Societies, and had to take out fidelity bond insurance to protect members' assets against theft and fraud.

At the time however, credit unions were regarded by government as small community enterprises and not as co-operative financial institutions that could grow to compete with banks or other financial service providers. The new Act had such a strong focus on mitigating risk that it resulted in legislation that itself restricted and limited growth. From the mid-1990s onwards therefore, British legislation began to be modified and, in some respects, relaxed. Larger common bond sizes were introduced around 1995, and credit unions serving towns of up to 50,000 people began to be accepted. In 1996, a new category of 'live or work' common bond was introduced and, for the first time, those who worked in an area could join a credit union alongside its residents.

After the 1979 Credit Unions Act, the single most important legislative advance for the credit union movement was the passing of the Financial Services and Markets Act (2000). This Act provided the framework for a single regulator for the financial services industry, the Financial Services Authority (FSA) which, in 2002, took over the regulation of credit unions from the Registry of Friendly Societies. A culture of compliance was introduced and credit unions had to meet defined and more rigorous operating standards. They were expected to provide timely and accurate financial returns to the FSA, maintain adequate levels of capital and meet defined standards in liquidity management and provision for loan losses.

The new legislation and regulatory regime brought a range of benefits for credit unions. For the first time, credit unions were no longer restricted to an upper limit on the number of members. The FSA also established the framework for a single Financial Ombudsman for handling complaints and the Financial Services Compensation Scheme (FSCS) to provide overall protection for members. Under the FSCS, for the first time credit union deposits were guaranteed with the same level of protection as the deposits of customers of banks and building societies. As of December 2010, this is now 100 % of the first £85,000 saved in a credit union. The reform implemented in 2002 also opened the way for credit unions to raise secondary capital through subordinated loans from external organisations.

A further legislative advance took place in 2006. Credit unions are the only credit provider in Britain that has by law an interest rate ceiling. Since the 1979 Act, this ceiling had been set at 12.68 % APR (or 1 % per month). This posed a problem for many credit unions operating in low-income communities, as their labour-intensive, low-value and often high-risk loans were not economically viable in any numbers at 12.68 % APR. The Credit Unions (Maximum Interest Rate on Loans) Order 2006 increased the limit on the maximum interest chargeable from 1 to 2 % per month (26.8 % APR). Unlike for all other credit providers however, an interest rate cap was maintained for credit unions. The cap was increased again in April 2014 from 2 to 3 % a month on the reducing balance of the loan (42.6 % APR).

In 2007, the opportunity for a further major advance in credit union legislation arose when the Government announced a review of co-operative and credit union legislation in Great Britain. Following consultation with the sector, this led, by July 2008, to firm proposals being made for legislative reform for both credit unions and industrial and provident societies (HMT 2008). The proposals made by the Government for credit unions were set out in the HM Treasury document, "Proposals for a Legislative Reform Order for Credit Unions and Industrial & Provident Societies in Great Britain" (HMT 2008) and, for the most part, already reflected the wishes of the credit union movement. Following several years of further negotiation, in January 2012, credit union legislation was finally significantly modernised.

From January 2012, the following new legislation came into force:

- The common bond: Credit unions still have to define their common bond or field of membership but they no longer have to prove that all the people able to join

the credit union have something in common. Credit union membership is more open, accessible and flexible. Credit unions can define multiple common bonds and thus be able to provide products and services to different groups of people within the one credit union. However, credit unions with a geographical common bond are limited to an area of two million potential members.
- Corporate membership: Credit unions are no longer limited to providing services to just individuals, they can now choose to offer membership to unincorporated associations and corporate bodies such as companies, partnerships and co-operatives. However corporate members can make up a maximum of 10 % of a credit union's total membership, hold a maximum of 25 % of shares and be granted a maximum of 10 % of the value of the loans in a credit union.
- Interest on savings deposits: All credit unions can now offer variable and guaranteed interest rates on savings deposits if they hold reserves of £50,000 or 5 % of total assets, whichever is higher, providing they can demonstrate to the FSA the capacity to manage and control interest-bearing accounts. Individual credit unions can choose to continue to offer dividends on shares instead of interest, or they can choose to offer dividend-bearing shares and interest-bearing deposits.
- Charging for ancillary services: Credit unions can now charge market rates for ancillary services. Previously credit unions could only pass on the cost of providing a service to members. However the ability to charge fees will only apply to future members, not those already in the credit union.
- Non-qualifying members: These are members who were once part of the common bond but are so no longer (e.g. they have moved away from the area). Previously there was a 10 % limit on non-qualifying membership as a proportion of the overall membership. This is now left to the discretion of the credit union which can set its own rules. This will prevent many people from losing access to financial services when they change their job or home.

4 Government Support for Credit Unions

As member-only, not-for-profit, socially-oriented organisations, credit unions do not pay tax on income from lending. This exemption from taxation reflects the fact that credit unions are recognised by government as serving only their members, as playing an important role in reaching out to people with low incomes and in promoting financial inclusion.

Political and financial support for credit unions by central and local government has gone well beyond providing tax exemptions however. Local government support was particularly high during the 1980s and 1990s when credit unions often formed part of local strategies to tackle poverty and disadvantage. It was with the support of publicly funded grants and resources and the intervention of local authority development staff that credit unions expanded rapidly during this period (Jones 1999; Goth et al. 2006).

Such support had both positive and negative effects. It certainly kick-started the registration of credit unions and assisted their development and growth in the early days. However, as local authorities ultimately recognised, it did not always lead to the longer-term stabilisation and strengthening of credit unions (Morris 1999; LGA 2001). External subsidies to cover costs could sometimes create a culture of grant dependency and confirm an image of credit unions as organisations funded to provide financial services to the poor. Grant funding could sometimes compromise the spirit of enterprise and leadership necessary to build an economically diverse membership: a key to success (McKillop et al. 2007).

It would be unfair, however, to argue that all external financial support undermined the development of credit unions. When properly targeted with defined measurable targets; such support, as confirmed in international studies, can facilitate the significant strengthening of credit unions (Arbuckle 1994; Arbuckle and Adams 2000).

4.1 Financial Inclusion Growth Fund

Progress in credit union development resulted in the UK Government growing in confidence in the ability of credit unions to serve low-income communities (see HCTC 2006). From 2006 to 2011, as part of a strategy to fight financial exclusion, the Labour Government created a Financial Inclusion Growth Fund to expand the availability of affordable credit through credit unions and community development financial institutions (CDFIs). The aim was to enable financially-excluded borrowers to avoid resorting to sub-prime, high-cost loan companies and to instead move into credit union or CDFI[5] membership. Nearly 100 million pounds was invested into the Growth Fund which provided credit unions and CDFIs with capital for on-lending and revenue to cover administrative costs.

Through the Growth Fund, 405,134 affordable loans to low-income members were made, to a total value of over 175 million pounds.[6] Around 90 % of Growth Fund loans were through the circa 100 credit unions contracted to deliver the programme.

Unlike some public subsidies of the past, the Growth Fund was tied to credit unions operating as market-oriented organisations and to their meeting defined targets and operating standards. Growth Fund contracts were awarded only to credit unions that were assessed to have the organisational capacity to deliver affordable credit to large numbers of low-income people. Significantly, the Growth Fund itself had a strengthening effect on these credit unions. Independent evaluation revealed

[5] Community Development Finance Institution—a form of social firm that offers loans in low-income communities. CDFIs are not member owned co-operatives as are credit unions.

[6] http://www.dwp.gov.uk/other-specialists/the-growth-fund/statistics/, accessed July 2012.

that 80 % of Growth Fund lenders improved operations and business practices as a result of the delivery of the programme (Collard et al. 2010).

Overall, the current UK Coalition Government has regarded the delivery of the Growth Fund to be a success. As a result, and to build on this success, in March 2011 it announced the creation of a new credit union modernisation and expansion fund of up to 73 million pounds to replace the Financial Inclusion Growth Fund, which ended the same month. The new fund would not provide further capital for on-lending but rather would aim to modernise delivery and customer support systems so that credit unions, and some CDFIs, could extend products and services to many more people on lower incomes.

Before committing to establishing the new modernisation and expansion fund, from April to September 2011 the Government commissioned a study to explore the potential and the feasibility of modernising those credit unions that are ready to expand (DWP 2011). The report confirmed that a market exists amongst over seven million people on lower incomes for locally provided banking, savings and loan services from trusted providers such as credit unions. More than 60 % of over 4500 people consulted in the study said they would use credit union services if they were available to them. The report concluded that, in order to modernise and expand, credit unions needed to demonstrate a commitment to change, to working more closely together and to making greater use of technology. On the basis of the study, the Government revised its figures and, through the Department of Work and Pensions (DWP), committed to make an investment of up to 38 million pounds over the 3 years 2012–2015. In April 2013, the Association of British Credit Unions Ltd was awarded the Credit Union Expansion Program (CUEP) contract to assist credit unions to sustainably provide services to a million more people and to develop a collaborative business model in order to provide an expanded and modernised service consistently across the country.

5 Current Models of Development

A changing approach to credit union organisation and management, together with the impact of new legislation and regulation and the renewed expectations of government, had already resulted in the emergence of a new vision of effective credit union development among many within the credit union sector. This vision is based on an understanding of credit unions as co-operative financial institutions having the capacity to offer a range of modern financial products and services to meet the varying needs of different segments of the low- and moderate-income market. Integral to the vision is organisational soundness and stability and an emphasis on operating efficiency, financial discipline, good governance and effective management. It envisages credit unions as serving the financial needs of an economically diverse population, within which a focus on low-income members can be preserved.

5.1 *Wide Variety in Organisational Capacity and Product Offerings*

In Britain, credit union are autonomous and independent financial institutions and, as such, take different approaches to organisational management and service delivery, and face distinct challenges and resource issues. The result is a wide variety of credit union models. Credit unions not only vary in size from around 200 members to over 30,000 members, they also vary in the products and services they are able to offer. All British credit unions offer savings and loans products; however, the terms and conditions of these can vary widely. Some credit unions offer just a simple loan and savings product, whilst other more modernised credit unions offer a wider range of savings products, including cash ISAs, and multiple loan and insurance products. A few credit unions have started to offer home equity loans or mortgages. Since 2006, 24 credit unions now offer a current transactional account.

There are now a large number of credit unions that are endeavouring to develop towards becoming modern professional financial co-operatives but have not yet established themselves fully as financially independent organisations. Many have received the financial support of local authorities or other funders and have not yet built the business sufficiently to become independent of external financial support. These credit unions also often have visible high-street premises and paid staff, and endeavour to offer a range of financial services to people on low and moderate incomes. Many still retain a number of volunteers as operational staff, even though most now employ a paid manager.

6 Economic and Organisational Challenges

Most credit unions in Britain face on-going economic and organisational challenges in developing the business and in expanding their membership and assets. Growth depends ultimately on economic strength, organisational capacity and operational efficiency. Recent research studies among London credit unions (Jones and Ellison 2011) and among credit unions in the North East of England and Cumbria (Jones 2012) have revealed a range of difficulties that credit unions typically face in establishing themselves as strong and efficient co-operative institutions.

In London, as elsewhere, there are major challenges for credit unions in maximising income and in reducing costs, in attracting savings and in ensuring effective lending. Many credit unions are not yet generating sufficient income to sustain and develop the business. Expense-to-asset ratios are high, often exacerbated through the operational demands of serving the low income market. As the London study demonstrated, credit unions are endeavouring to develop efficiencies in systems and procedures. This is, however, not easy: many credit union directors and managers lack the experience, staff or resources to make rapid progress in re-engineering the business. The result is that most London credit unions still depend to some extent on external financial or in-kind support to cover basic operating costs (Jones and Ellison 2011).

Long-term development depends on maximising savings, for it is the savings of members that creates the funds to on-lend and thus to generate income. Maximising savings involves attracting an increasing number of people on more moderate incomes with the capacity to save. But the ability to attract a more economically diverse membership depends on offering quality products and services that people want and on using the kinds of modernised, electronic delivery channels that more moderate-income members find attractive. In London, as elsewhere, variations in approach and capacity have resulted in credit unions offering products and services that are so dissimilar from one another as to be inconsistent in quality and in efficiency of service delivery. Even though there are notable exceptions, most individual credit unions lack the resources to develop an attractive range of products and services and to introduce modern IT and electronic systems.

The new credit union legislative reform offers credit unions a new range of new opportunities to maximise savings: these include the introduction of corporate deposits, deferred shares and the ability to pay interest on savings deposits. The possibility of attracting organisations, groups and companies into membership for the first time could be particularly significant for credit unions. However, in the London study not all credit unions had yet developed the capacity, expertise or technology to take full advantage of the new legislation.

Another area of challenge that emerged strongly in the London study was the need for credit unions to develop effective lending at realistic prices both to attract higher-value borrowers and to meet the cost of serving high-maintenance borrowers with low-value loans. For most London credit unions, the lending business was not performing at a rate or size to achieve optimum financial return. The average loan-to-asset ratio among live-or-work credit unions was around 56 %, whereas the World Council of Credit Union recommends that 70–80 % of assets need to be out on loan in order to achieve financial stability (Jones and Ellison 2011).

The challenges faced by credit unions are not just economic, but also concern governance and operational management. There is not always the common vision and focus throughout the credit union sector that is needed to drive credit unions forward—neither is there sufficient staffing in credit unions, particularly at the middle management level, to operate the business effectively. The London study (Jones and Ellison 2011) argued that the expansion of credit union financial services would require significantly higher-level skills and competencies in leadership and strategic planning; organisational management and systems, financial and asset management; credit administration and debt recovery; and human resources. The study maintained that a step change in the strategic thinking of boards and in the overall competence of management would be needed if credit unions as a whole were to develop as co-operative financial institutions with the capacity to serve large numbers of low and moderate income members.

7 The Future of the British Credit Union Movement

The London study revealed a problem with the current model of credit union development. Despite growth and expansion, credit unions overall are finding it difficult to break through as major players in the national financial market. The problem is that development currently depends on each credit union as an autonomous financial co-operative independently strengthening its own management and operational systems. This is resource intensive and expensive, and it results in developments in processes and procedures having to be replicated time and time again in individual credit unions.

This also puts a strain on each individual credit union. Many credit union managers in the London interviews described how credit unions were often understaffed, how existing staff were over-worked, and how difficult it was for them to think strategically whilst being themselves immersed in day-to-day operations. With some notable exceptions, very few credit unions had sufficient staff to develop a middle management structure and sometimes even to fill key roles and responsibilities. This left senior management with little time and energy to concentrate on expanding the business.

Added to this, credit unions are under financial as well as organisational strain. Managers in London explained the ongoing challenges of driving down costs and of generating sufficient income from lending to free themselves from dependency on external subsidies. Even the largest credit unions still had to count on some external financial support.

As credit unions endeavour to manage these organisational and financial challenges, they do so within an increasingly competitive context. To compete in the market place, credit unions need modern and efficient systems in place to deliver quality products and professional and responsive services to their members. The current model of credit union development may be under too much strain to deliver the kind of consistent and accessible service that people seek.

Such challenges have led an increasing number of credit unions to transfer engagements (merge) into another credit union. Through merger the aim has been to achieve economies of scale and to build capacity to operate in a competitive marketplace. Undoubtedly this process of consolidation is set to increase as smaller credit unions question the viability of an independent future. However, it does not solve the problem of enabling credit unions as a whole to build the systems that would make a radical difference to the organisation and service delivery.

7.1 Rethinking the Credit Union Development Model

Rather than continuing mergers, there is another (better?) solution to credit union development. This is to be found in greater collaboration and in the development of a cohesive and comprehensive system of shared services. Internationally, co-operative banks and credit unions have adopted various collaborative approaches to development. These vary greatly from country to country, from the nationally centralised federated systems of France, Austria and French-speaking Canada, to the more decentralized, voluntarily-integrated models of Australia, US, Spain, and English-speaking Canada.

This focus on the importance of collaborative systems for successful development has also been argued by Fischer (2002), Desrocher and Fischer (2005). Following extensive research into the performance of financial co-operatives operating on a federated network as opposed to an atomized-competitive network model, Fischer (2002) demonstrated that those operating on a federated network (collaborative) model displayed either equal or superior performance to those operating on a more atomised model. In a later study, Desrocher and Fischer (2005) argued that integrated, collaborative models tended to reduce the volatility of efficiency and performance and to control costs more effectively. They maintained that research also showed that, despite the high costs of running hub-like organisations in collaborative systems, these systems still operated at lower costs than less integrated systems.

The range of back-office activities that are suitable for such a collaborative approach can vary. Michael (2007), in conducting research with credit union managers in the US, found that those of keenest interest to credit union managers included compliance and internal audit, consumer lending and marketing, accounting and information technology, human resources, and facilities management and planning. When the idea of collaboration was discussed with managers in the London study, there was particular interest in greater collaborative approaches to technological innovation, credit administration and control, internal auditing and a credit union call centre.

Collaboration and the development of integrated systems will call for a cultural shift in the way boards and managers think about credit union organisation and operations. As argues, collaboration involves a primary focus on commonality rather than uniqueness, and on a radical increase in the role of operational excellence in the credit union culture. In fact, it will involve a major sea-change and restructuring in the way credit unions operate and do business (cf. Filene 2008)

Internationally, the benefits of collaboration are tangible. Collaboration generates economies of scale, enables technical expertise to be shared across credit unions, enables a wider range of products and services for small as well as larger credit unions, and offers greater stability and security within the sector. In some cases, collaboration also leads to the development of a central credit union organisation with which partner organisations and other bodies can do business.

7.2 The Emergence of a Collaborative Approach to Development

An electronic hub is the sine qua non of any credit union collaborative system. This fact led ABCUL to explore the feasibility of the development of a central services organisation containing a core electronic banking platform. This would enable extensive collaboration on back-office functions throughout the credit union sector. It would assist the operation of loan, savings and transaction accounts, including internet access and SMS messaging, and enable the development of a range of collaborative services, including treasury management, along with the possibility of general ledger accounting and internal audit.

Such a platform would facilitate the development of new credit union products and services—even for those credit unions that are not using the new platform—and is adaptable to support new functions as required, such as bill payment accounts and pre-paid debit cards. It would enable a central customer service centre, open outside of office hours, and allow a link with the Post Office Horizon platform[7] and other external platforms as they arise. The link with the Post Office has major potential benefits for the credit union movement, as it would assist many more people to access their accounts, including both deposits and withdrawals, without the need to visit a credit union branch.

Given the experience of other co-operative financial institutions world-wide, there is every reason to believe that collaboration via an electronic hub would assist in progressing towards greater professionalism and quality standards throughout the credit union movement. The core electronic banking platform is not in itself collaboration; it is the necessary technical condition for collaboration, and the long term scope of this collaboration is the choice of participating credit unions. Greater consistency in products and services would also allow such developments as a central marketing facility, something often desired in the credit union movement but still not attained.

7.3 Credit Union Expansion Project

The UK Government's commitment to make a further investment of up to 38 million pounds into the credit union sector offered the possibility of developing a collaborative business operating model to enable credit unions to modernise and to expand their products and services consistently across the country. Following an open tender process, the DWP awarded ABCUL in April 2013 the contract to develop the credit union expansion project (CUEP), now being delivered through ABCUL's subsidiary company, Cornerstone Mutual Services (CMS) This

[7] The branch office accounting system currently operating throughout the British post office system.

strengthening programme aims to build the sustainable development of the sector and to ensure that credit unions will be able to provide services to 794,000 more members by March 2015 (ABCUL 2013). It also aims to support cumulative loan and savings deposit growth by 437 million pounds and 473 million pounds respectively.

Since its launch on May 1st, 2013, 82 credit unions have signed up to be part of CUEP. Around 30 of these 82 credit unions are participating in the first phase of the project. They will be required to define their business and financial plans for increasing growth, improving efficiency and profitability, and ensuring that they are no longer dependent on any external publically-funded subsidy by 2015. The project aims to nearly double the membership of the British credit union sector, but the success of the project will be assessed more in terms of progress in sustainable development. ABCUL's approach will focus on four key performance indicators, which include the increase in the economic diversity of the membership, the increase in the average loan income ratio for the sector to 17.5 %, the reduction of operating expenses to below 5 % and a similar reduction in the delinquency ratio. These targets were to be achieved by March 2015.

The project is structured as a programme of interrelated interventions based on the promotion of collaboration among participating credit unions and founded on the development of a shared business operating model. These interventions include a marketing strategy, new centralised products and services, the development of automated account services, new electronic channels for credit union members (including a new automated membership and product on-boarding portal), along with centralised business support, back-office services and training for credit unions. These will necessitate the development and implementation of a new IT infrastructure—the electronic hub discussed in the previous section. In 2014, it was decided that the new IT platform would be hosted on Fiserv Agilit, a service retail bank technology solution.

As a minimum requirement, the DWP has identified that CUEP must deliver shared support services in the areas of credit, control, accountancy, marketing and human resources; and ensure the provision of automated account services for all participating credit unions, which include basic transaction accounts, current accounts, budgeting and bill payment accounts, loan accounts and savings accounts. DWP has agreed on a budget of up to 35.6 million pounds, to provide the majority of funding towards the project costs of centralised products, services and marketing. However 20 million pounds of this funding will go directly to participating credit unions, to incentivise growth through payment for the achievement of particular targets.

CUEP presents a major opportunity to the British credit union sector. There is little evidence that the traditional atomistic business model will enable credit unions to develop the range of quality products and services that are needed to attract large numbers of people into membership. World-wide, atomised systems seem to grow to a certain size and then stagnate. On the other hand, the move to greater collaboration and shared back-office systems holds a real possibility of modernising and professionalising the sector, driving down individual credit union costs and ensuring that credit union products and services are accessible to many more people.

It must be emphasized, however, that collaboration is not a hand-over of control of the management of the credit union to a third party. Overall responsibility for each individual credit union remains firmly with each credit union's directors and management. It is for this reason that the development of a governance strengthening programme will also form a central part of CUEP. Collaboration is based on an agreement between credit unions that their collective future is best served by sharing back-office and sometimes front-office services. This depends, of course, on the development of a high level of trust between credit unions as they learn to compromise and to delegate tasks to a centralised organisation. It will require a high-level of maturity in governance and management processes to achieve success.

Realistically, individual credit union expansions and mergers will continue. Some credit unions are still so small that meeting performance standards sufficiently to collaborate will be difficult, and some larger credit unions will still need to open up to new and emerging markets. However, the business case for greater collaboration and shared back offices is compelling. With the support of the Government, there is now a real opportunity for British credit unions to take a major leap forward. Only time will tell if CUEP is the kind of project that can make that leap forward happen.

References

ABCUL (2013) Credit union expansion project. Project definition report. Association of British Credit Unions Ltd, Manchester

Arbuckle L (1994) The road to success another crossroads. Experiences from the Honduras Cooperative Strengthening Project. World Council of Credit Unions, Madison

Arbuckle L, Adams (2000) Reforming credit unions in Honduras. In: Westley GD, Branch B (eds) Safe money. Building effective credit unions in Latin America. John Hopkins University Press, Washington, DC

Branch B, Cifuentes M (2001) The road to Jinotega, part II: Towards maximising credit union financial sustainability. World Council of Credit Unions, Madison, WI

Collard S, Hale C, Day L (2010) Evaluation of the DWP growth fund. Revised final report. Personal Finance Research Centre University of Bristol and Ecorys

Desrocher M, Fischer KP (2005) The power of networks: integration and financial cooperative performance. Ann Public Coop Econ 76(3):307–354

DWP (2011) Credit Union Expansion Project, Feasibility Study Report to: the Minister for Welfare Reform, the Minister for Pensions and copied to the Secretary of State for Work and Pensions. CUEP Project Steering Committee, Department of Work and Pensions, HM Government, London

Filene Research Institute (2008) Connecting the dots on credit union collaboration: a colloquium at the Wharton School of the University of Pennsylvania. Filene Research Institute, Madison, WI

Fischer KP (2002) Governance, regulation and mutual financial intermediaries performance: the foundations of success. CREFA working paper no. 01-11. CREFA, Laval, Quebec

Goth P, McKillop DG, Ferguson C (2006) Building better credit unions. Joseph Rowntree Foundation, York

HMT (2008) Proposals for a legislative reform order for credit unions and industrial and provident societies in Great Britain, London

House of Commons Treasury Committee (2006) Banking the unbanked: banking services, the post office card account, and financial inclusion: thirteenth report of session 2005–06, vol 2. The Stationery Office, London

Jones PA (1999) Towards sustainable credit union development. ABCUL, Manchester. ISBN 9506281-6-6

Jones PA (2004a) Changing British credit unions: learning lessons from Latin America. In: Harafolas S, Spear R, Stryjan Y (eds) Local society and global economy. Editions Hellin, Greece

Jones PA (2004b) Growing credit unions in the West Midlands. J Coop Stud 37: 1 (No 110)

Jones PA (2008) From tackling poverty to achieving financial inclusion: the changing role of British credit unions in low-income communities. J Socio-Econ 37:2141–2154

Jones PA (2012) Strategies for growth. A research study into the progress and development of credit unions in the North East of England and Cumbria. LJMU and The Northern Rock Foundation, Newcastle

Jones PA, Ellison A (2011) Community finance for London, Scaling up the credit union and social finance sector. A report for Santander. Policies and Liverpool JMU

Local Government Association (2001) Changing credit unions: paying dividends in community finance. LGA, London

McKillop DG, Ward A-M, Wilson JOS (2007) The development of credit unions and their role in tackling financial inclusion. Public Money Manag 27(1):37–44

Michael SC (2007) A preliminary study on credit union franchising. Filene Research Institute, Madison, WI

Morris K (1999) Using credit unions as on-lending agents for external lines of credit, Chapter 3. In: Balkenhol B (ed) Credit unions and the poverty challenge: extending outreach, enhancing sustainability. International Labour Organisation, Geneva

O'Connell S (2005) Alternatives to money lenders? Credit unions and their discontents. History and Policy. www.historyandpolicy.org

Richardson DC (2000a) Unorthodox microfinance: the seven doctrines of success. Microfinance Bull 4:3–7

Richardson DC (2000b) Model Credit Unions into the twenty-first century. In: Westley GD, Branch B (eds) Safe money. Building effective Credit Unions in Latin America. John Hopkins University Press, Washington, DC

Treasury HM (2011) The legislative reform (industrial and provident societies and credit unions) order 2011. The Stationery Office Limited, London

Ward A-M, McKillop DG (2005) An investigation into the link between UK credit union characteristics: location and their success. Ann Public Coop Econ 76(3):461–489

Dr. Paul A Jones is a heads up the Research Unit for Financial Inclusion (RUFI) at Liverpool John Moores University (UK). RUFI undertakes academic, action and evaluative research in a wide range of areas related to the development of financial services for lower and moderate-income households, money and debt advice and credit union development. He has published widely in the field of financial inclusion and credit union development.

Part II
Credit Cooperative Systems in Eastern Europe

Bulgarian Cooperative Banking

Matteo Cotugno and Valeria Stefanelli

Abstract The chapter describes the peculiar characteristics of the Bulgarian economic system, with reference to the trend of the major macroeconomic variables. In this context, the analysis point out the features of the Bulgarian cooperative credit system, determining its profile based on the type of network taken into consideration and the two different entities: the Central Cooperative Bank Plc (CCB) and the Agriculture Credit Cooperatives (ACCs). The study highlights a substantial fragility of the Bulgarian cooperative system and outlines the hope of a better regulation to support it in the recent contest of EU Cooperative regulation changes.

1 Introduction

Because of their business model, which is based on proximity to local communities, stable relationships with clients and members, expertise, long-term perspective and a joint liability system, co-operative banks are a key element of systemic stability. During the crisis, the co-operative banking model has performed reasonably well. This performance was emphasized by the notably positive results obtained by co-operative banks in the comprehensive assessment exercise (stress test and asset Quality Review) that was conducted. This exercise showed that the general capitalisation conditions of the EU banking system were aligned with co-operative banks' tradition of soundness and high capitalisation (EACB 2015).

In the EU panorama, the Bulgarian Credit Cooperative system could be further developed with more adequate legislation. The cooperative credit system has played an important role in the Bulgarian economy, both before World War Two and during the Soviet period, when the financial intermediation function was

M. Cotugno (✉)
Department of Economics and Business, University of Catania, Catania, Italy
e-mail: matteo.cotugno@unict.it

V. Stefanelli
Department of Economic Science, University of Salento, Lecce, Italy
e-mail: valeria.stefanelli@unisalento.it

S. Karafolas (ed.), *Credit Cooperative Institutions in European Countries*, Contributions to Economics, DOI 10.1007/978-3-319-28784-3_13

monopolized by the State. However, at present, particularly due to an inadequate regulatory structure, the system has lost its leading role. The cooperative credit system in Bulgaria is built around a number of different realities. A number of these systems are the outcome of private initiatives (Central Cooperative Bank Plc), a portion are financed by government organizations (Agriculture Credit Cooperatives), and others are financed by non-governmental organizations (Nachala Cooperative) as micro-credit schemes in support of several sectors of the Bulgarian economy.

This chapter is organized as follows. The initial part describes the peculiar characteristic of the Bulgarian economic system, with reference to the trend of the major macroeconomic variables. The subsequent paragraph analyzes the characteristics of the Bulgarian cooperative credit system, determining its characteristics based on the type of network taken into consideration and the two different entities: the Central Cooperative Bank Plc (CCB) and the Agriculture Credit Cooperatives (ACCs). The last paragraph outlines the hope of a better regulation to support the Bulgarian Credit Cooperatives in the recent contest of EU Cooperative regulation changes.

2 The Bulgarian Economic System

Until November 1989, the Bulgarian economy was based on the Soviet system, with State control over all economic sectors (including financial intermediation). The fall of Communism and the transition process has resulted in a remarkable economic recovery that nonetheless was not strengthened by the requisite structural and legislative reforms. After the financial crisis of 1996–1997, the progress made in recent years by the Bulgarian economy is clearly outstanding such that it meets most of the parameters established by the Maastricht Treaty for accession to the EU.

The real GDP of Bulgaria, after the sharp downturn of 2009 (Table 1), recorded average growth rates higher than that of the Euro Area. The entry of Bulgaria into the European Union and the need to adhere to strict public balance sheet parameters imposed by the European convergence has produced an extremely positive effect on inflation rates. During the period of 1997–2006, the average annual inflation was 36.2 % compared with an average of 2 % in the Euro area. As shown in Table 1, since 2009, inflation rates in Bulgaria have been progressively reduced, reaching the levels of deflation recorded in 2014 and expected for 2015.

To reduce the risks of the devaluation of the local currency (the Lev), on 27 November 2008, the government decided to maintain a fixed exchange rate between the Lev/Euro at 1.95583 Lev (Lev/Euro). The country's fiscal system is extremely favourable for investment; since 2008, the government has introduced a flat tax of 10 % for earned income and income from economic activity.

Despite the considerable efforts of the Bulgarian government, the gap between the income level of Bulgaria and the countries of the European Union remains marked. In fact, Bulgaria is the poorest country in the European Union with a high

Table 1 Real GDP and consumer prices (annual percent change)

	Average 1997–2006	2007	2008	2009	2010	2011	2012	2013	2014	2015 f
Real GDP (annual percent change)										
Bulgaria	3.8	6.9	5.8	−5.0	0.7	2.0	0.5	1.1	1.7	1.2
Euro area	2.3	3.0	0.5	−4.5	2.0	1.6	−0.8	−0.5	0.9	1.5
Consumer prices (annual percent change)										
Bulgaria	36.2	7.6	12.0	2.5	3.0	3.4	2.4	0.4	−1.6	−1.0
Euro area	2.0	2.2	3.3	0.3	1.6	2.7	2.5	1.3	0.4	0.1

Source: our processing based on IMF (2015a, b)

level of structural unemployment and significant disparities in terms of age, gender, and region.

Macroeconomic imbalances in Bulgaria are concentrated on a devaluation of the real exchange rate (deflated by the CPI), a negative Net International investment position and more than the 75 % established by the Treaty of Maastricht. According to the Convergence Report of 2014, containing inflation, is the result of the sharp slowdown in economic growth. The absence of structural reforms of the country's economic recovery would lead to a major turnaround and reach the CPI target rate of change.

Bulgarian public finance conditions are relatively strong, although the country suffered a sharp deterioration during 2014. The deficit-to-GDP ratio was maintained during 2014 at −3.7 % (−1.5 % for the previous year; −2.4 % was the average for the Euro Area) and the Government debt-to-GDP ratio in 2014 was equal to 27.6 % (18.1 % in 2013), well below the 60 % established by the Treaty of Maastricht and the level registered by the major EU countries (91.9 % was the average for the Euro Area).

3 The Financial and Banking System

3.1 From the Soviet Period to the 1996–1997 Crisis

Similar to how the Bulgarian economy and the development of the financial and banking system has been affected by a Communist regime (1944–1989), the country was moulded on the characteristic traits of the monopolistic model present in other countries (Poland, USSR, Czechoslovakia, Romania and East Germany). During that period, the banking system was composed of a single bank, the *Bulgarska Narodna Banka,* BNB (Bulgarian National Bank), that through a territorial network of branches, operated in the dual capacity as central bank and commercial bank. In contrast to other Soviet-type regimes, the Bulgarian banking system featured the variant of a second institution that lacked a bank statute and that was responsible for gathering Bulgarian household savings: the State Savings Bank (currently, DSK). In 1964, the Bulgarian government recognized the need to externalize the BNB regulation of international trade, leading to the establishment of the Bulgarian Foreign Trade Bank (BFTB—currently, Bulbank), which addressed international banking operations (Koford and Tschoegl 2002).

The function of intermediation between savers and investors was internalized in the State-owned banking system because the assets gathered through the State Savings Bank were employed by the BNB in State-owned industrial enterprises to finance investments in capital assets and to circulate capital. The risk management function was utterly non-existent in such a system because the capital allocation was centralized and pertained to the State. In addition, such a banking system failed to allow the formation of those competences that in addition to evaluating and managing risks, are indispensable to selecting deserving entrepreneurial initiatives and to determining prices based on riskiness. Conversely, that banking system had led to exchange risk management competences, although rudimentary (Bonin 2001).

The first signs of an opening of the banking system appeared in 1981, the year Mineralbank was established; Mineralbank specialized in providing credit to small and medium-sized enterprises in the mining sector. Actually, the major change in the organization of the banking system occurred with the end of the Soviet period in 1989 when the BNB lost its monopolist commercial bank role and confined its competences to monetary and currency policies.

Therefore, the banking system still needed to be built from scratch because there were no institutions, no adequate legislative system, and no banking culture. Furthermore, even the competences that are typical of those who must allocate capital to create shareholder value were missing. The initial steps taken during the transition were the establishment of seven new sectoral banks in 1989, which replaced a few BNB branches.[1] The year 1990 is acknowledged as the year of maximum expansion of the Bulgarian banking system; by that year's end, the latter was composed of 70 banks, of which seven were sectoral banks, two were specialized banks (Bulgarian Foreign Trade Bank and State Savings Bank) and 59 were commercial banks.

In spite of its major progress, the Bulgarian banking system remained fragile. There was no suitable regulatory structure for both the banking sector and bankruptcy regulations, most banks were owned by the State, and the level of overdue bills inherited from the Soviet era in bank portfolios was huge, given the limited capitalization of many banks. In 1992, to eliminate this deficiency, the State established the Banking Consolidation Company (BCC), which was entrusted with the task of reducing the undercapitalization of State-owned banks (71 % in

[1] The Agricultural and Cooperative Bank, the Biochemical Bank, the Construction Bank, the Economic Bank, the Electronics Bank, the Transportation Bank, and the Transport, Agricultural, and Building Equipment Bank, which was also known as Balkan Bank. Refer to Koford and Tschoegl (2002).

1991) through the direct subscription of equity stakes in the banks and the merger of many banks (Vincelette 2001).

The first results were timely. In 1992, 22 state-owned banks were consolidated into the United Bulgarian Bank. In 1993, 12 additional state-owned banks were consolidated into a single bank, the Express Bank. The system was gradually consolidating, and it reached the brink of the economic and financial crisis (1996–1997) with 35 banks. Throughout the transition years, the most urgent reform had been delayed; in total asset terms, the State maintained an extremely high equity stake in the banking system (84.8 % in October 1996). Additionally, there was a notably close connection between banks and enterprises.

Many economic sectors remained monopolistic and under state control. In particular, the mechanics, chemistry, transport and telecommunications, and energy sectors continued to benefit from bank loans despite lacking creditworthiness (Gomel 2002). Furthermore, under the law, the BNB was required to rectify the losses generated by the system's banks, discouraging risk management and credit selection activity. Thus, the economic crisis rapidly became a financial and monetary crisis. For two consecutive years, the GDP had been utterly negative (−10.1 % in 1996 and −7.0 % in 1997). At the same time, the devaluation of the Bulgarian Lev (BGN) had caused prices to increase in an exponential manner; the CPI was equal to +310.4 % in 1996 and to +578.6 % in 1997. In addition, the BGN had been considerably devaluated with respect to the dollar.[2]

The government performed innumerable measures to rise out of this deep crisis; most importantly, the government passed renewed prudential and supervisory legislation to regulate the banking system. In particular, the introduction of the Law on Banks on June 25, 1997 considerably reformed prior regulations in force since 1992. This law introduced: the minimum capital adequacy requirement of 12 % of total risk-weighted assets; limits to the concentration of assets; as well as rules for evaluating guarantees, classifying assets and calculating appropriated surplus. In addition, the accounting standards were modified and new rules regarding currency reserves were introduced. In contrast, the International Monetary Fund established the Currency Board, which was entrusted with the task of supervising public spending to consolidate the State's national debt.

3.2 The Current Situation

Currently, the Bulgarian financial system has been completely renewed and benefits the banking channel, rather than direct channels, as the means of resource intermediation. Non-banking financial intermediaries represent a small percentage of banking intermediaries.

---

[2] By the end of 1995, 65 BGN were needed for a US Dollar. By the end of 1996, 178 BGN were needed for a USD and by the end of 1997, 1674 BGN were required for a USD. Cf., BNB Statistics.

Table 2 Structure of the Bulgarian banking system

Bulgarian banking system	2009	2010	2011	2012	2013	2014
Commercial banks licensed in Bulgaria	23	22	23	22	22	21
Commercial foreign banks' branches	6	6	7	7	7	6
Cooperative bank under law on bank[a]	1	1	1	1	1	1
Agriculture credit cooperatives	33	n.d.	n.d.	n.d.	15	15

Source: our processing based on the BNB, Decree n. 343/1998, Amersdorffer et al. (2015)
[a]It is the Cooperative Central Bank, the only Bulgarian bank operating according to the Law on Banks

Table 3 Market share of domestic and foreign banks

Market share of domestic and foreign banks	2010	2011	2012	2013	09.2014
Non EU bank branches	0.7	0.8	0.7	0.8	0.1
Non EU-banks	2.2	2.3	1.5	1.3	1.4
EU bank branches	4.1	3.7	6.1	5.5	6.6
Domestic banks	19.3	23.5	26.4	30.2	23.2
EU bank subsidiaries	73.7	69.7	65.3	62.2	68.7

Source: our processing based on the BNB Data

In particular, the total quantity of assets in Bulgaria's financial system reached BGN 109.05 billion by the end of September 2014. Of this, 74.9 % are derived from the banking sector, and 25 % is attributable to other areas of the financial system (insurance companies and funds managed by pension insurance companies, leasing companies, and financial vehicle corporations) (BNB 2004). The deleveraging of the stock-exchange market has resulted in a significant reduction of market capitalization in the GDP. In 2007, the market capitalization to GDP ratio was equal to 49.9 %, whereas in 2013 the ratio was equal to 12.6 % (The World Bank indicator).

Furthermore, since the crisis of 1996–1997, the number of banks in the Bulgarian system has generally stabilized, rarely exceeding a total of 35 (including foreign bank branches) (Table 2). The 2008–2009 global financial crisis has had major repercussions in Bulgaria, although stronger tensions registered during 2014. In particular, in June 2014, the Corporate Commercial Bank (CCB), the fourth largest bank in the country, failed to write off huge losses on loans (approximately 2/3 of the total assets). After a bank run concern, which also involved the First Investment Bank AD, the banking system has stabilized because of the intervention of the BNB and the help of EU funds, which were used to increase liquidity in the banking system.

The ownership of most Bulgarian banks is foreign, as shown in Table 3. In particular, the market share of the subsidiaries of EU banks in 2014 is equal to 68.7 %, representing a significant increase following the failure of the Corporate Commercial Bank. The market share of the subsidiaries, in fact, had been steadily reduced since 2010; however, the events recorded in June of 2014 have reduced the market share of domestic banks, to the benefit of branches of EU banks or subsidiaries of EU banks licensed in Bulgaria.

Table 4 Loans to nonfinancial corporations, households and NPISHs by economic activity

	2010 (%)	2011 (%)	2012 (%)	2013 (%)	2014 (%)	I—2015 (%)
Agriculture, forestry and fishing	2.1	2.4	2.6	2.7	3.1	2.8
Manufacturing	12.4	12.6	13.0	13.3	14.0	14.5
Trade	20.1	20.1	20.4	20.7	18.8	18.4
Construction and real estate activity	13.9	13.5	12.8	13.5	12.7	12.7
Other service activities	16.1	17.7	19.1	17.7	17.4	17.3
Total non-financial corporations	62.5	63.9	65.2	65.3	62.9	63.0
Total households and NPISHs	37.5	36.1	34.8	34.7	37.1	37.0
Perc. variation of loans to non financial corporations	2.48	5.45	4.96	0.13	−11.48	−0.43
Perc. variation of loans to households	−8.34	−4.12	2.90	1.97	1.26	−0.18

Source: our processing based on BNB (2015)

Table 5 Risk, profitability and capital adequacy of Bulgarian banking system

	2010	2011	2012	2013	09.2014
Non-performing loans/net loans	11.9	9.7	10.6	10.3	10.5
Return on assets	0.86	0.78	0.71	0.70	1.03
Return on equity	6.7	6.1	5.71	5.64	8.26
Total capital adequacy	17.48	17.53	16.7	16.9	19.47

Source: our processing based on BNB (2015)

The banking system concentration level increased sharply during 2014 after several years of a steady decrease. In fact, the first five Bulgarian banks hold a market share, in total asset terms, of 54.05 %. The same banks, at the end of 2013, held market share equal to 49.5 % (our processing based on BNB data).

Regarding the distribution and the change in the quantity of credit extended to non-financial corporations and households, we emphasize the following main trends (Table 4). The share of funding allocated to non-financial corporations represents 63 % in the I-quarter of 2015. This result is fairly steady over time. Over time, the manufacturing sector has observed a major allocation of credit at the expense of trade and real estate. Regarding the rates of change, in 2014, primarily because of the failure of the Corporate Commercial Bank, the amount of credit granted to non-financial corporation decreased by approximately 11.5 %. However, in other years, there was no lack of support of the economy by the banking system with regard to non-financial corporations. However, the loans to households situation appears more difficult, if the change in the credit stock is related to the change in nominal GDP.

In profitability terms, the Bulgarian banking system as a whole denotes an improvement in profit performance and the capital adequacy ratio (Table 5). The non-performing loans ratio (net-impairment) in the last three years remained steady at approximately 10.5 %. Note that the BNB classification of non-performing loans also included past due exposure of more than 90 days, emphasizing a rigorous identification of non-performing exposure.

4 The Cooperative Credit System in Bulgaria

The origins of the cooperative credit system in Bulgaria date to the beginning of the twentieth century through the intervention of farmers and small and medium-sized agricultural firms. The saving and credit cooperatives based on the Raffaisen approach represented an important link of the Bulgarian banking system until the end of World War Two. The cooperative credit system continued working in rural areas during the Soviet era, particularly to compensate for the desires of a highly centralized banking system based on a single central and commercial bank. Most important, the BNB branches were solely present in major towns, leaving a considerable supply vacuum in those rural areas that were not served by financial intermediaries. The lack of competences, the perception of high riskiness in the agricultural business, and the unclear definition of the legal framework with respect to the examination of guarantees caused the utter failure of any initiative to re-launch the agricultural system that used commercial banks (Popov 2003; Cotugno 2010).

The first Bulgarian cooperative credit bank dates to 1910 when the *Bulgarska Zemedelska Banka* presided over a spin-off of the cooperative-type banking activities to form the *Bulgarska Centralna Kooperativna Banka* (Bulgarian Central Cooperative Bank). In fact, the origins of the Bulgarian Central Cooperative Bank were based on the rural world and date to 1862 when a large number of autonomous rural credit associations established the bank to serve as a treasury for the local administrations and as a deposit and lending bank for local agricultural farms (Koford and Tschoegl 2002). The cooperative movement acquired greater local characteristics during the communist period, although it did so without referring to national associations or federations, given that the entire banking system remained under State control. Currently, the cooperative movement is built around two different entities:

- The Central Cooperative Bank Plc (CCB);
- The Agriculture Credit Cooperatives (ACCs);

As previously noted, the main obstacle to adequate growth of the cooperative credit system in Bulgaria has been the desire for an appropriate regulatory framework. Given the structured and modern banking rules and regulations enacted in response to the 1996–1997 crisis, the Bulgarian governments that followed, as with the BNB, failed to promote non-commercial development of the banking system. In fact, the BNB's need to ensure the full governance of the monetary and credit policies has required, through the revision of the Cooperative Act, the prohibition by Cooperatives of the acceptance of deposits from their customers.

Therefore, the bank regulations currently in force provide for a two-tiered banking system.

1. Banks can be established in compliance with the Law on Banks, subject to the prior authorization of the BNB and the district court having jurisdiction. For all purposes, these are commercial banks; however, these banks can work according to the rationale that is typical of the cooperative credit system, should this be required. In such a case, these banks shall be subject to BNB supervision and shall not benefit from any facility because it uses the cooperative form. Because the Law on Banks has been crafted for commercial banks, its intermediary subjects that desire to work under a cooperative scheme are required to recreate in their statutes the typical provisions of the cooperative model.
2. Although the banks established in compliance with the Cooperative Act have a legal framework that previously includes provisions for the cooperative model, in contracts, they are subject to considerable limitations because they are not allowed to accept deposits from their customers. Indeed, this limits their growth to the amount of their equity. In fact, Article 38 of the Cooperative Act passed in 1991 had specified that "a cooperative shall be free to engage in savings and loan activities by virtue of a resolution of its General Meeting". The crisis in 1996–1997 has led to a reformulation of this provision whereby "The cooperative may engage in depositary and crediting operations by resolution of the General Meeting and with the authorization of the Bulgarian National Bank and as provided for in a separate law". In fact, the text is connected with article 2 of the Law on Banks that states that "the provisions of this Law shall not apply to mutual aid funds of cooperatives extending loans only to their members on the account of contributions made by them and cooperative funds".

The more recent Decree No. 343 of 30 December 2008 of the Council of Ministers confirms this role related to Credit Cooperatives.

In other words, a cooperative bank cannot conduct a deposit-taking activity unless it is authorized to do so by the BNB; in addition, a cooperative bank is subject to the Law on Banks, thereby falling within the case referred to in paragraph 1 above. "Mutual aid credit cooperatives of private farmers, established as per the agricultural capital fund scheme in compliance with the agreements for utilization of the financial grant, concluded between the government of the Republic of Bulgaria and the Commission of the European Union", are not required to apply for the authorization because article 17 of the final and transitional provisions of the Law on Banks explicitly provides for their exemption.

Despite the pressures placed by the Cooperatives registered under the Cooperative Act on the Bulgarian Parliament and the BNB, the latter have not yet approved ad hoc regulation for deposit and credit cooperatives, leaving the credit intermediation sector mainly in the hands of commercial banks and confining cooperative credit to a narrow market niche.

The current regulatory and supervision is assigned to the Ministry of Agriculture, which, as discussed below, does not grasp the real needs of business development of ACCs in Bulgaria.

4.1 The Central Cooperative Bank Plc

The Central Cooperative Bank Plc is a commercial bank registered in the Republic of Bulgaria with a head office and administration address in Sofia. The Central Cooperative Bank Plc was established in 1991 through the Central Cooperative Union (the national federation of Bulgarian Cooperatives), which is composed of a few regional cooperative unions and nearly 1100 cooperative-type enterprises. Their objective was to succeed in unifying the financial resources of the Bulgarian cooperative system to enable its proper development (Central Cooperative Bank, Annual Report). The Central Cooperative Bank Plc is the sole Bulgarian cooperative bank registered under the Law on Banks and, therefore, is subject to BNB supervision. The bank's organizational structure is as follows: there are no local or regional banks that participate in a federation or a central bank; however, there are 266 branches that cover the national territory as well as abroad (Central Cooperative Bank, Presentation 2014).

Since March 1999, the CCB Plc has been listed on the Bulgarian Stock Exchange and is currently controlled by CCB Group Assets Management EAD, a company that, in turn, is 100 % owned by Chimimport JSC, a financial holding that has equity interests in the financial sector as well as in such sectors as legal consulting services, chemical product trade, rubber by-products and fertilizers and transport. The acquisition by Chimimport occurred at the beginning of 2002, when the Bank Consolidation Company AD divested 32.77 % of its CCB capital (Central Cooperative Bank Plc 2013) ownership. Today the capital of CCB Plc is 68.5 % owned by CCB Group Assets Management EAD and 5.1 % directly owned by Chimimport (Central Cooperative Bank Plc 2014).

The CCB Plc has a two-tier governance system, at the top of which is the General Meeting of Shareholders. The Supervisory Board consists of a few members that are elected directly by the General Meeting and is responsible for appointing the Management Board and the Procurator. The Management Board elects the Executive Directors with the approval of the Supervisory Board (with respect to the National Code of Corporate Governance).

The CCB Plc is a full member of European Association of Cooperative Banks and of the International Cooperative Banking Association.

The CCB Plc is growing rapidly and has a focus on retail segments, including individual clients and small and medium sized enterprises. The CCB Plc has strong market positions in the card business, payment systems and lending to agricultural producers. From a marketing perspective, the CCB Plc provides easy access to its product/services through a branch network; the Bank is developing its fee-based services and other non-interest income activities. Based on article 1 and 3 of General Terms and Conditions of Central Cooperative Bank, "*The Bank provides to its Clients the following services: (1) services, related to depositing cash to a payment account, as well as the associated operations for servicing the payment account; (2) services, related to withdrawing cash from a payment account, as well as the associated operations for servicing the payment account; (3) the performance of payment operations, including transferring funds to a payment account of the Client with the bank or with another provider of payment services: a) the performance of direct debits, including one off direct debits; b) the performance of payment operations via payment cards or other similar instruments; c) the performance of credit transfers, including orders for periodic transfers; (4) the performance of payment operations, when the funds are part of a loan granted to the Client: a) the performance of direct debits, including oneoff direct debits; b) the performance of payment operations* via *payment cards or other similar instruments; c) the performance of credit transfers, including orders for periodic transfers; (5) issurance of payment instruments and/or accepting payments with payment instruments; (6) performance of available money transfers; (7) the performance of payment operations, upon which the consent of the Client, as a payer, for the performance of the payment operation is given* via *telecommunication, digital or information means and the payment is made to the operator of the telecommunication or information system or network, acting only as an intermediary between the Client and the provider of the goods or services. (...) Art.3. With regard to the payment operations performed on the account, the Client of the bank may be in the quality of a payer and/or a beneficiary. (...)"*.

The CCB Plc has a strong relationship with a number of correspondent banks, which allow it to improve its business contacts. In fact, the Bank has 360 correspondents and 22 Nostro accounts, as well as a number of lines for documentary operations for various amounts and trade finance for the imports of investment product produced in EU (refer to the CCB Plc Profile reported in its website).

In recent years, the evolution of the CCB market share has been extremely favourable. In 2004, CCB had market share of 2.4 % in total asset terms; however, 2013 data shows market share of 4.6 %.

The CCB Plc has a diversified portfolio of products and a partiality for the agricultural sector.

In total asset terms, CCB Plc in 8th place in the BNB classification for the banking system as of 31.12.2013. In December 2013, The Bulgarian Credit Rating Agency confirmed the rating awarded to CCB Plc; the long-term rating is BBB-, and the short-term rating is A-3 (Central Cooperative Bank Plc 2013).

In performance terms, the CCB registered a growth rate of 11.82 % in balance sheet assets in 2013 (Table 6). The growth rate in the past two years is better than ever before because of more conservative policies for granting credit. In fact, the results of this policy have produced a net reduction of non-performing loans from 9.7 to 4.6 %.

Growth in equity has not had the same magnitude as growth in the total financial statement assets. In fact, overall, the financial leverage has increased, and the level of equity to total assets over time has decreased.

The company's profitability level over time has decreased, from a ROE of 8.17 % in 2010 to 2.85 % in 2013.

Table 6 Central Cooperative Bank Plc, performance

	2010	2011	2012	2013
CCB total asset (rate of change %)	24.22	31.43	11.53	11.82
CCB total equity (rate of change %)	8.98	21.46	4.34	2.62
ROE (%)	8.17	3.79	2.90	2.85
ROA (%)	0.98	0.42	0.30	0.27
Equity/total assets (%)	11.99	11.08	10.37	9.51
NPL/loans (%)	9.74	7.16	5.59	4.58

Source: our processing based on CCB Plc (2013)

4.2 The Agriculture Credit Cooperatives

In early 1996, a few groups of agricultural enterprises established Agriculture Credit Cooperatives (ACCs), working within the legal context of the Cooperative Act, to grant credit to their members according to rationale typical of the cooperative models. In the same year, the Ministry of Agriculture and the European Union[3] had launched the Agricultural Capital Fund Scheme (ACAS), a program to sustain the Bulgarian agriculture, by appropriating a fund of 14 million euro for initiatives in support of the agricultural world. In May 1996, 33 Agriculture Credit Cooperatives benefited from the funds placed at their disposal by the Ministry and European Union. After a brief period required for recruiting and training staff, towards the end of 1996 the Cooperatives began to disburse the first loans to their members (Dimitre 2006).

In recent years, the Ordinance No. 26 of 23 April 2009 on Financial Institutions, at par. 6, provides as follow: "*The cooperatives under par. 12 of the Law on Credit Institution incumbent upon the entry into force of this Ordinance shall be registered on the grounds of a certificate for compliance with the requirements of Decree No. 343 of 30 December 2008 of the Council of Ministers issued by the Minister of Agriculture or a person authorised by him, and continue their activity under the procedure established by the Council of Ministers*".

The Decree No. 343 of 30 December 2008 of the Council of Ministers determines the manner in which the Mutual-Aid Credit Cooperatives for Private Farmers-Producers (Agriculture Credit Cooperatives or ACCs) shall continue their activity as financial institutions within the meaning of the Credit Institutions Act.

The ACC shall be a legal entity registered under the Cooperatives Act. At least half of the Credit Cooperative members shall be agricultural producers. An ACC member may be any legally capable natural person who is familiar with its Articles of Association and the ensuing rights and obligations, who agrees to observe these and who is willing to collaborate on the further development of the Cooperative's

[3] The European Funds refer to the Poland/Hungary Assistance for Restructuring Economy (PHARE) Program.

activity. One person may be a member of only one ACC. The typical organization of each Cooperative consists of a variable number of members and generally includes between 200 and 600 members. The ACC shall conduct activities for: granting loans to their members, marketing and providing services in the economic and financial sectors, providing social and health insurance and other services related to agriculture, fisheries and aquacultures, and developing rural regions solely in favour of their members. The ACC may grant loans of no more than BGN 5000 for activities other than those previously listed. In addition, a CC loan cannot be granted to a member, for example, who has outstanding obligations related to his membership and has not deposited the minimum share capital in accordance with the ACC Law.

The ACC's governance system is composed of a General Meeting that manages the ACC, which shall directly elect a Chairperson and a Supervisory Board; the Supervisory Board shall elect a Management Board and an Audit Committee.

The General Meeting includes all the members of the Cooperative and meets at least once a year to outline the strategic policies and adopt the yearly balance sheet and income statements. As specified in article 21 of the Cooperative Act, "each member shall be entitled to one vote which shall be cast personally, regardless of his share of the nominal capital". However, there is no mandatory provision to appropriate the accumulated year-end profits. In fact, it is mandatory to appropriate 20 % of the profits generated, whereas the general meeting must determine the allocation of the remainder and, possibly, its distribution in the form of dividends (Cooperative Act, article 35, 1996). ACC's governance is based on the Supervisory board, which is intended to provide a monitoring role for ACC management.

The organizational structure of each individual ACC also provides for the presence of a Chairman of the Agriculture Credit Cooperative, who is the person responsible for the bank and who acts as a liaison with the outside, the chairman of the management board and the coordinator of human resources. Generally, in each ACC, there is at least one loan inspector who is responsible for credit operations, as well as an accountant and a lawyer who are responsible for maintaining the branch accounting and for debt collection, respectively. In addition to coordinating the personnel working in each branch, the Chairman participates in the national federation of the cooperative credit banks' meetings. In fact, each local cooperative joins a national federation (Federal Agriculture Credit Cooperative, FACC), which represents the interests of the ACC with respect to national and local authorities. Currently, this is a closed system that does not accept new members. The Federation is registered under the Act for Legal Persons with Non-Profit Activities, according to the agreements entered into by the Bulgarian government and the EU (Popov 2003).

The highest body of the federation is its General Meeting, composed of the chairmen of the 16 ACCs.[4]

[4] At the moment, they are: "Agroimpuls"—Sliven; "Maritsa invest"—Plovdiv; "Doverie"—Dobrich; "Saglasie 96"—Russalya, Veliko Turnovo; "Perelik"—Smolyan; "Solidarnost"—

Each chairman is entitled to one vote to elect the Federation managing bodies, with special reference being provided to the Management Board (composed of five members) and the Chairman of the Federation, as well as an executive director of the Federation who is entrusted with day-to-day management tasks and the coordination of the unitary management of the 33 ACCs. Each ACC contributes an amount toward the Federation's costs relative to that ACC's assets.

The prohibition to not accept deposits from their customers represents a significant limitation and considerably deters the ACCs' development in Bulgaria. In fact, the major obstacles for the development of the ACCs were previously specified at that time. First, financial services were solely restricted to lending. Deposits were explicitly prohibited. Second, as often observed with regard to early formation phases of rural credit cooperatives, the regulation and supervision were assigned to the Ministry of Agriculture. However, it quickly became evident that the Ministry was not well-suited for this task. Third, technical support, e.g., by the German Cooperative and Raiffeisen Foundation (DGRV), was limited to the training of key persons of the cooperatives, i.e., managers and staff members. The DGRV could have assisted in establishing a supportive legal framework for cooperative financial intermediation but did not receive appropriate support by the Ministry of Agriculture or other authorities.

These shortcomings led to the failure of a number of ACCs. The ACCs deviated from their initial mission or/and accumulated poorly performing loans. Nevertheless, 15 ACCs joined forces in establishing the National Cooperative Union 'Evrostart' (NCU), which continues to operate. The NCU organizes external audits, trainings and is active in lobbying, but is not assigned a supervisory function. Since 2011, all NCU cooperatives are registered as "financial institutions" within the registry of the Bulgarian National Bank4. The ACCs' operation is regulated by Ordinance No. 26 (Bulgarian National Bank) and the Law on Credit Institutions (Bulgarian National Bank). Most ACCs are located in remote rural areas but also in semi-urban provincial towns. Nevertheless, their clientele mainly consists of small private farmers.

Because the cooperatives, compared with microfinance institutions in other parts of the world, serve a small number of members, all operations, i.e., screening, monitoring and enforcing repayment, are based on personal relationships within the social networks of rural communities, which were noted previously. Although the lending strategy does not support well-known group lending approaches, similar processes can be observed. For instance, the functioning of the credit cooperative relies heavily on informal information flows in the social network of the cooperative members and on social pressure (in case of delayed loan repayment). One of the largest growth impediments for the ACCs is the limited funding base because they

---

Plovdiv; "Aetos"—Aytos, Burgas; "Mizia"—Pleven; "Pomoriiski stopanin"—Pomorie, Burgas; "Stopanin 1"—Haskovo; "Samokov 96"—Samokov, Sofia; "General Toshevo"—General Toshevo, Dobrich; "Momina voda"—Momchilovtsi, Smolyan; "Kaynardzha"—Kaynardzha, Silistra; "Nadezhda"—Pliska, Shumen; "Smilyan"—Smilyan, Smolyan.

are not allowed to collect savings and can barely refinance in the Bulgarian financial system. However, since 2002, Oikocredit International, a socially responsible investor, began to refinance certain ACCs. However, such socially oriented investors, which depend on attracting funds from donors or private investors, are motivated to document the positive and so-called "social" impact of their investments. These investors strongly engage in the application of Social Performance Measurement (SPM) by educating their clients, i.e., operating microfinance institutions such as the ACCs, and requiring them to conduct SPM as a self-assessment or as an external audit. To implement an SPM, Social Performance Indicators (SPI) should be included in the ACCs' management.

5 Conclusions

Until 1989, the banking system had been inspired by the typical rationale of the planned economy with centralization of the resources' trading services and the presence of a single State-owned bank. The opening of the economic system to market logics has occurred swiftly, but because there was no adequate legislative context, from 1996 to 1997, problems inherent in the system led to a bank panic that, in turn, led to an impressive financial crisis that caused considerable depreciation of the national currency, strong inflationary tensions and total reorganization of the financial system.

Considerable relevance has been attached to the cooperative credit system in the years prior to the Soviet-era and, to a lesser extent, to the Soviet era. The system's current role has decreased in importance, particularly because of a largely unfavourable legal context. The main Bulgarian cooperative bank is the Central Cooperative Bank Plc, which is a single entity that manages branches throughout the territory. In sum, the bank is not a federation of local banks because it is a single national bank, as commercial banks are. In addition to the Central Cooperative Bank Plc, another cooperative credit system has become operational; this refers to a national federation and is composed of many Agriculture Credit Cooperatives. The federation's registration under the Cooperative Act and, recently, the requirements of Decree No. 343 of 30 December 2008 of the Council of Ministers issued by the Minister of Agriculture imply that it is not allowed to accept deposits from the public, and this considerably limits the movement's expansion.

A reformulation of the regulatory framework is a critical issue for the life of cooperative credit in Bulgaria, although to date, this has been avoided because of the desire to centralize the banking system on an exclusively commercial-type model.

Thus, EACB remains an active player in the European Social Dialogue on Banking (ESDB), which is the dialogue between employer associations (EACB and ESDB) and employees (UNI Finance) in the banking sector. The EACB's recent projects strived to enhance social dialogue in 'enlargement countries' such as Bulgaria (and Romania and Croatia) by sharing the best practices of other 'new' member states, such as Malta and Cyprus, and those of older Member States, through the dissemination of one of the best results of the European Social Dialogue (EACB 2015).

Therefore, it is hoped that the attention of the international cooperative institutions and the recent changes in EU Credit Cooperative Regulation may enable greater support of the Bulgarian Credit Cooperatives. It is also hoped that the attention will enhance reflection on growth within the European banking sector, in which financial cooperatives play an important role.

References

Bonin JP (2001) Financial intermediation in Southeast Europe: banking on the Balkans. Working paper, Department of Economics, Wesleyan University

Bulgarian National Bank (2004) Commercial banks in Bulgaria, various years, www.bnb.bg

Bulgarian National Banks (2015) Financial supervision reports - Data. www.bnb.bg

Central Cooperative Bank Plc (2013) Annual report, various years. www.ccbank.bg

Central Cooperative Bank (2014) Annual report. www.ccbank.bg

Cotugno M (2010) The Bulgarian cooperative banking system. In: Boscia V, Carretta A, Schwizer P (eds) Cooperative banking in Europe, Studies in banking and financial institutions. Palgrave Macmillan, Basingstoke

Dimitre NN (2006) Possibilities of agricultural credit cooperatives for creating tenable small farming in Bulgarian rural areas. Contributed paper presented at the IAMO Forum 2006, June, Germany

European Central Banking (ECB) (2014) Convergence report, April

European Association of Co-operative Banking (EACB) (2015) Leveraging the co-operative banks' difference, 2014. Annual report

Gomel G (2002) Banking and financial sector in transition countries and convergence towards European Integration, Banca d'Italia, May

International Monetary Found (2015a) World economic outlook, uneven growth, short and long term factors, April

International Monetary Found (2015b) IMF country report no. 15/119

Koford K, Tschoegl AE (2002) Foreign banks in Bulgaria, 1875–2002. Working paper series, Department of Economics College of Business & Economics University of Delaware, no. 2002–06

Amersdorffer F, Buchenrieder G, Bokusheva R, Wolz A (2015) Financial and social performance of rural credit cooperatives in Bulgaria. J Oper Res Soc 66:57–65

Popov I (2003) The cooperative system in Bulgaria. Report on the occasion of the IRU-Law Seminar, Berlin, November

Vincelette GA (2001) Bulgarian banking sector development, post-1989. SE Eur Polit 2(1):4–23

The Changing Role of Cooperatives and Credit Unions in Czech Economy

Magdalena Hunčová and Martin Mikeska

Abstract Within the Czech Republic, the history of credit unions, savings and loan co-operatives and other types of credits and mutuals was very rich till the beginning of World War II. However, these days there are only a few "credit cooperatives/credit unions" left many of which are gradually changing under the Basel European regulations and the supervision of the Czech National Bank into banking institutions.

1 Introduction

Cooperatives as well as credit ones, and mutuals are known as a significant part of social economy (Anheier 2005). In countries where market economy is traditional, all cooperatives and mutuals have been in operation up till now and they have usually played an important role in sustainable local and regional development. They are a specific part of a not-for-profit economy and non-risk finance related to social aspects of the economy. Generally, they support the social capital development and local economies based on initiatives of like-minded people. Within the Czech Republic, the history of credit unions, savings and loan co-operatives, and other types of credit cooperatives and mutuals was very rich till the beginning of World War II. However, these days the original credits or mutuals are hard to find here. There are only a few "credit cooperatives/credit unions" left many of which are gradually changing into banking institutions, with reference to the Basel European regulations and under the supervision of the Czech National Bank. Recently they do not and cannot carry out their specific role in financing of the

M. Hunčová
Faculty of Social and Economic Studies, J. E. Purkyně University in Ústí and Labem, Ústí and Labem, Czech Republic
e-mail: mhuncova@hotmail.com

M. Mikeska (✉)
Faculty of Management and Economics, Tomas Bata University, Zlín, Czech Republic
e-mail: mikeska@fame.utb.cz

S. Karafolas (ed.), *Credit Cooperative Institutions in European Countries*, Contributions to Economics, DOI 10.1007/978-3-319-28784-3_14

social economy sector. The chapter maps the historical development of Czech credit cooperatives till today, bringing a view about their position at nowadays financial market in the Czech Republic and attempts to explain the reasons for certain developmental trends. It also suggests what we can expect on this field in the near future.

While historically the first (authentic) cooperative, distinctive by the rules in its articles, was established in Rochdale, England, in 1846 for collective work, sale and consumption, in Central Europe the first cooperatives were established at about the same time as a response to the lack of cheap capital. From 1846 until the beginning of World War II, there in Bohemia and Moravia the basis of the cooperative idea was an attempt to solve social problems without violence caused by the failure of the "self-regulatory market place" and "taming of risk capital", by means of reversing the factors of a principle into "work employs and controls the capital democratically" (Hunčová 2006). The cooperatives were members' economic associations open to anybody who wanted to respect the basic regulations regardless of their origin, religion or political persuasion. The mutual relations of the cooperative members were based on democratic decision making by equal voting rights (1 member 1 vote) on the basis of the same small capital contribution. The purpose of the association and cooperative economy was and remains to be the economic, social and cultural benefit for cooperative members. Cooperatives looked after the education of its members, their cultural improvement as well as community development, as well. Economic gain wasn't distributed. In that way, the cooperative system filled the gaps in the labor market, stimulated citizens in the process of collective care for their social welfare, increased competitiveness of the local economy, humanized the market and was *the school of prime democracy and small business* (Hunčová 2010a).

Czech cooperatives, credit cooperatives included, historically, have gone through two extensive and deep reforms imposed by the State till now, namely the forcible submission to the central economic plan firstly and then obligatory submission to the market secondary. Because the recent cooperatives in the Czech Republic are under regulation of the Commercial Code (1992–1993)/Corporate Code (from 2014) only, we can meet there also some untypical cooperatives being established and work today, for example with only one member-owner, or motivated only for profit, no legal problem. Credit unions have their own legislation nowadays, but they don't become to be a source of "small finance" yet. Mutuals, with only a few minor exceptions, do not exist in the Czech Republic today.

Nowadays the European Union appreciates cooperatives and mutuals as an important part of the social economy and as an engine of local and regional development. Meanwhile in the Czech Republic (and in other post-totalitarian countries), due to their specific historic and institutional heritage, the cooperatives are being suppressed or merely tolerated. In spite of that, the cooperative system has not ceased to exist; in case of productive and social cooperatives it is even possible to observe certain positive trends in their development.

2 Cooperatives and Credit Unions in Czech Republic: Historical Overview

2.1 First Period Till 1938

In Bohemia and Moravia (the pre-1918 Austrian part of Austro-Hungarian Monarchy), the first credit unions and loan and savings cooperatives came into existence in the second half of nineteenth century in two forms (Hunčová 2004), namely:

1. Rural loan and savings cooperatives ("kasas")—the *Raiffeisen* type. In Bohemia, they were called "kampelička" in honor of their promoter, František Cyril Kampelík, MD (1805–1872). In the Austrian Raiffeisen system the same "kasas" have been working up till now; they have been covered by their banks and selling centre. The purpose of cooperative "kasas" was the financial support for small rural farming. Apart from small provision of loans their importance was also to teach people to be thrifty. The membership rights were based on 1 vote 1 member; the volunteering principle and voluntary work (self-help) was applied; the only paid employee was a cashier; potential profit was deposited in a reserve fund. Deposits were usually very small and that is why liability was unlimited. Loans, which were mostly operational, were provided at low interest rates for up to 4 years. The basis of this economic association was created by rural communities where people knew each other well.
2. Urban credit unions (also some rural or municipal ones)—the type of *Schulz-Delitsch*. Their purpose was financial support for craftsmen and small industry owners. They breached the principle of mutuality by employing also non-members—professionals. They also provided loans to non-members. Non-members could deposit their free capital at limited interest (hire). Votes were relatively linked to the amount of deposit which means that shares as deposits could be unequal. Liability was limited to the amount of deposit. The purpose of urban credit unions was to support crafts, competitiveness, and housing by provision of low interest (investment) loans.

In the Czech Lands, the urban credit unions as well as the rural loan and saving cooperatives ("kasas") grew up fully on the basis of self-help; they were self-governed in their activities and they mostly relied only on their own members' financial means. Despite that, they gradually managed to become not only partners of big banking houses but, primarily, the base for development of Czech agriculture and crafts. Other small and medium-size businesses cooperated with the credit unions and cooperative kasas as well. In Bohemia, thanks to loan and savings cooperatives ("kampelička" in Bohemia, and "raifeisenka" in Moravia), it was possible, among other things, for peasants to pay their debts dated back to the time of abolition of serfdom and statute labor. The most significant development of credit unions in Czechoslovakia was achieved in the two decades before World War II (Hunčová 2004).

Some dates (Hunčová 2012):

- 1920 there were in the Czech region 3820 credits with 409,000 of members
- 1925 there were in the Czech region 4006 credits with 506,000 of members
- 1930 there were in the Czech region 4269 credits with 646,000 of members

In contrast to that, insurance cooperatives did not develop in Czechoslovakia. However, there were a wide range of mutuals, company subsidy funds (especially for sickness and unemployment benefits, for example Křižík's fund) as well as foundations based upon membership or non-membership (for the purpose of philanthropy, such as the Hlávka siblings' foundation for backing of gifted students, science and art).

During the annexation of the border areas of Czechoslovakia (1938) and World War II (1938–1945) parts of the internal bonds and nets of credit cooperatives were severed, particularly because the credit unions were taken over and passed into the German Reich legal system together with their members, assets and liabilities. At the same time once autonomous credit cooperatives were obligatorily submitted to the cooperative headquarters.

2.2 *Second Period 1945–1989*

After the liberation in 1945, the credit unions managed to revitalize successfully and they effectively took part in the Czechoslovak currency reform in the beginning of 1950s. After 1953 all assets and liabilities in the credit union sector were transferred under the Česká národní spořitelna (Czech National Savings Bank) and brought under the State ownership; the membership base ceased to exist. By that the credit cooperatives sector in Czechoslovakia was virtually eliminated. Družstevní banka (The Cooperative Bank) faced similar fate when it was nationalized in 1953. The only credit-union type of bank that worked during the communist regime was called Živnostenská banka (Trade Bank). In 1992 it was privatized by a foreign investor and later fused with other banks.

Former members of these credit unions have never been compensated (not even after 1990 or later) because of major difficulties connected with potential identification of the members and their heirs, including their rights and duties.

Some dates (Hunčová 2012):

- 1945 there were in the Czech region 3625 credits with about 1,070,000 of members
- 1947 there were in the Czech region 4248 credits with about 1,306,000 of members

After 1953 mutually subsidizing funds and foundations were also abolished and liability for providing support in case of social need, sickness, disablement, unemployment and old age was taken over by the Czechoslovak state (by means of tax collection and state budget expenses).

3 Current Model: The New Era of Credit Unions

3.1 The First Phase: 1995–2005: The Overly Liberal Market

After 1989, in the Czech Republic there a general Commercial Code was passed (1992), which also regulated cooperatives, instead specific cooperatives laws. The so-called Transformation Law of the same period compelled the cooperatives to "transform into the market environment" with no reference to the standards of the Statement on the Co-operative Identity (ICA 1995). Credit cooperatives had not existed in the Czech Republic at that time (they were abolished in 1953), the Transformation Law did not affect them.

The new Act No. 87/1995 Coll. on credit unions should have filled the gap in the field of financial market. Richard Mandelík, the executive chairman of the Czech Credit Unions Association and an initiator of the Act, welcomed the passage of the Act by saying: "*This passage, in defiance of the government's will, is a significant success of all who see a modern state as a richly structured civil society*" (Mandelík 1998). The Association became a WOCCU (World Council of Credit Unions) member. Based on this membership the Association adopted some working principles, e.g., running without the umbrella of the cooperative central bank. The membership in the Association of Cooperative Credit Unions was not obligatory. The new Czech credit unions did not restore offering services in the original format to other type of coops, nor to craftsmen, small entrepreneurs, retailers or farmers.

The Act No. 87/1995 enabled establishing credit unions in a strongly liberal way. The minimum capital was determined to be only 500,000 CZK.[1] No specific requirements for the knowledge of the founders were assigned. The credit unions could freely establish daughter companies and accept members from anywhere. The umbrella cooperative bank was not proponed. The supervision of the credit unions was supposed to be done by a state-founded Úřad pro dohled nad družstevními záložnami (Office for the Supervision of Cooperative Unions). For the purposes of consolidation a Zajišťovací fond družstevních záložen (Security Fund for Cooperative Unions) was founded.

In the first phase of the new era only the credit union members (natural as well as legal persons) could use their services. After submitting an application and payment of the membership dues the applicant could become a credit union member. The membership dues were individual with every credit union; it could vary from 1 CZK to 1000 CZK. A contract on establishing a current or a saving account was signed with every account opening, which was similar to a regular bank account opening. The advantages and duties of credit union membership resulted from the credit union articles. Among the basic membership rights belonged the right to participate in the Meeting of the Members, the right for information on the credit union economic activities and the right to ask questions to the top managers

[1] The average exchange rate of the Czech Koruna and American Dollar in 1995 was approximately 26.5 CZK to 1 USD so 500,000 CZK equaled 18,870 USD.

of the credit union. The basic duties comprised the member participation in the loss cover of the credit union up to the amount of the membership dues; the loss participation did not include the account deposits. Contrary to the banks the credit unions offered low or null account charges yet higher interest rates on the savings or fixed term deposits. Compared to the banks, they also offered more advantageous loans to their members. On the other hand, the credit unions created only a small branch net. These branches often filled the local market gaps following closures of some bankrupt commercial banks. At the end of 1996 overall 57 credit unions of varying focus, potential and quality existed in the Czech Republic. Three years later their number rose to 130.

Three basic variations of credit unions could be identified in 1999:

A. A-type, enterprise credits as *small associations being established by* a closed group of entrepreneurs *who* used this form as their own *"banking institution"* within the gaps in the bank market. This type was not originally acknowledged to be orthodox but it most often survived the later upheavals. This type of credits best corresponded to the original purpose of the authentic loan and savings cooperatives. Some of them staid out of the Czech Credit Unions Association
B. *B-type, urban credit unions, oriented to their members' benefits in the form of favorable* **credit** *joined with* **other services** (obtaining a flat, car lease purchase, etc.). This type of credit unions also seemed to stand close to the original idea, although they were not stable due to often ill-considered and unsecured large and long-term credits and relatively ill-defined terms for making use of credit.
C. C-type, large credit unions *being established by capable or ambitious individuals and groups without territorial, membership or social limits.* A **"hunt" for inhabitants' deposits** at high deposit interest rates of up to 35 % became their distinctive feature. These deposits were evaluated in a risky way which made this type of credit union a stand-in for risky investment funds. They recruited their members from the whole area of the Czech Republic. This type of unions was the most vulnerable to intentional "tunneling out" (unseen stealing from the company). It also suffered from the lack of control from its members. The majority of such credit unions went bankrupt at the end of the first phase, the rest goes to transform into banks later (Hunčová 2006).

The overly liberal market of the credit unions between 1996 and 2000 brought first significant problems. Credit unions were founded by people without experience in financial sector. Credit unions lacked mid-term and long-term business plans which would take economic stability and efficiency into consideration. In its benevolence the Act No. 87/1995 in its original wording created prerequisites for the future credit union bankruptcies by enabling an unlimited property participation for the legal persons. There was no functional regulation nor supervision of credit exposure against the debtors. Until the year 2000 eleven credit unions operating with one third of all credit union deposits were under the receivership. Bankruptcy was declared on six credit unions with 60 % of total deposits. Further six credit unions with over 20 % of total deposits were under the receivership in the end of 2001 (see Table 1).

Table 1 Development of credit unions between 1996 and 2013

Year	Assets (in CZK)	The number of members	The number of credit unions	The number of credit unions (business register)	Active credit unions	Compulsory liquidation	Bankruptcy petition	Receivership
1996	176,000,000.00	7092	45					
1997	1,267,000,000.00	25,160	66					
1998	4,484,000,000.00	63,301	75					
1999	10,450,000,000.00	126,486	127	133	127	3	0	3
2000	10,480,000,000.00	111,744	73	134	73	44	6	11
2001	10,980,000,000.00	N/A	55	134	55	54	19	6
2002	952,835,000.00	N/A	46	127	46	50	30	1
2003	1,128,408,000.00	N/A	42	119	42	45	32	0
2004	2,146,000,000.00	19,077	33	111	33	44	34	0
2005	4,190,000,000.00	30,611	20					
2006	6,977,000,000.00	42,451	20					
2007	9,000,000,000.00	35,942	19					
2008	7,899,400,000.00	35,921	17					
2009	11,994,200,000.00	34,006	17					
2010	19,934,200,000.00	34,006	14					
2011	28,297,300,000.00	44,696	14					
2012	39,279,000,000.00	54,408	13					
2013	31,622,000,000.00	53,595	12					

Source: www.cnb.cz

As a reaction to this situation the Act No. 100/2000 Coll. changed and amended the Act No. 87/1995. The Office for the Supervision of Cooperative Unions gained the competence to revoke the credit union license to those credit unions which committed serious failings in the activities of credit unions or which obviously did not perform any long-term activities. Further tightening of credit unions operations came with the Czech entrance to the European Union. The Act No. 280/2004 Coll. came into effect on May 1, 2004 which was an umbrella norm for the legislation changes initiated by the Act No. 100/2000 Coll. This norm reflecting the necessity of the harmonization with the European law dramatically changed the current situation in the sector of credit unions.

The Act No. 280/2004 Coll. changed the minimum capital requirement for credit unions from 500,000 CZK to 35,000,000 CZK, which disabled further activities of unions with limited membership managing limited amount of deposits. Based on this dilemma it was clear that credit unions would have to abandon the principle of equal property shares and accept asymmetric vote rights. This should happen by creating a direct link between the settlement amount and economic results and by enabling profit distribution that would reflect principles of loss coverage duties of their members.

In comparison with almost 130 credit unions in 1999, there were only 33 consolidated credit unions left in the Czech Republic by December 31, 2005 with 18,700 members; 1569 million CZK of deposits; and 1364 million of credits. Furthermore, there were 44 credit unions under liquidation and 34 were declared bankrupt. Meanwhile, the new legal limitations, which should prevent further instability of this segment, negatively influenced the remaining credit unions. In that period, the whole credits sector in the Czech Republic went through fundamental consolidation. With reference to EU regulations (BASEL) credit unions were imposed to increase their foundation capital.

Since April 1, 2006 credit unions have been under financial supervision of the *Czech National Bank* (CNB). A year later there were only 21 credit unions left in the Czech Republic; by 2013 their number decreased to 12. They keep standing out of cooperative nets and do not have their own umbrella bank. Under pressure of law they themselves keep changing into commercial banks. In assessment, credit unions in the first phase of the new era did not fulfill their role of financing institutions as a part of social economy in the Czech Republic.

3.2 The Second Phase 2006–2013: The Credit Unions Legislative Changes

The second phase begins with the new supervisor of credit unions—the Czech National Bank, and with new conditions for their activities. From 2006 the credit unions have to obtain the license from the CNB and they have information duty according to the Decree No. 123/2007 Coll. All the deposits in the credit unions are secured up to €100,000 for each depositor.

Based on the amendment of the Act on Banks (No. 21/1992 Coll.) a necessity arose to issue licenses to banks and branches of foreign banks (from countries out of the European economic area). Some competences regarding mergers, transferring of property to the associates or closing of a bank have been newly assigned to the Czech National Bank. Banks and branches of foreign banks have new duties in connection with fight against legalization of yield from criminal activities and for the purposes of preserving international peace and safety, protection of human rights and fight against terrorism.

Based on the amendment of the Act on Credit Unions (No. 87/1995 Coll.) the savings and credit cooperatives (credit unions) have been placed on the same level as banks, by applying principles such as the supervision by the Czech National Bank, justified as the "consolidation of the banking sector".

The named norms adjusted the conditions and tightened the requirements for establishment, granting the license, organization, management (including the requirement for the specialized qualifications of top managers) and gaining qualified interest on the legal person. The emphasis is also placed on appropriate capital endowment and capital structure of savings and credit cooperatives; adherence to the rules of liquidity; and performance prudence. A full involvement in the domestic payment system brings new duties as well. Similarly to banks and branches of foreign banks rules are applied.

4 Credit Cooperatives in the National Banking Market

4.1 The Influence of the Crisis 2007–2011: The Birth of a New Sector

Previous tightening of the conditions has brought strengthening of the whole sector of low-cost banks and credit cooperatives at the expense of standard banks since the 2007 financial crisis created demand for a new type of financial institution. Clients demanded a bank with deposits secured equally to a standard bank but offering cheaper services. The Czech banking fees, the highest ones in the EU in a long-term perspective, forced clients to look for cheaper alternatives. It was credit cooperatives and other low-cost banks that offered low fees and multiple higher interest rates on deposits. More than a million clients changed their standard bank over for a low-cost bank or a credit union. The increase of the membership in the credit cooperatives from 2007 to 2011 indicated new tendencies on the Czech financial market. It was enabled by a new Client Mobility Code, which allowed clients to flexibly transfer their account among the financial institutions. According to some surveys only one quarter of the clients would nowadays choose one of the Big Five standard banks (ČSOB, ČS, KB, RB, Unicredit). The dynamics of the growth of low-cost banks and credit unions clients was enormous. It can be illustrated with an example of FIO bank (a former credit union), where the number of clients exceeded 416,000 in 2014. In the case of standard banks the situation can be illustrated on the following examples: Česká spořitelna (ČS) claims it serves 5.3 million clients; ČSOB serves 3.1 million clients; GE Money Bank (the largest medium-sized bank) serves 1.1 million clients.

Naturally, the volume of clients' deposits is more important for the banks than their number. From the point of view of the balance sum development it is necessary to state that the low-cost banking segment does not comprise more than 5 % of the total financial sector.

In the upcoming years the standard banks will fight with the low-cost banks mainly when it comes to the rich clients. Credit unions should take a different path, though. Their mission is primarily to offer services to their own members (cooperators); these services being cheap loans and secure deposits. The Czech mass media and the Czech National Bank evaluate financial services exclusively from the financial and economic point of view of the banking sector and not from the social-economy, solidarity and mutual point of view. This creates negative public opinion and distorts the view of the whole credit union segment in the Czech Republic. The standard banks can be expected to create effort for clients not to deposit all their money with the low-costs and credit unions. The following development of the financial markets in the Czech Republic will be driven not only by the price factors but also by the portfolio of the offered services.

To summarize the development trends of the Czech credit unions between 1998 and 2011 through data, here is a short factual overview: There were 75 credit unions in 1998 with 63,301 members and CZK 4,484,000 worth of deposits. The total of provided credits to members was CZK 1,900,000. In 2011, the total number of credit unions was down to 14; the total number of members has decreased to 44,696. Additional 23 credit unions were in liquidation and 16 were in bankruptcy process. The total of deposits by members increased to CZK 25,060,000 and the total of provided credits to members rose to CZK 19,293,000.

4.2 Interventions of the Czech National Bank 2011–2013: Attempts to Eliminate Risks in the Credit Union Sector

Due to the interventions of the CNB an initiation of administrative procedure and the following license revocation in two significant cases took place in the second phase between the years 2011 and 2013. In case of the Unibon credit union the CNB initiated the administrative procedure on license revocation based on unsatisfactory economic results. The ratio of capital to risk weighted assets dropped below the 8 % level. Further on, the CNB found out that this credit union in a long term perspective violated exposure limits against some of its members and economically connected groups of people despite repeated Central bank warnings. In the second case the credit union Metropolitní spořitelní družstvo (MSD) significantly violated its obligation to have a functional management and inspection system including the risk-management system, especially the credit risk management system. Credit risk of MSD was only managed formally thus the credit union faced significant risk of having unrepaid credits provided in a considerable volume which endangered its stability and the property of depositors.

2012 was declared to be the year of cooperatives, credit unions included. Credit union significance was emphasized even by the European Parliament when it approved of a report in 2013 claiming the contribution of credit unions in overcoming the financial crisis. According to experience of economists and politicians of the world and according to the opinion of the representatives of the European Parliament cooperative banks and cooperatives in the sphere of industry and services demonstrated to be more resistant in the time of crisis in comparison with other banks and businesses. On the other hand, the IMF criticized credit unions in the previous periods for not fulling their social roles; IMF suggested the need for restructuring. The Czech government and the CNB reacted with further measures affecting credit cooperatives. They have tightened the rules for credit unions beyond the rules valid for regular banks. For the intended consolidation of financial markets the CNB also used the fact that a part of the *sector* of credit cooperatives got into economic problems in the period of 2011–2014. The CNB based their Unibon and MSD license revocation on the critical voices that failing credit rate reaches 6–7 % in regular banks while it is 20–30 % with credit unions. Even if the CNB is indisputably right, the problems of credit unions appeared due to the dysfunctional Act on Credit Unions after 1995, because that law did not take into consideration cooperative principles and values, specific features of credit unions and the situation of credit unions in the Czech Republic, nor the economic turbulence of the period.

Reporting of credit unions is regulated by the Decree No. 426/2013 Coll. on reporting of credit unions to the Czech National Bank and the Regulation (EU) No. 680/2014 of April 16, 2014 laying down implementing technical standards of institutions reporting for the purposes of supervision according to the Regulation (EU) No. 575/2013 (ITS) of the European Parliament and of the Council on prudential requirements for credit institutions and investment firms.

4.3 The Third Phase 2014–2018: Prevention of the Credit Union Growth

Another wave of fundamental legislative changes for credit unions took place in 2014. As a reaction to the situation and to adaptation of the CRR4 Decree the Czech Ministry of Finance prepared the amendments of the Act on Banks, Act on Credit Unions, Capital Market Undertaking Act and the Act on Czech National Bank. The amendments were passed in 2014, taking effect on January 1, 2015. This change has had a dramatic effect on the whole sphere of entrepreneurship, especially so on the business activities of credit unions. The positive point can be seen in the fact that in the amendments the CNB stated its aim for the credit unions to be managed under the cooperative principles and not offering the complex portfolio of banking services. The amendment of the Act No. 87/1995 Coll. on Credit Unions defined cardinal limits for activities of credit unions, which are stricter than the limits for regular banks. These are valid from 2015 in this form:

1. A doubled contribution to the Deposits Insurance Fund. The new rules set that credit unions quarterly contribute 0.08 % of the volume of the insured deposits while banks pay 0.04 %. One-member-equals-one-vote rule. Previous amendments allowed asymmetric voting in credit unions where one member could easily override votes of others provided he or she knew the value of their credit shares. Such practice, according to the CNB, leads to the lower efficiency of control mechanisms inside credit unions.
2. Balance sheet sum of maximum CZK 5 billion, credit limit to members maximum CZK 30 million. The amendment tightens the conditions for business activities of credit unions. It limits the maximum balance sheet sum to CZK 5 billion. If the credit union exceeds this limit, it has to transform into a bank as of 2018. The amount of credit loans offered by a credit union is limited to CZK 30 million as of 2018. Since 2015 the credit unions cannot offer their services and products to the persons who are not the credit union members.
3. Higher membership dues 1:10; minimum membership dues CZK 1000. The proposal is to strengthen joint responsibility of members for economic activities of the credit union by defining the maximum membership duties and defining its links to the sum of interest-bearing deposits. Since 2018 the minimum duties are defined to be CZK 1000 (it is one tenth of the sum of interest-bearing deposits of one member).

On the one hand, these new principles can lead to strengthening of the credit union identity as cooperatives. On the other hand they can force the existing credit unions to transform into banks thus significantly weakening the cooperative segment. The Association of Cooperative Credit Unions that unites credit cooperatives in the Czech Republic (including the ones not constituting their cooperative character, such as the credit unions owner of which is a foreign person) opposed the CNB with the claim that equal voting principle caused the collapse in the sector of credit unions in 2002–2004. Its re-introduction may be in conflict with the interest to strengthen sector stability. The Association has protested in the form of an open letter to the members of Czech Parliament especially against the 1:10 rule which it considers to be unconstitutional. The Association has also filed a complaint with the European Commission and it hopes that the Commission will order the Czech amendment to be invalidated. According to the Association, the measures accepted in the amendment limit the ability of credit cooperatives to accept deposits from coop members down to one tenth. The persons interested in cooperative savings have so far paid only symbolic membership dues which are not insured as they participate at a potential credit union loss. The amendment, however, states, that since July 1, 2015, only a tenfold deposit of the membership dues can be interest-bearing. The membership dues are also exempted from the legal deposit insurance so in case of bankruptcy the client can lose them. These limits and the reduction of the deposit guarantee will most probably negatively reflect in the willingness of depositors to deposit their money in a credit cooperative. By lowering of state guarantees and defining limits for interest-bearing deposits the benefit of the financial product as such has ceased to exist. With the existing limit of membership dues of CZK 20,000 and adhering to the 1:10 rule it is possible to deposit maximum of CZK 200,000 for one member of a credit union. Yet membership dues are not insured and they participate at potential loss of a credit union. Such conditions can deter anybody willing to deposit bigger amounts of money.

Despite the stated problems the Association does not consider establishing new, small credit unions that would satisfy the given conditions. The Association claims the main aim of credit unions is to provide favorable interest for the secured deposits. The possible linking of credit unions and other cooperatives and fulfilling other roles of credit unions and cooperative banks which are common abroad have not been considered yet by the Association. Nevertheless, credit unions which would be forced to transform to banks can gradually develop into cooperative banks or the umbrella banks for credit unions.

5 The Future of Czech Credit Cooperatives: Transformation to Banks?

Despite being based on the US credit union model, the Czech credit unions restored after 1995 more or less comprised the character of credit unions based on Schulz-Delitsche principle.

In the three basic phases of credit cooperative market development the situation in the Czech Republic has shifted from overly liberal and uncontrolled model of the 1990s to the financial market strictly based on strict regulation. The effort of the CNB to "restore" credit unions in the sense of their cooperative principles is devastating for the current sector of Czech credit unions. The measures taken to limit the growth of credit cooperatives implemented in 2015 in the amendment of the Act No. 87/1995 Coll. forces some credit unions to leave the sector by transforming to banks or gradually terminate their existence.

Credit unions look for ways how to harmonize the new strict rules with their further existence. The two largest credit unions, Creditas and Moravský peněžní ústav (MPÚ) with balance sheet sum around CZK 10 billion each, have no other option than voluntarily transform into banks by 2018 or resign on their further growth. To accomplish the transformation to bank they have to obtain a bank license from the CNB.

However, it is quite possible that the remaining credit unions under the CNB pressure will manage to gradually fulfill the role of cooperatives that pertains to their character of supporting the social economy and regional development. They have the potential to develop new sectors of social economy and enable their prospective members to develop cooperative networks based on democratic management of the Czech economy. Present conditions do not make it easy. Nevertheless, the cooperative sector in the Czech Republic is still viable and cooperatives in their legal form are still attractive for many Czech inhabitants (Hunčová 2010b).

References

Anheier H (2005) Nonprofit organizations—theory, management, policy. Routledge, London, p 54. ISBN 0-415-31419-4

Czech National Bank. Financial market supervision reports 2006–2013. https://www.cnb.cz/cs/dohled_financni_trh/souhrnne_informace_fin_trhy/zpravy_o_vykonu_dohledu/index.html

Hunčová M (2004) The Czech co-operative reality and its social aspects: trends and challenges for co-operatives and social enterprises in developed and transition countries. ISSAN, Trento, pp 6–7. ISBN 88-88224-19-4

Hunčová M (2006) Družstva a jejich role v tržní ekonomice (Cooperatives role in the market economy). UJEP, Ústí nad Labem. ISBN 80-7044-810-5

Hunčová M (2010a) Ekonomický rozměr občanské společnosti (Economic dimension of the civil society). Prague, Wolters Kluwer CR. ISBN 978-80-7357-545-8

Hunčová M (2010b) Success of the Czech workers' co-operatives: fiction, mistake, or reality? Lyon's ICA European research conference—co-operatives contributions to a plural economy, Lyon, 2–4 Sept 2010

Hunčová M (2012) Co-operatives in the Czech Republic recently. XVII international conference on cooperative studies—cooperatives in the focus of a new economic policy, Wien/Vienna, 18–20 Sept

Mandelík R (1998) Obnova a rozvoj peněžního družstevnictví a nová právní úprava peněžního družstevnictví (Reconstruction and development of credits system and new legislation regarding the credits system). UJEP Academic conference Družstevnictví v tržní ekonomice (Cooperative system in the market economy), Ústí nad Labem, 1998

Office for the Supervision of Cooperative Unions reports 1999–2004. https://www.cnb.cz/cs/dohled_financni_trh/souhrnne_informace_fin_trhy/archiv/druzstevni_zalozny/index.html

Credit Unions in Estonia

Andro Roos and John Õun

Abstract The aim of credit unions and co-operative banks is collocating member deposits to allocate them as loans, so that capital could circulate among members. Market share of credit unions in Estonia is marginal at the moment (*ca.* 0.2 % of overall banking market). There exist 22 credit unions in Estonia, which have 6770 members altogether (31.07.2015). Before WWII the situation was very different. There existed 189 credit unions and two co-operative banks (central credit unions) in 1939. They had 79,100 members altogether. Market share of credit unions in overall banking market in Estonia was 52 % on that period. The article will give overview about the situation of nowadays credit union sector in Estonia, including statistical data and description development problems.

1 Introduction

The aim of credit unions and co-operative banks is collocating member deposits to allocate them as loans, so that capital could circulate among members. Comparing with other financial institutions, idiomaticalness of co-operative banking is that customers are owners/members of the institution at the same time. These members of a credit union or co-operative bank have entire control over the management of their co-operative and they attend on profit splitting according to their activeness consuming credit union services. Commercial banks at the same time are often owned by a small circle of investors and their aim is to earn profit for them. These are two main differences between commercial banking and co-operative banking.

Market share of credit unions in Estonia is marginal at the moment (*ca.* 0.2 % of overall banking market). There exist 22 credit unions in Estonia, which have 6770 members altogether (31.07.2015). Before WWII the situation was very different. There existed 189 credit unions and two co-operative banks (central credit unions) in 1939. They had 79,100 members altogether. Market share of credit unions in

A. Roos (✉) • J. Õun
University of Tartu, Tartu, Estonia
e-mail: andro@lkm.ee; John.oun@yhistupank.ee

S. Karafolas (ed.), *Credit Cooperative Institutions in European Countries*,
Contributions to Economics, DOI 10.1007/978-3-319-28784-3_15

overall banking market in Estonia was 52 % on that period (Roos 2007). The article will give overview about the situation of nowadays credit union sector in Estonia, including statistical data and description development problems.

2 Main Characteristics of Estonian Credit Unions and Co-operative Banking Sector

Theoretically, co-operative banking system consists of two levels in Estonia: credit union and central credit union (co-operative bank) level. According to the credit institution law and credit union law, banks are defined as credit institutions whereas credit unions are defined as financial institutions. In that sense, Estonia is different from other EU member states, as credit unions are not credit institutions. Hence, only commercial and co-operative banks are defined as credit institutions. There exist no co-operative bank in Estonia at the moment.

Credit unions are based on individuals and firms in Estonia. At the same time, central credit unions can be formed from credit unions and they help member unions to provide broader range of services and make greater investments in banking technology. Alternative way of establishment and functioning of a co-operative bank is that a co-operative bank itself is built up on the principle of credit union, but has the status of bank (credit institution)—it may not be central cooperative, which bases on credit unions, but can also consist of individuals and firms, like an ordinary credit union.

Relative importance (market share of credit unions is *ca.* 0.2 % of overall Estonian banking market) of co-operative banking and credit unions in Estonia is small due to the fact that there are small number of credit unions operating—at the end of 2011 there were only 18 credit unions operating and only 10 of them were operating actively. Nine credit unions belong to Estonian Union of Credit Co-operatives (EUCC), which functions mainly nominally. Actively functioning credit unions are: Loo CU (does not belong to EUCC), Eesti Korteriühistute CU (*Credit Union of Estonian House Cooperatives*) (does not belong to EUCC), Leie CU, Kehtna CU, Kambja CU, Põlvamaa CU, Tartu CU, Saaremaa CU, Eesti Evangeelne Luterlik CU (*Estonian Evangelical Lutheran Credit Union*) Maaelu Edendamise CU (*Rural Development Credit Union*) and Metsa CU (*Forestry Credit Union*). Three last mentioned credit unions function as profession-based cooperatives and all others as territory-based. These two types are allowed also by Estonian credit union law, which also states that if a credit union is established as profession-based cooperative, it may have 1000 members maximum. If a credit union is established as territory-based cooperative, it may have members from municipality the credit union is positioned, including neighboring municipalities. Still, this restriction is often interpreted in the way that these cooperatives are active all around Estonia, as all municipalities are neighboring.

On the one hand, the number of credit unions is small because of the complexity of establishment procedures of credit unions in Estonia. Complexity of establishing a credit union is influenced by high rate of minimum share capital and minimum number of founding members. Estonia has validated high rate of founding members—25. Estonia has validated also high rate of credit union share capital—EUR 32,000. In Estonia the minimum rate of credit union share capital is over ten times greater than in the case of an ordinary co-operative. In the case of establishing a co-operative bank, it is necessary to fulfil all the same obligations set by the credit institutions law as in the case of establishing a commercial bank. The most important obligation is the requirement of minimal share capital—five million euros. A co-operative bank has to have minimum of 50 founding members. These may be credit unions, if the co-operative bank is built up as central credit union or 50 legal and natural persons, if the co-operative bank is built up on the principle of credit union.

3 Development Problems of Estonian Credit Unions

First credit unions in Estonia were established by Baltic-German people. Regaining economical and cultural independence, Estonians started to establish their own credit unions, which were not supported by special laws or state support, like in developed countries nowadays. First Estonian credit union was established in Tartu in 1902. After successful Independence war in 1918, credit unions of Republic of Estonia started to grow fast and by 1940, the share of co-operative banking was over 50 % in Estonia. After losing independence to the Soviet Union, soviet powers proscribed private ownership, including credit unions and other co-operatives. Powers of post-soviet Estonia (since 1990) have not banned co-operation, but co-operation has also not been the first priority of any post-soviet government of Estonia.

In theoretical studies, three stages of development are proposed: nascent, transitions and mature industry phases. A specific stage is achieved when distinctive attributes can be ascertained. These attributes are: asset and membership size, strength of common bond, emphasis on voluntarism, sections of society being served, range of services, central organizational development, technological development and system of deposit and loan guarantee. Analyzing credit union systems of Estonia, one can conclude that Estonian credit unions are positioned in nascent industry phase in general.

Second important problem, which has impeded the development of Estonian credit unions, is lack of state guarantee for credit union deposits. Hence, Estonian credit unions may not seem very trustworthy for public. Still, according to objective criterions, this is not true. If we compare summarized balance sheets of Estonian credit unions and commercial banks, one can see, that equity of credit unions exceeds amount of deposits four times. In the case of commercial banks it is vice versa. The amount of deposits exceeds equity six times. Hence, inter-bank risks for depositors are much smaller in the case of Estonian credit unions than in the case of commercial banks.

In the other hand, holding free resources of money in the case of Estonian credit unions, increases the risks for depositors. In the case of Estonian commercial banks it is vice versa again. According to Estonian credit union law, credit unions are required to deposit their money resources in some domestic commercial bank. These resources that Estonian credit unions hold in commercial banks can get lost in the case of bankruptcy of a commercial bank, because credit union deposits in commercial banks are not guaranteed. Commercial banks in the same time deposit their money on correspondent account of Bank of Estonia. These deposits are fully guaranteed by the government.

Collecting deposits is the main basis of loan giving activities and through that, the basis of credit union growth. International empirics has shown that to efficiently collect deposits, there are three premises: a depositor has to have full overview and quick access to his/her deposit, deposits have to be guaranteed, depositor has to be paid highest interest possible for his/her deposit. In Estonia only the third premise is enforced. Hence, in first priority in Estonia, deposits have to be state guaranteed to achieve the second premise. Right now deposits hold in credit unions are not guaranteed by state guarantee fund. In the case of deposits held in credit unions, deposit interest go under 21 % income tax. Depositors of commercial banks do not have to by income tax from interest revenue at the same time.

Nowadays IT-based economy demands banks and also credit unions, if they want to be competitive, to offer internet banking, ATM, debit and credit card services, so that a member could have immediate access to his/her bank account in credit union. In Estonia technological development of credit unions have not been taken as first priority, although speaking of credit union sector development, it is inevitable. The first step towards this goal would be implementing electronic customer service and accounting system for credit unions, so that they could make transactions and conduct clearing within themselves, in perspective also with Bank of Estonia and commercial banks. Following second step would be implementing on-line banking for credit unions. Technological development of credit unions gives also better chances to expand their range of services as well as target group. All these factors are important for moving to higher development phase. EUCC started to develop its own internet banking system in 2010. Following implementation of credit union internet banking system, ATM and card payment systems will be future goals.

4 Statistical Overview of Estonian Credit Union Sector

Based on the statistics of Bank of Estonia, there were 26 credit unions active from 2004 to 2011. Two credit unions went into bankruptcy in 2010, two was liquidated in 2013 and 2014. By the end of July 2015 there were 22 credit unions which have revealed statistical data about themselves. Credit unions have great potential for

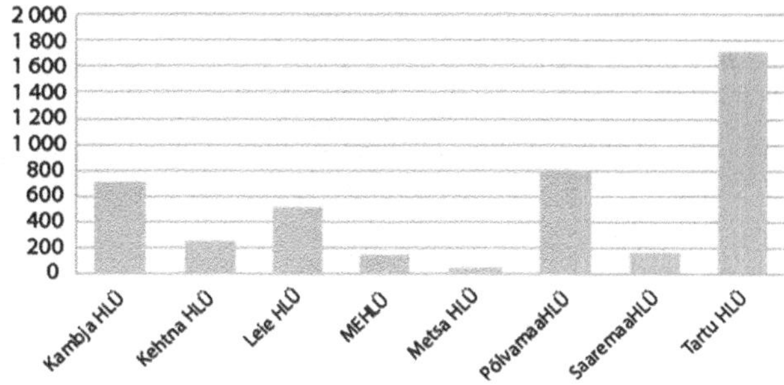

Fig. 1 Members of member-CUs of EUCC on 31.03.2015

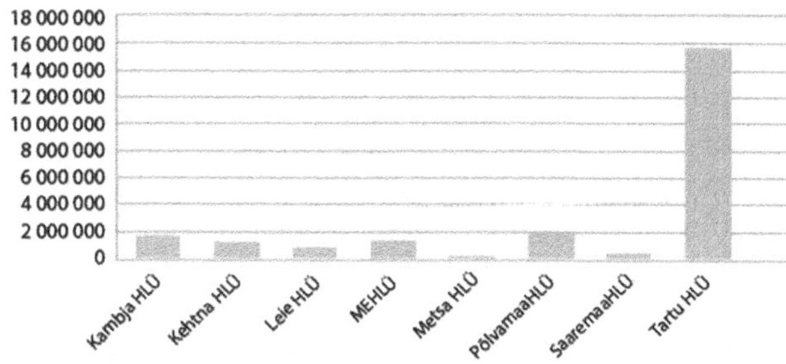

Fig. 2 Total assets of member-CUs of EUCC on 31.03.2015

expansion, due to the general economic environment being favourable. Also another advantage is the tendency of foreign commercial banks (99 % of total banking market in Estonia) as market leaders to export their profits abroad in a situation where the clients have trouble with their finances.

The total assets managed by credit unions in Estonia amounted to 47.5 million euros by the end of July 2015. Thereof 36.7 million euros was served as demands to clients (loans granted). Total equity of credit unions summated to 11.7 million (Fig. 1).

By the end of July 2015 there were a total of 6770 members in Estonian credit unions. The number of members varies considerably between different co-operatives. Largest CU—Tartu Credit Union—has 1900 members. Other larger credit unions have 500–800 members individually, where as smaller credit unions involve less than 200 members. Generally the fact is that the more members a credit union has, the more assets it manages. Largest credit union manage assets up to 17.7 million euros, compared to smaller CUs which are managing less than 0.5–1 million euros (Fig. 2).

All the credit unions operate accordingly the same regulations. However some have focused on specific areas of management. Areas have been specified by Metsa Credit Union (*Forestry Credit Union*), where the members are mainly private forest owners, and by Estonian Cooperative Housing Credit Union, which manages different Cooperative Housings' finances.

Besides focusing on different areas of management, some credit unions have also defined themselves by the territory, where they operate. Examples of that kind of credit unions are brought above in the article. One credit union which has shown

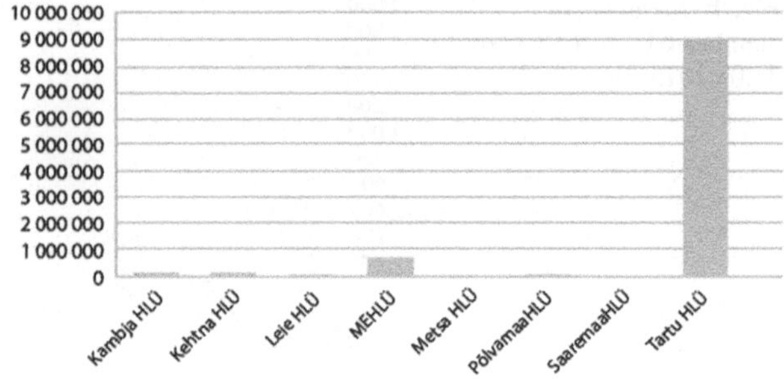

Fig. 3 Loans to business of member-CUs of EUCC on 31.03.2015

great growth in last 2 years, is Tartu Credit Union, which has HQ in Tartu (second largest city in Estonia) and branches in Tallinn (capital) and Narva (third biggest city). Tartu Credit Union also has its own monthly newspaper and weekly broadcast in radio and monthly show in TV. Due to following of the co-operative principle, the competition between credit unions is minimized. This in turn allows to focus on offering of competitive services compared to services commercial financial institutions offer.

In most credit unions there are both, natural persons and legal persons, who use financial services. The market can be segmented in different ways, but most common practice in Estonian CUs is making difference in three separate segments: private clients, businesses and non-profit companies. Most of the clients value the most: low credit costs, personal relationship between the directors and members and the support offered to local businesses to flourish (Fig. 3).

Financing local businesses is an integral part and goal of credit unions. The largest business financiers are Tartu Credit Union, Loo Credit Union and Maaelu Edendamise Credit Union. Estonian credit union all together serve 23.5 million euros in loans to local businesses.

Another goal of credit unions is to provide means to people to pool their savings and provide lending opportunities. The largest share of private loans is provided by Põlvamaa Credit Union, followed by Kambja Credit Union and Loo Credit Union. Estonian credit union all together serve 11.6 million euros in loans to private persons (Fig. 4).

To understand how rapid the growth of credit unions has been, we can take a look at Estonian largest Tartu Credit Union progress during the past 2 years. At the end of 2013 total assets managed by Tartu Credit Union was 8,074,739 €, number of members 1107 private and legal persons. At the end of July 2015 total assets managed was 17,550,706 €, number of members 1857 (Figs. 5 and 6).

This will also increase the income and costs of the credit union operations. Right now the yearly interest from deposits is 5 % and loan interest is 7 %, the increase in members will also allow for higher profits in the future. With an increase in the amount of deposits the amount of loans granted will also be able grow (Fig. 7).

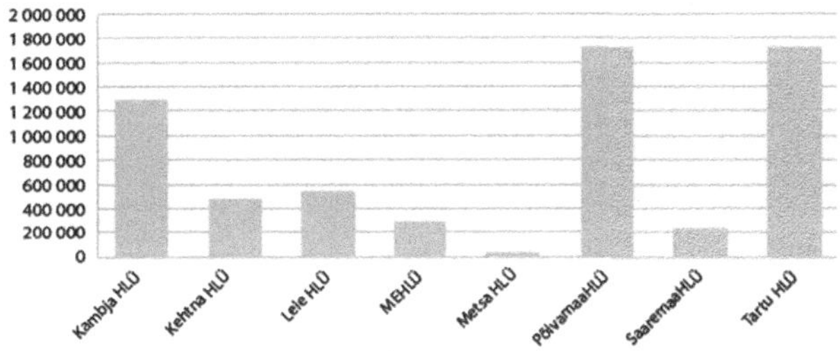

Fig. 4 Loans to persons of member-CUs of EUCC on 31.03.2015

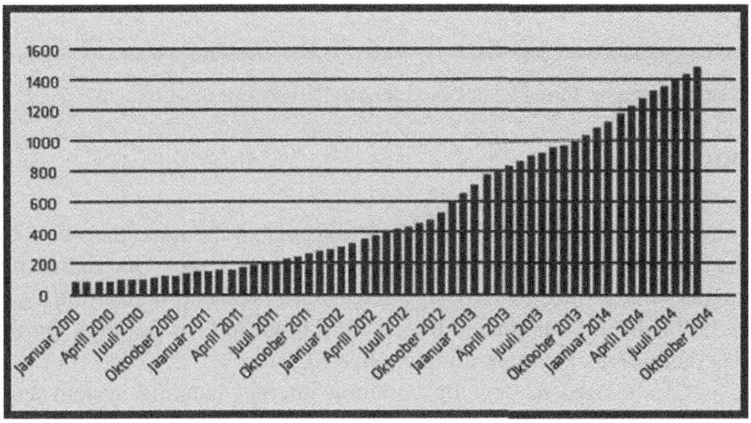

Fig. 5 Number of members of Tartu Credit Union January 2010–October 2014

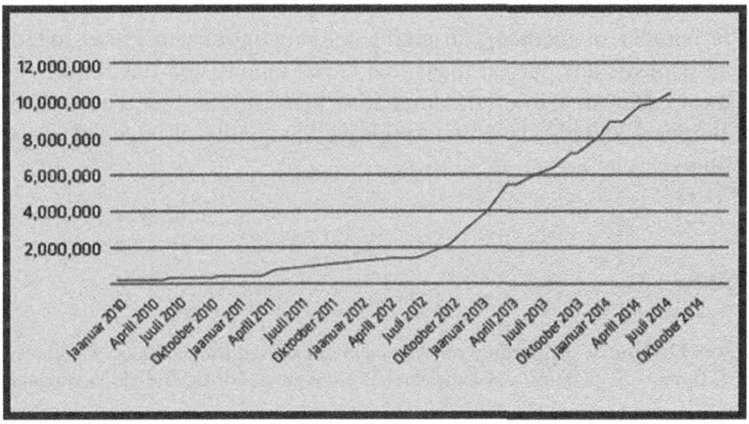

Fig. 6 Deposits of Tartu Credit Union January 2010–October 2014

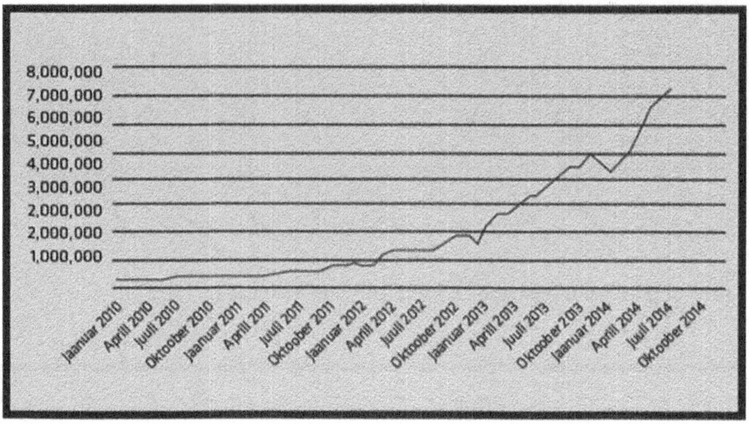

Fig. 7 Loans granted of Tartu Credit Union January 2010–October 2014

5 Conclusion

Market share of credit unions in Estonia is marginal at the moment (*ca.* 0.2 %), but it was the opposite in 1939—52 % of overall banking market. One reason for this is governments policy (in CUs deposit interests are taxed, in banks not; deposits in commercial banks are guaranteed by the state fund, in CUs not etc). On the other hand CUs themselves are been quite passive to date.

Still, as CUs started to develop common internet banking system and as the second largest CU Tartu Credit Union has started to offer innovative services to members as factoring, leasing, issuance of alternative currency, guarantee letters, insurance etc, there is much potential for fast growth in Estonian credit union sector.

As the number of members in credit unions continue to grow, together with amount of deposits and served loans, the credit unions will have more options to finance local businesses, to offer competitive interest rates that are suited better for specific purposes and also be able to improve the quality of financial services they are offering.

Reference

Roos A (2007) Ühistulise panganduse roll ja arenguvõimalused Balti riikides. MA thesis, University of Tartu, 150 p. http://www.metsaraha.ee/dokumendid/Artiklid/Hoilaenumagistritoeoe.pdf

The History, the Current System and the Special Features of Savings Cooperatives in Hungary

Attila Moizs and Gábor G. Szabó

Abstract Recently 260 Savings and Credit Cooperatives existed and worked in Hungary, the number of its members was about two million. In our days about 110 Cooperatives are registered at the Hungarian Financial Supervisory Authority, 106 are Savings Cooperatives of them. What is the reason of decrease? What sort of internal and external reasons cause, that five Savings-Cooperatives leave off on the average a year? The dilemmas of the development alternatives also support the assumption, that in the future model of savings cooperatives, a reorganized and efficient integration collaboration has an important role to play. The purpose of this writing is the promotion of the collective thinking, and by the help of this the Savings Coop's will be successful and active participants of the sector.

1 The Establishment and Evolution

The political era following the failure of the revolution of 1848–1849 did not favour the unraveling of the cooperative movement. None of the forms of volunteer organizations were desirable for the Austrian authorities. For the reorganization of the economy, capital was needed, both in the industry and in the agriculture—which was in the process of change after the liberation of the serves—but the institutional system of this was not at hand. Although the economics in Hungary in the second half of the nineteenth century (general poverty, lack of capital, later the challenges of the capitalist development) was very much similar to the

A. Moizs (✉)
"MECSEK" Savings Cooperative, Mecseknádasd, Hungary

Supervisory Board of National Interest Representation Alliance of Savings Cooperatives, Budapest, Hungary
e-mail: moizs@freemail.hu

G.G. Szabó
Institute of Economics, Center for Economic and Regional Studies, Hungarian Academy of Sciences, Budapest, Hungary
e-mail: szabo.gabor@krtk.mta.hu

S. Karafolas (ed.), *Credit Cooperative Institutions in European Countries*, Contributions to Economics, DOI 10.1007/978-3-319-28784-3_16

circumstances German farmers were at and which has generated the Raiffeisen movement, the chance for the establishment of credit institutions came to reality in that part of Transylvania which was mainly inhabited by Saxons who possessed over a relative large independence. This means that the first Hungarian credit institutions were the Transylvanian credit cooperatives, whose organizations was mainly based on nationality (Hungarian, Saxon). The Saxons established the first credit cooperative, being recognized by most people, in Beszterce in 1851.

Around the very same time of the formation of the Transylvanian credit cooperatives the credit cooperative in Győr (1864) and the First Hungarian General Officers' Society (1865)—which has also carried some features of cooperatives—came into existence.

The Hungarian credit cooperative movement followed the principles of Delitzsch mainly.

Antal Csengery has already urged by the time of the Austrian-Hungarian Compromise of 1867, the establishment of such a Raiffeisen-type credit cooperative system, where the cooperatives, operating in different villages and towns are held together by a kind of "Central Volksbank". For the sake of the assurance of the wide range of agricultural loans, the Credit Cooperative of Pest County (Pestmegyei Hitelszövetkezet) came into existence in 1886 under the management of Count Sándor Károlyi. This cooperative followed the pattern of credit cooperatives which have been successfully operating in great cities of other Hungarian regions (Győr, Székesfehérvár, Debrecen), and it later gained national authority. Soon, as the result of the organization started in smaller towns and villages, by the year 1894 several credit cooperatives were operating in Hungary, 80 in Pest county and 72 nationwide, with about 300,000 members.

The legislation passed Act XXIII on the economic and industrial credit banks in 1898, this way the National Central Credit Cooperative (OKH) came into existence in the very same year, which harmonized with the ambitions of the Alliance of Smallholders (Gazdaszövetség). The credit and industrial cooperative movement started by count Sándor Károlyi merged in OKH.

For the establishment of OKH the state provided significant capital and ensured significant allowances. Its task was the organizing of the operation of credit cooperatives, the supervision, and the fulfillment of credit claims which were in connection with activities of rural agricultural and small-scale industry. It played a great role not only in the coordination and monitoring of credit cooperatives, but it also played an immense role in the execution of the agrarian reform in 1920, in the sale of agricultural crops, the spreading of the cooperative ideology and in the synchronization of the activity of various typed cooperatives.

While the OKH held 964 credit cooperatives together by the turn of the century, by the year 1917 this number grew to 2430. By the end of WW I, this number—thanked mainly to the Peace Treaty of Trianon—decreased to 1000 and it did not change until 1938. Between 1939 and 1942 this number increased significantly to about 1500. The number of members increased from 200,000, registered in 1900, to 635,000 by the year 1917. Although the number of members went back dramatically with more than 50 % in 1919, in 1942 the number of members came close to approximately 800,000, and the financial services were in 4360 settlements available.

The OKH took an essential pat in the extension of the Hungarian Cooperative Movement and it showed a good example of the positive role taking of the State. It was a rather unfortunate circumstance that the constant increase of the state influence until the end of WW II, which was due to the lack of capital, and the dictatorship following WW II, broke the pioneering role of OKH, as the Hungarian cooperative movement defined by great thinkers and creators.

WW II meant a very unfortunate turning point for the Hungarian cooperative movement from various aspects, this way in the development of credit cooperatives too. The war has destroyed a significant amount of personal staff and infrastructure, due to the reorganization of borders the number of credit cooperatives fell back to 943, whereas the number of members fell back to 548,832. Although 3860 new cooperatives has been established until 1948 (from which 26 were credit cooperatives), those economic organizations became inoperative due to the hyperinflation they had to go through.

There were some other damages, much larger than the economical problems; the cooperative movement had to go through. With the ideology of the new dictatorship the idea of cooperative autonomy and cooperative self-management based on private property, did not harmonize. The meanwhile established Constitution has acknowledged the cooperative property, but it made also clear, that the most efficient device in the hand of the executive power will be a state-owned bank system in order to reach their goals. The most important events of the liquidation of the credit cooperatives is the taking over and the liquidation of the management of central cooperatives, the appointment of governmental commissioners, the establishment of the Hungarian National Cooperative Center in the place of the formal centers, with state management and with the expropriation of their wealth. After the wealth has been taken away from the formal cooperatives, they all had been closed down. The process came in 1952 to an end, when the National Savings Bank (OTP) received an exclusive license for providing banking services for private individuals, this way credit cooperatives were forced to hand over the transactions of individuals to OTP. The systematic liquidation of credit cooperatives was by 1953 accomplished.

It became soon obvious, that OTP was not able to fulfill the role of credit cooperatives in rural regions. The possibility and necessity for the establishment of savings cooperatives has been first articulated in the Decree 1956/1091 of the Ministerial Council on the Development *of the agricultural cooperative movement*. The Decree contained regulations regarding the establishment, operation, its organizations, deposit collection of savings cooperatives. It also defined orders regarding the lending of money by savings cooperatives, and also orders about the management and supervision.

Savings cooperatives were strictly connected to villages. The savings cooperatives coming into existence with the special permission of the Minister of Finance, were allowed to collect deposits publicly (with state guarantee), but it was allowed to provide loans, similarly to current credit cooperatives, only to its members. The savings cooperative was forced to keep the sums of money, which extended beyond the amount defined by the administrative regulations, at OTP. According to decree 23/1959 (X.15) of the Minister of Finance savings cooperatives were allowed to provide loan exclusively for agricultural purposes. The setup of membership was defined by strict central proportions. Savings cooperatives had a complete tax and duty exemption in the field of their basic activity. In 1958 there were cooperatives in 212 Hungarian settlements, a year later the number changed to 264. As the legislative barrier came to an end in 1959, savings cooperatives opened branches. This way, showing a constant growth, 1143 branches were ran by 388 cooperatives in year 1971, and the number of members reached 800,000, which was similar to year 1942 (881 people equated 20.6 % of the total population).

The number of savings cooperatives showed a decreasing tendency after Act III/1971 and decree 29/1971 (VII.23.) of the Minister of Finance came into force, which can be explained with the, this time occurring, mutually advantageous mergers. According to the Statutory rule 22/1978 (XI.29.) savings cooperatives have been allowed to collect deposits among private individuals.

The change in regime, the reorganization of the two-levelled banking system in 1987, and Act LXIX./1991 about the financial institutions and about the activities of financial institutions, has forced the savings cooperatives to face fundamentally new challenges. The economical environment, the conditions of the market and the fundamental changes in the regulation required faster decision making and a stronger representation of interests. By the time Law I/1992 came into force (20 January 1992) altogether 260 savings cooperatives in 1752 branches were providing a growing range of services (they possessed over a 5 % market share), and the number of its members was reaching the total amount of 1,780,000.

The economic liberalism, which has been strengthened politically, put a such weight on the bank system, for which banks could have not been prepared (e.g. they had to decide about the creditworthiness of small, inexperienced enterprises, in completely new fields, in a new market environment for the granting of credits whose interest has been state supported, and were meant to cure the situation caused by the general lack of capital). This general situation led directly to the necessity of bank and debtor consolidation of 1992–1993.[1] The savings cooperatives have also drawn their consolidation consequences. It became obvious that they are less and less able to suit the requirements of the competition independently, and it is necessary, as international practices have shown before, to centralize a certain part of tasks. They have recognized, that a shared product development, the establishment of a single image, the investments in information technology, the capital allocation, the handling of national and international accounting and financial tasks, the institution defense, and the enforcement of interest are such activities, which can be carried out in a form of collaboration more efficiently and with

[1] Following the establishment of the multi leveled bank system, an involvement of the state became important soon, for the consolidation of many banks and financial institutions and for their re-capitalization.

smaller costs. Due to this, certain integrative ambitions became stronger. The first success was reached in 1989, when Takarékbank (Bank of Hungarian Savings Co-operatives Co. Ltd.) was founded by the savings cooperatives. Takarékbank suffered through a significant capital loss in 1992.

Another significant result of the collaboration was the signing of the integration contract in 1993. This contract was signed by 246 savings cooperative from the 256. The tasks of the National Savings Co-operational Security Fund (which came into existence in 1991) were carried out by the National Saving Co-operative Institutional Representative Fund (OTIVA) following the signing of the contract, which provided first from the consolidation capital and later from the sums given by the savings cooperatives, support for its members. Those savings cooperatives which did not want to join the integration, created their own interest defense alliance and their own institution defense in 1993. In the previous years, a new strategically cooperating group was formed with the participation of six savings cooperatives and a commercial bank (which was actually established from a savings cooperative)[2]. This group was built around a certain financial investor group. This way, the 3rd Hungarian institutional fund came into existence.

In spite of the establishment of collective organizations and the articulation of collective aims, savings cooperatives have had various reactions to the constantly changing external forces. This could have been the result of the differing features and the differing quality of the management. Due to the selection and polarization which is still happening, the number of savings cooperatives has decreased to 108 until 30 July 2015 (besides these there are two credit cooperatives), and this tendency could go on with the merges, unions and transformations into commercial banks.

2 The Previous Model (Until 2013)

2.1 The Cooperative Credit Bank System in Hungary Until 2013

The institutions of the cooperative credit bank system in Hungary are the following and they can be seen on Fig. 1:

1. Savings cooperatives
2. Credit cooperatives
3. Regional savings cooperative alliances
4. National interest representational alliances (OTSZ, TÉSZ)
5. Institutional defense funds (OTIVA, TAKIVA, REPIVA, HBA)
6. Central bank (Takarékbank Zrt.)

[2] These savings cooperatives also have an independent institution defense fund from 1994.

local level:	
1. Savings cooperatives	*2. Credit cooperatives*
regional level:	
3. Regional savings cooperative alliances	-
national level:	
4. National associations OTSZ, TÉSZ and outsiders (investor owners and independents)	-
5. Institutional defense funds OTIVA, TAKIVA, REPIVA	HBA
6. TAKARÉKBANK Zrt (central bank, commercial bank, investment bank – mostly for members of OTSZ)	

Fig. 1 The sector of co-operative banks in Hungary until 2013

2.1.1 Savings Cooperatives

Savings cooperatives are the dominant representational forms of the Hungarian cooperative credit bank system. They are legally independent credit banks which possess over an independent management and follow independent business policies, and have almost the same licenses and rights as commercial banks. In theory its fundamental principles are identical with the principles being published by the International Alliance of Cooperative Banks on 20 October 2008[3], but the practical appearance of these is very variable and it often shows a contradictory picture. Originally savings cooperatives were created locally from 1956; this meant that they were each connected to village. The geographical separation and the inviolability of their territories were included in the integration contract. The minimum number of members should be 200 (from which at least 67 % has to be a natural person), the value of one share cannot be more than 10,000 HUF (app. 320 EUR), one member—one vote. One member can only represent one other member in the general assembly. Limiting and keeping the value of the share on a low level has been recently put in the chapter of Act on credit institutions and financial enterprises. The aim of this was to prevent the exclusion of traditional members with the increase of the par value of the share.

2.1.2 Credit Cooperatives

Until their political liquidation in 1953, credit cooperatives had been widely popular in Hungary. They not only possessed over a rich history and a large basis, but they also represented classical, traditional values.

[3] International definition of Cooperative Banks adopted by the ICBA (International Co-operative Banking Association) general assembly of October 20th 2008.

The most significant difference between savings cooperatives and credit cooperatives is that the latter is only allowed to provide services for its members (except changing money).

2.1.3 Regional Savings Cooperative Alliances

These are organizations somewhere between the national and local level, spreading over more counties. They have an independent budget and independent tasks.

2.1.4 Institutional Defense Funds

The compulsory participation in institution defense came to an end in 2003, but many of the cooperatives supported the restoration of the compulsoriness, because outsiders carry a great reputational risk regarding the whole sector. Independently from the abolition of the compulsoriness, cooperative credit banks were members of an institution defense fund. Each fund has been built up around the interest representational organizations.

2.1.5 Central Bank

The largest owner and business basis of Takarékbank was formed by the members of OTSZ integration, but a large portion of the other savings cooperatives were owners too, respectively they use the services of Takarékbank. For example the members of TÉSZ group decided on cooperation in 2011, in terms of shared bank cards and ATM (POS) machines.

Takarékbank manages the accounts of most savings cooperatives, and they carry out a strong cooperation in every field of business. For example: shared product development, allocation of sources on savings, through consortium loans and foreign exchange activities, a complete cooperation in bank card business, in the field of information technology, national and international money transfers, providing cash etc.

Moreover an economic cooperation was launched in 2008 (Takarékpont network), with the participation of Takarékbank 21 savings cooperatives from different parts of the country and with two banks which formally have been savings cooperatives. Although the members have kept their legal independence, they have established a stronger and more efficient form of cooperation. They offer the same products; they have a single image and marketing policy.

3 Internal Operation, Management

The most important internal organs of savings cooperatives are the general assemblies, which are very often held in the form of partial general meetings, because of the large number of members. The partial meetings are held according to territorial principles, usually based on the members of one or two branches. It is even more usual the calling of a general assembly with a minimum of 50 members together, because practically all important decisions regarding the normal management can be handed over to this staff due to the authority of the general assembly. There are certain other things which are excluded from this authority, such as the definition of the authority of the general assembly. Actual decisions (the acceptance of the balance, the election of officials) are made by the meetings of delegates. This means that those general assemblies are rather formal, only giving out some information.

The board of directors of savings cooperatives has to consist of at least three members, and it has at least one fully employed, manager member (internal member.) The chairman is elected by the general assembly (the meeting of delegates) for the maximum of 5 years. This is similar to the election of members. The supervisory committee should also have at least three members. There is a minimum of a double management. The managers has to fulfill the professional requirements (education, experience, good reputation) defined in law.

4 Membership Policies

The theory which lasted until the first part of the 1990's was obviously inaccurate. It stated that more and more member should join the cooperative as a stipulation for selling the products. This was reached by agitation and this way a large mass basis has been created. Raising the number of members has appeared in the yearly agenda of cooperatives as a general cooperative aim. Savings cooperatives have really gained a large number of new members this way, without these having any practical advantage. In contrary, the untreatable number of members was not only for the new members formal, who treated their symbolic financial contributions as some kind of credit fee and with the discontinuance of the business relation their genuine relationship with the cooperative has come to an end, but also for the "real" members, whose authority gained through their membership and their influence became insignificant with the large amount of members. Beside this, the management had to face itself with a large amount of administrative duties. For dealing with these a number of makeshift arrangements came into existence which also decreased the cooperative nature of ownership. As the orders of cooperative policies (together with the cooperative policy) have faded away, the downsizing of the cooperative basis has started to take place.

In the first place, with the increase of the minimal amount of cooperative shares, most savings cooperatives were able to decrease the number of their membership, very often to the minimum number defined by the legislation of the time. This had actually various advantages: on the one hand the administrative duties of cooperatives have decreased immensely, the organization became efficient again, on the other hand the membership of the cooperative comprised of such members more and more, who have taken greater financial risk than just a symbolic amount and due to this they started to behave as real owners.

At the same time with the decrease of membership the capital supplement ability of the cooperative has also decreased. The legislative authorities have evaluated this process rather negative, and in order to avoid an extremely strong owner concentration, have very soon increased the necessary minimum number of members to 200 people.

5 Business Policy

Savings cooperatives provide an almost full scale of banking services, their risk taking opportunities are at the same time limited, this means that besides the retail, micro and small enterprises, respectively more and more local governments form the client basis of savings cooperatives characteristically. Savings cooperatives make their business decision completely on their own, for their decisions they are responsible with their whole wealth. In case of insolvency, institute defense funds help their members. This worked differently in the various funds. For example there was a fund where an aid fund has been reserved with the constant payments of the members, and there are funds where only in case of insolvency were some decisions made regarding involvement (for example providing subordinated loan capital).

In Hungary the average amount of members in cooperatives has shown a decreasing tendency in recent years, which can be also brought back to the fact, that the low par value of shares became disproportionately tiny compared to the decades long reserved wealth of cooperatives (*intergenerational endowment*)[4]. The individual wealth responsibility of members is not significant compared to the amount of wealth their put at stake with their decisions. This has caused the increase of the par value of fundamental shares, which resulted in the decrease of the number of members. At the same time the wealth interest transforming from formal to real, has enlarged the desire of members for a larger amount of dividend. This way we can make the assumption, that the business policy is more and more defined by profit orientation. At the same time, the total par value of shares owned by the members only means a tiny proportion of the cooperative wealth, and of the own equity capital of the cooperative.

---

[4] See Fonteyne 2007.

Saving cooperatives are characteristically deposit makers in inter-bank markets, their sources coming from clients is much larger than the loans they provide for their clients. The loan/deposit proportion of the sector was, on 31 December 2014, 38 %, which means they possessed almost three times as much deposits as loans given to their clients. A significant part of their sources covering loans are put in Hungarian government securities and in inter-bank deposits. They do not have a relationship to the stock market.

6 Cooperative Principles in Savings Cooperatives

Hungarian savings cooperatives have followed that practice, stemming from the roots of credit cooperatives, where they prescribed for their new clients to become members of the given cooperative. This has been compulsory for every new client. This practice, according to our view, has not only violated the fundamental principle of volunteerism, but it has not reached its original aim either. Due to the fact that the membership has been formed this way, it remained formal, there was no content it, and it has not gone beyond a simple bank-client relationship. The management seeks the establishment of such membership consciously, with whom they can reach their aims more easily. This way they try to limit the phenomenon of open membership (for example in order to exclude investors with bad intentions) to an extent. This is possible according to the legislation being in force. The "directed" setup of membership has decreased the efficiency of member supervision based on internal democracy.

In connection with this, the phenomenon "entrenching" of the management is neither typically cooperative nor Hungarian. The directed membership and the low member participation, respectively the lack of direct involvement, enables top leaders of cooperatives to be elected periodically (characteristically in every 5 years) without having any other candidate at hand. This is also strengthened by the non-defined termination of the appointed management. Bonding the management this manner is far away from the traditional values of cooperatives and it can harm the competitiveness of the cooperative.

Another characteristic feature of classical cooperatives is that members take active part in the economic activities of the cooperative. These so called "partnerships" features has been less dominant from the beginning (compared to other, e.g. agricultural cooperatives) in case of credit cooperatives, because banking activities are, due to their nature, capital unifying. In today's saving cooperatives the personal involvement is carried out by those workers who are at the same time members. This only means a tiny part of the membership. Carrying out banking activities is not only a field which requires special training, but it is also true that the reachable profit cannot be efficient with the increase of the amount of members. *The above findings result in the fact, that a participation of a wide range of members in the management is not possible.*

Care and social risk taking, having been regarded as cooperative values, can be interpreted in the relationship among the members or in the relationship between the member and the community. In classical examples it was still possible to find an active, real care between the members and their families, but for modern cooperatives a rather financial care is characteristic. For example they establish a community fund, for the support of certain, earlier defined aims (social, sport, cultural etc.). Due to the fact that this fund can be created from the profit, it, mutatis mutandis, decreases the assets of the cooperative; it harms its efficiency and profitability. This means the management, if it is really profit oriented, can put these activities in the background.

According to the above written, it has to be admitted, that in case of savings cooperatives the cooperative principles are very often violated. This can put the cooperative values to the background, those values which actually make them different from other financial organizations operating in other forms, especially from joint stock companies.

7 Changes in the External Regulation

Hungarian Parliament has accepted a new, general regulation regarding savings and credit cooperatives and some banks with cooperative identity (hereafter *cooperative credit institutions*, short for CCI's) in 2013. The Act X/2006 on Cooperatives (hereafter Coop Law) has been changed; some of its main elements have been regulated newly in Act V/2013 (Civil Code), a new Act on Credit Institutions (CCXXXVII/2013, hereafter *Credit Institution Law*) has come into force and most importantly Act CXXXV/2013, the so called Law on Integration of Savings Cooperatives (hereafter *Integration Law*) has been published which has a tremendous impact on savings and credit cooperatives in Hungary. The Civil Code has modified a bit the definition of cooperative and included obligatory and liability of the members as parts of it. According to the new regulations, the cooperative is an organisation with legal entity which is established with the members' share-note equity and operating according the principles of open membership and variable capital; the objective of the organisation is to promote meeting the economic and other societal (cultural, educational, social and health care) needs of the members, whereas the obligations of a member include providing equity investment for the cooperative and "personal contribution" regulated by the by-law (founding document) as well. Members have limited liability regarding obligations of the cooperative.

Limitation of liability of the member is closely connected to the new definition, which can be found in a separate chapter on liability circumstances in the Coop Law. According to the new legislation member has no obligation to fulfil the cooperative's commitment, his or her liability is limited to the amount of his or her cooperative share based on the old regulation. Since the cooperative share is part of the coop equity and can be involved to settling its obligation, the new legislation makes no real difference, it only emphasise the limited liability.

Obligatory elements of by-laws can be found among joint regulations concerning legal entities in Civil Code[5] as well as in 3:321§ which part strictly concerns cooperatives only. The latter one left out the detailed description of membership legal relations and contents of the organisation like can be found in Coop Law. Representative rules are regulated by the Law (3:29§–3:31§) and not by inner specification given usually in the by-laws. However, indication of names of founding members and their seat addresses is mandatory rule, as well as the possible forms of personal contributions of members; regulations regarding services can be carried out from the mutual found and terms of rules of conflict of interest regarding members and officials of the cooperative.

Regarding organisational regulation significant modification only concerned terms of references of the general meeting. Exclusion of a member and the review of resolution of exclusion, starting sue for damages caused by leader officials of the cooperative, the decision about membership in an association of cooperatives, acceptance of membership of investor members, changes in the nominal value of cooperative shares and the date of payment of share premium are no longer in the scope of authority of the general meeting.

While the obligatory minimum number of founding members did not change, there is a significant alteration in the composite of membership according to the new regulation. In the past the only limit was that legal persons and companies without legal entities could not exceed the half of membership, according to the regulation in the new Civil Code demands more requirements to fulfil. One most important one is that the number non-natural persons (not taking into account legal persons working in cooperative form, but only legal persons and companies without legal entities) cannot exceed 1/5th of the membership. Also, members with personal contribution should reach at least 4/5th of the membership. There is a restriction on the equity provided by a single member, it could not exceed the 15 % of the capital, in case of legal persons the maximum share is 1/3.

The Coop Law restricted the share of solely investment property in 30 % of cooperative share capital and the number of "investor members" in 10 % of the (total) membership. The Coop Law left the principles (like "investor members", members with personal contribution etc. named in the law) of allocation of profit (surplus) in scope of authority of general assembly, however according Civil Code[6] half of the profit (surplus) has to be distributed among members according to their personal contributions. While Coop Law declares the concrete forms of personal contributions, the new regulation refers the decision about what can accepted as personal contribution to terms of reference of general meeting. An interesting feature of Civil Code that protection of minorities has a separate title (Title XIX)

[5] 3:5§ of Act V/2013 (Civil Code).

[6] 3:356§ (2).

and it declares that members with 5 % of votes can initiate of getting together the general assembly or one-off financial audit.

Important feature of the Coop Law that it has lower emphasis on the regulation of associations of cooperatives (as a pressure group organisation) which is can be seen clearly from the fact that there is only one paragraph and not a full chapter devoted to this topic and more importantly it has no reference to the legal status of the above mentioned associations. It is even more important change that former elements of guarantee (see 97§ in the former regulation) allocated appraisal and legislative initiative rights for association of cooperatives while they disappeared from the recent legislation.

One of the relevant changes of Credit Institution Law regarding CCI's is the legal requirement of establishing them as private limited companies apart from cooperative form. The other important change is that unlike 8§ (Sect. 6) of Credit Institution Law, new legislation allows CCI's to carry out a wide variety of activities; however 17/B§ of the Integration Law limits the possible actions.

After Credit Institution Law come into force the minimum founding equity requirement is higher (HUF 300 million) compared to the previous minimum equity of HUF 250 million.

One can state that new Civil Code and its new regulation on cooperatives together with the Credit Institution Law which come into force recently established a solid and adequate base for the reform. The main elements of the Integration Law:

The Law establishes and regulates the Organisation of Integration (hereafter Organisation) which is legal person and unlike the voluntary funds in the past it is an obligatory institutional protection organisation with (legally obliged) membership of every CCI which existed at the date the Law come into force, as well as memberships of Takarékbank Zrt. (private limited company), Hungarian Development Bank Zrt. (hereafter HDB) and all persons and organisations (had been) accepted as members of the Organisation. Operating licence terminates if a CCI put an end to its membership in the Organisation or it is no longer owner of preferred share (stock).

The equity of Organisation consists of contribution of HDB (HUF 1 billion), membership fees and the equity of former institutional defense funds which had ceased to exist according to the Law. The above assets together with equities of Takarékbank Zrt. and CCI's are parts of the consolidated prudential own funds. The Organisation is partly responsible of the solvency and equity allocation of Takarékbank Zrt. and cooperative credit organisations and in special cases—in order to maintain them—it could acquire property in above organisations; however it has to be alienated in 2 years.

Takarékbank Zrt. as central bank of the integration accepts obligatory regulation (containing for example detailed rules of risk management concerning overall operation, business policy to follow, joint marketing activities, unified information technology system etc.) regarding CCI's, control their activities and it can give them instructions in order to maintain their adequate operation. The Law determines consequences regarding implementation of instruction(s) as well as concerning possible disoperation of CCI's (e.g. not following legal rules and regulation).

Board of Directors of Takarékbank Zrt. can make decisions about suspension of charges of leader officials of CCI as well it can initiate suspension of integration membership or exclusion from the membership regarding the CCI (Similarly the Organisation can make the same decisions as can read above).

If according to Board of Directors of Takarékbank Zrt. the CCI is in crisis then it can make decisions about the suspension of charges of managing leaders of the institution, determine new temporary charges of officers or it can initiate suspension of integration membership or exclusion from the membership regarding the cooperative (Exclusion from the integration membership regarding the CCI is also a right of the Organisation).

CCI's are obliged to hold their bank and securities accounts at Takarékbank Zrt. and they can only use their free financial resources to invest into assets provided by Takarékbank Zrt. The Law made compulsory the implementation of unified information technology system for Takarékbank Zrt. and CCI's as well from 1 July 2016.

Prior approval of Takarékbank Zrt. is needed to accept of the accounting report, to appoint leader officers and to carry out acquisition in or to sell assets of other business organisations (or legal entities) as well[7].

There is a prior and ex-post obligation to provide information on behalf of the cooperative credit institution towards to Takarékbank Zrt. regarding many issues like sending invitation to the meetings and setting up the agenda of them; as well as reporting about general and other meeting meetings with the possible risk of loosing validity of the decisions made there if they would not meet with above requirements. Representative of Takarékbank Zrt. has the right of consultation in general meeting of the CCI.

The most important rules regarding CCI's are the backbones of the regulation concerning them. Important rule of capital requirements is that the minimum level of requested prudential own funds is determined by the Organisation individually and if it sinks below it the Organisation can determine selling non-banking operational assets of CCI, can set other individual capital requirement or other operational measures like setting up the maximum of the interest to be paid, forbidding business among owners and CCI as well paying out deposits and other financial resources. The Organisation has the right to call together the general meeting and it also has license to direct attention of the board of directors or the general assembly to make decisions about certain issues and it can call upon bigger owners (with more influence like higher share of votes than 5 % and owners with qualifying holding) to carry out certain measures.

According to the Law CCI can only be established by an approved sample by-law determined by Takarékbank Zrt. (and the Organisation) and only in legal forms as credit cooperative, savings cooperative and public limited liability

[7] If it exceeds the 0.1 % of the consolidated own funds of the integration.

company. In case of choosing cooperative form it can only operate as a member of the Organisation with minimum number of 200 members and the maximum number of legal entities has to be less than 1/3 of the total membership.

The Law contains regulation on the legal entity (with membership in it of Takarékbank Zrt., CCI's and the Organisation) who has joint liability for any debts. To pay out members or in any other cases of reduction of the subscribed capital, apart from the decisions of the relevant decision body of the cooperative, prior approval of Takarékbank Zrt. is needed. It can only refuse the approval if paying interest undermines the solvency of the cooperative, it hampers the fulfilment of the business plan or it can jeopardise reaching the level of unique prudential own funds.

The Law obliged already operating CCI's to accept the new by-law determined by the Organisation in 45 days and it obligated Takarékbank Zrt. to review assets and liabilities of the above institutions in 1 year and propose exclusion from the integration membership if it is necessary. Finally the Law sets up the rules of exiting from the integration membership, securing the rule that the liability of quitting organisation lasts only until day of exit.

8 The Current Model

The institutions of the cooperative credit bank system in Hungary are the following and they can be seen on Fig. 2:

1. Savings cooperatives
2. Credit cooperatives
3. Banks within integration
4. Regional savings cooperative alliances
5. National associations (SZHISZ, OTSZ, TÉSZ)
6. Common Capital Cover Fund (TFKA)
7. Central bank (Takarékbank Zrt.)

9 The Importance of the Cooperative Sector in Hungary[8]

Savings cooperatives shared 1448 billion HUF from the 32,866 billion HUF balance sheet total in year 2014 and possessed 7.6 % (1213 billion HUF) of all bank (16,045 billion HUF) deposits. The amount of loans (462 billion HUF) given by cooperatives was 2.9 % of the bank sector[9]. This proportions were 10.5 and

[8] On 31 December 2014, Source: MAGYAR NEMZETI BANK (The Central Bank of Hungary). http://felugyelet.mnb.hu/bal_menu/jelentesek_statisztikak/statisztikak/bankszektor

[9] Without Takarékbank and other Cooperative Banks which are members of integration.

local level:
1. Savings cooperatives *2. Credit cooperatives 3. Banks*
(Together: Cooperative Credit Institutions)

regional level:
4. Regional savings cooperative alliances (minimal or formal role)

national level:
5. National associations
SZHISZ – Integration Organisation of Cooperative Credit Institutions
(members: Takarékbank Zrt., Hungarian Development Bank Zrt. and CCI's)
OTSZ, TÉSZ (minimal or formal role)

6. Institutional defense funds
TFKA – Common Capital Cover Fund of Cooperative Credit Institutions
(members: Takarékbank Zrt., SZHISZ and CCI's)

7. TAKARÉKBANK Zrt.
(central-, commercial-, investment bank whit regulatory and supervisory functions)

Fig. 2 The sector of co-operative banks in Hungary

3.5 % in 2010. Savings cooperatives run 1486 branches (48 % of the total number of branches bank), in every 3rd settlement only they offer services, employ more than 6800 people, which means the 18 % of the whole banking sector. They possessed over a 105 billion HUF large capital in average (3.5 % of the sector) their average, annual capital equivalence indicator was 19.5 %. By the end of the 1980s, the amount of the members of cooperative credit institutions has reached two billion, however this amount of members has decreased to about 150,000 people until today. About 15 % of the population of Hungary is client of one of the savings cooperative.

10 Summary

The collective European thinking puts a great emphasis on savings cooperatives in the process of the elimination of social and economical differences.

Thanks to its conservative business policies, the savings cooperative sector remained stable and liquid, even during the time of crisis. In spite of the fact that the amount of their shares has not grown significantly, their business, social, and political judgment, their popularity and good reputation has grown rapidly since the end of 2008.

Although the search for a solution has speeded up in the past few years, and there has been some attempts carried out for the reformation of cooperative integration, they have not brought any breakthrough due to the lack of a unified view of the future and the lack of the particular aims. Putting and emphasis on the possibility of a distinctive role played the management, which is rather strange for savings cooperatives, has not helped to define the common strategic aims. This is even the dead-end of collaboration and it is against international trends.

The present government has articulated a few times, that it intends an important role for the sector in the execution of programs which aim the stimulation of the economy. They have defined a total amount of 10–15 % share from the market in the long run.

Birth of the Integration Law was almost necessary according to the processes analysed above. The Law aimed to strengthen the cooperative network and not to cut back member institutions or change them to commercial bank offices. Therefore only aspects which serve the above aim can be enforceable during the reconstruction of the network. It would be a big mistake to reconstruct the sector in a way (and it is not a derivable solution from the Law) to classify present cooperatives and its branch offices as only bank offices belonging Takarékbank Zrt. holding formal settings but distracting the contents of a legal entity like competences, sources, financial results etc.

Members of the integration are very much depending on each other and the success or failure of the model is based on their collaboration.

Bibliography

Desrochers M, Fischer KP (2005) The power of networks: integration and financial cooperative performance. Working paper 05–14, CIRPÉE, Quebec

Di Salvo R (2002) La gouvernance des systèmes bancaires mutualistes et coopératifs en Europe. Revue d'économie financière 67:165–177

Fonteyne W (2007) Cooperative banks in Europe—policy issues (July 2007). IMF working paper no 07/159, published in SSRN: http://ssrn.com/abstract=1007908

ICA (1995) The international co-operative alliance statement on co-operative identity. Review of International Co-operation 3:3–4 (Downloadable internet source: Statement on the co-operative identity: cooperative principles for the 21st century. http://www.ica.coop/ica/info/enprinciples.html based on ICA News, No. 5/6, 1995)

ICBA (2008) International definition of cooperative banks adopted by the ICBA (International Co-operative Banking Association) general assembly of October 20th 2008

Kiss Gy (2008) Trend and paradigm shift? Bank Stock Mark (1–2): 22–27

Moizs A (2009) Possible directions of development for savings cooperatives. PhD studies 8, Doctoral School of the University of Pécs—Faculty of Law, Pécs, Hungary

Moizs A (2009) The ethical and legal problems of property registration in savings cooperatives. JURA 15(1), pp 86–93

Moizs A (2010) Heterogenesis. In: Ph.D. studies (Ph.D. Tanulmányok) no. 9. Doctoral School, Faculty of Law of University of Pécs, Pécs, pp 487–523

Moizs A (2011) The reorganisation of ownership relations in savings cooperatives. JURA 1:90–98

Moizs A, Szabó GG (2012) Cooperative credit institutions in Hungary (A szövetkezeti hitelintézetek Magyarországon). Hitelintézeti Szemle 1:67–85

Partl M (2009) Presentation held in 14.10.2009 at the ÖGV-TÉSZ meeting in Vienna

Prime Minister's Office (2003) Material of the Cooperative Political Committee of the Prime Minister's Office (Hungary, 2003)

Rabobank Nederland Economic Research Department (2008) Countervailing power of cooperative banks 2008 (working paper)

Réti M (2007) What does the legal background provide today in Hungary in terms of social cooperatives? (The supplemented material of the conference held in 5 Nov 2007 with the title: New opportunities of social development—an open discussion about social cooperatives

Cooperative Savings and Credit Unions in Latvia

Tatjana Mavrenko

Abstract Cooperative Savings and Credit Unions (CSCUs) in Latvia are formal cooperative financial institutions operating on financial market. CSCUs provide basic financial services—savings, loans and money transferring—to their members at reasonable price. CSCUs are mutual help organizations, which mostly serve unbankable people. CSCUs are the key social enterprises and microfinance institutions on Latvian financial market. Financial cooperation in Latvia has long history. CSCUs (historically also called savings societies, credit cooperatives) were widely spread and well developed in Latvia before the II World War, but in 1940 had to cease their operation. CSCUs network was renewed in 1995 after Latvia had regained its independence. Since that time, CSCUs provide necessary services to the people who are not interested or able to obtain financial services in other credit and financial institutions. At the end of 2014 Latvian CSCUs network united 32 CSCUs, more than 26,000 members and almost 23 MEUR in assets.

1 Establishment and Evolution of Latvian CSCUs

1.1 Latvian CSCUs Before II World War

CSCUs in nowadays Latvia continue traditions established by the first German credit cooperatives in the nineteenth century. Credit cooperatives were organized by people to ensure access of small farmers and entrepreneurs to financial resources, accumulating members' savings and providing loans to the ones in need. Credit cooperatives could offer better rates because of low costs of operation. They could operate in farmers' premises and use volunteers' work; costs of gathering information about borrowers were low because members knew each other very well. Cooperatives followed the idea of mutual help and got broad recognition both in rural and urban areas (Caprio and Vittas 1997: 155–156). Nowadays

T. Mavrenko (✉)
BA School of Business and Finance, Riga, Latvia
e-mail: mavrenko.tatjana@inbox.lv

S. Karafolas (ed.), *Credit Cooperative Institutions in European Countries*, Contributions to Economics, DOI 10.1007/978-3-319-28784-3_17

financial cooperatives continue to follow the same traditions and operation principles as their ancestors. Today there are several definitions of CSCUs, but all of them have roots in operation principles of the first cooperative organizations. CSCU is a democratically managed member-owned, not-for-profit cooperative financial institution. Its members pool their savings, lend money to each other, and obtain other related financial services. CSCU is a mutual help organization with the main goals to provide necessary financial services to their members, to educate members in wise and economic use of their funds, to assist members in improvement of their life quality (Lee 1990: 1–3; Jerving et al. 1994: 1–3; Grace and Branch 2000: 16; Kučinskis 2004: 18; Witzeling 1993: 17).

Similar to other European countries, first attempts to organize CSCUs in Latvia appeared in the end of nineteenth century. However, in the beginning growth of the first credit cooperatives was very slow. Demand for cooperative credits increased because of repurchasing of houses and unbearable interest rates demanded by other informal lenders. Latvian CSCUs have shown successful growth and in the beginning of 1914 there were already 236 CSCUs with 112,000 members. In the following years, CSCUs continued their fast growth. In 1913–1914, Riga—the capital of Latvia—became financial centre of the Baltic States. Local banks, mutual credit societies, CSCUs, branches of big Russian banks provided lending services to production, trade and construction fields; broad number and high volume of financial services helped to bust economic growth in the country. The same institutions managed to attract the most part of savings of Latvian people (Aizsilnieks 1968: 37). Historical events, changes of political power in the country, struggle for state independence—all this unrest in external environment strongly affected financial and credit market. In 1918, when Latvia regained its independence and German troops left the country, people were afraid of threats coming from the East, and big volume of money and valuables left the country (Aizsilnieks 1968: 125). In 1919, after occupation of Latvia by the Soviets, the People's Bank of Soviet Socialist Republic of Latvia was established and all other financial and credit institutions were nationalized, transferring all their assets to the People's Bank, which became the state monopolist in provision of financial and credit services in the country. All savings exceeding 10,000 Rubls were nationalized, smaller savers still could take out their savings not exceeding 400 Rubls per month. Despite the rather independent position of Latvian People's Bank, it still was considered a regional department of Soviet Russia's People's Bank (Aizsilnieks 1968: 94). The year of 1920 again was considered the rebirth year of CSCUs. A new state has restarted its growth and needed financial resources to heat economy of the country. After all political collusions all these resources had to be accumulated from the beginning (Aizsilnieks 1968: 208). Development of Latvian CSCUs in 1923–1940 is shown on Figs. 1 and 2 [developed by the author based on (Aizsilnieks 1968: 319, 469,663)].

Figure 1 shows that number of CSCUs in Latvia was growing fast until 1927, then growth became very slow and starting from the year 1933 number of CSCUs went down from 634 CSCUs to 419 in 1940. Number of CSCUs members was growing fast until 1931, and then stayed almost unchangeable. The biggest number

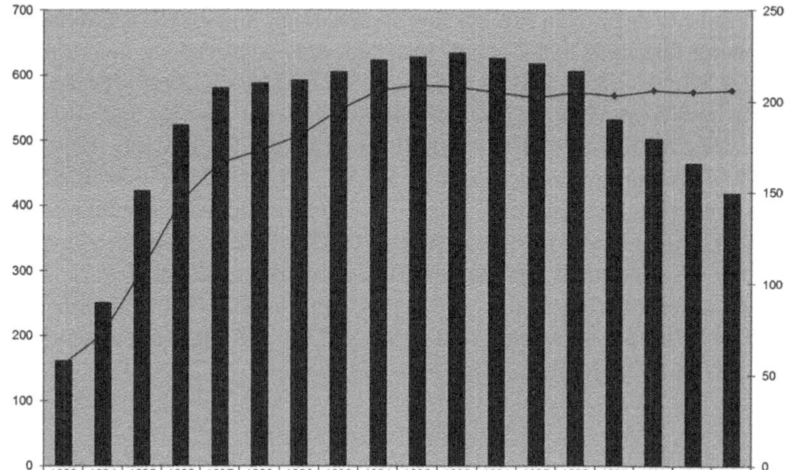

	1923	1924	1925	1926	1927	1928	1929	1930	1931	1932	1933	1934	1935	1936	1937	1938	1939	1940
SCU number	161	251	422	524	580	588	592	605	623	628	634	626	618	606	532	503	404	419
SCU members, thsd.	56	72	108	145	166	173	181	195	206	209	208	205	202	205	203	206	205	206

Fig. 1 Development of Latvian CSCUs in 1923–1940 (data on 01.01.xx.): Number of members and CSCUs [based on Aizsilnieks (1968: 319, 469,663)]

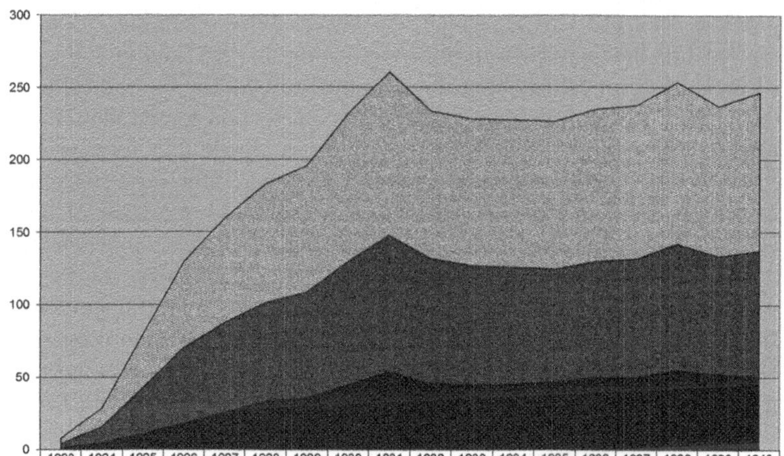

	1923	1924	1925	1926	1927	1928	1929	1930	1931	1932	1933	1934	1935	1936	1937	1938	1939	1940
Assets, MLVL	3,5	12,8	36,6	59,3	72,2	82,1	87,3	101,8	112,9	101,8	101,3	101,4	102,1	104,7	105,7	111,6	103,1	109,4
Loans, MLVL	2,5	10,8	31,8	51,9	61,6	68,1	72,7	85,3	94,2	85,7	82,2	80,6	77,5	79,7	81,7	86,8	81,4	86,4
Savings&Shares, MLVL	1,7	4,7	10,7	18,1	25,6	33,2	36	44,8	53,9	46,1	44,9	45,3	47	50,4	50,2	55,3	52,3	51

Fig. 2 Development of Latvian CSCUs in 1923–1940 (data on 01.01.xx.), LVL: Financial Statistics [based on Aizsilnieks (1968: 319, 469,663); to recalculate to EUR use exchange rate 1 EUR = 0.702804 LVL]

of CSCUs—634—was operating in 1933, but the biggest number of members—209,000—was achieved already a year before, in 1932.

Financial statistics of Latvian CSCUs in 1923–1940 is shown in Fig. 2.

Figure 2 shows that savings and shares, loans and assets of Latvian CSCUs were growing fast until 1931, when total amounts achieved the maximum volumes—112.9 MLVL (160.6 MEUR) in assets, 94.2 MLVL (134.0 MEUR) in outstanding loans and 53.9 MLVL (76.7 MEUR) in attracted savings and shares. In 1932 all positions decreased to 101.8 MLVL (144.8 MEUR) in assets, 85.7 MLVL (121.9 MEUR) in outstanding loans, 46.1 MLVL (65.6 MEUR) in savings and shares. In the next years level of assets, loans, savings and shares was rather constant without any big fluctuations. In 1940, when all CSCUs had to cease their operation because of the new political regime, CSCUs network represented very strong national financial and social capital: 419 CSCUs united 206,000 of members, 109.4 LVL (155.7 MEUR) in assets, 86.4 LVL (122.9 MEUR) in outstanding loans and 51 MLVL (72.6 MEUR) in savings and shares.

1.2 Latvian CSCUs After 1991

After more than 50 years-long gap new attempts to re-establish financial cooperatives in Latvia appeared in 1992, when the I Congress of Railroad Trade Union supported the idea to re-establish Railroad CSCU, continuing traditions of the previous Railroad CSCU, which was successfully operating before 1940. Latvia regained its independence from Soviet Union in 1991, and in 1992, there still was no legal basis for establishing and operation of CSCUs. Railroad CSCU got license to its operation on 9 February 1995. This date is considered the rebirth date of the modern network of CSCUs in Latvia. Credit Institution Law was approved on 5 October 1995 and came into force on 24 October 1995 (Law on Credit Institutions of the Republic of Latvia 1995). The law regulated operation of both banks and CSCUs. Banks became the key credit institutions in newly independent Latvia and in the following years were strongly supported and lobbied by the state. CSCUs were organized by initiative groups of volunteers, who did huge work to continue Railroad CSCU tradition and bring public interest to opportunities provided by CSCUs. Reestablishment of CSCUs in Latvia was strongly supported by international aid organizations and leading global CSCUs networks. In July 1994 World Council of Credit Unions with funding provided by United States Agency for International Development (USAID) started to implement CSCUs supporting project "Introducing Democratic Financial Institutions into the Latvian and Lithuanian Marketplace", which until September 1997 assisted initiative groups in formation of CSCUs and building of capability of local CSCUs by providing training, technical assistance and supervision (WOCCU 1996). During the mentioned project, five more CSCUs were started in Latvia and at the end of 1997 CSCU network already united 3.24 thousands members and 0.50 millions EUR in assets (see Figs. 3 and 4). Major banking crisis of 1995 has forced interest of people about alternative credit and financial institutions. The crisis was caused by fraud and low control in banking sector and resulted in bankruptcy of 15 commercial banks, accounting up to 40 % of the banking assets and 53 % of household deposits (Aaslund and

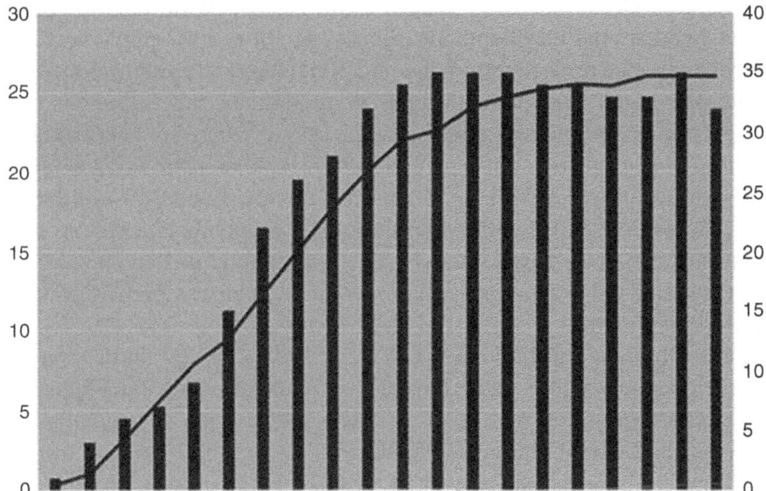

	1995	1996	1997	1998	1999	2000	2001	2002	2003	2004	2005	2006	2007	2008	2009	2010	2011	2012	2013	2014
SCU number	1	4	6	7	9	15	22	26	28	32	34	35	35	35	34	34	33	33	35	32
SCU members, thsd.	0,3	1	3,2	5,6	7,9	9,5	12,3	15	17,7	20	22	22.6	24,1	24,7	25,2	25,5	25,4	26	26	26

Fig. 3 Development of Latvian CSCUs in 1995–2014 (data on 31.12.xx.): Number of members and CSCUs (developed by the author based on Quarterly Statistics of Latvian CSCUs and Banks, and Statistics of Latvian CSCUs—members of LACSCU)

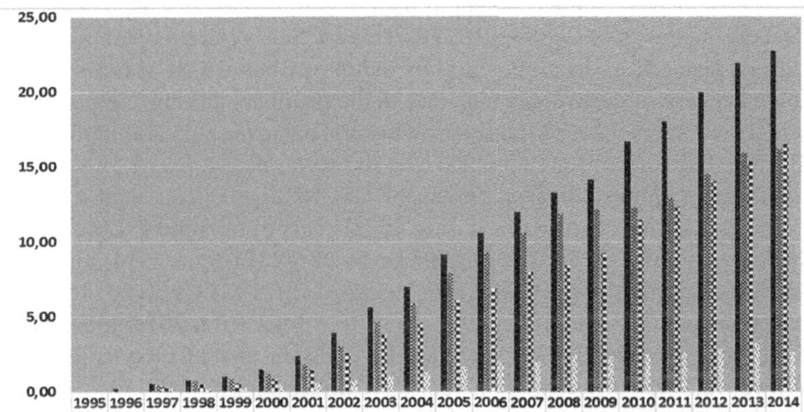

	1995	1996	1997	1998	1999	2000	2001	2002	2003	2004	2005	2006	2007	2008	2009	2010	2011	2012	2013	2014
Assets, MEUR	0,04	0,20	0,50	0,77	0,97	1,47	2,35	3,86	5,56	6,92	9,09	10,5	11,9	13,2	14,0	16,6	17,9	19,9	21,9	22,7
Loans, MEUR	0,04	0,13	0,43	0,68	0,81	1,18	1,75	2,99	4,58	5,85	7,87	9,25	10,5	11,8	12,0	12,2	12,8	14,4	15,9	16,1
Savings, MEUR	0,03	0,09	0,27	0,46	0,54	0,80	1,44	2,55	3,74	4,55	6,05	6,83	7,97	8,39	9,25	11,3	12,2	14,0	15,3	16,5
Shares, MEUR	0,01	0,07	0,14	0,18	0,23	0,41	0,53	0,71	0,98	1,29	1,59	1,99	1,99	2,42	2,28	2,42	2,62	2,79	3,2	2,6

Fig. 4 Development of Latvian CSCUs in 1995–2014 (data on 31.12.xx.): Financial statistics (developed by the author based on Quarterly Statistics of Latvian CSCUs and Banks, and Statistics of Latvian CSCUs—members of LACSCU)

Dombrovskis 2011: 11). It caused high mistrust of population to the banks and gave chance to foster development of CSCUs. Initiative of World Council of Credit Unions was continued by Development International Desjardins. This international division of Desjardins CSCUs network in Quebec, with funding provided by Canadian International Development Agency, in 1998–2002 implemented CSCUs technical assistance project "Strengthening of Savings and Credit Cooperatives in Latvia" with the major goal to contribute to mobilizing the economic potential of the population by providing Latvians with access to secure cooperative financial services (DID 2011). Canadian financial and technical aid helped Latvian CSCUS network to grow from 7 CSCUs with 5.55 thousands members and 0.77 millions EUR in assets in 1998 to 26 CSCUs with 14.96 thousands of members and 3.86 millions EUR in assets in 2002 (see Figs. 3 and 4). Then foreign aid to Latvian CSCUs was ceased. The country did big progress in development and was preparing itself to enter the European Union.

Development of Latvian CSCUs in 1995–2014 is shown on Figs. 3 and 4 (developed by author based on statistic data provided by Financial and Capital Market Commission of Latvia (FCMC) and Latvian Association of Cooperative Savings and Credit Unions (LACSCU)).

Figure 3 shows that number of CSCUs in Latvia was growing fast during the periods of both foreign aid projects. Increase in number of CSCUs in 2003–2005 was also mostly based on the initial work done during Development International Desjardins Project. Project staff met initiative groups all around the country, provided awareness meetings, specific training, and financial resources for lending services. Starting with the year 2005 number of CSCUs in Latvia is rather constant—33–35 CSCUs. One CSCU started its operation and decided not to continue it because of very limited potential membership. Another CSCU ceased its operation during the crisis 2008–2010. Three new CSCUs started operation, two of them did not succeed in development. One employer-based CSCU has ceased its operation because of bankruptcy situation in the members uniting company. Number of CSCU members was constantly growing and achieved ~26,000 in the end of 2014. Financial growth of Latvian CSCUs is shown on Fig. 4.

Figure 4 shows constant growth of CSCUs assets, loans and total amount of members' savings and shares during all 20 years of operation. Total CSCUs assets increased form 0.04 MEUR in 1995 up to 22.7 MEUR in 2014, total outstanding loans increased from 0.04 MEUR in 1995 up to 16.1 MEUR in 2014, total members savings from 0.03 MEUR in 1995 up to 16.5 MEUR un 2014, total shares—from 0.01 MEUR up to 2.6 MEUR. Despite constant annual growth in all positions, growth rate was different from year to year (see Fig. 5).

Figure 5 shows that the highest growth rates were in the beginning of establishing of CSCU network in Latvia and in the following years of foreign aid projects. Total assets of the CSCU network had grown by 366.7 % in the first year 1996, and then growth rate decreased to 150 % in 1997, 54.3 % in 1998. The next highest growth rate in total CSCU assets was in 2001–2002, relatively 60.2 % and 64.2 %. Later increase in assets varied between 3.7 % (2014) and 44.3 % (2003). Number of CSCUs continued to grow significantly up to the year 2004, and then number of CSCUs became rather constant. Increase in membership was extremely high in the first years of operation, starting from 233.3 % in 1996 and finishing with 22 % in 2002. Later growth in membership was lower than 20 % per year. In the last 2 years change in total number of members was insignificant. Increase in total

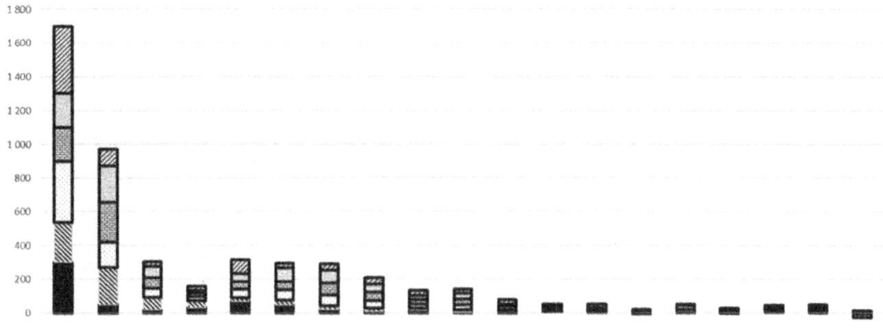

	1996	1997	1998	1999	2000	2001	2002	2003	2004	2005	2006	2007	2008	2009	2010	2011	2012	2013	2014
Shares growth %	400	100	30	23,1	81,3	27,6	35,1	38	31,9	23,1	25	0	21,4	-5,9	6,2	8,2	6,5	14,7	-18,8
Savings growth %	200	216,7	68,4	18,8	47,4	80,4	77,2	46,9	21,7	32,8	12,9	16,7	5,4	10,2	23,1	7,8	14,3	9,2	7,8
Loans growth %	200	233,3	60	18,8	45,6	48,2	70,7	53,3	27,6	34,5	17,5	13,8	12,2	2,4	1,1	5,4	12,3	10,0	1,3
Assets growth %	366,7	150	54,3	25,9	51,5	60,2	64,2	44,3	24,3	31,5	15,8	13,5	10,7	6,5	18,0	8,1	10,9	9,9	3,7
SCU members growth %	233,3	220	75	41,1	20,3	29,5	22	18	13	10	2,7	6,6	2,5	2,0	1,2	-0,4	2,4	0	0
SCU number growth %	300	50	16,7	28,6	66,7	46,7	18,2	7,7	14,3	6,3	2,9	0	0	-2,9	0	-2,9	0	6,1	-8,6

Fig. 5 CSCU growth, % to previous year, 1996–2014

outstanding loans was extremely high in the first years of operation, achieved 233.3 % in 1997 and 53.33 % in 2003. In other years, growth of outstanding loans fluctuated below 20 %. Total savings were growing since the first CSCU, starting with 200 % in 1996 and finishing with 7.8 % in 2014. Increase in share capital varied from year to year, starting from growth 400 % in 1996 and finishing with decrease 18.8 % in 2014. CSCUs growth dynamic leads to both positive and negative conclusions. The positive one makes it obvious that existing CSCUs have shown stable growth also without any external aid. It proves that Latvian CSCUs were not established just because of foreign aid of US and Canadian CSCUs networks, but it was real local initiative and local demand for cooperative financial services. That is why Latvian CSCUs continue their operation and show increase in financial statistics. The negative conclusion is that existing Latvian CSCUs are not ambitious in their growth and new CSCUs are not established in the country.

2 Current Model and Operation of CSCUs in Latvia

Latvian CSCUs are the part of Latvian Financial and Capital Market (LFCM) and are licensed, regulated and supervised by Financial and Capital Market Commission (FCMC). Figure 6 shows position of CSCUs among participants of LFCM.

Banks and CSCUs are the only institutions in Latvia, who are eligible to attract clients' deposits. Both institutions also provide credit and payment services. While banks are providing broader number of services in bigger scale, CSCUs are involved in provision of basic financial services—savings, credits, and payment services—to people with low income. CSCUs compete with banks in provision of savings and credit services, with insurance and financial market companies—in

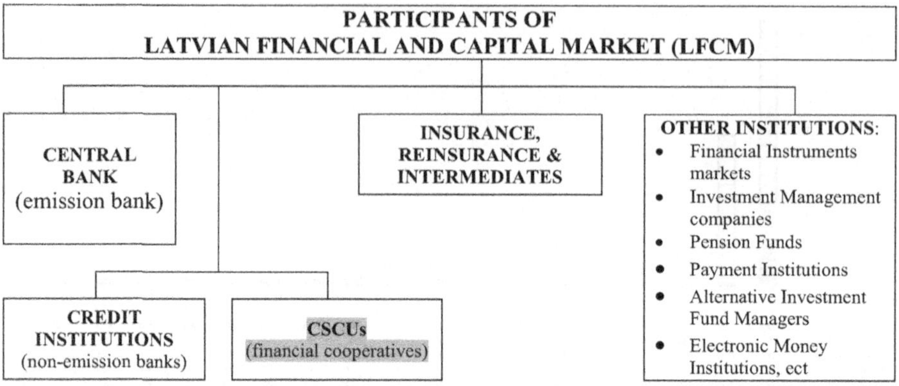

Fig. 6 CSCUs position on Latvian financial and capital market [developed by the author based on Participants of the Financial and Capital Market of Latvia (2015)]

attraction of people savings. There are few more institutions, which are operating outside LFCM but provide high competition to CSCUs. These institutions are leasing and factoring companies, credit companies, lombards, special lending programs. CSCUs play important role in provision of financial and credit services to people who are unable or not interested to use services of banks, other financial institutions, leasing or credit companies.

Taking into account huge difference in capital level of banks and CSCUs, on 29 March 2001 Latvian Parliament—Saeima—has approved a special Law on Savings and Credit Unions of the Republic of Latvia, which came into force on 1 January 2002. This legal act was developed in order to enforce access to financial resources and to foster regional development, activating participation of individuals in the economic processes of the country (Law on Savings and Credit Unions §1).

The Law defines CSCU as a cooperative organization with changing number of members and volume of capital, which provides the following services to its members: attract savings and deposits, issue credits, provide money transferring and payment services, upon member's request buy and sell financial instruments and currencies, provide guarantees for members in the face of creditors; keep members' valuables, consult members in financial questions, provide information about members' loans repayment capability, provide other services defined by Financial and Capital Market Commission (Law on Savings and Credit Unions, §2.1). The Law defines such main goals of CSCUs as development of members' capability to work jointly in order to foster their wealth through mutual help and self-government principles, accumulation of resources for lending purposes to members, satisfaction of individual and entrepreneurial needs of CSCU members (Law on Savings and Credit Unions, §2.2). The main features of CSCU operation are: democratic structure, fair interest rates, constant education and training possibilities, financial stability, fostering of social goals, and social responsibility.

CSCUs are serving clients related to the definite membership, which is defined in CSCU Law and CSCU By-Laws. The main types of CSCU membership, defined in the Law on CSCUs, are the following:

- based on territory principle: all members live, work or have property on the definite territory of the definite self-government(s),
- based on employment principle: all members are employed by the same employer,
- based on interest unity principle: all members of CSCU are members of the related trade union, non-government organization, professional or sports association.

In Latvia, CSCUs serve only individuals within the definite membership, but in case, if it is approved by CSCU Law and CSCU Bay-Laws, CSCUs can serve also legal entities, for example, micro, small and medium enterprises, where CSCU members are owners. Spouses of CSCUs members are also eligible to join CSCUs. CSCUs, based on territory principle, can accept members-uniting self-government as a member. CSCUs, which are based on interest unity principle, can accept members-uniting organization as a member (Law on Savings and Credit Unions, §4–5).

To start an CSCU in Latvia at least 20 members and 2500 EUR in share capital are required (Law on Savings and Credit Unions, §8.1, 15.1). This number of members and amount of start capital is affordable not to limit CSCUs establishing opportunities, but it is not sufficient to satisfy demand for loans in local communities. One of the primary goals of the start-up CSCUs is to ensure growth-oriented operating and financial plans, and strictly follow them.

Organization structure of Latvian CSCUs is based on cooperative organization principles. To become a CSCU member it is enough to buy at least one share. CSCU members are owners, clients and managers of their financial cooperative. Number of shares owned by a member does not influence his or her participation in decision making. The main principle is one member—one vote. Members come together at least once a year to the general assembly, where they discuss and approve all key decisions. Members take decisions about main fields of operation and management of CSCU: development policy, budget, evaluation of performance, changes in By-Laws, election of Credit Committee, Supervisory Committee, Information and Training (I&T) Committee, Board of Directors. CSCU organization structure is shown in Fig. 7.

CSCU Board represents and manages CSCU operation between Members General Assemblies. Credit Committee reviews loan applications and takes decision about lending based on CSCU Credit Policy approved by Members General Assembly. Supervisory Committee is an internal audit of CSCU. Information and Training Committee informs members about existing and new CSCU services, promotes financial cooperation idea and fulfils marketing function of CSCU. Members are elected in all committees and this is the main reason why CSCU is called the most democratic institution on financial market—members are involved in daily decision-making. Volunteer work is highly appreciated and broadly used in CSCU, very often elected bodies are volunteers; mostly employees are paid for the work.

CSCU financial mechanism is shown on Fig. 8. CSCUs accumulate members resources in savings and shares, then lend out to the members for definite purposes.

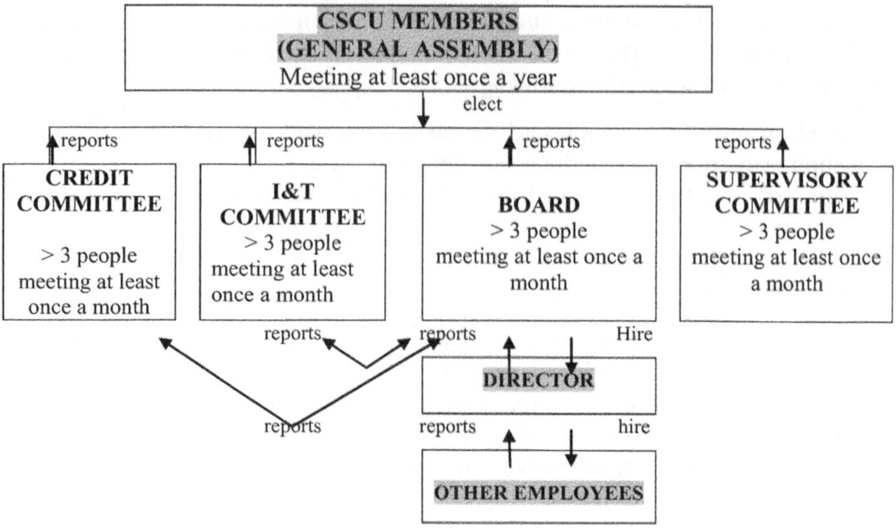

Fig. 7 CSCU organization structure [Developed by Author based on Lee (1990: 5), Law on Cooperative Organizations of the Republic of Latvia, Mavrenko (2002: 209)]

It is important that CSCU is self-sufficient and can operate only with internal resources of its members. It means that 80–95 % of CSCUs funds should be lent out to the members, and attracted savings should be 55–70 % of total funds of the CSCUs (LACSCU). Very often CSCUs are forced to attract external funds from banks to satisfy demand for loans. Some CSCUs may suffer from exceed of cash and in this case can lend to other SCUs, deposit in the bank, CSCU or invest in state bonds. Latvian CSCUs can get profit, but this is not the main goal. The main goal of any CSCU is to satisfy members' needs with financial services. Usually interest rates for savings and loans are defined in the way, that CSCU earns enough to cover resource costs and operation costs without any profit goal. Latvian CSCUs have no any exemption from taxes.

Organization structure of Latvian CSCUs very often consists of Board, Credit Committee, and Supervisory Committee, but Information and Training Committee is not elected. In big CSCUs training and marketing function is fulfilled by employees, in territory based and interest unity based CSCUs this role may be played by self-government or uniting organization.

Network of Latvian CSCUs has all preconditions for stable growth and niche in the country. Law on CSCUs was developed to regulate operation of CSCUs in the country in accordance with all CSCU peculiarities. Latvian CSCUs are included in the formal financial market, are eligible to attract savings. Savings in CSCUs are guaranteed by the state in accordance with Deposit Guarantee Law (DGL) with the maximum amount 100,000 EUR per depositor (DGL §3). 29 of 32 Latvian CSCUs are united by Latvian Association of Cooperative Savings and Credit Unions (LACSCU), which represents CSCUs interests and rights on national and international levels. All these mentioned factors construct the basis of any successful CSCUs network in any country. But there are still some unsolved issues. There is no Central

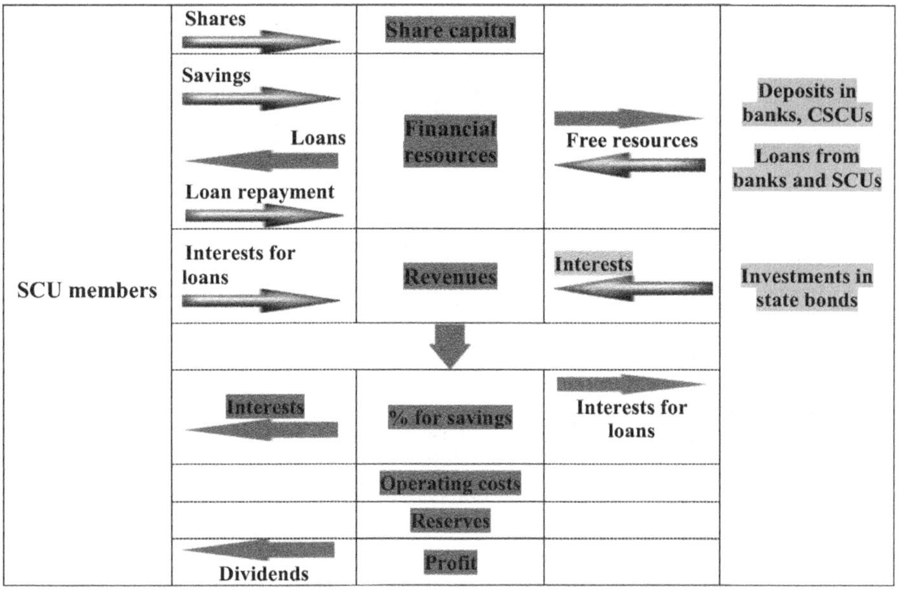

Fig. 8 CSCU financial mechanism [developed by Author based on Latvian Law on Savings and Credit Unions and Law on Cooperative Organizations of the Republic of Latvia, (Mavrenko 2002: 209)]

CSCU for CSCUs in Latvia, and in case of lack or exceed of cash CSCUs cannot solve this problem using centralizes approach in the network. They need to use services of the external institutions or use direct communication and negotiations with each other. At this moment it is difficult to forecast when Central CSCU may appear on Latvian market, CSCUs do not put much effort in this direction.

LACSCU is non-government organization, which was established on 10 October 1997 as a uniting organization of Latvian CSCUs. The main goal of LACSCU is to foster CSCUs operating and development policy in the country. LACSCU unites knowledge and experience of all Latvian CSCUs, represents and protects CSCUs interests and rights, foster development of CSCUs legal basis. LACSCU provides consultancies to initiative groups in establishment of their CSCUs, ensures consultancies and training to existing CSCUs, provides information about Latvian and international CSCU networks, organizes experience exchange events for CSCUs. LACSCU has good cooperation with Latvian CSCUs abroad—12 in USA, 1 in Canada and 1 in Australia. Since 10 February 2000, LACSCU has close cooperation with Mortgage Bank of Latvia, which is involved in different development projects in the country (LACSCU).

Operation statistics of Latvian CSCUs—members of LACSCU at the end of the 3rd quarter of 2014 is shown in Table 1. 29 from 32 CSCUs are members of LACSCU. There are only two types of CSCU membership represented in Latvian network—interest unity and territory basis (see Table 1).

Table 1 Operation results of CSCUs members of LACSCU, 31 December 2014

Nr.	*Trade union based CSCUs*	*Members persons*	*Assets EUR*	*Loans EUR*	*Shares EUR*	*Savings EUR*
1	Seaman CSCU	2,544	9,288,417	6,133,415	872,175	7,531,189
2	Railroad CSCU	12,877	8,728,045	6,222,281	1,767,772	6,356,527
3	CSCU "LAKRS KS" (public service and transport industry employees)	538	136,966	89,516	32,227	76,958
4	Teachers CSCU	922	126,995	90,297	24,497	83,571
5	LABA CSCU	1,116	48,827	7,216	32,715	6713
6	LVSAD CSCU (Medicine and Health Care Industry employees)	302	42,408	29,964	20,351	21,562
7	Cesu CSCU (retailing employees)	17	21,352	20,669	14,549	6000
	TOTAL trade union based CSCUs	18,316	18,393,010	12,593,358	2,764,286	14,082,520
	% from total	71 %	81 %	78 %	73 %	86 %
Nr.	*Regional (rural) CSCUs*	*Members*	*Assets*	*Loans*	*Shares*	*Savings*
1	CSCU "Allazu saime"	851	992,421	785,175	236,081	525,186
2	CSCU "Dzese pluss"	264	597,831	478,779	266,132	190,099
3	Kandava CSCU	611	449,754	384,522	69,659	272,579
4	Zoseni CSCU	552	409,939	370,425	53,805	301,062
5	Kauguri CSCU*	635	355,603	295,660	51,138	100,653
6	CSCU "Ligatnes druva"	440	249,414	233,086	41,967	156,568
7	Pure CSCU	509	239,296	184,662	51,982	163,639
8	Taurene CSCU	514	214,140	201,527	32,602	118,918
9	CSCU "Avots 37"	158	148,486	140,088	31,816	95,097
10	Nitaure CSCU	237	127,862	122,013	34,285	74,960
11	Punu CSCU	416	90,564	80,923	8,152	2,432
12	Veselava CSCU	181	67,080	49,121	21,516	45,424
13	Straupe CSCU	129	65,413	47,303	19,650	34,706
14	Vecpiebalga CSCU	286	59,163	47,008	16,080	43,953
15	Sala CSCU	328	51,688	36,320	12,395	37,888
16	Rundale CSCU	286	54,965	27,053	7,969	27,359
17	Lielvarde CSCU	253	44,667	42,403	16,717	26,720
18	Rujiena CSCU	406	38,025	36,275	8,537	14,452
19	Rucava CSCU	214	19,110	15,715	11,434	7,180
20	CSCU "Nigrande"*	92	9,038	7,890	3,913	4,126
21	CSCU "Skilbeni"	89	8,308	5,717	4,155	449
22	CSCU "AlfaBeta"*	21	5,391	4,059	4,091	0

(continued)

Table 1 (continued)

TOTAL regional CSCUs	7,472	4,298,158	3,595,724	1,004,076	2,243,450
% from total	29 %	19 %	22 %	27 %	14 %
TOTAL CSCUs—LACSCUs members	25,788	22,691,168	16,189,082	3,768,362	16,325,970

*Data on December 2013
Developed by the author based on Statistics of Latvian CSCUs—members of LACSCU, for year 2014

There is obvious disproportion in development of CSCUs inside the LACSCU network. 7 CSCUs, which are based on interest unity, represent 71 % of the total membership, 81 % of total assets, 78 % of total outstanding loans, 73 % of total shares and 86 % of total savings. 22 territory-based CSCUs represent only 29 % of the total membership of the network, 19 % of total assets, 22 % of total outstanding loans, 27 % of total share capital and 14 % of total savings. The first group of CSCUs is mostly represented by trade union-based CSCUs, including two the biggest ones of the network—Seamen and Railroad CSCUs in Riga. The second group is represented mostly by rural CSCUs. Big difference in size, location, membership peculiarities, growth strategies and future potential development—all these factors do not let Latvian CSCUs to get united in goals and common development strategy. The biggest CSCU by assets is Seamen CSCU with 9.3 MEUR, the smallest one—CSCU AlfaBeta with only 5391 EUR in assets. In attempt to find an optimal size of CSCU, the Author has calculated that in order to be self-sufficient and to work full time, CSCU should have around 800,000 EUR in outstanding loans. In this case CSCU will be able to keep four full-time employees, pay market price for the rent of premises, acquire its own equipment and software, and afford marketing costs and employee training. As it is shown in Table 1, only two—the biggest ones SCUs—are able to fulfil this requirement. Other CSCUs have to cut costs. Usually they are open just few days a week, benefit from support of the uniting organization or self-government, for example, use their premises, equipment, labour force at low or without costs (Mavrenko 2011: 95).

The Author provides SWOT analysis of Latvian CSCUs at the end of 2014 in Table 2.

Despite positive development of CSCUs in Latvia in 2005–2014 (see Figs. 3 and 4), impact of the existing CSCUs to the economy of the country in absolute numbers is still insignificant. At the same time, Latvian CSCUs have good opportunities to strengthen their positions, being a part of microfinance market and providing a serious alternative to banks and other credit and financial institutions. Still broad political support is needed to foster development of CSCUs network all around the country both on macro and mezzo levels. CSCUs need to grow faster, plan higher growth and become self-sufficient as soon as possible, ensuring stability on micro level. On Author's opinion, all mentioned threats and weaknesses, mentioned in Table 2, can be diminished step by step, if CSCUs will get more

Table 2 SWOT analysis of Latvian CSCUs, 2014

External environment	
Opportunities	Threats
– Political and financial support to microfinance all around the world and especially in EU – Positioning of CSCUs as Microfinance Institutions – Strong global CSCUs network – Strong lobby of CSCUs on international level – Separate law on CSCUs in Latvia – European Investment Fund is providing financing to Microfinance development – State strategic development program recognizes necessity for solving social problems and development of microenterprises – Overall support of CSCUs in Latvia from government and public institutions – Strong regulation and supervision outside the network: Commission on Financial and Capital Market – Fast loan market becomes more regulated	– Strong lobby of banks in the country – Society is oriented on profit maximization and development of cooperative organizations is not so popular anymore – Broad emigration opportunities, which more motivate people to go abroad than to organize cooperatives – CSCUs are not members of interbank payment system and can do payments only with bank intermediation – Risk of fraudulent operation of newcomers trying to benefit from network's assets and cooperative status – High competition with fast loan companies
Internal environment	
Strengths	Weaknesses
– Latvian CSCU network has long history, constant growth trend since re-establishing of the network in 1995, good reputation – LACSCU unites 29 CSCUs from 32, represents most of the network – WOCCU and International Development Desjardins institutional development and technical assistance projects were implemented in Latvia, providing support and training to staff, elected bodies and members of CSCUs – Savings in CSCUs are guaranteed by the state based on Deposit Guarantee Law (Law on Deposit Guarantees of the Republic of Latvia) – Low risk of CSCUs operation	– Latvian CSCUs network is not homogenous, there are 2 big CSCUs and 30 small CSCUs – Trade Union- based CSCUs and rural CSCUs have different strategic goals and work scale – There is no strong leader in Latvian CSCUs network to unite all of them – CSCU network is so different by members and interests, that it is not possible to launch a uniting Central CSCU – Poor CSCUs marketing and lack of strategic goals in regional CSCUs – Low funding of LACSCU, and in the result limited training and promotion activities – There is rather slow growth in CSCUs' membership and assets, CSCUs are poor in growth-oriented planning – CSCUs are not fully self-sufficient and need to cut costs because of low scale of operation and income; usually cuts affect marketing, training and representation – Low technical basis in most CSCUs

serious support from the government, self-governments and other united organizations, as also put their own efforts in pro-growth planning and marketing.

3 Latvian CSCUs and Financial Crisis 2008–2010

Latvia is one of the countries which where hit the most by the financial crisis 2008–2010. Financial shocks and economic downturn had impact on Latvian CSCUs, too. Many CSCUs finished the year 2010 with losses. One regional CSCU was forced to cease operation. Nevertheless, at the same time, comparing operation of CSCUs with operation of banks and leasing companies, it is obvious that CSCUs did much better than competing for-profit institutions and kept their supportive function also in difficult times. Operation of CSCUs in 2005–2010, which was shown on Figs. 3 and 4, should be compared with the performance of banks and leasing companies in the same period, which is shown on Figs. 9 and 10 (developed by the author based on statistic data 2005–2010 provided by CFCM).

Figure 9 shows that in 2005–2010, number of banks and branches of foreign banks in Latvia increased from 23 up to 29. Total assets of banks continued to grow until 2008, starting with 15,570 MEUR in 2005 and achieving 33,072 MEUR in 2008. Then in 2009 total banking assets decreased until 30,845 MEUR and showed small growth in 2010 up to 31,256 MEUR. Banking outstanding loans were growing during economic boom period from 9903 MEUR in 2005 until 23,604 MEUR in 2008. Affected by deep financial crisis banks strongly diminished lending, and volume of outstanding loans in 2010 decreased to 20,395 MEUR. At

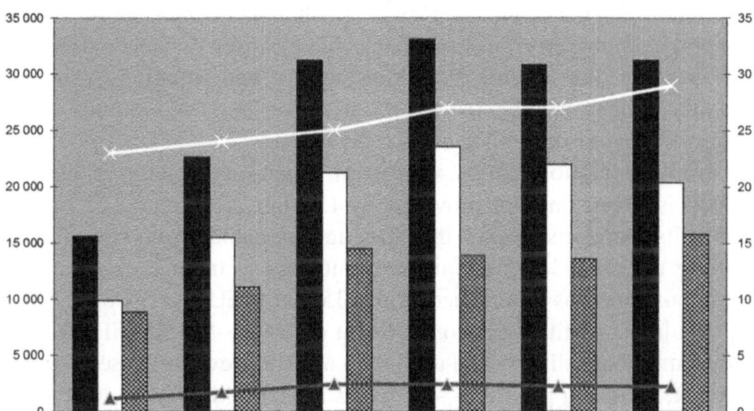

	2005	2006	2007	2008	2009	2010
Assets, MEUR	15 570	22 634	31 184	33 072	30 845	31 256
Loans, MEUR	9 903	15 471	21 224	23 604	21 953	20 395
Savings, MEUR	8 822	11 037	14 483	13 887	13 588	15 810
Capital&Reserves, MEUR	1 187	1 720	2 470	2 423	2 271	2 277
Banks and foreign branches	23	24	25	27	27	29

Fig. 9 Operation Statistics of Banks and Branches of Foreign Banks in Latvia, 2005–2010 (developed by the author based on Quarterly Statistics of Latvian CSCUs and Banks, and Statistics of Latvian CSCUs—members of LACSCU, statistical data 2005–2010) (Mavrenko 2011: 89)

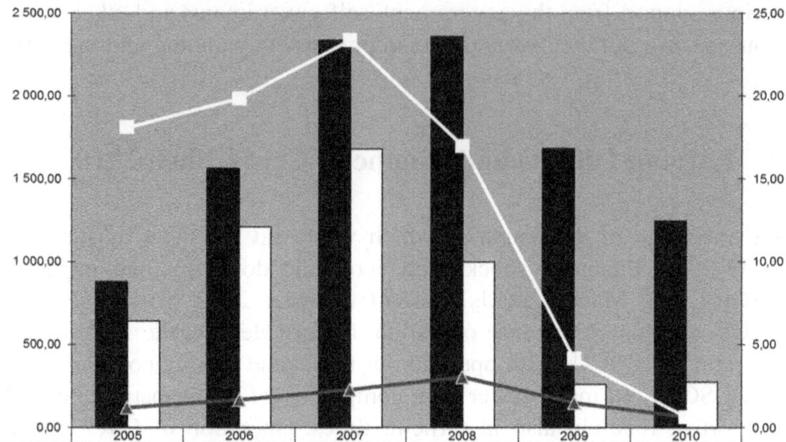

	2005	2006	2007	2008	2009	2010
Lease portfolio, MEUR	881,48	1 561,59	2 334,79	2 356,29	1 682,70	1 244,64
New purchases, MEUR	640,04	1 210,07	1 678,05	999,89	262,29	273,82
Factoring portfolio, MEUR	119,51	165,95	227,30	302,49	149,44	63,62
Consumer loans, MEUR	18,08	19,83	23,34	16,96	4,14	0,63

Fig. 10 Operation Statistics of Members of Latvian Association of Leasing Companies, 2005–2010 (developed by the author based on Statistics of Members of the Latvian Association of Leasing Companies 2005–2010) (Mavrenko 2011: 90)

the same time volume of attracted savings was constantly growing and achieved 14,483 MEUR in 2007, then in 2009 decreased until 13,588 MEUR and started to grow again, achieving 15,810 MEUR in 2010. Total capital and reserves did not show significant fluctuation, staying close to 2271 MEUR during the whole period. In the growing phase of economy, banks were very active in lending and caused overheating of the economy. However, when their funds became the most needed to support economy in crisis time, banks have chosen distance position. When savings are growing, but lending is decreasing is a bad situation in the economy of the country, money is collected but not used for the growing purpose, in other words, money is not working (Mavrenko 2011: 88).

Similar situation can be viewed in leasing and factoring business. Figure 10, which is based on data provided by Latvian Association of Leasing Companies about its members, shows that leasing companies followed the banks' example. During the crisis leasing companies stopped to finance new purchases at all; and lease portfolio has diminished from 2356.29 MEUR in 2008 till 1244.64 MEUR in 2010, almost getting back to the result of 2005—881.48 MEUR in lease portfolio. Consumer loans diminished until 0.33 MEUR, new purchases decreased till 273.82 MEUR, factoring portfolio—till 63.62 MEUR (Mavrenko 2011: 89).

How it can be seen on Figs. 3 and 4, operation statistics of Latvian CSCUs in the same period 2005–2010 had very different dynamics. Operation of CSCUs was rather stable both in economic boom and in crisis. CSCUs with their conservative policy, social goals, not-for-profit principle and high risk aversion could survive during the crisis and showed low dependence between their operation results and macroeconomic situation, causing less shocks to their members. CSCUs were the only institutions, which during 2005–2010 showed growth both in attraction of savings and provision of loans (Mavrenko 2011: 89).

4 Conclusions

CSCU financial statistics data looks rather insignificant in comparison with banking sector. At the same time, it is important to see the difference in clientele of both types of institutions. CSCUs serve unbankable or financially excluded people. Services provided by CSCUs are the only opportunity for these people not to stay outside economic and social processes in the country. Based on definite membership, CSCUs serve local society; accumulate national capital to benefit regional development and social welfare in the country. There is a huge potential hidden in CSCUs, but still big work should be done to strengthen and broaden CSCUs network in Latvia. Successful growth is possible only in case if CSCUs will get strong support on all three levels—macro, mezo and micro. Political support is needed to strengthen the idea of financial cooperation on the national level. Involvement of self-governments is necessary to position and use CSCUs as a tool for regional development. CSCUs themselves should be pro-active in planning of their operation and put higher goals for future development.

References

Aaslund A, Dombrovskis V (2011) How Latvia came through the financial crisis. Peterson Institute for International Economics, Washington, DC, 140 p

Aizsilnieks A (1968) Latvijas tautsaimniecības vēsture 1914–1945.g.g. (History of Latvian Economy 1914–1945, in Latvian language). Daugava, Rīga, 983 p

Caprio G Jr, Vittas D (eds) (1997) Reforming financial systems: historical implications for policy. Cambridge University Press, Cambridge, 222 p

Current WOCCU Development Projects (1996). Available at: http://www.uwcc.wisc.edu/icic/orgs/copac/member/WOCCU-World-Council-of-Credit-Unions1/Current-WOCCU-Development-Projects--19961.html. Accessed 20 Aug 2011

Jerving et al (eds) (1994) Credit Union handbook. WOCCU, Madison, 132 p

Kučinskis J (2004) Krājaizdevu sabiedrību ceļvedis: kopdarbības iespējas Latvijā (Credit Union Roadmap: Cooperation Opportunities in Latvia, in Latvian language). Hipotēku banka, Rīga "Elpa-2", 160 p

LACSCU, Information about LACSCU. Available at http://www.lkkss.lv. Accessed 20 Aug 2015

Law on Savings and Credit Unions (in Latvian), LR likums "Krājaizdevu sabiedrību likums", Latvijas Vēstnesis, 162 (1223), 03.06.1998., Ziņotājs, 13, 02.07.1998., with actual amendments, 20.08.2015.

Law on Cooperative Organizations of the Republic of Latvia (in Latvian), LR likums "Kooperatīvo sabiedrību likums", Latvijas Vēstnesis, 48/49 (1109/1110), 24.02.1998., Ziņotājs, 6, 19.03.1998., with actual amendments, 20.08.2015

Law on Credit Institutions of the Republic of Latvia (in Latvian), LR likums "Kredītiestāžu likums", of the Republic of Latvia Latvijas Vēstnesis, 163 (446), 24.10.1995., Ziņotājs, 23, 07.12.1995., with actual amendments, 20.08.2015

Law on Deposit Guarantees of the Republic of Latvia (in Latvian), LR likums "Noguldījumu garantiju likums" (ex- "Fizisko personu noguldījumu garantiju likums"), Vēstnesis, 48/49 (1109/1110), 24.02.1998., Ziņotājs, 6, 19.03.1998., with actual amendments, 20.08.2015

Leasing companies—members of Latvian Association of Leasing Companies (in Latvian), Līzinga kompānijas—LLDA biedri. Available at: http://www.llda.lv/par/biedri.html. Accessed 10 Jan 2011

Lee PA (ed) (1990) Introduction to Credit Unions. CUNA, Kendall & Hunt Publishing Company, Dubuque, 265 p

Mavrenko T (2002) Krājaizdevu sabiedrība kā kreditēšanas aktivizēšanas instruments ārpus lieliem regionālajiem centriem (Credit Union as a Credit Activating Tool Outside Big Regional Centers, in Latvian language), Starptautiskās zinātniskās konferences "Tradicionālais un novatoriskais sabiedrības ilgtspējīgā attīstībā, konkurētspējas problēmas ilgtspējīgā ekonomikas attīstībā" materiāli, Rēzekne, Rēzeknes Augstskola, 28/02-02/03/2002, pp 207–215

Mavrenko T (2011) Development of microfinance in Latvia: new look at savings and credit unions. J Bus Manag 4:85–100

Participants of the Financial and Capital Market of Latvia. Available at: http://www.fktk.lv. Accessed 25 Aug 2015

DID' s Professional Experience, pp 42. Available at: http://www.did.qc.ca/documents/DID-Professional-Experience.pdf. Accessed 10 Sept 2011

Quarterly Statistics of Latvian CSCUs and Banks. Available at http://www.fktk.lv. Accessed 25 Aug 2015

Statistics of Latvian CSCUs—members of LACSCU. Available at http://www.lkkss.lv. Accessed 25 Aug 2015

Statistics of Members of the Latvian Association of Leasing Companies 2005–2010 (in Latvian), Latvijas līzinga devēju asociācijas biedru statistika 2005–2010 gados. Available at: http://www.llda.lv/par/statistika.html. Accessed 2 Jan 2011

Witzeling R (1993) People not profit: the story of the Credit Union movement. CUNA, Kendall & Hunt Publishing Company, Dubuque, 128 p

Грэйс Д, Бранч Б (ред) (2000) Примерный закон для кредитных союзов (Example of Credit Union Law, in Russian language). WOCCU, 88 с

Credit Unions in Lithuania

Jurgita Liutvinskiene and Jurgita Meskauskaite-Cilliers

Abstract Over 20 years since its beginnings in 1995, the movement of Lithuanian credit unions has grown into a large network of financial co-operatives. At the beginning of 2015, the Lithuanian credit unions had more than 149,800 members and accounted for a 2.5 % market share of the retail banking market. Lithuanian credit unions were created and developed in line with the model of a two-level Desjardins credit unions' system of Quebec (Canada) but also have some unique characteristics as a result of the Lithuanian legal and business environment. Therefore, at the beginning of 2015 the majority of Lithuanian credit unions (63 out of 74) were united under the two-level co-operative system, which may be classified as a consensual network. As a result of a weak mutual integration of another 11 credit unions, they should be classified as an atomized network. The financial crisis of 2008 and its aftermath created new challenges to the further development of credit unions that are discussed in this paper.

1 The Establishment and Evolution of Credit Unions' Network in Lithuania

1.1 Historical Background of Credit Unions in Lithuania

Credit co-operation in Lithuania started at the end of nineteenth century, almost at the same time when co-operation ideas spread in Germany, Italy and other European countries. The first credit co-operatives in Lithuania were established in 1871–1873 and were called "taupomosios skolinamosios draugijos" ("savings borrowing societies") (Terleckas 2011).

J. Liutvinskiene (✉)
Business Development Department, Lithuanian Central Credit Union, Kaunas, Lithuania
e-mail: j.liutvinskiene@lku.lt

J. Meskauskaite-Cilliers
London, United Kingdom
e-mail: jurga.cilliers@gmail.com

S. Karafolas (ed.), *Credit Cooperative Institutions in European Countries*,
Contributions to Economics, DOI 10.1007/978-3-319-28784-3_18

The number of financial cooperatives grew relatively quickly: there were 437 credit co-operatives in 1928. As a result of an increasing pressure to provide services more effectively, credit co-operatives started to consolidate. In 1939 there were 310 active credit co-operatives, which had 119,000 members (Terleckas 2000). The World War II and the resulting occupation of Lithuania by the Soviet Union meant a complete termination of the activity of credit unions.

In 1994, several years after Lithuania regained its independence (1990), the idea of credit co-operation returned. It was promoted and supported by such foreign aid organizations as the Canadian International Development Agency (CIDA), the Open Society Fund-Lithuania, USAID, and also local leaders. As a result, two international organizations, Développement International Desjardins (DID) and World Council of Credit Unions (WOCCU), launched two separate projects to support and assist with the development of credit co-operatives in Lithuania.

Canada (Quebec province) and the US, where credit unions are successfully established as significant players of the financial system, provided the majority of financial, technical and know-how support for the development of the Lithuanian credit unions' (Lt: *kredito unijos*) network. Step by step the model of Desjardins credit unions (Canada), with some exceptions, was adopted as the most appropriate form of credit union co-operation to Lithuanian market environment.

1.2 Evolution of Legal Environment for Credit Unions

After a year of intensive co-operation of DID and WOCCU projects with the working group at the Lithuanian Parliament (Seimas of the Republic of Lithuania) the first Law on Credit Unions was passed in 1995. The law stipulated that a credit union could be established by at least 50 real members that are connected by a certain membership criteria, a common bond. It could be based on one of the following characteristics:

- Employment by the same company, institution;
- Belonging to the same professional group;
- Belonging to a certain formal, registered association;
- Residing in the same location—a town or village.

Only natural persons could become members of a credit union. The minimum share capital requirement for credit unions was set at 4344 €. The minimum value of a single share was set at 87 €.

By law, credit unions could:

- Receive term and demand deposits from its members, other credit unions, associations of credit unions, public organizations, religious communities, institutions authorized by the Government of Lithuania and/or local municipalities, and international charitable (sponsorship) foundations and/or such foundations of foreign states;

- Provide short-term and long-term loans to its members only for the purposes provided for in law;
- Lend money to other credit unions or associations of credit unions, or borrow money from other credit unions or associations of credit unions and invest liquid funds of a credit union into government-backed securities.

The law also stipulated that until 31st of December 1997 credit unions were exempted from the profit tax of legal persons for the first 2 years of their operation. From 1st of January 1998 the profit tax was introduced, but it was still reduced by 70 % (Igaryte 2003).

Although credit unions could perform their main functions: accept deposits and lend to their members, the legislation for credit unions still had several serious shortcomings (Igaryte and Bubnys 2011):

- Deposits in credit unions were not covered by the state deposits' insurance scheme while the deposits in commercial banks were insured;
- Credit unions were not eligible for receiving emergency loans from the Central Bank in case of impaired liquidity/ solvency (except from other credit unions or their associations);
- Credit unions were lending to each other in the form of term deposits without any real guaranties;
- Credit unions did not have access to the payments and clearing system of the Central Bank;
- Minimum value of a single member share was too high in relation to real incomes of the Lithuanians at that time;
- Credit unions were not able to lend to small businesses, established by members of credit unions;
- Credit unions could include only one membership criteria in their by-laws.

Therefore, amendments to the existing credit unions' legislation were initiated with a goal to introduce the best practice of Desjardins credit unions in Lithuania. At a result of this initiative, a new Law on the Central Credit and amendments to three important laws were adopted by the Parliament in 2000: the Law on Credit Unions, the Law on Deposits' Insurance, the Law on Legal Persons' Profit Tax (see Table 1 for the main amendments).

Another important achievement of Lithuanian credit unions was an exemption from the EU directive on Credit institutions Nb. 2000/12/EB (2000) in regards to the minimum capital requirement, which was negotiated before joining the European Union. As a result, the EU requirement for the minimum initial capital of one million euros was imposed only on the Central Credit Union, excluding credit unions (Igaryte 2003).

Nevertheless, Lithuanian credit unions could not raise the initial capital of the Central Credit Union without help of the Lithuanian Government. Therefore, a clause that the Government could be accepted as a member of the Central Credit Union was laid down in the law. The Government was set to participate in the following way:

Table 1 Amendments to the credit unions' legislation in 2000

Name of the law	The scope
Amendments of the Law on Credit Unions	The share price of a single member (natural person) share was reduced from 87 € to 29 € Permission to accept small enterprises that are established by members of the credit unions (up to 49 employees) as associate members was included The share price for a single legal person share was set at 290 €
Amendments of the Law on Legal Persons Profit Tax Law	Exemption from the profit tax was extended. From 1st January 2000 until 1st January 2003 credit unions were exempted from the profit tax. From 1st January 2003 the reduced rate of profit tax (by 70 %) was applied to credit unions
Amendments of the Law on Deposits Insurance	Credit unions were included in the state deposits insurance scheme The annual rate of an insurance premium was set as follows: 1. 0.45 % for banks and branches of banks 2. 0.2 % for credit unions
Law on the Central Credit Union	The Central Credit Union is a credit institution operating on a co-operative basis, established by credit unions and the Government of Lithuania, and functioning as a co-operative society The Central Credit Union shall operate on the basis of share capital and fulfil the functions of the supporting of liquidity and restoration of solvency of credit unions, accepting deposits, providing loans and assuming responsibility for managing risks resulting from it

Source: Igaryte and Bubnys (2011)

- The Government should acquire one main share and 5299 additional shares at the price of 290 € each. Total amount of the Government-owned shares added up to 1.53 million euros;
- Over a set period of time, credit unions should buy-back the shares from the Government until the complete repayment;
- Although the Government owned the largest part of the share capital, it did not receive exclusive voting rights.

From 1st July 2003 the Law on Financial Institutions came into power in Lithuania. This law has defined financial services and set up the requirements for the founders, participants and heads of the financial undertakings and credit institutions engaged in the provision of financial services, pursuit of business, procedure for and peculiarities of supervision of the activities of the financial institutions providing licensed financial services. This law was a part of package of harmonizing Lithuanian laws with the EU legislation.

Since the law introduced new rules for credit institutions, the laws regulating activities of credit unions and the Central Credit Union had to be adapted. The initial draft of the new Law on Credit Unions, which was prepared by the Central

Bank in 2004, was rejected by the Parliament as a result of an appeal of credit unions. The main reason for returning this draft law was the proposed inadequately strict regulation of credit unions activities. However, the Lithuanian Central Credit Union was subject to the EU regulation and the amendments of the Law on the Central Credit Union were passed by the Parliament. It came into effect on 1st May 2004 (the first day of Lithuania's membership in the EU). The law established very strict qualification requirements for the managers of LCCU, a requirement to establish the internal audit service, etc.

After long discussions, a new Law on Credit Unions was prepared and the Parliament approved it. The new law came into effect on 1st of January 2009.

Its effect on the legal environment of credit unions is summed up by these main points (Igaryte and Bubnys 2011):

- New membership requirements were created. Credit unions could be established only on a territorial basis (the original municipality and its neighboring municipalities);
- A broader range of legal persons was allowed to become members of a credit union;
- The price of the membership share was leveled for both natural and legal persons to a 29 €. The minimum capital requirement for credit union remained the same at 4344 €;
- New prudential requirements were set for lending: the size of the maximum loan could not be higher than 25 % of the credit union's capital. This requirement was postponed until 1 January 2013 for credit unions with capital that does not exceed 0.58 million euros;
- Strict requirements were set for the lending to the managers of a credit union;
- Qualification requirements were set to the managers of elected bodies;
- For the credit unions, which assets' size exceeded 2.9 million euros, a requirement to have both an external and internal audit was introduced.

A three levels procedure for the establishment of a credit union was set. The establishment requirements were made stricter. Credit unions also became regulated by the Law on Co-operative Entities, which was passed by the Parliament in 1993, but was not applied to credit unions until 2009.

The Law on Credit Unions was amended again in 2014. The most important changes included:

- The right to provide payment, currency exchange and some other services to non-members;
- The right to accept medium-sized enterprises as associate members;
- A membership criterion was extended by allowing to accept members based not only on the territorial criteria, but also on the basis of employment in the same enterprise or belonging to the same trade union;
- Minimum number of members was increased from 50 until 150 members;
- A new type of preferred shares with cumulative and non-cumulative dividend was introduced. These shares may not exceed 1/3 of the total share capital;

- Credit risk manager must be hired if the assets of the credit union exceed 14.5 million euros.

Another important amendment to credit unions' regulation was made in 2008, when the exemption from the profit tax was abolished by the Parliament. This was partly a result of the economic crisis and was a part of an austerity package that affected different parts of the economy.

1.3 Growth of Credit Unions in Lithuania

As of 1st of January 2015, 74 credit unions operated in Lithuania. On this date, 63 credit unions were members of the Lithuanian Central Credit Union and the Association of Lithuanian Credit Unions. Credit unions had 149,800 members at the beginning of 2015. Out of them, more than 136,300 were members of LCCU credit unions.

The growth of credit unions and their clients in 2002–2014 is presented in Chart 1.

Chart 1 demonstrates that the number of credit unions was increasing fast until 2004. After 2004, the establishment of new credit unions slowed down, but a steady growth of membership was maintained. In 2010–2013 another boom of establishing credit unions was observed. However, this period was also marked by the first ever insolvencies of credit unions. In 2013 the Central Bank cancelled licenses of three non LCCU member credit unions. At the beginning of 2014 one LCCU-member credit union and one non-member credit union were also recognized as insolvent. At the end of 2014, 74 credit unions remained in operation in Lithuania.

At the end of 2014 credit unions in Lithuania had more than 535 million euros of accumulated savings and lent out more than 263.5 million euros in loans. The assets of credit unions amounted to 617.2 million euros.

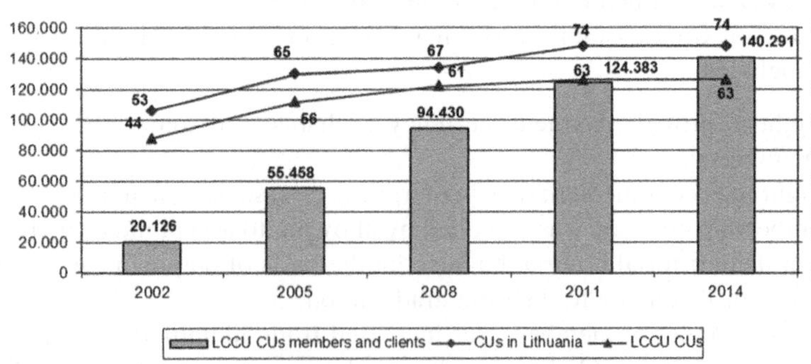

Chart 1 Credit unions and their clients in Lithuania, 2002–2014. *Source*: Central Bank of Lithuania, LCCU, 2015

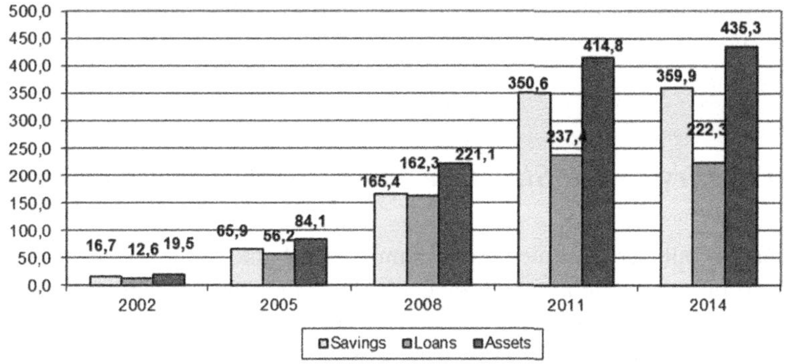

Chart 2 Assets, savings and loans growth of LCCU member credit unions, 2002–2014. *Source*: LCCU, 2015

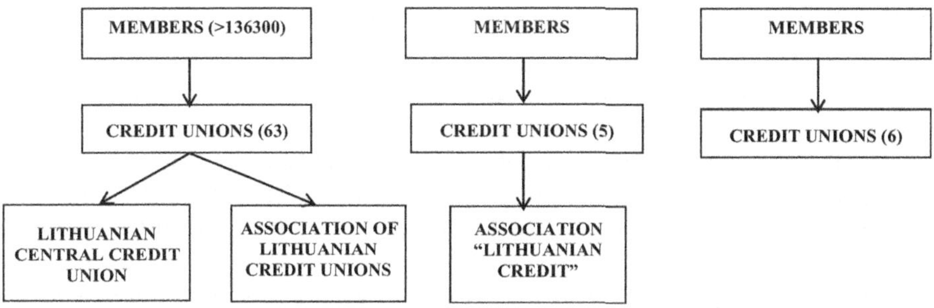

Chart 3 Structure of credit unions' network in Lithuania. *Source*: The Bank of Lithuania, LCCU, ALCU, ALC, 2014

Chart 2 demonstrates the growth of 63 LCCU-member credit unions.

2 The Current Model of Credit Unions' Network in Lithuania

The structure of the Lithuanian credit unions' network is presented in Chart 3. At the mid of 2014 63 credit unions were unified under the umbrella of the Association of Lithuanian credit unions (*Asociacija Lietuvos kredito unijos*) and the Lithuanian Central Credit Union (*Lietuvos centrinė kredito unija*). Five credit unions were allied by the Association "Lithuanian Credit" (*Asociacija "Lietuvos kreditas"*) and six credit unions acted independently.

According the classification of financial networks (Desrochers and Fischer 2005) only 63 credit unions that are members of the Lithuanian Central Credit Union may be treated as a *consensual network* (medium level of integration). As a result of lack of real mutual integration other 11 credit unions shall be classified as an *atomized network* (no or very low integration).

2.1 The First Level: Structure and Activities of Credit Unions

In Lithuania, only credit unions and commercial banks have the legal status of a credit institution and are allowed to accept deposits from the public. Credit unions together with commercial banks are covered by the state deposits insurance system and their activities are supervised by the Central Bank.

The structure of a credit union is presented in Chart 4. By law the General Members Assembly elects the following governing bodies: Supervisory Board, Board of Directors, Loan Committee and Commission of Inspectors.

The Commission of Inspectors (or at least one inspector) shall be elected by General Members Assembly to appraise credit union's annual financial statements. When the assets of a credit union exceed 2.9 million euros its financial statements must be verified by an independent audit and it also has to establish an Internal Audit Unit, which is elected and supervised by the Supervisory Board.

The Law on Credit Unions states that the General Members Assembly may not be replaced by the meeting of representatives. This is a key difference from other co-operative entities in Lithuania, as this is allowed by the Law on Co-operative Entities.

The profit at the end of the year may be distributed either by allocating dividends proportional to the turnover of a member's business with the credit union or by allocating dividends in proportion to shares in the credit union. However, the

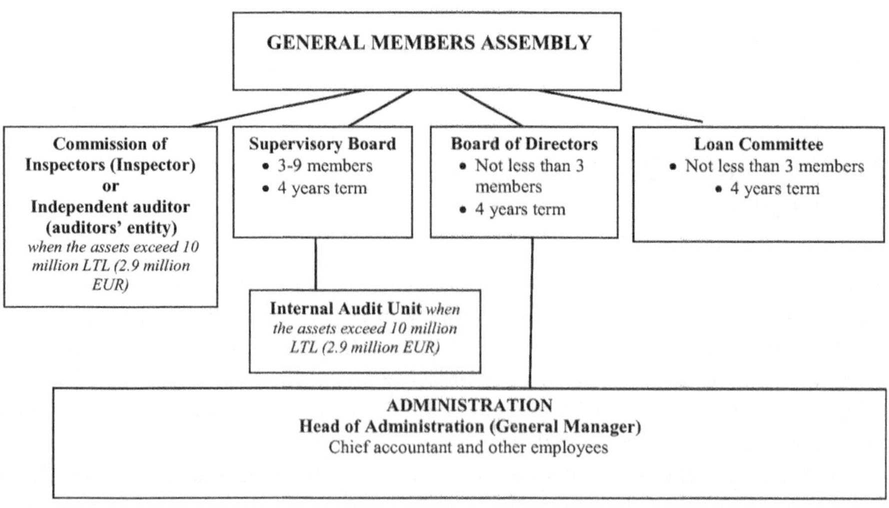

Chart 4 Organizational structure of a credit union. *Source*: The Law on Credit Unions, 2008

dividends are rarely paid as the members prefer to receive the benefits in the form of favorable interest rates or reduced service fees.

By law, the main activities of credit unions are the following:

1. Collection of term and demand deposits from members and other clients;
2. Lending to members;
3. Payment services to members and clients.

Lending services may be provided only to the members of a credit union. Saving services, with some exceptions, may also be provided to clients:

- Natural persons: children or foster-children, when at least one of their parents or foster-parents is a member of a credit union;
- Legal persons: state or municipal institutions, associations, religion communities, professional trades and charity and sponsorship funds from Lithuania, as well as international and foreign charity and sponsorship funds;
- Legal entities that are being established by members of a credit union.

At the beginning of 2015, 97 % of the clients of the LCCU credit unions were members of credit unions.

The law allows credit unions to provide a wide range of services. However, only LCCU member credit unions are able to provide payment services such as money transfers, internet banking, international payment cards and payments for utilities. Providing additional services requires large investment and ongoing technological support. As a result, independent credit unions can offer only basic services to their members: loans and deposits. All credit unions, regardless of their membership in the second level organization, are local and act exclusively in the Lithuanian market.

2.2 *The Evolution of a Second Level of Credit Unions' System*

The leaders of Lithuanian credit unions soon realized that the dependency on foreign grants was not sustainable. The DID project's funding was extended twice: in 1997 and 2000, but on a condition that credit unions will set up a consultancy center which will be fully supported by credit unions. As a result, the Association of Lithuanian credit unions (ALCU) was established in 1997 on the premises of the DID project. From the very beginning it started to collect a small fee from credit unions that helped credit unions to get used to the idea that the consultancy services needed to be financed by their own funds (Igaryte 2008).

Until the establishment of the Central Credit Union in Lithuania, ALCU in parallel with the DID project provided all the necessary services to credit unions: marketing, training, IT systems and support, general business consultancy, assistance with licensing, lobbying, as well as credit lines and liquidity management assistance, monitoring of activities. Later almost all of these functions were transferred to LCCU. ALCU retained its lobbyist function (Igaryte 2008).

The other association, the National association of credit unions (*Nacionaline kredito uniju asociacija*), was also established in 1997 by credit unions, which were set up with a help of the WOCCU project. But this association decreased its operations when the financing from USAID stopped. Quite recently this association renewed its activities under a different name: Association "Lithuanian Credit" (*Asociacija "Lietuvos kreditas"*). This association advises not only credit unions, but also other companies that provide credit to the public.

In 1999 credit unions and politicians decided to create a centralized financial center to manage the liquidity of credit unions and provide emergency loans. A model of the Central Credit Union was designed in line with the model of a two-tier Desjardins credit unions' system in Quebec (Canada) with some variations relevant to the Lithuanian legal environment (Igaryte 2008). The law on the Central Credit Union was passed on 18th of May 2000. The Lithuanian Central Credit Union (LCCU) was established by 28 credit unions and the Government of Lithuania in 2001 and licensed by the Central Bank at the end of 2002.

The Lithuanian Central Credit Union is a member-based, co-operative financial institution, which provides services to credit unions and their members. The same voting principle "one member—one vote" is applied at General Assembly of the LCCU, regardless of the size of a credit union or the State's role of the dominant shareholder.

Organizational structure of the LCCU is slightly different from the structure of a credit union. These bodies are elected by the General Members Assembly: Supervisory Board, Board of Directors, Stabilization Fund Commission and Head of the Internal Audit Service.

The profit at the end of the year may be allocated to members in the same form, as in credit unions: turnover related dividends and share capital related dividends.

By law, LCCU main functions are the following (LCCU, 2015):

- *Maintaining credit unions' liquidity.* In order to ensure the implementation of this function, the LCCU has accumulated a reserve for maintaining credit unions' liquidity. Credit unions hold 1 % of their deposits in this reserve. The amount of the Liquidity Reserve was 4.2 million euros as of 1st January 2015. Funds from the liquidity maintenance reserve can be used for extending liquidity loans to member credit unions.
- *Maintaining credit unions' solvency.* To maintain credit unions' solvency, the LCCU set up the Stabilization Fund. As of 1st of April 2015 credit unions paid annual fee of 0.3 % from their deposits. The amount of the Stabilization Fund was 1.9 million euros as of 1st January 2015. In case of a probable insolvency member credit unions may receive funds from the Stabilization Fund in the form of subordinated loans or through gratuitous allocation of funds, which have to be included into the reserve capital of the credit union. A credit union has a right to receive support from the Stabilization Fund, but there is no obligation for the LCCU to recover the losses of an insolvent credit union.
- *Auxiliary supervision and monitoring of credit union activities.* The Board elected by the LCCU General Member Assembly ensures the supervision and

monitoring of activities of member credit unions. The Board and the Stabilization Fund Commission organize a continuous monitoring of credit unions' activities and provides recommendations on how to minimize key risks.

- *Financial center activities.* The LCCU provides a wide range of financial services to credit unions: accepts deposits and repayable funds, grants loans and takes on the related risks. Via the LCCU, credit unions are connected to the payment and clearing center of the Central Bank and the payment cards' authorization center, owned by a private company.
- Provides other support to credit unions (risk management, IT systems' support, marketing, training, business consultations, etc.).

While providing these and other centralized services to credit unions LCCU plays an important role in ensuring a better stability of the credit unions' sector as well as ensures the cost efficiency at the operational level.

3 The Importance of Credit Unions in the Lithuanian Banking Market

At the beginning of 2015, 74 credit unions, one Central Credit Union, seven banks and eight branches of the foreign banks were operating in Lithuania. The market share of credit unions amounted to 2.5 % as of 1st of January 2015 (2.7 % as of 1st of January 2014). One large credit union terminated its activities at the beginning of 2014, so the market share of credit unions has shrunk slightly.

Market share indicators of credit unions and banks at the end of 2014 are presented in Table 2. These data were provided by the Lithuanian Central Credit Union and the Association of Lithuanian Banks, therefore only the data of the 63 credit unions, seven banks and two foreign bank branches are presented.

The contribution of credit unions to the Lithuanian economy is particularly visible in rural areas and small towns, where they account for more than half of the local financial services. The market share, calculated in the number of clients is larger than in assets and constituted 3.7 % as of 1st January 2015. Measuring by the density of service points (excluding ATMs) within the network, which consisted of

Table 2 Credit unions and banks indicators at the end of 2014

Indicator	Credit unions (LCCU members)	Banks (ALB members)
Branches and sales points	187	367
Number of employees	586	8835
Number of clients	140,291	3,668,281
Number of private clients	135,134	3,477,490
Number of corporate clients	5157	190,791
Payment cards	15,407	3,462,025
Internet banking users	39,543	3,968,901

Source: LCCU and the Association of Lithuanian Banks, 2015

63 credit unions' headquarters and 124 distant service points as of, the common market share of the LCCU member credit unions was even 33.6 %.

Credit unions focus on rural areas because the population there has no access to adequate financial services. Credit unions became a strategic partner of farmers in many Lithuanian regions and successfully contributed to the sustainable growth of the agribusiness sector. Answering the specific needs of agricultural sector, credit unions provide very favorable and competitive credit conditions. It's estimated that credit unions have 20–25 % of the agricultural loans market share in rural areas. Providing credit to micro and small enterprises is another focus of credit unions. At the end of 2011, 57 credit unions (LCCU members) offered a new product: business loans for start-ups through the Entrepreneurship Promotion Fund. During the after-crisis period banks almost stopped the lending to business start-ups. This business loans program is another example of the important role credit unions play in the growth of the community wealth.

4 Economic Crisis Effects and the Future of Credit Unions Network in Lithuania

In 2015 the growth of the Lithuania's economy decelerated due to the challenging external environment. The Bank of Lithuania forecasts that GDP in 2015 should grow by 2 % and another 3.4 % in 2016 (The Bank of Lithuania 2015-06-10). Due to the current country's economic circumstances a domestic demand remains the key factor of economic growth in the country. According the Bank of Lithuania a private consumption expenditure in 2015 should increase by 3.4 % (and by additional 4 % in 2016) and the unemployment rate should fall to 10 % (and down to 9.2 % in 2016). However, it is expected that credit unions will grow gradually and expand their services in line with the country's economic situation.

Table 3 demonstrates assets, loans and deposits growth indicators of credit unions and banks in 2010 and 2013. The growth of credit unions and banks in 2010 was very different: banks were very reluctant to lend, while credit unions significantly increased their loan portfolios and assets. In 2013, the growth of credit unions has slowed down significantly and the growth ratio of loans was negative.

Table 3 Comparison of credit unions and banks by main indicators at the end of 2013

Indicator	Credit unions, 2013 (million, EUR)	Change of the indicator for credit unions		Banks, 2013 (million, EUR)	Change of the indicator for banks	
		2010	2013		2010	2013
Assets	621	+36.9 %	+4.3 %	22468.2	−3.0 %	+3.0 %
Loans	297.7	+25.5 %	−8.5 %	14775.2	−5.2 %	+0.4 %
Deposits	541.1	+40.0 %	+2.5 %	13787.2	+10.6 %	+9.2 %

Source: The Central Bank of Lithuania, 2011, 2014

The banks also did not try to grow their business and as a result, stagnation was felt in the crediting market.

The slow-down of the growth of credit unions was not only affected by the economic crisis, but also by the new requirements imposed by the Central Bank in the mid of 2013. The key new requirements, which had direct negative impact on the growth of credit unions, were new liquidity and capital adequacy ratios. The liquidity ratio for the fast growing credit unions was increased from 30 % up to 60 %, while capital adequacy ratio for some credit unions increased from 13 % up to 25 % in case the loans to associate members comprise a large proportion in the total loans portfolio.

In 2011–2014, the Lithuanian financial sector was exposed to several serious crises: two commercial banks and five credit unions were declared insolvent by the Central Bank. The closures of credit unions has proved the importance and need for more professional risk management and established internal control procedures combined with more active member involvement in the management process.

The other weaknesses of credit unions, which were highlighted in the study by the Central Bank (2014), are low level of credit unions' capitalization and insufficient mutual guarantee system in the case of serious losses. Consolidation of credit unions into co-operative banks was proposed by the Central Bank as one of possible ways to increase the capital of credit unions. In March 2014, the guidelines for the strengthening of credit unions' sector were presented by the Central Bank for public consultation. Responding to the Central Bank's proposals to the changes of legislation regulating credit unions, LCCU member credit unions drafted their own recommendations. The proposal includes the extending of the present guarantee system from the current, paid-up fund (LCCU Stabilization Fund) to a mixed cross-guarantee system, which would include a paid-up fund (Stabilization Fund) and a call-up fund (Ayadi et al 2010). The call-up fund would be used in the case of losses that could not be covered by the Stabilization Fund. However, it remains unclear whether these changes will be approved of.

Although the credit unions' system in Lithuania does not have a clear vision of its future just yet, it is very obvious that in the next few years the most important strategic issue will be finding an acceptable model for further mutual integration as well as re-organization of the operations of credit unions to ensure they are well-capitalized and more competetive in the Lithuanian market.

5 Conclusions

The main positive factors that influenced the establishment and growth of credit unions' network in Lithuania could be summed up as:

1. Strong community leaders that inspired the establishment and growth of credit unions.
2. Know-how support from Desjardins credit unions' movement.
3. The reluctance of commercial banks to finance agricultural and small business sectors.

4. Favorable legal environment, defined by:
   - Status of a credit union as a credit institution, which allowed them to accept deposits from the public, and the inclusion of credit unions in the State system of deposits' insurance;
   - Profit tax exemption that was applied to credit unions for more than 10 years;
   - Exemption from a minimum capital requirement from the EU directive on Credit institutions.
5. The establishment of the second level of integration: the Lithuanian Central Credit Union (LCCU) that manages credit unions' liquidity and can step in and provide emergency funds and management advice in the case of solvency problems.

Despite the fact that credit unions in Lithuania have a relatively small market share, they are an important part of social economy, especially in the regions where they provide access to financial services. Credit unions also play an important role in financing farmers and micro or small entrepreneurs.

Economic crisis and the closure of several credit unions have brought to light several weaknesses of the credit unions' system in Lithuania, which must be addressed in a near future:

- The closer involvement of members in the management process of credit unions and their financial education;
- The sustainable capitalization of credit unions;
- The improvement of mutual guarantee system and an extension to the mixed cross-guarantee system, which would include a paid-up fund (Stabilization Fund) and a call-up fund.

Although the credit unions' network in Lithuania does not have a clear vision of its future just yet, it is very obvious that in the next few years the most important strategic issue will be finding an acceptable model for further mutual integration as well as re-organization of the operations of credit unions to ensure they are well-capitalized and more competetive in the Lithuanian market.

References

Ayadi R, Llewellyn DT, Schmidt RH, Arbak E, De Groen WP (2010) Investigating diversity in the banking sector in Europe: key developments, performance and role of cooperative banks. Centre for European Policy Studies, Brussels, p 184. ISBN 978-94-6138-042-5

Desrochers M, Fischer KP (2005) The power of networks: integration and financial cooperative performance. Ann Public Coop Econ 76(3):307–354

Igaryte J, Bubnys S (2011) Legislation and structure of Lithuanian credit unions system. Les Cahiers de l'economie sociale, no. 7. ICA European research conference "Co-operatives contribution to a plural economy", Lyon, 2–4 Sept, 2010. L'Harmattan, Paris, ISBN 978-2-296-07625-9

Igaryte J (2003) Lithuanian Credit Unions: overview of legal environment. Microfinance Centre for Central and Eastern Europe and the New Independent States. Policy Monitor, Nb. 4

Igaryte J (2008) The governance of credit unions system in Lithuania: at the crossroad towards atomized or centralized credit unions system. Les Cahiers de l'economie sociale, no. 6. ICA XXII international research conference "Cooperative challenges: food, credit, democracy and development", Dourdan, 19–22 Oct, 2006. L'Harmattan, Paris, ISBN 978-2-296-07625-9

Terleckas V (2011) Bankininkystė Lietuvoje 1795–1915. Lietuvos bankas, Vilnius, p 622. ISBN 978-9986-651-62-8

Terleckas V (2000) Lietuvos bankininkystės istorija 1918–1941. Lietuvos bankas, Vilnius, p 444. ISBN 9986-651-26-3

The Bank of Lithuania (2014) Kredito unijų sektoriaus stiprinimas: dokumentas viešai diskusijai (Strengthening of Credit Unions' sector: a document for the public discussion). http://lb.lt/kredito_uniju_sektoriaus_stiprinimas, 2014-03-19

The Bank of Lithuania (2015) Lithuania's economic development and outlook, 10 Jun 2015. https://www.lb.lt/macroeconomic_forecast, 2015-06-10

The Law on Credit Unions, 1995, 2000, 2008, 2014, Seimas of the Republic of Lithuania. http://www3.lrs.lt/pls/inter3/dokpaieska.showdoc_l?p_id=479323, 2015-06-05

The Law on the Central Credit Union, 2000, 2004, Seimas of the Republic of Lithuania. http://www3.lrs.lt/pls/inter3/dokpaieska.showdoc_l?p_id=416516, 2014-05-01

The Law on Co-operative Entities, 1993, 2002, Seimas of the Republic of Lithuania http://www3.lrs.lt/pls/inter3/dokpaieska.showdoc_l?p_id=430845, 2014-05-01

The Law on Financial Institutions, 2002, Seimas of the Republic of Lithuania. http://www3.lrs.lt/pls/inter3/dokpaieska.showdoc_l?p_id=452549, 2014-05-01

Statistical data of LCCU member credit unions. Lithuanian Central Credit Union. www.lku.lt

Statistical data of Lithuanian banks. The Association of Lithuanian Banks. www.lba.lt

Statistical data of Lithuanian credit unions. The Bank of Lithuania. www.lb.lt

The Polish Credit Co-operative System: Historical and Contemporary Experiences

Zofia Chyra-Rolicz

Abstract This paper describes the long, over 150 years old tradition on saving and credit co-operation on the Polish territory during the time of political dependence, the middle world's war time in the II Republic of Poland and period of real socialism. Against the repressive policy, saving and credit co-operatives survived, changing organizational shape and functions, serving not only particular for members, also for society and common interests.

The new epoch for co-operative banking arrived with the time of political transformation in 1989. Co-operative banks survived the time of agricultural crisis at the beginning of 1990 in good economic conditions with the governmental support, saving property of their members and clients. Today they are important factor supporting local enterprising in agriculture and processing and local small industry. New political forces jointed with Solidarity movement established, or rather revive the old form of co-operative saving and credit chases named of Franciszek Stefczyk, well known co-operative leaders at nineteenth and twentieth centuries. This new movement SKOK win a great success during transformation, 1599 chases are acting in country-wide net with 2.1 million members (and with their families—it would be about six to seven million people) among the employees earning small salary. It creates important part of social economy enterprises and try to support the different forms of co-ops.

1 Historical Heritage

Polish saving and credit co-ops had had long tradition in Poland, over 150 years old.[1] This new economic and social idea appeared in time of political dependency under three empires: Russian, German and Austria–Hungary, as a local movement jointed

[1] Historical informations from: Zarys historii polskiego ruchu spółdzielczego, 1971, (ed. Ingot S.), ZW CRS, Warszawa, vol. I; Rusiński 1980, Zarys historii polskiego ruchu spółdzielczego, ZW CZSR, Warszawa, vol. II 1918–1939.

Z. Chyra-Rolicz
Department of Humanities, Siedlce University of Natural Sciences and Humanities, Siedlce, Poland
e-mail: CHYROL@op.pl

S. Karafolas (ed.), *Credit Cooperative Institutions in European Countries*, Contributions to Economics, DOI 10.1007/978-3-319-28784-3_19

economic reasons with long time perspectives supporting the national spirit in many different organizations as peasant's circle, libraries, national houses with educational self-help program. Polish society in nineteenth century had not only adapted the foreigners co-operative patterns, also was able to create own organization serving for common interests. The main role on this field belonged to priest Stanisław Staszic (1755–1826) which established THR (The Hrubieszów Agricultural Society for Common Rescue in Adversity) in 1816 as a private foundation for supporting and educating peasants, but with own management: manager, advisory council and auditory units. This organization, associated peasants, had own saving and credit bank and also other useful institutions as library, hospital, social help houses, and was oriented into developing the progress in agriculture and cultural-educational activity addressed to peasants' members and their families. The founder was a distinguished person of the Polish Enlightenment and his idea became from the utopian project of better society, but in spite of other utopian project, it was a successful and permanent archetype of an agricultural co-operative and it had worked for several decades. This pre-co-operative society had acting since very long time in different political and socio-economic circumstances, up to 1952. Results of its activity was clear and clever to compare the civilization level with outside villages and their habitants. So Stanisław Staszic can be accounted into the narrow group of early pioneers of co-operative' ideas and movement, which had grow up in the nineteenth and twentieth centuries, but he has been well known only on Polish territory but not in worldwide scope, perhaps because of political situation—political dependency and language not popular as, French German or English. Without doubting Staszic deserved to be called one of the precursors of co-operative movement in the world, and certainly the father of the Polish co-operative movement. Staszic's ideas had lived in the circle of Polish society as a way for future generation working for common benefit. His name had been used by many societies jointed economic work with educational and cultural activity for very long time. On the Polish land annexed by the three empires (Germany, Russia and Austria) the first wave of co-operative initiatives had arrived at the 1860–1870 nineteenth century as a modern social pattern of economic struggle against capitalism from the high developed countries—the British Empire and Germany. We adopted the patterns of consumer co-operatives from England and saving and credit societies of Herman Schulze von Delitzch and Friedrich Wilhelm Raiffeisen from Germany. In the Polish political circumstances this movement of associations had a very strong national meaning, very important for supporting the national spirit and tradition, also economic position for generation living in political dependency.

The trend of liberal oriented co-operatives connected with organization of Peoples' Banks (Volksbanken) had developed early in the Wielkopolska Region, also Pomerania and Silesia—occupied by Prussia. This was also connected with the considerably high economic level of a country and restrictive policy against Poles and Polish nationality. The new idea was adapted and developed by the large group of economic and social dynamic activists recruited from landlords, urban intelligentsia, bourgeois, craftsmen and rich peasants The great hope of the Polish society, oppressed by Germans, were ideas of so called "organic work", which created the simply, everyday work for civilization progress in countryside in economic and social meaning, education and economic development. These ideas had particular response in the society and were based on three patterns: social and economic modernization by jointed forces, establishing various type of Polish associations and solidarity between different group of society. Wielkopolska, formed in such atmosphere, was the type of co-operatives referring to models of Herman Schulze von Delitzch, and its basic objectives was to provide Polish merchants, craftsmen and later also peasants, credit funds that would enable them to developed their businesses or farms, which by itself formed a type of resistance against ruler. They had followed new patterns of social and economic activity looking forward high developed countries and modern peoples. Herman Schultze von Delitz, himself stayed for a certain period of time in 1850 in Września, as a judge. His banks were observed by Polish society leaders. Such co-operatives were called People's Banks (Banki Ludowe), and the first was established in 1861 in Poznań among bourgeois. Over the next 10 years a few dozen of analogous initiatives had appeared, and just before the outbreak of the I World War there were 221 People's Banks in this region which associated almost 140,000 members. Many of them still have existed (Zarys historii 1971, p. 92–97).

Particular banks need support, specially capitals. An institutional cooperation between them was established in 1871 (The year of proclamation the German Empire, after the German-French war), when the oppressive politic against Poles were increased. During the meeting of 44 delegates from co ops acting in countryside the Union of Polish Co-operatives were establish in Poznań on April. There were representatives from 28 co-ops: 19 from Wielkopolska, 8 from Pomerania and 1 from High Silesia among delegates. At the beginning they tried to find the good area for economic business and social activity reaching the Polish society in the national spirit. The Union later was renamed into the Associations of Commercial and Economic Companies and associated not only banks, buy also peasant circles and its agricultural shops, companies for dividing the lands of big manors or developing nets of electricity and making even another activity. The People's Banks had supported them as a sources of capitals form becoming from saving by members (Zarys historii 1971, pp. 145–148). The first leader of The Union, pioneer in such activity in Polish territory, was catholic priest—Rev. Augustyn Szamarzewski (1832–1891), the next leader, which developed the organization of Polish co-ops was Rev. Piotr Wawrzyniak (1849–1910). The scope of business grew up quickly and it was necessary joint the forces and capitals for bugger plans. The Bank of the Union of Commercial Companies Union was established in 1886 in Poznań and became the financial base of co-operatives, working under the spirit of solidarism. The director was Józef Kusztelan (1843–1907), he was former teacher, which lost job by German restrictive policy and was forced to find the new area of activity among Polish people. Due to the activity of the Bank and the Union itself—the whole crediting system could perfectly cooperate with each other, and proper financial resources could be assigned to where particularly need at certain point in time. Both these institutions played an enormous role in the development of Polish loan societies on the Polish territory, occupied by German. Due to their scope, dynamism, good cooperation and role that they had played in protecting the Polish environment against German pressure—they were often referred to as "Wielkopolska Co-operative System" covering also agricultural marketing co-operatives, parcel co-operatives (established for buying out deteriorating estates and dividing land among Polish peasants), dairy co-operatives or housing co-ops in towns (After decades Ukrainians had followed these co-operative experiences on their way to political independency). The total number of different Polish co-ops was 313 associated 125,868 members in 1913 (Zarys historii 1971, p. 136). Among the pioneers and leaders of this system were many Catholic priests following generations: as mentioned above Rev. Augustyn Szamarzewski, Rev. Piotr Wawrzyniak and Rev. Stanisław Adamski (1875–1967), who later on (in 1930) was the Bishop of Katowice on Silesia and the leader of the Union of Poles in Germany, and also Rev. Bolesław Domański (1872–1939), the next Patron of Union Polish Co-operatives and the Union of Poles in Germany in the middle wars time. They had behaved their work in co-operative movement as a social service according the Christian solidarism expressed later on in the encyclical "Rerum novarum" of pope Leon XIII (1891) and social science of the Church. They and belonged to the wide group of "father-founders" adapting and creating this movement on Polish lands. During 50 years their activity, the Wielkopolska Province remained a leading co-operative centre of Poland, also after the independence was regained in 1918. It was the result of everyday so called "organic work" leading towards the economic and cultural developing the country. The character of banks were changed with the time: At first decades bans worked generally in towns associated small and middle shopkeepers and craftsmen. Later on co-operative banks entered into villages and were oriented for credit needs of peasants. As far in nineteenth century rich peasants constituted almost 25 % in all their members, inasmuch before the I world war peasants were 2/3 of members. The co-operative activity in countryside grow in specially important for Polish society oppressed in their national life by government and the German Colonization Commission, which had expulsed Poles from their lands. It was appraised, that every 1/10 Poles in Wielopolska district belonged and put their deposit in Polish co-operative banks. These capitals allowed to develop the Polish economic and cultural activity, also keep lands in Polish hands. The scope of their activity was growing with the time and social acceptation. There were banks associated on the average 617 members, sometimes even 1000 members acting in not far in an administrative district. So dynamic grow needed the bigger sources of capitals collected in co-operative banks, so the own bank (mentioned above) was established in 1886 in Poznań (Zarys historii 1971, p. 102–106). It was not only the financing centre for banks, but also the centre of co-operative instructions, publishing house and propaganda showing new possibilities of common co-operative activity as diary, housing, electrical, agricultural trade. This bank also supported new types of co-operatives. Polish co-operatives supported also many libraries and reading rooms, orchestras, chorus, amateur's theatres propagated the Polish language and knowledge of Polish history and culture. The Polish Theatre in Poznań was financed by the Polish co-operatives earning the sources from renting apartments in co-operative houses and hotel. Co-operatives were points of resistance for Polish society against the Germanizing policy. Before the I world war there were 221 so called popular banks (Volk Banks) worked only in Wielkopolska, Pomerania and High Silesia, associating 140,000 of members. In this time (1871–1913) also German people establisher their co-operative banks, and at the beginning the national division was not so strong marked, but with the progress of oppressive policy against the Polish society, the two parallel systems were existing associated Polish or German members.

Another branch of banking co-operatives developed on Polish territory was connected with experiences of Friedrich Wilhelm Raiffeisen, also German leader, activist working with peasants. Initially he tried to create various charitable organizations, however finally he came to the conclusion that in order for these associations to be durable, it is necessary that the recipients of such support show commitment and self organization, and not count on mercy of wealthier classes. It was the main principle of mutual support of the most destitute on which he based his the first rural loan societies established since 1960 of nineteenth century. This way went Franciszek Stefczyk (1861–1924), philosopher and historian, also the peasant movement's leader in Galicia, the province included into Austria Empire. At the beginning he was a teacher in agricultural school in countryside, in Czernichów near Kraków and—according the ethos of social work—he became a social leader among peasants. He had the opportunity to know ideas and practices of agricultural co-operatives of Friedrich Wilhelm Raiffeisen during his studies in Vienna and scientific trips to Germany and Habsburg's Empire. After the turn in his place of work in Poland, he established the first loan bank based on these models in Czernichów, and over the next years lead to establishing many similar rural savings—loan societies, that over time they began to called by his name, and Franciszek Stefczyk was seen as one of the co-operative leaders, pioneers in this part of Polish land. The usury was a great economic and social problem of hundred thousands peasant's farms in this time and region, conducting them to the bankruptcy and many families to extreme poverty and homeless. The Raiffeisen model of saving—loan chaise, adapted by Franciszek Stefczyk to the Polish circumstances, helped them to solve this tragic chain of economical dependency, beggary and became to lead a healthy economy in their farms. Franciszek Stefczyk was also the leader of peasant' circle and leader in peasant's popular political movement, conducting them to education on politic activity in parties and parliaments (provincial in Lvov, and countrywide in Vienna). He also created agricultural and commercial co-operatives, promoted dairy and craftsmen co-operatives. Stefczyk was also the promoter of co-operative vision for supporting the poor economy in this region and created plans of economic developing it on the co-operative way and self-help among peasants and other group of society in the spirit of solidarity. In 1899 he established the national Patronage for co-operatives, which was an organization for this whole co-operative system with support of government (Witalec 2008, p. 138). The National Patronage had managed training and courses, developed propaganda of hew pattern of common activity, published books and brochures, provided financial and organizational support in creating new co-operatives. In 1909 he established their National Central Fund in the capital of Austrian Galicia-Lvov. Very quickly saving-loans societies became popular in Galicia. There were only 26 registered chases, when The National patronage began its activity, before the I World War—in 1913 there were 1397 this kind of co-operatives, associated over 321,800 members. The main group of them were peasants—91.3 %, another social groups engaged in these societies: teachers—0.6 %, priests—0.5 %, landowners—0.2 % and different category of people—7.4 %. It means that they familiarized themselves this tool for modern farming economy and other business. The great value of these co-ops was also the good memory and socials links between people, which helped to rebuild such enterprises in future (Zarys historii 1971, pp. 210–212).

Co-operative propaganda overcame the border of Russia Empire and at the beginning of twentieth century, after the revolution of 1905–1907, it was boom of co-operative initiatives similar to Stefczyk's pattern in savings and loan societies, peasant's circles, dairy and agricultural trade co-operative.

The great I world war was very destructive in this part of Europe, ruinous the political reality and economic life. Collapsing of three empires—Russia, Germany and Austrian—Hungary took floor for independent Polish state as a democratic state. After regained independence in November 1918, co-operatives established in the three annexed Polish territories, from various ideological trends, different legal system, traditions and social-economic conditions were capable of coexisting with each other, and even were able to create large and efficient organism unified from three parts. This fact certainly was caused by the co-operative law voted by the Polish Parliament on October 20 1920, acting form 1921. In scale of Europe it was the most modern, democratic in those time legal regulation connecting co-operatives as a independent, voluntary movement, open for everybody without any limitations. Over the whole period between the world wars the co operative movement maintained a pluralistic nature, developing from different ideological trends and organizational branches, in those economic areas where it was previously present, but also entered new areas. Consumer and agricultural co-operatives developed large educational activity, organizing many courses and training for staff and people, which gained new possibilities to catch jobs in co-operatives mainly in countryside. The area of co-operatives were growing up with the time. It was generally estimated, that every fifth grown-up citizen in Poland was a member of some type of co-operative before the II World War. In economic terms, in 1938 the market share of co-operatives in retails sale equal 4–5 % of all sales, in purchasing of agricultural products—according to various calculations—from 1.5 % to even 12 % (Rusiński 1980, p. 192; Stawarz 2006).

During the II Republic of Poland (1918–1939) different forms of co-operative banks had possibility of spectacular development. They had existed as saving and credit chases concerning the rules of Herman Schulze von Delitzsch, also as national peasant's banks following the patterns of F. W. Raiffeisen. These co-operative branches were very popular and had played very important role changing the condition of better live in villages and towns among peasants, craftsmen, shopkeepers, tradesmen. Saving and loans co-operatives were the basis for widely economic activation of society, rather poor, after so long political dependency and oppressive politics in majority part of the territory of the state, great post—war collapsing economy, changing the borders and monetary systems in condition of undeveloped regions. After monetary reform in 1924, giving Polish złoty as a valid currency, it was the good time for establishing this kind of co-operatives strongly connected with circulation of currency. In the middle war decades an extremely dynamic development of the movement initiated by Franciszek Stefczyk occurred, which spread all over the country, before the outbreak of the second World War about 5000 Stefczyk's chases existed. They were seen as solid, trustfully institutions. More or less one fifth of savings deposit was placed in co-operatives banks or funds.

Co-operatives became not only an important landscape element of the Polish economy, but also an element of creating a civil society, particularly in those regions of Poland, where co-operatives had long tradition of 2–3 generations and were much more developed as in Wielkopolska, Pomerania, and partially areas of former Galicia. At the end of this period co-operatives was a hope for better life in undeveloped regions of the country. It (mainly consumer, banks, housing, agricultural co-ops) was include to the great state's plan building an industrial area on The East and South provinces, so called the Central Industrial Region.

The Second World War brought the total devastation of hitherto existing possessions of Polish co-operatives. They were included in German war economy or were closed. The Polish co-operatives' banks were liquidated on the territory annexed into the Third Reich. Many co-operatives leaders were killed from occupants as a leader of Polish society. In the middle part of Poland—in German—occupied Poland (1919–1945) Polish banks were existed but they received repayment of credits in debasement currency, what spoiled their economy. On the Eastern territory annexed by Soviet Union all Polish enterprises, including co-operatives were liquidated or became a soviet state or co-operatives' property. Very quickly the great deportations of Polish citizens changed national and social relations there and broke the links among Polish people.

The history of post-war Polish savings and credit co-operatives we can divide into a few periods, in which its conditions of activity and results were different (Księga Polskiej Spółdzielczości 2006, pp. 160–161).

At first, after the end of the war up to 1948 main efforts were conducted into restoration the pre-war co-operatives and establishing new ones and association them into new organizational structures as also including them into the frame of social and economical life of the country overcoming the big lost of national property, devastation and big chaos connected with changing the borders and people.

Next years—from 1948 to 1956 brought the central planned economy and centralization of political and social life in Poland adapting the soviet patterns of the real socialism. In economy it means the deeply reform of banking system, regulation of currency, nationalization of many private and co-operative banks. There was only allowed to work the National Polish Bank (NBP), another banks were liquidated. This area of social services were open only for state's banks. The co-operatives' banking system lost its spirit. Earlier existing saving and loan co-operatives were changed into urban, workers' and local village commune chases in countryside. Co-operative banking organization were included into central planned economy and became a part of state's saving and credit systems. Co-operatives lost its independence, full voluntary spirit and democratic character. Reorganized co-operatives became the part of so called "social economy", leading people into classless socialist society. The main dogma of this time was equality in rather law level condition of life. In these circumstances co-operatives useful for owners of small enterprises had not possibility to exist and develop. After the first 15 years after the II world's war co-operative banking had not been good seen by government as a factor supporting the private sector of national economy.

The better time for this co-operative branch arrived in 1956 with the political change, when the private initiatives in economy was allowed. The banking reform was annulated, the old name of savings and loan co-operatives came back. Renovated, established again co-operatives were divided into acting in urban or agricultural environment. Co-operatives regained earlier voluntary and democratic character. The Union of Savings and Loan Co-operatives was establish on August 1957 and it associated primary co-ops, but the function of financial centre was still played by the national state bank (Złota Księga 2004, pp. 8–9). It was the time of quickly developing of co-ops. In 1960 there were 1359 such co-ops, associated 1.88 million members, in 1970–1645 with 2.78 million members and in 1975–1664 with 3.46 million members. These figures shown how much they were useful for different group of society, in towns and countryside: employed, small businessmen, peasants (Spółdzielczość w liczbach 1989, pp. 10–13).

Next years—1975–1989 were the period of came back the tendency towards centralization in a national economy and in politic life. The new administrative division of Poland acted in 1975 leaded in consequence the reorganization of many institution, also changes in co-operative structures. The new reform of 1975 allowed to use the name "co-operative's bank" for savings and loan co-operatives and associated in the new bank, which jointed two different organization: the state Land Bank and Union of Savings and Loan Co-operatives. From 1975 co-operative banks, acting in rural environment had been associated in BGŻ (The Bank of Food Economy) under the pressure of new governmental policy serving the development of agriculture and also private farms (Księga Polskiej Spółdzielczości 2006, p. 161). Capitals in this new established bank were mixed—belonged to state and co-operatives. This bank was also a financial centre for associated co-ops. Co-operative banks created the primary level in the banking system of People Republic of Poland, acting in central planned economy. The area of their activity was large, at first they served for developing farming, food-processing, agricultural industry and it was allowed them to distribute states' sources for support it and also co-ops banks has possibility to credit private business. The basic goals of co-operative banking were to serve at realization the national economic plans. In spite of central planned socialist economy and governmental strategy leading towards the collective farms and developing food processing industry, BGŻ had distributed credits for private peasants helping them to modernize their family farms, buying agricultural machines, equipments, lands and building new better houses. Co-operative banks also supported socio-cultural activity in their environment.

The beginning of political and economical transformation in 1989/1990 brought the big change for Polish co-operatives. The new Act of 20 January 1990 voted by the Parliament destroyed hitherto organizational structure of socialist co-operatives, put into liquidation all co-operatives union and associations over level of primary co-ops all branches. The BGŻ was not only a co-operative union, didn't put into liquidation and co-operative banks stood there without breaking their links (Chyra-Rolicz 2005, pp. 13–14).

2 The Credit Co-operative System in the Time of Free: Market Transformation

The new epoch for co-operative banking arrived with the time of political transformation in 1989. It was a come back into co-operative banking, growing from authentically economic needs, worked at its origin in free market conditions. The BGŻ survived, as a financial centre but the association in it was not more obligatory for co-operative banks.

The beginning of transformation brought economic chaos and very difficult situation in agriculture, what had bed influence on co-operatives' banks. They had many so called "bed doubts" leading to the bankruptcy. The governmental financial help was necessary against collapsing the whole system. The price of it was high, the BGŻ was restructured, privatized as share-holders company. According the act from 24th June 1994 about the modification of co-operative banks and BGŻ, BGŻ was transformed into joint stock company associated co-ops. The procedure of transforming lasted until 9th October 1994 and co-operative banks full voluntary voted about changing their shares in former (state and co-operative) BGŻ into shares (stocks) in the new BGŻ S.A. (Złota Księga 2004, p. 9). The capital of the new joint stock company BGŻ S.A. was 228,954, 000.000 (old value of currency, before denomination) Polish złoty (PLN) and was divided between the state and co-ops: 150,881 shares (66 % of capital stocks) belonged to the State Treasure, and 78,073 shares (34 % of capital stocks) belonged to co-operative banks. The price of one share was one million PLN (before denomination, after denomination it means 100 new PLN).[2] The State Treasure received important shares in this bank, but co-operatives' banks kept its character as a voluntary partner in this legal form of financial enterprises. There were 1662 co-operatives existing in this time in the structure of the BGŻ. Almost 95 % from it took collaboration with this new Bank on the basis of voluntary civil agreement. At the end of 1995 BGŻ S.A. provided the banking activity in 49 provincial departments, 52 operational units and 32 - sub-offices. It employed 9276 persons, in the central—543. In this time it was the second bank in Poland, after the state's PKO BP.[3]

[2] Tokarzewski (1996, p. 86).

[3] Tokarzewski (1996, p. 87, 88).

The law of 20th January 1990 and the amendments of banking law from 20th September 1991 opened also the way to establish the regional groups of co-operative banks and the firth regional associations of co-operative banks working as joint stock company appeared in 1990–1991.[4] The first was Gospodarczy Bank Wielkopolski S.A. in Poznań (Commercial Bank Wielkopolski SA). The next was Bank Unii Gospodarczej S.A. in Warsaw (Economic Union Bank SA) and Bank Południowo-Zachodni S.A. in Wrocław (Economic Bank South-West SA).

After 1990 co-operatives' banks have established full voluntary their associations and the membership in its is also full voluntary. At the beginning there were three such structures: Beskids' Audit Union in Kęty, Franciszek Stefczyk's Audit Union Co-operatives' Banks in Warsaw and Regional Audit Union of Co-operatives' Banks in Poznań. Main tasks of these unions are: frequently audit of associated banks according rules of the Co-operative law; audit of their financial reports according the rules of book-keeping; analyses of economical and financial banks' situation; experts' reports internal and external, advisory, teaching, training and other tasks, described in statutes (Złota Księga 2004, p. 9).

Another co-operatives banks associated themselves into three regional banks, established by them in form of joint stock company Ltd (but not co-operative of legal person!). There were: Mazovia Regional Bank, Bank of Polish Co-operatives an Economic Bank of Wielkopolska. Co-operative banks survived the time of agricultural crisis at the beginning of 1990 with the governmental support, saving property of their members and clients. Today they are the serious factor supporting local enterprising in agriculture and processing and local small industry. There were the fusion of two groups of associated banks at the end of June 2011 (27–28.08 2011); groups of co-operative banks from Economic Bank of Wielkopolska and Mazovian Regional Bank joint together and today exists two associations of co-operative banks; the Bank of Polish Co-operatives Ltd Company and Co-operative Banks' Group. There is only one unassociated bank—Cracovian Co-operative Bank in Kraków.

The Bank of Polish Co-operatives Ltd Company was established on March 1992, by the unification the six regional banks (Econimic Bank South West, Bank of Economic Union, also Lublin's, Małopolska's, Resovia, Warmia and Mazury Regional Banks, associated the co-operative banks for strengthening the capitals and scope of business. It was the time for looking for the new formula of banking activity, lack of capitals and not good condition of agriculture. The bank BPS S.A. provides its services to both individual as well as business customers—privates companies, agricultural sector and public sector entities through 79 outlets located in the whole country. This bank affiliated 359 co-operative banks at the end of 2009, what constitutes 62.33 % of the Polish co-operative banking sector. BPS SA maintained its position as the first among associating banks. The Bank's gross financial result for 2009 amounted to PLN 70.1 million, an increase of 3.8 % over 2008 and net profit totaled PLN 57.2 million, by 6.7 % exceeded the previous year.

[4] Tokarzewski (1996, p. 65).

Later on, in May 2011 the number of associated banks was diminished—into 274 banks, because of fusions. Among the shareholders of Bank BPS S.A. dominated co-operative banks which own together 87.3 % shares. The bank total balance reached 12.5 billion PLN at the end of 2009. Total balance of affiliated co-operatives banks exceeded 34.6 billion PLN and shareholders equity 3.5 billion PLN.[5] In spite of crisis' circumstances in the Polish economy, next years brought intensification of co-operation with subsidiary companies in scope of products offering with expands the Bank's products. The balance sheet value of BPS S.A. at the end of 2012 amounted to 18.6 billion PLN and it was higher than in 2011 by 1.0 billion PLN, i. e. 5.9 %.[6]

Bank BPS S.A. had celebrated the 10th anniversary of its activity in 2012. At the end of 2012 Bank BPS S.A. associated 365 banks, i. e. 63.81 % of total number of Co-operative Banks in Poland. In comparison with December 2011, the number of Co-operative Banks decreased by two units, what was the result of conducted merger proceedings.[7] The net financial result of Co-operative Banks in 2012 amounted to 570.8 million PLN and was by million PLN 23.4, about 4.28 % higher than in 2011. Balance of the associated Banks in 2012 there was an increase of activity scale performed by associated Co-operative Banks measured with the level of balance sheet value of the associated banks amounted to million PLN 52,086. In comparison with the end of 2011 it grew by 8.74 %, i. e. million PLN 4187.[8]

Among organizations associated co-operative banks the main role has played very quickly the Countrywide Union of Co-operative Banks (Krajowy Związek Banków Spółdzielczych) established on 2nd March 1991 in Ciechocinek as an association (Monografia 2001, pp. 8–16). This Union had helped co-operatives banks to buy the shares in regional banks, created in this time. The main goals of the new union were wide: creation the modern system of co-operative banking in Poland and renewal the old good tradition of savings-credit cooperation. It was decided that modernize co-operatives banks would be own property of their members and will accelerate development of agriculture and food processing. The countrywide new established banks' union would help every co-operative banks, witch have been interested in activity in this direction—to create regional structures—banks' associations, to coordinate their organizational efforts; to get information about systems of co-operative banks in countries of European Common Market (in this time); to assistance in localization of financial sources; to initiative establishing new co-operative banks. KZBS has published its monthly *Głos Banków Spółdzielczych* (The Voice of Co-operative Banks), concerning very useful information for them from country and abroad. It is also the way of modernization of banking system and occasion for sharing good experiences.

[5] http://www.bankbps.pl—annual report 2009, p. 5.

[6] http://www.bankbps.pl—annual report 2012, p. 23, 75, 111—data 2013-01-06 15:20.

[7] http://www.bankbps.pl—annual report 2012, p. 111, 132—data 2013-01-06 15:20.

[8] http://www.bankbps.pl—annual report 2012, p. 111, 132—data 2013-01-06 15:20.

During two decades KZBS has executed these goals, leading Polish co-operative to the modernization in technical meaning and also in openly activity oriented towards needs of small business in agriculture and in different kind of entrepreneurship. KZBS became play the role of leader of co-operative banking and integrated them. The great importance has every year so called "Forum of co-operatives banks", organized in different places with help of one of the oldest bank in this region and celebrate the professional fest . Usually it is a great event in the cultural life in this town, jointing the presentation of banks' activity with concerts or another popular amusement open for habitants, not only members of bank. Every year, in the end of June or beginning of July KZBS organizes the pilgrimage tour to Lvov in Ukraine with meeting at the tomb-stone of Franciszek Stefczyk on Łyczakowski Cemetery in anniversary of his death. This excursion, integrating the people form co-operative banks, has also a patriotic meaning in sense of positivism "organic work" for better future in the past time of political dependency, but actual today.

In 1994 the reform of whole national banking system was voted in the Parliament,[9] adapting it to the free market rivalry. Co-operative Banks entered to the new reality as good organized structures.

In the middle of 1990 the great problem appeared before Polish economy and co-operatives—preparation to the nearly accession into Common Europe. For co-operatives' banks it means the necessary to keep and concentrate capitals according the plan of accession, signed by Polish government. The 1998 year—was a turning-point on this way. Co-operatives' banks were obliged collected as own capitals 300,000 ECU according with mentioned agreement. If they would didn't collected such money, the menace of liquidation, closing the activity, was real. In the middle of 1998 only 19.5 % of acting banks were able to rich this level. Co-operative banks had begun fusions, bank stronger in capitals rescued small ones by jointed them in one structure, with several local units. This way was not easy, not every banks went this way with success. Only in 1999 29 banks collapsed and 11 were joint into five great banks formed as Company Ltd.

Big challenges appeared before Polish co-operatives' banks with enter into UE connected with so called—the second UE's directions, which means that any financial enterprises, using in their name word "bank" is obliged to have own capitals on the level minimum one million euros, and—if it would acting independently—it must have own capitals five million euros. The deadline for reaching this level was so short, negotiated on 2007. This agreement signed by the Polish negotiators before the accession to UE was too much difficult in Polish circumstances, in the post-communist country with rather poor society, transforming barely its economy. This instruction forced many fusion of co-operatives banks and diminished their number as independent ones.

[9] Tokarzewski (1996, pp. 64–65).

There were 572 co-operative banks working in Poland in the end of 2012,[10] after the long way of adaptation the free market economy and adaptation to UE instructions. They are much more stronger in own capitals and cultivate the spirit of voluntary, democratic organization, according co-operative rules. Contemporary Polish co-operatives' banks went deeply modernization, they are well equipped in modern electronic devices working in the net. They provide their activity in 3487 units in good looking new or renovated houses or rooms, but their meaning is not in big numbers or external view. Their the most important value and force is close contacts, relations with small and medium scale enterprises in countryside, the knowledge of their problems and needs, which bear interests and may be transfer on grow up riches, reduction of unemployment and economical and social development of whole region obtained by activity of the bank (Jakubowska 2009, pp. 39–55; Stawarz 2006, p. 86).

For the modernization and spirit of rivalry among co-operative banks important meaning has the special ranking of co-operative banks every year. This rivalry takes in account not only financial result of their activity, but also the scope of social or cultural activity of their environments. It is very strong rivalry for choosing the best 100 banks in the country taking in advantage all these activities.

Krakowski Bank Spółdzielczy (Cracovian Co-operative Bank in Kraków) has occupied the front place in these rankings for several years. It is very deep rooted in its environment, its origin has dated 1898, when it was established as the Society Advanced Payment for Clarks of Kraków and next many time had changed the name. The most dynamic and expansive period of its develop became after 1994. Only in 1994–1999 this bank jointed 22 smaller co-operatives banks in nearly towns and villages. Today it is very strong bank with 27 units, 16 sub-offices, 3 chases' points and large scope of activity in the city and countryside. This is an universe bank, attending not only sphere of agriculture, also small and medium size different type enterprises, not only agricultural or food-processing. It credits agricultural Stock Exchanges, assistances in establishing the groups of agricultural producers, local trade, auto-business, building of new houses, different services and deferred payment retail. It collaborates with EUROPAY INTERNATIONAL, initiates using credit cards Maestro also another credit cards. It win several prestige rewards because of results in stimulation of economic development and assistance in many cultural initiatives for public and health. care, hospitals, houses for pensioners and disabled persons. The bank is also well known as a great patron of contemporary art and artists. It has even own art gallery in the center of the city!

Many co-operative bank took success during the time of transformation. One of them was the Co-operative Bank in Siedlce, established in 1924 as the Stefczyk's chase by leader of peasant movement Szczepan Ciekot and received his name in its name. Earlier, the tradition shown the chase had acted from 1902. During of 80 years of activity co-operative idea and spirit of common business were cultivated here. All the time the saving and credit chase (using different names) was very

[10] http://www.bankbps.pl—annual report 2012, p. 111 data 2013-01-06 15:20.

closed to needs of local community in the town and agricultural region. It has served well for local community for many decades supporting peasants and small business: shopkeepers and craftsmen. The time of post communist transformation and breaking down central planned economy solved many initiatives. The bank took the risk of managing its matters themselves, fighting with strong former structures of bureaucracy's dependence. This straggle was successful. The bank has developed very quickly as a strong financial centre, jointing four units, former independent co-operative banks, which couldn't collected enough own capitals according the UE instruction. The spectacular success was seen in the spirit of self-dependence and the new modern building at 5/7/9 Pusta street, built from the surpluses at the beginning of 1990 twentieth century Shareholders, employees and clients are very much attached to their bank, deeply rooted in the town and its environment for three generations. To-day this bank is a modern and strong financial centre for the neighbourhood, it co operatives as good with big enterprises like the Co-operative Dairy in Sielce or the Housing Co-operative here, as well like with small shareholders. Mentioned above co-operative dairy is a big scope enterprise, sending its milk products to post-soviet countries and into internal country-wide market. The local housing co-operative is also a big enterprise, half of habitants of the town has lived in the modern houses, which were built after 1957. It has a great meaning of civilization progress in housing.

Another good example we can find in the Co-operative Bank in Brańsk, small bank acting in agricultural region of North Podlasie, near Białystok. This bank has also long tradition from 1920 twentieth century. It jointed also another co-operative banks in environment, creating the strong financial enterprises. The bank supported many cultural initiatives, helps to organize concurs of co-operative knowledge for school children, artistic exhibition, support publishing books concerning this regions. It plays not only financial role stimulating the develop of business but also a centre of culture in local scope. This bank propagate an ethical business, supports school saving and loan chases as the first step towards adult co-operative. It develop co-operative education of children, what was forgotten in the time of transformation.

The great dimension of business characterized also the District Co-operative Bank in Sokołów Podlaski, which joint many smaller banks and today is acting as a financial center for environment, serving capitals for district dairies, meat-processing factory and governmental local administration and authorities self-government.

Co-operative banks entered into distribution the UE funds for individual peasants and agricultural enterprises, as for example groups of agricultural producers, which have close relation of co-operative banks as their members. It strengthened their position in the national economy and local society and free market. It is necessary to underline, that co-operative banks doesn't executed their debts as commercial banks, leading creditors to bankruptcy, so they are really friendly banks for small and medium business, understanding their needs and problems.

3 The New Movement: The Past Inspired Again

New political forces jointed with Solidarity's movement established, or rather revived the older form of co-operative saving and credit chases named of mentioned above Franciszek Stefczyk, well known co-operative leaders in nineteenth and twentieth centuries. The beginning of this movement was very simple and prosaic, chases were established on basis of workers and employed self-help organizations—saving and credit chases, acting in enterprises. This form organizational form was also very old, with long tradition going from nineteenth century, which survived the time of real socialism and beginning of political and economic transformation connected with privatization of big industrial enterprises and collapsing many of them. The revival of these chases started in 1990 in the cradle of "Solidarity" movement in Gdańsk at the seaside and was supported by funds of World Council of Credit Unions Inc. (WOCCU). There was established the Polish Credit Unions in this time, which has helped by funds and organizational instructions, training developing of this old-new movement. It has associated rather poor people, which can not receive the loans in another banks, commercial or even co-operatives ones, without satisfactory guaranty of credits. This movement, built from the top into down, has organized members in Co-operative Saving Credit-Chases (SKOK) using the name of Franciszek Stefczyk as a trade mark of former solidity. People with law an medium salary associated themselves in these chases, which established big organizational structure countrywide with own financial central—The Main Chase—SKOK (The Countrywide Co-operative Saving-Credit Chase). This organization is acting as co-operative of legal persons, associated all regional and local chases in Poland on basis of own law concerning chases activity of SKOKs. The countrywide chase is a central financial organization for all chases and play the auditory and instructional role towards them. It is the member of WOCCU and International Co-operative Alliance (ICA). The financial operations in system of SKOK are safety. There are special the Program of Protection of Savings and Fund of Stabilization the Countrywide Chase also insurances of deposits are obligatory.

At the beginning the force of this movement depended not on big capitals but in popular character of organizations, mass acceptation and collecting common funds by multiplied small members' shares as it was at the beginning of the co-operative movement. These chases are very close to ordinary people, not businessmen, existing from their salary on rather law level condition of living often with families. Loans from SKOKs help them to solve temporary difficulties of everyday life, to renovate apartments, to buy technical equipments, to go on holidays—for example. There is the Polish branch of great, large international movement associated over 100 millions people in over 90 countries in the world (Węcławski 2000, p. 34).

The SKOK movement grew up very quickly in the time of transformation in Poland, which brought quickly the deeply social stratification and growing number of people living in worse condition of living, near the line of poverty or even under it. After 10 years of activity in Poland (at the beginning of twenty-first century)

SKOKs are the fourth financial institution in the country consideration the number of chases and other associated organizations. They jointed over one million members (and calculating with their families—over three millions people), which were attending in 1325 units. This success is amazing as an answer for real social needs and based on voluntary work of uncalculated mass of volunteers and leaders, form whom the work for chases became the passion of a life (Węcławski 2000, p. 45).

From the beginning the SKOK movement in Poland it was open for international relation. The collaboration the Countrywide Chase SKOK with international-world and European movement of credits unions is very rich and useful for Polish organizations. On November 2000 the chairman of The Countrywide Chases Mr Grzegorz Bierecki became the member of Council of Directors WOCCU with the headquarters in Madison, Wisconsin, USA. It was the terms of compliments for his personal activity and for results of all Polish SKOK movement, which was seen as a leader of this movement in East Europe region. At 7th June was signed the agreement between the Ukrainian State Commission of Regulation the market of Financial Assistance and Polish the Countrywide Chase SKOK. The main goal was collaboration in establishing efficient system of regulation and audit over savings and credits Ukrainian chases and sharing the Polish experiences and patterns of success in this area. Quickly this movement have appeared in the post-soviet Baltic States, which gain the political independency. Spectacular success it had also in Lithuania.

Another the test of appreciation took place in Warsaw in 24–28 June 2002, when deliberated the VI International Conference and Generally Assemble of WOCCU. There were 724 participants—leaders of credit unions form 31 countries with Mr Arthur Arnold, the president and general director and Mr Gerry Foley, the chairman of WOCCU at the had. This big conference was organized with the help of WOCCU, The Countryside Chase SKOK, The Society of Mutual Insurance SKOK, the Foundation of Polish Credits Unions, CUNA and California Credit Union League.

This new movement win a great success after almost 24 years of transformation, almost 1600 chases are working in countrywide net with 2.19 million members (in 31st December 2014) among the people earning small salary. Table 1 shows the developing of this movement.

4 Struggle for Independence

So quickly development of the new credit-saving co-operative movement, associated hundreds of thousands and millions members (multiplied by members of their household, families using these funds) had awaked strong reactions of different groups of interests and politicians liberal orientation, which tried to control this movement and kept it into very narrow frame of chase's operation similar to former scope of employees self-help chases working at many factories and entrepreneurs during the time of real socialism. Private commercial banks with foreigners capitals

Table 1 Co-operative saving–credit chases (SKOK) in 1992–2014

Year	Number of chases (with units)	Number of members (in thousands)	Assets (in thousands PLN)+	Deposits (in thousands PLN)+	Loans (in thousands PLN)+
1992	13	14	4277	3565	2985
1993	32	21	11,173	8528	8697
1994	106	46	35,446	29,362	25,650
1995	137	85	100,752	91,570	83,431
1996	168	138	219,443	190,446	160,843
1997	237	194	368,260	312,562	280,598
1998	290	259	590,376	528,376	412,482
1999	420	306	882,727	740,056	668,386
2000	560	394	1,199,362	995,251	865,748
2001	680	525	1,752,316	1,558,436	1,235,554
2002	923	703	2,455,086	2,253,906	1,659,780
2003	1285	924	3,343,652	3,111,630	2,212,939
2004	1461	1169	4,228,673	3,937,924	2,856,265
2005	1553	1395	5,329,024	4,989,570	3,502,929
2006	1589	1551	5,969,789	5,552,966	4,047,299
2007	1663	1669	7,324,988	6,705,001	5,147,320
2008	1757	1856	9,446,921	8,604,073	6,932,627
2009	1801	2026	11,637,339	10,842,415	8,411,273
2010	1851	2177	14,014,363	13,028,073	9,792,675
2011	1934	2315	15,598,200	14,518,197	10,906,655
2012	1987	2591	16,805,349	15,491,190	11,090,601
2013	1892	2660	13,890,225	17,431,805	12,035,777
2014	1599	2192	13,668,443	12,533,069	8,487,735

+ notice: 1 Polish złoty (PLN) = 25 eurocents; 1 euro = approximately more or less 4 PLN
Source: www.SKOK.com.pl (SKOK in figures) and http://www.skok.pl/o-skok/skok-w-liczbach data 2015-04-29 22:49

and private enterprises offering credits in condition of usurious tried to fight against national credit institution established on the Polish roots and growing by its own forces with spirit of self-help. The minimal rate of percentage created the strong competition for commercial institutions. In fact, SKOK's members–clients were not good wanted clients of commercial banks or another credit entrepreneurs because of low scope of interest and input. The SKOK' s movement had enlarged the scope of their activity according the social needs. This new movement started from rather narrow scope of loans according the level of small deposits and answered for new social challenges entered into area of social, life and sickness also accident insurances, as well as currency operations. It edited own credit-cards and it built the countywide net of cash-machines. Liberal oriented political parties (Unia Demokratyczna, Unia Wolności, Platforma Obywatelska) several times in 90 and at the beginning of twenty-first century tried to prepare acts in the parliament leading the legislation toward the hard and fast audit into chases' interests of the

Chief Inspectorate of Banking Supervision. The strong press campaign was provided in the very popular newspapers (*Gazeta Wyborcza, Fakt, Super Express*) giving black publicity for SKOK's movement. The act limiting SKOK's activity was voted in Parliament and the former President of the III Republic Lech Kaczyński appealed it in the Supreme Court of Justice (Constitutional). President Kaczyński was very much attached to this movement from the origin of his political activity in Solidarity movement in Gdańsk and posterior leadership of the party Prawo i Sprawiedliwość (PiS—Law and Justice), which is interested in developing of national entrepreneurship and grow of the Polish capitals leading to the economic and political independency. This matter has been proceeded long time, the president Kaczyński tragically died on 10th April 2010 in plane-crash and the next President Bronisław Komorowski, attached to the liberal oriented party Platforma Obywatelska (PO—Citizens'Platform), made few steps back and removed his objections from the Court concerning the auditory of the Commission of Finance Control. The President's motions to the Court treat at last to rather marginal matters under the strong pressure of commercial banks' lobby. The same standpoint presented also the prime-minister Donald Tusk. Anyway of long lasting judicial procedure, we can observed the affaire leading to the bankruptcy of the south-west department of SKOK, which looked as well organized criminal provocation in spring 2008. Next year, there were a strange into the another unit of SKOK - "Kopernik" and "unknown perpetrators" steal here computers' data-basis. Malevolent political and criminal actions against SKOKs are multiplied last time.[11] The goal of these pressure is hostilely taking possession of this well organized country-wide banking structure with whole network of institutions by commercial entrepreneurship.

5 Supporting Social Economy

Both branches of co-operative banking—Co-operative Banks (BS) and SKOKs have gone a difficult way of transformation into modern banking system, close to different groups of people—their clients or members in other environments. Going from another patterns, supported by another political forces, both find the place on the free market and are useful for people needs. Both have assisted in changing the country, condition of living, creating jobs and opening wider space for social activity. Today both are the solid pillars of credit system in Poland, propagating the ethical way of business. All of it has important meaning in situation, when 80 % of the Polish banking sector was sold to foreigners organization of commercial banks, oriented only into get the biggest surplus.

[11] Pawlak (2008, p. 24), Gmyz (2011, pp. 86–88), "Wniosek do TK w sprawie SKOK ograniczony" (2011, p. 33).

The special mission of saving and credit co-operative has been support the social economy, mainly other co-operatives branches, which had found big difficulties trying to catch credits.

Social economy has had also a long tradition on the Polish territory, concerning the developing of co-operative movement in the second half of nineteenth century. These experiences were rich in the independent state the II Republic of Poland (1918–1939). During the II world's war legal acting co-ops were the important part of The Polish Underground Country. Next, in over 40 years of the state of real socialism, co operative sector acted in the planned economy as a sector of so called "social economy", strongly dependent from state authority but without spirit authentic co-operative movement.

The collapsing of system of real socialism opened the possibility of wide activity many different types of NPO (foundations, associations) and minimised role of co-ops on these area. After 1989/1990 socialist co-operative sector survived heavy transformation. International conferences of social economy (2002 in Prague, 2004 and 2005 in Cracow) as well as the UE policy interesting in possibility of the social economy, help to change the view on co-operative movement as a useful part of social policy and social economy leading to minimisation the big unemployment. It is a new discovery of co-operative idea via social policy of UE. Presentations of examples of social co-ops during mentioned above conferences allowed understand that we have a long and reach tradition of these activity under another name. There are approximately 40,000 registered different NPO in Poland, buy not all are acting. Social co-ops are seen as a new idea useful in solving the problem of unemployment of weak category of people at the labour market as youth, women, disabled persons, ex-prisoners, long lasted unemployed. They organised work in production and many types of services. Computer services are the new area of activity for these co-ops, easy to reach for disabled persons. Usually Polish social co-ops try to find the space for them on the market organising work as an answer for new needs of different groups of society. At the beginning they look for support from NPO, specific associations, local authorities. There were about 150 social co-ops registered in the Countrywide Cooperative Council at the end of 2010. The lack of legislation was the strong barrier in their developing. Liberal oriented political forces wanted to minimised the scope of governmental support for enterprises and groups of person, which have right to ask of help. After long lasting discussion the Polish Parliament voted the special act concerning this kind of co-ops in April 2006. It facilitates problems of support them by public sources but many of social co-ops are looking for UE assistance funds. On May 2006 social co-ops established their countrywide union for articulate their interests. In 2007 the new law concerning social co-ops were voted in the Parliament. It opened the field of organisation new social co-ops, which established their own auditory union. The saving and credit co-operative (Co-operative Banks) try to support this new movement at the spirit of solidarity. These law regulations have opened the possibility of legal co-operation between different forms of co-operatives or social enterprises, but the real scope of financial support at last depends of banks' economic situation. It gives the new perspective social activity rather for local banks and chases.

6 Conclusion

The Polish co-operative banking system survived many reorganization changes, transformations, repressive policies—and still have existed and developed. It has been seen as a important part of national economy, own Polish capitals collected by people and serving them. Co-operative banks and chases enjoy good opinion as a solid enterprises which try to help their debtors, not lead them to bankruptcy. Members feel links with their bank, especially in small towns and countryside. These organizations, democratically managed, create the civil society. Experiences of the last two decades has shown that this sector, acting in very difficult condition of strong struggle with liberal oriented policy and dogma of privatization, was able to grow, to decide about its matters themselves, according economic and social needs. It was also able to modernize the bank-system according the challenges of twenty-first century and technical e-revolution from own sources. This sector came into contacts with many notorious foreign banks and with their help in training our staffs, Polish co-operative banks and chases reduced the big distance in backwardness our banking system comparing with high developed countries. Today, the modern co-operative banking system serves as a good example of social economy jointed the care about social goals with good management and economy results.

References

Chyra-Rolicz Z (ed) (2004, 2005) Pomoc czy przeszkoda? Rola tradycji w odbudowie polskiej spółdzielczości (Collected studies). Wydawnictwo Akademii Podlaskiej, Siedlce, pp. 13–14

Gmyz C (2011) Zamach na SKOK. Uważam Rze 16:86–88

Jakubowska A (2009) Lokalne i ponadlokalne instytucje finansowe w warunkach transformacji systemowej. Spółdzielczy Kwartalnik Naukowy 1:39–55

Księga Polskiej Spółdzielczości (2006) (ed) vol II. Agencja Reklamowo-Wydawnicza "Promocja Polska", Bydgoszcz, pp. 160–161

Monografia Krajowego Związku Banków Spółdzielczych 1991–2001 (2001) KZBS, Warszawa, pp. 8–16

Pawlak M (2008) Zamach na SKOK-i. Gazeta Polska 27(780):24

Rusiński W (1980) Zarys historii polskiego ruchu spółdzielczego, vol. II 1918–1939. ZW CZSR, Warszawa

Spółdzielczość w liczbach (1989) (ed) NRS/GUS, Warszawa, pp. 10–13

Stawarz A (2006) Rola bankowości i przedsiębiorczości w ochronie miast postindustrialnych w warunkach rozwoju demokracji lokalnej. Polskie Towarzystwo Etnologii Miasta 9, Warszawa, p. 86

Tokarzewski T (1996) Polskie Banki Spółdzielcze. BGŻ SA, Warszawa, pp. 86–88

Węcławski J (2000) System bankowy w Polsce. MIG, Rzeszów

Witalec P (2008) Spółdzielczość kredytowa systemu Schulzego w Małopolsce w latach 1873–1939. IPN/MHPRL, Warszawa, p. 138

Wniosek do TK w sprawie SKOK ograniczony (2011) Gazeta Polska 17(925): 33

Złota Księga Banków Spółdzielczych (2004) vol II. KZBS, Warszawa, p. 9

Zarys historii polskiego ruchu spółdzielczego (1971) (ed. Ingot S) vol I. ZW CRS, Warszawa (up to 1918), pp. 92–97, 145–148

http://www.kzbs.pl/index.php?strona76

http://www.skok.com.pl

http://www.bankbps.pl

The Credit Cooperative System in Romania

Daniela Pirvu and Logica Banica

Abstract Credit cooperatives in Romania are a category of non-banking financial institutions. The first forms of credit cooperatives emerged in nineteenth century. The credit cooperative system has its own cooperative self-help mechanism. Central House of Credit Cooperatives represents a credit institution established by the association of credit cooperatives, in order to manage their common interests, to track compliance with applicable laws and regulations for all affiliated cooperatives, by exercising administrative, technical and financial supervision and control on their operations.

Loan products offered by credit cooperatives (CREDITCOOP network) have a low level of complexity. They are mainly offered to individual customers, having a short-term maturity. The overwhelming majority of loans are aimed at individuals. The CREDITCOOP network has a lending activity predominantly in rural space. The arrangement of units especially in small towns and rural areas aims the proximity to low-income customers and small and medium farmers. Credit cooperatives want to provide them with a wide range of products, from paying various types of bills to granting credits and keeping their economies.

Credit cooperatives in Romania were faced with internal fraud, in recent years. In order to manage information risk more effectively, all transactions of secondary locations shall obtain approval from the head office, by authorized persons.

1 The Establishment and Evolution of the Credit Cooperative System in Romania

The first Romanian credit cooperative organizations were established in 1891, under the name of popular banks, adopting the German model systems. Mainly, popular banks had to provide loans to small rural households, but compared with the existing credit needs, the activity of these organizations was appreciated

D. Pirvu (✉) • L. Banica
University of Pitesti, Pitesti, Romania
e-mail: ddanapirvu@yahoo.com; olga.banica@upit.ro

S. Karafolas (ed.), *Credit Cooperative Institutions in European Countries*,
Contributions to Economics, DOI 10.1007/978-3-319-28784-3_20

unsatisfactory (Muresan and Muresan 1998). The number of popular banks, number of cooperative members and amount of subscribed capital increased considerably, in subsequent decades. Other credit institutions with cooperative character called "lease congregations" were established in order to satisfy the credit needs of farmers, in the early twentieth century. After World War I, credit cooperative organizations remained the most accessible types of banks for the largest social class in Romania—the peasantry. The Cooperative Central Bank (institute of financing all credit cooperatives) was created after adoption of the Law of cooperatives (1929). Public authorities have supported the credit cooperative system in Romania through grants and rediscounted loans (Galan 1935). The economic crisis from 1929 to 1933 has affected popular banks in Romania, but before the start of World War II these institutions contributed significantly to attracting Romanian peasantry in the savings and credit system. In 1940, there were over 7000 popular banks, compared with the 700 banks operating in 1903 (Madgearu 1940). The institutional structure of the credit cooperative system in Romania includes the following links:

- central national bodies with guidance and control role;
- credit cooperatives. They could join to form federations or unions. Federations executed only economic operations, having no right in control or guidance of member cooperatives. Unions had no share capital.

In 1948, the communist regime in Romania has decided to liquidate the credit cooperative organizations abusively (popular bank assets have not been returned to members; they were taken by a state-controlled institution—the Central Organization of Consumer Cooperatives).

In 1954, credit cooperatives have been re-established under the name of credit and savings cooperatives. These bodies had an upward trend in terms of organizational and financial development because they have proven utility in supporting associate members with loans and other services.

Credit cooperatives sector underwent major transformations, since 1989. Credit cooperatives have regained as "popular banks", since 1996. The credit cooperative system operated on three organizational levels (Law no. 109/1996 on organization and operation of consumer cooperatives and credit cooperatives):

- credit cooperatives;
- local houses of credit cooperatives: credit cooperative associations at regional level (county);
- Central House of Credit Cooperatives: a national association of local houses.

Credit unions were not forced to join a central authority that could provide them an adequate supervision and control so that, during 1997–1998 there have been many popular independent banks. They took advantage of the system imperfections, violating the principles of cooperative and carrying out illegal banking activities.

Concerns about the health of banking system was extended to credit unions whose licensing, regulation and supervision have entered in the National Bank of

Romania's tasks, since 2000. In this way, it ended the application of previous legal framework, whose main weakness was the ignoring of credit character for credit cooperatives (popular banks) that, in fact, carry out banking activities. The legal framework established in 2000, supplemented and amended in 2002, ensured the imposition of standards aligned with the relevant Community provisions (Isarescu 2006). The excessive regulation of the sector and the introduction of some prudential measures imposed by the National Bank of Romania have limited the activity of credit cooperatives.

In 2000, a process of credit cooperatives network' authorization began as a result of change in banking law. The new legislation (Government Emergency Ordinance no. 97/2000 on credit cooperative organizations) stipulated that credit cooperatives will operate in networks consisting of a central house, its branches and credit cooperatives affiliated to the central house. Each credit cooperative could have chosen for affiliation to a central house. In order to set up a central house, at least 50 credit cooperatives were needed. The central bodies had responsibilities relating to the representation, supervision, control and financial and logistical support of credit. Also, these institutions provided e-banking services, internal rules or regulations and the necessary software.

During 2002–2004, the credit cooperative system in Romania has undergone a comprehensive process of fusion, because under the new legislation (Law no. 200/2002 for approving Government Emergency Ordinance no. 97/2000 on credit cooperative organizations), a minimum threshold limit has been set.

In late 2002, only one network (CREDITCOOP) received the authorization to operate (ten credit cooperative networks had made requests for authorization). In late 2003, the number of credit cooperatives affiliated to CREDITCOOP was 565. The number of territorial units of CREDITCOOP decreased to 133 at the end of 2004, then to 124 in late 2006 and to 50 in late 2009, as a result of an extensive restructuring process. Reducing the number of credit cooperatives provided better conditions for their development. Thus, conditions for obtaining some bank prudential indicators within the limits set by legal regulations were created and the decision-making process was concentrated in one central body with a proper management (Morar 2010). The lending activity of credit cooperative organizations has declined, since 2002, when credit cooperatives were placed under the supervision of National Bank of Romania. In 2000 loans granted by credit cooperative organizations represented about 9 % and in 2004 about 2 % of all loans granted to individuals and companies in Romania.

The credit cooperatives in Romania currently operate in accordance with the law that was adopted in 2006 (Government Emergency Ordinance no. 99/2006 on credit institutions and adequacy of capital).

2 The Current Credit Cooperative System in Romania

2.1 The Establishment and Organization of Credit Cooperative Organizations in Romania

According to current legislation, a **credit cooperative** is a credit institution established as an autonomous association of persons united voluntarily to meet their common economic and social needs and aspirations. The credit cooperative activity takes place mainly on the principle of mutual aid between cooperative members. Credit cooperatives in Romania are forced to join a central house by subscription and payment of the share capital, representing at least the value of the shares set out in the Constitutive Act of the central house. Credit cooperatives are subordinated to the central house under the conditions established by the affiliate. Central House of Credit Cooperatives and affiliated credit cooperatives form a credit cooperative network.

The **Central House of Credit Cooperatives** is a credit institution established by the association of credit cooperatives in order to manage their common interests and to monitor the compliance with laws and regulations applicable to all affiliated credit cooperatives by supervision and administrative, technical and financial control over the way of organizing and operating credit cooperatives.

Central houses are constituted according to the provisions of the Constitutive Act by the association of at least 30 founding credit cooperatives. Each of the affiliated credit unions must subscribe and pay an amount representing at least 20 % of its share capital in favor of the central house.

The Central House of Credit Cooperatives promotes the interests of affiliated credit cooperatives. It has the following main tasks:

(a) representing the economic, financial, legal, social-cultural common interests of affiliated credit cooperatives to the National Bank of Romania, public institutions and justice courts;
(b) monitoring and ensuring the cohesion and proper functioning of the entire network; for this purpose the central house takes all necessary measures to ensure the liquidity and adequacy of the capital to risks for each credit cooperative organization and network as a whole, including, where appropriate, financial assistance to affiliated credit cooperatives;
(c) issuing Constitutive Act and other regulations for organizing the activity within the network;
(d) supervising affiliated credit cooperatives with regard to compliance with the legal provisions and regulations issued by the National Bank of Romania, the Constitutive Act and regulations of central house; exercising administrative, technical and financial control over the way of organizing and operating affiliated credit cooperatives;
(e) guarantying all obligations of affiliated credit cooperatives, so it take the necessary measures to ensure the payment of contributions owed by them;

(f) liquidating affiliated credit cooperatives;
(g) reporting data and information required by the National Bank of Romania, in accordance with legal regulations;
(h) informing affiliated credit cooperatives about existing legal regulations and issuing regulations for ensuring compliance with national laws in the entire network;
(i) ensuring management of network's available resources;
(j) offering e-banking services in relations between affiliated credit cooperatives, state treasury and other credit institutions, through the current account opened at National Bank of Romania;
(k) training staff and organizing common social-cultural activities.

Credit cooperatives are formed by free association of individuals, without any discrimination based on nationality, ethnic origin, language, religion, political affiliation, wealth, social status, race or sex. Cooperative member may be any individual who has the full legal capacity, domicile/residence/workplace in the territorial jurisdiction of the credit cooperative, signed or accepted, as appropriate, its Constitutive Act and subscribed and paid an amount representing at least the minimum number of shares set by the Constitutive Act.

The minimum number of cooperative founding members, established by the Constitutive Act cannot be less than 1000. The Constitutive Act may provide the possibility of forming a credit cooperative with a minimum of 100 cooperative founding members, if they subscribe and pay a total amount representing at least 1000 shares. Each cooperative member is entitled to one vote, regardless of the number of shares held. The validity of decisions taken by the general meeting of shareholders requires the presence of majority of co-operators. The decisions are taken by an absolute majority vote of those present.

Credit cooperatives are organized on a territorial area of its own operation, established by the Constitutive Act. In this territorial area they may establish branches. This includes specific areas of the county where the credit cooperative has its registered office and surrounding counties. Operating territory of a credit cooperative affiliated to a central house is unique.

It should be noted that the shares are indivisible, they cannot be sold, assigned or pledged than between cooperate members and they cannot be represented by negotiable instruments. Defining for credit cooperatives is that banking in a credit cooperative network is conducted (mainly and with priority) with and for cooperate members and credit cooperatives in the network. In fact credit cooperatives have the characteristics of a bank carrying out specific activities to attract financial resources and to lend but customers will be the cooperative members. However, the law does not prohibit accessing from other people to services offered by the cooperative. The legislator pointed out that the credit cooperatives aimed "especially" to support cooperative members through self-help and co-operation. Therefore we conclude that providing services by a credit cooperative to other natural or legal persons are not excluded.

The Central House of Credit Cooperatives has a role of intermediary between credit cooperatives and the National Bank of Romania, public institutions and justice courts, reporting data and information required by these institutions. It also plays a role of central bank for affiliated credit cooperatives in the sense that the law gives a part of its task, namely monitoring and ensuring cohesion and proper functioning of the entire credit cooperative network. So, the central house of credit cooperatives acts, with some exceptions, like the National Bank of Romania, which was strengthened by the following duties: supervising affiliated credit cooperatives and exercising administrative, technical and financial control over the organization and administration of the entire credit cooperative network. Moreover, the Central House of Credit Cooperatives guarantees all obligations of affiliated credit cooperatives and ensures its liquidation.

The minimum amount of the initial capital and, respectively, that of the own funds of Central House of Credit Cooperatives is set out at the EUR 5 million lei equivalent. The minimum limit of own funds of a credit cooperative is set out at the EUR 75,000 million lei equivalent. The minimum amount of total capital, respectively, of the own funds of a credit cooperative network is set out at the EUR 10 million lei equivalent (Regulation no. 18 of 14.12.2006 on the own funds of credit institutions and investment firms).

2.2 Functioning of Credit Cooperative Networks in Romania

The Central House of Credit Cooperatives should be authorized, collectively, with all credit cooperatives of the network which will be established. The National Bank of Romania has responsibilities in authorizing credit cooperative networks in Romania.

Credit cooperatives may conduct the following activities:

- collecting deposits or other reimbursable funds from their members and individuals, firms or other entities who have the domicile/residence/workplace or registered office in the territorial jurisdiction of the credit cooperative;
- granting credits to: (1) cooperative members, with priority, (2) individuals, legal persons or other entities without legal personality who have the domicile/residence/workplace or registered office in the territorial jurisdiction of the credit cooperative at a level not exceed 25 % of the assets of the credit cooperative;
- payment transactions;
- issuing and administering payment instruments such as: credit cards, traveller's checks including the issuance of electronic money;
- issuing guarantees and assuming commitments;
- operating transactions on own account and/or on behalf of clients, under the law: (1) currency, (2) securities and other transferable financial instruments;

- consulting services related to capital structure, business strategy and other business aspects, providing services related to mergers and acquisitions and other consulting services;
- renting safe deposit boxes;
- providing any other activities or services, if they are circumscribed financial sector, in compliance with special legal provisions governing those activities, if any.

Credit cooperatives cannot issue bonds. They can finance their activities through inter cooperative loans or loans from other credit institutions.

The Central House of Credit Cooperatives may carry out, within the existing authorization, any of the activities allowed a credit institution, under the law. The activity is carried out, mainly and predominantly, in the interests of affiliated credit cooperatives and to ensure the adequacy of capital and the liquidity across the credit cooperative network. Loans granted to legal entities by a Central House of Credit Cooperatives, other than affiliated credit cooperatives, may not exceed 20 % of the assets of the Central House of Credit Cooperatives. Central House of Credit Cooperatives may issue bonds under the conditions specified by law for joint stock companies.

In order to start operations, each credit cooperative organization should open a current account within 30 days after obtaining the operating authorization, as follows:

(a) the Central House of Credit Cooperatives opens a current account at National Bank of Romania;
(b) credit cooperatives open current accounts at the Central House of Credit Cooperatives to which they are affiliated.

Each central house of credit cooperatives elaborates (with the approval of the National Bank of Romania) regulations of payment transactions between affiliated credit regulations of payment.

Each cooperative member is entitled to request for a loan but he must contribute to the social fund of credit cooperative, in the spirit of mutual aid. The contribution is at least a tenth of the loan amount requested. For these contributions, cooperative members receive an annual interest. The annual interest is approved by the General Assembly when approving the Balance Sheet and it depends on economic and financial results of the credit cooperative. The social fund may not be withdrawn until 1 year after paying the last loan rate and interest thereon, except in cases provided for in the Constitutive Act.

Credit cooperatives distribute 25 % of their net profit annually for the establishment a pool of mutual aid. It is designed to create the necessary conditions for reducing banking transaction costs of credit cooperative.

Cooperative credit organizations in Romania do not receive preferential tax regime.

2.3 CREDITCOOP Network

2.3.1 Organizing CREDITCOOP Network

The CREDITCOOP Central Cooperative Bank and affiliated cooperative banks form the only credit cooperative network currently authorized in Romania. In 2013, the network CREDITCOOP was formed by the CREDITCOOP Central Cooperative Bank and 46 affiliated cooperative banks. These have 763 secondary locations situated especially in small towns and rural areas. In the past 3 years, two affiliated cooperative bank and 21 secondary locations have been closed. The organizational structure of the cooperative credit organizations in the CREDITCOOP network includes:

1. **General meeting of shareholders** has powers to: (1) discuss, approve and modify the annual financial statements, (2) establishing work program, budget of revenues and expenditures for next fiscal year, (3) adopting of various decisions.
2. **The Board of Directors** has, inter alia, the following duties: (1) reviewing and confirming annual financial statements, (2) approving policy loans, the bank's obligations and commitments, (3) approving loans that do not comply with bank's lending policies and approving loans that exceed a amount representing 10 % of own funds or involve a high risk, (4) approving measures to recover bad loans, (5) setting some acceptable levels for significant risks, assessing, monitoring and managing these risks, (6) approving the annual internal audit plan, (7) approving procedures for establishing the powers and responsibilities in the field of risk management, (8) establishing the conditions for using the bank's patrimony, approving the organizational and personnel structure of the bank, (9) approving the internal work rules, (10) establishing and approving the competencies of Risk Management Committee, Credit Committee, Audit Committee and Labor Security Committee, (11) approving the establishment of branches, (12) establishing competencies of Steering Committee, (13) approving responsibilities of executive management, (14) establishing the internal auditor, approving his competencies and examining his reports. In addition to the duties listed, the Board of Directors of Cooperative Central Bank approves the annual plan to monitor affiliated cooperative banks.
3. **Credit cooperatives leaders** propose for Board's approval, the Operating Rules of cooperative credit organization which establishes at least: the organizational structure, responsibilities of each compartment and relations between them, responsibilities of agencies and other secondary locations, powers and duties of directors.

Developing and maintaining good business management practices required establishment of the following bodies:

- the Risk Management Committee assists credit cooperatives in fulfilling their duties in the field of risk management;

- the Committee of Loans, Guarantees and Risk assists credit cooperatives in fulfilling their duties in lending activity and customer identification;
- in addition, an Audit Committee and a Supervisory Committee operates in the Cooperative Central Bank; it assists the Board of Directors in fulfilling the assessment and monitor activities regarding functioning of cooperative banks in terms of asset quality, financial performance and monitoring the banking prudence indicators.

2.3.2 The Main Activities of Cooperative Credit Organizations in CREDITCOOP Network

The main activities of cooperative credit organizations in CREDITCOOP network are:

- granting credits to cooperative members and individuals other than cooperative members of affiliated cooperative banks;
- granting credits to legal persons who have the domicile/residence or registered office or operates through an entity without legal personality in the territorial jurisdiction of the central house;
- collecting deposits;
- making investments in the interbank market;
- making payments and settlement, including settlement of receipts and payments take place.
- transferring funds;
- consulting activity;
- effecting transactions on behalf of a client.

Cooperative banks in the CREDITCOOP network grant loans to cooperative members in lei exclusively on short and medium term. The main types of loans are:

- loans for real estate investments;
- consumer credits;
- refinancing loans.

In order to qualify for credits, cooperative members contribute with the "social found", an amount that should be made available to cooperative bank. It is determined by the Constitutive Act. This approach has the character of mutual aid and cooperative members receive interest on "social found". Loans granted by cooperative banks in CREDITCOOP network with shall be refunded with interest thereon, in the form of rate, within the time limits set by contract. These are established by negotiation between bank and customer depending on the amount of credit, the evolution of customer's revenues and maximum time limits provided in the rules of credit issued by CREDITCOOP Central Cooperative Bank. Annual interest rates on loans are approved by the Board of each cooperative bank, within the limits of circulars sent by the central house in the network. They are unique to each credit limit and for all cooperative members.

Cooperative banks may charge loan fees to cover part of the costs of credit risk management and expenses of management and accounting of loans. The level of these fees is determined by Board of each cooperative bank and they must be within the limits provided by the circulars of CREDITCOOP Cooperative Central Bank.

Individuals who are not cooperative members and they have the domicile or residence in the territorial jurisdiction of CREDITCOOP Cooperative Central Bank can receive credits if they meet the following conditions: (1) realize permanent income, (2) open a liquidity account at the agency of CREDITCOOP Cooperative Central Bank which will make the payments and receipts, (3) guarantee the repayment of loans and payment of interests with their income and personal/collateral guarantee.

Loans granted to non-members of cooperative banks and firms by a cooperative bank in CREDITCOOP network cannot exceed 15 % of its assets. This limit can be changed by decisions of the Board of Directors but it cannot exceed 25 % of the cooperative bank's assets.

Cooperative banks in CREDITCOOP network and agencies of CREDITCOOP Cooperative Central Bank grant short and medium term loans to microenterprises, consumer and handicraft cooperatives, public and religious organizations, family associations and individuals with liberal professions, which have the registered office the territorial jurisdiction of cooperative banks. In order to qualify for credits, legal persons mentioned above must meet the following conditions: (1) to have a liquidity account at the cooperative bank and to conduct receipts and payments through this account, (2) to conduct a profitable activity. It has proven with accounting documents, (3) to have credibility and a good financial and patrimonial situation.

Interests and loans fees charged by cooperative banks in CREDITCOOP network for legal person's loans must be within the limits set by the Central Cooperative Bank circulars. Insurance guarantees are income's legal person and personal/collateral guarantee.

Cooperative banks and the CREDITCOOP Central Cooperative Bank can support each other with fixed-term funds for the conduct of current and investments activities, modernization works, the purchase of fixed assets etc. Only cooperative banks which are credible and offer sufficient guarantees to honor the maturity of obligations under can benefit from it. The value of loans, interest charged and other conditions included in contracts will be approved by the boards of directors of lender cooperatives and beneficiary cooperatives. Only credible cooperative banks which offer sufficient guarantees to honor the obligations of contracts can benefit from these funds. The value of loans, interests and other contractual terms will be approved by the Boards of Directors of lending and debtor cooperative banks.

2.3.3 Analysis of Credit Cooperative Organizations in CREDITCOOP Network

In terms of target customer segment, cooperative banks in CREDITCOOP network grant loans to cooperative members (with priority) because these are credit institutions established as autonomous association of individuals voluntarily united in order to meet common needs and economic, social and cultural aspirations of cooperative members.

The arrangement of units especially in small towns and rural areas aims approaching banks to low and middle income customers and farmers. Credit cooperative organizations offer them a wide range of banking products, from paying bills to various types of loans and deposits. The main customers of credit cooperative organizations in CREDITCOOP network are individuals and small and medium enterprises. The distribution of exposures by type of customer during 2011–2013 is presented in Table 1.

As noted, credit cooperatives in Romania provide loans, mainly to individuals. Mainly, Romanian credit cooperative organizations are lenders because the value of claims on customers is higher than the value of deposits (Fig. 1).

The loan portfolio registered an upward trend during 2007–2013, across the CREDITCOOP network. During 2009–2013, the value of deposits increased. The CREDITCOOP network's need for financial resources was largely covered by deposits.

During 2007–2012, the CREDITCOOP network's activity was profitable (Fig. 2).

The low level of consolidated profit in 2009 is justified in economic crisis manifested virulent in Romania. Even though in 2010 the damage of economic and financial environment continued, the CREDITCOOP network obtained a higher consolidated profit compared to last year. The profit growth trend has accentuated in 2011. Amid worsening performance indicators of the banking system in Romania (50 % of Romanian credit institutions recorded losses on the income statement), during 2012–2013, net profit of the CREDITCOOP network decreased considerably.

Table 1 The distribution of exposures by type of customer (2011–2013)

	2011		2012		2013	
Type of customer	The balance of credits (million lei)	(%)	The balance of credits (lei)	(%)	The balance of credits (lei)	(%)
Individuals	544.2	99.8	563.9	99.4	611.3	99.3
Legal person	1.3	0.2	3.7	0.6	4.2	0.7
Total	551.8	100	567.6	100	615.5	100

Source: CREDITCOOP Central Cooperative Bank (2011–2013), Annual Reports made to meet the requirements of transparency and publishing

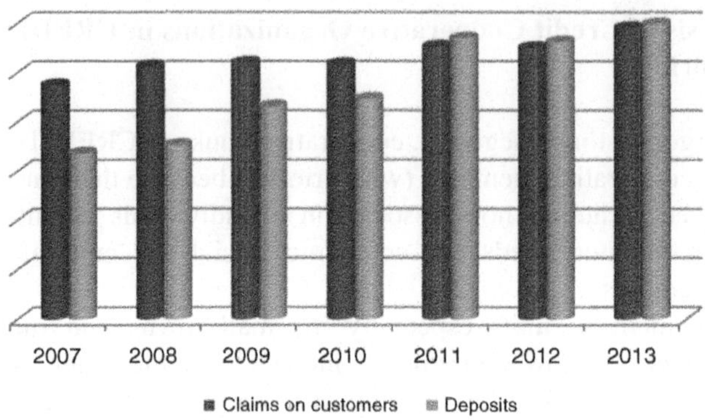

Fig. 1 Claims on customers and Deposits in Romanian credit cooperative organizations (based on the information in the consolidated balance sheet of CREDITCOOP Central Cooperative Bank)

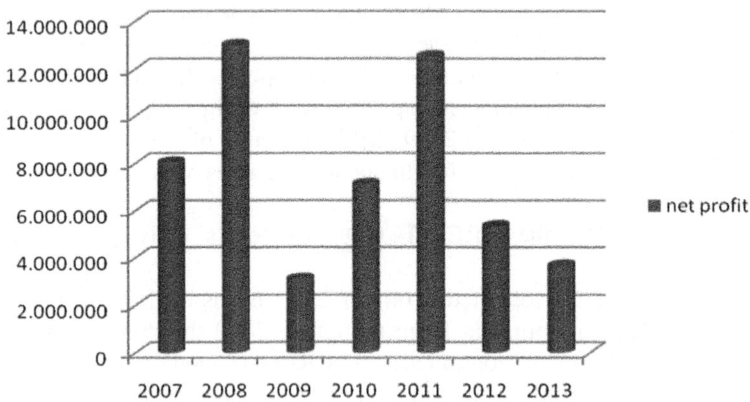

Fig. 2 Evolution of Romanian credit cooperative organizations' profit (based on the information in the consolidated balance sheet of CREDITCOOP Central Cooperative Bank)

3 The Part (Importance) of the Romanian Credit Cooperative System in the National Banking Market

Romanian banking system is a two-tier system, including the National Bank of Romania and credit institutions. In late 2013, in Romania operated 40 credit institutions (two fully or majority state-owned banks, three banks with majority privately-owned domestic capital, 25 banks with majority privately-owned foreign capital, nine branches of foreign banks and one cooperative network—CREDITCOOP).

54.4 % of banking assets are concentrated in the top five banks of the Romanian banking market (three banks with fully foreign capital, one bank with fully public capital and one bank with majority privately-owned domestic capital). Market share

Table 2 The market share of CREDITCOOP network

Year	2005	2006	2007	2008	2009	2010	2011	2012	2013
Net asset balance sheet—CREDITCOOP (% of total)	0.31	0.35	0.27	0.22	0.24	0.23	0.24	0.23	0.25

Source: National Bank of Romania, Annual Report (2005–2013)

Table 3 Loans granted to private sector by cooperative banks in CREDITCOOP network (2007–2013)

Year	2007	2008	2009	2010	2011	2012	2013
Loans (% of total)	0.30	0.25	0.26	0.25	0.26	0.76	0.80

Source: National Bank of Romania, Annual Report (2007–2013)

Table 4 Share capital: the banking system in Romania versus CREDITCOOP network (2007–2013) (million lei)

Year	2007	2008	2009	2010	2011	2012	2013
Share capital—CREDITCOOP	108.5	119.4	121.5	122.7	126	132.6	133.4
Share capital—total of credit institutions	11,124.3	13,309.8	14,385.4	16,944.1	18,289.3	25,043.8	25,273.9

Source: National Bank of Romania, Annual Report (2007–2013)

of credit institutions with majority privately-owned foreign capital is 90 %. Market share of credit institutions with majority privately-owned domestic capital is 10 % (including the cooperative network).

The market share of CREDITCOOP network is very small and it has recorded a downward trend during 2005–2013 (Table 2).

The share of credits granted by Romanian cooperative banks in the aggregate private sector credit demonstrates the little importance of credit cooperative organizations in the Romanian banking market (Table 3).

Regarding the degree of capitalization of cooperative banks in CREDITCOOP network, one can notice that the share capital increased during 2007–2013, following the nationwide tendency (Table 4).

The share capital of cooperative banks in CREDITCOOP network represented 0.97 % of aggregate share capital in 2007 and 0.53 % of aggregate share capital in 2013. The volume of activity undertaken by the cooperative banks in CREDITCOOP network is low compared to the human potential and infrastructure available. In Fig. 3 are shown some discrepancies in size between the Romanian bank that ranks first in terms of assets and customers (Romanian Commercial Bank) and CREDITCOOP.

Analysis of some banking indicators highlight differences and similarities between the activity of cooperative banks in CREDITCOOP network and banking system in Romania viewed as a whole (Table 5).

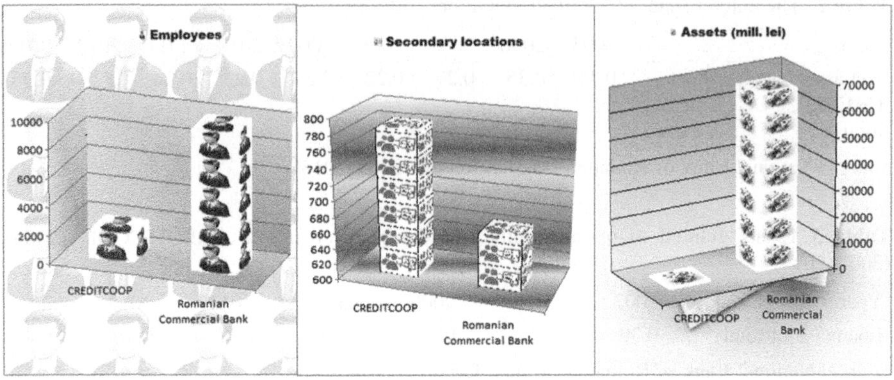

Fig. 3 CREDITCOOP against Romanian Commercial Bank

Table 5 Banking indicators: the banking system in Romania versus CREDITCOOP network (2011–2013) (%)

Banking indicators	Banking system in Romania			CREDITCOOP network		
	2011	2012	2013	2011	2012	2013
Solvency ratio	15.02	14.94	15.46	32.4	32.4	26.77
Capital-leverage ratio (tier 1 capital divided by total average assets)	8.11	8.02	7.96	21.8	22.6	20.82
Loans granted to customers/total assets	58.64	60.78	58.63	65.53	64.75	68.8
Economic rate of return	−0.16	−0.64	0.01	0.78	0.63	0.41
Return on equity	−1.73	−5.92	0.13	2.24	1.96	1.33
Loans granted to customers/deposits from customers	113.46	117.37	104.59	115.71	97.73	104.54

Source: National Bank of Romania, Annual Report (2011–2013) and CREDITCOOP Central Cooperative Bank, Consolidated balance sheet (2011–2013)

The banking indicators in the case of CREDITCOOP network are better compared to the indicators in the case of Romanian banking system.

Romanian banks adopted a cautious position regarding the risk taking, because of tensions in international financial markets and uncertainties in the domestic economic environment. These were determined largely by austerity measures promoted by the Romanian Government. With a solvency ratio higher than that the solvency ratio recorded in the banking system in Romania, the CREDITCOOP network proves a risk aversion. The loan-portfolio quality of CREDITCOOP network is better than that found in the banking system in Romania. This proves the existence of an efficient monitoring system of credit.

The year 2010 was marked by passing on losses of banking system in Romania. These results were attributed to the unprecedented growth in spending provisions.

The CREDITCOOP network obtained positive financial results, even if the amount of provisions has doubled.

Currently, the network CREDITCOOP position in the Romanian banking system is minor. This situation is generated by the following factors:

- the huge competition made by the commercial banks (especially foreign capital banks) that promoted aggressive policies to attract money and to grant credits (especially in the case of individuals);
- credibility problems for credit cooperative organizations before 2000. During this period, several administrators of credit cooperatives were involved in acts of deception, theft and forgery. In recent years, several cases of embezzlement, forgery and deception that were involved employees of cooperative banks were publicized. As a result of on-site inspections performed by the National Bank of Romania, in 2009 all 50 cooperative banks in CREDITCOOP network received penalties addressing Board members and leaders of cooperative banks (213 people). Sanctions have been applied in relation to the lending activity of secondary locations, reporting operational risk events, internal auditing, as well as outsourced activities. During 2011–2013, the number of penalties received by the cooperative banks in CREDITCOOP network decreased significantly and the sanctions have been applied in relation to the internal auditing.
- reluctance of Romanians from any form of cooperative organization because the general perception on cooperative system is obstructed by the communist system's sequelae. It used the cooperative system by force to achieve its objectives, so that cooperative principles and rules of organization were distorted.

Maintaining current marketing strategies of CREDITCOOP network (promoting its banking services in rural areas) will be limited the future development of cooperative system in Romania, because there are significant disparities between urban and rural areas in terms of economic growth and development. Most Romanian villagers (who are not near cities) are retirees or people who practice the subsistence agriculture.

A more active marketing policy (focused on attracting small businesses in the cooperative system) could be a part of the success formula for cooperative credit organizations in Romania.

References

CREDITCOOP Central Cooperative Bank (2007–2013) Annual report made to meet the requirements of transparency and publishing

CREDITCOOP Central Cooperative Bank (2007–2013) Consolidated balance sheet

Galan AG (1935) Monograph of credit cooperatives in Romania: 1906–1935, Bucharest, p 15

Government Emergency Ordinance no. 97/2000 on credit cooperative organizations.

Government Emergency Ordinance no. 99/2006 on credit institutions and adequacy of capital.

Isarescu M (2006) Economic reflections. Contributions to the theory of macro stabilization. Expert Publishing House, Bucharest, p 217

Law no. 109/1996 on organization and operation of consumer cooperatives and credit cooperatives.
Law no. 200/2002 for approving Government Emergency Ordinance no. 97/2000 on credit cooperative organizations.
Madgearu V (1940) Romanian economy after the World War. Economic Independence Publishing House, Bucharest, p 6
Morar A (2010) Analysis of financial activity in Romanian credit cooperative. PhD thesis, Cluj Napoca
Muresan M, Muresan D (1998) Economic history. Economic Publishing House, Bucharest, p 161
National Bank of Romania (2005–2013) Annual Report
Regulation no. 18 of 14.12.2006 on the own funds of credit institutions and investment firms.

Credit Co-operatives in Serbia: Retrospect and Prospect

Richard Simmons and Marija Nikolic

Abstract This chapter takes an overview of credit co-operatives in Serbia in retrospect and prospect. It starts by examining the legal frameworks that have regulated their work, from the first Law on agricultural and handicraft co-operatives from 1898, through to the most recent Law on Banks from 2005. It moves on to consider different phases of development of credit co-operatives; before the second world war (when numbers peaked during the 1930s); during the post-war period (when the sector declined in the face of state socialism); and during the more recent period of transition (leading to the dissolution of credit co-operatives in 2005). To conclude the paper, the current situation (which places significant legal obstacles in the way of credit co-operatives) is then assessed and the possibility of the revitalization of credit co-operatives is considered. Special attention will be given to how the revitalization of credit co-operatives might play a role in the survival and effectiveness of other co-operative sectors in Serbia, particularly agriculture (since agricultural co-operatives account for 67 % of the total number of registered co-operatives in Serbia today). This analysis suggests that the situation is now critical, and an urgent review of the current position is required.

1 Introduction

The co-operative movement in Serbia is among the oldest in Europe and the world, and has historical significance as one of the founder members of the International Co-operative Alliance. The first co-operative on today's territory of Republic of Serbia, "Gazdovský spolok", was founded as a credit agricultural co-operative in 1846 by immigrant Slovakians in the economically more developed province of

R. Simmons (✉)
University of Stirling, Stirling, UK
e-mail: r.a.simmons@stir.ac.uk

M. Nikolic
University of Belgrade, Belgrade, Serbia
e-mail: mnikolic@agrif.bg.ac.rs

S. Karafolas (ed.), *Credit Cooperative Institutions in European Countries*, Contributions to Economics, DOI 10.1007/978-3-319-28784-3_21

Vojvodina. In the Kingdom of Serbia, the first was the "Co-operative for mutual help and savings", founded in 1894 in the village of Vranovo according to Raiffeisen principles. Credit co-operatives are therefore among the oldest forms of co-operative in Serbia.

Given the dominance of small family farms and the heavy indebtedness of small and medium-sized family farms, agricultural credit co-operatives had special significance in the development of the co-operative movement in Serbia at the end of the nineteenth century. Once the first society was founded, the number of agricultural credit co-operatives increased exponentially. At the beginning of the twentieth century there were over 400, and in the period between two world wars there were as many as 1173 credit agricultural co-operatives. After the Second World War the co-operative movement experienced a number of ups and downs in Serbia, as will be explored later. However, despite this chequered context, credit co-operatives managed to survive until they were discouraged by law in 2005. Even so, some of them (such as the Railway Saving and Credit Co-operative) have not been wound up until very recently.

The evolution of credit co-operatives in Serbia is presented in this chapter. It starts by examining the legal frameworks that have regulated their work, from the first Law on agricultural and handicraft co-operatives from 1898, through to the most recent Law on Banks from 2005. It moves on to consider different phases of development of credit co-operatives; before the second world war (when numbers peaked during the 1930s); during the post-war period (when the sector declined in the face of state socialism); and during the more recent period of transition (leading to the dissolution of credit co-operatives in 2005). To conclude the paper, the current situation is then assessed and the possibility of the revitalization of credit co-operatives considered, particularly in the light of developments since the global financial crisis in 2008. Special attention will be given to how the revitalization of credit co-operatives might play a role in the survival and effectiveness of other co-operative sectors in Serbia, particularly agriculture (since agricultural co-operatives account for 67 % of the total number of registered co-operatives in Serbia today). This analysis suggests that the situation is now critical, and an urgent review of the current position is required.

2 Setting the Scene: The Legal Framework for Credit Co-operatives in Serbia

Before we embark on a more detailed history of the evolution of credit co-operatives in Serbia, it is helpful to set the scene by examining the evolution of the legal frameworks for credit co-operatives over the last century or so. The aim in putting these different laws in one section is to allow the reader to familiarise themselves quickly with some of the key milestones, and then to also provide a pictorial guide for readers to use for reference throughout the rest of the chapter.

The first law to regulate the work of co-operatives in the Kingdom of Serbia was The Law on Agricultural and Handicraft Co-operatives in 1898. This law aimed to remove unnecessary obstructions to the further development of co-operatives. Two types of co-operatives were recognised: agricultural and handicraft co-operatives. Amongst the provisions of this law, Article 1 authorised agricultural co-operatives to "*...give their members credit and take savings for keeping*".[1]

In 1925, the Law on Agricultural Credit was enacted. Newly-formed entities known as 'local and district co-operatives' were created under the management of a Directorate for Agricultural Credit, to provide credit to farmers with state support. The new 'co-operatives' were to operate in parallel with existing 'genuine' credit co-operatives. This can be evaluated as the first attempt of the state to take over the control of the credit co-operative system in Serbia.

A new General Law on Co-operatives in 1937 extended the role of credit co-operatives to "*...receiving saving deposits, raising loans, granting credits, interceding in insurance for their members, as well as providing agricultural inputs for their members and sale of their products on commission*".[2] Credit co-operatives were authorised to take deposits from non-members, not just from their members.[3] The law also enabled other types of co-operative to be involved in credit activities.

The aftermath of the second world war saw considerable turmoil for the co-operative movement. Credit co-operatives suffered in this environment, but access to savings and credit services (SCS) were offered by the general agricultural co-operatives established under the system of 'self management' after 1953.[4] Some time later, in 1977, the Law on Saving-Credit Organisations and Businesses with Saving Deposits created a legal basis for the foundation and development of SCS.[5] In collaboration with a state bank, *Agrobanka*, this led to a relatively 'golden' period of growth for SCS in the early 1980s.

In 1989, two co-operative laws were adopted: the general Law on Co-operatives, and a special Law on Agricultural Co-operatives. When the Law on Co-operatives came into effect several others were rescinded, among them the Law on Saving-Credit Organisation and Business with Saving Deposits (1977). These laws promoted a return to true international co-operative principles, with the Law on Co-operatives regulating the work of saving-credit co-operatives and services in a special chapter. Then, in January 1990, a new federal Law on Co-operatives was

---

[1] Article 1 Paragraph 1 Law on agricultural and handicraft cooperatives (1898).

[2] Article 1 Paragraph 7 Law on commercial cooperatives (1937).

[3] Article 1 Paragraph 6 Law on commercial cooperatives (1937).

[4] Following WW2 agricultural co-operatives were first organised on the Soviet kolkhoz model. However, resistance from the peasantry was strong. By 1953, the Yugoslav communist elite introduced a 'softer' version of the communist ideology and social system called 'self management' (Sljukic 2002).

[5] SCS can be distinguished from saving-credit cooperatives by legal status—contrary to cooperatives, SCS were not legal entities. SCS were formed by another cooperative that was usually called a "founder cooperative". Founder cooperatives were usually agricultural cooperatives, but were sometimes also handicrafts and housing cooperatives.

enacted. The aim of this law was a reaffirmation of the co-operative movement. Therefore it was created in a more liberal spirit compared to previous laws on co-operatives, with a special emphasis on the business and market role of co-operatives.

However, these developments came at a particularly testing time in the nation's history, and soon the situation changed again. In 1993 a new Law on Banks and other Financial Organizations was enacted. This law effectively eliminated credit co-operatives from the co-operative system and left their management to the state authorities. A new federal Law on Co-operatives was enacted in 1996. This law allowed both for farmers to found saving-credit co-operatives and for agricultural co-operatives to provide SCS. However, these provisions conflicted with the Law on Banks and other Financial Organizations (1993). More specifically, Article 21, paragraph 2 of the 1993 Law allowed only legal persons with the special permission of the National Bank of Yugoslavia to be involved in deposit, credit and other banking businesses. This presented a considerable obstacle to agricultural co-operatives seeking to start a saving-credit service.

Any remaining possibility for the formation of saving-credit co-operatives and services was removed following the enactment in 2005 of the Law on Banks. The Law on Banks (2005) compelled all kinds of financial organizations other than banks to, within 1 year, transform into a bank, merge with a bank or cease working. The effects of this law were considerable: by late 2005 only eight credit co-operatives were still operating, and in 2008 all of them stopped working. Thus, after a long and fruitful tradition, one kind of co-operative is prohibited by law. Later, we will see that despite a number of draft co-operative laws being prepared since 1996, none of these have been enacted (Fig. 1).

3 A Detailed History of Credit Co-operatives in Serbia

Having briefly reviewed the key legislative milestones in the history of development of credit co-operatives in Serbia, it is now possible to undertake a more detailed commentary. In doing so, the chapter will consider this development in three key phases:

(i) The period prior to the Second World War
(ii) The period after the Second World War until 1989
(iii) The transition period from 1989

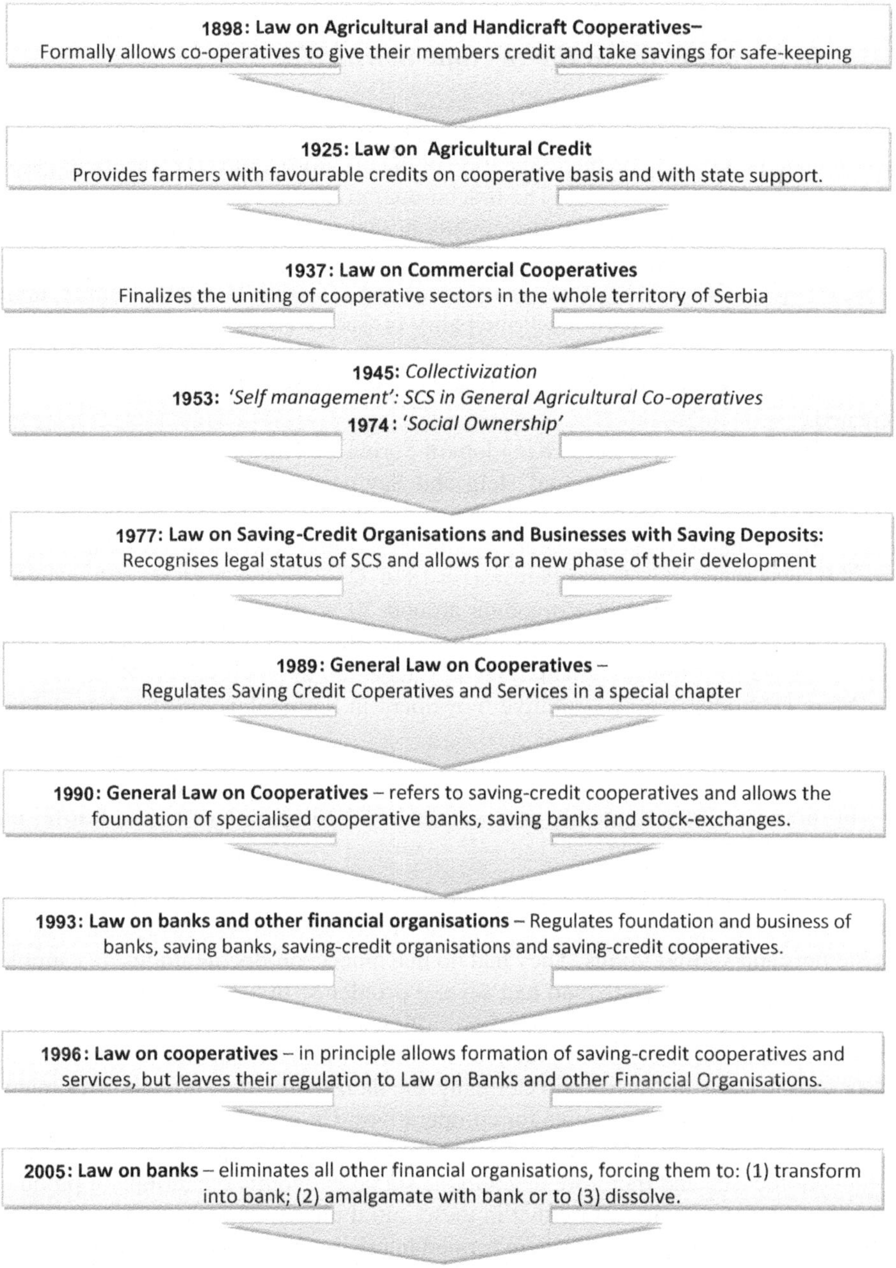

Fig. 1 Timeline for the legal framework for credit co-operatives in Serbia

3.1 The Development of Saving and Credit Co-operatives in Serbia Prior to the Second World War

The literature abounds with papers on the early history of the Serbian co-operative movement, particularly on the foundation of the first co-operatives (Vuckovic 1957; Ranđelović 1999; Zakić 2000). The first co-operatives appeared in Serbia at around the same time as co-operative movements in many developed Western European countries. At that time, today's Republic of Serbia consisted of two parts: the northern part (Vojvodina) that was part of the Austrian-Hungary Empire until 1918 and the southern part, the Principality of Serbia (which was proclaimed the Kingdom of Serbia in 1882). These territories formed a new country in 1918 and, after many integration and disintegration processes, today's Republic of Serbia was created.

The first co-operative in the Kingdom of Serbia was formed in Vranovo in 1894 as the "Co-operative for Mutual Help and Savings".[6] There is therefore a long tradition of credit co-operatives in the Kingdom of Serbia. The first co-operatives in Vojvodina emerged even earlier: credit-agricultural co-operative "Gazdovský spolok" was founded in Bački Petrovac in 1846. Co-operatives whose only activity was credit were formed in Vojvodina around 20 years later: in Pivnice in 1868 Vojvodina Slovakians formed an exclusively credit co-operative, and the first Co-operative for Mutual Help and Savings appeared in Novi Sad in 1870.

More generally, the co-operative movement in Serbia developed in parallel on two levels:

- In cities, where handicrafts and consumer co-operatives dominated
- In rural areas, where mainly credit-agricultural co-operatives on the Raiffeisen principles were formed.

In cities, co-operatives were put forward as way of uniting small craftsmen with a common purpose. Many dwellers in urban areas had small workshops for making basic pots and similar things. They had no machinery, producing things in a simple manner. These small craftsman had several problems; first, producing enough for the market and then being able to make a sufficient profit (as their products had high production costs). A common practice (for those who could afford it) was to send their sons to study in Austria and Germany. On their return, they brought back many ideas—including early concepts for co-operatives. Co-operatives were proposed to help the craftsmen buy machines, improve the quality of their products, reduce their production costs, and therefore develop the social-economic conditions of production. However, it is interesting that in these initial phases of co-operative development, few credit co-operatives were formed in urban areas, despite the co-operative thinkers of the time elaborating ideas for their foundation and development (Ranđelović 1999: 82).

[6] This cooperative later changed name into "Vranovo agricultural credit cooperative" and it is better known under this name.

This is exemplified in the short history of another important cooperative founded in Belgrade in 1882, known as *The Belgrade Cooperative*. The purpose of the cooperative was to provide services to merchants, craftsmen, and clerks. It had two departments: for banking and insurance. During 1882 and 1883 the collection of deposits was very slow, due to fear that the co-operative might collapse, but also because of the negative propaganda of local loan-sharks who did not welcome this competition. The management of the cooperative asked for help from one of the most distinguished businessmen of that time, Djordje Vajfert. Vajfert supported the idea and became the first chairman of the cooperative in 1883. This boosted the progress of the cooperative, which collected a significant amount of capital by 1887, gaining increasing popularity amongst the local population. However, a sense of nervousness regarding the cooperative's capital liquidity accompanied the right of depositors to ask, at any time, for the return of 75 % of their deposit. The wealthiest members, who were the strongest in cooperative, unsuccessfully proposed transforming the cooperative into a investor-owned business on two occasions in 1886 and 1888. With the eventual withdrawal of Djordje Vajfert, The Belgrade Cooperative finally lost its cooperative roots on January 6th 1890 (Aleksic 2012).[7]

In rural areas, it was easier to persuade people to start co-operatives. In Serbia at this time there was a transitional movement from feudalistic, subsistence farming to a more developed capitalistic market economy. There were very few big farms; the majority were small, individual farms. Only the small minority of wealthy people (usually traders and craftsmen, although some larger farmers) were able to take loans from banks, leaving small farmers to take private loans at very high rates of interest. There was a continual lack of money and yet a great need for it to modernise and develop agricultural production, smooth the effects of agricultural risks and allow small farmers to move beyond subsistence. This unfavourable agrarian structure, along with the generally small scale of family farms, the heavy indebtedness of farmers that resulted from expensive credit conditions, and increasing numbers of landless villagers due to the forced sale of their farms, were the driving factors behind the foundation of credit-agricultural co-operatives in rural areas. Co-operatives recognised the needs of these people. For example, the first agricultural producer co-operative founded in Ruma in 1883 gave credit to its members to lease land (Kišgeci and Vitez 1994: 27).

In this way, credit co-operatives represented one of the earliest forms of co-operatives in Serbia, growing out of the strong need for favourable agricultural loans, directed at the development of capitalism and the intensification of agricultural production. An important example was the credit-agricultural co-operative in Vranovo, the foundation treaty of which underlines that its goal is to "*...provide to its members money for agricultural works, to develop and acclimatize*

[7] Although this organisation had a short cooperative life, it continued to be one of the most important financial institutions in Belgrade until the Second World War. http://www.gradnja-online.com/index.php?view=magazine_detail&type=arhitektura&id=4783

consciousness on savings among them ... To grant loans based on jointly obligations of its members and to collect savings from members and other individuals"[8] (Pantić and Nikolov 1994: 202). This example served as a model for defining the main activity of many other co-operatives formed at that time. Therefore, while co-operatives were involved in other activities such as the provision of necessary inputs for agricultural farms, their role in collecting savings and giving credit was fundamental.

In spite of slightly different dynamics in the foundation and activities of co-operatives in Vojvodina and Kingdom of Serbia, a mutual characteristic was this combination of agricultural and credit activities. It was common that cooperatives were involved in providing credit, but also selling food, cattle, and inputs for agricultural production (Nikolic 2009). The connection was officially recognised in the Law on Agricultural and Handicraft Co-operatives in 1898, the first law to regulate the work of co-operatives in the Kingdom of Serbia. This Law recognised two types of co-operatives—agricultural and handicraft co-operatives—and specifically allowed for co-operatives to take savings and give credit to their members. The aim of this law was to enable the regular and successful development of co-operatives and to create a legal base for further unobstructed development.

In the period between the two World Wars there was still a significant need for favourable credit in the rural areas of Serbia. Despite their increasing number, credit co-operatives were unable to satisfy this need. To solve this problem, the government enacted the Law on Agricultural Credit in 1925, according to which local and district co-operatives were formed under the management of the Directorate for Agricultural Credit. This can be evaluated as the first attempt of the state to take over the control of credit co-operatives in Serbia. The goal of local and district co-operatives was to provide the necessary credit to farmers with state support. At its heart, this was an attempt to create a new co-operative movement under the authority of the state, in parallel with the already existing system of genuine credit co-operatives. The Law on Agricultural Credit envisaged that these newly-formed local and district co-operatives would provide the foundation of the credit system—existing credit co-operatives were obligated to adjust their activities to comply with the requirements of this law. In practice, this meant that the Directorate for Agricultural Credit pooled money from the government and savings from the existing co-operatives and then decided who would be given credit. Primary credit co-operatives had to give all the money they received in savings to the Directorate and could no longer decide by themselves how these savings were invested. Instead, the Directorate made these decisions, with the goal of spreading credit more evenly. As part of this process, the Directorate could decide to give credit to co-operatives, to their unions and/or to some other associations of agricultural producers. However, representatives of the existing credit co-operative movement were vigorously opposed to this move, and 4 years after its foundation

[8] All citations from laws are translations of M. Nikolic, co-author of this paper.

Table 1 Types of co-operatives in Serbia between two world wars

	Credit coops		Buying-selling coops		Others		
Year	Number	%	Number	%	Number	%	Total
1920	800	54	621	42	47	3	1468
1921	808	52	694	44	61	4	1563
1922	1258	62	700	35	62	3	2020
1923	1227	61	716	36	63	3	2006
1924	1220	61	708	36	65	3	1993
1925	1181	60	707	36	72	4	1960
1926	1165	60	718	37	74	4	1957
1927	1183	60	727	37	66	3	1976
1928	1059	56	746	39	85	4	1890
1929	1087	54	806	40	102	5	1995
1930	1187	53	880	40	152	7	2219
1931	1096	48	903	40	287	13	2286
1932	1139	45	1018	41	352	14	2509
1933	1173	43	1153	42	394	14	2720
1934	1156	40	1325	46	425	15	2906
1935	1109	37	1424	48	446	15	2979
1936	1109	35	1558	49	490	16	3157
1937	1096	33	1632	49	595	18	3323
1938	1098	32	1731	50	654	19	3483
1939	1077	30	1819	50	751	21	3647

Source: Zakić (2000: 263)

the Directorate for Agricultural Credit was terminated. Instead, two bodies were formed:

- Main co-operative for agricultural credit and
- Preferential Agricultural Bank (PAB).

Credit co-operatives in Serbia were at their most numerous in the period 1922–1939. Numbers peaked at 1187 in 1930, but by the Second World War there were still 1077 credit co-operatives, representing 29.5 % of the total number of co-operatives (Zakić 2000: 263) (Table 1).

Where credit co-operatives were active, they were very important for farmers. First, while they usually controlled only limited resources (which restricted their impact on the intensification of agriculture and development of the village), they granted more favourable credits than the competition and helped the surviving family farms. Second, just before the Second World War, they also invested heavily in the provision of agricultural machinery and tools, and this significantly contributed to technical progress in agriculture (Pavlović 1994: 41). Third, many credit co-operatives were in fact multifunctional organisations, widely involved in providing inputs for agriculture and selling agricultural products. Finally, credit co-operatives often had a significant social role. Hence, while some credit co-operatives divided any surplus,[9] in many cases they did not. Instead, surpluses were directed into a reserve fund for (i) covering future losses, (ii) rewarding eminent farmers and savers, and (iii) other educational and charitable purposes.

The role and potential of credit co-operatives was recognised in a new law in 1937, the Law on Commercial Co-operatives. This law singled out credit co-operatives, saying that they could be involved in "*...receiving saving deposits, raising loans, granting credits, interceding in insurance for their members, as well as providing agricultural inputs for their members and sale of their products on commission*".[10] The same law also stated that other types of co-operatives could be involved in credit activities, and that co-operatives could receive saving deposits not just from their members, but also from non-members.[11]

In sum, despite their perceived potential, the credit co-operative movement was at that time too underdeveloped to meet farmers' needs, and the role of credit co-operatives remained relatively marginal between the two world wars.[12] However, farmers had to take money from somewhere, and most of them were forced to take credit from private persons (46 %) and private banks (32 %) (Pavlović 1994: 34). This reinforced the high indebtedness of many small farmers.

3.2 Credit Co-operatives in Serbia in the Period After Second World War Until 1989

After the Second World War the co-operative movement in Serbia was subjected to drastic reforms, in order to eliminate residual elements of the capitalist system. For example, in the immediate aftermath of WW2, agricultural co-operatives were organised on the Soviet *kolkhoz* model. Again, however, resistance from the peasantry was strong. By 1953, the Yugoslav communist elite introduced a 'softer' version of the communist ideology and social system called 'self management' (Sljukic 2002). Under 'self-management' private ownership was limited but co-operatives managed to accumulate land, as well as machinery and facilities for food processing. However, between 1974 and 1976, the politicians decided to transfer all co-operative assets into social ownership. This included 194,000 ha of

---

[9] For example, the Cooperative for Credit and Savings in Niš, after taking 15 % of any surplus for rewards for members of the committee and 3 % for clerks' wages, paid out the rest to members as a dividend (Jovančić 1991: 62).

[10] Article 1 Paragraph 7 Law on commercial cooperatives (1937).

[11] Article 1 Paragraph 6 Law on commercial cooperatives (1937).

[12] Similarly, while the Preferential Agricultural Bank was established to (1) collect significant resources and to give it to agriculture, and (2) to make it possible for farmers to receive credit, not based on the mortgage of land, but on a personal guarantee, in the end these goals were quickly diminished. Increasingly, the PAB also based credit on mortgages, meaning that the money usually went to farmers with big farms. Farmers with small farms could not receive credit because they did not have enough estate for a mortgage.

land purchased by co-operatives during the 1960s, to which peasant members lost all their legal rights.

During this period, the saving-credit activity of the co-operative movement developed on two levels: in saving-credit co-operatives (SCC) and in saving-credit services in other types of co-operatives (SCS). During the 1950s state-run banks and other saving-credit organisations were getting stronger, and there was a gradual reduction in the activity and number of saving-credit co-operatives. This had particularly negative consequences for agriculture, since the saving-credit *co-operatives* had previously helped to activate members' free resources and provide access to a favourable source of finance. However, from 1953 to 1974, saving-credit *services* (SCS) did exist in general agricultural co-operatives.[13] During much of the 1960s, these self-managed producer co-operatives were important as a way of organising for around 100,000 'middle stratum' peasant families (Mrksic 1987). The main activity of these general agricultural co-operatives was to organise agricultural production on members' farms and co-operative farms and to develop cooperation with small farmers that were not members of the co-operative. To support this, they also collected small savings and other free resources from farmers and rural inhabitants and steered them in favourable credits to support productive activities amongst co-operative members.

In the following decade the role of credit co-operatives was marginalised, but during the 1970s a gradual revitalisation started. The constitution of SFR of Yugoslavia from 1974 introduced a different concept of co-operative savings. An important step was enacting the Law on Saving-Credit Organisations and Businesses with Saving Deposits in 1977, which enabled the foundation of saving-credit services in co-operatives and the organisation of associated members. This created a legal basis for the foundation and development of SCS. SCS were distinguished from saving-credit co-operatives first of all by legal status—contrary to saving-credit co-operatives, SCS were not legal entities. SCS were formed by another co-operative that was usually called a "founder co-operative". Founder co-operatives were usually agricultural co-operatives, but were sometimes also handicrafts and housing co-operatives. The objectives of saving-credit services were to:

- Give favourable interest rates on saving deposits;
- Grant credits at favourable rates; and
- Use surpluses to promote the work of the founder co-operative.[14]

The foundation of SCS in co-operatives was mainly supported by some commercial bank, whereby the commercial bank gave some form of deposit guarantee, and other supports (usually people and in some cases offices). Most of them were founded with the cooperation and help from one particular bank: Agrobanka.

[13] This was a specific cooperative form that existed in former Yugislavia in period 1953–1974.

[14] These services also built on earlier co-operative traditions of commitment to a social role. For example, many held funds both to support members through unfortunate circumstances (e.g funeral costs in case of bereavement, or medical costs in case of illness) and to help them celebrate exceptional events (e.g. when members' children achieved something of particular note).

Box 1: Case Study of Agrobanka and Concept of Co-operative Savings and Crediting of Farmers

Agrobanka originated in 1929 as the Preferential Agricultural Bank, which operated until the beginning of World War II. In 1959 the Yugoslav Agricultural Bank '*Poljobanka*' emerged from its foundations. *Agrobanka* was its legal successor, created in 1978 as '*Basic Agricultural Bank Agrobanka*' (and transformed again in 1981 into '*Specialized Agricultural Bank Agrobanka*').

Agrobanka signed an agreement in 1978 with the Co-operative Union of Serbia, after the enactment of the Law on Saving-Credit Organisations and Businesses with Savings Deposits (1977) had created the legal environment for the formation of SCS. This agreement regulated the foundation of SCS, the conditions of business cooperation, the standards and models of warranty, the maintenance of liquidity, how much money of total fund for credits could be allocated for credits for co-operative member and how much of that money could be given to people just saving in the bank and are not members of coops and other important aspects of their business.

This was an important development, and at the beginning this agreement was not very well received by the other commercial banks. By the end of 1979 an agreement was signed by ten more banks, which formally ended any difficulty with the further development of SCS. However, in practice, apart from *Agrobanka*, other commercial banks showed no interest in this development.

In 1979 there were just three co-operatives with saving-credit services that worked successfully, but then their number increased rapidly. *Agrobanka* helped the foundation of SCS in all types of co-operatives, but particularly in agricultural co-operatives. *Agrobanka* provided logistic support in the founding and business of the SCS, prepared all legal bylaws, and conducted control regarding the proportion of use of resources. However, conditions of awarding credit, interest rates on credit deposits and other relevant factors were determined by the founder co-operative.

The more favourably the saving conditions compared with the banks, the more money became available for awarding credit and improving the work of famer members. Both members and non-members could save in SCS. Both could also raise loans, if that was allowed by the provisions of the SCS. In the first place SCS guaranteed savings themselves, although they usually held only limited resources. In the second place, the founder co-operative provided this guarantee. *Agrobanka* provided the final guarantee, since at the beginning of business it was a standard practice to sign a contract of guarantee between *Agrobanka* and the founder co-operative. Aggregated resources were divided in the following proportions: 10 % of resources was retained in the transfer account as a minimal reserve of liquidity, and the rest of the resources were steered as credits to savers and to the founder co-operative in the ratio of a maximum of 40 % of credit to the founder and at least 60 % of credit to saver members.

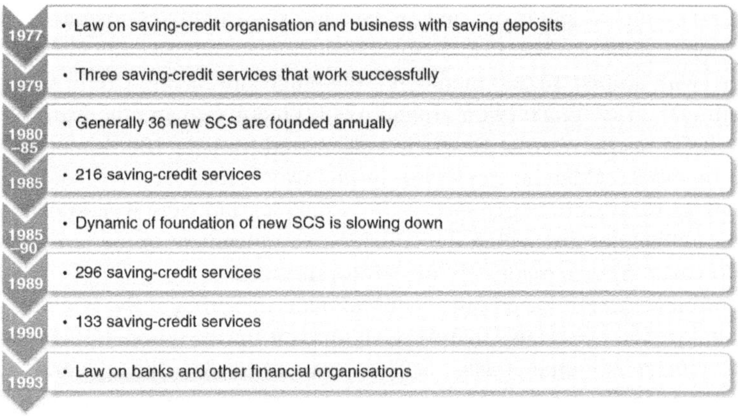

Fig. 2 Foundation, development and dissolution of credit co-operatives in Serbia in 1977–1993

In what might be seen as something of a 'golden' period between 1980 and 1985, around 36 new SCS were founded annually, with about 30,000 new savers each year amongst farmers and villagers. At the end of this period there were 216 SCS with around 180,000 savers, and more than half (56 %) of farmers organisation took credits from SCS (Agrobanka 2001). After 1985 the dynamic of the foundation of new SCS started slowing down. This is the period when political crises in the former SFR of Yugoslavia started to emerge. By 1990, the political situation had deteriorated critically: in 1990 Slovenia separated, in 1991 Serbia entered into conflict with Croatia. The economic consequences of these developments started around 1985, but things became increasingly serious as the 1990s approached. At the end of 1989 there were 296 SCS in total, but just a year later only 133 SCS, with half the number of savers. Disintegration of the political and economic system and the unique economic area of the former SFR of Yugoslavia, in addition to economic sanctions and the international isolation of Serbia, led to an extended economic crisis especially hyperinflation and complicated conditions of founding and working, resulted in the total eradication of saving-credit services by the middle 1990s (Fig. 2).

3.3 *Credit Co-operatives in Serbia in the Transition Period from 1989*

By the early 1990s (at the beginning of transition period) there were around 70 saving-credit co-operatives.[15] On the one hand, there were some remaining

[15] Monograph "Century and a half of cooperative movement", Co-operative Union of Yugoslavia (2005: 38).

agricultural credit co-operatives, and on the other some credit co-operatives based on a professional 'common bond'. Examples include the Saving-Credit Co-operative of Teachers (with around 13,000 members); the Yugoslav Saving-Credit Co-operative "Jugozadruga" in Belgrade (with around 67,000 members) and the Railway Saving and Credit Co-operative from Belgrade that existed for over 100 years (with around 120,000 members) (Mandić 1994: 56). In this way it may be seen that some credit co-operatives were particularly successful businesses and were well known amongst the wider public, not just within the co-operative movement or the territory of their work. However, by this point only the strong survived.

Several new system-based laws were adopted in Serbia at the beginning of the transitional period. Two laws that were significant for the co-operative sector were adopted almost simultaneously at the end of 1989: the general Law on Co-operatives, and a special Law on Agricultural Co-operatives. When the Law on Co-operatives came into effect several others were rescinded, among them the Law on Saving-Credit Organisation and Business with Saving Deposits (1977). These newly-adopted laws were important first of all because they promoted a return to true international co-operative principles, but also—from the point of view of credit businesses, because the Law on Co-operatives (1989) regulated the work of saving-credit co-operatives and services in a special chapter.

After these two laws in the Republic of Serbia, a new federal Law on Co-operatives was enacted in January 1990. The aim of this law was a reaffirmation of the co-operative movement. Therefore it was created in a more liberal spirit compared to previous laws on co-operatives, with a special emphasis on the business and market role of co-operatives. The federal Law on Co-operatives (1990) included provisions for saving-credit co-operatives; it gave the opportunity for co-operatives to form specialised co-operative banks, saving banks and a stock exchange for their own needs (Article 21, Paragraph 2). However, as we will explain, these provisions de jure applied only until the Law on Banks and other Financial Organisations (1993) came into effect.

A particularly important law referring to the co-operative sector that was adopted in the transitional period was the federal Law on Co-operatives (1996). Although several draft laws were presented in following years, none of them were enacted until very recently (December 2015), and this new law has changed nothing in relation to the credit co-operatives. The Law on Co-operatives (1996) states that farmers can form saving-credit co-operatives,[16] and that agricultural co-operatives can organise saving-credit business for their members' needs.[17] Agricultural co-operatives were therefore enabled to form saving-credit services as a part of the co-operative.[18] However, in a key stipulation of the federal Law on Co-operatives

[16] Article 3 Paragraph 3 Law on cooperatives (1996).

[17] Article 3 Paragraph 1 Law on cooperatives (1996).

[18] It is interesting that such an opportunity was given only to agricultural cooperatives; some claim that the same principle could have been used for other types: manufacturing, consumer, housing co-operatives, and so on (Marković 1998: 61).

(1996), Article 2 states that co-operatives can be formed as saving-credit, but that upon their foundation their "*. . . organisation, work and management are subject to the provisions of the federal law that regulates banks and other financial organisations.*"[19]

In this way, the federal Law on Co-operatives (1996) was subjected to the same constraints that had befallen the federal Law on Co-operatives (1990), in that its provisions for saving-credit co-operatives were subject to the provisions of the Law on Banks and other Financial Organizations (1993): a law emanating from quite a different perspective. Indeed, the enactment of the 1993 Law began a process of elimination of saving-credit co-operatives. At the time the Law on Banks and Other Financial Organisations (1993) came into effect, saving-credit co-operatives were included in a unique banking system in the Republic of Serbia, which until 2005 consisted of:

- Central bank (today National Bank of Serbia),
- Commercial banks and
- Other financial organisations.

From 1993, the foundation and work of saving-credit co-operatives—as a type of 'other financial organisation'—became subject to the new Law on Banks and other bylaws created by the National Bank of Serbia—which was in charge for all 'other financial organisations'.[20] Prior to this, credit co-operatives could decide themselves how to allocate resources, what to invest in, whether to divide any surplus, and what interest rates to charge. After the 1993 law was adopted, the work of any organisation that wanted to conduct savings and credit business was regulated according to the practise of the National Bank, which was subject to direct government influence. In practice, the National Bank dictated everything including interest rates, how much a credit co-operative must hold in its reserve fund, how much could be invested and so on—effectively placing saving-credit co-operatives under state control.

After the Law on Banks and Other Financial Organisations (1993) had been brought in to force, the Union of Saving-Credit Co-operatives of Serbia[21] expressed their disagreement and suggested a group of measures for the survival and revival of credit co-operatives. They insisted primarily that the regulation of the foundation and business of saving-credit co-operatives should be returned to the Law on Co-operatives. However, in contrast with earlier episodes of resistance, this action did not achieve its desired effect.

With the enactment of the Law on Banks and Other Financial Organisations (1993), co-operatives faced a choice—to harmonise their business with the Law

[19] Article 2 Paragraph 3 Law on cooperatives (1996).

[20] Beside saving-credit cooperatives, this category included post-office savings banks, other savings banks and saving-credit organisations. Post-office savings banks were founded in 1923 as state financial institutions.

[21] The Union of Saving-Credit Cooperatives were formed in 1991 according to Law on cooperatives (1990) (Nikolic 2009: 148).

(1993) within a deadline of 6 months or to stop working. In December 1993, 6 months after the enactment of this law, 224 saving-credit co-operatives were erased from the Register of Organisations, because they did not manage to harmonise their work with this law within the prescribed period.[22] According to the Union of Saving-Credit Co-operatives of Serbia, over 300 saving-credit co-operatives and services did not fulfil the commitment to adjust their work to the Law on Banks and Other Financial Organisations (1993) and these were forbidden to keep working. One group of saving-credit co-operatives, like the Railway Saving and Credit Co-operative, did manage to survive through this period. They dissolved into two legal entities and moved their non-financial activities in newly-formed companies related to the co-operative. In that way they fulfilled the legal provisions for continuance of their work.

Box 2: Case Study of Railway Saving and Credit Co-operative
The Co-operative for Mutual Help and Savings for Railway Staff was founded on May 4th 1891 with its head office in Belgrade, less than 7 years after the opening of the first railway in Serbia. Over the years the co-operative has changed its name several times and moved head office, but has never stopped working, not even during the First and Second World Wars.

Savings were collected through a membership fee which depended on the incomes of co-operative members. 70 % of the membership fee was directed into savings, and 30 % into co-operative funds. Co-operative members could pay one or more deposit per month, and at the end of the year savings were increased by interest on capital. The level of interest was defined by the Board of Directors based on business results in the previous year. During its work, the co-operative also had a significant social role: it helped members in case of illness or death, provided them with fundamental necessities, enabled them to take a vacation in co-operative hotels with subsidised prices, and so on.

Although formed as a co-operative solely for railway staff, membership was broadened (after 1945) to staff from other types of transport, and later to all economically active people. The Railway Saving and Credit Co-operative integrated in 1945 with the Credit Co-operative of State Transport Staff from Belgrade. During its existence, this co-operative created significant assets, with, for example, an office building in Belgrade and an hotel in Vrnjačka banja. It also had over 55,000 active accounts. The value and prosperity of the Railway Saving and Credit Co-operative is demonstrated by the increase in its members over time (Table 2). At the Annual Assembly in 1982 new regulations were adopted and new representatives were selected, which led to a renewed membership and savings drive. The biggest annual increase in numbers of members was recorded in 1987, due to a positive set of financial

(continued)

[22] Interview with Mr Pero Radović, liquidation director in Railway saving and credit cooperative, conducted in November 2009 in Belgrade.

results. 9605 new members joined the coop in that year, giving a total of 105,437 members. One reason for this increase in 1987 was the approval of all appeals from members to use the recreation and holiday capacities in the hotels that were owned by the cooperative (or in hotels rented by the cooperative). None of the members were rejected. In the next year the funeral fund was increased, and the cooperative again helped everyone that asked for such help. From 1981 to 1990 the number of members was continually increasing. However, in 1990, for the first time, the numbers of members decreased as political and economic crises started to hit.

The environment for doing business and the material position of the members both started getting progressively worse (particularly in the South of the country). The enactment of the Law on Banks and Other Financial Organisations (1993) followed, and in 1994 the co-operative was divided into two legal entities:

(i) "Railway saving and credit co-operative 1981"—whose activity was solely saving-credit business, and
(ii) Co-operative company "Maj-komerc", LLC—which was involved in other non-financial businesses.

The Law on Banks (2005) had two further effects: first, the withdrawal of working permission by the National Bank of Serbia and second, commencement of the liquidation process. Accordingly, the Commercial Court of Belgrade started liquidation proceedings on 04.01.2007. The process of liquidation is ongoing, but the organization has not been providing services for some years now.

Table 2 Number of co-operative members in Railway saving and credit co-operative from its foundation until 1990

Year	Number of members
1892	413
1914	1820
1921	1754
1931	5625
1941	5453
1945	7148 (after integration)
1955	13,443
1960	21,624
1970	29,440
1981	70,574
1990	117,957

Source: 100 years of Solidarity, Monograph of Railway saving and credit co-operative, Belgrade, 1991

In sum, saving-credit co-operatives could exist in the period 1993–2005, but only within a very strict legal environment. In the literature the dominant opinion is that the work of these co-operatives was suppressed by unfavourable legal provisions. However, it should be noted that co-operative unions themselves were not active in the promotion of credit co-operatives—the most significant of them, the Co-operative Union of Serbia was predominantly interested in agricultural co-operatives. So, although they could exist according to the law, all these factors led to the almost complete disappearance of saving-credit co-operatives. For 10 years the number of saving-credit co-operatives continuously decreased.

This was the beginning of the end for this form of co-operative, a process that was completed when the Law on Banks came into effect in 2005. This law decreed that only banks could collect saving deposits and grant loans. In practice, this meant that all other forms of financial organisations were abolished, including saving-credit co-operatives. Article 142 of the Law on Banks prescribed that within 1 year (or by December 10th 2006) all forms of other financial organisations would have to transform into a bank, merge with a bank or stop working. Saving-credit co-operatives that wanted to transform into a bank faced a major obstacle—in the Law on Banks (2005) it was defined that the minimal starting capital would be 10,000,000 € (in dinars),[23] and most saving-credit co-operatives were not able to provide this. The effects of this law were considerable: by late 2005 only eight credit co-operatives were still operating, and in 2008 all of them stopped working.

4 What Next for Credit Co-operatives in Serbia?

Having examined where we have come from, this chapter will conclude with a review of where we are now and some suggestions of where we might be going: the need and potential for credit co-operatives in Serbia; an innovative integrated rural co-operative system; a proposal a credit co-operative network with a central apex body; and an assessment of the remaining obstacles in Serbia to the revitalisation of credit co-operatives.

4.1 The Need and Potential for Credit Co-operatives in Serbia

The global financial crisis since 2008 (GFC) has made a difficult situation worse for the economy in Serbia, and there continues to be widespread economic concern. The effects of this are particularly visible in the rural areas. Yet even before the

[23] Article 12 Paragraph 3 Law on banks (2005).

GFC many of these problems were apparent. Bogdanov (2008: 135–140) showed that:

- Households that own farms account for 30.1 % of all Serbian households;
- The number of agricultural households living below the poverty line in 2007 was very high (36.7 %);
- Households and regions with a greater share of resources from agriculture are more at risk of vulnerability and poverty than those whose incomes derive significantly from non-agricultural sources.

Small agricultural producers lack the possibility to improve their own production with modest resources. Co-operatives and their members are finding access to credit a particular problem. It can be hard for smaller-scale enterprises to get credit at all, as they are less attractive to the banks (the potential returns are smaller, and the perceived risks higher). In addition, agricultural co-operatives do not always have the capacity to present business plans of the sophistication often required by the banks. Even when they are able to get credit, the rate of interest charged by the banks is very high.

A face-to-face survey of 150 agricultural co-operatives conducted in 2008–2009 showed that credit was one of the biggest problems for them and their members; 58 % of co-operative managers stated that better access to finance/credit would most help their co-operative society to perform better (Simmons et al. 2010). Without credit, farmers face an unhealthy reliance on 'middle men' that further squeezes their profitability. Equally importantly, they are unable to 'scale up' their businesses, either by diversifying their business activity (SIPRU 2013) or by doing more of what they were doing already. This is important. Satellite accounts research conducted by the Statistical Office of the Republic of Serbia (2011) shows that there is still a core of around 900 agricultural co-operatives that are operating successfully. This independently verifies the findings of the sample survey conducted by Simmons et al. (2010), which found that 60 % of (the 1500 registered) agricultural co-operatives in Serbia served to raise their members' incomes. Considering the very poor conditions for both co-operatives (legal and enabling environment) and farmers (e.g. no credit from the commercial banks and no ability to self-organise credit through credit co-operatives), the resilience and success of these 900 is worthy of significant scientific and policy interest. While 60 % of co-operatives feel they could do more to raise their members' incomes, 91 % recognise that they require some form of 'outside help' to do so (Simmons et al. 2010). Nevertheless, in line with their philosophy of self-help, co-operatives are not looking for any 'free handouts'. Asked what outside help their co-operative needed, managers instead identify the provision of 'reasonably-priced' loans.

Vázquez Barquero (1999) observes that successful local economic development depends on the development of economic '*hardware*' (e.g. infrastructure) and '*software*' (e.g. upgrading of human capital). Interestingly, however, Vazquez Barquero (1999) adds a third essential category; that of '*orgware*'. This refers to the organizational and institutional capacity to deliver local economic development. Elsewhere we have argued that agricultural and credit co-operatives represent a vitally important part of this 'orgware' (Simmons 2012). Internationally, agricultural co-operatives are increasingly recognised as important avenues through which small-scale rural farmers, by leveraging the power of collective action, can be linked to markets, access affordable farm inputs, increase their agricultural productivity and collectively negotiate for better terms of trade (e.g. Birchall 2010). A question remains as to how far Serbia can afford to continue to ignore these organisations if it is to encourage rural entrepreneurship.

Saving-credit co-operatives represent a legitimate response from agricultural producers to providing a favourable source of credit. Historically, these co-operatives have concentrated small amounts of extra resources and directed them towards businesses chosen by the needs of their members and not just by the expectation of profit (Birchall 2013). Despite popular sentiment to the contrary in Serbia, credit co-operatives can be an important part of Serbia's future—not just its past.

4.2 Credit Co-operatives in an Integrated Rural Co-operative System

SIPRU (2013) states that 'Economic well-being for all those engaging [only] in agriculture in Serbia cannot be achieved nowadays, and it will most certainly not be possible in the future. *Economic diversification is hence necessary*, namely diversification at the levels of village, farm and individual economics. The first step in this direction would be *to find for a village a role integrated in a specific spatial whole*. The integrated concept entails considering an area with all its potentials' (emphasis original).

Simmons (2011) has developed an integrated model for local economic and social development in rural Serbia, linking the savings and credit function of co-operatives to both (i) the productive capacity of local agriculture and/or tourism producers, and (ii) the social development capacity of separate local associations (see Fig. 3).

This model creates an upward spiral for sustainable local development, whereby the savings and credit function becomes the engine for local economic development. Co-operative businesses focus on being businesses, while the association focuses on social well-being. Community assets are owned and/or governed by the association on behalf of the community, who engage the local community in inclusive decision-making processes. Conflicts of interest can be minimised through the specification of rules that the leadership of the co-operative and association are different. This model also allows for further economic growth through the well-established co-operative practice of federation. The model has been presented to expert audiences in Serbia and internationally and has received strong support for its ability to strengthen the self-help and self-governance capacities of rural agricultural communities.

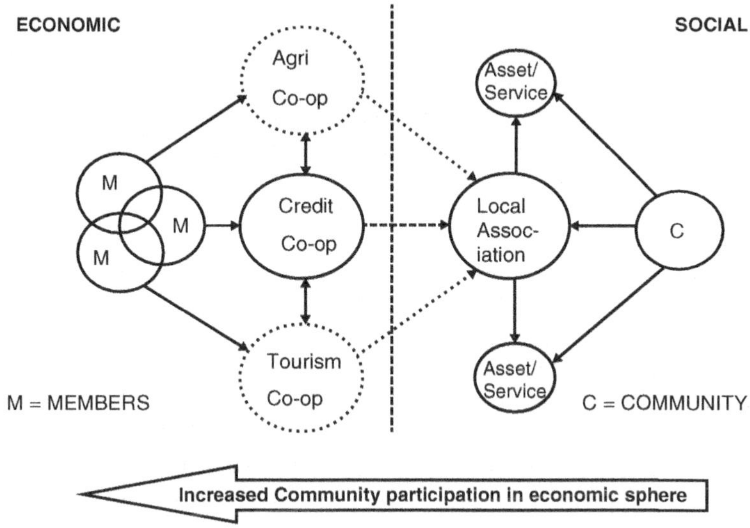

Fig. 3 A model for Credit Co-operatives in rural economic and social development in Serbia

4.3 Building a Credit Co-operative Network

In principle, it is not difficult to provide the necessary *legal and regulatory* environment for such credit co-operatives to be established. However, as we will discuss, this continues to prove a challenging proposition in Serbia. If this can be resolved, progress can be made with *technical and practical* support for setting up credit co-operatives (updating for the modern era the kind of service provided by *Agrobanka* in the late 1970s and early 1980s). This support could be provided, for example, by the development foundations of banks such as Raiffeisen or Rabobank. This would be a very positive **first step.** However, the capital that credit co-operatives are each able to raise at the local level is limited by the amounts invested by their members. While this has provided significant levels of growth in many countries, it is often insufficient to sustain a large-scale programme of co-operative support and development.

A **second step** would be to link up the credit co-operatives to a more substantial banking structure. In some countries there is a central co-operative bank. This provides access to more substantial funds by linking up the resources of the credit co-operatives and co-operative banks across the whole country. In some cases, the central co-operative bank can also raise money in other ways—for example harnessing increased flows of remittances from its diaspora, or raising money on the financial markets. Hence, while credit co-operatives are important in providing localised support in terms of savings and loans within communities—particularly agricultural communities—linking them up to this more substantial banking structure could provide the necessary answer to the problem of credit.

It would be unrealistic to establish from scratch a new central co-operative bank with the necessary reach across Serbia. A tentative solution would be to use an existing bank to provide full-scale banking facilities to smaller-scale credit co-operatives. In this model, deposits taken by the credit co-operative are held in a ring-fenced account at the bank. If the bank collapses, the credit unions' money is therefore safe. The advantage is that the Bank can provide the credit co-operatives with the ability to conduct more complex financial transactions, including clearing services and foreign exchange payments. Another advantage is that the bank would be able to administer and supervise the on-lending of capital from external sources directly via its network of credit union and rural co-operative bank accounts. Small loans, of the kind that are so necessary to the co-operative sector and yet so unattractive to the big banks, could then be approved and serviced effectively by credit co-operatives.

Until recently, *Agrobanka* had suggested itself as well placed to play this role nationally. Its on-the-ground knowledge from its branch network from Vojvodina right down to the South, would have been a real advantage in knowing the markets in which co-operatives work. When the above ideas were tentatively explored with the bank in 2010, there was also a keen interest at Board level. Sadly, *Agrobanka* went into administration in December 2011 following financial irregularities. Other candidates now need to be explored for this role.

4.4 Remaining Obstacles for Saving-Credit Co-operatives in Serbia

There remain two important obstacles to the revitalisation of saving-credit services in Serbia. First, agricultural co-operatives are not currently in a solid economic position, primarily because of unsolved ownership issues (Ševarlić 2006). The improvement of agricultural co-operatives is also dependent on greater specialisation of production and expanding the scope of work into processing industry within the co-operative movement. Therefore, in general we do not recommend re-establishing saving-credit services as a part of agricultural co-operatives, especially in view of the human resource skills and capacities available in them. Ideally, agricultural co-operatives should be focused on their main activity. Hence, it would be more efficient to revive saving-credit co-operatives as separate legal entities. This said, the local context is important. There are some excellent examples of existing agricultural co-operatives where trust and human capabilities are high. The co-location of saving-credit services in these co-operatives may well be a good solution, at least in the short term.

Second, in today's legal environment, revitalisation of saving-credit co-operatives and saving-credit services in other types of co-operatives would be in contradiction of the Law on Banks (2005). The legal environment is currently the most important obstacle in this process. The Law on Co-operatives from 1996 was created and enacted in a different socio-political environment. However, starting from 2002 several draft laws on co-operatives have been presented. Only recently has a new law been enacted and it changes very little in relation to the credit co-operatives. Regular changes of government have hindered any significant change, and this situation continues to be hampered by a lack of political will.

The status of saving-credit co-operatives has changed in the seven draft laws on co-operatives that have been created in the previous 8 years. The first, widely recognised as a good step forward, was the *Draft Law on Co-operatives* from 2002, created by the Federal Ministry of Economy and Domestic Trade. Prof. Hagen Henry, a leading expert in co-operative legislation, participated in the preparation of this draft. The special status of saving-credit co-operatives in this document is indicated in three ways:

- *First*, the foundation and business of these co-operatives is regulated more severely than other types of co-operative, for example through territorial limitation in line with the Raiffeisen principles traditionally applied in credit co-operatives in Serbia.
- *Second*, there is provision that saving-credit co-operatives must be founded by at least 30 private persons capable for business and two legal entities of which one has to be co-operative.[24] This means that more founders are required for saving-credit co-operatives—since other types of co-operatives can be founded by ten persons.
- *Third*, starting capital for saving-credit co-operatives is defined as a minimum of 10,000 US$ (in dinars), while for other types of co-operative starting capital is define as a minimum of 2000 US$ (in dinars by banking rate on the day of payment).[25]

In 2004, the Co-operative Union of Vojvodina presented a *Draft Law on Agricultural Co-operatives*. Although this was a special law by focus (i.e. it was created only for agricultural co-operatives), this draft is also significant because it stated that agricultural co-operatives can, beside their main activity, be engaged in saving-credit business for their members.[26]

As administrative and ministerial responsibilities changed, further new draft laws were presented in 2005 and 2006. The co-operative sector directed severe criticisms at these documents and among them was the fact that saving-credit co-operatives were excluded. In 2009 a new working group was created under the management of the Ministry of Economy and Regional Development. Its task was to create new draft law on co-operatives. In its first version, credit cooperatives were listed as one of the types of cooperatives that could exist. However, a later revision made some severe changes, and it was not clear if credit cooperatives would keep their position. Again, this draft law was not enacted before a change of government terminated the process.

[24] Article 10 Paragraph 4 Draft law on cooperatives (2002).

[25] Article 52 Paragraphs 2 and 3 Draft law on cooperatives (2002).

[26] Article 3 Paragraph 3 Draft law on agricultural cooperatives (2004).

During 2012 and early 2013 the latest version of draft law on cooperatives was presented to the public. Article 11 of the draft law listed all the types of cooperatives regulated by this document, including agricultural, housing, consumer, social, youth co-operatives and so on. However, credit cooperatives were conspicuously absent. In this way, the position of saving-credit co-operatives in recent drafts did not raise much hope that this form of co-operative was likely to be revived. This was confirmed when the new law of 2015 was enacted.

5 Conclusion

Saving-credit co-operatives are the oldest form of co-operative in Serbia. In the early stage of their foundation and development, these co-operatives were dominantly connected with agriculture—since there was a significant lack of capital—collecting small savings and free resources and directing them in favourable loans to 'good risks' in their community. From the end of the Second World War their position almost continuously deteriorated, except for a short period of renaissance in the early 1980s. Their position does not appear to have moved forward since Sljukic (2002: 201) observed that: 'The co-operative movement remains relatively weak, fragile and exposed to the will of much stronger actors: large commercial companies, agro-industrial companies and large landowners, (all of whom) have established links with the new political elite in order to preserve their dominant position'.

Yet nowadays it is hard to find a country in which there is both (i) such a reliance on agricultural production and (ii) an agrarian structure where small individual farms dominate (as is the case in rural Serbia) where there are no saving-credit cooperatives. The legal environment in Serbia does not allow the existence of saving-credit co-operatives and restrains other types of co-operatives from collecting savings and granting loans. This gives a monopoly to the private commercial banks in these activities, and yet these banks have little interest in serving this sector of the market. The non-existence of saving-credit co-operatives therefore results in both a diminished agricultural community and an emaciated co-operative sector, since small farmers and members of other types of co-operatives have no viable sources of credit for expanding their production. They are forced to apply to a banking sector which is almost completely unwilling to work with them or their co-operative organisations. There are strong but uncoordinated appeals from co-operative organisations, regional unions and co-operative supporters for the revival of saving-credit co-operatives. Despite this apparent necessity, saving-credit co-operatives have not returned in the new law on co-operatives that has been enacted.

This paper asserts that this situation should be kept under urgent review. It is often said about co-operatives that if they did not exist they would have to be invented (Birchall 2004). Serbia is now in a position where credit co-operatives do not exist, but it can be persuasively argued that they need to be reinvented for the modern era. Today's economic conditions in the rural areas have many similarities with those of the heyday of agricultural co-operatives in the early twentieth century. We now have the benefit of more than 150 years of international experience and considerable scientific enquiry into 'what works' upon which to draw in building a modern and effective co-operative sector. The possibilities for this are exciting. Moreover, the emphasis on self-help behind this development is in perfect tune with an economic situation in which the market is too busy rebuilding its balance sheets and the state lacks sufficient financial resources to act. All can contribute to putting Serbia's resources (human, land, capital) back to work and start to increase productivity. In this way, SIPRU's (2013) vision of a new future for rural Serbia might very well include a new future for credit co-operatives.

References

Agrobanka (2001) Concept of revitalisation of co-operative savings and crediting farmers. Agricultural bank Agrobanka A.D, Belgrade

Aleksic V (2012) Belgrade cooperative and its role in economic development of Serbia from the late 19th to early 20th Century. Journal Bankarstvo 6:108–133

Birchall J (2004) Co-operatives and the millennium development goals. ILO, Geneva

Birchall J (2010) People-centred businesses. Palgrave, Basingstoke

Birchall J (2013) Finance in an age of austerity: the power of customer-owned banks. Edward Elgar, Cheltenham

Bogdanov N (2008) Living standards measurement study, Serbia 2002–2007(Agriculture). Statistical Office of the Republic of Serbia, Belgrade, pp 133–152

Co-operative Union of Yugoslavia (2005) Century and a half of co-operative movement. Co-operative Union of Yugoslavia, Belgrade

Jovančić B (1991) Co-operative for credit and savings in Niš from 1849 till 1910. Journal Ekonomika 1:59–66

Kišgeci J, Vitez M (1994) Social-economic conditions of foundation and characteristics of first co-operatives in Vojvodina—co-operatives of Serbs and Slovakians. In: 100 years of agricultural co-operative movement in Serbia. Co-operative Union of Serbia, Belgrade, pp 19–27

Law on Agricultural and Handicraft Co-operatives (1898) Special edition, Niš

Law on Banks (2005) Official Journal RS, number 107/05

Law on Banks and other Financial Organisations (1993) Official Journal SRJ, number 32/93, 61/95, 44/99 and 36/02 and Official Journal RS, number 72/03 and 61/05

Law on Commercial Co-operatives (1937) Official Journal of Kingdom of Yugoslavia 217: LXII

Law on Co-operatives (1996) Official Journal SRJ, number 41/96, 12/98 and Official Journal RS, number 101/2005

Law on Saving-Credit Organisation and Business with Saving Deposits (1977) Official Journal SRS, number 53/77, 9/78, 66/81 and 18/88

Mandić S (1994) Significance of saving-credit co-operatives and services for work of consumer co-operatives. Journal Nova trgovina 9–10:56–57

Marković V (1998) Cooperation and connection of consumer and saving-credit co-operatives. Journal Nova trgovina 5–6:60–62

Mrksic D (1987) Srednji slojevi u Jugoslaviji. IIC SSO, Belgrade

Nikolic M (2009) Evolution of cooperative legislation in Europe. The Serbian Association of Agricultural Economics, Belgrade

Pantić V, Nikolov N (1994) Credit agricultural co-operative in Vranovo. In: 100 years of agricultural co-operative movement in Serbia. Co-operative Union of Serbia, Belgrade, pp 202–205

Pavlović M (1994) Serbian agricultural co-operative movement in Kingdom of Yugoslavia (1918–1941). In: 100 years of agricultural co-operative movement in Serbia. Co-operative Union of Serbia, Belgrade, pp 30–47

Ranđelović V (1999) Co-operative movement and agricultural co-operatives. Faculty of Agriculture and Co-operative Union of Serbia, Belgrade

Ševarlić M (2006) Breakdown of collective ownership. http://www.politika.co.yu/rubrike/Ekonomija/t1458.sr.html Date of last review 02.03.2010

Simmons R (2011) Co-operatives and rural economic and social development in Serbia. Paper to ICA global research conference 'new opportunities for co-operatives', Mikkeli, Finland, 24–27 Aug

Simmons R (2012) Economic and social development in Rural Serbia: the role of agricultural co-operatives. Background Report for Serbian Ministry of Agriculture, World Bank-funded project for a National Strategy for Agricultural Co-operatives

Simmons R, Ševarlić M, Nikolic M (2010) The role and potential of co-operatives for poverty reduction and local economic development in Serbia [Роль и Потенциал КооПеРативов в СоКРащении БедноСти и Развитии МеСтной ЭКоноМиКи в СеРБии] Business. Education. Rights. BULLETIN Volgograd Institute, 2011, № 1 (14) (in English and Russian)

SIPRU (Social Inclusion and Poverty Reduction Unit) (2013) The future of rural Serbia. SIPRU, Belgrade

Sljukic S (2002) Sociological aspects of peasant co-operation in post-socialist Romania. NEC Yearbook 2001–2002. New Europe College, Buchares

Statistical Office of the Republic of Serbia (2011) Satellite accounts for cooperative economy of the Republic of Serbia. Statistical Office of the Republic of Serbia, Belgrade

Vázquez Barquero A (1999) Desarrollo, redes y innovación: lecciones sobre desarrollo endógeno. Pirámide, Madrid

Vuckovic M (1957) Cooperative movement. Zadruzna stampa, Belgrade

Zakić Z (2000) Coop-management. Dunav grupa, Dunav preving a.d., Belgrade

Credit Co-operatives in Slovakia

Elena Šúbertová

Abstract Nowadays approximately half a million (approximately 9 %) people in the Slovak Republic are individual members of a co-operative. According to their specialization the co-operatives are divided into agricultural, production, consumer or housing co-operatives. They are associated in the Co-operative Union of the Slovak Republic. It is a pity that our current legislation does not allow to set up credit co-operatives. It was in Slovakia where the first credit co-operative in the world was established.

The first organization operating on co-operative principles was founded by Samuel Jurkovič in the village of Sobotište on February 9th, 1845. The first co-operative in Slovakia, and simultaneously first credit co-operative in the world was called "Spolok gazdovský" (Farmers' Unit).

1 The Developmental Stages of Credit Co-operatives in Slovakia

The development of credit co-operatives in Slovakia was not straightforward; it was complicated and can be divided into several main stages:

1.1 The Beginnings of Credit Co-operatives in Slovakia

In the first stage, which began by setting up co-operatives in our country and ended by World War I, the process of setting up co-operatives began in the country as well as activities of people to solve poor economic and social conditions. The establishment of the first credit co-operative in the world, and the first co-operative in

This scientific contribution was prepared within the project VEGA number 1/0709/15, of the Ministry of Education of the Slovak Republic under the title "The Evaluation of the of Efficiency of Funding the Projects Aimed at Support of Development of Newly Established Small and Medium-sized Enterprises in the Slovak Republic".

E. Šúbertová
Faculty of Business Management, University of Economics in Bratislava, Bratislava, Slovakia
e-mail: elena.subertova@euba.sk; subertova@gmail.com

S. Karafolas (ed.), *Credit Cooperative Institutions in European Countries*, Contributions to Economics, DOI 10.1007/978-3-319-28784-3_22

Table 1 The developmental stages of credit co-operatives in Slovakia

Period	Stage	Years	Characteristic
1st stage	Early co-operatives	1845–1918	Formation of credit co-operatives
2nd stage	Development of co-operatives	1919–1948	Development of credit co-operatives and establishment of farmers' common treasuries
3rd stage	Deformation of co-operatives	1949–1989	Socialist period, gradual disappearance of credit co-operatives and farmers common treasuries
4th stage	Transformation of co-operatives	1990–1992	Transformation of collective co-operatives into co-operatives of individual members
5th stage	Operation of co-operatives under the Commercial Code	1993–up to now	Activities of four main types of co-operatives, discussions on setting up credit co-operatives, setting up non banks

Reference: author

Slovakia by Samuel Jurkovič was the most important event of the first stage (Table 1).

The life of Samuel Jurkovič, the founder of Slovak co-operatives, as well as the foundation of the first co-operative in the Slovak territory can be briefly outlined as follows:

Samuel Jurkovič was born on February 9th, 1796 in a peasant family in Brezová pod Bradlom. After he had graduated from secondary school, he decided to study theology in Bratislava. As he was not awarded a scholarship, he accepted a post of teacher in Nové Mesto nad Váhom where he also worked as a notary. From July 1817 to August 1831, Jurkovič worked in Nové Mesto nad Váhom. As a teacher he liked studying new and interesting things.

The Lutheran Church in Sobotište offered him the post of teacher. At the same time Jurkovič also worked as a notary to be able to support his family. Gradually, in daily contacts with people, he concluded that people needed both spiritual and material support. The lack of money was causing an increase in poverty, especially during the years of scarcity and famine. At that time, the official interest rate was 6 %. However, loans were provided only by individuals, such as publicans, at usurious interests of about 50 % a year. Therefore, Jurkovič considered the possibility of establishing financial institutions similar to savings banks. The savings banks at that time demanded, in accordance with the so-called Commercial Act XVIII of 1840, as many as 30,000 guilders of subscriber principal. It was impossible for inhabitants of a small town such as Sobotište to obtain such amount. So, Jurkovič wanted to set up an organization—a co-operative more accessible to the poor and he started *'Spolok gazdovsky'* (*Farmers' Association*). He prepared a draft proposal for statutes and submitted it to the local citizens for approval.

The co-operative was based on principles of self-help and reciprocity. The aim of the co-operative was not to make a profit, it only used to co-ordinate deposits and loans for those who were interested in them. Under the proposed statutes, the financial means of the co-operative were to be obtained by regular weekly deposits, the interest on loans were to be 6 %. The basic amount when joining the co-operative was 30 guilders and each member deposited three guilders every Sunday. All members deposited the same amount and they adopted the principle that one member had one vote. The interest rate on deposits was also 6 %. The task of the co-operative was to receive regular deposits from its members and if necessary to assist them financially. It kept records of all financial transactions in the accounts as well as in membership cards. The co-operative was characterized by joint liability of all members. The association could also accept as their members the citizens from other villages.

On the day of Jurkovič's 49th birthday, on February 9th, 1845, 'Spolok gazdovsky (Farmers' Unit)' was founded. It had 12 founder members. Within a year the membership increased to 60 members. Under the statutes of the co-operative the membership was limited to 6 years. The co-operative was founded in the period of feudalism in Slovakia; however, the revolutionary years of 1848–1849 came soon. Jurkovič had to hide because of his national beliefs and activities. After 3 year of its existence the co-operative had 600 guilders in silver in the treasury.

The credit co-operative in Sobotište existed for 6 years until January 28th, 1851 and then it was revoked under the statutes.

After that Jurkovič worked as an official in Vrbovice and Turá Lúka where he organized various cultural events. Samuel Jurkovič died on July 13th, 1873. However, the development of co-operatives did not stop after his death.

Based on the model of Sobotište other credit co-operatives were founded by villages and towns, such as Vrbovce in 1845, Myjava, Brezová pod Bradlom, Mošovce, Blatnica, Važec, Brezno, Tisovec a Nový Sad in 1846 and Vrbice, Ratková, Revúca etc. in 1847.

In the first stage, the special law regulated the activity of co-operatives. In Slovakia Hungarian Act No XXXVII/1875 influenced the legislation on co-operatives.

At the beginning the credit co-operatives met the financial needs of capital-poor agricultural enterprises and tradesmen in small, short-term credit amounts at favourable or zero interest rates. Number of Credit co-operatives (of the Central Co-operative) in Slovakia from 1894 to 1918 is in Chart 1.

The common feature of the co-operatives in Europe is merging into co-operative unions and thereby accumulating their financial resources.

Together with creating unions the co-operative central treasuries were founded that were gradually transformed into universal banks and their activity was governed by co-operative banks acts.

Number of members of Credit co-operatives (of the Central Co-operative) in Slovakia from 1894 to 1918 is in Chart 2.

Chart 1 Number of Credit co-operatives (of the Central Co-operative) in Slovakia from 1894 to 1918. Collective (1995)

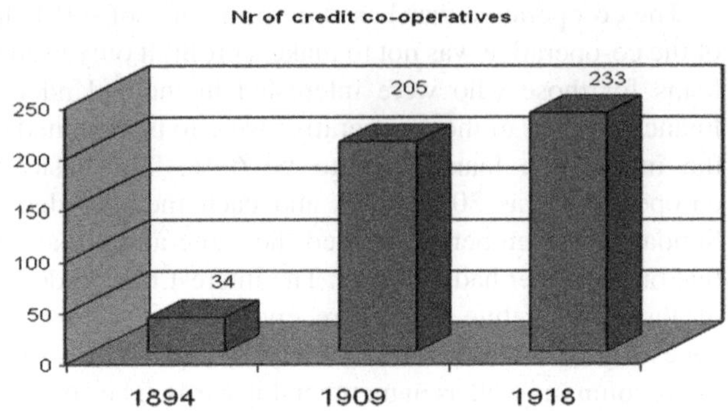

Chart 2 Number of members of Credit co-operatives (of the Central Co-operative) in Slovakia from 1894 to 1918. Collective (1995)

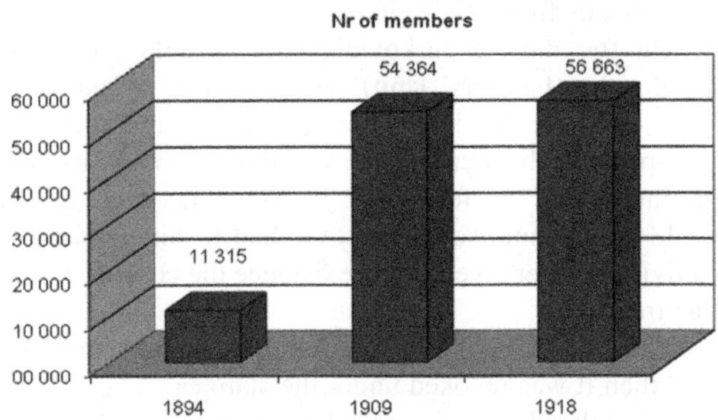

1.2 *Development of Credit Co-operatives in Slovakia*

In the second stage, mainly after World War I, the co-operatives represented a strong movement in Slovakia when 997 co-operatives joined the so-called Central Co-operative (co-operative headquarters).

That strong movement was not united and divided into:

- *Credit co-operatives, and*
- *Farmers' Financial Co-operatives.*

Number of Credit co-operatives (of the Central Co-operative) in Slovakia from 1936 to 1947 is in Chart 3.

Since Samuel Jurkovič's era the co-operatives used to be founded from the bottom by their members while the peasants' mutual treasuries used to be founded from the top, i.e. firstly they founded the Union of Farmers' Common Treasuries and after that farmers' common treasuries themselves. Both types of co-operatives provided available economic and personal loans at a low interest rate on the principle of reciprocity, under common control, quickly, without bureaucracy. The credit co-operatives underwent dynamic development since their inception. Number of members of Credit co-operatives (of the Central Co-operative) in Slovakia from 1936 to 1947 is in Chart 4.

Chart 3 Number of Credit co-operatives (of the Central Co-operative) in Slovakia from 1936 to 1947. Collective (1992)

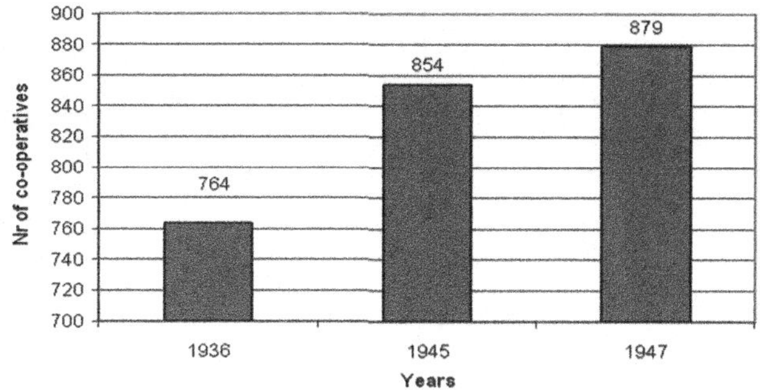

Chart 4 Number of members of Credit co-operatives (of the Central Co-operative) in Slovakia from 1936 to 1947. Collective (1992)

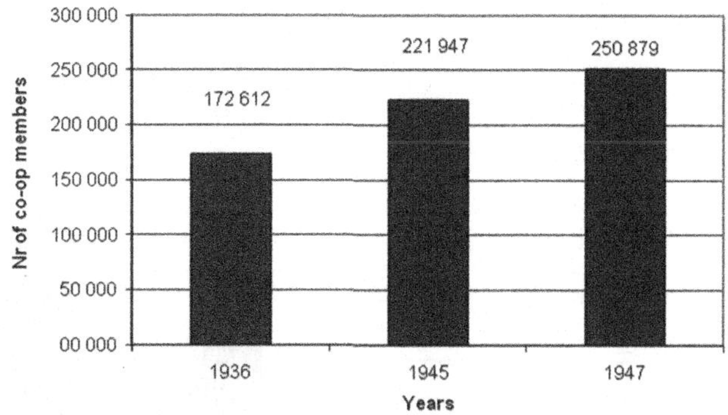

Further the peasants' mutual treasuries were developing from the interwar period in twentieth century to 1947. For example the peasants' mutual treasuries reached the amount of 562,809,910 Slovak crowns from 100,047 depositors in 1936. They granted loans amounting to 481,851,242, their net profit was 839,344 Slovak crowns. Farmers' Financial Co-operatives (FFC) in Slovakia in the period 1924–1947 is in Chart 5.

World War II affected badly the development of co-operatives in Slovakia by reducing the number of workers and lack of capital. After the war, the boom of co-operatives began again.

After World War II there were 912 financial co-operatives with 342,237 members and until 1947 the number of Farmers' Financial Co-operatives increased to 957 with 439,432 members (Charts 5 and 6).

The aims and forms of credit co-operatives were changed after 1945 with regard to extent of provided service and introduction of cashless payment. The professional bank officials began to work in those co-operatives.

The structure of Credit co-operatives in Slovakia in 1947 is in Charts 7 and 8.

The disunity of co-operatives also resulted from other problems in the Slovak territory (national, political problems) see Table 2.

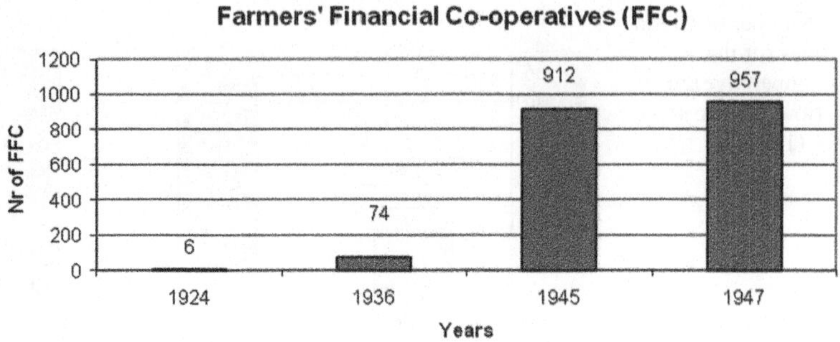

Chart 5 Farmers' Financial Co-operatives (FFC) in Slovakia in the period 1924–1947. Collective (1995)

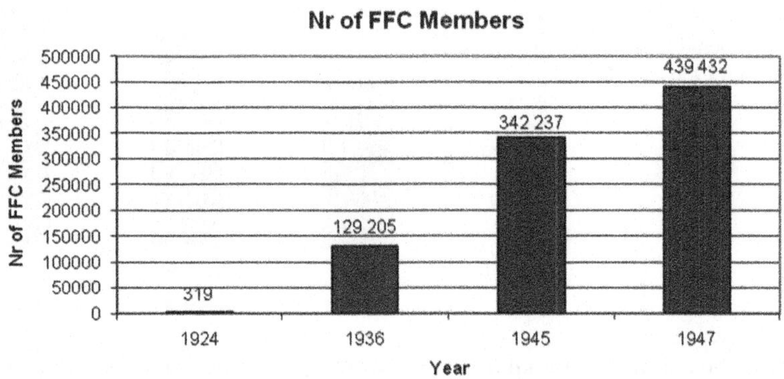

Chart 6 Farmers' Financial Co-operatives Members in Slovakia in the period 1924–1947. Collective (1995)

1.3 *Deformation of Credit Co-operatives in Slovakia*

In the third stage, after 1948, especially since 1949 the co-operatives were seen as a semi-private form of business that would merge gradually with the state sector. In the middle of twentieth century *there was an attempt from the state to distort co-operatives, and later to control them by various regulations or orders* (e.g. entry into co-operatives not on a voluntary basis, or liquidation of credit and trade co-operatives, etc.). The regulation of co-operatives was realized through the Uniform Agricultural Co-operatives Act No. 69/1949 Zb., under which 'the collectivisation' was implemented in the former Czechoslovak Republic. The Act on Co-operatives was passed for non-agricultural co-operatives as late as in the mid fifties.

The financial means of the co-operatives were transferred to the Postal Bank and Slovak Savings Bank.

Chart 7 Structure of Credit co-operatives in Slovakia in 1947. *Source*: Šúbertová (2004)

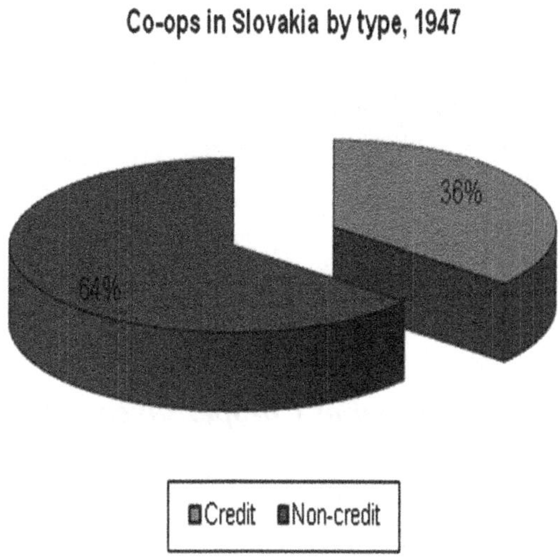

Source: Šúbertová,E., 2004 „Družstevníctvo v procese globalizácie", KARTPRINT Bratislava, ISBN 80-88870-34-8, p. 17

Chart 8 Structure of members Credit co-ops in Slovakia in 1947. *Source*: Šúbertová (2004)

Source: Šúbertová,E., 2004 „Družstevníctvo v procese globalizácie", KARTPRINT Bratislava, ISBN 80-88870-34-8, p. 17

Table 2 Co-operative enterprises from 1945 to 1947

Co-operatives	Year	Number of co-operatives	Number of members
Credit	1945	912	342,237
	1947	957	439,432
Not-for credit	1945	1339	263,587
	1947	1704	373,819
Total	1945	2251	716,056
	1947	2661	813,251

Šúbertová (2004)

1.4 Transformation of Co-operatives in Slovakia

In the fourth stage, after 'the velvet revolution' in 1989, the co-operatives were blamed for not having a place in the market economy because they were relics of socialism. However, they were the co-operatives that began to get rid of various deformations of the previous period.

In this stage, *the co-operatives were transformed* from collectivist enterprises into *shareholding co-operatives,* i.e. *private companies.* The transformation was realized under the so-called transformation act into business partnerships in accordance with the Commercial Code.

At the beginning of 1990 the co-operatives held new democratic elections to all co-operatives bodies. The Acts No 162/1990 Zb. 'On Agricultural Co-operatives' and No 176/1990 Zb. 'On Housing, Consumer, Production and Other Co-operatives', which were adopted in April 1990, became the basis for removal of legislative barriers. Under the above acts the co-operatives became equal and independent of the state, on the basis of their own new statutes approved democratically by all members of the co-operative.

The following adopted laws contributed to the maintenance and development of co-operatives in the early 1990s:

- Constitutional Law No 100/1990 Zb, and
- Constitutional Charter of Civil Rights and Freedoms of 1991.

The above-mentioned laws recognized the equality of all forms of ownership, including co-operative ownership.

2 Present Operation of Co-operatives Under the Commercial Code

The following acts were extremely important for development of co-operatives from a legal standpoint:

(a) ***Act No 513/1991 Zb. Commercial Code***. The Commercial Code regulated legal relationships and internal organization of co-operatives in order to conform to internationally recognized principles and values of co-operatives as well as to the standard of European co-operatives. ***The nineteenth amendment to the Commercial Code No 530/2003 is effective from February 1st, 2004*** and articles 221–260 of the given Act refer to co-operatives (Mačerinskienė and Šúbertová 2008).
(b) ***Act No 42/1992 Zb on the adjustment of property relations and settlement of property claims of co-operatives, the so-called transformation act.*** The Transformation Act was passed by the Federal Assembly of CSFR on 30th November 1991 and published in the Collection of Laws on February 28th, 1992. The given act ***was only a temporary legislative measure with limited effect in one year since its publication in the Collection of Laws.*** So the co-operatives in accordance with the transformation act were obliged to transform themselves into companies under the Commercial Code within a year. It was necessary to take an inventory of property and its valuation, make a list of beneficiaries, prepare and approve the transformation project, determine the equity shares for beneficiaries, adopt the co-operative statutes in accordance with the Commercial Code. Under the transformation act a beneficiary was a person that put assets into a co-operative and had not been settled yet or a person that was employed in the co-operative on the date of approval of the act (November 30th, 1991).
(c) ***Act No 182/1993 Zb. 'on ownership of flats and business premises governing the transfer of flats and business premises in the ownership' and Act No 151/1995 Z.z.*** as amended.
(d) ***Act No 264/1995 Z.z.' amendment to the so-called transformation act'*** that referred only to transformed agricultural co-operatives. The Commercial Code as a generally binding legal regulation became a legal basis for transformation of co-operatives, which amended the Act on the adjustment of property relations and settlement of property claims in co-operatives, i.e. 'transformation act'.

In accordance with the Commercial Code ***'The co-operative is a society with an open number of members established for the purpose of doing business or ensuring economic, social and other needs of its members'.***

It means that the main motive for joining the co-operative is to ensure its members' their needs not to make profits (Hesková et al. 2008).

The co-operative ought to be in accordance with co-operative principles and unlike the other societies it ought to be **an open society**. In other words, during its existence, the members can join or leave it according to their needs. The co-operative ought to have at least five members—individuals. This does not apply if there are at least two legal entities as its members (For joint-stock companies—one legal entity, for limited companies—the founder can be either one physical or legal entity).

To set up a co-operative it is necessary to conduct an inaugural meeting which:

1. **Determines the amount of subscribed capital (a minimum of EUR 1250)**
2. **Approves the statutes that have to contain:**
   - Co-operative name and address
   - Business activities
   - Establishment and termination of membership, rights and responsibilities of members to the co-operative
   - Amount of basic membership contribution, or amount of capital and method of payments of the membership contribution and settlement of shares after dissolution of the co-operative
   - Co-operative bodies, number of its members, the length of tenure, way of their appointment, convening for meetings
   - How to use profits and how to cover possible losses
   - Creation and use of indivisible fund
   - Other provisions.

3 The Inaugural Meeting Elects the Co-operative Bodies: The Board and Control Commission

The Membership Meeting is the Highest Authority of the Co-operative In small co-operatives (up to 50 members) the board and control commission can be replaced by membership meeting.

The membership meeting is held at least once a year. Under the Commercial Code all questions can be decided by more than half number of present members and for approval the majority of present voters is required.

The act of voting shall apply ***the membership principle,*** **i.e.** ***one vote per member*** if the statutes do not determine otherwise.

The Board is the Statutory Body of the Co-operative The board implements the resolutions of the membership meeting and is accountable to it for its activities. The boards meet if necessary. ***It elects the president*** (director) or vice-president unless they are elected by the membership meeting. *The president* manages and organizes the co-operative activities under the statutes; he or she chairs the board meetings and represents the co-operative outside.

The Control Commission Supervises Activities of the Co-operative and Handles Complaints of the Co-operative Members It comments on annual accounts. It reports to the membership meeting. It has at least three members; it also elects its own president. The board members cannot be members of the control commissions. The two posts are incompatible.

Chart 9 Co-operative enterprises (agricultural, production, housing, consumer) in Slovakia from 1990 to 2010. Šúbertová (2001), The Co-operative Union of the Slovak Republic (2011), own calculations

Co-operative enterprises (agricultural, production, housing, and consumer) in Slovakia from 1990 to 2010 are in Chart 9.

At present, there are no credit co-operatives in Slovakia as there is no legislation allowing their existence (see Chart 9).

The Bank Act does not allow the operation of credit co-operatives; it only allows banks in the form of joint stock companies. But there is a draft of 'Act on savings and credit co-operatives', which was prepared by experts in the field of law and co-operatives as well as by AXA, a.s. Bratislava—a company that is oriented towards the development, projecting and supply of bank information systems.

Under the Commercial Code 513/1991 Zb as amended and under Act No 566/2001 Z.z. on securities and investment services there were several no-banks like co-operatives, however, investment services were provided by other companies (e.g. Capital Invest, stockbroker, a.s. for the Shareholding co-operative Slovenské investície) under the Act on portfolio of securities management. They provided the following investment services:

I. **Main investment services:**

- Accepting a client's orders for buying or selling or other dealings with investment tools,
- Accepting client's orders for buying or selling of investment tools and its realization to the account different from the service provider's account,
- Accepting client's orders for buying or selling investment tools and its realization to their own account.

II. **Ancillary investment services:**

- Safekeeping and administration of one or several investment tools,
- Providing loans or credits to clients for purposes of realization of client's orders for buying or selling investment tools. As providers of loans and credits they are trade participants,
- Ensuring the issuance of securities for issuers and services relating to underwriting, placement, paying incomes and repaying investment tools,
- Advisory activities referring to investment into investment tools.

There were various subjects that had been operating as *unlicensed non-banks* in the financial market in the Slovak Republic. They collected about a billion Slovak crowns from Slovak inhabitants (also in foreign currencies, e.g. USD). The above-mentioned "*Podielové družstvo Slovenské investície*" operated as a subject of the financial market. It provided loans and simultaneously purchased financial means from inhabitants. The basic contribution of a member amounted to SKK 14,000 (USD 300, EUR 330). The highest member shares reached as many as 15.22 % in 2001, later 14 % p.a.

One disadvantage of these subjects is that the deposits from citizens are not protected (Deposit Protection Fund) like in the licensed banks. So the non-banks disappeared rather quickly. They ceased to exist because people lost confidence in non-banks after collapse of the first such co-operatives.

4 Conclusions

During the present economic crisis the co-operatives that will react flexibly and actively to the needs of co-operative members and growing consumer needs will be successful. The collaboration ought to be developed on principles of reciprocity not only within the frames of one co-operative on the local level in production of goods and provision of services, but also in *provision of credit services in the co-operatives.* These co-operatives have their positives and negatives.

The advantages of credit co-operatives include:

- Lower interest rates,
- Availability of loans for lower and middle classes,
- Possibility to support small and medium-sized enterprises.

The disadvantages include:

- The accumulation of funds depends on the number of co-operative members,
- Some problems with providing long-term loans,
- Higher overhead compared to other types of co-operatives.

The credit co-operatives in Slovakia were successful in the past and became models for formation of co-operatives in the world. It is a paradox that Slovakia, which was the first country with credit co-operatives in the world, has not adopted the relevant legislation allowing the establishment of credit co-operatives again and thereby encourages the economic development in the Slovak country.

References

Collective (1992) Vývoj družstevnictví na území ČSFR. Družstevní unie Praha, pp 206–212

Collective (1995) 150 years of Slovak co-operatives. Družstevná únia SR, VOPD Prúdy Bratislava, pp 8–18, ISBN 80-85355-22-1

Hesková M, Pícha K, Šúbertová E (2008) Evropská družstva: vzdělávání a výchova. Profess Consulting, Zeleneč, pp 9–10

Mačerinskiené I, Šúbertová E (2008) Present role of development co-operative society in Lithuania and in the Slovak Republic. In Podnikanie a konkurencieschopnosť firiem: zborník z medzinárodnej vedeckej konferencie. Katedra podnikovohospodárska FPM EU, Bratislava, pp 257–263

Šúbertová E (2001) Družstevné podnikanie v treťom tisícročí. KARTPRINT, Bratislava, p 24, 41. ISBN 80-88870-20-8

Šúbertová E (2004) Družstevníctvo v procese globalizácie. KARTPRINT, Bratislava, p 17. ISBN 80-88870-34-8

The Co-operative Union of the Slovak Republic (2011) "Internal papers" of Družstevná únia SR, Bratislava. http://www.dusr.sk/download/dokumenty/DU_SR_novinky_2012.pdf. Accessed 20 Feb 2012

From Credit Cooperatives to Cooperative Bank in Slovenia

Franci Avsec

Abstract The cooperative movement in Slovenia began with credit cooperatives which successfully solved the indebtedness problem of numerous farmers in the second half of the nineteenth century. In the period between the two world wars, the cooperative movement was divided according to political lines and was seriously affected by the economic depression in the 1930s. After the Second World War, all credit cooperatives were administratively wound up and never resumed their activity as grass root organisations. Their mission was continued for a very short period by the second level cooperatives of agricultural cooperatives in the 1950s, and after another break, lasting one decade, by the savings and loan services of agricultural cooperatives. Since the banks were permitted to carry out a wider range of banking services than savings and loan services, these services, their Union and agricultural and forestry cooperatives founded the *Slovenska zadružna kmetijska banka d.d.* (Slovenian Agricultural Cooperative Bank Ltd) in 1990. In the view of Slovenia's adhesion to the European Union, stricter banking legislation standards were implemented and nearly all savings and loan services transferred their banking activity and assets to the Slovenian Agricultural Cooperative Bank Ltd which had been meanwhile renamed as *Deželna banka Slovenije d.d.* (Country Bank of Slovenia Ltd). In return, the former Union of savings and loan services which transformed itself into a cooperative named *Kapitalska zadruga*, became the largest shareholder of Deželna banka Slovenije Ltd.

1 Introduction

The cooperative movement in Slovenia has a long history with many ups and downs. The development of credit cooperatives is probably the most interesting story of the movement and can be roughly divided into three periods.

F. Avsec
Cooperative Union of Slovenia, Ljubljana, Slovenia
e-mail: franci.avsec@siol.net

S. Karafolas (ed.), *Credit Cooperative Institutions in European Countries*, Contributions to Economics, DOI 10.1007/978-3-319-28784-3_23

The first and the longest period in which the credit cooperatives represented the backbone of the whole cooperative movement, began in the second half of the nineteenth century, when credit and other cooperatives, firstly organised after the Schulze Delitzsch model and then after the Raiffeisen model spread across the whole ethnic territory, enabling the access of farmers, craftsmen, and workers to credit and other services. Paradoxically, as cooperatives had saved numerous farmers from usury at the end of the nineteenth century, the economic crisis in the 1930s imposed governmental protection of farmers in relation towards their creditors who were, inter alia, also credit cooperatives as one of the main credit suppliers of farmers so that they could only gradually resume their activity. During the Second World War, the activity of credit cooperatives and their central institutions was practically blocked due to the war operations and destruction.

The second period began after the Second World War and ended with the gaining of independence of Slovenia. At the beginning of this period, credit cooperatives were administratively wound up and never resumed their activity as genuine grass root cooperatives with individuals as members. Cooperatives were assigned a role of associating and gradual transforming of private small scale production, especially in agriculture. Since private farmers owned the major part of agricultural land and forests, farmers' supply and marketing cooperatives became the most numerous and economically important cooperatives.

After the introduction of a more liberal self-management system and so called social ownership at the beginning of the 1950s, the credit cooperatives, i.e. cooperative savings and loan associations emerged as the second degree cooperatives to which agricultural and forestry cooperatives were affiliated, but only for a few years. They were soon administratively merged with the municipal banks.

After the agricultural policy assumed a more friendly position towards private farmers at the end of the 1960s, Slovenia adopted the first Act relating to the so called savings and loan services of agricultural cooperatives. In the following two decades agricultural cooperatives and their savings and loan services, with the important support of the government, contributed to the modernisation of private farms, although still within the limits provided for private property in agriculture. The end of this period is marked by the economic crisis in Yugoslavia in the late 1980s when the transition to a market economy was initiated. As savings and loan services were not allowed to carry out all kinds of banking activity, the agricultural and forestry cooperatives established Slovenian Agricultural Cooperative Bank Ltd (*Slovenska zadružna kmetijska banka d.d.*) in 1990.

The third period covers the time after Slovenia gained independence (1991). Savings and loan services which were established with unlimited liability of their founders, turned out to be a specific, rather curious legal form compared with the former system of primary credit cooperatives, which are a well-known form of credit institution in market economies.

Savings and loan services were required to adjust themselves to the requirements of banking legislation before Slovenia joined the European Union. In this time, the present organisational model of the cooperative bank as the sole financial institution of the cooperative system was shaped.

The development of cooperative financial institutions in these periods is described in more detail in Chap. 2.

In view of the accession of Slovenia to the EU, the banking legislation provided for an adjustment of savings and loan services to stricter requirements. It did not provide for any institutional changes; for instance for transformation of savings and loan services into credit cooperatives, for widening of the potential membership base, and/or permitted activities. Such an institutional setting had a decisive influence on the cooperative bank in the form of the joint stock company prevalently owned by agricultural and forestry cooperatives and their central organisations which is analysed in Chap. 3.

The financial and economic crisis which erupted in 2008, has already had a profound impact on the whole banking system in Slovenia. The recent consolidation measures in this sector are discussed in Chap. 4.

The recent signs of recovery in the banking system and the economy as a whole are briefly shown in Chap. 5.

The present shareholders' structure of the Slovenian cooperative bank and its future vision are discussed in Chap. 6.

The paper ends with some concluding remarks regarding credit cooperatives in the Slovenian legal and financial system.

2 The Development of Cooperative Financial Institutions in Slovenia

2.1 Credit Cooperatives as a Backbone of the Slovenian Cooperative Movement Before WWII

The first successful credit cooperative was the Association for Financial Assistance to Artisans and Craftsmen in Ljubljana (*Društvo za denarno pomoč obrtnikom in rokodelcem v Ljubljani*), founded in 1856 by Jan Nepomuk Horak and other artisans in Ljubljana (Schauer 1940). For years, this organisation which followed a model of a similar association founded in 1851 in Celovec, the capital of Carinthia (a province within the today Austria), remained a successful, but lonely trial of cooperative self-help.

The circumstances for more numerous credit cooperatives ripened in the 1870s. The first period of credit cooperatives is called "a national period" by Slovenian historians since the movement was led by the patriotic intelligentsia, which, in its striving for economic independence of the Slovenian nation, considered credit cooperatives as an appropriate tool for economic emancipation (Schauer 1940). The movement was focused on the north-eastern part of the Slovenian ethnic territory, which was at that time most exposed to the pressure of foreign capital.

Dr. Josip Vošnjak (1834–1911), a physician and a member of the Provincial Diet, became acquainted with loan associations in Bohemia during his visit to Prague in 1868, and was impressed by the idea that mutual loan associations could gather and retain important capital in the hands of the nation. Therefore, he propagated the idea of credit cooperatives in several newspapers and books. At first trials in various towns failed, but in the beginning of the 1870s the first credit cooperatives in the Slovenian ethnic territory were established (Loan Association in Ljutomer, Styria, 1872). A year later, the Austrian Act on Cooperatives was adopted which considerably alleviated the establishment of cooperatives (Postava od pridobilnih in gospodarstvenih društvih ali tovarištvih 1873). Before the Act entered into force, cooperatives had been obliged to assume a legal form of association and their incorporation was uncertain since it depended on approval of political authorities (the concession system). The legislation on cooperatives from 1873 provided, however, that each legal entity satisfying the requirements laid down by the act, was entitled to be incorporated as a cooperative by the competent court (the so called normative system). By the beginning of 1883 there were 14 credit co-operatives in business and a year later there were already 25 (Schauer 1945).

The engineer Mihael Vošnjak (1837–1920), a brother of Jože Vošnjak, established the first association of credit co-operatives in the Slovenian territory on 23 January 1883 (*Zveza slovenskih posojilnic v Celju,* the Association of Slovenian Loan Associations in Celje). The association offered assistance to its members for transactions, and already in 1888, 15 years before the enactment of the Austrian Co-operative Auditing Act, began to perform regular audits in affiliated cooperatives (Schauer 1945, p. 113). During this period the Slovene co-operative movement had a strong national focus and was underpinned by the belief that political freedom required an effective economic framework (Table 1).

By the turn of the century, credit co-operation in Slovenia had acquired an important social dimension. This period is called the "social period" by historians since its main goal was to improve the position of farmers, artisans, and workers, especially through access to credit on the basis of mutual help in cooperatives.

The need for credit was triggered after the land discharge in 1848 when farmers became free owners of the land. On one hand, farmers needed money to pay taxes and compensation for land discharge as well as hereditary indemnities due to the introduction of the free division of land. On the other hand, they lost revenues from transport and home industry activities due to the development of the industrial and railway systems. Many usurers took advantage of the increased demand for loans. Due to the high expenses involved, city banks and savings banks did not provide loans for farmers.

A severe economic recession triggered the failure of many farms as well as massive migration. In response to this situation numerous credit and other types of co-operatives emerged with a low sharebase, while the members assumed joint and several liability. The main initiator of the cooperative movement in this period was Dr. Janez Evangelist Krek (1865–1917), the leader of the Christian Social movement, who was influenced by Raiffeisen's principles.

Table 1 The territorial development of the Slovenian credit cooperatives in the initial period of the movement

Year/Province	Carniola	Styria	Carinthia	Littoral	Total
1856	1	–	–	–	1
1872	1	1	–	–	2
1873	1	1	1	–	3
1874	1	3	1	–	5
1875	3	3	1	–	7
1876	3	4	1	–	8
1881	3	6	6	–	15
1882	6	8	1	–	15
1883	6	9	1	–	16
1884	6	14	1	2	23
1885	9	14	3	2	28
1886	9	14	3	2	28
1887	9	16	3	2	30
1888	11	16	5	2	34
1889	11	16	7	3	37
1890	12	19	8	3	42
1891	14	22	11	4	51
1892	14	23	13	7	57
1893	18	24	16	9	67
1894	28	27	16	10	81

Source: Schauer (1945, p. 119)

Krek actively took part at the first Catholic Political Convention in Ljubljana in 1892, and later published an essay with a title The Black Book of Peasantry (Sovran/pen name for Krek/ 1895) where he described and substantiated his views on how to solve the social problems of the Slovenian working classes. As a priest and professor of theology, Krek was of the opinion that a man is a free being and responsible for his deeds, but that there were also other factors which influenced man's will, with one of the most influential being economic life. He thought that private ownership should be respected, but not absolutely, and blamed the monetary economy which enabled the speculation and usury as the cause of all social evils. The solution of the problem would be the restoration of the natural economy which required, firstly, the so called steady farmers' homes which might not be divided or forcedly sold, and secondly, a cooperative system which would protect farmers from unforeseeable market oscillations and which enabled self-government of farmers. However, Krek was realistic enough to initiate the starting with Raiffeisen credit cooperatives "as the most appropriate", since "the money has disassociated all, so the organisation should be started in money affairs" (Sovran/pen name for Krek/ 1895).

Krek was a tireless organiser, writing articles, speaking at various gatherings on Sundays and holidays, personally taking part in the establishment of numerous credit cooperatives. The first credit cooperative after Raiffeisen's model was established in 1894 in Trnovo near Ilirska Bistrica and the second one in Dobrepolje (Lukan 1989, p. 84).

In 1895, a first cooperative union within Krek's movement was established (*Zveza kranjskih posojilnic,* the Union of Carniolan Loan Societies). Three years later a new federation for furthering cooperative thought in Slovenian territory beyond Carniola was founded (*Gospodarska zveza*, the Economic Union). In 1900, both unions were reorganised in *Gospodarska zveza*, which in 1903 changed its name to *Zadružna zveza v Ljubljani* (Cooperative Union in Ljubljana). According to the Act on Auditing of Cooperatives (Zakon z dne 10. junija 1903), which prescribed a mandatory periodic (biannual) auditing of cooperatives, either by their unions or auditors nominated by the court, cooperative unions in Celje and in Ljubljana began to perform regular audits in affiliated cooperatives. By the end of 1902, the number of affiliated cooperatives in the cooperative union of Ljubljana surpassed the membership of the union in Celje (Lukan 1989, p. 84) (Table 2).

While successful in establishing the second cooperative school in Europe (in 1908), Krek was not successful in centralising the cooperative movement, since several cooperative unions were founded following regional and political divisions.

Thus, for instance, cooperatives from the western part of the Slovenian ethnic territory established the cooperative union in Gorica in 1904, while liberal politicians founded the Union of Slovenian cooperatives (*Zveza slovenskih zadrug*) in Ljubljana in 1907. The latter union was the third audit union of Slovenian cooperatives and emerged as a consequence of the split in the liberal party. While the Cooperative union in Celje continued to associate cooperatives in Styria and Carinthia, its members from Carniola and the Littoral left it and affiliated to the newly established union in Ljubljana.

Krek also strove for a concession for a cooperative bank in order to make cooperatives independent from the capitalist banking system; in spite of preparations, the concession for the bank was not issued until 1920 (Lukan 1989, p. 87).

Credit cooperatives were an institutional innovation in the field of financial intermediation in Slovenia. By accumulating investors' savings and drawing on their in-depth knowledge of local conditions, they were able to make a realistic assessment of borrowers' loan capacity and reduce the associated risks. By the mid-1890s, co-operatives had reduced the interest rate from approximately 20 % to around 6 %, due to the increased availability of credit (Hočevar 1987). The introduction of liquidity balances and the establishment of co-operative auditing associations further reduced risk.

After the First World War and the collapse of the Austro-Hungarian Empire, the major part of the Slovenian territory belonged to the newly established Kingdom of Serbs, Croats, and Slovenes (later Kingdom of Yugoslavia). Since some territories with a nationally mixed population became part of other states, the number of Slovenian cooperatives affiliated to the cooperative unions with seat in the newly established South Slavic state was reduced compared with the numbers before the war. However, already in the first decade after the end of the First World War, the

Table 2 The development of credit and other cooperatives belonging to the Cooperative union in Ljubljana (*Zadružna zveza v Ljubljani*) and its predecessors, 1900–1912

	Credit cooperatives		Other cooperatives		All cooperatives	
Year	Number	Membership	Number	Membership	Number	Membership
1900	58	n.a.	32	n.a.	90	n.a.
1901	104	27,309	53	11,376	157	38,685
1902	107	31,158	69	13,888	176	45,046
1903	113	34,065	68	13,475	181	47,540
1904	131	41,498	93	16,342	224	58,256
1905	159	49,200	126	16,275	285	65,475
1906	183	53,069	139	18,875	322	71,940
1907	225	64,729	135	19,574	360	84,203
1908	303	78,150	150	21,343	453	99,493
1909	349	90,490	131	19,763	483	110,253
1910	378	103,249	144	21,968	522	125,217
1911	397	108,813	150	22,527	557	131,340
1912	405	115,114	170	22,330	575	137,444

Source: Lukan (1989, p. 86)

activities of about 500 Slovenian credit cooperatives achieved and surpassed the pre-war level (Lazarević 2006, p. 183).

In 1920, the Cooperative union in Ljubljana (Zadružna zveza v Ljubljani), the auditing union and business central organisation of credit cooperatives of the Catholic political movement founded *Zadružna gospodarska banka d.d.* (the Cooperative Economic Bank Ltd) which, according to its balance sheet, occupied alternatively the second and third place among Slovenian banks between the two world wars (Lazarević 2006, p. 190).

Credit cooperatives emerged also within the workers' social democratic movement, although later. Thus, some workers' consumer cooperatives accepted also savings deposits. In 1920, the workers' cooperatives founded their Union of Economic Cooperatives for Slovenia (*Zveza gospodarskih zadrug za Slovenijo*), later renamed the Union of Economic Cooperatives for Yugoslavia (*Zveza gospodarskih zadrug za Jugoslavijo*). From 1920 to 1930, workers' cooperatives were supported also by *Zadružna banka d.d.* (Cooperative Bank) as a central financial organisation of this movement (Kristan 1956).

After the cooperative union in Celje merged with the liberally oriented Zveza slovenskih zadrug, there were three auditing unions of Slovenian cooperatives (Table 3).

After a decade of successful industrialisation and economic conjuncture, the economic crisis worsened the indebtedness of farmers, due to unfavourable price oscillations. Several credit institutions refused to repay savings deposits. The Act relating to the protection of farmers from 1932 proclaimed a moratorium on farm debts (Zakon o zaščiti kmetov 1932). Although the act was conceived as a short-term measure, it was not until 1936, when after several moratorium prolongations,

Table 3 Auditing unions of Slovenian cooperatives in 1937

Name of the union	Number of affiliated cooperatives
Zadružna zveza v Ljubljani	687
Zveza slovenskih zadrug v Ljubljani	380
Zveza gospodarskih zadrug za Jugoslavijo	45

Source: Valenčič (1939, p. 459)

the government adopted a Regulation which provided for conversion of farmers' debts and sanitation of credit institutions. According to the Regulation, the Privileged Agrarian Bank (*Privilegirana Agrarna Banka, PAB*) took over all credit claims of financial institutions against farmers, and the claims were reduced by half. The credit institutions had to write off 50 % of the reduction and for the other 50 % bonds were issued. The reduced loans were to be repaid in 12 years in annual instalments (Uredba o likvidaciji kmetskih dolgov 1936) (Table 4).

According to some critical remarks, the credit cooperative system should have focused more on financial needs of their members and not on speculative investments (Gosar 1935, p. 437).

The Privileged Agrarian Bank took over the credit claims of 455 Slovenian credit cooperatives against 39,851 debtors which owed 375 million dinars (Grafenauer 1970, p. 641).

2.2 The Period from the End of the Second World War to Slovenian Independence (1945–1991)

2.2.1 The Winding Up of the Pre-war System and a Short Period of Cooperative Savings Associations

The political and economic system of Slovenia was radically changed after the Second World War. The pre-war cooperative unions and banks which had been organised following the political divisions, were considered to be an instrument for social exploitation in the former regime and therefore wound up administratively, while their property was mainly confiscated.

For the same reason, all credit co-operatives in Slovenia were liquidated by the government in 1947 (Uredba o likvidaciji kreditnih zadrug 1947).

Politically, the main role in the cooperative movement was assigned to agricultural cooperatives. The political campaign to establish the agricultural working cooperatives after the example of the Soviet kolchoses (1948–1953) failed and the major part of the agricultural land and forests remained in private property, which was, however, limited (the so called agrarian maximum).

After the introduction of the self-management system, the agricultural cooperatives began to develop as supply and marketing cooperatives for private farmers. In a more liberal environment for cooperatives, the Regulation on banks and saving

Table 4 The restructuring plan for a farmer's debt in the amount of 100 Yugoslav dinars, according to the Regulation from 1936

Number of years	Date	Interest	Principal	Amount balance
0	15.XI.1936	3.00	–	100.00
1	15.XI.1937	2.79	7.01	92.99
2	15.XI.1938	2.58	7.22	85.77
3	15.XI.1939	2.35	7.45	78.32
4	15.XI.1940	2.12	7.68	70..64
5	15.XI.1941	1.88	7.92	62.72
6	15.XI.1942	1.64	8.16	54.56
7	15.XI.1943	1.38	8.42	46.14
8	15.XI.1944	1.12	8.68	37˙46
9	15.XI.1945	0.86	8.94	28.52
10	15.XI.1946	0.58	9.22	19.30
11	15.XI.1947	0.30	9.50	9.80
12	15.XI.1948	–	9.80	–

Source: Uredba o likvidaciji kmetskih dolgov (1936)

banks from 1954 allowed agricultural cooperatives to form cooperative saving associations with the permission of the competent people's committee (Uredba o bankah in hranilnicah 1954). In 1955, the Union of cooperative savings associations began to work. At the end of 1958, this Union had ten members (in Brežice, Celje, Nova Gorica, Koper, Kranj, Ljubljana, Maribor, Murska Sobota, Novo mesto, and Ptuj) with 620 members—agricultural cooperative organisations and 1033 shares with the nominal value of 11 million YUD (Zveza zadružnih hranilnic in posojilnic 1959, Čičerov 2011, p8). However, after some years of activities, these associations and their newly established union had to cease their activities as the Act on Banks from 1961 provided that cooperative saving associations had to transfer their activity on the municipal banks and cease to work (Zakon o bankah 1961).

In 1962, the legislation was adopted according to which all cooperatives unions had ceased to operate as self-standing legal entities.

2.2.2 The First Slovenian Act About Savings and Loan Services (1969)

Towards the end of the 1970s the agricultural policy in Slovenia took a more friendly and favourable position towards private agriculture and cooperatives. In spite of the remaining administrative limitation for private agriculture (the so called agrarian maximum fixing the maximum surface of agricultural areas and forests that might be owned by farmers and other citizens), the political prejudices towards the mechanisation of private farms disappeared and resulted in a very intensive process for modernisation of private farms.

One of the first signs of the changed political attitude towards private agriculture and cooperatives was the Act on establishing of savings and loan services of agricultural and forestry labour organisations, adopted by the Slovenian Assembly in 1969 (Zakon o ustanavljanju hranilno kreditnih služb kmetijskih in gozdnogospodarskih delovnih organizacij 1969). This act allowed agricultural cooperatives, other agricultural and forestry organisations to establish internal organisational units called savings and loan services which were permitted to collect savings from members and employees as well as other rural population and to grant loans to their founders and farmers.

Although the savings and loan service was not a legal entity according to the Act from 1969, it enjoyed, to a certain extent, organisational and business autonomy in relation to its founder.

Thus, the highest governance body of the founder elected a committee and a manager of the savings and loan service.

A savings and loan service had to invest an amount equal to at least 10 % of savings deposits at a commercial bank as sight deposit for liquidity reserve. This reserve was allowed to be used only for repayment of savings deposits if there was not enough coverage from current reserves and assets.

A savings and loan service had to earmark for reserves at least 25 % of the surplus remaining after the payment of interests, wages, and other operational expenses. This obligation expired after the reserves reached an amount equal to 5 % of the total saving deposits.

Savings and loan services were prohibited from granting loans to their founders at conditions more favourable than to other persons. A founder was allowed to get a loan from its service only to one third of the total deposits, while for granting further loans the assent of the highest founder's governance body was required.

The Act prescribed the unlimited liability of the founding agricultural cooperative or forestry organisation for deposits collected by the savings and loan service. Subsidiarily, the Republic of Slovenia was liable for savings deposits.

Already in 1971, the agricultural cooperatives and forestry organisations as founders of savings and loan services, established a voluntary representative and central business organisation of savings and loan services (*Zveza hranilno kreditnih služb Slovenije*, Union of Savings and Loan Services of Slovenia).

A year later (1972) the Cooperative Union of Slovenia (*Zadružna zveza Slovenije*) was re-established after a 10 years' hiatus.

In 1975, the Slovenian Republic adopted legislation to subsidy the interest for investment loans in private agriculture. This measure supported further development of savings and loan services.

2.2.3 The Legislation Regarding Savings and Loan Services from 1980 to 1990 and the Establishment of the Slovenian Agricultural Cooperative Bank (1990)

In the 1970s, the institutional structure of the whole economy became fragmented with the introduction of the so called "basic organisations" as legal entities within the labour organisations (formerly called social enterprises). As agricultural cooperatives had in principle, according to the constitutional provisions, the position of labour organisations, their farmer members and employees could also organise basic organisations within an agricultural cooperative. Therefore, the second Act on Savings and Loan Services and on Mutual Help Funds (Zakon o hranilno kreditnih službah in blagajnah vzajemne pomoči 1980) defined a savings and loan service as a financial legal entity which might be founded either by one or more agricultural cooperative(s), their basic organisations and other organisations entering into business transactions with farmers.

The agricultural cooperatives of that time might not deal with forest management which was performed jointly for forests in social as well as in private ownership. The forest management was carried out by the forestry organisations, which had, at that time, the exclusive right to place forestry products (from all forests, regardless of their private or social ownership) on the market (the forest owners being granted the right to receive wood for domestic use within the productive capability of their forests, to perform the cutting in their forests, and to receive a certain part of sale price for the wood cut down in their forests). As savings and loan services were endowed with legal personality, a possibility for their concentration and a certain rationalisation was open.

The Act from 1980 provided for joint and several liabilities of founders for savings deposits gathered by their savings and loan service. Assets deposited by the service at a bank, enjoyed the same guarantees as other savings deposits at banks, while the Republic of Slovenia assumed a subsidiary liability for saving deposits at the savings and loan service.

According to the Act from 1980, each savings and loan service had to form a reserve fund and fund of fixed assets. Every year, the service had to earmark at least 0.1 % of all placements shown in the annual account in the reserve fund until it amounted to 1 % of this basis.

However, an increasing inflation rate and the first signs of a deepening economic crisis were not so favourable to banking activities of savings and loan services as before.

In 1980, the Republic of Slovenia ceased to subsidy interest of investment loans in private agriculture.

The third Slovenian Act on savings and loan services [Zakon o hranilno kreditnih službah (ZHKS) 1990] was adopted in the period of transition towards a market economy.

According to the Act from 1990, a savings and loan service was allowed to enter into transactions only to the extent of the assets it had gathered as deposits and credits. The service might use for long-term placements at most 50 % of deposits and at least 5 % of deposits had to be invested into liquidity reserve, available for use at any moment.

The founders of a credit and loan service were liable jointly and severally for savings deposits in domestic currency, current accounts at savings and loan services. In addition, the Republic of Slovenia was liable for savings deposits, but only subsidiarily.

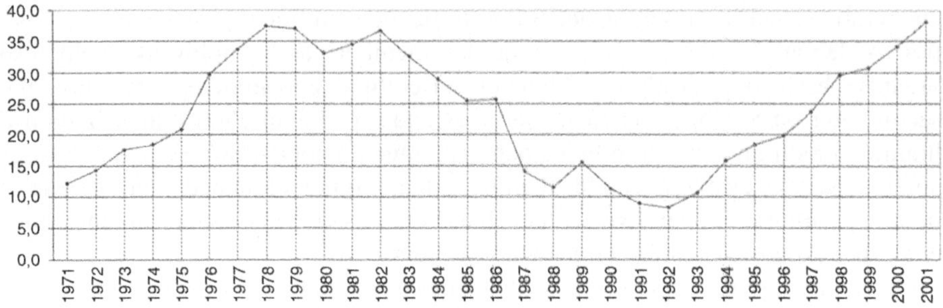

Graph 1 The amount of saving deposits gathered by savings and loan services affiliated to the Union of Savings and Loan Services of Slovenia, 1971–2001 (as of the end of each year, in Slovenian tolar (SIT) billion, prices 2001). *Sources*: Zveza hranilno kreditnih služb Slovenije (1971–2001)

This provision was amended already in the same year when the Act had been passed. The amendment stipulated that the State guaranteed for deposits at a savings and loan service only if the service had acquired a guarantee of a commercial bank. According to the transitory provisions, savings and loan services did not need to get a bank's guarantee up to the amount of their deposits at the time when the amendment entered into force (18 August 1990) (Graph 1).

The Act from 1990 broadened the activities of the savings and loan services, which were permitted to gather savings and other deposits from individuals and legal entities, but their range of activities was still decidedly narrower than that of banks.

Therefore, agricultural and forestry cooperative organisations, their savings and loan services, the Union of these services, Cooperative Union of Slovenia, and some other organisations, mostly from the agrifood and forestry sector, established Slovenska zadružna kmetijska banka (the *Slovenian Agricultural Cooperative Bank Ltd*) on 18 January 1990, in Celje.

3 The Current Model After Adjustment to the Banking Legislation

Slovenia gained independence in 1991.

In 1991 and 1992, Slovenia adopted legislation about privatisation and restitution of formerly nationalised private property. The Act on Cooperatives from 1992 provided also for the restitution of property nationalised into cooperative organisations. Since there were no credit cooperatives, the Act foresaw that the nationalised property of former credit cooperatives and their unions might be restituted on application of the Union of Savings and Loan Services and the Slovenian Agricultural Cooperative Bank (Zakon o zadrugah (ZZad) 1992).

The economists estimate that the losses of the Yugoslav banking system at the end of the 1980s exceeded the capital of all banks by a factor of 3.5 (Lazarević 2011, p. 263). The restructuring of large banks became an urgent need after Slovenia had gained independence. In 1993, two largest banks representing half the domestic banking sector and with around 45 % non-performing loans were placed under the control of the Bank Rehabilitation Agency (OECD 1997, p. 74). After the restructuring, asset quality and financial performance in the sector significantly improved (Lazarević 2006, pp. 267–270).

Neither savings and loan services nor the newly established Slovenian Agricultural Cooperative Bank Ltd were included by these measures since their overall financial position was much healthier.

In 1996, Slovenia and the European Union signed the European Association Agreement, which declared Slovenian membership in the EU as its final goal. Slovenia formally applied for membership immediately after signing the Agreement. The accession negotiations started in March 1998 and were successfully concluded at the Copenhagen European Council Summit in December 2002.

In the meantime, Slovenia harmonised its legislation with the *acquis communautaire*.

The first Slovenian Banking Act (Zakon o bančništvu (ZBan) 1999) provided for a 5 year period during which the existent savings and loan services should adjust their organisation and activities to the requirements of the banking legislation regarding minimum capital, risk management, deposit guarantee scheme, control, and reporting. Detailed provisions were laid down by a decree issued by the Bank of Slovenia (Sklep o usklajevanju hranilno kreditnih služb z določbami zakona o bančništvu 1999) (Table 5).

In accession negotiations, Slovenia, however, applied neither to exempt the savings and loan services from the scope of banking directives nor to provide a standing derogation in certain aspects. Instead, it got a transitional period of only 8 month after the accession date to align the business of savings and loan services with the banking standards of the EU.[1]

In the period of adjustment to the banking legislation requirements, savings and loan services sought connection with other financial institutions. The vast majority of savings and loan services decided to merge with their Union which had itself a status of savings and loan service, being established by agricultural and forestry cooperatives as founders of local savings and loan services.

[1] See, *ANNEX XIII* (List referred to in Article 24 of the Act of Accession: Slovenia) to Act concerning the conditions of accession of the Czech Republic, the Republic of Estonia, the Republic of Cyprus, the Republic of Latvia, the Republic of Lithuania, the Republic of Hungary, the Republic of Malta, the Republic of Poland, the Republic of Slovenia and the Slovak Republic and the adjustments to the Treaties on which the European Union is founded (Official Journal of EU L 236, 23 September 2003, p. 908):

»In Slovenia, Directive 2000/12/EC shall not apply until 31 December 2004 to savings and loans undertakings established before 20 February 1999.«

Table 5 The requirements and deadlines for adjustment of savings and loan services to the banking legislation from 1999

Requirement	Deadlines
Minimum share capital (186 million SIT, approximately one million euros at the then currency rate), fully paid in cash	The first half amount of the minimum capital had to be paid in until 31 December 2001, the second half was due on 31 December 2003 at the latest
Capital adequacy ratio	The first report on capital adequacy had to be submitted as of 31 December 2001, the final adjustment had to take place on 31 December 2003, at the latest
Risk management	Risk management plans had to be prepared by 30 June 2001, providing at least one quarter of prescribed reservations by 31 December 2000, one half by 31 December 2001, three quarters by 31 December 2002, and the full amount by 31 December 2003
Great exposures	All exposures exceeding the permitted levels had to be established immediately after the decree entered in force and gradually reduced to the permitted level by 31 December 2003 at the latest, with semi-annual reporting
Liquidity risk	The liquidity ratio of the first class had to be achieved by 31 December 2001, the liquidity ratio of other classes by the end of the adjustment period, while the reporting started on 31 December 2001
Investments in shares and immovables	Fulfilment of requirements until the end of the adjustment period
Business books and annual accounts	Accounting records had to be kept and annual accounts prepared in accordance with the provisions for banks: until the end of the adjustment period
Internal audit	Internal audit had to be organised by the end of adjustment period
Auditing according to the banking legislation	Auditing according to the banking legislation had to be organised starting on the date of adjustment, at the latest from December 2003 onwards
Inclusion in a deposit guarantee scheme	From 31 December 2001 til 31 December 2003 at the latest

Source: Sklep o usklajevanju hranilno kreditnih služb z določbami zakona o bančništvu (1999)

Some savings and loan services merged with the Slovenian Agricultural Cooperative Bank Ltd, while a few others merged with other banks.

Some savings and loan services, in particular those that did not adhere to the Union of Savings and Loan Services of Slovenia were wound up or went into bankruptcy proceedings.

Table 6 Adjustment of savings and loan services in Slovenia to the banking legislation, 2001–2006

Adjustment measure/year	2001	2002	2003	2004	2005	2006	Total
Merger	14	12	12	2	–	–	40
Transfer of activity	4	3	4	3	1		15
Ordinary liquidation	1	–	1	2	–	–	4
Compulsory liquidation	1	–	–	8	–	–	9
Bankruptcy proceedings	1	2	1	–	–	–	4
Cancellation	–	4	–	–	1	1	6
Transformation into a savings bank	–	–	–	–	1	–	1
Total	21	21	18	15	3	1	79

Sources: Banka Slovenije (2004, pp. 16–19, 2005, p. 9, 2006, p. 46)

Only one savings and loan service transformed itself into a joint stock company—with an agricultural cooperative and some other shareholders—and obtained a licence from the National Bank to continue its activity as a savings bank. However, the founders gradually sold their shares to two municipalities (Vipava and Ajdovščina), two credit cooperatives (local cooperative banks) from neighbouring Italy, Deželna banka Slovenije Ltd, and some minor shareholders (Hranilnica in posojilnica Vipava d. d 2015) (Table 6).

At first, the Slovenian Union of Savings and Loan Services intended itself to transform into a credit institution, specialised for the agrifood sector. However, after the efforts to obtain a special legislative regulation in Slovenia failed, the Union decided to transfer its banking activity as well as its assets to the Slovenian Agricultural Cooperative Bank Ltd that had been renamed as Deželna banka Slovenije Ltd. This bank, in turn increased its share capital issuing additional shares to the Union of Savings and Loan Services which became the (relatively) greatest shareholder of Deželna banka Slovenije Ltd. As both institutions covered the same sector, the operation lead to important synergistic effects.

After there was no active savings and loan service in 2006, the second Slovenian Banking Act from 2006, repealed the Act on savings and loan services from 1990 (Zakon o bančništvu (ZBan-1) 2006) (Graph 2).

In 2004, the Slovenian Agricultural Cooperative Bank Ltd changed its name into the Deželna banka Slovenije (Country Bank of Slovenia).

After the transfer of banking activities on the cooperative bank the Union of Savings and Loan Services of Slovenia transformed itself into a cooperative and changed its name to *Kapitalska zadruga (Capital Cooperative)*, a cooperative for promotion of members' interests.

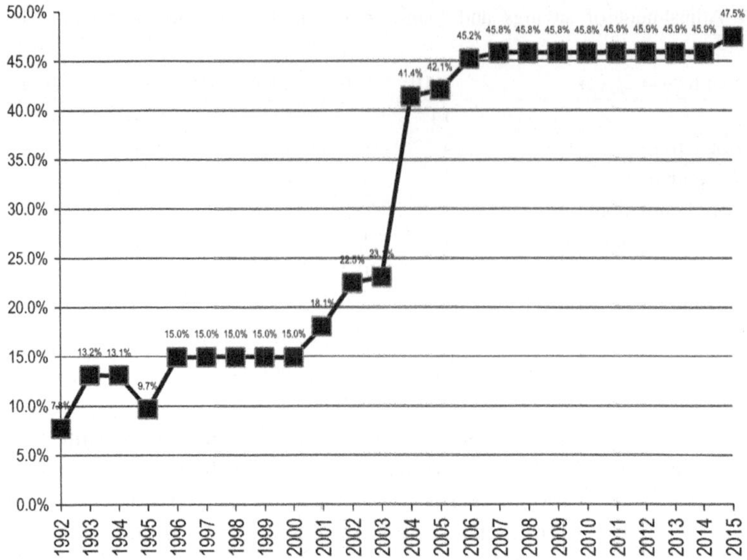

Source: Deželna banka Slovenije, 2015 a, b.

Graph 2 Share of the Union of Savings and Loan Services of Slovenia, now, Kapitalska zadruga, in the capital of the Slovenian Agricultural Cooperative Bank, now Deželna Banka Slovenije from 1990–2015 (as of 31 December of years 1990–2014 and of 6 March 2015). *Source*: Deželna Banka Slovenije (2015a, b)

4 Additional Measures in Deželna banka Slovenije Ltd and Extraordinary Measures in the Banking System After the Outbreak of the Financial Crisis (2008)

The Slovenian banking system is one of the smallest in the euro area. Total assets amounted to 40 billion euros at the end of 2013, equivalent to 123.4 % of GDP (European Commission 2015).

Before the outbreak of the financial crisis in 2008, the Slovenian economy had one of the highest growth rates.

The banking crisis in Slovenia emerged, according to a report of the Bank of Slovenia, due to three key factors.

The first one was a fast, unsustainable ("overheated") growth before the crisis. After entering the European Union and adoption of the Euro (1 January 2007), the lowered interest rates and large supply of assets on international financial markets triggered an increased competition among banks as lenders and contributed to lowering the loan standards for corporate loans. In the period from 2004 to 2008, the exposure of domestic banks to foreign banks increased from less than 4 billion euros to more than 16 billion euros (Banka Slovenije 2015c).

The second factor was the excessive indebtedness of non-financial corporations. The banks tied an exceptionally high percentage of loans to the value of pledged real estate, which was aggravated by the act that the debt increased at the fastest pace in cyclical economic sectors, above all in construction and real estate. In addition, a privatisation model that relied on borrowing and planning the payment of the debts through future monetary flows of acquired companies was widely used.

The third factor was the increasing rate of non-performing loans during the crisis (Banka Slovenije 2015c).

In only 1 year—2009, the Slovenian gross domestic product decreased by 7.8 %, while the number of unemployed increased from 46,000 in 2008 to 102,000 in 2013 (Statistical Office of the Republic of Slovenia 2015a, b).

After the outbreak of the financial crisis in 2008, the Slovenian banks have had to make provisions for expected losses which eroded the banks' capital base so they lacked capital for normal operations.

In order to solve this problem, the Slovenian Parliament passed the Measures of the Republic of Slovenia to Strengthen the Stability of Banks Act (MSSBA, Zakon o ukrepih Republike Slovenije za krepitev stabilnosti bank 2012). According to the Act, the Government founded the Bank Asset Management Company (BAMC) to promote stability of the Slovene financial system and restore trust in its functioning. The Act allows business banks with head office in the Republic of Slovenia to transfer non-performing assets to BAMC. These assets originate mainly from past loans not being serviced by the debtors due to the economic crisis.

In exchange for the transfer of non-performing assets banks may receive money or other assets in the form of BAMC bonds with government guarantee or government bonds that can be sold later on the market. The banks can sell bonds immediately upon receipt or refinance them in euro system meaning receiving a soft loan from the European Central Bank insured with these bonds. Liquid funds are thus obtained mostly in the form of short-term loans providing the capital for domestic economy.

A lot of speculation as to the total cost of the recapitalisation of banks in Slovenia was circulating for a number of years. The Slovenian monetary authorities therefore opted for a comprehensive review of the banking system through bank asset quality reviews (AQR) and stress tests (STs)[2] which were conducted in a representative sample of ten banks,[3] not including Deželna Banka Slovenije Ltd.

---

[2] The asset quality review (AQR) included verification of data completeness and integrity, a review of individual loans, collateral valuation and identification of the adequacy of impairments.

The objective of the stress tests was the assessment of the eventual capital requirements under the conditions of the baseline scenario (more favourable) and the adverse scenario (the scenario of sharply increased macroeconomic imbalances: a cumulative 9.5 % fall in GDP from 2013 to 2015 which is 1 percentage point higher than the fall from 2009 to 2012; the cumulative fall of private consumption by 18 % in comparison with the 2.5 % fall in the period 2009–2012) over a 3-year projection period, i.e. 2013–2015 (Banka Slovenije 2013a, b, p. 8).

[3] The AQR included the following ten banks (or 70 % of the assets of the banking system): NLB d. d., NKBM d.d., Abanka Vipa d.d., Banka Celje d.d., Gorenjska Banka d.d., Probanka d.d., Factor

According to the European Commission rules on eligibility for state aid for banks in distress, the Banking Act was amended in November 2013 with a provision stipulating that qualified liabilities (that include equity, hybrid capital and subordinated debt instruments) of a bank are either be written off or converted into the highest-quality form of capital, i.e. ordinary shares before any state aid is given to the bank or government-funded capital of the bank increases (Zakon o spremembah in dopolnitvah Zakona o bančništvu (ZBan-1L) 2013).

In accordance with the amended Banking Act and taking into account the conditions for state-funded recapitalisation, the Bank of Slovenia adopted decisions on 18 December 2013 imposing two extraordinary measures on five banks (NLB, NKBM, Abanka, Factor banka and Probanka):

- The termination of qualified liabilities (equity and subordinated liabilities of the aforementioned banks)[4]; and
- The recapitalisation of the banks in question in the form of state aid to cover outstanding losses and ensure capital adequacy (Banka Slovenije 2015b).

Following the approval from the European Commission from 18 December 2013, the Slovenian government carried out capital increase in five Slovenian banks (Banka Slovenije 2013a).

Banks that were excluded from the aforementioned tests had to close their 2013 balance sheets by applying the methodology used in the asset quality review (AQR) and the stress tests. If the tests revealed a capital deficit, banks had to disclose it.

Deželna Banka Slovenije Ltd could not stay unaffected by the unfavourable economic trends during the crisis.

On 1 July 2014, Deželna Banka Slovenije Ltd received a Bank of Slovenia Decree on additional measures to increase the share capital. According to the Decree, the Management Board of Deželna Banka Slovenije Ltd convened a general Meeting on 14 October 2014 and proposed to meeting to pass a resolution to increase the Bank's paid-up share capital by issuing new no par value shares so that the Bank's capital adequacy ratio will reach at least 11.4 % and its tier 1 capital ratio at least 9.1 %.

The resolution foresaw the share capital increase by maximally 4,636,588.28 €(maximum of 1,111,112 new ordinary shares, each sold at 9.00 €). The Securities

---

banka d.d., Raiffeisen banka d.d., Hypo Alpe-Adria-Bank d.d., and UniCredit banka d.d. The stress tests included eight banks, excluding Factor banka and Probanka, which have been undergoing an orderly wind-down process since the autumn of 2013 (Banka Slovenije 2013a, b, p. 15).

[4] Several shareholders and creditors challenged the constitutionality of the provision before the Constitutional Court. The challenged provision of the Banking Act is based on the Communication from the Commission on the application, from 1 August 2013, of State aid rules to support measures in favour of banks in the context of the financial crisis, the so called "Banking Communication"). On 6 November 2014, the Slovenian Constitutional Court submitted the question to the European Court of Justice whether the Banking Communication of the European Commission should be interpreted as binding upon Member States and whether the measures are obligatory if state aid is subsequently to be deemed legal (Ustavno sodišče Republike Slovenije 2014).

Market Agency approved the Prospectus for the public offering of shares of Deželna Banka Slovenije Ltd on 24 October 2014 (record date).

The shares of Deželna Banka Slovenije Ltd were offered to the public from 4 November 2014. Round one lasted until 3 December 2014 when existing shareholders—who had the right of pre-emption—had subscribed and paid 225,546 newly issued shares in the total issue value of 2,029,914.00 €.

During the second round (from 8 to inclusive 31 December 2014) when the shares were offered to the entire interested public, 259,702 newly issued shares were subscribed and paid, in the total issue value of 2,337,318.00 €.

In both rounds of the capital increase, a total of 98 existing shareholders and external investors together subscribed and paid 485,248 shares in the total issue value of 4,367,232.00 €.

Since the resolution of the general meeting declared that the offering would be successful if at least 444,445 newly issued shares in the total amount of at least 4,000,005.00 € were subscribed and paid, Deželna Banka Slovenije Ltd announced in January 2015 that the capital increase had been successfully completed (Deželna Banka Slovenije 2015a, b).

5 First Signs of Recovery

The banking system and the whole economy of Slovenia showed signs of recovery in 2013 and 2014.

The GDP, while still decreasing (by 1 %) in 2013, increased in 2014 by 2.6 % (Statistical Office of the Republic of Slovenia 2015a). At the end of April 2015, a total of 114,923 persons were registered in the unemployment register, 7.0 % fewer than in April 2014 (UMAR 2015a, b). Current account balance has been steadily increasing from −26 million euros in 2010 to 2187 million euros in 2014 (UMAR 2015a) (Table 7).

One of the signs of economic improvement was also a decrease in required yields on government bonds. The maximum value of 7.45 % was reached in mid-August 2013 and decreased to 6.7 % in October 2013 when the banks' stress tests were carried out. After the recapitalisation of five banks, it decreased to 1.3 % at the end of February 2015 (Banka Slovenije 2015b).

The restored confidence in the banking system is most evidently shown through the increased household deposits, that rose by 4 % (or by 729 million euros) in the whole banking system, while their growth in Deželna Banka Slovenije Ltd was even higher—by 14 % (or by 70 million euros). The household deposits at the Cooperative Bank reached the highest amount (590 million euros) in the last decade (Deželna Banka Slovenije 2015a, b).

However, the banks' balance sheets contracted from 2010 till 2014, while the Cooperative Bank increased its balance sheet in 2014 first after the decreasing after 2010 when it achieved its peak (Banka Slovenije 2015a, b, c; Deželna Banka

Table 7 Gross domestic product of the Republic of Slovenia, 2008–2014

Category/year	2008	2009	2010	2011	2012	2013	2014
Gross domestic product, current prices (million euros)	37,951	36,166	36,220	36,868	36,006	36,144	37,246
Gross domestic product, real growth rate (%)	3.3	−7.8	1.2	0.6	−2.6	−1.0	2.6
Gross domestic product per capita, current exchange rate (EUR)	18,769	17,714	17,678	17,960	17,506	17,550	18,065
Gross domestic product per capita, current exchange rate (USD million)	27,606	24,708	23,436	25,000	22,492	23,308	24,000

Source: Statistical Office of the Republic of Slovenia (2015a)

Slovenije 2015a). Deželna Banka Slovenije Ltd could, although not essentially, improve its market share (Graph 3).

The performance of the banking system has improved recently. Although the system as a whole reported a net loss for financial year 2014, the net loss was the lowest (−67 million euros) in the last 5 years, while the Cooperative Bank reported even 1.6 million euros of profit before tax.

Deželna Banka Slovenije Ltd managed to increase the number of active corporate transactional accounts by 18 % in 2014 due to a favourable trend in E-banking and improved several business indicators (like interest margin and financial intermediation margin) (Table 8).

The income position of the whole banking sector is still characterised by the high level of non-performing loans and low credit demand from creditworthy firms (European Commission 2015; Banka Slovenije 2015b).

6 Cooperatives as Shareholders of Deželna Banka Slovenije Ltd and the Bank's Vision for the Future

At the end of 2014 Deželna Banka Slovenije Ltd successfully completed the capital increase according to the additional measure decreed by the Bank of Slovenia. During this operation, the shareholding cooperatives managed to increase also their relative shares: the greatest shareholder Kapitalska zadruga increased its share by some percentage points, not exceeding the 50 % limit of its qualified share, while the total dispersed participation of individual cooperatives from Slovenia and abroad (two cooperative banks, one from Austria and the other from Italy) increased to 23.72 % (Table 9).

The Cooperative Bank's vision is to be a successful and safe, effective, universal, medium-sized bank with offices throughout Slovenia.

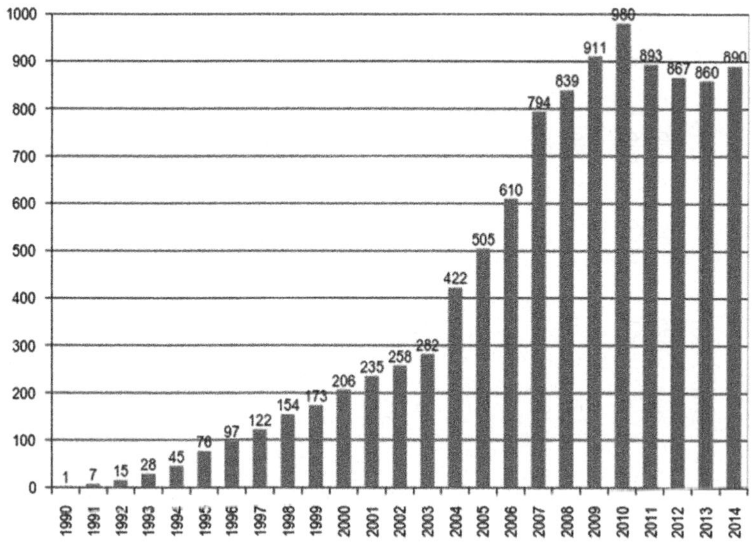

Graph 3 The balance sheet of Deželna Banka Slovenije Ltd (til 2004: Slovenska zadružna kmetijska banka Ltd) from 1990 to 2014 (million euros)

The strategy of the bank is focused on a streamlined, technically and organisationally updated network, an extensive range of competitive banking and non-banking products (for instance, leasing, insurance policies, factoring, real estate), while the bank business should remain cost-effective and competitive in terms of quality assurance and productivity. In the nearest future, the bank wants to focus its business strategy on citizens, small and medium-sized enterprises, agro-food sector and securities transactions in all forms (Deželna Banka Slovenije 2015a, b).

In last years, the bank improved its relative position compared to the Slovenian banking system as a whole (Table 10).

The future development will depend on the overall economic situation in Slovenia and on the ability of the cooperatives to remain the major shareholders of the bank, since the shareholding (but also other) cooperatives have limited capital strength to provide funds for higher capital increases within a short period of time. However, the Bank of Slovenia envisages further tightening of capital adequacy ratio as very probable (Banka Slovenije 2015b).

It will also be important whether and how the Cooperative Bank will manage to use its advantages. These advantages are the third most extensive branch network among banks in Slovenia (with 85 local offices), good knowledge of its customers, and relatively high discipline of farmers in repaying loans. From about 65,000 clients of the bank, half of them receive agricultural subsidies from the EU (Anadolli 2014). The bank tries to adapt its financial products to the needs of its customers also, through a cooperation with insurance companies and cooperatives.

Table 8 Key financial data of Deželna Banka Slovenije Ltd for the decade 2005–2014

Data/Year	2005	2006	2007	2008	2009	2010	2011	2012	2013	2014
Total assets (in million euros)	459	610	757	839	911	980	893	867	856	890
Total deposits by non-banking sector measured at amortised cost (in million euros)	338	354	525	580	620	665	661	617	646	703
– Corporates	100	47	161	149	152	172	170	126	126	112
– Retail	238	307	364	431	468	493	491	491	520	591
Total loans to non-banking sector measured at amortised cost (in million euros)	191	257	390	514	502	502	504	633	646	622
– Corporates	160	218	318	436	417	402	394	520	530	498
– Retail	31	39	72	78	85	100	110	113	116	124
Total capital (in million euros)	35	39	80	76	78	39	69	62	45	47
Net interest income (in million euros)	11	13	16	20	16	22	18	21	21	21
Impairments of financial assets measured at amortised cost, and provisions (in million euros)	−1	1,5	1	3	5	9	15	17	30	13
Share capital (in million euros)	30	35	70	78	85	83	73	66	53	56
Interest margin (in %)	2.55	2.28	2.33	2.48	1.87	2.36	1.85	2.37	2.49	2.55
Financial intermediation margin (in %)	3.83	4.15	4.41	3.02	2.88	3.26	2.44	3.03	3.09	3.49
Return on assets (ROA) before tax (in %)	0.18	0.62	1.36	0.14	0.05	0.18	−1.15	−0.85	−2.01	0.15
Return on equity (ROE) before tax (in %)	2.08	8.73	18.78	1.44	0.53	2.13	−14.47	−11.78	−32.03	3.42
Return on equity (ROE) after tax (in %)	1.63	6.36	14.48	1.25	0.44	1.73	−11.63	−11.14	−28.40	2.84
Capital adequacy ratio (in %)	11.20	10.00	14.30	12.20	13.40	13.20	11.90	11.47	10.04	12.03
No. of employees (at the end of period)	402	401	411	422	405	361	362	352	355	355

Source: Deželna Banka Slovenije (2015b)

Table 9 Shareholders of the Deželna Banka Slovenije Ltd as of 6 March 2015

Shareholders	Shares (%)
Kapitalska zadruga	47.53
Other cooperatives from Slovenia and their subsidiaries	14.99
Cooperatives from abroad (Austria and Italy)	8.73
All shareholding cooperatives	71.25
Other shareholders	28.75
All shareholders	100.00

Source: Deželna Banka Slovenije (2015a, b)

Table 10 Some indicators about financial position of Deželna Banka Slovenije Ltd compared with the Slovenian banking system

Indicator	Entity	2008	2014
Total	Deželna Banka Slovenije Ltd (million euros)	839	890
Assets	All banks (million euros)	47,948	38,754
	Share of Deželna Banka Slovenije Ltd (in %)	1.75	2.30
Interest	Deželna Banka Slovenije Ltd	2.48	2.55
Margin (in %)	All banks	2.20	2.18
Financial	Deželna Banka Slovenije Ltd	3.02	3.49
Intermediation margin (in %)	All banks	3.00	3.10

Sources: Banka Slovenije (2009, 2015a), Deželna Banka Slovenije (2015b)

7 Concluding Remarks

The story of credit cooperatives in Slovenia is interesting since one can trace three paths to the establishment of a financial system for cooperatives.

The first period is characterised by the leading role of credit cooperatives in the whole cooperative system. Their prevalence is due to a large membership base, while supply, marketing, consumer, housing, and other cooperatives could not reach so many people.

In the second period, credit cooperatives and their unions were wound up. As cooperatives in many sectors vanished, farmers' cooperatives gradually took the leading role, followed by housing and crafts cooperatives. At that time special financial institutions emerged within the agricultural cooperation, taking the form of specialised credit sections or secondary financial organisations of agricultural cooperatives.

While the first cooperative financial system was administratively wound up after the Second World War, rather unique financial cooperative institutions afterwards could not succeed to become a durable solution due to unsuitable legal form of savings and loan services with unlimited liability of their founders and unsatisfactory external supervision (what increased risks in a liberalised economic environment). In addition, a limited range of permitted financial services became a serious competitive disadvantage during market-oriented economic reforms and triggered the establishment of the Cooperative Bank (first named Slovenian Agricultural Cooperative Bank Ltd and after that the Country Bank of Slovenia Ltd) in 1990.

On the other hand, Slovenia has not provided for establishment of credit cooperatives in its legislation so far. Maybe the institutional innovations introduced by the European cooperative society and corresponding options allowed in national legislation about cooperatives (regarding minimum capital, transferability of shares, etc.) will finally allow to open this area of activity to cooperatives.

References

Anadolli S (2014) Deželna banka Slovenije še ni rubila nobenega kmeta. Delo, tor, 21.01.2014. http://www.delo.si/gospodarstvo/potrosnik/sonja-anadolli-dezelna-banka-slovenije-se-ni-rubila-nobenega-kmeta.html. Accessed 30 May 2015

Banka Slovenije (2004) Poročilo o nadzoru bančnega poslovanja v letu 2003 in prvi polovici leta 2004. Banka Slovenije, Ljubljana

Banka Slovenije (2005) Poročilo o nadzoru bančnega poslovanja v letu 2004. Banka Slovenije, Ljubljana

Banka Slovenije (2006) Poročilo o finančni stabilnosti. Banka Slovenije, Ljubljana

Banka Slovenije (2009) Poslovanje bank v tekočem letu, gibanja na kapitalskem trgu in obrestne mere, avgust 2009. Banka Slovenije, Ljubljana

Banka Slovenije (2013a) Frequently asked questions and answers regarding the reorganisation of the Slovenian banking system. Banka Slovenije, Ljubljana, http://www.bsi.si/library/includes/datoteka.asp%3FDatotekaId%3D5423. Accessed 30 May 2015

Banka Slovenije (2013b) Government carries out capital increases at five banks following European Commission approval. Banka Slovenije, Ljubljana, https://www.bsi.si/iskalniki/sporocila-za-javnost-en.asp?VsebinaId=16263&MapaId=202#16263. Accessed 30 May 2015

Banka Slovenije (2015a) Letno poročilo 2014. Banka Slovenije, Ljubljana

Banka Slovenije (2015b) Poslovanje bank v tekočem letu, gibanja na kapitalskem trgu in obrestne mere, marec 2015. Banka Slovenije, Ljubljana, http://www.bsi.si/publikacije-in-raziskave.asp?MapaId=1329. Accessed 30 May 2015

Banka Slovenije (2015c) Report of the Bank of Slovenia on the causes of the capital shortfalls of banks and the role of the Bank of Slovenia as the banking regulator in relation thereto, the recovery of banks in 2013 and 2014, the efficiency of the system of corporate governance of banks under state ownership and the manner of resolving the consequences of the capital inadequacy of commercial banks. Banka Slovenije, Ljubljana

Čičerov S (2011) Zbornik Deželne banke Slovenije d. d. ob 20-letnici delovanja. Deželna banka Slovenije, Ljubljana

Deželna banka Slovenije (2014) Bank of Slovenia decree on additional measures to increase capital. Deželna banka Slovenije, Ljubljana, http://www.dbs.si/obanki/novice/vsebina.asp?MapaID=311&NewsId=590. Accessed 30 May 2015

Deželna banka Slovenije (2015a) Results and conclusion of the capital increase. Deželna banka Slovenije, Ljubljana, http://www.dbs.si/obanki/novice/vsebina.asp?MapaID=311&NewsId=626. Accessed 30 May 2015

Deželna banka Slovenije (2015b) Poslovanje. Letna poročila 2003–2014. Deželna banka Slovenije, Ljubljana, http://www.dbs.si/o-banki/poslovanje.html. Accessed 30 May 2015

European Commission (2015) Country report Slovenia 2015. Commission staff working document, Brussels, 18.3.2015, SWD(2015) 43 final/2. http://ec.europa.eu/europe2020/pdf/csr2015/cr2015_slovenia_en.pdf. Accessed 30 May 2015

Gosar A (1935) Za nov družabni red, Knjiga 2. Družba sv. Mohorja, Celje

Grafenauer B (1970) Gospodarski obrat kmetije. In: Blaznik P, Grafenauer B, Vilfan S (eds) Gospodarska in družbena zgodovina Slovencev, Agrarno gospodarstvo, zvezek I. SAZU, Ljubljana, pp 619–651

Hočevar T (1987) Slovensko poslovno bančništvo kot inovacijski dejavnik, 1900–1930, *Zgodovina denarništva in bančništva na Slovenskem* (The History of Monetary and Banking Institutions in Slovenia). Zveza zgodovinskih društev Slovenije, Ljubljana, pp 61–74

Hranilnica in posojilnica Vipava d. d. (2015) Letno poročilo. http://www.hranilnica-vipava.si/files/Letno%20porocilo%202012.pdf. Accessed 30 May 2015

Kristan C (1956) Radničko zadrugarstvo u Sloveniji. In: Zadružni leksikon FNRJ, Knjiga II. Zadružna štampa, Zagreb, pp 1193–1199

Lazarević Ž (2006) Slovenian banking until the end of the second world war. Megatrend Rev: Int Rev Appl Econ 3(1):177–199

Lazarević Ž (2011) Banking transition in Slovenia in the 1990s. Megatrend Rev: Int Rev Appl Econ 8(1):259–274

Lukan W (1989) The second phase of Slovene cooperativism (1894–1918). Slov Stud, J Soc Slov Stud 1–2:83–96

OECD (1997) OECD economic surveys: Slovenia 1997. OECD Publishing, Paris, 158 p

Postava od pridobilnih in gospodarstvenih društvih ali tovarištvih (1873) Državni zakonik za kraljevine in dežele v državnem zboru zastopane. št. postave 70, kos XXV, Dunaj, pp 273–289

Schauer D (1940) Naša prva zadruga. Samozaložba, Ljubljana

Schauer D (1945) Prva doba našega zadružništva. Samozaložba, Ljubljana

Sklep o usklajevanju hranilno kreditnih služb z določbami zakona o bančništvu (1999) Uradni list RS, No. 109

Sovran J (Krek JE) (1895) Črne bukve kmečkega stanu. Samozaložba, Ljubljana

Statistical Office of the Republic of Slovenia (2015a) Active population by Labour Force Survey by measures and year. http://pxweb.stat.si/pxweb/Dialog/viewplus.asp?ma=H261E&ti=&path=../Database/Hitre_Repozitorij/&lang=1

Statistical Office of the Republic of Slovenia (2015b) Gross domestic product and economic growth. http://www.stat.si/StatWeb/en/field-overview?id=29&headerbar=10

UMAR (2015) Slovenian economic mirror: continuation of favourable economic trends in the first months of the year; cost competitiveness continues to improve. http://www.umar.gov.si/en/public_info/press_releases/release/zapisi/ekonomsko_ogledalo_nadaljevanje_ugodnih_gospodarskih_gibanj_v_prvih_mesecih_letosnjega_leta_stro/1/. Accessed 30 May 2015

UMAR (2015a) Slovenian economic mirror. No. 3/vol. XXI/2015. http://www.umar.gov.si/fileadmin/user_upload/publikacije/eo/2015/SEM_marec2015_splet.pdf. Accessed 30 May 2015

Uredba o bankah in hranilnicah (1954) Uradni list FLRJ, No. 4

Uredba o likvidaciji kmetskih dolgov (1936) Službeni list kraljevske banske uprave Dravske banovine, No. 33, pp 752–760

Uredba o likvidaciji kreditnih zadrug (1947) Uradni list LRS, No. 16

Ustavno sodišče Republike Slovenije (2014) Sklep št. U-I-295/13-132 z dne 6. 11. 2014. http://www.us-rs.si/media/u-i-295-13-132.pdf. Accessed 30 May 2015

Valenčič V (1939) Pregled našega zadružnega gibanja in stanja. In: Lavrič J et al (eds) Spominski zbornik Slovenije. Jubilej, Ljubljana, pp 461–467

Zakon o bančništvu (ZBan) (1999) Uradni list RS, No. 7

Zakon o bančništvu (ZBan-1) (2006) Uradni list RS, No. 131

Zakon o bankah (1961) Uradni list FLRJ, No. 10

Zakon o hranilno kreditnih službah (ZHKS) (1990) Uradni list RS, No. 14

Zakon o hranilno kreditnih službah in blagajnah vzajemne pomoči (1980) Uradni list SRS, No. 4.

Zakon o spremembah in dopolnitvah Zakona o bančništvu (ZBan-1L) (2013) Uradni list RS, No. 96

Zakon o ukrepih Republike Slovenije za krepitev stabilnosti bank (2012) Uradni list RS, No. 105

Zakon o ustanavljanju hranilno kreditnih služb kmetijskih in gozdnogospodarskih delovnih organizacij (1969) Uradni list SRS, No 22

Zakon o zadrugah (ZZad) (1992) Uradni list RS, No. 13 (For amendments of the Act, see Uradni list RS, No. 7/1993, 13/1993-ZP-G, 22/1994, 68/1995 Odl.US: U-I-78/93, 35/1996, 41/2007, 87/2009; for the last official consolidated text: Uradni list RS, No. 97/2009)

Zakon o zaščiti kmetov (1932) Službeni list kraljevske banske uprave Dravske banovine, No. 33, 27 Apr 1932, pp 653–655

Zakon z dne 10. junija 1903 o pregledu pridobitnih in gospodarskih zadrug ter drugih društev (1903) št. 133, kos LXIII, Državni zakonik za kraljevine in dežele, v državnem zboru zastopane, Dunaj, pp 409–411

Zveza zadružnih hranilnic in posojilnic (1959) Poročilo za IV. redni občni zbor. Zveza zadružnih hranilnic in posojilnic, Ljubljana

Zveza hranilno kreditnih služb Slovenije (1971–2001) Letna poročila. Zveza hranilno kreditnih služb Slovenije, Ljubljana

The manufacturer's authorised representative in the EU is Springer Nature Customer Service Centre GmbH, Europaplatz 3, 69115 Heidelberg, Germany. If you have any concerns regarding our products, please contact ProductSafety@springernature.com

Printed and bound by CPI Group (UK) Ltd, Croydon, CR0 4YY
22/09/2026
02221051-0002